4.00

The Library
INTERNATIONAL CHRISTIAN
GRADUATE UNIVERSITY

Presented to:

Edward Hill

June 16, 1963

St Peter's Episcapal Church
Rialto, Calif.

Edward B. Olander, Jr
— Vicar

D1547462

THE BOOK OF COMMON PRAYER

and Administration of the Sacraments
and Other Rites and Ceremonies
of the Church

ACCORDING TO THE USE OF THE
PROTESTANT EPISCOPAL CHURCH
IN THE UNITED STATES OF AMERICA

Together with The Psalter
or Psalms of David

THE CHURCH PENSION FUND
20 Exchange Place
New York

CERTIFICATE.

I CERTIFY that this edition of the Book of Common Prayer has been compared with a certified copy of the Standard Book. as the Canon directs, and that it conforms thereto.

JOHN WALLACE SUTER

Custodian of the Standard Book of Common Prayer

September, 1945.

BX
5943
P967

The Library
INTERNATIONAL CHRISTIAN
GRADUATE UNIVERSITY

Table of Contents

26246

THE RATIFICATION OF
THE BOOK OF COMMON PRAYER.

BY THE BISHOPS, THE CLERGY, AND THE LAITY OF THE PROTESTANT EPISCOPAL CHURCH IN THE UNITED STATES OF AMERICA, IN CONVENTION, THIS SIXTEENTH DAY OF OCTOBER, IN THE YEAR OF OUR LORD ONE THOUSAND SEVEN HUNDRED AND EIGHTY-NINE.

This Convention having, in their present session, set forth *A Book of Common Prayer, and Administration of the Sacraments, and other Rites and Ceremonies of the Church,* do hereby establish the said Book: And they declare it to be the Liturgy of this Church: And require that it be received as such by all the members of the same: And this Book shall be in use from and after the First Day of October, in the Year of our Lord one thousand seven hundred and ninety.

Preface

IT is a most invaluable part of that blessed "liberty wherewith Christ hath made us free," that in his worship different forms and usages may without offence be allowed, provided the substance of the Faith be kept entire; and that, in every Church, what cannot be clearly determined to belong to Doctrine must be referred to Discipline; and therefore, by common consent and authority, may be altered, abridged, enlarged, amended, or otherwise disposed of, as may seem most convenient for the edification of the people, "according to the various exigency of times and occasions."

The Church of England, to which the Protestant Episcopal Church in these States is indebted, under God, for her first foundation and a long continuance of nursing care and protection, hath, in the Preface of her Book of Common Prayer, laid it down as a rule, that "The particular Forms of Divine Worship, and the Rites and Ceremonies appointed to be used therein, being things in their own nature indifferent, and alterable, and so acknowledged; it is but reasonable that upon weighty and important considerations, according to the various exigency of times and occasions, such changes and alterations should be made therein, as to those that are in place of Authority should, from time to time, seem either necessary or expedient."

The same Church hath not only in her Preface, but likewise in her Articles and Homilies, declared the necessity and expediency of occasional alterations and amendments in her Forms of Public Worship; and we find accordingly, that, seeking to keep the happy mean between too much stiffness in refusing, and too much easiness in admitting variations in things once advisedly established, she hath, in the reign of several Princes, since the first compiling of her Liturgy in the time of Edward the Sixth, upon just and weighty considerations her thereunto moving, yielded to make such alterations in some particulars, as in their respective times were thought convenient; yet so as that the main body and essential parts of the same (as well in the chiefest materials, as in the frame and order thereof) have still been continued firm and unshaken.

Her general aim in these different reviews and alterations hath been, as she further declares in her said Preface, to do that which, according to her best understanding, might most tend to the preservation of peace and unity in the Church; the procuring of reverence, and the exciting of piety and devotion in the worship of God; and, finally, the cutting off occasion, from them that seek occasion, of cavil or quarrel against her Liturgy. And although, according to her judgment, there be not any thing in it contrary to the Word of God, or to sound doctrine, or which a godly man may not with a good conscience use and submit unto, or which is not fairly defensible, if allowed such just and favourable construction as in common equity ought to be allowed to

v

Preface

all human writings; yet upon the principles already laid down, it cannot but be supposed that further alterations would in time be found expedient. Accordingly, a Commission for a review was issued in the year 1689: but this great and good work miscarried at that time; and the Civil Authority has not since thought proper to revive it by any new Commission.

But when in the course of Divine Providence, these American States became independent with respect to civil government, their ecclesiastical independence was necessarily included; and the different religious denominations of Christians in these States were left at full and equal liberty to model and organize their respective Churches, and forms of worship, and discipline, in such manner as they might judge most convenient for their future prosperity; consistently with the constitution and laws of their country.

The attention of this Church was in the first place drawn to those alterations in the Liturgy which became necessary in the prayers for our Civil Rulers, in consequence of the Revolution. And the principal care herein was to make them conformable to what ought to be the proper end of all such prayers, namely, that "Rulers may have grace, wisdom, and understanding to execute justice, and to maintain truth"; and that the people "may lead quiet and peaceable lives, in all godliness and honesty."

But while these alterations were in review before the Convention, they could not but, with gratitude to God, embrace the happy occasion which was offered to them (uninfluenced and unrestrained by any worldly authority whatsoever) to take a further review of the Public Service, and to establish such other alterations and amendments therein as might be deemed expedient.

It seems unnecessary to enumerate all the different alterations and amendments. They will appear, and it is to be hoped, the reasons of them also, upon a comparison of this with the Book of Common Prayer of the Church of England. In which it will also appear that this Church is far from intending to depart from the Church of England in any essential point of doctrine, discipline, or worship; or further than local circumstances require.

And now, this important work being brought to a conclusion, it is hoped the whole will be received and examined by every true member of our Church, and every sincere Christian, with a meek, candid, and charitable frame of mind; without prejudice or prepossessions; seriously considering what Christianity is, and what the truths of the Gospel are; and earnestly beseeching Almighty God to accompany with his blessing every endeavour for promulgating them to mankind in the clearest, plainest, most affecting and majestic manner, for the sake of Jesus Christ, our blessed Lord and Saviour.

Philadelphia, October, 1789.

Concerning the
Service of the Church

THE Order for Holy Communion, the Order for Morning Prayer, the Order for Evening Prayer, and the Litany, as set forth in this Book, are the regular Services appointed for Public Worship in this Church, and shall be used accordingly; *Provided*, that in addition to these Services, the Minister, in his discretion, subject to the direction of the Ordinary, may use other devotions taken from this Book or set forth by lawful authority within this Church, or from Holy Scripture; and *Provided further*, that, subject to the direction of the Ordinary, in Mission Churches or Chapels, and also, when expressly authorized by the Ordinary, in Cathedral or Parish Churches or other places, such other devotions as aforesaid may be used, when the edification of the Congregation so requires, in place of the Order for Morning Prayer, or the Order for Evening Prayer.

For Days of Fasting and Thanksgiving appointed by the Civil or Ecclesiastical Authority, and for other special occasions, for which no Service or Prayer hath been provided in this Book, the Bishop may set forth such form or forms as he shall see fit, in which case none other shall be used.

NOTE, That in the directions for the several Services in this Book, it is not intended, by the use of any particular word denoting vocal utterance, to prescribe the tone or manner of their recitation.

THE USE OF THE PSALTER AND THE LECTIONARY.

THE Old Testament is appointed for the First Lessons, and the New Testament for the Second Lessons, at Morning and Evening Prayer throughout the year.

The Psalms and Lessons to be read every day are to be found in the following Table of Psalms and Lessons for the Christian Year; except only those for the Immovable Holy Days, the Proper Psalms and Lessons for all which days are to be found in the Table for the Fixed Holy Days.

On the following days, and their eves, if any, the Proper Psalms appointed in the Tables shall be used: Christmas, Epiphany, Purification, Ash Wednesday, Annunciation, Good Friday, Easter Day, Ascension Day, Whitsunday, Trinity Sunday, Transfiguration, All Saints, and Thanksgiving Day.

But NOTE, That on other days, the Minister shall use the Psalms appointed in the Tables; or at his discretion he may use one or more of those assigned in the Psalter to the day of the month, or from the Table of Selections of

Service of the Church

Psalms. And NOTE *further*, That in the case of a Psalm which is divided into sections, the Minister may use a section or sections of such Psalm.

The Psalms and Lessons printed on the same line are intended to be used together. At any service for which more than one such set of Psalms and Lessons are appointed, the choice thereof is at the discretion of the Minister.

Any set of Psalms and Lessons appointed for the evening of any day may be read at the morning service, and any set of morning Psalms and Lessons may be read in the evening.

The starred Lessons provided for Sundays are particularly appropriate for use when Morning Prayer with one Lesson precedes the Holy Communion.

Upon any Sunday or Holy Day, the Minister may read the Epistle or the Gospel of the Day in place of the Second Lesson at Morning or Evening Prayer.

Upon any weekday, other than a Holy Day, the Psalms and Lessons appointed for any day in the same week may be read instead of those appointed for the Day.

When an Octave is observed for any Holy Day, the Psalms and Lessons for the Day may be used upon the Sunday within the Octave.

Upon special occasions the Minister may select such Psalms and Lessons as he may think suitable.

Any Lesson may be lengthened or shortened at the Minister's discretion.

HYMNS AND ANTHEMS.

HYMNS set forth and allowed by the authority of this Church, and Anthems in the words of Holy Scripture or of the Book of Common Prayer, may be sung before and after any Office in this Book, and also before and after Sermons.

Selections of Psalms

Psalms and Lessons

Days	Psalms	First Lesson	Second Lesson
FIRST SUNDAY	50	Mal. 3:1–6 & 4:4–6	Luke 1:5–25
IN ADVENT	46, 97	*Isa. 28:14–22	Heb. 12:14
Monday	1, 3	Isa. 1:1–9	Mark 1:1–13
Tuesday	7	Isa. 1:21–28	Mark 1:14–28
Wednesday	9	Isa. 2:6–19	Mark 1:29–39
Thursday	10	Isa. 4:2	Mark 1:40
Friday	22	Isa. 5:8–29	Mark 2:1–12
Saturday	28, 29	Isa. 7:1–9	Mark 2:13–22
SECOND SUNDAY	25	Isa. 52:1–10	Luke 1:26–56
IN ADVENT	119:1–16	*Isa. 55	2 Tim. 3
Monday	33	Isa. 8:5–8, 11–20	Mark 2:23—3:6
Tuesday	48	Isa. 9:18—10:4	Mark 3:7–19
Wednesday	50	Isa. 11:1–10	Mark 3:20
Thursday	62, 63	Isa. 13:1–5, 17–22	Mark 4:1–20
Friday	73	Isa. 24:16b	Mark 4:21–29
Saturday	80	Isa. 28:1–13	Mark 4:30
THIRD SUNDAY	22:23 & 99	Jer. 1:4–10, 17–19	Luke 1:57
IN ADVENT	85, 107:1–16	*Isa. 35	1 Thess. 5:12–22
Monday	84	Isa. 29:1–4, 9–14	Mark 5:1–20
Tuesday	90	Isa. 30:8–17	Mark 5:21
Ember Wednesday	1, 15	Jer. 23:9–15	Luke 12:35–48
Thursday	96	Isa. 32:1–4, 15–20	Mark 6:1–6
Ember Friday	40:1–16	Jer. 23:23–32	2 Cor. 5:5
Ember Saturday	42, 43	Mal. 2:1–9	Matt. 9:35—10:15
FOURTH SUNDAY	80	*Isa. 40:1–11	Luke 3:1–17
IN ADVENT	77, 100	Jer. 33:7–16	1 Thess. 1
Monday	116	Isa. 33:13	Luke 1:5–25
Tuesday	130, 131	Isa. 25:1–9	Luke 1:26–38
Wednesday	132	Zech. 8:1–8, 20–23	Luke 1:39–45
Thursday	144	2 Sam. 7:18	Luke 1:46–56
Friday	147	1 Sam. 2:1b–10	Luke 1:57–66
Christmas Eve	50	*Baruch* 4:36—5:9	Luke 1:67
CHRISTMAS DAY	89:1–30	Isa. 9:2–7	Luke 2:1–20
ST. STEPHEN	118	2 Chron. 24:17–22	Acts 6

x

for the Christian Year

Psalms and Lessons

MORNING PRAYER

Days	Psalms	First Lesson	Second Lesson
ST. JOHN EVAN-GELIST	23, 24	Exod. 33:12	John 13:20–26, 31–35
HOLY INNOCENTS	8, 26	Jer. 31:1–6, 15–16	Matt. 18:1–14
FIRST SUNDAY	145	*Isa. 9:2–7	Luke 2:1–20
AFTER CHRISTMAS	98, 138	Isa. 49:8–13	Heb. 2
December 29	27	Isa. 56:1–8	1 John 1
December 30	33	Isa. 59:1–3, 15b–21	1 John 2:1–17
December 31	147	Isa. 62	1 John 2:18
CIRCUMCISION	103	Deut. 30:1–10	Eph. 2:11
SECOND SUNDAY	65, 121	*Micah 4:1–5 & 5:2–4	Luke 2:21–32
AFTER CHRISTMAS	89:1–30	Isa. 44:1–8, 21–23	Col. 2:6–17
January 2	37:26	Isa. 63:7–14	1 John 3:1–11
January 3	66	Isa. 64:4	1 John 3:13
January 4	92	Isa. 65:17	1 John 4
January 5	144	Isa. 66:18–23	1 John 5
EPIPHANY	46, 100	Isa. 60:1–9	2 Cor. 4:1–6
January 7	85	Isa. 42:1–9	Matt. 3:13
January 8	65	Isa. 45:20	Mark 9:2–13
January 9	22:23 & 24	Isa. 49:8–13, 22–23	1 John 1:1–9
January 10	67, 87	Isa. 19:19	Col. 2:6–17
January 11	102:15	Jonah 4	1 Pet. 1:1–9
January 12†	50	Mal. 1:11	2 Thess. 1
FIRST SUNDAY	72, 97	Isa. 60:1–9‖	Matt. 2:1–12
AFTER EPIPHANY	92, 93	*Prov. 8:22–35	Col. 1:9
Monday	1, 3	Prov. 1:7–19	Eph. 1
Tuesday	5	Prov. 2:1–9	Eph. 2:1–10
Wednesday	7	Prov. 3:1–7, 11–12	Eph. 2:11
Thursday	9	Prov. 3:13–20	Eph. 3:1–13
Friday	10	Prov. 3:27	Eph. 3:14
Saturday	16	Prov. 4:7–18	Eph. 4:1–16
SECOND SUNDAY AFTER	118	*Zech. 8:1–8, 20–23	1 Cor. 12:12–31a
EPIPHANY	29, 99	Exod. 34:29	Mark 9:2–13
Monday	17	Prov. 4:20	Eph. 4:17

† NOTE, That the Psalms and Lessons for the dated days after the Epiphany are to be used only until the following Sunday.

‖ On January 13, read Isa. 60:10.

xii

for the Christian Year

EVENING PRAYER

Days	Psalms	First Lesson	Second Lesson
ST. JOHN EVAN-GELIST	97	Isa. 6:1–8	Rev. 1
HOLY INNOCENTS	19, 126	Isa. 54:1–13	Mark 10:13–16, 23–31
FIRST SUNDAY	68 or 27	Isa. 63:7–16	2 Pet. 1:1–12
AFTER CHRISTMAS	8, 113	Job 28:12	Matt. 11:25
December 29	20, 21:1–6	Isa. 57:13	Heb. 1
December 30	111, 112	Isa. 60:13	Heb. 2
December 31	90, 150	Deut. 10:12—11:1	Heb. 3
CIRCUMCISION	148	Deut. 30:11	Rev. 19:11–16
SECOND SUNDAY	111, 112	Prov. 9:1–6, 10	2 Cor. 4:1–6
AFTER CHRISTMAS	132	Haggai 2:1–9	Luke 2:34–40
January 2	2, 110	Isa. 63:15—64:1	Heb. 4:1–13
January 3	34	Isa. 65:8–16	Heb. 4:14—5:14
January 4	91	Isa. 66:1–2, 5–13	Heb. 6:1–12
Epiphany Eve	29, 98	Isa. 49:1–7	Luke 3:15–22
EPIPHANY	72	Isa. 61	Rom. 15:8–21
January 7	97, 99	Isa. 43:1–12	Acts 11:1–18
January 8	93, 96	Isa. 48:12–21	Acts 26:1, 13–23
January 9	48, 117	Isa. 54:1–10	Acts 28:23
January 10	138, 146	Zech. 8:11–13, 20–23	Rom. 10:1–20
January 11	147	*Tobit* 13:1b–5, 7–11	Rom. 11:13–27
January 12†	145	Isa. 9:2–7	Gal. 3:27—4:7
FIRST SUNDAY	84, 122	1 Sam. 1:21	Matt. 18:1–14
AFTER EPIPHANY	19, 67	Isa. 49:1–7	1 John 1:1–9
Monday	4, 8	Ezek. 1:2–6, 24–28	John 1:1–18
Tuesday	11, 12	Ezek. 2	John 1:19–34
Wednesday	13, 14	Ezek. 3:4–14	John 1:35
Thursday	15, 21	Ezek. 3:16–21	John 2:1–12
Friday	6, 26	Ezek. 7:10–15, 23–27	John 2:13
Saturday	27	Ezek. 11:14–20	John 3:1–13
SECOND SUNDAY	102:15 & 117	Isa. 45:1–15	Rom. 9:14–26
AFTER EPIPHANY	62, 127	Isa. 54:11	John 1:35
Monday	18:1–20	Ezek. 12:21	John 3:14–21

† NOTE, That the Psalms and Lessons for the dated days after the Epiphany are to be used only until the following Sunday.

xiii

Psalms and Lessons

MORNING PRAYER

Days	Psalms	First Lesson	Second Lesson
Tuesday	23, 24	Prov. 6:12–19	Eph. 5:1–14
Wednesday	28	Prov. 8:1–11	Eph. 5:15
Thursday	30	Prov. 8:12–20	Eph. 6
Friday	32	Prov. 8:22–35	Phil. 1:1–11
Saturday	36	Prov. 9:1–6, 13–18	Phil. 1:12–26
THIRD SUNDAY	42, 43	*Isa. 41:8–10, 17–20	John 4:1–14
AFTER EPIPHANY	11, 12	Deut. 16:18–20 & 17:8–11	James 2:1–13
Monday	39	Prov. 10:12–14, 18–21	Phil. 1:27—2:11
Tuesday	41	Prov. 10:22–29	Phil. 2:12–18
Wednesday	44	Prov. 11:9–14, 24–30	Phil. 2:19
Thursday	45	Prov. 14:26	Phil. 3:1–16
Friday	51	Prov. 15:16–23, 27–29	Phil. 3:17—4:3
Saturday	55	Prov. 16:25	Phil. 4:4
FOURTH SUNDAY	66	Isa. 61	Luke 4:16–32
AFTER EPIPHANY	18:1–20	*Deut. 4:5–13, 32–40	Eph. 2
Monday	56, 60:1–5	Prov. 20:9–12, 17–22	Col. 1:1–17
Tuesday	61, 62	Prov. 21:21	Col. 1:18—2:5
Wednesday	63, 64	Prov. 22:1–6, 17–25	Col. 2:6–19
Thursday	68:1–19	Prov. 23:20–21, 29–35	Col. 2:20—3:11
Friday	69:1–22, 30–37	Prov. 24:23	Col. 3:12–17
Saturday	77	Prov. 25:11–15, 17–22	Col. 3:18—4:6
FIFTH SUNDAY	15, 85	Ruth 1:1–17	Col. 3:5–11
AFTER EPIPHANY	112, 113	*Hab. 1:12—2:4, 9–14	Luke 12:35–48
Monday	79	Prov. 26:17	1 Pet. 1:1–12
Tuesday	82, 101	Prov. 27:1–6, 10–12	1 Pet. 1:13
Wednesday	86	Prov. 28:1–13	1 Pet. 2:1–10
Thursday	89:1–19	Prov. 29:11–25	1 Pet. 2:11–17
Friday	92	Prov. 30:4–9	1 Pet. 2:18
Saturday	97	Prov. 31:10	1 Pet. 3:1–12
SIXTH SUNDAY	75, 138	Isa. 2:6–19	Matt. 25:14–29
AFTER EPIPHANY	93, 98	*Isa. 66:1–2, 10, 12–16, 18–23	2 Thess. 1

for the Christian Year

EVENING PRAYER

Days	Psalms	First Lesson	Second Lesson
Tuesday	25	Ezek. 13:1–9	John 3:22
Wednesday	31	Ezek. 14:1–11	John 4:1–14
Thursday	33	Ezek. 14:12–20	John 4:15–26
Friday	40:1–16	Ezek. 18:1–4, 19–23	John 4:27–42
Saturday	34	Ezek. 18:26	John 4:43
THIRD SUNDAY	27, 134	Isa. 56:1–8	John 2:13
AFTER EPIPHANY	103	Isa. 54:1–8	Rom. 14:1—15:3
Monday	37:1–24	Ezek. 27:1–5, 26–36	John 5:1–15
Tuesday	46, 47	Ezek. 33:1–9	John 5:16–29
Wednesday	49	Ezek. 33:10–20	John 5:30
Thursday	50	Ezek. 33:23	John 6:1–14
Friday	54, 57	Ezek. 34:1–10	John 6:15–29
Saturday	29, 99	Ezek. 34:11–16	John 6:30–40
FOURTH SUNDAY	145	Isa. 45:20	Rom. 10
AFTER EPIPHANY	30, 36:5	Dan. 10:10–19	Mark 6:45
Monday	65	Ezek. 34:25	John 6:41–59
Tuesday	71	Ezek. 36:22–28	John 6:60
Wednesday	72	Ezek. 37:1–14	John 7:1–13
Thursday	73	Ezek. 37:21b	John 7:14–24
Friday	75, 76	Ezek. 39:21	John 7:25–36
Saturday	19, 67	Ezek. 43:1–9	John 7:37
FIFTH SUNDAY	21, 22:23	Joel 3:9–17	Matt. 13:36–52
AFTER EPIPHANY	7	Amos 5:14–24	Gal. 6:1–10
Monday	81	Isa. 14:3–11	1 Thess. 1
Tuesday	90	Isa. 14:12–20	1 Thess. 2:1–13
Wednesday	91	Isa. 22:1–5, 12–14	1 Thess. 2:17—3:13
Thursday	94	Isa. 24:1–6, 10–16a	1 Thess. 4:1–12
Friday	102	Isa. 31	1 Thess. 4:13
Saturday	84, 122	Isa. 47:1, 7–15	1 Thess. 5:1–11
SIXTH SUNDAY AFTER EPIPHANY	9	Gen. 19:1–3, 12–17, 24–28	Luke 17:20
	76, 96	2 Esdras 8:63—9:13	2 Pet. 3:1–14, 17–18

Psalms and Lessons

MORNING PRAYER

Days	Psalms	First Lesson	Second Lesson
Monday	99, 100	Lam. 1:1–6	1 Pet. 3:13
Tuesday	107:1–16	Lam. 1:15	1 Pet. 4:1–6
Wednesday	111, 112	Lam. 2:1–10	1 Pet. 4:7–11
Thursday	115	Lam. 4:1–6, 9	1 Pet. 4:12
Friday	106	Lam. 4:11–20	1 Pet. 5:1–7
Saturday	118	Lam. 5	1 Pet. 5:8
SEPTUAGESIMA	20, 121	*Joshua 1:1–9	2 Tim. 2:1–13
SUNDAY	1 & 18:21–35 or 1 & 125	Ezek. 3:4–11	Matt. 5:1–16
Monday	123, 127	Gen. 1:1–19	Mark 6:7–13
Tuesday	135	Gen. 1:20—2:3	Mark 6:14–29
Wednesday	137:1–6 & 140	Gen. 2:4–9, 16–25	Mark 6:30–44
Thursday	141	Gen. 3	Mark 6:45
Friday	143	Gen. 4:1–16	Mark 7:1–13
Saturday	149	Gen. 6:5–8, 13–22	Mark 7:14–23
SEXAGESIMA	71	*Isa. 50:4–10	2 Cor. 12:1–12
SUNDAY	33	Isa. 30:8–21	Mark 4:26–34
Monday	2, 3	Gen. 7:1, 7–10, 17–23	Mark 7:24
Tuesday	5	Gen. 8:6	Mark 8:11–26
Wednesday	7	Gen. 9:8–17	Mark 8:27—9:1
Thursday	9	Gen. 11:1–9	Mark 9:2–13
Friday	22	Gen. 11:27—12:8	Mark 9:14–29
Saturday	16	Gen. 13:2, 5–18	Mark 9:30–37
QUINQUAGESIMA	103	*Wisdom 7:7–14*	John 15:1–17
SUNDAY	19, 23	*Deut. 10:12–15, 17—11:1	1 John 2:1–17
Monday	18:1–20	Gen. 18:1–16	Mark 9:38
Tuesday	18:21–36	Gen. 18:20	Mark 10:1–16
ASH WEDNESDAY	32, 143	Isa. 58:1–12	Heb. 12:1–14
Thursday	27	Gen. 19:1–3, 12–17, 24–28	1 Cor. 1:1–17
Friday	95 & 40:1–16	Gen. 21:9–21	1 Cor. 1:18
Saturday	28	Gen. 22:1–14, 19	1 Cor. 2
FIRST SUNDAY	50	*Isa. 58	Matt. 6:1–18
IN LENT	3, 62	*Ecclus. 2*	Rom. 7:14
Monday	36	Gen. 24:1–27	1 Cor. 3:1–17

for the Christian Year

Psalms and Lessons

MORNING PRAYER

Days	Psalms	First Lesson	Second Lesson
Tuesday	37:1–24	Gen. 24:28–38, 49–51, 58–67	1 Cor. 3:18—4:5
Ember Wednesday	26	Ezek. 2	Matt. 9:1–13
Thursday	37:26	Gen. 25:28	1 Cor. 4:6
Ember Friday	95 & 84	Ezek. 34:1–16	Matt. 10:24–33, 37–42
Ember Saturday	101	Ezek. 34:17–25, 30–31	2 Tim. 2:1–15
SECOND SUNDAY IN LENT	86, 142 30, 32	*1 Kings 8:37–43 Ezek. 18:1–4, 25–32	Col. 3:12–17 Matt. 5:27–37
Monday	39	Gen. 27:1–29	1 Cor. 5
Tuesday	41	Gen. 27:30–40	1 Cor. 6:1–11
Wednesday	56	Gen. 27:46—28:4, 10–22	1 Cor. 6:12
Thursday	62	Gen. 29:1–13, 18–20	1 Cor. 7:1–17
Friday	95 & 54, 61	Gen. 32:22–31	1 Cor. 8
Saturday	63	Gen. 35:1–7, 16–20	1 Cor. 9:1–14
THIRD SUNDAY IN LENT	25 34	*Deut. 6:1–9, 20–25 Zech. 1:1–6, 12–17	1 Cor. 3 Mark 8:27—9:1
Monday	68:1–19	Gen. 37:3–28, 36	1 Cor. 9:15
Tuesday	74	Gen. 40	1 Cor. 10:1–13
Wednesday	75, 76	Gen. 41:1a, 8, 14–24	1 Cor. 10:14–22
Thursday	85	Gen. 41:25–40	1 Cor. 10:23—11:1
Friday	95 & 79	Gen. 42:1–26, 29a, 35–38	1 Cor. 11:17
Saturday	89:1–19	Gen. 43:1–5, 11–16, 26–34	1 Cor. 12:1–11
FOURTH SUNDAY IN LENT	147 18:1–20	Exod. 16:4–15 *Ezek. 39:21	John 6:27–40 2 Cor. 3:12
Monday	90	Gen. 44	1 Cor. 12:12–31a
Tuesday	93, 96	Gen. 45	1 Cor. 12:31b—13:13
Wednesday	94	Gen. 47:29–31 & 48:8–20	1 Cor. 14:1–12
Thursday	104	Gen. 49:33—50:26	1 Cor. 14:13–25

for the Christian Year

EVENING PRAYER

Days	Psalms	First Lesson	Second Lesson
Tuesday	46, 47	Jer. 4:1–9	John 9:24
Ember Wednesday	4, 16	Ezek. 3:16	2 Cor. 4
Thursday	49	Jer. 4:11–22	John 10:1–10
Ember Friday	77	Ezek. 37:1–14	1 Tim. 4
Ember Saturday	19, 23	Ezek. 37:21b	1 Tim. 6:6
SECOND	26, 119:1–16	2 Sam. 12:1–10,	1 Cor. 6:9
SUNDAY		13–14	
IN LENT	31	*Ecclus.* 51:1–12	Luke 18:1–8
Monday	50	Jer. 4:23	John 10:11–21
Tuesday	51	Jer. 5:1–9	John 10:22–38
Wednesday	65, 67	Jer. 5:10–19	John 11:1–16
Thursday	66	Jer. 5:20	John 11:17–27
Friday	69:1–22, 30–37	Jer. 6:1–8	John 11:28–44
Saturday	72	Jer. 6:9–21	John 11:45
THIRD	119:113–128 &	Amos 5:4–15	Gal. 5:16–24
SUNDAY	143		
IN LENT	27	Prov. 4:7–18	Luke 11:29–36
Monday	71	Jer. 7:1–15	Mark 10:17–31
Tuesday	73	Jer. 7:21–29	Mark 10:32–45
Wednesday	77	Jer. 8:4–13	Mark 10:46
Thursday	80	Jer. 9:2–16	Mark 11:12–26
Friday	86	Jer. 9:17–24	Mark 12:1–12
Saturday	103	Jer. 10:1–13	Mark 12:13–17
FOURTH SUNDAY	116	Isa. 55	John 6:41–51
IN LENT	46, 122	2 Esdras 2:15–32	Rev. 3:1–12
Monday	91	Jer. 13:15	Mark 12:18–27
Tuesday	92	Jer. 14:1–10	Mark 12:28–37
Wednesday	97, 98	Jer. 15:1–9	Mark 12:38
Thursday	99, 100	Jer. 15:10	Mark 13:1–13

Psalms and Lessons

MORNING PRAYER

Days	Psalms	First Lesson	Second Lesson
Friday	95 & 102	Exod. 1:8–14, 22	1 Cor. 14:26
Saturday	108:1–6 & 112	Exod. 2:1–22	1 Cor. 15:1–11
FIFTH SUNDAY	51	*Isa. 1:10–20	1 Pet. 4:12
IN LENT	71	Deut. 18:15	Luke 20:9–18
Monday	119:1–16	Exod. 3:1–15	1 Cor. 15:12–19
Tuesday	123, 127	Exod. 4:10–18, 27–31	1 Cor. 15:20–34
Wednesday	128, 129	Exod. 5:1–9, 19—6:1	1 Cor. 15:35–49
Thursday	144	Exod. 11:1–8	1 Cor. 15:50
Friday	95 & 141:1–4, 146	Exod. 12:21–28	1 Cor. 16:1–14
Saturday	147	Exod. 12:29–39, 42	1 Cor. 16:15
SIXTH SUNDAY	24, 97	*Zech. 9:9–12	Mark 11:1–11
IN LENT	22	Isa. 52:13—53:12	Matt. 26
Mon. before Easter	71	Isa. 42:1–7	John 14:1–14
Tues. before Easter	6, 12	Hosea 14	John 15:1–16
Wed. before Easter	94	Zech. 12:9–10 & 13:1, 7–9	John 16:1–15
Maundy Thursday	116	Jer. 31:31–34	John 13:18
GOOD FRIDAY	22, 40:1–16, 54	Gen. 22:1–18 or *Wisdom* 2:1, 12–24	John 18
Easter Even	14, 16	Job 14:1–14	John 19:38 or Heb. 4
EASTER	93, 111	*Isa. 25:1–9	Matt. 28:1–10, 16–20
DAY	57	Exod. 12:1–14	Rev. 14:1–7, 12–13
Easter Monday	2	Isa. 61:1–3, 10–11	Luke 24:1–12
Easter Tuesday	30	Dan. 12:1–4, 13	1 Thess. 4:13
Wednesday	97, 99	Micah 7:7–9, 18–20	1 Tim. 6:11–19
Thursday	149, 150	Ezek. 37:1–14	Phil. 3:7
Friday	124, 125, 126	Isa. 65:17	Rev. 1:4–18
Saturday	145	Isa. 25:1–9	Rev. 7:9

for the Christian Year

EVENING PRAYER

Days	Psalms	First Lesson	Second Lesson
Friday	107	Jer. 16:5–13	Mark 13:14–23
Saturday	118	Jer. 17:5–14	Mark 13:24
FIFTH SUNDAY	42, 43	Hosea 6:1–6	Heb. 10:1–25
IN LENT	40:1–16	Jer. 14:7–21	John 10:17–38
Monday	119:17–32 & 117	Jer. 20:7–13	John 12:1–11
Tuesday	120, 121, 122	Jer. 22:10–23	John 12:12–19
Wednesday	132	Jer. 28:1–2, 10–17	John 12:20–33
Thursday	133, 134, 137:1–6	Jer. 30:12–17, 23–24	John 12:34–43
Friday	139	Jer. 32:36–42	John 12:44
Saturday	145	Jer. 33:1–9, 14–16	John 13:1–17
SIXTH SUNDAY	130, 138	Jer. 8:9–15, 18—9:1	1 Cor. 1:17
IN LENT	77	Isa. 59:1–3, 9–21	John 12:20–36
Mon. before Easter	42, 43	Lam. 1:7–12	John 14:15
Tues. before Easter	51	Lam. 2:10, 13–19	John 15:17
Wed. before Easter	74	Lam. 3:1, 14–33	John 16:16
Maundy Thursday	142, 143	Lam. 3:40–58	John 17
GOOD FRIDAY	69:1–22 & 88	Isa. 52:13—53:12	1 Pet. 2:11
Easter Even	27	Job 19:21–27a	Rom. 6:3–11
EASTER	98, 114	Isa. 51:9–16	Luke 24:13–35
DAY	118	Isa. 12	John 20:11–18
Easter Monday	103	Exod. 15:1–13	John 20:1–10
Easter Tuesday	115	Isa. 30:18–21	John 20:11–18
Wednesday	148	Isa. 26:12–16, 19	John 20:19–23
Thursday	147	Isa. 52:1–10	John 20:24
Friday	110, 114	Zeph. 3:14	John 21:1–14
Saturday	18:1–20	Jer. 31:10–14	John 21:15

Psalms and Lessons

MORNING PRAYER

Days	Psalms	First Lesson	Second Lesson
FIRST SUNDAY	66	*Wisdom* 2:23—3:9	Rom. 1:1–12
AFTER EASTER	103	*Isa. 43:1–12	Luke 24:36–49
Monday	1, 3	Exod. 13:3–16	Heb. 1
Tuesday	5	Exod. 13:17—14:4	Heb. 2:1–8
Wednesday	22:23	Exod. 14:5–14, 19–21, 24–28, 30	Heb. 2:9
Thursday	28	Exod. 15:20	Heb. 3
Friday	40:1–16	Exod. 16:1–7, 13b–15	Heb. 4:1–13
Saturday	42, 43	Exod. 17:1–7	Heb. 4:14—5:14
SECOND SUNDAY	23, 146	*Isa. 40:1–11	John 10:1–10
AFTER EASTER	34	*Baruch* 4:21–30	Phil. 3:7–16
Monday	49	Exod. 17:8	Heb. 6:1–12
Tuesday	50	Exod. 18:1–12	Heb. 6:13
Wednesday	63	Exod. 18:13	Heb. 7:1–11
Thursday	66	Exod. 19:1–7, 16–20	Heb. 7:12
Friday	51	Exod. 20:1–21	Heb. 8
Saturday	72	Exod. 24:1–11, 16–18	Heb. 9:1–14
THIRD SUNDAY	36:5 & 138	2 Sam. 12:15b–23	John 14:1–14
AFTER EASTER	113, 124	*1 Sam. 2:1b–10	Acts 2:22–36
Monday	85	Exod. 25:1–11, 17–22	Heb. 9:15
Tuesday	86	Exod. 28:1–4, 29–38	Heb. 10:1–14
Wednesday	89:1–19	Exod. 32:1–7, 15–20	Heb. 10:15–25
Thursday	91	Exod. 32:21–24, 30–34	Heb. 10:26
Friday	94	Exod. 33:7	Heb. 11:1–16
Saturday	99, 100	Exod. 34:1–10, 29–35	Heb. 11:17–31
FOURTH SUNDAY	116	*Job 19:21–27a	John 12:44
AFTER EASTER	107:1–16	Ezek. 37:1–14	Acts 3:1–21
Monday	110, 114	Num. 10:29	Heb. 11:32
Tuesday	124, 126	Num. 11:4–6, 10–15, 23, 31–32	Heb. 12:1–17
Wednesday	128, 129	Num. 12	Heb. 12:18

for the Christian Year

EVENING PRAYER

Days	Psalms	First Lesson	Second Lesson
FIRST SUNDAY	33	Zeph. 3:14	John 20:19
AFTER EASTER	30, 121	2 Esdras 2:33	Rev. 1:4–18
Monday	4, 11	Isa. 40:1–11	1 Pet. 1:1–12
Tuesday	15, 24	Isa. 40:12–17	1 Pet. 1:13
Wednesday	25	Isa. 40:18, 21–31	1 Pet. 2:1–10
Thursday	29, 46	Isa. 42:1–9	1 Pet. 2:11–17
Friday	39	Isa. 42:10–17	1 Pet. 2:18
Saturday	93, 111	Isa. 43:1–7	1 Pet. 3:1–12
SECOND SUNDAY	145	Ezek. 34:11–16, 30–31	John 21:1–19
AFTER EASTER	16, 100	2 Esdras 8:20–30, 46, 51–54	1 Cor. 15:12–23
Monday	47, 48	Isa. 43:8–13	1 Pet. 3:13
Tuesday	61, 62	Isa. 43:15–21 & 44:1–3	1 Pet. 4:1–6
Wednesday	65	Isa. 44:6–8, 21–23	1 Pet. 4:7–11
Thursday	71	Isa. 44:9–20	1 Pet. 4:12
Friday	73	Isa. 44:24—45:4	1 Pet. 5:1–7
Saturday	33	Isa. 45:5–12, 15–19	1 Pet. 5:8
THIRD SUNDAY	68:1–20	Isa. 26:12–16, 19	2 Cor. 5
AFTER EASTER	115	*Wisdom* 5:1–6, 14–16	Luke 20:27–39
Monday	77	Isa. 45:20	Eph. 1:1–14
Tuesday	84, 117	Isa. 46:3–4, 9–13	Eph. 1:15
Wednesday	90	Isa. 48:12–21	Eph. 2:1–10
Thursday	97, 98	Isa. 49:1–12	Eph. 2:11
Friday	103	Isa. 49:13–23	Eph. 3:1–12
Saturday	23, 30	Isa. 50:4–10	Eph. 3:13
FOURTH SUNDAY	18:1–20	Dan. 12:1–4, 13	1 Thess. 4:13
AFTER EASTER	27	Isa. 60:13	John 8:12–30
Monday	111, 113	Isa. 51:1–11	Eph. 4:1–16
Tuesday	121, 122	Isa. 51:12–16	Eph. 4:17
Wednesday	135	Isa. 52:1–2, 7–12	Eph. 5:1–14

Psalms and Lessons

MORNING PRAYER

Days	Psalms	First Lesson	Second Lesson
Thursday	132	Num. 13:17–26, 30–33	Heb. 13:1–8
Friday	143	Num. 14:1–10	Heb. 13:9–16
Saturday	146, 149	Num. 14:11–25	Heb. 13:17
FIFTH SUNDAY	65, 67	*Ezek. 34:25	Luke 11:1–13
AFTER EASTER	118	2 Esdras 14:27–35	Acts 4:1–13, 33
Rogation Monday	104	Deut. 8:1–11, 17–20	Matt. 6:5–15
Rogation Tuesday	80	Deut. 11:10–17	Matt. 6:24
Rogation Wednesday	144	Jer. 14:1–9	1 John 5:5–15
ASCENSION DAY	96	Dan. 7:9–10, 13–14	Eph. 4:1–16
Friday	15, 108:1–5	Micah 4:1–7	Rom. 8:31
Saturday	45	Gen. 49:1–2, 8–10	2 Thess. 2:13
SUNDAY	21:1–6 & 24	*Isa. 33:5–6, 17, 20–22	John 17
AFTER	8, 108:1–5	Isa. 4:2	Heb. 4:14—5:10
ASCENSION	72	Isa. 65:17	Rev. 21:1–14, 21–27
Monday	2	1 Sam. 2:1b–10	Rev. 5
Tuesday	92	2 Sam. 7:18	Rev. 11:15
Wednesday	21:1–6 & 23	Isa. 4:2	Rev. 19:11–16
Thursday	66	2 Kings 2:1–15	Rev. 21:1–8
Friday	115	Isa. 35	Rev. 21:9
Saturday	81	Zech. 8:1–8, 20–23	Rev. 22:1–17
WHITSUNDAY	68 or 18:1–20	*Wisdom* 1:1–7	John 4:19–26
	145	*Joel 2:28	Rom. 8:1–11
Whit Monday	139	*Wisdom* 9:1–6	1 Cor. 3:9–17
Whit Tuesday	148	Ezek. 36:22–28	1 Cor. 12:1–13
Ember Wednesday	132	*Ecclus.* 39:1–8	1 Cor. 2
Thursday	48	Isa. 44:1–8, 21–23	Gal. 5:16–25
Ember Friday	122, 125	Isa. 61:1–9	2 Cor. 3
Ember Saturday	19	Micah 3:5–8	2 Tim. 1:1–14
TRINITY	29, 99	*Isa. 6:1–8	1 Pet. 1:1–12
SUNDAY	33	Gen. 1:1—2:3	John 1:1–18

for the Christian Year

EVENING PRAYER

Days	Psalms	First Lesson	Second Lesson
Thursday	145	Isa. 54:1–10	Eph. 5:15
Friday	130, 138	Isa. 54:11	Eph. 6:1–9
Saturday	148, 150	Isa. 55	Eph. 6:10
FIFTH SUNDAY	147	Isa. 48:12–21	Rev. 5
AFTER EASTER	144	Ezek. 36:25	Mark 11:22–26
Rogation Monday	34	Deut. 28:1–14	James 1:1–17
Rogation Tuesday	65, 67	1 Kings 8:22–30	James 4:8
Ascension Eve	93, 99	*Three Children* 29–37	Luke 24:44
ASCENSION DAY	24, 47	Isa. 33:5–6, 17, 20–22	Heb. 4:14—5:10
Friday	20, 29	Isa. 12	Acts 1:12
Saturday	8, 98	Jer. 23:5–8	Acts 2:1–21
SUNDAY	93, 96	*Wisdom 9*	Eph. 1
AFTER	46, 47	Isa. 32:1–4, 15–20	John 3:16–21, 31–36a
ASCENSION	97, 110	Dan. 7:9–10, 13–14	Rev. 22
Monday	147	Isa. 66:1–2, 10–13	Acts 2:22–36
Tuesday	57, 138	Isa. 26:1–7	Acts 2:37
Wednesday	33	Isa. 25:1–9	Acts 3:1–10
Thursday	72	Isa. 9:2–7	Acts 3:11
Friday	116, 117	2 Sam. 22:32–34, 44–51	Acts 4:1–12
Whitsun Eve	46, 133	Deut. 16:9–12	Rom. 8:12–18
WHITSUNDAY	104	*Wisdom 7:22—8:1*	1 Cor. 2
	48, 122	Isa. 11:1–9	John 6:53–69
Whit Monday	103	Jer. 31:31–34	Acts 4:13–22
Whit Tuesday	145	Num. 11:16–17, 24–30	Acts 4:23
Ember Wednesday	84	*Wisdom 9:9–11, 17–18*	Acts 5:12–28
Thursday	18:1–20	*Wisdom 11:21—12:2*	Acts 5:29
Ember Friday	43, 134	Isa. 52:1–10	Acts 6
Trinity Eve	111, 113	Num. 6:22	2 Cor. 13:5
TRINITY	98, 100	*Ecclus.* 43:1–12, 27–33	Eph. 4:1–16
SUNDAY	148, 150	Job 38:1–11, 16–18 & 42:1–6	John 1:29–34

Psalms and Lessons

MORNING PRAYER

Days	Psalms	First Lesson	Second Lesson
Monday	2, 3	Num. 16:1–14	Luke 1:1–25
Tuesday	5	Num. 16:15–35	Luke 1:26–38
Wednesday	7	Num. 17:1–11	Luke 1:39–56
Thursday	9	Num. 20:1–13	Luke 1:57–66
Friday	10	Num. 20:14	Luke 1:67
Saturday	13, 14	Num. 21:4–9	Luke 2:1–20
FIRST SUNDAY	73	*Jer. 23:23–32	Matt. 7:13–14, 21–29
AFTER TRINITY	89:1–19	Isa. 5:8–12, 18–24	James 5
	90	Gen. 3	Rom. 5
Monday	28	Num. 22:2–14	Luke 2:21–40
Tuesday	32	Num. 22:15–21, 36–40	Luke 2:41
Wednesday	37:1–24	Num. 22:41—23:12	Luke 3:1–22
Thursday	37:26	Num. 23:13–26	Luke 4:1–13
Friday	40:1–16	Num. 23:27—24:13, 25	Luke 4:14–30
Saturday	44	Deut. 34	Luke 4:31–41
SECOND SUNDAY	15, 19	Job 31:13–28	1 Cor. 13
	76, 125	*Deut. 20:1–9	Luke 9:57
AFTER TRINITY	11, 12	Gen. 6:5–8, 13–22	Matt. 24:32–42
Monday	48	Joshua 1	Luke 4:42—5:11
Tuesday	49	Joshua 3:1–6, 13–17	Luke 5:12–26
Wednesday	57	Joshua 4:1–8	Luke 5:27
Thursday	63	Joshua 6:1–7, 11, 14–20	Luke 6:1–11
Friday	71	Joshua 14:6	Luke 6:12–26
Saturday	73	Joshua 23:1–3, 11–16	Luke 6:27–38
THIRD SUNDAY	145	*Jer. 31:1–14	Matt. 9:9–13
	25	Prov. 16:18–24, 32	Phil. 1:27—2:4
AFTER TRINITY	27	Gen. 9:1–17	1 Pet. 3:17—4:6
Monday	86	Judges 5:1–18	Luke 6:39
Tuesday	89:1–19	Judges 5:19	Luke 7:1–10
Wednesday	92	Judges 6:1, 11–16, 33–35	Luke 7:11–17
Thursday	94	Judges 7:1–8	Luke 7:18–35
Friday	102	Judges 7:16	Luke 7:36
Saturday	107:1–16	Judges 10:17, 11:29–40	Luke 8:1–15

xxvi

for the Christian Year

EVENING PRAYER

Days	Psalms	First Lesson	Second Lesson
Monday	4, 8	Ezra 1:1–8	Acts 7:1–16
Tuesday	16, 20	Ezra 4:7,11–24	Acts 7:17–34
Wednesday	25	Haggai 1:1–8, 12–15	Acts 7:35–53
Thursday	27	Haggai 2:1–9	Acts 7:54—8:4
Friday	6, 26	Zech. 1:7–17	Acts 8:5–25
Saturday	29, 30	Zech. 2	Acts 8:26
FIRST SUNDAY	119:33–48	Deut. 30:11	John 13:1–17, 34–35
AFTER	49	Job 21:17–33	Luke 16:19
TRINITY	85	1 Sam. 1:1–11, 19–20	Acts 6
Monday	31	Ezra 5:1–2, 6–17	Acts 9:1–19
Tuesday	33	Ezra 6:1–12	Acts 9:20–31
Wednesday	34	Ezra 6:13–18	Acts 9:32
Thursday	39	Zech. 7:8	Acts 10:1–23
Friday	41, 54	Zech. 8:1–13	Acts 10:24–33
Saturday	46, 47	Zech. 8:14	Acts 10:34
SECOND	112, 113	1 Sam. 20:1–7, 12–42	1 Pet. 1:17
SUNDAY	138, 146	2 Kings 4:8–17	Luke 14:12–24
AFTER TRINITY	147	1 Sam. 3:1–18	Acts 7:44—8:4
Monday	42, 43	Ezra 7:1, 6–16, 25–28	Acts 11:1–18
Tuesday	50	Ezra 8:15a, 21–23, 31–36	Acts 11:19
Wednesday	61, 62	Neh. 1	Acts 12:1–24
Thursday	65	Neh. 2:1–8	Acts 12:25—13:12
Friday	77	Neh. 2:9	Acts 13:13–25
Saturday	66	Neh. 4:6	Acts 13:26–43
THIRD	32, 36:5	Jer. 23:1–8	Luke 19:2–10
SUNDAY	103	Ezek. 34:20–24	Luke 15:1–10
AFTER TRINITY	72	1 Sam. 8	Acts 8:5–25
Monday	84, 85	Neh. 5:1–13	Acts 13:44—14:7
Tuesday	90	Neh. 8:1–3, 5–6, 9–12	Acts 14:8–18
Wednesday	104	Neh. 9:5–15	Acts 14:19
Thursday	111, 114	Neh. 9:32	Acts 15:1–12
Friday	116	Neh. 13:15–22	Acts 15:13–21
Saturday	93, 99	1 Macc. 1:1, 7–15	Acts 15:22–35

Psalms and Lessons

MORNING PRAYER

Days	Psalms	First Lesson	Second Lesson
FOURTH	91	*Lam. 3:22–33	Matt. 10:24–39
SUNDAY	75, 82	Deut. 32:1–4, 34–39	Rom. 2:1–16
AFTER TRINITY	22:23 & 67	Gen. 12:1–9	Gal. 3:1–9
Monday	119:49–64	Judges 13:2–14, 24	Luke 8:16–25
Tuesday	123, 124	Judges 16:4–14	Luke 8:26–39
Wednesday	125, 138	Judges 16:15–22]	Luke 8:40
Thursday	136	Judges 16:23	Luke 9:1–17
Friday	142, 143	Ruth 1:1–14	Luke 9:18–27
Saturday	147	Ruth 1:15	Luke 9:28–45
FIFTH	62, 63	*Eccles. 2:1–11, 18–23	Matt. 19:16
SUNDAY	34	Prov. 15:1–10, 26	James 3
AFTER TRINITY	1, 121	Gen. 17:1–8	Heb. 11:1–16
Monday	11, 12	Ruth 2:1–13	Luke 9:46
Tuesday	17	Ruth 2:14	Luke 10:1–24
Wednesday	20, 21:1–6	Ruth 3:1–13	Luke 10:25–37
Thursday	25	Ruth 4:1–8	Luke 10:38—11:13
Friday	26	Ruth 4:9–17	Luke 11:14–28
Saturday	28	1 Sam. 1:1–11	Luke 11:29–36
SIXTH	85	2 Sam. 19:16–23	Matt. 5:38
SUNDAY	16, 111	*Isa. 57:13b–19	2 Tim. 2:7–13
AFTER TRINITY	71	Gen. 18:1–16	Rom. 4:13
Monday	39	1 Sam. 1:12–20	Luke 11:37
Tuesday	45	1 Sam. 1:21–28, 2:11	Luke 12:1–12
Wednesday	56	1 Sam. 2:18–26	Luke 12:13–21
Thursday	65	1 Sam. 3:1–18	Luke 12:22–34
Friday	69:1–22, 30–37	1 Sam. 4:1b–11	Luke 12:35–48
Saturday	72	1 Sam. 4:12	Luke 12:49
SEVENTH	18:1–20	*Hosea 14	Rom. 6:12–18
SUNDAY	133, 134, 138	*Ecclus.* 6:5–17	John 15:12
AFTER TRINITY	40:1–16	Gen. 22:1–18	Heb. 6
Monday	75, 76	1 Sam. 8:4	Luke 13:1–9
Tuesday	77	1 Sam. 9:1–10	Luke 13:10–21

for the Christian Year

EVENING PRAYER

Days	Psalms	First Lesson	Second Lesson
FOURTH	51	Isa. 29:9–15	Matt. 15:1–20
SUNDAY	139	Prov. 27:1–6, 10–12	Luke 6:36–42
AFTER TRINITY	80	1 Sam. 9:1–10, 18–19, 26—10:1	Acts 8:26
Monday	119:65–80 & 117	*1 Macc.* 1:41–53	Acts 15:36—16:5
Tuesday	126, 127, 130	*1 Macc.* 1:54	Acts 16:6–15
Wednesday	132, 134	*1 Macc.* 2:1–14	Acts 16:16–24
Thursday	144	*1 Macc.* 2:15–30	Acts 16:25
Friday	145	*1 Macc.* 2:31–43	Acts 17:1–15
Saturday	148, 150	*1 Macc.* 2:49–52, 61–70	Acts 17:16
FIFTH	66	Prov. 3:1–7, 11–12	Luke 14:25
SUNDAY	65	Judges 6:11–23	Luke 5:1–11
AFTER TRINITY	97, 98	1 Sam. 11	Acts 9:1–20
Monday	8, 19	*1 Macc.* 3:1–9	Acts 18:1–11
Tuesday	13, 14	*1 Macc.* 3:42–54	Acts 18:12–23
Wednesday	27	*1 Macc.* 4:36–51	Acts 18:24—19:7
Thursday	30, 31:1–6	*1 Macc.* 4:52	Acts 19:8–20
Friday	32, 36:5	Dan. 1:1–7, 17–21	Acts 19:21
Saturday	47, 48	Dan. 2:1–6, 10–13	Acts 20:1–16
SIXTH	57, 130	Exod. 24:1–11, 16–18	Heb. 9:18
SUNDAY	94:1–22	Gen. 4:1–16	Matt. 5:20–26
AFTER TRINITY	104	1 Sam. 16:1–13	Acts 11:1–18
Monday	42, 43	Dan. 2:14–24	Acts 20:17
Tuesday	49	Dan. 2:25–35	Acts 21:1–14
Wednesday	62, 63	Dan. 2:36–45	Acts 21:15–26
Thursday	66	Dan. 3:1–7	Acts 21:27–36
Friday	71	Dan. 3:8–18	Acts 21:37—22:16
Saturday	15, 46	Dan. 3:19	Acts 22:17–29
SEVENTH SUNDAY	50	Dan. 5:1–9, 13–30	Rom. 1:17–21, 28–32
AFTER TRINITY	116	Micah 7:14	Mark 8:1–21
	24, 29	1 Sam. 17:1–11, 32, 40–50	Acts 11:19
Monday	73	Dan. 4:4–5, 10–18	Acts 22:30–23:11
Tuesday	74	Dan. 4:19–27	Acts 23:12–24

Psalms and Lessons

MORNING PRAYER

Days	Psalms	First Lesson	Second Lesson
Wednesday	80	1 Sam. 9:11–21	Luke 13:22
Thursday	85	1 Sam. 9:22	Luke 14:1–14
Friday	86	1 Sam. 10:1–11	Luke 14:15–24
Saturday	90	1 Sam. 10:17	Luke 14:25
EIGHTH	119:33–48	*Ecclus.* 1:18–27	John 7:14–24
SUNDAY	126, 127	Zech. 4:1–10	Gal. 3:24—4:7
AFTER TRINITY	84	Gen. 24:1–27	Eph. 5:22
Monday	104	1 Sam. 11:1–13	Luke 15:1–10
Tuesday	111, 114	1 Sam. 11:14—12:5	Luke 15:11
Wednesday	119:81–96	1 Sam. 12:19	Luke 16:1–18
Thursday	128, 129	1 Sam. 15:1–9	Luke 16:19
Friday	139	1 Sam. 15:10–23	Luke 17:1–10
Saturday	145	1 Sam. 15:24–34	Luke 17:11–19
NINTH	115	Ezek. 14:1–11	1 Thess. 4:1–12
SUNDAY	103	*Wisdom* 11:21—12:2	John 8:1–11
AFTER TRINITY	91	Gen. 28:10	2 Cor. 9
Monday	2, 3	1 Sam. 16:1–13	Luke 17:20
Tuesday	5	1 Sam. 16:14	Luke 18:1–14
Wednesday	9	1 Sam. 17:1–11	Luke 18:15–30
Thursday	10	1 Sam. 17:17–27	Luke 18:31
Friday	22	1 Sam. 17:28–40	Luke 19:1–10
Saturday	18:1–20	1 Sam. 17:41–51	Luke 19:11–28
TENTH	145	*Ecclus.* 1:1–10	John 8:25–36
SUNDAY	147	Jer. 26:1–7, 10–15	Matt. 23:34
AFTER TRINITY	144	Gen. 32:22–31	2 Cor. 4:7
Monday	40:1–16	1 Sam. 18:1–9	Luke 19:29–40
Tuesday	41	1 Sam. 20:1–7, 12–23	Luke 19:47–20:8
Wednesday	44	1 Sam. 20:24–39	Luke 20:9–26
Thursday	49	1 Sam. 22:6	Luke 20:27–40
Friday	51	1 Sam. 23:7–18	Luke 20:41–21:4
Saturday	66	1 Sam. 28:3–19	Luke 21:5–19
ELEVENTH	124, 125	*Isa.* 26:12–16, 19	Rom. 8:26
SUNDAY	33	Job 5:8–18	Matt. 23:13–31
AFTER TRINITY	62, 63	Gen. 37:3–4, 12–35	James 1:1–15
Monday	71	1 Sam. 31	Luke 21:20
Tuesday	73	2 Sam. 1:1–16	Luke 22:1–13

for the Christian Year

EVENING PRAYER

Days	Psalms	First Lesson	Second Lesson
Wednesday	81	Dan. 4:28	Acts 23:25—24:9
Thursday	89:1–19	Dan. 5:1–9	Acts 24:10–23
Friday	91	Dan. 5:10–16	Acts 24:24–25:12
Saturday	96, 98	Dan. 5:17–30	Acts 25:13
EIGHTH	25	*Ecclus.* 6:22	Luke 10:38
SUNDAY	92	Prov. 11:24	Matt. 7:15–21
AFTER TRINITY	148, 150	1 Sam. 26:1–7, 12–17, 21–25	Acts 12:1–17
Monday	116	Dan. 6:1–8	Acts 26:1–23
Tuesday	118	Dan. 6:9–15	Acts 26:24—27:8
Wednesday	119:97–112 & 117	Dan. 6:16–23, 25–27	Acts 27:9–26
Thursday	132, 134	Esther 2:5–8, 17–23	Acts 27:27
Friday	138, 146	Esther 3:1–12	Acts 28:1–15
Saturday	147	Esther 4:1, 5–17	Acts 28:16
NINTH	119:9–24	Prov. 4:1–4, 20–27	Heb. 12:1–13
SUNDAY	51	Lam. 3:40–58	Luke 15:11
AFTER TRINITY	93, 96	1 Sam. 31	Acts 13:1–3, 14–31, 38, 44–49
Monday	4, 8	Esther 5	Rom. 1:1–17
Tuesday	16, 20	Esther 6	Rom. 2:1–16
Wednesday	19, 23	Esther 7	Rom. 2:17
Thursday	21:1–6 & 24	Micah 1:1–7a	Rom. 3:1–20
Friday	25	Micah 2	Rom. 3:21
Saturday	84	Micah 3:1–8	Rom. 4:1–12
TENTH	15, 46	Isa. 44:1–8, 21–23	Rom. 12:1–9
SUNDAY	42, 43	Lam. 1:1–12	Luke 19:41
AFTER TRINITY	47, 48	2 Sam. 1:17	Acts 14:8
Monday	37:1–24	Micah 4:1–8	Rom. 4:13
Tuesday	37:26	Micah 4:9—5:1	Rom. 5
Wednesday	39	Micah 6:1–8	Rom. 6
Thursday	50	Micah 6:9	Rom. 7:1–13
Friday	54, 57	Micah 7:1–9	Rom. 7:14
Saturday	65, 67	Micah 7:14	Rom. 8:1–17
ELEVENTH	68 or 123, 142	*Ecclus.* 35:10–19	Mark 12:38
SUNDAY	100, 101	Eccles. 5:1–7	Luke 18:9–14
AFTER TRINITY	30, 121	2 Sam. 7:18	Acts 15:1–21
Monday	77	Nahum 1:3–8, 15	Rom. 8:18–27
Tuesday	78	Nahum 2	Rom. 8:28

Psalms and Lessons

MORNING PRAYER

Days	Psalms	First Lesson	Second Lesson
Wednesday	87, 101	2 Sam. 1:17	Luke 22:14–30
Thursday	92	2 Sam. 4:1, 5, 7–12	Luke 22:31–46
Friday	94	2 Sam. 5:1–10	Luke 22:47–62
Saturday	96	2 Sam. 6:1–11	Luke 22:63— 23:12
TWELFTH	139	**Ecclus.* 15:11	Phil. 2:12–18
SUNDAY	102:15 & 146	*Ecclus.* 38:1–14	Luke 4:31
AFTER TRINITY	72	Gen. 41:1a, 8, 14–40	Col. 3:22—4:6
Monday	107:1–16	2 Sam. 6:12–15, 17–19	Luke 23:13–25
Tuesday	115	2 Sam. 7:1–11, 16–17	Luke 23:26–38
Wednesday	125, 127, 130	2 Sam. 7:18	Luke 23:39–49
Thursday	137:1–6 & 138	2 Sam. 9:1–9, 13	Luke 23:50–24:12
Friday	142, 143	2 Sam. 11:1–13	Luke 24:13–35
Saturday	147	2 Sam. 11:14	Luke 24:36
THIRTEENTH	104	**Ecclus.* 17:1–15	Mark 3:20–21, 31–35
SUNDAY			
AFTER	73	Hab. 1:12—2:4, 14	Heb. 10:35
TRINITY	118	Gen. 43:1–5, 11–16, 26–34	Heb. 13:1–21
Monday	7	2 Sam. 12:1–10, 13–15a	2 Cor. 1
Tuesday	16	2 Sam. 12:15b–23	2 Cor. 2
Wednesday	17	2 Sam. 15:1–12	2 Cor. 3
Thursday	25	2 Sam. 15:13–29	2 Cor. 4
Friday	32	2 Sam. 15:30—16:4	2 Cor. 5:1–10
Saturday	31	2 Sam. 16:5–19	2 Cor. 5:11
FOURTEENTH	19, 24	*Micah 6:1–8	Phil. 4:4–13
SUNDAY	65	1 Chron. 29:10–17	Luke 17:5–10
AFTER TRINITY	85	Gen. 45:1–15, 25–28	Rom. 12:9
Monday	39	2 Sam. 16:23—17:14	2 Cor. 6:1–10
Tuesday	40:1–16	2 Sam. 17:15–23	2 Cor. 6:11—7:1
Wednesday	45	2 Sam. 18:1–17	2 Cor. 7:2
Thursday	56	2 Sam. 18:19	2 Cor. 8:1–15
Friday	69:1–22, 30–37	2 Sam. 19:1–10	2 Cor. 8:16
Saturday	68:1–19	2 Sam. 19:11–23	2 Cor. 9

for the Christian Year

EVENING PRAYER

Days	Psalms	First Lesson	Second Lesson
Wednesday	85, 98	Nahum 3	Rom. 9:1–5, 14–24, 30–33
Thursday	90	Hab. 1:2–4, 12—2:4	Rom. 10
Friday	103	Hab. 2:9–14, 19–20	Rom. 11:1–21
Saturday	112, 113	Hab. 3:2–6, 10–13, 18–19a	Rom. 11:22
TWELFTH	27	*Tobit* 13:1b–5, 7–11	Rom. 15:14–21
SUNDAY	32, 126	Isa. 29:18	Mark 7:31
AFTER TRINITY	67, 122	2 Sam. 15:1–23	Acts 15:36—16:5, 9–15
Monday	111, 114	Zeph. 1:2–3, 7, 14–18	Rom. 12
Tuesday	116	Zeph. 3:1–8	Rom. 13
Wednesday	121, 123, 124	Zeph. 3:9	Rom. 14:1–12
Thursday	144	*Ecclus.* 1:1–10	Rom. 14:13
Friday	145	*Ecclus.* 1:11–20, 26–27	Rom. 15:1–16
Saturday	148, 150	*Ecclus.* 2	Rom. 15:17
THIRTEENTH	11, 12	Deut. 15:7–15	Matt. 26:6–13
SUNDAY	112, 113	Deut. 24:10	Luke 10:23–37
AFTER TRINITY	20, 23	2 Sam. 18:1, 6–14, 19–33	Acts 16:16–34
Monday	4, 8	*Ecclus.* 3:17	Matt. 1:18
Tuesday	13, 14	*Ecclus.* 4:1–18	Matt. 2:1–12
Wednesday	18:1–20	*Ecclus.* 4:20—5:7	Matt. 2:13
Thursday	27	*Ecclus.* 15:11	Matt. 3
Friday	22	*Ecclus.* 16:17	Matt. 4:1–11
Saturday	29, 30	*Ecclus.* 19:4–18	Matt. 4:12
FOURTEENTH	50	Jer. 7:1–11	Luke 13:18–30
SUNDAY	92	Deut. 8:1–14, 17–20	Luke 17:11–19
AFTER TRINITY	42, 43	1 Kings 3:4–15	Acts 17:16
Monday	33	*Ecclus.* 19:20	Matt. 5:1–16
Tuesday	36:5 & 47	*Ecclus.* 20:9–20	Matt. 5:17–26
Wednesday	62, 63	*Ecclus.* 24:1–9, 18–22	Matt. 5:27–37
Thursday	66	*Ecclus.* 28:13	Matt. 5:38
Friday	51	*Ecclus.* 31:12–18, 25—32:2	Matt. 6:1–18
Saturday	67, 93	*Ecclus.* 34:1–8	Matt. 6:19

Psalms and Lessons

MORNING PRAYER

Days	Psalms	First Lesson	Second Lesson
FIFTEENTH	49	*Ecclus. 5:1–10	Luke 12:13–21
SUNDAY	103	Deut. 7:6–13	Gal. 2:15–20
AFTER TRINITY	1, 15	Exod. 2:1–22	James 4
Monday	75	2 Sam. 19:24–39	2 Cor. 10
Tuesday	76	2 Sam. 23:8–17	2 Cor. 11:1–15
Wednesday	77	2 Sam. 24:1, 10–25	2 Cor. 11:16
Thursday	81	1 Kings 2:1–4, 10–12	2 Cor. 12:1–13
Friday	85	1 Kings 3:4–15	2 Cor. 12:14
Saturday	92	1 Kings 3:16	2 Cor. 13
SIXTEENTH	116	*Isa. 12	John 11:21–44
SUNDAY	91	Jer. 32:36–42	Rom. 11:25
AFTER TRINITY	145	Exod. 3:1–15	1 Pet. 5:1–11
Monday	103	1 Kings 8:1–11	1 Thess. 1
Tuesday	118	1 Kings 8:12–21	1 Thess. 2:1–13
Wednesday	119:113–128	1 Kings 8:22–30	1 Thess. 2:17—3:13
Thursday	126, 128	1 Kings 8:54–63	1 Thess. 4:1–12
Friday	102	1 Kings 9:1–9	1 Thess. 4:13
Saturday	143, 149	1 Kings 11:26–31, 34–37	1 Thess. 5:1–11
SEVENTEENTH	25	*Jer. 13:15–21	Mark 10:35–45
SUNDAY	10	Ecclus. 8:1–9	2 Tim. 2:19
AFTER TRINITY	107:1–16	Exod. 5:1–9, 19—6:1	Heb. 3
Monday	18:1–20	1 Kings 12:1–11	1 Thess. 5:12
Tuesday	20, 23	1 Kings 12:12–20	2 Thess. 1
Wednesday	21:1–6 & 28	1 Kings 12:25	2 Thess. 2:1–12
Thursday	27	1 Kings 16:29	2 Thess. 2:13—3:5
Friday	37:1–24	1 Kings 17:1–16	2 Thess. 3:6
Saturday	37:26	1 Kings 17:17	James 1:1–11
EIGHTEENTH SUNDAY	48, 112	Prov. 2:1–9	1 Tim. 3:14—4:16
AFTER	62, 63	*Amos 8:4–12	John 7:37
TRINITY	77:11 & 114	Exod. 14:5–14, 19–21, 24–28, 30	Heb. 11:23–29, 32–40
Monday	41	1 Kings 18:1–15	James 1:12–21

for the Christian Year

EVENING PRAYER

Days	Psalms	First Lesson	Second Lesson
FIFTEENTH	26, 128	Eccles. 5:8	1 Tim. 6:1–10
SUNDAY	34	Joel 2:21–27	Matt. 6:24
AFTER TRINITY	84	1 Kings 8:22–30, 54–63	Acts 18:1–17
Monday	71	*Ecclus.* 34:18—35:3	Matt. 7:1–12
Tuesday	72	*Ecclus.* 36:1–17	Matt. 7:13
Wednesday	73	*Ecclus.* 37:6–15	Matt. 8:1–13
Thursday	80	*Ecclus.* 38:24	Matt. 8:14–27
Friday	89:1–19	*Ecclus.* 42:15–21	Matt. 8:28—9:8
Saturday	46, 96	*Ecclus.* 43:1–12	Matt. 9:9–17
SIXTEENTH	90	Ezek. 33:1–9	Matt. 24:37
SUNDAY	142, 146	1 Kings 17:8–9, 17–24	Luke 7:11–17
AFTER TRINITY	66	1 Kings 12:1–20	Acts 19:21
Monday	104	*Ecclus.* 43:13–19	Matt. 9:18–35
Tuesday	111, 113	*Ecclus.* 43:20	Matt. 9:36–10:15
Wednesday	119:129–144 & 117	*Ecclus.* 44:1–15	Matt. 10:16–31
Thursday	121, 122, 138	Job 1:1–12	Matt. 10:32—11:1
Friday	139	Job 1:13	Matt. 11:2–19
Saturday	97, 98	Job 2	Matt. 11:20
SEVENTEENTH	36:5 & 130	Mal. 2:1–10	Luke 13:10–17
SUNDAY	33	*Ecclus.* 10:7–18	Luke 14:1–11
AFTER TRINITY	144	1 Kings 18:1–2, 17–39	Acts 20:17
Monday	7	Job 3:1–10, 13–20	Matt. 12:1–13
Tuesday	11, 12	Job 4:12	Matt. 12:14–30
Wednesday	29, 30	Job 5:8–18	Matt. 12:31
Thursday	31	Job 10:1–9, 12–18	Matt. 13:1–23
Friday	22	Job 11:7	Matt. 13:24–30, 36–43
Saturday	145	Job 12:1–10	Matt. 13:31–35, 44–52
EIGHTEENTH SUNDAY	147	Deut. 11:18–21, 26–28, 32	Gal. 1:1–12
AFTER TRINITY	119:89–104	Deut. 5:1–21	Matt. 22:34
	139	1 Kings 19	Acts 21:7–19, 27–39
Monday	33	Job 12:13–22	Matt. 13:53—14:12

XXXV

Psalms and Lessons

MORNING PRAYER

Days	Psalms	First Lesson	Second Lesson
Tuesday	42, 43	1 Kings 18:16–24	James 1:22
Wednesday	44	1 Kings 18:25–30, 36–46	James 2:1–13
Thursday	49	1 Kings 19:1–8	James 2:14
Friday	51	1 Kings 19:9	James 3
Saturday	71	1 Kings 21:1–10	James 4:1–12
NINETEENTH	72	*Job 24:1–17	Titus 2
SUNDAY	34	Jer. 30:12–22	John 5:1–16
AFTER TRINITY	29, 99	Exod. 19:1–7, 16–19 & 20:1–3	Rom. 3:1–2, 19–31
Monday	89:1–19	1 Kings 21:11–22	James 4:13—5:11
Tuesday	90	1 Kings 22:1–12	James 5:12
Wednesday	94	1 Kings 22:13–28	1 Tim. 1:1–11
Thursday	100, 110	1 Kings 22:29–40	1 Tim. 1:12
Friday	119:145–160	2 Kings 1:2–8, 17a	1 Tim. 2:1–10
Saturday	120, 122, 123	2 Kings 2:1–15	1 Tim. 3:1–13
TWENTIETH	11, 12	Mal. 2:14	Matt. 19:3–9a, 13–15
SUNDAY			
AFTER	1, 15	*Eccles. 9:4–10	Eph. 6:1–9
TRINITY	115	Exod. 32:1–6, 15–20, 30–34	1 Cor. 10:14–22
Monday	124, 128	2 Kings 4:8–17	1 Tim. 3:14—4:5
Tuesday	125, 126	2 Kings 4:18–25a	1 Tim. 4:6
Wednesday	127, 130	2 Kings 4:25b–37	1 Tim. 5:1–16
Thursday	141:1–4 & 142	2 Kings 5:1–8	1 Tim. 5:17
Friday	143	2 Kings 5:9–19	1 Tim. 6:1–11
Saturday	149	2 Kings 5:20	1 Tim. 6:12
TWENTY-FIRST	76, 121	*Isa. 59:15b	2 Cor. 10:1–7, 17–18
SUNDAY			
AFTER	27	*Baruch 3:14–15, 29–37	John 9:1–38
TRINITY	91	Exod. 33:1, 12–23	Heb. 4:1–13
Monday	2, 3	2 Kings 6:8–14	2 Tim. 1:1–14
Tuesday	5	2 Kings 6:15–23	2 Tim. 1:15—2:13

for the Christian Year

EVENING PRAYER

Days	Psalms	First Lesson	Second Lesson
Tuesday	39	Job 14:1–14	Matt. 14:13–21
Wednesday	50	Job 18:5–7, 14–21	Matt. 14:22
Thursday	73	Job 21:7–20, 29–33	Matt. 15:1–20
Friday	85, 86	Job 24:1–4, 12–20	Matt. 15:21
Saturday	93, 98	Job 25:2–6 & 26:6–14	Matt. 16:1–12
NINETEENTH	80	Jer. 5:7–19	2 Cor. 13
SUNDAY	103	*Wisdom* 12:12–19	Matt. 9:1–8
AFTER TRINITY	19, 46	1 Kings 21:1–22	Acts 22:24— 23:11
Monday	92	Job 28:12	Matt. 16:13
Tuesday	104	Job 38:1–11, 16–18	Matt. 17:1–13
Wednesday	113, 114	Job 38:19–30	Matt. 17:14
Thursday	116	Job 38:31–38	Matt. 18:1–14
Friday	119:161–176 & 117	Job 39:19	Matt. 18:15
Saturday	144	Job 42:1–9	Matt. 19:1–15
TWENTIETH	145	Jer. 31:31–37	John 13:31–35
SUNDAY	107:1–9, 33–43 or 84	Jer. 2:1–9, 13	Matt. 22:1–14
AFTER			
TRINITY	111, 112	2 Kings 2:1–15	Acts 24:10
Monday	131, 133, 134	Eccles. 1:2–11	Matt. 19:16
Tuesday	132	Eccles. 2:1–11	Matt. 20:1–16
Wednesday	135	Eccles. 2:18	Matt. 20:17
Thursday	137:1–6 & 138	Eccles. 3:1–2, 9–15	Matt. 21:1–16
Friday	139	Eccles. 3:16	Matt. 21:17–32
Saturday	19, 46	Eccles. 5:1–7	Matt. 21:33
TWENTY-FIRST	25	Gen. 15:1–6	Rom. 4:1–8
SUNDAY	30, 146	2 Kings 5:1–15a	John 4:46b
AFTER TRINITY	118	2 Kings 6:8–23	Acts 25:1–22
Monday	4, 8	Eccles. 5:8	Matt. 22:15–33
Tuesday	11, 12	Eccles. 6:1–2, 7–12	Matt. 22:34

Psalms and Lessons

MORNING PRAYER

Days	Psalms	First Lesson	Second Lesson
Wednesday	9	2 Kings 9:1–6, 10b–16	2 Tim. 2:14
Thursday	10	2 Kings 9:17–28	2 Tim. 3
Friday	22	2 Kings 9:30	2 Tim. 4:1–8
Saturday	21:1–6 & 23	2 Kings 11:1–4, 9–16	2 Tim. 4:9
TWENTY-SECOND	32, 43	*Ecclus.* 27:30—28:7	Matt. 18:7–20
SUNDAY	147	*Baruch* 5	1 John 2:24
AFTER TRINITY	71	Num. 20:14	2 Tim. 1:3–14
Monday	18:21–36	2 Kings 17:6–8, 12–18	Titus 1
Tuesday	25	2 Kings 21:1–3, 10–18	Titus 2
Wednesday	28	2 Kings 22:3–13	Titus 3
Thursday	30	2 Kings 22:14	Philemon
Friday	40:1–16	2 Kings 23:1–4, 11–14, 21–23	2 John
Saturday	31	2 Kings 23:24–30	3 John
TWENTY-THIRD	33	Jer. 29:1, 4–14	Titus 3:1–8
SUNDAY	8, 138	*Isa. 64	Matt. 23:1–12
AFTER TRINITY	23, 102:15	Deut. 34	2 Tim. 4:1–8
Monday	41	Jer. 35:1–11	Col. 1:1–17
Tuesday	44	Jer. 35:12	Col. 1:18—2:5
Wednesday	50	Jer. 36:1–8	Col. 2:6–19
Thursday	52, 53	Jer. 36:11–19	Col. 2:20—3:11
Friday	54, 61	Jer. 36:20–26	Col. 3:12–17
Saturday	55	2 Kings 25:8–11, 22, 25–26	Col. 3:18—4:6
TWENTY-FOURTH	66	*Mal. 3:13—4:3	Luke 10:17–24
SUNDAY	20, 28	*Ecclus.* 36:1–17	1 Tim. 2:1–8
AFTER TRINITY	136	Joshua 23:1–3, 11–16	Luke 13:1–9
Monday	63, 64	Lev. 19:1–2, 9–18	Phil. 1:1–11
Tuesday	68:1–19	Lev. 19:26	Phil. 1:12–26
Wednesday	71	Lev. 20:1–8	Phil. 1:27—2:18
Thursday	74	Lev. 25:23–31	Phil. 2:19
Friday	69:1–22, 30–37	Lev. 26:1–13	Phil. 3
Saturday	79	Lev. 26:27–42	Phil. 4

for the Christian Year

EVENING PRAYER

Days	Psalms	First Lesson	Second Lesson
Wednesday	13, 14	Eccles. 8:12—9:1	Matt. 23:1–12
Thursday	16, 17	Eccles. 9:11	Matt. 23:13–23
Friday	6, 26	Eccles. 11	Matt. 23:25
Saturday	18:1–20	Eccles. 12	Matt. 24:1–14
TWENTY-SECOND	51	1 Kings 8:46–53	Luke 7:36
SUNDAY	7	Zech. 7:8	Matt. 18:21
AFTER TRINITY	65	2 Kings 9:1–6, 10b–13, 16–26	Acts 26
Monday	20, 24	Deut. 4:1–9	Matt. 24:15–28
Tuesday	29, 36:5	Deut. 4:15–24	Matt. 24:29–41
Wednesday	34	Deut. 4:25–31	Matt. 24:42
Thursday	37:1–24	Deut. 4:32–40	Matt. 25:1–13
Friday	37:26	Deut. 5:1–21	Matt. 25:14–30
Saturday	27	Deut. 5:22	Matt. 25:31
TWENTY-THIRD	19, 67	Ezek. 33:30	1 Cor. 4:8–16
SUNDAY	72	*Wisdom* 6:1–11	Matt. 22:15–22
AFTER TRINITY	99, 100	2 Kings 23:1–4, 11–14, 21–23	Acts 27:1–20, 27–32, 39–44
Monday	42, 43	Deut. 6:1–9	Matt. 26:1–16
Tuesday	46, 85	Deut. 6:10–16, 20–25	Matt. 26:17–30
Wednesday	47, 48	Deut. 7:6–13	Matt. 26:31–46
Thursday	49	Deut. 8:1–10	Matt. 26:47–56
Friday	51	Deut. 8:11	Matt. 26:57
Saturday	93, 98	Deut. 9:7–17, 25–29	Matt. 27:1–10
TWENTY-FOURTH	139	Deut. 33:1–3, 26–29	Jude 1–4, 17–25
SUNDAY	86	2 Kings 4:18–37	Matt. 9:18–26
AFTER TRINITY	73	2 Chron. 36:11	Acts 28:16
Monday	56, 57	Deut. 10:12	Matt. 27:11–26
Tuesday	67, 84	Deut. 13:1–11	Matt. 27:27–44
Wednesday	72	Deut. 15:7–15	Matt. 27:45–56
Thursday	77	Deut. 17:14	Matt. 27:57
Friday	80	Deut. 18:15	Matt. 28:1–10
Saturday	65	Deut. 19:11	Matt. 28:11

Psalms and Lessons

MORNING PRAYER

Days	*Psalms*	*First Lesson*	*Second Lesson*
THIRD SUNDAY	15, 85	Ruth 1:1–17	Col. 3:5–11
BEFORE ADVENT	112, 113	*Hab. 1:12—2:4, 9–14	Luke 12:35–48
Monday	81	Obadiah 1–9	1 Pet. 1:1–12
Tuesday	82, 101	Obadiah 10	1 Pet. 1:13
Wednesday	86	Mal. 1:6–11	1 Pet. 2:1–10
Thursday	94	Mal. 2:1–10	1 Pet. 2:11–17
Friday	88	Mal. 3:1–15	1 Pet. 2:18
Saturday	104	Mal. 3:16—4:6	1 Pet. 3:1–12
SECOND SUNDAY	75, 138	Isa. 2:6–19	Matt. 25:14–29
BEFORE ADVENT	93, 98	*Isa. 66:1–2, 10, 12–16, 18–23	2 Thess. 1
Monday	105	Lam. 1:1–6	1 Pet. 3:13
Tuesday	106	Lam. 1:15	1 Pet. 4:1–6
Wednesday	113, 114	Lam. 2:1–10	1 Pet. 4:7–11
Thursday	115	Lam. 4:1–6, 9	1 Pet. 4:12
Friday	116, 117	Lam. 4:11–20	1 Pet. 5:1–7
Saturday	120, 123	Lam. 5	1 Pet. 5:8
SUNDAY NEXT	39	Jer. 4:23	Matt. 25:31
BEFORE ADVENT	145	*Jer. 3:14–18	1 Cor. 11:17–32
Monday	124, 128	Joel 1:13	2 Pet. 1:1–11
Tuesday	129, 130	Joel 2:1–11	2 Pet. 1:12
Wednesday	136	Joel 2:12–19	2 Pet. 2:1–10a
Thursday	137:1–6 & 138	Joel 2:21	2 Pet. 2:10b
Friday	142, 143	Joel 3:1–8	2 Pet. 3:1–10
Saturday	146, 149	Joel 3:9–17	2 Pet. 3:11

OPTIONAL PSALMS AND LESSONS FOR THE AUTUMNAL EMBER DAYS

Ember Wednesday	1, 15	Deut. 18:15	1 Cor. 1:1–18
Ember Friday	48	2 Kings 2:1–15	1 Cor. 9:7
Ember Saturday	132	Ezek. 33:1–9	2 Cor. 6:1–10

xl

for the Christian Year

EVENING PRAYER

Days	Psalms	First Lesson	Second Lesson
THIRD SUNDAY BEFORE ADVENT	21, 22:23	Joel 3:9–17	Matt. 13:36–52
	7	Amos 5:14–24	Gal. 6:1–10
Monday	90	Deut. 24:10–18	1 Thess. 1
Tuesday	91	Deut. 25:1–3, 13–16	1 Thess. 2:1–16
Wednesday	92	Deut. 26:1–11	1 Thess. 2:17—3:13
Thursday	103	Deut. 28:1–14	1 Thess. 4:1–12
Friday	102	Deut. 29:2, 9–21	1 Thess. 4:13
Saturday	145	Deut. 30:11	1 Thess. 5:1–11
SECOND SUNDAY BEFORE ADVENT	9	Gen. 19:1–3, 12–17, 24–28	Luke 17:20
	76, 96	2 Esdras 8:63—9:13	2 Pet. 3:1–14, 17–18
Monday	107	*Wisdom* 1:1–7	1 Thess. 5:12
Tuesday	111, 112	*Wisdom* 6:1–11	2 Thess. 1
Wednesday	118	*Wisdom* 6:12–21	2 Thess. 2:1–12
Thursday	121, 122	*Wisdom* 7:7–14	2 Thess. 2:13—3:5
Friday	125, 126, 127	*Wisdom* 7:15–22a	2 Thess. 3:6
Saturday	99, 100	*Wisdom* 7:22—8:1	Jude
SUNDAY NEXT BEFORE ADVENT	90	Eccles. 11:9—12:8, 13–14	Heb. 13:1–21
	103	Isa. 25:1–9	John 5:17–29
Monday	131, 133, 134	*Wisdom* 9:1–4, 9–11	Rev. 1:1–8
Tuesday	132	*Wisdom* 9:13	Rev. 1:9
Wednesday	139	*Wisdom* 10:1–4, 15–21	Rev. 2:1–11
Thursday	140, 141:1–4	*Wisdom* 11:21—12:2	Rev. 2:12–17
Friday	144	*Wisdom* 12:12–19	Rev. 3:1–6
Saturday	148, 150	*Wisdom* 13:1–9	Rev. 3:7–13

OPTIONAL PSALMS AND LESSONS FOR THE AUTUMNAL EMBER DAYS

Ember Wednesday	24, 26	Jer. 42:1–6	1 Tim. 3
Ember Friday	84, 134	Ezek. 13:1–9	2 Tim. 2:19
Ember Saturday	99. 100	Isa. 6:1–8	Heb. 13:7–21

Psalms and Lessons

MORNING PRAYER

Occasions	Psalms	First Lesson	Second Lesson
THE DEDICATION OF A CHURCH	132	1 Kings 8:22–30	John 10:22–30
PATRONAL FESTIVAL (OF A BISHOP)	132	Isa. 61	Matt. 10:1–20
PATRONAL FESTIVAL (OF A CONFESSOR)	3, 8	Jer. 15:15	Eph. 4:1–13
PATRONAL FESTIVAL (OF A MARTYR)	30	Job 19:23–27	Luke 6:20–36
PATRONAL FESTIVAL (OF A VIRGIN)	96, 97	Isa. 54:1–5, 11–14	Luke 10:38
PATRONAL FESTIVAL (OF A MATRON)	85	Prov. 31:10	Rom. 12
INDEPENDENCE DAY	18:1–20	Isa. 26:1–4, 7–8, 12	John 8:31–36
THANKSGIVING DAY	65	Deut. 8:1–11, 17–20	1 Thess. 5:12–23
	145	Deut. 26:1–11	John 6:26–35

MORNING OR EVENING PRAYER

A MEMORIAL DAY	148	*Ecclus.* 44:1–15	Heb. 11:32—12:2
A NATIONAL OR STATE FESTIVAL	145 or 46, 47	Isa. 25:1–9 & 26:1–4	Heb. 11:8–16 & 12:28
A NATIONAL OR STATE FAST	3, 20 or 80	Dan. 9:3–19	1 Pet. 2:9
THE END OF THE YEAR	90	Eccles. 11:1–4, 6–10 & 12:13–14	Rev. 21:1–7
BEFORE A CONFIRMATION	143:1–10	Isa. 11:1–9	Acts 19:1–7
	1, 15	Ezek. 36:25–28	Eph. 3:14
BEFORE ORDINATIONS:			
OF A DEACON	36:5 & 63	Isa. 6:1–8	Mark 10:32–45
OF A PRIEST	132	Ezek. 3:1–11	2 Cor. 5:11—6:10
OF A BISHOP	23, 100	Isa. 61	2 Tim. 2:1–15, 19–26
AT THE INSTITUTION OF A MINISTER	99, 100	Ezek. 33:1–9	John 10:1–18
AT THE LAYING OF A CORNERSTONE	118	Isa. 28:14–22	1 Pet. 2:1–10

for Special Occasions

EVENING PRAYER

Occasions	Psalms	First Lesson	Second Lesson
THE DEDICATION	84	Haggai 2:1–9	1 Cor. 3:9–17
OF A CHURCH	48, 122	Gen. 28:10–12, 16–17	Heb. 10:19–25
PATRONAL FESTIVAL	23, 100	*Ecclus.* 50:5, 11–21	John 21:15–17
(OF A BISHOP)	111, 112	Isa. 52:1–10	John 20:19–23
PATRONAL FESTIVAL	121, 124	*Ecclus.* 2:1–11	Luke 12:1–12
(OF A CONFESSOR)	118	Isa. 49:1–12	Acts 4:5–13
PATRONAL FESTIVAL	138, 146	*Ecclus.* 51:7–12	Luke 21:10–19
(OF A MARTYR)	116	Job 5:8–21	Rev. 7:9
PATRONAL FESTIVAL	45	Jer. 31:1–14	Matt. 25:1–13
(OF A VIRGIN)	113, 122	Joel 2:28	Matt. 13:44–52
PATRONAL FESTIVAL	148	Esther 4:1, 5–17	Luke 23:50—
(OF A MATRON)			24:10
	34	Isa. 49:14–21	2 John
INDEPENDENCE DAY	121, 122	Deut. 4:1–14	Gal. 4:26—5:1
THANKSGIVING	147	Isa. 12	Phil. 4:4–7
DAY	104	Deut. 11:8–21	1 Tim. 6:6–16

MORNING OR EVENING PRAYER

AT A CHURCH	48	Isa. 55	Acts 15:22–31
CONVENTION	27	Isa. 60	1 Cor. 12:1–26
AT	67, 138	Isa. 43:1–12	Matt. 28:16
SERVICES	65	Isa. 49:5–13	Luke 10:1–9
IN THE	46, 47	Isa. 55:1–11	Luke 24:44–49
INTEREST	102:15	Isa. 9:2–7	John 12:20–32
OF	72	Isa. 52:1–10	Rom. 10
CHURCH	96	Isa. 45:20	Eph. 2:10
MISSIONS	97	Isa. 60:1–11	Eph. 3:1–12
AT SERVICES IN	41	Prov. 11:24	Matt. 7:15–21
THE INTEREST	112, 146	Deut. 24:10	Luke 10:23–37
OF	107:1–9,	Zech. 8:9–17	2 Cor. 9:1, 6–15
SOCIAL	33–43		
SERVICE	34	Eccles. 9:4–10	Eph. 6:1–9
AT SERVICES	19, 63	Deut. 11:18–21,	Matt. 18:1–14
IN THE		26–28, 32	
INTEREST	111, 112	Job 28:12	Gal. 3:24—4:7
OF	25	Deut. 6:1–9, 20–25	2 Tim. 3:14—
CHRISTIAN			4:2
EDUCATION	27	Isa. 28:9–17	1 Pet. 2:1–10
CHRISTIAN UNITY	85 or 122, 133	Isa. 35	John 17

Psalms and Lessons for the Fixed Holy Days

WHICH ARE NOT IN THE TABLE OF LESSONS FOR THE CHRISTIAN YEAR

Days	MORNING PRAYER			EVENING PRAYER		
	Psalms	First Lesson	Second Lesson	Psalms	First Lesson	Second Lesson
ST. ANDREW *Eve* November 30	34	Isa. 55:1-5	John 1:35-42	102:15 & 117 96, 100	Isa. 49:1-6 Zech. 8:20	1 Cor. 4:1-16 John 12:20-36
ST. THOMAS *Eve* December 21	27	Job 42:1-6	John 14:1-7	23, 121 112, 113	2 Sam. 15:17-21 Isa. 43:8-13	John 11:1-16 1 Pet. 1:3-9
ST. PAUL *Eve* January 25	66	Isa. 45:18	2 Cor. 12:1-9	1, 19 67, 138	*Ecclus.* 39:1-10 Jer. 1:4-10	Gal. 1:1-5, 11-24‡ Acts 26:1-23
PURIFICATION *Eve* February 2	84	1 Sam. 1:21	Gal. 4:1-7†	113, 122 48, 134	Exod. 13:11-16 Haggai 2:1-9	Heb. 10:1-10 1 John 3:1-8
ST. MATTHIAS *Eve* February 24	15, 24	1 Sam. 2:27-35	Matt. 7:15-27	33 145	1 Sam. 16:1-13 1 Sam. 12:1-5	1 John 2:15 Acts 20:17-35
ANNUNCIATION *Eve* March 25	8, 113	Isa. 52:7-10	Heb. 2:5††	111, 131 36:5 & 138	Gen. 3:1-15 1 Sam. 2:1-10	Rom. 5:12 Matt. 1:18-23
ST. MARK *Eve* April 25	102:15	Isa. 62:6	Rom. 15:4-13	67, 96 19, 112	*Ecclus.* 51:13-22 *Ecclus.* 2:1-11	Acts 12:25—13:3 2 Tim. 4:1-11, 16-18
ST. PHILIP AND ST. JAMES *Eve* May 1	139	Job 23:3-12	John 1:43	119:33-48 27	Prov. 4:7-18 Isa. 30:18-21	John 12:20-26 John 17:1-8
ST. BARNABAS *Eve* June 11	1, 15	Job 29:11-16	Acts 9:26-31§	112, 146 97, 100	*Ecclus.* 31:3-11 Isa. 42:5-12	Acts 4:32 Acts 14:8‡‡

	Psalms	1st Lesson	2nd Lesson	Psalms	1st Lesson	2nd Lesson
ST. JOHN BAPTIST *Eve* June 24	82, 98	Mal. 3:1-6	Matt. 3	103 / 24, 96	*Ecclus.* 48:1-10 / Mal. 4	Luke 1:5-23§§ / Matt. 11:2-19
ST. PETER *Eve* June 29	22:23 & 67	Ezek. 2:1-7	Acts 11:1-18¶	118 / 23, 146	Ezek. 3:4-11 / Ezek. 34:11-16	Acts 4:8-20 / John 21:15-22
ST. JAMES *Eve* July 25	34	Jer. 45	1 Pet. 1:22—2:10	112, 113 / 33	Exod. 3:1-15 / Jer. 26:8-15	Mark 1:14-20 / Matt. 10:16-32
TRANSFIGURATION *Eve* August 6	27	Exod. 34:29	2 Cor. 3	97, 99 / 29, 93	1 Kings 19:1-12 / Exod. 24:12	2 Cor. 4:1-6 / Phil. 3:13
ST. BARTHOLOMEW *Eve* August 24	91	Gen. 28:10-12, 16-17	John 1:43	1, 15 / 46, 102:15	Deut. 18:15-19 / Isa. 66:1-2, 18-23	Luke 6:12-23 / 1 Pet. 5:1-11
ST. MATTHEW *Eve* September 21	119:1-16	1 Kings 19:15-16, 19-21	Matt. 19:16	65, 117 / 19, 112	1 Chron. 29:9-17 / Job 28:12	Rom. 10:1-15 / 1 Tim. 6:6-19
ST. MICHAEL AND ALL ANGELS *Eve* September 29	8, 91	Job 38:1-7	Heb. 1:13—2:10	148, 150 / 34	Dan. 12:1-3 / 2 Kings 6:8-17	Rev. 5 / Acts 12:1-11
ST. LUKE *Eve* October 18	67, 96	Isa. 52:7-10	Acts 1:1-8	103 / 147	Ezek. 47:1-2, 6-8, 12 / *Ecclus.* 38:1-14	Luke 1:1-4 / Col. 4:2
ST. SIMON AND ST. JUDE *Eve* October 28	118	Isa. 28:9-16	Eph. 2:11-18	66 / 62, 121	Isa. 4:2 / Deut. 32:1-4	Acts 1:6-14 / John 14:15
ALL SAINTS *Eve* November 1	1, 15	*Wisdom* 3:1-9	Rev. 19:1-16	97, 112 / 148, 150	*Ecclus.* 44:1-15 / *Wisdom* 5:1-5, 14-16	Heb. 11:32—12:2 / Rev. 21:1-4, 22—22:5

† After Septuagesima, read Rom. 8:14-21.
†† After Easter, read 1 John 4:7-14.
§ In the week of Trinity I, read Luke 14:25.
¶ Before Trinity III, read Acts 3.

‡ After Septuagesima, read Acts 22:1-21.
‡‡ After Trinity III, read Rom. 10:1-15.
§§ In the week after Trinity, read Matt. 21:23-27.

The Calendar

JANUARY	FEBRUARY	MARCH
1 A *Circumcision*	1 d	1 d
2 b	2 e *Purification of Virgin Mary*	2 e
3 c	3 f	3 f
4 d	4 g	4 g
5 e	5 A	5 A
6 f *Epiphany*	6 b	6 b
7 g	7 c	7 c
8 A	8 d	8 d
9 b	9 e	9 e
10 c	10 f	10 f
11 d	11 g	11 g
12 e	12 A	12 A
13 f	13 b	13 b
14 g	14 c	14 c
15 A	15 d	15 d
16 b	16 e	16 e
17 c	17 f	17 f
18 d	18 g	18 g
19 e	19 A	19 A
20 f	20 b	20 b
21 g	21 c	21 c
22 A	22 d	14 22 d
23 b	23 e	3 23 e
24 c	24 f *St. Matthias*	24 f
25 d *Conversion of St. Paul*	25 g	11 25 g *Annunciation of Virgin Mary*
26 e	26 A	26 A
27 f	27 b	19 27 b
28 g	28 c	8 28 c
29 A	29	29 d
30 b		16 30 e
31 c		5 31 f

xlvi

The Calendar

APRIL		MAY		JUNE	
	1 g	1 b	*St. Philip and St. James*	1 e	
13	2 A	2 c		2 f	
2	3 b	3 d		3 g	
	4 c	4 e		4 A	
10	5 d	5 f		5 b	
	6 e	6 g		6 c	
18	7 f	7 A		7 d	
7	8 g	8 b		8 e	
	9 A	9 c		9 f	
15	10 b	10 d		10 g	
4	11 c	11 e		11 A	*St. Barnabas*
	12 d	12 f		12 b	
12	13 e	13 g		13 c	
1	14 f	14 A		14 d	
	15 g	15 b		15 e	
9	16 A	16 c		16 f	
17	17 b	17 d		17 g	
6	18 c	18 e		18 A	
	19 d	19 f		19 b	
	20 e	20 g		20 c	
	21 f	21 A		21 d	
	22 g	22 b		22 e	
	23 A	23 c		23 f	
	24 b	24 d		24 g	*Nativity of St. John Baptist*
	25 c *St. Mark*	25 e		25 A	
	26 d	26 f		26 b	
	27 e	27 g		27 c	
	28 f	28 A		28 d	
	29 g	29 b		29 e	*St. Peter*
	30 A	30 c		30 f	
		31 d			

The Calendar

JULY		AUGUST		SEPTEMBER	
1 g		1 c		1 f	
2 A		2 d		2 g	
3 b		3 e		3 A	
4 c	Independence Day	4 f		4 b	
5 d		5 g		5 c	
6 e		6 A	*Transfiguration*	6 d	
7 f		7 b		7 e	
8 g		8 c		8 f	
9 A		9 d		9 g	
10 b		10 e		10 A	
11 c		11 f		11 b	
12 d		12 g		12 c	
13 e		13 A		13 d	
14 f		14 b		14 e	
15 g		15 c		15 f	
16 A		16 d		16 g	
17 b		17 e		17 A	
18 c		18 f		18 b	
19 d		19 g		19 c	
20 e		20 A		20 d	
21 f		21 b		21 e	*St. Matthew*
22 g		22 c		22 f	
23 A		23 d		23 g	
24 b		24 e	*St. Bartholomew*	24 A	
25 c	*St. James*	25 f		25 b	
26 d		26 g		26 c	
27 e		27 A		27 d	
28 f		28 b		28 e	
29 g		29 c		29 f	*St. Michael and all Angels*
30 A		30 d		30 g	
31 b		31 e			

The Calendar

OCTOBER	NOVEMBER	DECEMBER
1 A	1 d *All Saints*	1 f
2 b	2 e	2 g
3 c	3 f	3 A
4 d	4 g	4 b
5 e	5 A	5 c
6 f	6 b	6 d
7 g	7 c	7 e
8 A	8 d	8 f
9 b	9 e	9 g
10 c	10 f	10 A
11 d	11 g	11 b
12 e	12 A	12 c
13 f	13 b	13 d
14 g	14 c	14 e
15 A	15 d	15 f
16 b	16 e	16 g
17 c	17 f	17 A
18 d *St. Luke*	18 g	18 b
19 e	19 A	19 c
20 f	20 b	20 d
21 g	21 c	21 e *St. Thomas*
22 A	22 d	22 f
23 b	23 e	23 g
24 c	24 f	24 A
25 d	25 g	25 b *Christmas Day*
26 e	26 A	26 c *St. Stephen*
27 f	27 b	27 d *St. John Evangelist*
28 g *St. Simon and St. Jude*	28 c	28 e *Innocents*
29 A	29 d	29 f
30 b	30 e *St. Andrew*	30 g
31 c		31 A

In addition to the above, in November, the first Thursday (or, if any other day be appointed by the Civil Authority, then such day) shall be observed as a Day of Thanksgiving to Almighty God, for the Fruits of the Earth, and all other Blessings of his merciful Providence.

Tables and Rules for the Movable and Immovable Feasts,

Together with the Days of Fasting and Abstinence, through the Whole Year.

RULES TO KNOW WHEN THE MOVABLE FEASTS AND HOLY DAYS BEGIN.

EASTER DAY, on which the rest depend, is always the First Sunday after the Full Moon, which happens upon or next after the Twenty-first Day of March; and if the Full Moon happen upon a Sunday, Easter Day is the Sunday after.

But NOTE, That the Full Moon, for the purposes of these Rules and Tables, is the Fourteenth Day of a Lunar Month, reckoned according to an ancient Ecclesiastical computation, and not the real or Astronomical Full Moon.

Advent Sunday is always the nearest Sunday to the Feast of St. Andrew, whether before or after.

Septuagesima Sunday is Nine Weeks before Easter.

Sexagesima Sunday is Eight Weeks before Easter.

Quinquagesima Sunday is Seven Weeks before Easter.

Quadragesima Sunday is Six Weeks before Easter.

Rogation Sunday is Five Weeks after Easter.

Ascension Day is Forty Days after Easter.

Whitsunday is Seven Weeks after Easter.

Trinity Sunday is Eight Weeks after Easter.

A TABLE OF FEASTS,

TO BE OBSERVED IN THIS CHURCH THROUGHOUT THE YEAR.

All Sundays in the Year
The Circumcision of our Lord JESUS CHRIST
The Epiphany
The Conversion of St. Paul
The Purification of the Blessed Virgin
St. Matthias the Apostle
The Annunciation of the Blessed Virgin
St. Mark the Evangelist
St. Philip and St. James, Apostles
The Ascension of our Lord JESUS CHRIST
St. Barnabas the Apostle
The Nativity of St. John Baptist
St. Peter the Apostle
St. James the Apostle
The Transfiguration of our Lord JESUS CHRIST

St. Bartholomew the Apostle
St. Matthew, Apostle and Evangelist
St. Michael and all Angels
St. Luke the Evangelist
St. Simon and St. Jude, Apostles
All Saints
St. Andrew the Apostle
St. Thomas the Apostle
The Nativity of our Lord JESUS CHRIST
St. Stephen, Deacon and Martyr
St. John, Apostle and Evangelist
The Holy Innocents
Monday and Tuesday in Easter Week
Monday and Tuesday in Whitsun Week

1

Tables and Rules

A TABLE OF FASTS.

Ash Wednesday   Good Friday

OTHER DAYS OF FASTING, ON WHICH THE CHURCH REQUIRES SUCH A MEASURE OF ABSTINENCE AS IS MORE ESPECIALLY SUITED TO EXTRAORDINARY ACTS AND EXERCISES OF DEVOTION.

I. The Forty Days of Lent.
II. The Ember Days at the Four Seasons, being the Wednesday, Friday, and Saturday after the First Sunday in Lent, the Feast of Pentecost, September 14, and December 13.
III. All the Fridays in the Year, except Christmas Day, and The Epiphany, or any Friday which may intervene between these Feasts.

DAYS OF SOLEMN SUPPLICATION.

The three Rogation Days, being the Monday, Tuesday, and Wednesday before Holy Thursday, or the Ascension of our Lord.

TABLES OF PRECEDENCE.

The Holy Days following have precedence of any other Sunday or Holy Day:

The Sundays in Advent
Christmas Day
The Epiphany
Septuagesima Sunday
Sexagesima Sunday
Quinquagesima Sunday
Ash Wednesday
The Sundays in Lent

All the days of Holy Week
Easter Day; and the seven following days
Rogation Sunday
The Ascension Day; and the Sunday after Ascension Day
Whitsunday; and the six following days
Trinity Sunday

If any other Holy Day fall on any day noted in the preceding Table, the observance of such Holy Day shall be transferred to the first convenient open day.

The following Holy Days have precedence of days not noted in the foregoing Table:

St. Stephen, Deacon and Martyr
St. John, Apostle and Evangelist
The Holy Innocents
The Circumcision of Christ
The Conversion of St. Paul
The Purification of St. Mary the Virgin

St. John Baptist
All Feasts of Apostles or Evangelists
The Transfiguration of Christ
St. Michael and all Angels
All Saints

On these Holy Days the Collect, Epistle, and Gospel for the Feast shall be used; but on Sundays the Collect for the Feast shall be followed by the Collect for the Sunday.

A TABLE

OF THOSE DAYS OR OCCASIONS FOR WHICH COLLECT, EPISTLE, AND GOSPEL ARE PROVIDED IN THIS BOOK AND WHICH, NOT BEING FIXED DAYS, DO NOT APPEAR IN THE CALENDAR.

The Ember Days
The Rogation Days
Thanksgiving Day

A Saint's Day
Feast of the Dedication of a
    Church

The Solemnization of Matrimony
The Burial of the Dead

Tables for finding Holy Days

TO FIND THE DATE OF EASTER DAY.

THE Numbers prefixed to the several Days, in the foregoing Calendar, between the twenty-first Day of March and the eighteenth Day of April, both inclusive, denote the Days upon which those Full Moons do fall, which happen upon or next after the twenty-first Day of March, in those Years of which they are respectively the Golden Numbers; and the Sunday Letter next following any such Full Moon points out Easter Day for that Year. All which holds until the Year of our Lord 2199 inclusive; after which Year, the places of these Golden Numbers will be to be changed, as is hereafter expressed.

To find Easter Day, look in the first column of the Calendar, between the twentieth Day of March and the nineteenth Day of April, for the Golden Number of the Year, against which stands the Day of the Paschal Full Moon. Then look in the third column for the Sunday Letter next after the Day of the Full Moon; and the Day of the Month standing against that Sunday Letter is Easter Day. If the Full Moon happen upon a Sunday, then (according to the first rule) the next Sunday after is Easter Day.

To find the Golden Number, or Prime, add 1 to the Year of our Lord, and then divide by 19; the Remainder, if any, is the Golden Number; but if nothing remain, then 19 is the Golden Number.

To find the Dominical or Sunday Letter, and the places of the Golden Numbers in the Calendar, see the General Tables which follow.

A TABLE TO FIND THE DOMINICAL OR SUNDAY LETTER.

To find the Dominical or Sunday Letter, according to the Calendar, for any given Year of our Lord, look for the next preceding Hundredth Year in the lower part of this Table, and for the Remainder of the number of the Year in the upper part; and against the Hundredth Year, under the Remainder, you have the Sunday Letter.

NOTE, That in all Bissextile or Leap-years, the Letter under the number marked with an asterisk is the Sunday Letter for the Months of January and February; and the Letter under the Number not so marked is the Sunday Letter for the Remainder of the Year.

Years in excess of Hundreds of Years.

0*	0	1	2	3	4*	4	5
	6	7	8*	8	9	10	11
	12*	12	13	14	15	16*	16
	17	18	19	20*	20	21	22
	23	24*	24	25	26	27	28*
	28	29	30	31	32*	32	33
	34	35	36*	36	37	38	39
	40*	40	41	42	43	44*	44
	45	46	47	48*	48	49	50
	51	52*	52	53	54	55	56*
	56	57	58	59	60*	60	61
	62	63	64*	64	65	66	67
	68*	68	69	70	71	72*	72
	73	74	75	76*	76	77	78
	79	80*	80	81	82	83	84*
	84	85	86	87	88*	88	89
	90	91	92*	92	93	94	95
	96*	96	97	98	99		

Hundreds of Years.

1600	2000	2400	2800	3200	B	A	G	F	E	D	C	B
1700	2100	2500	2900	3300		C	B	A	G	F	E	D
1800	2200	2600	3000	3400		E	D	C	B	A	G	F
1900	2300	2700	3100	etc.		G	F	E	D	C	B	A

lii

Tables for finding Holy Days

A TABLE TO FIND EASTER DAY,
FROM THE YEAR OF OUR LORD 1786, TO THE YEAR OF OUR LORD 2013, BOTH INCLUSIVE, BEING THE TIME OF TWELVE CYCLES OF THE MOON.

Golden Number	Year of our Lord	Easter Day	Year of our Lord	Easter Day	Year of our Lord	Easter Day
1	1786	April 16	1824*	April 18	1862	April 20
2	1787	April 8	1825	April 3	1863	April 5
3	1788*	March 23	1826	March 26	1864*	March 27
4	1789	April 12	1827	April 15	1865	April 16
5	1790	April 4	1828*	April 6	1866	April 1
6	1791	April 24	1829	April 19	1867	April 21
7	1792*	April 8	1830	April 11	1868*	April 12
8	1793	March 31	1831	April 3	1869	March 28
9	1794	April 20	1832*	April 22	1870	April 17
10	1795	April 5	1833	April 7	1871	April 9
11	1796*	March 27	1834	March 30	1872*	March 31
12	1797	April 16	1835	April 19	1873	April 13
13	1798	April 8	1836*	April 3	1874	April 5
14	1799	March 24	1837	March 26	1875	March 28
15	1800	April 13	1838	April 15	1876*	April 16
16	1801	April 5	1839	March 31	1877	April 1
17	1802	April 18	1840*	April 19	1878	April 21
18	1803	April 10	1841	April 11	1879	April 13
19	1804*	April 1	1842	March 27	1880*	March 28
1	1805	April 14	1843	April 16	1881	April 17
2	1806	April 6	1844*	April 7	1882	April 9
3	1807	March 29	1845	March 23	1883	March 25
4	1808*	April 17	1846	April 12	1884*	April 13
5	1809	April 2	1847	April 4	1885	April 5
6	1810	April 22	1848*	April 23	1886	April 25
7	1811	April 14	1849	April 8	1887	April 10
8	1812*	March 29	1850	March 31	1888*	April 1
9	1813	April 18	1851	April 20	1889	April 21
10	1814	April 10	1852*	April 11	1890	April 6
11	1815	March 26	1853	March 27	1891	March 29
12	1816*	April 14	1854	April 16	1892*	April 17
13	1817	April 6	1855	April 8	1893	April 2
14	1818	March 22	1856*	March 23	1894	March 25
15	1819	April 11	1857	April 12	1895	April 14
16	1820*	April 2	1858	April 4	1896*	April 5
17	1821	April 22	1859	April 24	1897	April 18
18	1822	April 7	1860*	April 8	1898	April 10
19	1823	March 30	1861	March 31	1899	April 2

*NOTE, That the Years marked with an asterisk are Bissextile or Leap-years.

Tables for finding Holy Days

Golden Number	Year of our Lord	Easter Day	Year of our Lord	Easter Day	Year of our Lord	Easter Day
1	1900	April 15	1938	April 17	1976*	April 18
2	1901	April 7	1939	April 9	1977	April 10
3	1902	March 30	1940*	March 24	1978	March 26
4	1903	April 12	1941	April 13	1979	April 15
5	1904*	April 3	1942	April 5	1980*	April 6
6	1905	April 23	1943	April 25	1981	April 19
7	1906	April 15	1944*	April 9	1982	April 11
8	1907	March 31	1945	April 1	1983	April 3
9	1908*	April 19	1946	April 21	1984*	April 22
10	1909	April 11	1947	April 6	1985	April 7
11	1910	March 27	1948*	March 28	1986	March 30
12	1911	April 16	1949	April 17	1987	April 19
13	1912*	April 7	1950	April 9	1988*	April 3
14	1913	March 23	1951	March 25	1989	March 26
15	1914	April 12	1952*	April 13	1990	April 15
16	1915	April 4	1953	April 5	1991	March 31
17	1916*	April 23	1954	April 18	1992*	April 19
18	1917	April 8	1955	April 10	1993	April 11
19	1918	March 31	1956*	April 1	1994	April 3
1	1919	April 20	1957	April 21	1995	April 16
2	1920*	April 4	1958	April 6	1996*	April 7
3	1921	March 27	1959	March 29	1997	March 30
4	1922	April 16	1960*	April 17	1998	April 12
5	1923	April 1	1961	April 2	1999	April 4
6	1924*	April 20	1962	April 22	2000*	April 23
7	1925	April 12	1963	April 14	2001	April 15
8	1926	April 4	1964*	March 29	2002	March 31
9	1927	April 17	1965	April 18	2003	April 20
10	1928*	April 8	1966	April 10	2004*	April 11
11	1929	March 31	1967	March 26	2005	March 27
12	1930	April 20	1968*	April 14	2006	April 16
13	1931	April 5	1969	April 6	2007	April 8
14	1932*	March 27	1970	March 29	2008*	March 23
15	1933	April 16	1971	April 11	2009	April 12
16	1934	April 1	1972*	April 2	2010	April 4
17	1935	April 21	1973	April 22	2011	April 24
18	1936*	April 12	1974	April 14	2012*	April 8
19	1937	March 28	1975	March 30	2013	March 31

* Note, That the Years marked with an asterisk are Bissextile or Leap-years.

Tables for finding Holy Days

A TABLE OF THE MOVABLE FEASTS,

ACCORDING TO THE SEVERAL DAYS THAT EASTER CAN POSSIBLY FALL UPON.

Easter Day	Sundays after Epiphany	Septuagesima Sunday	First day of Lent	Ascension Day	Whitsunday	Sundays after Trinity	Advent Sunday
March 22	1	Jan. 18	Feb. 4	April 30	May 10	27	November 29
March 23	1	Jan. 19	Feb. 5	May 1	May 11	27	November 30
March 24	1	Jan. 20	Feb. 6	May 2	May 12	27	December 1
March 25	2	Jan. 21	Feb. 7	May 3	May 13	27	December 2
March 26	2	Jan. 22	Feb. 8	May 4	May 14	27	December 3
March 27	2	Jan. 23	Feb. 9	May 5	May 15	26	November 27
March 28	2	Jan. 24	Feb. 10	May 6	May 16	26	November 28
March 29	2	Jan. 25	Feb. 11	May 7	May 17	26	November 29
March 30	2	Jan. 26	Feb. 12	May 8	May 18	26	November 30
March 31	2	Jan. 27	Feb. 13	May 9	May 19	26	December 1
April 1	3	Jan. 28	Feb. 14	May 10	May 20	26	December 2
April 2	3	Jan. 29	Feb. 15	May 11	May 21	26	December 3
April 3	3	Jan. 30	Feb. 16	May 12	May 22	25	November 27
April 4	3	Jan. 31	Feb. 17	May 13	May 23	25	November 28
April 5	3	Feb. 1	Feb. 18	May 14	May 24	25	November 29
April 6	3	Feb. 2	Feb. 19	May 15	May 25	25	November 30
April 7	3	Feb. 3	Feb. 20	May 16	May 26	25	December 1
April 8	4	Feb. 4	Feb. 21	May 17	May 27	25	December 2
April 9	4	Feb. 5	Feb. 22	May 18	May 28	25	December 3
April 10	4	Feb. 6	Feb. 23	May 19	May 29	24	November 27
April 11	4	Feb. 7	Feb. 24	May 20	May 30	24	November 28
April 12	4	Feb. 8	Feb. 25	May 21	May 31	24	November 29
April 13	4	Feb. 9	Feb. 26	May 22	June 1	24	November 30
April 14	4	Feb. 10	Feb. 27	May 23	June 2	24	December 1
April 15	5	Feb. 11	Feb. 28	May 24	June 3	24	December 2
April 16	5	Feb. 12	March 1	May 25	June 4	24	December 3
April 17	5	Feb. 13	March 2	May 26	June 5	23	November 27
April 18	5	Feb. 14	March 3	May 27	June 6	23	November 28
April 19	5	Feb. 15	March 4	May 28	June 7	23	November 29
April 20	5	Feb. 16	March 5	May 29	June 8	23	November 30
April 21	5	Feb. 17	March 6	May 30	June 9	23	December 1
April 22	6	Feb. 18	March 7	May 31	June 10	23	December 2
April 23	6	Feb. 19	March 8	June 1	June 11	23	December 3
April 24	6	Feb. 20	March 9	June 2	June 12	22	November 27
April 25	6	Feb. 21	March 10	June 3	June 13	22	November 28

NOTE, That in a Bissextile or Leap-year, the number of Sundays after Epiphany will be the same as if Easter Day had fallen one Day later than it really does. And, for the same reason, one Day must, in every Leap-year, be added to the Day of the Month given by the Table for Septuagesima Sunday, and for the First Day of Lent: unless the Table gives some Day in the Month of March for it; for in that case, the Day given by the Table is the right Day.

Tables for finding Holy Days

GENERAL TABLES

FOR FINDING THE DOMINICAL OR SUNDAY LETTER, AND THE PLACES OF THE GOLDEN NUMBERS IN THE CALENDAR.

TABLE I.

TO find the Dominical or Sunday Letter for any given Year of our Lord, add to the Year its fourth part, omitting fractions, and also the Number, which, in TABLE I., standeth at the top of the column wherein the number of Hundreds contained in that given Year is found; divide the sum by 7, and if there be no Remainder, then A is the Sunday Letter; but if any number remain, then the Letter which standeth under that Number at the top of the Table, is the Sunday Letter.

NOTE, That in all Bissextile or Leap-years, the Letter found as above will be the Sunday Letter from the first Day of March inclusive, to the End of the Year.

TABLE I.

6	5	4	3	2	1	0
B	C	D	E	F	G	A
				1600	1700	1800
1900 2000	2100	2200	2300 2400	2500	2600	2700 2800
2900	3000	3100 3200	3300	3400	3500 3600	3700
3800	3900 4000	4100	4200	4300 4400	4500	4600
4700 4800	4900	5000	etc.			

TABLE II.

To find the Days to which the Golden Numbers ought to be prefixed in the Calendar in any given Year of our Lord, consisting of entire Hundred Years, and in all the intermediate Years betwixt that and the next Hundredth Year following, look in the first column of this Table for the given Year, consisting of entire Hundreds, and against it, under each Golden Number, you will find the Day of the Month to which that Golden Number ought to be prefixed in the Calendar, during that period of One Hundred Years: and if the number of the Day be greater than 20, it is a Day of March; but if it be less than 20, it is a Day of April.

The asterisk, affixed to certain Hundredth Years, denotes those Years which are still to be accounted Bissextile or Leap-years in the new Calendar; whereas all the other Hundredth Years are to be accounted only common Years.

lvi

Tables for finding Holy Days

TABLE II.

THE GOLDEN NUMBERS

Years of our Lord	1	2	3	4	5	6	7	8	9	10	11	12	13	14	15	16	17	18	19
1600*	12	1	21	9	29	17	6	26	14	3	23	11	31	18	8	28	16	5	25
1700, 1800	13	2	22	10	30	18	7	27	15	4	24	12	1	21	9	29	17	6	26
1900. 2000*, 2100	14	3	23	11	31	18	8	28	16	5	25	13	2	22	10	30	17	7	27
2200, 2400*	15	4	24	12	1	21	9	29	17	6	26	14	3	23	11	31	18	8	28
2300, 2500	16	5	25	13	2	22	10	30	18	7	27	15	4	24	12	1	21	9	29
2600, 2700, 2800*	17	6	26	14	3	23	11	31	18	8	28	16	5	25	13	2	22	10	30
2900, 3000	18	7	27	15	4	24	12	1	21	9	29	17	6	26	14	3	23	11	31
3100, 3200*, 3300	18	8	28	16	5	25	13	2	22	10	30	17	7	27	15	4	24	12	1
3400, 3600*	21	9	29	17	6	26	14	3	23	11	31	18	8	28	16	5	25	13	2
3500, 3700	22	10	30	18	7	27	15	4	24	12	1	21	9	29	17	6	26	14	3
3800, 3900, 4000*	23	11	31	18	8	28	16	5	25	13	2	22	10	30	17	7	27	15	4
4100	24	12	1	21	9	29	17	6	26	14	3	23	11	31	18	8	28	16	5
4200, 4300, 4400*	25	13	2	22	10	30	18	7	27	15	4	24	12	1	21	9	29	17	6
4500, 4600	26	14	3	23	11	31	18	8	28	16	5	25	13	2	22	10	30	17	7
4700, 4800*, 4900	27	15	4	24	12	1	21	9	29	17	6	26	14	3	23	11	31	18	8
5000, 5200*	28	16	5	25	13	2	22	10	30	18	7	27	15	4	24	12	1	21	9
5100, 5300	29	17	6	26	14	3	23	11	31	18	8	28	16	5	25	13	2	22	10
5400, 5500, 5600*	30	18	7	27	15	4	24	12	1	21	9	29	17	6	26	14	3	23	11
5700, 5800	31	18	8	28	16	5	25	13	2	22	10	30	17	7	27	15	4	24	12
5900, 6000*, 6100	1	21	9	29	17	6	26	14	3	23	11	31	18	8	28	16	5	25	13
6200, 6400*	2	22	10	30	18	7	27	15	4	24	12	1	21	9	29	17	6	26	14
6300, 6500	3	23	11	31	18	8	28	16	5	25	13	2	22	10	30	17	7	27	15
6600, 6800*	4	24	12	1	21	9	29	17	6	26	14	3	23	11	31	18	8	28	16
6700, 6900	5	25	13	2	22	10	30	18	7	27	15	4	24	12	1	21	9	29	17
7000, 7100, 7200*	6	26	14	3	23	11	31	18	8	28	16	5	25	13	2	22	10	30	17
7300, 7400	7	27	15	4	24	12	1	21	9	29	17	6	26	14	3	23	11	31	18
7500, 7600*, 7700	8	28	16	5	25	13	2	22	10	30	18	7	27	15	4	24	12	1	21
7800, 8000*	9	29	17	6	26	14	3	23	11	31	18	8	28	16	5	25	13	2	22
7900, 8100	10	30	18	7	27	15	4	24	12	1	21	9	29	17	6	26	14	3	23
8200, 8300, 8400*	11	31	18	8	28	16	5	25	13	2	22	10	30	17	7	27	15	4	24

Tables for finding Holy Days

TABLE II.

THE GOLDEN NUMBERS

Morning and Evening Prayer

together with

Prayers and Thanksgivings

The Litany

A Penitential Office

The Order for
Daily Morning Prayer

¶ *The Minister shall begin the Morning Prayer by reading one or more of the following Sentences of Scripture.*

¶ *On any day, save a Day of Fasting or Abstinence, or on any day when the Litany or Holy Communion is immediately to follow, the Minister may, at his discretion, pass at once from the Sentences to the Lord's Prayer, first pronouncing,* The Lord be with you. *Answer.* And with thy spirit. *Minister.* Let us pray.

¶ *And* NOTE, *That when the Confession and Absolution are omitted, the Minister may, after the Sentences, pass to the Versicles,* O Lord, open thou our lips, *etc., in which case the Lord's Prayer shall be said with the other prayers, immediately after* The Lord be with you, *etc., and before the Versicles and Responses which follow, or, in the Litany, as there appointed.*

THE LORD is in his holy temple: let all the earth keep silence before him. *Hab. ii.* 20.

I was glad when they said unto me, We will go into the house of the LORD. *Psalm cxxii.* 1.

Let the words of my mouth, and the meditation of my heart, be alway acceptable in thy sight, O LORD, my strength and my redeemer. *Psalm xix.* 14.

O send out thy light and thy truth, that they may lead me, and bring me unto thy holy hill, and to thy dwelling. *Psalm xliii.* 3.

Thus saith the high and lofty One that inhabiteth eternity, whose name is Holy; I dwell in the high and holy place, with him also that is of a contrite and humble spirit, to revive the spirit of the humble, and to revive the heart of the contrite ones. *Isaiah lvii.* 15.

The hour cometh, and now is, when the true worshippers shall worship the Father in spirit and in truth: for the Father seeketh such to worship him. *St. John iv.* 23.

Morning Prayer

Grace be unto you, and peace, from God our Father, and from the Lord Jesus Christ. *Phil. i.* 2.

Advent. Repent ye; for the Kingdom of heaven is at hand. *St. Matt. iii.* 2.

Prepare ye the way of the LORD, make straight in the desert a highway for our God. *Isaiah xl.* 3.

Christmas. Behold, I bring you good tidings of great joy, which shall be to all people. For unto you is born this day in the city of David a Saviour, which is Christ the Lord. *St. Luke ii.* 10, 11.

Epiphany. From the rising of the sun even unto the going down of the same my Name shall be great among the Gentiles; and in every place incense shall be offered unto my Name, and a pure offering: for my Name shall be great among the heathen, saith the LORD of hosts. *Mal. i.* 11.

Awake, awake; put on thy strength, O Zion; put on thy beautiful garments, O Jerusalem. *Isaiah lii.* 1.

Lent. Rend your heart, and not your garments, and turn unto the LORD your God: for he is gracious and merciful, slow to anger, and of great kindness, and repenteth him of the evil. *Joel ii.* 13.

The sacrifices of God are a broken spirit: a broken and a contrite heart, O God, thou wilt not despise. *Psalm li.* 17.

I will arise and go to my father, and will say unto him, Father, I have sinned against heaven, and before thee, and am no more worthy to be called thy son. *St. Luke xv.* 18, 19.

Good Friday. Is it nothing to you, all ye that pass by? behold, and see if there be any sorrow like unto my sorrow which is done unto me, wherewith the LORD hath afflicted me. *Lam. i.* 12.

In whom we have redemption through his blood, the forgiveness of sins, according to the riches of his grace. *Eph. i.* 7.

4

Morning Prayer

Easter. He is risen. The Lord is risen indeed. *St. Mark xvi.* 6; *St. Luke xxiv.* 34.

This is the day which the LORD hath made; we will rejoice and be glad in it. *Psalm cxviii.* 24.

Ascension. Seeing that we have a great High Priest, that is passed into the heavens, Jesus the Son of God, let us come boldly unto the throne of grace, that we may obtain mercy, and find grace to help in time of need. *Heb. iv.* 14, 16.

Whitsunday. Ye shall receive power, after that the Holy Ghost is come upon you: and ye shall be witnesses unto me both in Jerusalem, and in all Judæa, and in Samaria, and unto the uttermost part of the earth. *Acts i.* 8.

Because ye are sons, God hath sent forth the Spirit of his Son into your hearts, crying, Abba, Father. *Gal. iv.* 6.

Trinity Sunday. Holy, holy, holy, Lord God Almighty, which was, and is, and is to come. *Rev. iv.* 8.

Honour the LORD with thy substance, and with the first-fruits of all thine increase: so shall thy barns be filled with plenty, and thy presses shall burst out with new wine. *Prov. iii.* 9, 10.

Thanksgiving Day.

The LORD by wisdom hath founded the earth; by understanding hath he established the heavens. By his knowledge the depths are broken up, and the clouds drop down the dew. *Prov. iii.* 19, 20.

¶ *Then the Minister shall say,*

DEARLY beloved brethren, the Scripture moveth us, in sundry places, to acknowledge and confess our manifold sins and wickedness; and that we should not dissemble nor cloak them before the face of Almighty God our heavenly Father; but confess them with an humble, lowly, penitent, and obedient heart; to the end that we may

5

obtain forgiveness of the same, by his infinite goodness and mercy. And although we ought, at all times, humbly to acknowledge our sins before God; yet ought we chiefly so to do, when we assemble and meet together to render thanks for the great benefits that we have received at his hands, to set forth his most worthy praise, to hear his most holy Word, and to ask those things which are requisite and necessary, as well for the body as the soul. Wherefore I pray and beseech you, as many as are here present, to accompany me with a pure heart, and humble voice, unto the throne of the heavenly grace, saying—

¶ Or he shall say,

LET us humbly confess our sins unto Almighty God.

A General Confession.

¶ To be said by the whole Congregation, after the Minister, all kneeling.

ALMIGHTY and most merciful Father; We have erred, and strayed from thy ways like lost sheep. We have followed too much the devices and desires of our own hearts. We have offended against thy holy laws. We have left undone those things which we ought to have done; And we have done those things which we ought not to have done; And there is no health in us. But thou, O Lord, have mercy upon us, miserable offenders. Spare thou those, O God, who confess their faults. Restore thou those who are penitent; According to thy promises declared unto mankind In Christ Jesus our Lord. And grant, O most merciful Father, for his sake; That we may hereafter live a godly, righteous, and sober life, To the glory of thy holy Name. Amen.

Morning Prayer

The Declaration of Absolution, or Remission of Sins.

¶ *To be made by the Priest alone, standing; the People still kneeling.*

¶ *But* NOTE, *That the Priest, at his discretion, may use, instead of what follows, the Absolution from the Order for the Holy Communion.*

ALMIGHTY God, the Father of our Lord Jesus Christ, who desireth not the death of a sinner, but rather that he may turn from his wickedness and live, hath given power, and commandment, to his Ministers, to declare and pronounce to his people, being penitent, the Absolution and Remission of their sins. He pardoneth and absolveth all those who truly repent, and unfeignedly believe his holy Gospel.

Wherefore let us beseech him to grant us true repentance, and his Holy Spirit, that those things may please him which we do at this present; and that the rest of our life hereafter may be pure and holy; so that at the last we may come to his eternal joy; through Jesus Christ our Lord. *Amen.*

¶ *Then the Minister shall kneel, and say the Lord's Prayer; the People still kneeling, and repeating it with him, both here, and wheresoever else it is used in Divine Service.*

OUR Father, who art in heaven, Hallowed be thy Name. Thy kingdom come. Thy will be done, On earth as it is in heaven. Give us this day our daily bread. And forgive us our trespasses, As we forgive those who trespass against us. And lead us not into temptation, But deliver us from evil. For thine is the kingdom, and the power, and the glory, for ever and ever. Amen.

¶ *Then likewise he shall say,*

O Lord, open thou our lips.
Answer. And our mouth shall show forth thy praise.

Morning Prayer

¶ *Here, all standing up, the Minister shall say,*

Glory be to the Father, and to the Son, and to the Holy Ghost;

Answer. As it was in the beginning, is now, and ever shall be, world without end. Amen.

Minister. Praise ye the Lord.

Answer. The Lord's Name be praised.

¶ *Then shall be said or sung the following Canticle; except on those days for which other Canticles are appointed; and except also, that Psalm 95 may be used in this place.*

¶ *But* NOTE, *That on Ash Wednesday and Good Friday the Venite may be omitted.*

✦ ✦ ✦

¶ *On the days hereafter named, immediately before the Venite may be sung or said,*

¶ *On the Sundays in Advent.* Our King and Saviour draweth nigh; * O come, let us adore him.

¶ *On Christmas Day and until the Epiphany.* Alleluia. Unto us a child is born; * O come, let us adore him. Alleluia.

¶ *On the Epiphany and seven days after, and on the Feast of the Transfiguration.* The Lord hath manifested forth his glory; * O come, let us adore him.

¶ *On Monday in Easter Week and until Ascension Day.* Alleluia. The Lord is risen indeed; * O come, let us adore him. Alleluia.

¶ *On Ascension Day and until Whitsunday.* Alleluia. Christ the Lord ascendeth into heaven; * O come, let us adore him. Alleluia.

¶ *On Whitsunday and six days after.* Alleluia. The Spirit of the Lord filleth the world; * O come, let us adore him. Alleluia.

¶ *On Trinity Sunday.* Father, Son, and Holy Ghost, one God; * O come, let us adore him.

¶ *On the Purification, and the Annunciation.* The Word was made flesh, and dwelt among us; * O come, let us adore him.

¶ *On other Festivals for which a proper Epistle and Gospel are ordered.* The Lord is glorious in his saints; * O come, let us adore him.

✦ ✦ ✦

8

Morning Prayer

Venite, exultemus Domino.

O COME, let us sing unto the LORD; * let us heartily rejoice in the strength of our salvation.

Let us come before his presence with thanksgiving; * and show ourselves glad in him with psalms.

For the LORD is a great God; * and a great King above all gods.

In his hand are all the corners of the earth; * and the strength of the hills is his also.

The sea is his, and he made it; * and his hands prepared the dry land.

O come, let us worship and fall down, * and kneel before the LORD our Maker.

For he is the Lord our God; * and we are the people of his pasture, and the sheep of his hand.

O worship the LORD in the beauty of holiness; * let the whole earth stand in awe of him.

For he cometh, for he cometh to judge the earth; * and with righteousness to judge the world, and the peoples with his truth.

¶ *Then shall follow a Portion of the Psalms, according to the Use of this Church. And at the end of every Psalm, and likewise at the end of the Venite, Benedictus es, Benedictus, Jubilate, may be, and at the end of the whole Portion, or Selection from the Psalter, shall be sung or said the Gloria Patri:*

G LORY be to the Father, and to the Son, * and to the Holy Ghost;

As it was in the beginning, is now, and ever shall be, * world without end. Amen.

¶ *Then shall be read the First Lesson, according to the Table or Calendar. And* NOTE, *That before every Lesson, the Minister shall say,* Here beginneth *such a* Chapter (*or* Verse of *such a* Chapter) of *such a* Book; *and after every Lesson,* Here endeth the First (*or* the Second) Lesson.

Morning Prayer

¶ *Here shall be said or sung the following Hymn.*

¶ *But* NOTE, *That on any day when the Holy Communion is immediately to follow, the Minister at his discretion, after any one of the following Canticles of Morning Prayer has been said or sung, may pass at once to the Communion Service.*

Te Deum laudamus.

WE praise thee, O God; we acknowledge thee to be the Lord.

All the earth doth worship thee, the Father everlasting.

To thee all Angels cry aloud; the Heavens, and all the Powers therein;

To thee Cherubim and Seraphim continually do cry,

Holy, Holy, Holy, Lord God of Sabaoth;

Heaven and earth are full of the Majesty of thy glory.

The glorious company of the Apostles praise thee.

The goodly fellowship of the Prophets praise thee.

The noble army of Martyrs praise thee.

The holy Church throughout all the world doth acknowledge thee;

The Father, of an infinite Majesty;

Thine adorable, true, and only Son;

Also the Holy Ghost, the Comforter.

THOU art the King of Glory, O Christ.

Thou art the everlasting Son of the Father.

When thou tookest upon thee to deliver man, thou didst humble thyself to be born of a Virgin.

When thou hadst overcome the sharpness of death, thou didst open the Kingdom of Heaven to all believers.

Thou sittest at the right hand of God, in the glory of the Father.

We believe that thou shalt come to be our Judge.

We therefore pray thee, help thy servants, whom thou hast redeemed with thy precious blood.

Morning Prayer

Make them to be numbered with thy Saints, in glory everlasting.

O LORD, save thy people, and bless thine heritage.
Govern them, and lift them up for ever.

Day by day we magnify thee;

And we worship thy Name ever, world without end.

Vouchsafe, O Lord, to keep us this day without sin.

O Lord, have mercy upon us, have mercy upon us.

O Lord, let thy mercy be upon us, as our trust is in thee.

O Lord, in thee have I trusted; let me never be confounded.

¶ *Or this Canticle.*

Benedictus es, Domine.

BLESSED art thou, O Lord God of our fathers: * praised and exalted above all for ever.

Blessed art thou for the Name of thy Majesty: * praised and exalted above all for ever.

Blessed art thou in the temple of thy holiness: * praised and exalted above all for ever.

Blessed art thou that beholdest the depths, and dwellest between the Cherubim: * praised and exalted above all for ever.

Blessed art thou on the glorious throne of thy kingdom: * praised and exalted above all for ever.

Blessed art thou in the firmament of heaven: * praised and exalted above all for ever.

¶ *Or this Canticle.*

Benedicite, omnia opera Domini.

O ALL ye Works of the Lord, bless ye the Lord: * praise him, and magnify him for ever.

11

Morning Prayer

O ye Angels of the Lord, bless ye the Lord: * praise him, and magnify him for ever.

O YE Heavens, bless ye the Lord: * praise him, and magnify him for ever.

O ye Waters that be above the firmament, bless ye the Lord: * praise him, and magnify him for ever.

O all ye Powers of the Lord, bless ye the Lord: * praise him, and magnify him for ever.

O ye Sun and Moon, bless ye the Lord: * praise him, and magnify him for ever.

O ye Stars of heaven, bless ye the Lord: * praise him, and magnify him for ever.

O ye Showers and Dew, bless ye the Lord: * praise him, and magnify him for ever.

O ye Winds of God, bless ye the Lord: * praise him, and magnify him for ever.

O ye Fire and Heat, bless ye the Lord: * praise him, and magnify him for ever.

O ye Winter and Summer, bless ye the Lord: * praise him, and magnify him for ever.

O ye Dews and Frosts, bless ye the Lord: * praise him, and magnify him for ever.

O ye Frost and Cold, bless ye the Lord: * praise him, and magnify him for ever.

O ye Ice and Snow, bless ye the Lord: * praise him, and magnify him for ever.

O ye Nights and Days, bless ye the Lord: * praise him, and magnify him for ever.

O ye Light and Darkness, bless ye the Lord: * praise him, and magnify him for ever.

O ye Lightnings and Clouds, bless ye the Lord: * praise him, and magnify him for ever.

Morning Prayer

O LET the Earth bless the Lord: * yea, let it praise him, and magnify him for ever.

O ye Mountains and Hills, bless ye the Lord: * praise him, and magnify him for ever.

O all ye Green Things upon the earth, bless ye the Lord: * praise him, and magnify him for ever.

O ye Wells, bless ye the Lord: * praise him, and magnify him for ever.

O ye Seas and Floods, bless ye the Lord: * praise him, and magnify him for ever.

O ye Whales, and all that move in the waters, bless ye the Lord: * praise him, and magnify him for ever.

O all ye Fowls of the air, bless ye the Lord: * praise him, and magnify him for ever.

O all ye Beasts and Cattle, bless ye the Lord: * praise him, and magnify him for ever.

O ye Children of Men, bless ye the Lord: * praise him, and magnify him for ever.

O LET Israel bless the Lord: * praise him, and magnify him for ever.

O ye Priests of the Lord, bless ye the Lord: * praise him, and magnify him for ever.

O ye Servants of the Lord, bless ye the Lord: * praise him, and magnify him for ever.

O ye Spirits and Souls of the Righteous, bless ye the Lord: * praise him, and magnify him for ever.

O ye holy and humble Men of heart, bless ye the Lord: * praise him, and magnify him for ever.

LET us bless the Father, and the Son, and the Holy Ghost: * praise him, and magnify him for ever.

Morning Prayer

¶ *Then shall be read, in like manner, the Second Lesson, taken out of the New Testament, according to the Table or Calendar.*

¶ *And after that shall be sung or said the Hymn following.*

¶ *But* NOTE, *That, save on the Sundays in Advent, the latter portion thereof may be omitted.*

Benedictus. St. Luke i. 68.

BLESSED be the Lord God of Israel; * for he hath visited and redeemed his people;

And hath raised up a mighty salvation for us, * in the house of his servant David;

As he spake by the mouth of his holy Prophets, * which have been since the world began;

That we should be saved from our enemies, * and from the hand of all that hate us.

To perform the mercy promised to our forefathers, * and to remember his holy covenant;

To perform the oath which he sware to our forefather Abraham, * that he would give us;

That we being delivered out of the hand of our enemies * might serve him without fear;

In holiness and righteousness before him, * all the days of our life.

And thou, child, shalt be called the prophet of the Highest: * for thou shalt go before the face of the Lord to prepare his ways;

To give knowledge of salvation unto his people * for the remission of their sins,

Through the tender mercy of our God; * whereby the day-spring from on high hath visited us;

To give light to them that sit in darkness, and in the shadow of death, * and to guide our feet into the way of peace.

14

Morning Prayer

¶ *Or this Psalm.*

Jubilate Deo. Psalm c.

O BE joyful in the LORD, all ye lands: * serve the LORD with gladness, and come before his presence with a song.

Be ye sure that the LORD he is God; it is he that hath made us, and not we ourselves; * we are his people, and the sheep of his pasture.

O go your way into his gates with thanksgiving, and into his courts with praise; * be thankful unto him, and speak good of his Name.

For the LORD is gracious, his mercy is everlasting; * and his truth endureth from generation to generation.

¶ *Then shall be said the Apostles' Creed by the Minister and the People, standing. And any Churches may, instead of the words,* He descended into hell, *use the words,* He went into the place of departed spirits, *which are considered as words of the same meaning in the Creed.*

I BELIEVE in God the Father Almighty, Maker of heaven and earth:

And in Jesus Christ his only Son our Lord: Who was conceived by the Holy Ghost, Born of the Virgin Mary: Suffered under Pontius Pilate, Was crucified, dead, and buried: He descended into hell; The third day he rose again from the dead: He ascended into heaven, And sitteth on the right hand of God the Father Almighty: From thence he shall come to judge the quick and the dead.

I believe in the Holy Ghost: The holy Catholic Church; The Communion of Saints: The Forgiveness of sins: The Resurrection of the body: And the Life everlasting. Amen.

¶ *Or the Creed commonly called the Nicene.*

I BELIEVE in one God the Father Almighty, Maker of heaven and earth, And of all things visible and invisible:

Morning Prayer

And in one Lord Jesus Christ, the only-begotten Son of God; Begotten of his Father before all worlds, God of God, Light of Light, Very God of very God; Begotten, not made; Being of one substance with the Father; By whom all things were made: Who for us men and for our salvation came down from heaven, And was incarnate by the Holy Ghost of the Virgin Mary, And was made man: And was crucified also for us under Pontius Pilate; He suffered and was buried: And the third day he rose again according to the Scriptures: And ascended into heaven, And sitteth on the right hand of the Father: And he shall come again, with glory, to judge both the quick and the dead; Whose kingdom shall have no end.

And I believe in the Holy Ghost, The Lord, and Giver of Life, Who proceedeth from the Father and the Son; Who with the Father and the Son together is worshipped and glorified; Who spake by the Prophets: And I believe one Catholic and Apostolic Church: I acknowledge one Baptism for the remission of sins: And I look for the Resurrection of the dead: And the Life of the world to come. Amen.

¶ *And after that, these Prayers following, the People devoutly kneeling; the Minister first pronouncing,*

The Lord be with you.
Answer. And with thy spirit.
Minister. Let us pray.

¶ *Here, if it hath not already been said, shall follow the Lord's Prayer.*

Minister. O Lord, show thy mercy upon us.
Answer. And grant us thy salvation.
Minister. O God, make clean our hearts within us.
Answer. And take not thy Holy Spirit from us.

Morning Prayer

¶ *Then shall follow the Collect for the Day, except when the Communion Service is read; and then the Collect for the Day shall be omitted here.*

A Collect for Peace.

O GOD, who art the author of peace and lover of concord, in knowledge of whom standeth our eternal life, whose service is perfect freedom; Defend us thy humble servants in all assaults of our enemies; that we, surely trusting in thy defence, may not fear the power of any adversaries, through the might of Jesus Christ our Lord. *Amen.*

A Collect for Grace.

O LORD, our heavenly Father, Almighty and everlasting God, who hast safely brought us to the beginning of this day; Defend us in the same with thy mighty power; and grant that this day we fall into no sin, neither run into any kind of danger; but that all our doings, being ordered by thy governance, may be righteous in thy sight; through Jesus Christ our Lord. *Amen.*

¶ *The following Prayers shall be omitted here when the Litany is said, and may be omitted when the Holy Communion is to follow.*

¶ *And* NOTE, *That the Minister may here end the Morning Prayer with such general intercessions taken out of this Book, as he shall think fit, or with the Grace.*

A Prayer for The President of the United States, and all in Civil Authority.

O LORD, our heavenly Father, the high and mighty Ruler of the universe, who dost from thy throne behold all the dwellers upon earth; Most heartily we beseech thee, with thy favour to behold and bless thy servant THE PRESIDENT OF THE UNITED STATES, and all others in authority; and so replenish them with the grace of thy Holy Spirit, that they may always incline to thy will, and walk in thy way.

Morning Prayer

Endue them plenteously with heavenly gifts; grant them in health and prosperity long to live; and finally, after this life, to attain everlasting joy and felicity; through Jesus Christ our Lord. *Amen.*

¶ *Or this.*

O LORD our Governor, whose glory is in all the world; We commend this nation to thy merciful care, that being guided by thy Providence, we may dwell secure in thy peace. Grant to THE PRESIDENT OF THE UNITED STATES, and to all in authority, wisdom and strength to know and to do thy will. Fill them with the love of truth and righteousness; and make them ever mindful of their calling to serve this people in thy fear; through Jesus Christ our Lord, who liveth and reigneth with thee and the Holy Ghost, one God, world without end. *Amen.*

A Prayer for the Clergy and People.

ALMIGHTY and everlasting God, from whom cometh every good and perfect gift; Send down upon our Bishops, and other Clergy, and upon the Congregations committed to their charge, the healthful Spirit of thy grace; and, that they may truly please thee, pour upon them the continual dew of thy blessing. Grant this, O Lord, for the honour of our Advocate and Mediator, Jesus Christ. *Amen.*

A Prayer for all Conditions of Men.

O GOD, the Creator and Preserver of all mankind, we humbly beseech thee for all sorts and conditions of men; that thou wouldest be pleased to make thy ways known unto them, thy saving health unto all nations. More especially we pray for thy holy Church universal; that it may be so guided and governed by thy good Spirit, that all who profess and call themselves Christians may be led into

Morning Prayer

the way of truth, and hold the faith in unity of spirit, in the bond of peace, and in righteousness of life. Finally, we commend to thy fatherly goodness all those who are any ways afflicted, or distressed, in mind, body, or estate; [* *especially those for whom our prayers are desired;*] that it may please thee to comfort and relieve them, according to their *This may be said when any desire the prayers of the Congregation.* several necessities; giving them patience under their sufferings, and a happy issue out of all their afflictions. And this we beg for Jesus Christ's sake. *Amen.*

A General Thanksgiving.

ALMIGHTY God, Father of all mercies, we, thine unworthy servants, do give thee most humble and hearty thanks for all thy goodness and lovingkindness to us, and to all men; [* *particularly to those who desire now to offer up their praises and thanksgivings for thy late mercies vouchsafed unto them.*] We bless thee for our creation, preservation, and all the blessings of *This may be said when any desire to return thanks for mercies vouchsafed to them.* this life; but above all, for thine inestimable love in the redemption of the world by our Lord Jesus Christ; for the means of grace, and for the hope of glory. And, we beseech thee, give us that due sense of all thy mercies, that our hearts may be unfeignedly thankful; and that we show forth thy praise, not only with our lips, but in our lives, by giving up our selves to thy service, and by walking before thee in holiness and righteousness all our days; through Jesus Christ our Lord, to whom, with thee and the Holy Ghost, be all honour and glory, world without end. *Amen.*

¶ NOTE, *That the General Thanksgiving may be said by the Congregation with the Minister.*

Morning Prayer

A Prayer of St. Chrysostom.

ALMIGHTY God, who hast given us grace at this time with one accord to make our common supplications unto thee; and dost promise that when two or three are gathered together in thy Name thou wilt grant their requests; Fulfil now, O Lord, the desires and petitions of thy servants, as may be most expedient for them; granting us in this world knowledge of thy truth, and in the world to come life everlasting. *Amen.*

2 Cor. xiii. 14.

THE grace of our Lord Jesus Christ, and the love of God, and the fellowship of the Holy Ghost, be with us all evermore. *Amen.*

Here endeth the Order of Morning Prayer.

The Order for
Daily Evening Prayer

¶ *The Minister shall begin the Evening Prayer by reading one or more of the following Sentences of Scripture; and then he shall say that which is written after them. But he may, at his discretion, pass at once from the Sentences to the Lord's Prayer.*

¶ *And* NOTE, *That when the Confession and Absolution are omitted, the Minister may, after the Sentences, pass to the Versicles,* O Lord, open thou our lips, *etc., in which case the Lord's Prayer shall be said with the other prayers, immediately after* The Lord be with you, *etc., and before the Versicles and Responses which follow.*

THE LORD is in his holy temple: let all the earth keep silence before him. *Hab. ii.* 20.

LORD, I have loved the habitation of thy house, and the place where thine honour dwelleth. *Psalm xxvi.* 8.

Let my prayer be set forth in thy sight as the incense; and let the lifting up of my hands be an evening sacrifice. *Psalm cxli.* 2.

O worship the LORD in the beauty of holiness; let the whole earth stand in awe of him. *Psalm xcvi.* 9.

Let the words of my mouth, and the meditation of my heart, be alway acceptable in thy sight, O LORD, my strength and my redeemer. *Psalm xix.* 14.

Advent. Watch ye, for ye know not when the master of the house cometh, at even, or at midnight, or at the cock-crowing, or in the morning: lest coming suddenly he find you sleeping. *St. Mark xiii.* 35, 36.

Christmas. Behold, the tabernacle of God is with men, and he will dwell with them, and they shall be his people, and God himself shall be with them, and be their God. *Rev. xxi.* 3.

Evening Prayer

Epiphany. The Gentiles shall come to thy light, and kings to the brightness of thy rising. *Isaiah lx.* 3.

Lent. I acknowledge my transgressions, and my sin is ever before me. *Psalm li.* 3.

To the Lord our God belong mercies and forgivenesses, though we have rebelled against him; neither have we obeyed the voice of the LORD our God, to walk in his laws which he set before us. *Dan. ix.* 9, 10.

If we say that we have no sin, we deceive ourselves, and the truth is not in us; but if we confess our sins, God is faithful and just to forgive us our sins, and to cleanse us from all unrighteousness. 1 *St. John i.* 8, 9.

Good Friday. All we like sheep have gone astray; we have turned every one to his own way; and the LORD hath laid on him the iniquity of us all. *Isaiah liii.* 6.

Easter. Thanks be to God, which giveth us the victory through our Lord Jesus Christ. 1 *Cor. xv.* 57.

If ye then be risen with Christ, seek those things which are above, where Christ sitteth on the right hand of God. *Col. iii.* 1.

Ascension. Christ is not entered into the holy places made with hands, which are the figures of the true; but into heaven itself, now to appear in the presence of God for us. *Heb. ix.* 24.

Whitsunday. There is a river, the streams whereof shall make glad the city of God, the holy place of the tabernacles of the Most High. *Psalm xlvi.* 4.

The Spirit and the bride say, Come. And let him that heareth say, Come. And let him that is athirst come. And whosoever will, let him take the water of life freely. *Rev. xxii.* 17.

Trinity Sunday. Holy, holy, holy, is the LORD of hosts: the whole earth is full of his glory. *Isaiah vi.* 3.

Evening Prayer

LET us humbly confess our sins unto Almighty God.

¶ Or else he shall say as followeth.

DEARLY beloved brethren, the Scripture moveth us, in sundry places, to acknowledge and confess our manifold sins and wickedness; and that we should not dissemble nor cloak them before the face of Almighty God our heavenly Father; but confess them with an humble, lowly, penitent, and obedient heart; to the end that we may obtain forgiveness of the same, by his infinite goodness and mercy. And although we ought, at all times, humbly to acknowledge our sins before God; yet ought we chiefly so to do, when we assemble and meet together to render thanks for the great benefits that we have received at his hands, to set forth his most worthy praise, to hear his most holy Word, and to ask those things which are requisite and necessary, as well for the body as the soul. Wherefore I pray and beseech you, as many as are here present, to accompany me with a pure heart, and humble voice, unto the throne of the heavenly grace, saying—

A General Confession.

¶ To be said by the whole Congregation, after the Minister, all kneeling.

ALMIGHTY and most merciful Father; We have erred, and strayed from thy ways like lost sheep. We have followed too much the devices and desires of our own hearts. We have offended against thy holy laws. We have left undone those things which we ought to have done; And we have done those things which we ought not to have done; And there is no health in us. But thou, O Lord, have mercy upon us, miserable offenders. Spare thou those, O God, who confess their faults. Restore thou those who are penitent; According to thy promises declared unto

23

mankind In Christ Jesus our Lord. And grant, O most merciful Father, for his sake; That we may hereafter live a godly, righteous, and sober life, To the glory of thy holy Name. Amen.

The Declaration of Absolution, or Remission of Sins.

¶ *To be made by the Priest alone, standing; the People still kneeling.*

ALMIGHTY God, the Father of our Lord Jesus Christ, who desireth not the death of a sinner, but rather that he may turn from his wickedness and live, hath given power, and commandment, to his Ministers, to declare and pronounce to his people, being penitent, the Absolution and Remission of their sins. He pardoneth and absolveth all those who truly repent, and unfeignedly believe his holy Gospel.

Wherefore let us beseech him to grant us true repentance, and his Holy Spirit, that those things may please him which we do at this present; and that the rest of our life hereafter may be pure and holy; so that at the last we may come to his eternal joy; through Jesus Christ our Lord. *Amen.*

¶ *Or this.*

THE Almighty and merciful Lord grant you Absolution and Remission of all your sins, true repentance, amendment of life, and the grace and consolation of his Holy Spirit. *Amen.*

¶ *Then the Minister shall kneel, and say the Lord's Prayer; the People still kneeling, and repeating it with him.*

OUR Father, who art in heaven, Hallowed be thy Name. Thy kingdom come. Thy will be done, On earth as it is in heaven. Give us this day our daily bread. And forgive us our trespasses, As we forgive those who trespass against

Evening Prayer

us. And lead us not into temptation, But deliver us from evil. For thine is the kingdom, and the power, and the glory, for ever and ever. Amen.

¶ Then likewise he shall say,

O Lord, open thou our lips.
Answer. And our mouth shall show forth thy praise.

¶ Here, all standing up, the Minister shall say,

Glory be to the Father, and to the Son, and to the Holy Ghost;
Answer. As it was in the beginning, is now, and ever shall be, world without end. Amen.
Minister. Praise ye the Lord.
Answer. The Lord's Name be praised.

¶ Then shall follow a Portion of the Psalms, according to the Use of this Church. And at the end of every Psalm, and likewise at the end of the Magnificat, Cantate Domino, Bonum est confiteri, Nunc dimittis, Deus misereatur, Benedic, anima mea, may be sung or said the Gloria Patri; and at the end of the whole Portion or Selection of Psalms for the day, shall be sung or said the Gloria Patri, or else the Gloria in excelsis, as followeth.

Gloria in excelsis.

GLORY be to God on high, and on earth peace, good will towards men. We praise thee, we bless thee, we worship thee, we glorify thee, we give thanks to thee for thy great glory, O Lord God, heavenly King, God the Father Almighty.

O Lord, the only-begotten Son, Jesus Christ; O Lord God, Lamb of God, Son of the Father, that takest away the sins of the world, have mercy upon us. Thou that takest away the sins of the world, receive our prayer. Thou that sittest at the right hand of God the Father, have mercy upon us.

Evening Prayer

For thou only art holy; thou only art the Lord; thou only, O Christ, with the Holy Ghost, art most high in the glory of God the Father. Amen.

¶ *Then shall be read the First Lesson, according to the Table or Calendar.*

¶ *After which shall be sung or said the Hymn called Magnificat, as followeth.*

¶ *But* NOTE, *That the Minister, at his discretion, may omit one of the Lessons in Evening Prayer, the Lesson read being followed by one of the Evening Canticles.*

Magnificat. St. Luke i. 46.

MY soul doth magnify the Lord, * and my spirit hath rejoiced in God my Saviour.

For he hath regarded * the lowliness of his handmaiden.

For behold, from henceforth * all generations shall call me blessed.

For he that is mighty hath magnified me; * and holy is his Name.

And his mercy is on them that fear him * throughout all generations.

He hath showed strength with his arm; * he hath scattered the proud in the imagination of their hearts.

He hath put down the mighty from their seat, * and hath exalted the humble and meek.

He hath filled the hungry with good things; * and the rich he hath sent empty away.

He remembering his mercy hath holpen his servant Israel; * as he promised to our forefathers, Abraham and his seed, for ever.

Evening Prayer

¶ *Or this Psalm.*

Cantate Domino. Psalm xcviii.

O SING unto the LORD a new song; * for he hath done marvellous things.

With his own right hand, and with his holy arm, * hath he gotten himself the victory.

The LORD declared his salvation; * his righteousness hath he openly showed in the sight of the heathen.

He hath remembered his mercy and truth toward the house of Israel; * and all the ends of the world have seen the salvation of our God.

Show yourselves joyful unto the LORD, all ye lands; * sing, rejoice, and give thanks.

Praise the LORD upon the harp; * sing to the harp with a psalm of thanksgiving.

With trumpets also and shawms, * O show yourselves joyful before the LORD, the King.

Let the sea make a noise, and all that therein is; * the round world, and they that dwell therein.

Let the floods clap their hands, and let the hills be joyful together before the LORD; * for he cometh to judge the earth.

With righteousness shall he judge the world, * and the peoples with equity.

¶ *Or this.*

Bonum est confiteri. Psalm xcii.

IT is a good thing to give thanks unto the LORD, * and to sing praises unto thy Name, O Most Highest;

To tell of thy loving-kindness early in the morning, * and of thy truth in the night season;

Upon an instrument of ten strings, and upon the lute; * upon a loud instrument, and upon the harp.

For thou, LORD, hast made me glad through thy works; *
and I will rejoice in giving praise for the operations of
thy hands.

¶ *Then a Lesson of the New Testament, as it is appointed.*

¶ *And after that shall be sung or said the Hymn called Nunc dimittis, as
followeth.*

Nunc dimittis. St. Luke ii. 29.

LORD, now lettest thou thy servant depart in peace, *
according to thy word.

For mine eyes have seen * thy salvation,

Which thou hast prepared * before the face of all people;

To be a light to lighten the Gentiles, * and to be the
glory of thy people Israel.

¶ *Or else this Psalm.*

Deus misereatur. Psalm lxvii.

GOD be merciful unto us, and bless us, * and show us the
light of his countenance, and be merciful unto us;

That thy way may be known upon earth, * thy saving
health among all nations.

Let the peoples praise thee, O God; * yea, let all the
peoples praise thee.

O let the nations rejoice and be glad; * for thou shalt
judge the folk righteously, and govern the nations upon
earth.

Let the peoples praise thee, O God; * yea, let all the
peoples praise thee.

Then shall the earth bring forth her increase; * and God,
even our own God, shall give us his blessing.

God shall bless us; * and all the ends of the world shall
fear him.

Evening Prayer

¶ *Or this.*

Benedic, anima mea. Psalm ciii.

PRAISE the LORD, O my soul; * and all that is within me, praise his holy Name.

Praise the LORD, O my soul, * and forget not all his benefits:

Who forgiveth all thy sin, * and healeth all thine infirmities;

Who saveth thy life from destruction, * and crowneth thee with mercy and loving-kindness.

O praise the LORD, ye angels of his, ye that excel in strength; * ye that fulfil his commandment, and hearken unto the voice of his word.

O praise the LORD, all ye his hosts; * ye servants of his that do his pleasure.

O speak good of the LORD, all ye works of his, in all places of his dominion: * praise thou the LORD, O my soul.

¶ *Then shall be said the Apostles' Creed by the Minister and the People, standing. And any Churches may, instead of the words,* He descended into hell, *use the words,* He went into the place of departed spirits, *which are considered as words of the same meaning in the Creed.*

I BELIEVE in God the Father Almighty, Maker of heaven and earth:

And in Jesus Christ his only Son our Lord: Who was conceived by the Holy Ghost, Born of the Virgin Mary: Suffered under Pontius Pilate, Was crucified, dead, and buried: He descended into hell; The third day he rose again from the dead: He ascended into heaven, And sitteth on the right hand of God the Father Almighty: From thence he shall come to judge the quick and the dead.

I believe in the Holy Ghost: The holy Catholic Church; The Communion of Saints: The Forgiveness of sins: The

Resurrection of the body: And the Life everlasting. Amen.

¶ *Or the Creed commonly called the Nicene.*

I BELIEVE in one God the Father Almighty, Maker of heaven and earth, And of all things visible and invisible:

And in one Lord Jesus Christ, the only-begotten Son of God; Begotten of his Father before all worlds, God of God, Light of Light, Very God of very God; Begotten, not made; Being of one substance with the Father; By whom all things were made: Who for us men and for our salvation came down from heaven, And was incarnate by the Holy Ghost of the Virgin Mary, And was made man: And was crucified also for us under Pontius Pilate; He suffered and was buried: And the third day he rose again according to the Scriptures: And ascended into heaven, And sitteth on the right hand of the Father: And he shall come again, with glory, to judge both the quick and the dead; Whose kingdom shall have no end.

And I believe in the Holy Ghost, The Lord, and Giver of Life, Who proceedeth from the Father and the Son; Who with the Father and the Son together is worshipped and glorified; Who spake by the Prophets: And I believe one Catholic and Apostolic Church: I acknowledge one Baptism for the remission of sins: And I look for the Resurrection of the dead: And the Life of the world to come. Amen.

¶ *And after that, these Prayers following, the People devoutly kneeling; the Minister first pronouncing,*

The Lord be with you.
Answer. And with thy spirit.
Minister. Let us pray.

¶ *Here, if it hath not already been said, shall follow the Lord's Prayer.*

Evening Prayer

Minister. O Lord, show thy mercy upon us.

Answer. And grant us thy salvation.

Minister. O Lord, save the State.

Answer. And mercifully hear us when we call upon thee.

Minister. Endue thy Ministers with righteousness.

Answer. And make thy chosen people joyful.

Minister. O Lord, save thy people.

Answer. And bless thine inheritance.

Minister. Give peace in our time, O Lord.

Answer. For it is thou, Lord, only, that makest us dwell in safety.

Minister. O God, make clean our hearts within us.

Answer. And take not thy Holy Spirit from us.

¶ *Then shall be said the Collect for the Day, and after that the Collects and Prayers following.*

A Collect for Peace.

O GOD, from whom all holy desires, all good counsels, and all just works do proceed; Give unto thy servants that peace which the world cannot give; that our hearts may be set to obey thy commandments, and also that by thee, we, being defended from the fear of our enemies, may pass our time in rest and quietness; through the merits of Jesus Christ our Saviour. *Amen.*

A Collect for Aid against Perils.

LIGHTEN our darkness, we beseech thee, O Lord; and by thy great mercy defend us from all perils and dangers of this night; for the love of thy only Son, our Saviour, Jesus Christ. *Amen.*

¶ *In places where it may be convenient, here followeth the Anthem.*

¶ *The Minister may here end the Evening Prayer with such Prayer, or Prayers, taken out of this Book, as he shall think fit.*

31

Evening Prayer

A Prayer for The President of the United States, and all in Civil Authority.

ALMIGHTY God, whose kingdom is everlasting and power infinite; Have mercy upon this whole land; and so rule the hearts of thy servants THE PRESIDENT OF THE UNITED STATES, *The Governor of this State,* and all others in authority, that they, knowing whose ministers they are, may above all things seek thy honour and glory; and that we and all the People, duly considering whose authority they bear, may faithfully and obediently honour them, according to thy blessed Word and ordinance; through Jesus Christ our Lord, who with thee and the Holy Ghost liveth and reigneth ever, one God, world without end. *Amen.*

A Prayer for the Clergy and People.

ALMIGHTY and everlasting God, from whom cometh every good and perfect gift; Send down upon our Bishops, and other Clergy, and upon the Congregations committed to their charge, the healthful Spirit of thy grace; and, that they may truly please thee, pour upon them the continual dew of thy blessing. Grant this, O Lord, for the honour of our Advocate and Mediator, Jesus Christ. *Amen.*

A Prayer for all Conditions of Men.

O GOD, the Creator and Preserver of all mankind, we humbly beseech thee for all sorts and conditions of men; that thou wouldest be pleased to make thy ways known unto them, thy saving health unto all nations. More especially we pray for thy holy Church universal; that it may be so guided and governed by thy good Spirit, that all who profess and call themselves Christians may be led into the way of truth, and hold the faith in unity of spirit, in the bond of peace, and in righteousness of life. Finally, we com-

Evening Prayer

mend to thy fatherly goodness all those who are any ways afflicted, or distressed, in mind, body, or estate; [* *especially those for whom our prayers are desired;*] that it may please thee to comfort and relieve them, according to their

* *This may be said when any desire the prayers of the Congregation.*

several necessities; giving them patience under their sufferings, and a happy issue out of all their afflictions. And this we beg for Jesus Christ's sake. *Amen.*

A General Thanksgiving.

ALMIGHTY God, Father of all mercies, we, thine unworthy servants, do give thee most humble and hearty thanks for all thy goodness and loving-kindness to us, and to all men; [* *particularly to those who desire now to offer up their praises and thanksgivings for thy late mercies vouchsafed unto them.*] We bless thee for our crea-tion, preservation, and all the blessings of

* *This may be said when any desire to return thanks for mercies vouchsafed to them.*

this life; but above all, for thine inestimable love in the redemption of the world by our Lord Jesus Christ; for the means of grace, and for the hope of glory. And, we beseech thee, give us that due sense of all thy mercies, that our hearts may be unfeignedly thankful; and that we show forth thy praise, not only with our lips, but in our lives, by giving up our selves to thy service, and by walking before thee in holiness and righteousness all our days; through Jesus Christ our Lord, to whom, with thee and the Holy Ghost, be all honour and glory, world without end. *Amen.*

¶ NOTE, *That the General Thanksgiving may be said by the Congregation with the Minister.*

Evening Prayer

A Prayer of St. Chrysostom.

ALMIGHTY God, who hast given us grace at this time with one accord to make our common supplications unto thee; and dost promise that when two or three are gathered together in thy Name thou wilt grant their requests; Fulfil now, O Lord, the desires and petitions of thy servants, as may be most expedient for them; granting us in this world knowledge of thy truth, and in the world to come life everlasting. *Amen.*

2 Cor. xiii. 14.

THE grace of our Lord Jesus Christ, and the love of God, and the fellowship of the Holy Ghost, be with us all evermore. *Amen.*

Here endeth the Order of Evening Prayer.

Prayers and Thanksgivings

PRAYERS.

¶ *To be used before the Prayer for all Conditions of Men, or, when that is not said, before the final Prayer of Thanksgiving or of Blessing, or before the Grace.*

A Prayer for Congress.

¶ *To be used during their Session.*

MOST gracious God, we humbly beseech thee, as for the people of these United States in general, so especially for their Senate and Representatives in Congress assembled; that thou wouldest be pleased to direct and prosper all their consultations, to the advancement of thy glory, the good of thy Church, the safety, honour, and welfare of thy people; that all things may be so ordered and settled by their endeavours, upon the best and surest foundations, that peace and happiness, truth and justice, religion and piety, may be established among us for all generations. These and all other necessaries, for them, for us, and thy whole Church, we humbly beg in the Name and mediation of Jesus Christ, our most blessed Lord and Saviour. *Amen.*

For a State Legislature.

O GOD, the fountain of wisdom, whose statutes are good and gracious and whose law is truth; We beseech thee so to guide and bless the Legislature of this State, that it may ordain for our governance only such things as please thee, to the glory of thy Name and the welfare of the people; through Jesus Christ, thy Son, our Lord. *Amen.*

For Courts of Justice.

ALMIGHTY God, who sittest in the throne judging right; We humbly beseech thee to bless the courts of

35

Prayers

justice and the magistrates in all this land; and give unto them the spirit of wisdom and understanding, that they may discern the truth, and impartially administer the law in the fear of thee alone; through him who shall come to be our Judge, thy Son, our Saviour Jesus Christ. *Amen.*

For Our Country.

ALMIGHTY God, who hast given us this good land for our heritage; We humbly beseech thee that we may always prove ourselves a people mindful of thy favour and glad to do thy will. Bless our land with honourable industry, sound learning, and pure manners. Save us from violence, discord, and confusion; from pride and arrogancy, and from every evil way. Defend our liberties, and fashion into one united people the multitudes brought hither out of many kindreds and tongues. Endue with the spirit of wisdom those to whom in thy Name we entrust the authority of government, that there may be justice and peace at home, and that, through obedience to thy law, we may show forth thy praise among the nations of the earth. In the time of prosperity, fill our hearts with thankfulness, and in the day of trouble, suffer not our trust in thee to fail; all which we ask through Jesus Christ our Lord. *Amen.*

A Prayer to be used at the Meetings of Convention.

ALMIGHTY and everlasting God, who by thy Holy Spirit didst preside in the Council of the blessed Apostles, and hast promised, through thy Son Jesus Christ, to be with thy Church to the end of the world; We beseech thee to be with the Council of thy Church *here* assembled in thy Name and Presence. Save *us* from all error, ignorance, pride, and prejudice; and of thy great mercy vouchsafe, we beseech thee, so to direct, sanctify, and govern *us* in *our* work, by the

Prayers

mighty power of the Holy Ghost, that the comfortable Gospel of Christ may be truly preached, truly received, and truly followed, in all places, to the breaking down the kingdom of sin, Satan, and death; till at length the whole of thy dispersed sheep, being gathered into one fold, shall become partakers of everlasting life; through the merits and death of Jesus Christ our Saviour. *Amen.*

¶ *During, or before, the session of any General or Diocesan Convention, the above Prayer may be used by all Congregations of this Church, or of the Diocese concerned; the clause,* here assembled in thy Name, *being changed to* now assembled (*or* about to assemble) in thy Name and Presence; *and the clause,* govern us in our work, *to* govern them in their work.

For the Church.

O GRACIOUS Father, we humbly beseech thee for thy holy Catholic Church; that thou wouldest be pleased to fill it with all truth, in all peace. Where it is corrupt, purify it; where it is in error, direct it; where in any thing it is amiss, reform it. Where it is right, establish it; where it is in want, provide for it; where it is divided, reunite it; for the sake of him who died and rose again, and ever liveth to make intercession for us, Jesus Christ, thy Son, our Lord. *Amen.*

For the Unity of God's People.

O GOD, the Father of our Lord Jesus Christ, our only Saviour, the Prince of Peace; Give us grace seriously to lay to heart the great dangers we are in by our unhappy divisions. Take away all hatred and prejudice, and whatsoever else may hinder us from godly union and concord: that as there is but one Body and one Spirit, and one hope of our calling, one Lord, one Faith, one Baptism, one God and Father of us all, so we may be all of one heart and of one soul, united in one holy bond of truth and peace, of faith and char-

37

Prayers

ity, and may with one mind and one mouth glorify thee; through Jesus Christ our Lord. *Amen.*

For Missions.

O GOD, who hast made of one blood all nations of men for to dwell on the face of the whole earth, and didst send thy blessed Son to preach peace to them that are far off and to them that are nigh; Grant that all men everywhere may seek after thee and find thee. Bring the nations into thy fold, pour out thy Spirit upon all flesh, and hasten thy kingdom; through the same thy Son Jesus Christ our Lord. *Amen.*

¶ *Or this.*

A LMIGHTY God, whose compassions fail not, and whose loving-kindness reacheth unto the world's end; We give thee humble thanks for opening heathen lands to the light of thy truth; for making paths in the deep waters and highways in the desert; and for planting thy Church in all the earth. Grant, we beseech thee, unto us thy servants, that with lively faith we may labour abundantly to make known to all men thy blessed gift of eternal life; through Jesus Christ our Lord. *Amen.*

For those who are to be admitted into Holy Orders.

¶ *To be used in the Weeks preceding the stated Times of Ordination.*

A LMIGHTY God, our heavenly Father, who hast purchased to thyself an universal Church by the precious blood of thy dear Son; Mercifully look upon the same, and at this time so guide and govern the minds of thy servants the Bishops and Pastors of thy flock, that they may lay hands suddenly on no man, but faithfully and wisely make choice of fit persons, to serve in the sacred Ministry of thy Church. And to those who shall be ordained to any holy function,

Prayers

give thy grace and heavenly benediction; that both by their life and doctrine they may show forth thy glory, and set forward the salvation of all men; through Jesus Christ our Lord. *Amen.*

¶ *Or this.*

ALMIGHTY God, the giver of all good gifts, who of thy divine providence hast appointed divers Orders in thy Church; Give thy grace, we humbly beseech thee, to all those who are to be called to any office and administration in the same; and so replenish them with the truth of thy doctrine, and endue them with innocency of life, that they may faithfully serve before thee, to the glory of thy great Name, and the benefit of thy holy Church; through Jesus Christ our Lord. *Amen.*

For the Increase of the Ministry.

O ALMIGHTY God, look mercifully upon the world which thou hast redeemed by the blood of thy dear Son, and incline the hearts of many to dedicate themselves to the sacred Ministry of thy Church; through the same thy Son Jesus Christ our Lord. *Amen.*

For Fruitful Seasons.

¶ *To be used on Rogation Sunday and the Rogation Days.*

ALMIGHTY God, who hast blessed the earth that it should be fruitful and bring forth whatsoever is needful for the life of man, and hast commanded us to work with quietness, and eat our own bread; Bless the labours of the husbandman, and grant such seasonable weather that we may gather in the fruits of the earth, and ever rejoice in thy goodness, to the praise of thy holy Name; through Jesus Christ our Lord. *Amen.*

Prayers

¶ *Or this.*

O GRACIOUS Father, who openest thine hand and fillest all things living with plenteousness; We beseech thee of thine infinite goodness to hear us, who now make our prayers and supplications unto thee. Remember not our sins, but thy promises of mercy. Vouchsafe to bless the lands and multiply the harvests of the world. Let thy breath go forth that it may renew the face of the earth. Show thy loving-kindness, that our land may give her increase; and so fill us with good things that the poor and needy may give thanks unto thy Name; through Christ our Lord. *Amen.*

For Rain.

O GOD, heavenly Father, who by thy Son Jesus Christ hast promised to all those who seek thy kingdom, and the righteousness thereof, all things necessary to their bodily sustenance; Send us, we beseech thee, in this our necessity, such moderate rain and showers, that we may receive the fruits of the earth to our comfort, and to thy honour; through Jesus Christ our Lord. *Amen.*

For Fair Weather.

A LMIGHTY and most merciful Father, we humbly beseech thee, of thy great goodness, to restrain those immoderate rains, wherewith thou hast afflicted us. And we pray thee to send us such seasonable weather, that the earth may, in due time, yield her increase for our use and benefit; through Jesus Christ our Lord. *Amen.*

In Time of Dearth and Famine.

O GOD, heavenly Father, whose gift it is that the rain doth fall, and the earth bring forth her increase; Behold, we beseech thee, the afflictions of thy people; increase the

Prayers

fruits of the earth by thy heavenly benediction; and grant that the scarcity and dearth, which we now most justly suffer for our sins, may, through thy goodness, be mercifully turned into plenty; for the love of Jesus Christ our Lord, to whom, with thee and the Holy Ghost, be all honour and glory, now and for ever. *Amen.*

In Time of War and Tumults.

O ALMIGHTY God, the supreme Governor of all things, whose power no creature is able to resist, to whom it belongeth justly to punish sinners, and to be merciful to those who truly repent; Save and deliver us, we humbly beseech thee, from the hands of our enemies; that we, being armed with thy defence, may be preserved evermore from all perils, to glorify thee, who art the only giver of all victory; through the merits of thy Son, Jesus Christ our Lord. *Amen.*

In Time of Calamity.

O GOD, merciful and compassionate, who art ever ready to hear the prayers of those who put their trust in thee; Graciously hearken to us who call upon thee, and grant us thy help in this our need; through Jesus Christ our Lord. *Amen.*

For the Army.

O LORD God of Hosts, stretch forth, we pray thee, thine almighty arm to strengthen and protect the soldiers of our country. Support them in the day of battle, and in the time of peace keep them safe from all evil; endue them with courage and loyalty; and grant that in all things they may serve without reproach; through Jesus Christ our Lord. *Amen.*

Prayers

For the Navy.

O ETERNAL Lord God, who alone spreadest out the heavens, and rulest the raging of the sea; Vouchsafe to take into thy almighty and most gracious protection our country's Navy, and all who serve therein. Preserve them from the dangers of the sea, and from the violence of the enemy; that they may be a safeguard unto the United States of America, and a security for such as pass on the seas upon their lawful occasions; that the inhabitants of our land may in peace and quietness serve thee our God, to the glory of thy Name; through Jesus Christ our Lord. *Amen.*

Memorial Days.

ALMIGHTY God, our heavenly Father, in whose hands are the living and the dead; We give thee thanks for all those thy servants who have laid down their lives in the service of our country. Grant to them thy mercy and the light of thy presence, that the good work which thou hast begun in them may be perfected; through Jesus Christ thy Son our Lord. *Amen.*

For Schools, Colleges, and Universities.

ALMIGHTY God, we beseech thee, with thy gracious favour to behold our universities, colleges, and schools, that knowledge may be increased among us, and all good learning flourish and abound. Bless all who teach and all who learn; and grant that in humility of heart they may ever look unto thee, who art the fountain of all wisdom; through Jesus Christ our Lord. *Amen.*

For Religious Education.

ALMIGHTY God, our heavenly Father, who hast committed to thy holy Church the care and nurture of thy

42

Prayers

children; Enlighten with thy wisdom those who teach and those who learn, that, rejoicing in the knowledge of thy truth, they may worship thee and serve thee from generation to generation; through Jesus Christ our Lord. *Amen.*

For Children.

O LORD Jesus Christ, who dost embrace children with the arms of thy mercy, and dost make them living members of thy Church; Give them grace, we pray thee, to stand fast in thy faith, to obey thy word, and to abide in thy love; that, being made strong by thy Holy Spirit, they may resist temptation and overcome evil, and may rejoice in the life that now is, and dwell with thee in the life that is to come; through thy merits, O merciful Saviour, who with the Father and the Holy Ghost livest and reignest one God, world without end. *Amen.*

For those about to be Confirmed.

O GOD, who through the teaching of thy Son Jesus Christ didst prepare the disciples for the coming of the Comforter; Make ready, we beseech thee, the hearts and minds of thy servants who at this time are seeking to be strengthened by the gift of the Holy Spirit through the laying on of hands, that, drawing near with penitent and faithful hearts, they may evermore be filled with the power of his divine indwelling; through the same Jesus Christ our Lord. *Amen.*

For Christian Service.

O LORD, our heavenly Father, whose blessed Son came not to be ministered unto, but to minister; We beseech thee to bless all who, following in his steps, give themselves to the service of their fellow men. Endue them

Prayers

with wisdom, patience, and courage to strengthen the weak and raise up those who fall; that, being inspired by thy love, they may worthily minister in thy Name to the suffering, the friendless, and the needy; for the sake of him who laid down his life for us, the same thy Son, our Saviour Jesus Christ. *Amen.*

For Social Justice.

ALMIGHTY God, who hast created man in thine own image; Grant us grace fearlessly to contend against evil, and to make no peace with oppression; and, that we may reverently use our freedom, help us to employ it in the maintenance of justice among men and nations, to the glory of thy holy Name; through Jesus Christ our Lord. *Amen.*

For Every Man in his Work.

ALMIGHTY God, our heavenly Father, who declarest thy glory and showest forth thy handiwork in the heavens and in the earth; Deliver us, we beseech thee, in our several callings, from the service of mammon, that we may do the work which thou givest us to do, in truth, in beauty, and in righteousness, with singleness of heart as thy servants, and to the benefit of our fellow men; for the sake of him who came among us as one that serveth, thy Son Jesus Christ our Lord. *Amen.*

For the Family of Nations.

ALMIGHTY God, our heavenly Father, guide, we beseech thee, the Nations of the world into the way of justice and truth, and establish among them that peace which is the fruit of righteousness, that they may become the Kingdom of our Lord and Saviour Jesus Christ. *Amen.*

Prayers

In Time of Great Sickness and Mortality.

O MOST mighty and merciful God, in this time of grievous sickness, we flee unto thee for succour. Deliver us, we beseech thee, from our peril; give strength and skill to all those who minister to the sick; prosper the means made use of for their cure; and grant that, perceiving how frail and uncertain our life is, we may apply our hearts unto that heavenly wisdom which leadeth to eternal life; through Jesus Christ our Lord. *Amen.*

For a Sick Person.

O FATHER of mercies and God of all comfort, our only help in time of need; We humbly beseech thee to behold, visit, and relieve thy sick *servant* [*N.*] for whom our prayers are desired. Look upon *him* with the eyes of thy mercy; comfort *him* with a sense of thy goodness; preserve *him* from the temptations of the enemy; and give *him* patience under *his* affliction. In thy good time, restore *him* to health, and enable *him* to lead the residue of *his* life in thy fear, and to thy glory; and grant that finally *he* may dwell with thee in life everlasting; through Jesus Christ our Lord. *Amen.*

For a Sick Child.

O HEAVENLY Father, watch with us, we pray thee, over the sick *child* for whom our prayers are offered, and grant that *he* may be restored to that perfect health which it is thine alone to give; through Jesus Christ our Lord. *Amen.*

For a Person under Affliction.

O MERCIFUL God, and heavenly Father, who hast taught us in thy holy Word that thou dost not willingly afflict or grieve the children of men; Look with pity,

45

Prayers

we beseech thee, upon the sorrows of thy *servant* for whom our prayers are offered. Remember *him*, O Lord, in mercy; endue *his soul* with patience; comfort *him* with a sense of thy goodness; lift up thy countenance upon *him*, and give *him* peace; through Jesus Christ our Lord. *Amen.*

For a Person, or Persons, going to Sea.

O ETERNAL God, who alone spreadest out the heavens, and rulest the raging of the sea; We commend to thy almighty protection, thy *servant*, for whose preservation on the great deep our prayers are desired. Guard *him*, we beseech thee, from the dangers of the sea, from sickness, from the violence of enemies, and from every evil to which *he* may be exposed. Conduct *him* in safety to the haven where *he* would be, with a grateful sense of thy mercies; through Jesus Christ our Lord. *Amen.*

For Prisoners.

O GOD, who sparest when we deserve punishment, and in thy wrath rememberest mercy; We humbly beseech thee, of thy goodness, to comfort and succour all prisoners [*especially those who are condemned to die*]. Give them a right understanding of themselves, and of thy promises; that, trusting wholly in thy mercy, they may not place their confidence anywhere but in thee. Relieve the distressed, protect the innocent, awaken the guilty; and forasmuch as thou alone bringest light out of darkness, and good out of evil, grant to these thy servants, that by the power of thy Holy Spirit they may be set free from the chains of sin, and may be brought to newness of life; through Jesus Christ our Lord. *Amen.*

46

Prayers

A Bidding Prayer.

¶ *To be used before Sermons, or on Special Occasions.*

¶ *And* NOTE, *That the Minister, in his discretion, may omit any of the clauses in this Prayer, or may add others, as occasion may require.*

GOOD Christian People, I bid your prayers for Christ's holy Catholic Church, the blessed company of all faithful people; that it may please God to confirm and strengthen it in purity of faith, in holiness of life, and in perfectness of love, and to restore to it the witness of visible unity; and more especially for that branch of the same planted by God in this land, whereof we are members; that in all things it may work according to God's will, serve him faithfully, and worship him acceptably.

Ye shall pray for the President of these United States, and for the Governor of this State, and for all that are in authority; that all, and every one of them, may serve truly in their several callings to the glory of God, and the edifying and well-governing of the people, remembering the account they shall be called upon to give at the last great day.

Ye shall also pray for the ministers of God's Holy Word and Sacraments; for Bishops [*and herein more especially for the Bishop of this Diocese*], that they may minister faithfully and wisely the discipline of Christ; likewise for all Priests and Deacons [*and herein more especially for the Clergy here residing*], that they may shine as lights in the world, and in all things may adorn the doctrine of God our Saviour.

And ye shall pray for a due supply of persons fitted to serve God in the Ministry and in the State; and to that end, as well as for the good education of all the youth of this land, ye shall pray for all schools, colleges, and seminaries of sound and godly learning, and for all whose hands are open for their maintenance; that whatsoever tends to the advancement of true religion and useful learning may for ever flourish and abound.

47

Prayers

Ye shall pray for all the people of these United States, that they may live in the true faith and fear of God, and in brotherly charity one towards another.

Ye shall pray also for all who travel by land, sea, or air; for all prisoners and captives; for all who are in sickness or in sorrow; for all who have fallen into grievous sin; for all who, through temptation, ignorance, helplessness, grief, trouble, dread, or the near approach of death, especially need our prayers.

Ye shall also praise God for rain and sunshine; for the fruits of the earth; for the products of all honest industry; and for all his good gifts, temporal and spiritual, to us and to all men.

Finally, ye shall yield unto God most high praise and hearty thanks for the wonderful grace and virtue declared in all his saints, who have been the choice vessels of his grace and the lights of the world in their several generations; and pray unto God, that we may have grace to direct our lives after their good examples; that, this life ended, we may be made partakers with them of the glorious resurrection, and the life everlasting.

And now, brethren, summing up all our petitions, and all our thanksgivings, in the words which Christ hath taught us, we make bold to say,

OUR Father, who art in heaven, Hallowed be thy Name. Thy kingdom come. Thy will be done, On earth as it is in heaven. Give us this day our daily bread. And forgive us our trespasses, As we forgive those who trespass against us. And lead us not into temptation, But deliver us from evil. For thine is the kingdom, and the power, and the glory, for ever and ever. Amen.

Prayers

COLLECTS.

¶ To be used after the Collects of Morning or Evening Prayer, or Communion, at the discretion of the Minister.

O LORD Jesus Christ, who saidst unto thine Apostles, Peace I leave with you, my peace I give unto you; Regard not our sins, but the faith of thy Church; and grant to it that peace and unity which is according to thy will, who livest and reignest with the Father and the Holy Ghost, one God, world without end. *Amen.*

ASSIST us mercifully, O Lord, in these our supplications and prayers, and dispose the way of thy servants towards the attainment of everlasting salvation; that, among all the changes and chances of this mortal life, they may ever be defended by thy most gracious and ready help; through Jesus Christ our Lord. *Amen.*

GRANT, we beseech thee, Almighty God, that the words which we have heard this day with our outward ears, may, through thy grace, be so grafted inwardly in our hearts, that they may bring forth in us the fruit of good living, to the honour and praise of thy Name; through Jesus Christ our Lord. *Amen.*

DIRECT us, O Lord, in all our doings, with thy most gracious favour, and further us with thy continual help; that in all our works begun, continued, and ended in thee, we may glorify thy holy Name, and finally, by thy mercy, obtain everlasting life; through Jesus Christ our Lord. *Amen.*

ALMIGHTY God, the fountain of all wisdom, who knowest our necessities before we ask, and our ignorance in asking; We beseech thee to have compassion upon our infirmities; and those things which for our unworthiness we dare not, and for our blindness we cannot ask, vouchsafe to give us, for the worthiness of thy Son Jesus Christ our Lord. *Amen.*

ALMIGHTY God, who hast promised to hear the petitions of those who ask in thy Son's Name; We beseech thee mercifully to incline thine ears to us who have now made our prayers and supplications unto thee; and grant that those things which we have faithfully asked according to thy will, may effectually be obtained, to the relief of our necessity, and to the setting forth of thy glory; through Jesus Christ our Lord. *Amen.*

THANKSGIVINGS.

¶ *To be used after the General Thanksgiving, or, when that is not said, before the final Prayer of Blessing or the Benediction.*

A Thanksgiving to Almighty God for the Fruits of the Earth and all the other Blessings of his merciful Providence.

MOST gracious God, by whose knowledge the depths are broken up, and the clouds drop down the dew; We yield thee unfeigned thanks and praise for the return of seed-time and harvest, for the increase of the ground and the gathering in of the fruits thereof, and for all the other blessings of thy merciful providence bestowed upon this nation and people. And, we beseech thee, give us a just sense of these great mercies; such as may appear in our lives by an humble, holy, and obedient walking before thee all our days; through Jesus Christ our Lord, to whom, with thee and the Holy Ghost, be all glory and honour, world without end. *Amen.*

Thanksgivings

The Thanksgiving of Women after Child-birth.

¶ To be said when any Woman, being present in Church, shall have desired
to return thanks to Almighty God for her safe deliverance.

O ALMIGHTY God, we give thee humble thanks for
that thou hast been graciously pleased to preserve,
through the great pain and peril of child-birth, *this woman*,
thy *servant*, who *desireth* now to offer *her* praises and thanksgivings unto thee. Grant, we beseech thee, most merciful
Father, that *she*, through thy help, may faithfully live according to thy will in this life, and also may be *partaker* of
everlasting glory in the life to come; through Jesus Christ
our Lord. *Amen.*

For Rain.

O GOD, our heavenly Father, by whose gracious providence the former and the latter rain descend upon
the earth, that it may bring forth fruit for the use of man;
We give thee humble thanks that it hath pleased thee to
send us rain to our great comfort, and to the glory of thy
holy Name; through Jesus Christ our Lord. *Amen.*

For Fair Weather.

O LORD God, who hast justly humbled us by thy late
visitation of us with immoderate rain and waters, and
in thy mercy hast relieved and comforted our souls by this
seasonable and blessed change of weather; We praise and
glorify thy holy Name for this thy mercy, and will always
declare thy loving-kindness from generation to generation,
through Jesus Christ our Lord. *Amen.*

For Plenty.

O MOST merciful Father, who of thy gracious goodness hast heard the devout prayers of thy Church, and
turned our dearth and scarcity into plenty; We give thee

Thanksgivings

humble thanks for this thy special bounty; beseeching thee to continue thy loving-kindness unto us, that our land may yield us her fruits of increase, to thy glory and our comfort; through Jesus Christ our Lord. *Amen.*

For Peace, and Deliverance from our Enemies.

O ALMIGHTY God, who art a strong tower of defence unto thy servants against the face of their enemies; We yield thee praise and thanksgiving for our deliverance from those great and apparent dangers wherewith we were compassed. We acknowledge it thy goodness that we were not delivered over as a prey unto them; beseeching thee still to continue such thy mercies towards us, that all the world may know that thou art our Saviour and mighty Deliverer; through Jesus Christ our Lord. *Amen.*

For Restoring Public Peace at Home.

O ETERNAL God, our heavenly Father, who alone makest men to be of one mind in a house, and stillest the outrage of a violent and unruly people; We bless thy holy Name, that it hath pleased thee to appease the seditious tumults which have been lately raised up amongst us; most humbly beseeching thee to grant to all of us grace, that we may henceforth obediently walk in thy holy commandments; and, leading a quiet and peaceable life in all godliness and honesty, may continually offer unto thee our sacrifice of praise and thanksgiving for these thy mercies towards us; through Jesus Christ our Lord. *Amen.*

For a Recovery from Sickness.

O GOD, who art the giver of life, of health, and of safety; We bless thy Name, that thou hast been pleased to deliver from *his* bodily sickness *this* thy *servant*, who now

Thanksgivings

desireth to return thanks unto thee, in the presence of all thy people. Gracious art thou, O Lord, and full of compassion to the children of men. May *his heart* be duly impressed with a sense of thy merciful goodness, and may *he* devote the residue of *his* days to an humble, holy, and obedient walking before thee; through Jesus Christ our Lord. *Amen.*

For a Child's Recovery from Sickness.

ALMIGHTY God and heavenly Father, we give thee humble thanks for that thou hast been graciously pleased to deliver from *his* bodily sickness the *child* in whose behalf we bless and praise thy Name, in the presence of all thy people. Grant, we beseech thee, O gracious Father, that *he*, through thy help, may both faithfully live in this world according to thy will, and also may be *partaker* of everlasting glory in the life to come; through Jesus Christ our Lord. *Amen.*

For a Safe Return from a Journey.

MOST gracious Lord, whose mercy is over all thy works; We praise thy holy Name that thou hast been pleased to conduct in safety, through the perils of the great deep (of *his* way), *this* thy *servant*, who now *desireth* to return *his* thanks unto thee in thy holy Church. May *he* be duly sensible of thy merciful providence towards *him*, and ever express *his* thankfulness by a holy trust in thee, and obedience to thy laws; through Jesus Christ our Lord. *Amen.*

The Litany

or General Supplication.

¶ *To be used after the Third Collect at Morning or Evening Prayer; or before the Holy Communion; or separately.*

O GOD the Father, Creator of heaven and earth;
Have mercy upon us.

O God the Son, Redeemer of the world;
Have mercy upon us.

O God the Holy Ghost, Sanctifier of the faithful;
Have mercy upon us.

O holy, blessed, and glorious Trinity, one God;
Have mercy upon us.

REMEMBER not, Lord, our offences, nor the offences of our forefathers; neither take thou vengeance of our sins: Spare us, good Lord, spare thy people, whom thou hast redeemed with thy most precious blood, and be not angry with us for ever.
Spare us, good Lord.

FROM all evil and mischief; from sin; from the crafts and assaults of the devil; from thy wrath, and from everlasting damnation,
Good Lord, deliver us.

From all blindness of heart; from pride, vainglory, and hypocrisy; from envy, hatred, and malice, and all uncharitableness,
Good Lord, deliver us.

From all inordinate and sinful affections; and from all the deceits of the world, the flesh, and the devil,
Good Lord, deliver us.

From lightning and tempest; from earthquake, fire, and flood; from plague, pestilence, and famine; from battle and murder, and from sudden death,
Good Lord, deliver us.

The Litany

From all sedition, privy conspiracy, and rebellion; from all false doctrine, heresy, and schism; from hardness of heart, and contempt of thy Word and Commandment,

Good Lord, deliver us.

By the mystery of thy holy Incarnation; by thy holy Nativity and Circumcision; by thy Baptism, Fasting, and Temptation,

Good Lord, deliver us.

By thine Agony and Bloody Sweat; by thy Cross and Passion; by thy precious Death and Burial; by thy glorious Resurrection and Ascension; and by the Coming of the Holy Ghost,

Good Lord, deliver us.

In all time of our tribulation; in all time of our prosperity; in the hour of death, and in the day of judgment,

Good Lord, deliver us.

WE sinners do beseech thee to hear us, O Lord God; and that it may please thee to rule and govern thy holy Church universal in the right way;

We beseech thee to hear us, good Lord.

That it may please thee so to rule the heart of thy servant, The President of the United States, that he may above all things seek thy honour and glory;

We beseech thee to hear us, good Lord.

That it may please thee to bless and preserve all Christian Rulers and Magistrates, giving them grace to execute justice, and to maintain truth;

We beseech thee to hear us, good Lord.

That it may please thee to illuminate all Bishops, Priests, and Deacons, with true knowledge and understanding of thy Word; and that both by their preaching and living they may set it forth, and show it accordingly;

We beseech thee to hear us, good Lord.

55

The Litany

That it may please thee to send forth labourers into thy harvest;

We beseech thee to hear us, good Lord.

That it may please thee to bless and keep all thy people;

We beseech thee to hear us, good Lord.

That it may please thee to give to all nations unity, peace, and concord;

We beseech thee to hear us, good Lord.

That it may please thee to give us an heart to love and fear thee, and diligently to live after thy commandments;

We beseech thee to hear us, good Lord.

That it may please thee to give to all thy people increase of grace to hear meekly thy Word, and to receive it with pure affection, and to bring forth the fruits of the Spirit;

We beseech thee to hear us, good Lord.

That it may please thee to bring into the way of truth all such as have erred, and are deceived;

We beseech thee to hear us, good Lord.

That it may please thee to strengthen such as do stand; and to comfort and help the weak-hearted; and to raise up those who fall; and finally to beat down Satan under our feet;

We beseech thee to hear us, good Lord.

That it may please thee to succour, help, and comfort, all who are in danger, necessity, and tribulation;

We beseech thee to hear us, good Lord.

That it may please thee to preserve all who travel by land, by water, or by air, all women in child-birth, all sick persons, and young children; and to show thy pity upon all prisoners and captives;

We beseech thee to hear us, good Lord.

That it may please thee to defend, and provide for, the

The Litany

fatherless children, and widows, and all who are desolate and oppressed;

We beseech thee to hear us, good Lord.

That it may please thee to have mercy upon all men;

We beseech thee to hear us, good Lord.

That it may please thee to forgive our enemies, persecutors, and slanderers, and to turn their hearts;

We beseech thee to hear us, good Lord.

That it may please thee to give and preserve to our use the kindly fruits of the earth, so that in due time we may enjoy them;

We beseech thee to hear us, good Lord.

That it may please thee to give us true repentance; to forgive us all our sins, negligences, and ignorances; and to endue us with the grace of thy Holy Spirit to amend our lives according to thy holy Word;

We beseech thee to hear us, good Lord.

Son of God, we beseech thee to hear us.

Son of God, we beseech thee to hear us.

O Lamb of God, who takest away the sins of the world;

Grant us thy peace.

O Lamb of God, who takest away the sins of the world;

Have mercy upon us.

O Christ, hear us.

O Christ, hear us.

Lord, have mercy upon us.

Lord, have mercy upon us.

Christ, have mercy upon us.

Christ, have mercy upon us.

Lord, have mercy upon us.

Lord, have mercy upon us.

The Litany

¶ *Then shall the Minister, and the People with him, say the Lord's Prayer.*

OUR Father, who art in heaven, Hallowed be thy Name. Thy kingdom come. Thy will be done, On earth as it is in heaven. Give us this day our daily bread. And forgive us our trespasses, As we forgive those who trespass against us. And lead us not into temptation, But deliver us from evil. Amen.

¶ *The Minister may, at his discretion, omit all that followeth, to the Prayer,* We humbly beseech thee, O Father, *etc.*

Minister.

O LORD, deal not with us according to our sins.
Neither reward us according to our iniquities.

Let us pray.

O GOD, merciful Father, who despisest not the sighing of a contrite heart, nor the desire of such as are sorrowful; Mercifully assist our prayers which we make before thee in all our troubles and adversities, whensoever they oppress us; and graciously hear us, that those evils which the craft and subtilty of the devil or man worketh against us, may, by thy good providence, be brought to nought; that we thy servants, being hurt by no persecutions, may evermore give thanks unto thee in thy holy Church; through Jesus Christ our Lord. *Amen.*

¶ *Minister and People.*

O Lord, arise, help us, and deliver us for thy Name's sake.

Minister.

O GOD, we have heard with our ears, and our fathers have declared unto us, the noble works that thou didst in their days, and in the old time before them.

The Litany

O Lord, arise, help us, and deliver us for thine honour.

Glory be to the Father, and to the Son, and to the Holy Ghost;

As it was in the beginning, is now, and ever shall be, world without end. Amen.

From our enemies defend us, O Christ.

Graciously look upon our afflictions.

With pity behold the sorrows of our hearts.

Mercifully forgive the sins of thy people.

Favourably with mercy hear our prayers.

O Son of David, have mercy upon us.

Both now and ever vouchsafe to hear us, O Christ.

Graciously hear us, O Christ; graciously hear us, O Lord Christ.

O Lord, let thy mercy be showed upon us;

As we do put our trust in thee.

Let us pray.

WE humbly beseech thee, O Father, mercifully to look upon our infirmities; and, for the glory of thy Name, turn from us all those evils that we most justly have deserved; and grant, that in all our troubles we may put our whole trust and confidence in thy mercy, and evermore serve thee in holiness and pureness of living, to thy honour and glory; through our only Mediator and Advocate, Jesus Christ our Lord. *Amen.*

¶ *The Minister may end the Litany here, or at his discretion add other Prayers from this Book.*

A Penitential Office

for Ash Wednesday.

¶ *On the First Day of Lent, the Office ensuing may be read immediately after the Prayer, We humbly beseech thee, O Father, in the Litany; or it may be used with Morning Prayer, or Evening Prayer, or as a separate Office.*

¶ *The same Office may be read at other times, at the discretion of the Minister.*

¶ *The Minister and the People kneeling, then shall be said by them this Psalm following.*

Miserere mei, Deus. Psalm li.

HAVE mercy upon me, O God, after thy great goodness; * according to the multitude of thy mercies do away mine offences.

Wash me throughly from my wickedness, * and cleanse me from my sin.

For I acknowledge my faults, * and my sin is ever before me.

Against thee only have I sinned, and done this evil in thy sight; * that thou mightest be justified in thy saying, and clear when thou art judged.

Behold, I was shapen in wickedness, * and in sin hath my mother conceived me.

But lo, thou requirest truth in the inward parts, * and shalt make me to understand wisdom secretly.

Thou shalt purge me with hyssop, and I shall be clean; * thou shalt wash me, and I shall be whiter than snow.

Thou shalt make me hear of joy and gladness, * that the bones which thou hast broken may rejoice.

Turn thy face from my sins, * and put out all my misdeeds.

Make me a clean heart, O God, * and renew a right spirit within me.

Cast me not away from thy presence, * and take not thy holy Spirit from me.

A Penitential Office

O give me the comfort of thy help again, * and stablish me with thy free Spirit.

Then shall I teach thy ways unto the wicked, * and sinners shall be converted unto thee.

Deliver me from blood-guiltiness, O God, thou that art the God of my health; * and my tongue shall sing of thy righteousness.

Thou shalt open my lips, O Lord, * and my mouth shall show thy praise.

For thou desirest no sacrifice, else would I give it thee; * but thou delightest not in burnt-offerings.

The sacrifice of God is a troubled spirit: * a broken and contrite heart, O God, shalt thou not despise.

Glory be to the Father, and to the Son, * and to the Holy Ghost;

As it was in the beginning, is now, and ever shall be, * world without end. Amen.

¶ *If the Litany hath been already said, the Minister may pass at once to* O Lord, save thy servants; *etc.*

Lord, have mercy upon us.
Christ, have mercy upon us.
Lord, have mercy upon us.

OUR Father, who art in heaven, Hallowed be thy Name. Thy kingdom come. Thy will be done, On earth as it is in heaven. Give us this day our daily bread. And forgive us our trespasses, As we forgive those who trespass against us. And lead us not into temptation, But deliver us from evil. Amen.

O Lord, save thy servants;
That put their trust in thee.
Send unto them help from above.
And evermore mightily defend them.

A Penitential Office

Help us, O God our Saviour.
And for the glory of thy Name deliver us; be merciful to us sinners, for thy Name's sake.

O Lord, hear our prayer.
And let our cry come unto thee.

Let us pray.

O LORD, we beseech thee, mercifully hear our prayers, and spare all those who confess their sins unto thee; that they, whose consciences by sin are accused, by thy merciful pardon may be absolved; through Christ our Lord. *Amen.*

O MOST mighty God, and merciful Father, who hast compassion upon all men, and who wouldest not the death of a sinner, but rather that he should turn from his sin, and be saved; Mercifully forgive us our trespasses; receive and comfort us, who are grieved and wearied with the burden of our sins. Thy property is always to have mercy; to thee only it appertaineth to forgive sins. Spare us therefore, good Lord, spare thy people, whom thou hast redeemed; enter not into judgment with thy servants; but so turn thine anger from us, who meekly acknowledge our transgressions, and truly repent us of our faults, and so make haste to help us in this world, that we may ever live with thee in the world to come; through Jesus Christ our Lord. *Amen.*

¶ *Then shall the People say this that followeth, after the Minister.*

TURN thou us, O good Lord, and so shall we be turned. Be favourable, O Lord, Be favourable to thy people, Who turn to thee in weeping, fasting, and praying. For thou art a merciful God, Full of compassion, Long-suffering, and of great pity. Thou sparest when we deserve punishment,

A Penitential Office

And in thy wrath thinkest upon mercy. Spare thy people, good Lord, spare them, And let not thine heritage be brought to confusion. Hear us, O Lord, for thy mercy is great, And after the multitude of thy mercies look upon us; Through the merits and mediation of thy blessed Son, Jesus Christ our Lord. Amen.

¶ Then the Minister shall say,

O GOD, whose nature and property is ever to have mercy and to forgive; Receive our humble petitions; and though we be tied and bound with the chain of our sins, yet let the pitifulness of thy great mercy loose us; for the honour of Jesus Christ, our Mediator and Advocate. *Amen.*

THE LORD bless us, and keep us. The LORD make his face to shine upon us, and be gracious unto us. The LORD lift up his countenance upon us, and give us peace, both now and evermore. *Amen.*

The Holy Communion

with

The Collects, Epistles, and Gospels

The Order for

The Administration of the Lord's Supper

or

Holy Communion

¶ *At the Communion-time the Holy Table shall have upon it a fair white linen cloth. And the Priest, standing reverently before the Holy Table, shall say the Lord's Prayer and the Collect following, the People kneeling; but the Lord's Prayer may be omitted at the discretion of the Priest.*

OUR Father, who art in heaven, Hallowed be thy Name. Thy kingdom come. Thy will be done, On earth as it is in heaven. Give us this day our daily bread. And forgive us our trespasses, As we forgive those who trespass against us. And lead us not into temptation, But deliver us from evil. Amen.

The Collect.

ALMIGHTY God, unto whom all hearts are open, all desires known, and from whom no secrets are hid; Cleanse the thoughts of our hearts by the inspiration of thy Holy Spirit, that we may perfectly love thee, and worthily magnify thy holy Name; through Christ our Lord. *Amen.*

¶ *Then shall the Priest, turning to the People, rehearse distinctly The Ten Commandments; and the People, still kneeling, shall, after every Commandment, ask God mercy for their transgressions for the time past, and grace to keep the law for the time to come.*

¶ *And* NOTE, *That in rehearsing The Ten Commandments, the Priest may omit that part of the Commandment which is inset.*

¶ *The Decalogue may be omitted, provided it be said at least one Sunday in each month. But* NOTE, *That whenever it is omitted, the Priest shall say the Summary of the Law, beginning,* Hear what our Lord Jesus Christ saith.

Holy Communion

The Decalogue.

GOD spake these words, and said:

I am the LORD thy God; Thou shalt have none other gods but me.

Lord, have mercy upon us, and incline our hearts to keep this law.

Thou shalt not make to thyself any graven image, nor the likeness of any thing that is in heaven above, or in the earth beneath, or in the water under the earth; thou shalt not bow down to them, nor worship them;

for I the LORD thy God am a jealous God, and visit the sins of the fathers upon the children, unto the third and fourth generation of them that hate me; and show mercy unto thousands in them that love me and keep my commandments.

Lord, have mercy upon us, and incline our hearts to keep this law.

Thou shalt not take the Name of the LORD thy God in vain;

for the LORD will not hold him guiltless, that taketh his Name in vain.

Lord, have mercy upon us, and incline our hearts to keep this law.

Remember that thou keep holy the Sabbath-day.

Six days shalt thou labour, and do all that thou hast to do; but the seventh day is the Sabbath of the LORD thy God. In it thou shalt do no manner of work; thou, and thy son, and thy daughter, thy man-servant, and thy maid-servant, thy cattle, and the stranger that is within thy gates. For in six days the LORD made heaven and earth, the sea, and all that in them is, and rested the seventh day: wherefore the LORD blessed the seventh day, and hallowed it.

Lord, have mercy upon us, and incline our hearts to keep this law.

Holy Communion

Honour thy father and thy mother;

that thy days may be long in the land which the LORD thy
God giveth thee.

*Lord, have mercy upon us, and incline our hearts to keep
this law.*

Thou shalt do no murder.

*Lord, have mercy upon us, and incline our hearts to keep
this law.*

Thou shalt not commit adultery.

*Lord, have mercy upon us, and incline our hearts to keep
this law.*

Thou shalt not steal.

*Lord, have mercy upon us, and incline our hearts to keep
this law.*

Thou shalt not bear false witness against thy neighbour.

*Lord, have mercy upon us, and incline our hearts to keep
this law.*

Thou shalt not covet

thy neighbour's house, thou shalt not covet thy neighbour's
wife, nor his servant, nor his maid, nor his ox, nor his ass, nor
any thing that is his.

*Lord, have mercy upon us, and write all these thy laws in
our hearts, we beseech thee.*

¶ *Then may the Priest say,*

Hear what our Lord Jesus Christ saith.

THOU shalt love the Lord thy God with all thy heart,
and with all thy soul, and with all thy mind. This
is the first and great commandment. And the second is like
unto it; Thou shalt love thy neighbour as thyself. On these
two commandments hang all the Law and the Prophets.

¶ *Here, if the Decalogue hath been omitted, shall be said,*

69

Holy Communion

Lord, have mercy upon us.
Christ, have mercy upon us.
Lord, have mercy upon us.

¶ *Then the Priest may say,*

O ALMIGHTY Lord, and everlasting God, vouchsafe, we beseech thee, to direct, sanctify, and govern, both our hearts and bodies, in the ways of thy laws, and in the works of thy commandments; that, through thy most mighty protection, both here and ever, we may be preserved in body and soul; through our Lord and Saviour Jesus Christ. *Amen.*

¶ *Here shall be said,*

The Lord be with you.
Answer. And with thy spirit.
Minister. Let us pray.

¶ *Then shall the Priest say the Collect of the Day. And after the Collect the Minister appointed shall read the Epistle, first saying,* The Epistle is written in the — Chapter of —, beginning at the — Verse. *The Epistle ended, he shall say,* Here endeth the Epistle.

¶ *Here may be sung a Hymn or an Anthem.*

¶ *Then, all the People standing, the Minister appointed shall read the Gospel, first saying,* The Holy Gospel is written in the — Chapter of —, beginning at the — Verse.

¶ *Here shall be said,*

Glory be to thee, O Lord.

¶ *And after the Gospel may be said,*

Praise be to thee, O Christ.

¶ *Then shall be said the Creed commonly called the Nicene, or else the Apostles' Creed; but the Creed may be omitted, if it hath been said immediately before in Morning Prayer; Provided, That the Nicene Creed shall be said on Christmas Day, Easter Day, Ascension Day, Whitsunday, and Trinity Sunday.*

Holy Communion

I BELIEVE in one God the Father Almighty, Maker of heaven and earth, And of all things visible and invisible: And in one Lord Jesus Christ, the only-begotten Son of God; Begotten of his Father before all worlds, God of God, Light of Light, Very God of very God; Begotten, not made; Being of one substance with the Father; By whom all things were made: Who for us men and for our salvation came down from heaven, And was incarnate by the Holy Ghost of the Virgin Mary, And was made man: And was crucified also for us under Pontius Pilate; He suffered and was buried: And the third day he rose again according to the Scriptures: And ascended into heaven, And sitteth on the right hand of the Father: And he shall come again, with glory, to judge both the quick and the dead; Whose kingdom shall have no end.

And I believe in the Holy Ghost, The Lord, and Giver of Life, Who proceedeth from the Father and the Son; Who with the Father and the Son together is worshipped and glorified; Who spake by the Prophets: And I believe one Catholic and Apostolic Church: I acknowledge one Baptism for the remission of sins: And I look for the Resurrection of the dead: And the Life of the world to come. Amen.

¶ *Then shall be declared unto the People what Holy Days, or Fasting Days, are in the week following to be observed; and (if occasion be) shall Notice be given of the Communion, and of the Banns of Matrimony, and of other matters to be published.*

¶ *Here, or immediately after the Creed, may be said the Bidding Prayer, or other authorized prayers and intercessions.*

¶ *Then followeth the Sermon. After which, the Priest, when there is a Communion, shall return to the Holy Table, and begin the Offertory, saying one or more of these Sentences following, as he thinketh most convenient.*

Holy Communion

REMEMBER the words of the Lord Jesus, how he said, It is more blessed to give than to receive. *Acts* xx. 35.

Let your light so shine before men, that they may see your good works, and glorify your Father which is in heaven. *St. Matt.* v. 16.

Lay not up for yourselves treasures upon earth, where moth and rust doth corrupt, and where thieves break through and steal: but lay up for yourselves treasures in heaven, where neither moth nor rust doth corrupt, and where thieves do not break through nor steal. *St. Matt.* vi. 19, 20.

Not every one that saith unto me, Lord, Lord, shall enter into the kingdom of heaven; but he that doeth the will of my Father which is in heaven. *St. Matt.* vii. 21.

He that soweth little shall reap little; and he that soweth plenteously shall reap plenteously. Let every man do according as he is disposed in his heart, not grudgingly, or of necessity; for God loveth a cheerful giver. 2 *Cor.* ix. 6, 7.

While we have time, let us do good unto all men; and especially unto them that are of the household of faith. *Gal.* vi. 10.

God is not unrighteous, that he will forget your works, and labour that proceedeth of love; which love ye have showed for his Name's sake, who have ministered unto the saints, and yet do minister. *Heb.* vi. 10.

To do good, and to distribute, forget not; for with such sacrifices God is well pleased. *Heb.* xiii. 16.

Whoso hath this world's good, and seeth his brother have need, and shutteth up his compassion from him, how dwelleth the love of God in him? 1 *St. John* iii. 17.

Be merciful after thy power. If thou hast much, give plenteously; if thou hast little, do thy diligence gladly to give of that little: for so gatherest thou thyself a good reward in the day of necessity. *Tobit* iv. 8, 9.

Holy Communion

And the King shall answer and say unto them, Verily I say unto you, Inasmuch as ye have done it unto one of the least of these my brethren, ye have done it unto me. *St. Matt.* xxv. 40.

How then shall they call on him in whom they have not believed? and how shall they believe in him of whom they have not heard? and how shall they hear without a preacher? and how shall they preach, except they be sent? *Rom.* x. 14, 15.

Jesus said unto them, The harvest truly is plenteous, but the labourers are few: pray ye therefore the Lord of the harvest, that he send forth labourers into his harvest. *St. Luke* x. 2.

Ye shall not appear before the LORD empty; every man shall give as he is able, according to the blessing of the LORD thy God which he hath given thee. *Deut.* xvi. 16, 17.

Thine, O LORD, is the greatness, and the power, and the glory, and the victory, and the majesty: for all that is in the heaven and in the earth is thine; thine is the kingdom, O LORD, and thou art exalted as head above all. 1 *Chron.* xxix. 11.

All things come of thee, O LORD, and of thine own have we given thee. 1 *Chron.* xxix. 14.

¶ *And* NOTE, *That these Sentences may be used on any other occasion of Public Worship when the Offerings of the People are to be received.*

¶ *The Deacons, Church-wardens, or other fit persons appointed for that purpose, shall receive the Alms for the Poor, and other Offerings of the People, in a decent Basin to be provided by the Parish; and reverently bring it to the Priest, who shall humbly present and place it upon the Holy Table.*

¶ *And the Priest shall then offer, and shall place upon the Holy Table, the Bread and the Wine.*

¶ *And when the Alms and Oblations are being received and presented, there may be sung a Hymn, or an Offertory Anthem in the words of Holy Scripture or of the Book of Common Prayer, under the direction of the Priest.*

73

Holy Communion

¶ *Here the Priest may ask the secret intercessions of the Congregation for any who have desired the prayers of the Church.*

¶ *Then shall the Priest say,*

Let us pray for the whole state of Christ's Church.

ALMIGHTY and everliving God, who by thy holy Apostle hast taught us to make prayers, and supplications, and to give thanks for all men; We humbly beseech thee most mercifully to accept our [*alms and*] oblations, and to receive these our prayers, which we offer unto thy Divine Majesty; beseeching thee to inspire continually the Universal Church with the spirit of truth, unity, and concord: And grant that all those who do confess thy holy Name may agree in the truth of thy holy Word, and live in unity and godly love.

We beseech thee also, so to direct and dispose the hearts of all Christian Rulers, that they may truly and impartially administer justice, to the punishment of wickedness and vice, and to the maintenance of thy true religion, and virtue.

Give grace, O heavenly Father, to all Bishops and other Ministers, that they may, both by their life and doctrine, set forth thy true and lively Word, and rightly and duly administer thy holy Sacraments.

And to all thy People give thy heavenly grace; and especially to this congregation here present; that, with meek heart and due reverence, they may hear, and receive thy holy Word; truly serving thee in holiness and righteousness all the days of their life.

And we most humbly beseech thee, of thy goodness, O Lord, to comfort and succour all those who, in this transitory life, are in trouble, sorrow, need, sickness, or any other adversity.

And we also bless thy holy Name for all thy servants departed this life in thy faith and fear; beseeching thee to

Holy Communion

grant them continual growth in thy love and service, and to give us grace so to follow their good examples, that with them we may be partakers of thy heavenly kingdom. Grant this, O Father, for Jesus Christ's sake, our only Mediator and Advocate. *Amen.*

¶ *Then shall the Priest say to those who come to receive the Holy Communion,*

YE who do truly and earnestly repent you of your sins, and are in love and charity with your neighbours, and intend to lead a new life, following the commandments of God, and walking from henceforth in his holy ways; Draw near with faith, and take this holy Sacrament to your comfort; and make your humble confession to Almighty God, devoutly kneeling.

¶ *Then shall this General Confession be made, by the Priest and all those who are minded to receive the Holy Communion, humbly kneeling.*

ALMIGHTY God, Father of our Lord Jesus Christ, Maker of all things, Judge of all men; We acknowledge and bewail our manifold sins and wickedness, Which we, from time to time, most grievously have committed, By thought, word, and deed, Against thy Divine Majesty, Provoking most justly thy wrath and indignation against us. We do earnestly repent, And are heartily sorry for these our misdoings; The remembrance of them is grievous unto us; The burden of them is intolerable. Have mercy upon us, Have mercy upon us, most merciful Father; For thy Son our Lord Jesus Christ's sake, Forgive us all that is past; And grant that we may ever hereafter Serve and please thee In newness of life, To the honour and glory of thy Name; Through Jesus Christ our Lord. Amen.

¶ *Then shall the Priest (the Bishop if he be present) stand up, and turning to the People, say,*

75

Holy Communion

ALMIGHTY God, our heavenly Father, who of his great mercy hath promised forgiveness of sins to all those who with hearty repentance and true faith turn unto him; Have mercy upon you; pardon and deliver you from all your sins; confirm and strengthen you in all goodness; and bring you to everlasting life; through Jesus Christ our Lord. *Amen.*

¶ Then shall the Priest say,

Hear what comfortable words our Saviour Christ saith unto all who truly turn to him.

COME unto me, all ye that travail and are heavy laden, and I will refresh you. *St. Matt.* xi. 28.

So God loved the world, that he gave his only-begotten Son, to the end that all that believe in him should not perish, but have everlasting life. *St. John* iii. 16.

Hear also what Saint Paul saith.

This is a true saying, and worthy of all men to be received, That Christ Jesus came into the world to save sinners. 1 *Tim.* i. 15.

Hear also what Saint John saith.

If any man sin, we have an Advocate with the Father, Jesus Christ the righteous; and he is the Propitiation for our sins. 1 *St. John* ii. 1, 2.

¶ After which the Priest shall proceed, saying,

Lift up your hearts.
Answer. We lift them up unto the Lord.
Priest. Let us give thanks unto our Lord God.
Answer. It is meet and right so to do.

¶ Then shall the Priest turn to the Holy Table, and say,

IT is very meet, right, and our bounden duty, that we should at all times, and in all places, give thanks unto thee, O Lord, Holy Father, Almighty, Everlasting God.

Holy Communion

¶ *Here shall follow the Proper Preface, according to the time, if there be any specially appointed; or else immediately shall be said or sung by the Priest,*

THEREFORE with Angels and Archangels, and with all the company of heaven, we laud and magnify thy glorious Name; evermore praising thee, and saying,

HOLY, HOLY, HOLY, Lord God of hosts, Heaven and earth are full of thy glory: Glory be to thee, O Lord Most High. Amen.

¶ *Priest and People.*

PROPER PREFACES.

CHRISTMAS.

¶ *Upon Christmas Day, and seven days after.*

BECAUSE thou didst give Jesus Christ, thine only Son, to be born as at this time for us; who, by the operation of the Holy Ghost, was made very man, of the substance of the Virgin Mary his mother; and that without spot of sin, to make us clean from all sin. Therefore with Angels, etc.

EPIPHANY.

¶ *Upon the Epiphany, and seven days after.*

THROUGH Jesus Christ our Lord; who, in substance of our mortal flesh, manifested forth his glory; that he might bring us out of darkness into his own glorious light. Therefore with Angels, etc.

PURIFICATION, ANNUNCIATION, AND TRANSFIGURATION.

¶ *Upon the Feasts of the Purification, Annunciation, and Transfiguration.*

BECAUSE in the Mystery of the Word made flesh, thou hast caused a new light to shine in our hearts,

77

Holy Communion

to give the knowledge of thy glory in the face of thy Son Jesus Christ our Lord.

Therefore with Angels, etc.

EASTER.

¶ *Upon Easter Day, and seven days after.*

BUT chiefly are we bound to praise thee for the glorious Resurrection of thy Son Jesus Christ our Lord: for he is the very Paschal Lamb, which was offered for us, and hath taken away the sin of the world; who by his death hath destroyed death, and by his rising to life again hath restored to us everlasting life.

Therefore with Angels, etc.

ASCENSION.

¶ *Upon Ascension Day, and seven days after.*

THROUGH thy most dearly beloved Son Jesus Christ our Lord; who, after his most glorious Resurrection, manifestly appeared to all his Apostles, and in their sight ascended up into heaven, to prepare a place for us; that where he is, thither we might also ascend, and reign with him in glory.

Therefore with Angels, etc.

WHITSUNTIDE.

¶ *Upon Whitsunday, and six days after.*

THROUGH Jesus Christ our Lord; according to whose most true promise, the Holy Ghost came down as at this time from heaven, lighting upon the disciples, to teach them, and to lead them into all truth; giving them boldness with fervent zeal constantly to preach the Gospel unto all nations; whereby we have been brought out of darkness and error into the clear

Holy Communion

light and true knowledge of thee, and of thy Son Jesus Christ.

Therefore with Angels, etc.

TRINITY SUNDAY.

¶ *Upon the Feast of Trinity only.*

WHO, with thine only-begotten Son, and the Holy Ghost, art one God, one Lord, in Trinity of Persons and in Unity of Substance. For that which we believe of thy glory, O Father, the same we believe of the Son, and of the Holy Ghost, without any difference of inequality.

Therefore with Angels, etc.

¶ *Or this.*

FOR the precious death and merits of thy Son Jesus Christ our Lord, and for the sending to us of the Holy Ghost, the Comforter; who are one with thee in thy Eternal Godhead.

Therefore with Angels, etc.

ALL SAINTS.

¶ *Upon All Saints' Day, and seven days after.*

WHO, in the multitude of thy Saints, hast compassed us about with so great a cloud of witnesses that we, rejoicing in their fellowship, may run with patience the race that is set before us, and, together with them, may receive the crown of glory that fadeth not away.

Therefore with Angels and Archangels, and with all the company of heaven, we laud and magnify thy glorious Name; evermore praising thee, and saying,

HOLY, HOLY, HOLY, Lord God of hosts, Heaven and earth are full of thy glory: Glory be to thee, O Lord Most High. Amen.

¶ *Priest and People.*

79

Holy Communion

¶ *When the Priest, standing before the Holy Table, hath so ordered the Bread and Wine, that he may with the more readiness and decency break the Bread before the People, and take the Cup into his hands, he shall say the Prayer of Consecration, as followeth.*

ALL glory be to thee, Almighty God, our heavenly Father, for that thou, of thy tender mercy, didst give thine only Son Jesus Christ to suffer death upon the Cross for our redemption; who made there (by his one oblation of himself once offered) a full, perfect, and sufficient sacrifice, oblation, and satisfaction, for the sins of the whole world; and did institute, and in his holy Gospel command us to continue, a perpetual memory of that his precious death and sacrifice, until his coming again: For in the night in which he was betrayed, (*a*) he took Bread; and when he had given thanks, (*b*) he brake it, and gave it to his disciples, saying, Take, eat, (*c*) this is my Body, which is given for you; Do this in remembrance of me. Likewise, after supper, (*d*) he took the Cup; and when he had given thanks, he gave it to them, saying, Drink ye all of this; for (*e*) this is my Blood of the New Testament, which is shed for you, and for many, for the remission of sins; Do this, as oft as ye shall drink it, in remembrance of me.

(a) Here the Priest is to take the Paten into his hands.

(b) And here to break the Bread.

(c) And here to lay his hand upon all the Bread.

(d) Here he is to take the Cup into his hands.

(e) And here he is to lay his hand upon every vessel in which there is any Wine to be consecrated.

WHEREFORE, O Lord and heavenly Father, according to the institution of thy dearly beloved Son our Saviour Jesus Christ, we, thy humble servants, do celebrate and make here before thy Divine Majesty, with these thy holy gifts, which we now offer unto thee, the memorial thy Son hath commanded

The Oblation.

80

Holy Communion

us to make; having in remembrance his blessed passion and precious death, his mighty resurrection and glorious ascension; rendering unto thee most hearty thanks for the innumerable benefits procured unto us by the same.

AND we most humbly beseech thee, O *The Invocation.* merciful Father, to hear us; and, of thy almighty goodness, vouchsafe to bless and sanctify, with thy Word and Holy Spirit, these thy gifts and creatures of bread and wine; that we, receiving them according to thy Son our Saviour Jesus Christ's holy institution, in remembrance of his death and passion, may be partakers of his most blessed Body and Blood.

AND we earnestly desire thy fatherly goodness, mercifully to accept this our sacrifice of praise and thanksgiving; most humbly beseeching thee to grant that, by the merits and death of thy Son Jesus Christ, and through faith in his blood, we, and all thy whole Church, may obtain remission of our sins, and all other benefits of his passion. And here we offer and present unto thee, O Lord, our selves, our souls and bodies, to be a reasonable, holy, and living sacrifice unto thee; humbly beseeching thee, that we, and all others who shall be partakers of this Holy Communion, may worthily receive the most precious Body and Blood of thy Son Jesus Christ, be filled with thy grace and heavenly benediction, and made one body with him, that he may dwell in us, and we in him. And although we are unworthy, through our manifold sins, to offer unto thee any sacrifice; yet we beseech thee to accept this our bounden duty and service; not weighing our merits, but pardoning our offences, through Jesus Christ our Lord; by whom, and with whom, in the unity of the Holy Ghost, all honour and glory be unto thee, O Father Almighty, world without end. *Amen.*

Holy Communion

And now, as our Saviour Christ hath taught us, we are bold to say,

OUR Father, who art in heaven, Hallowed be thy Name. Thy kingdom come. Thy will be done, On earth as it is in heaven. Give us this day our daily bread. And forgive us our trespasses, As we forgive those who trespass against us. And lead us not into temptation, But deliver us from evil. For thine is the kingdom, and the power, and the glory, for ever and ever. Amen.

¶ *Then shall the Priest, kneeling down at the Lord's Table, say, in the name of all those who shall receive the Communion, this Prayer following.*

WE do not presume to come to this thy Table, O merciful Lord, trusting in our own righteousness, but in thy manifold and great mercies. We are not worthy so much as to gather up the crumbs under thy Table. But thou art the same Lord, whose property is always to have mercy: Grant us therefore, gracious Lord, so to eat the flesh of thy dear Son Jesus Christ, and to drink his blood, that our sinful bodies may be made clean by his body, and our souls washed through his most precious blood, and that we may evermore dwell in him, and he in us. *Amen.*

¶ *Here may be sung a Hymn.*

¶ *Then shall the Priest first receive the Holy Communion in both kinds himself, and proceed to deliver the same to the Bishops, Priests, and Deacons, in like manner, (if any be present,) and, after that, to the People also in order, into their hands, all devoutly kneeling. And sufficient opportunity shall be given to those present to communicate. And when he delivereth the Bread, he shall say,*

THE Body of our Lord Jesus Christ, which was given for thee, preserve thy body and soul unto everlasting life. Take and eat this in remembrance that Christ died for thee, and feed on him in thy heart by faith, with thanksgiving.

82

Holy Communion

¶ And the Minister who delivereth the Cup shall say,

THE Blood of our Lord Jesus Christ, which was shed for thee, preserve thy body and soul unto everlasting life. Drink this in remembrance that Christ's Blood was shed for thee, and be thankful.

¶ If the consecrated Bread or Wine be spent before all have communicated, the Priest is to consecrate more, according to the Form before prescribed; beginning at, All glory be to thee, Almighty God, and ending with these words, partakers of his most blessed Body and Blood.

¶ When all have communicated, the Priest shall return to the Lord's Table, and reverently place upon it what remaineth of the consecrated Elements, covering the same with a fair linen cloth.

¶ Then shall the Priest say,

Let us pray.

ALMIGHTY and everliving God, we most heartily thank thee, for that thou dost vouchsafe to feed us who have duly received these holy mysteries, with the spiritual food of the most precious Body and Blood of thy Son our Saviour Jesus Christ; and dost assure us thereby of thy favour and goodness towards us; and that we are very members incorporate in the mystical body of thy Son, which is the blessed company of all faithful people; and are also heirs through hope of thy everlasting kingdom, by the merits of his most precious death and passion. And we humbly beseech thee, O heavenly Father, so to assist us with thy grace, that we may continue in that holy fellowship, and do all such good works as thou hast prepared for us to walk in; through Jesus Christ our Lord, to whom, with thee and the Holy Ghost, be all honour and glory, world without end. *Amen.*

¶ Then shall be said the Gloria in excelsis, all standing, or some proper Hymn.

Holy Communion

GLORY be to God on high, and on earth peace, good will towards men. We praise thee, we bless thee, we worship thee, we glorify thee, we give thanks to thee for thy great glory, O Lord God, heavenly King, God the Father Almighty.

O Lord, the only-begotten Son, Jesus Christ; O Lord God, Lamb of God, Son of the Father, that takest away the sins of the world, have mercy upon us. Thou that takest away the sins of the world, receive our prayer. Thou that sittest at the right hand of God the Father, have mercy upon us.

For thou only art holy; thou only art the Lord; thou only, O Christ, with the Holy Ghost, art most high in the glory of God the Father. Amen.

¶ *Then, the People kneeling, the Priest (the Bishop if he be present) shall let them depart with this Blessing.*

THE Peace of God, which passeth all understanding, keep your hearts and minds in the knowledge and love of God, and of his Son Jesus Christ our Lord: And the Blessing of God Almighty, the Father, the Son, and the Holy Ghost, be amongst you, and remain with you always. *Amen.*

GENERAL RUBRICS.

¶ *In the absence of a Priest, a Deacon may say all that is before appointed unto the end of the Gospel.*

¶ *Upon the Sundays and other Holy Days, (though there be no Sermon or Communion,) may be said all that is appointed at the Communion, unto the end of the Gospel, concluding with the Blessing.*

¶ *And if any of the consecrated Bread and Wine remain after the Communion, it shall not be carried out of the Church; but the Minister and other Communicants shall, immediately after the Blessing, reverently eat and drink the same.*

¶ *If among those who come to be partakers of the Holy Communion, the Minister shall know any to be an open and notorious evil liver,*

Holy Communion

or to have done any wrong to his neighbours by word or deed, so that the Congregation be thereby offended; he shall advertise him, that he presume not to come to the Lord's Table, until he have openly declared himself to have truly repented and amended his former evil life, that the Congregation may thereby be satisfied; and that he hath recompensed the parties to whom he hath done wrong; or at least declare himself to be in full purpose so to do, as soon as he conveniently may.

¶ *The same order shall the Minister use with those, betwixt whom he perceiveth malice and hatred to reign; not suffering them to be partakers of the Lord's Table, until he know them to be reconciled. And if one of the parties, so at variance, be content to forgive from the bottom of his heart all that the other hath trespassed against him, and to make amends for that wherein he himself hath offended; and the other party will not be persuaded to a godly unity, but remain still in his frowardness and malice; the Minister in that case ought to admit the penitent person to the Holy Communion, and not him that is obstinate. Provided, That every Minister so repelling any, as is herein specified, shall be obliged to give an account of the same to the Ordinary, within fourteen days after, at the farthest.*

THE EXHORTATIONS.

¶ *At the time of the Celebration of the Communion, after the prayer for the whole state of Christ's Church, the Priest may say this Exhortation. And* NOTE, *That the Exhortation shall be said on the First Sunday in Advent, the First Sunday in Lent, and Trinity Sunday.*

DEARLY beloved in the Lord, ye who mind to come to the holy Communion of the Body and Blood of our Saviour Christ, must consider how Saint Paul exhorteth all persons diligently to try and examine themselves, before they presume to eat of that Bread, and drink of that Cup. For as the benefit is great, if with a true penitent heart and lively faith we receive that holy Sacrament; so is the danger great, if we receive the same unworthily. Judge therefore yourselves, brethren, that ye be not judged of the Lord; repent you truly for your sins past; have a lively and stedfast faith

85

Holy Communion

in Christ our Saviour; amend your lives, and be in perfect charity with all men; so shall ye be meet partakers of those holy mysteries. And above all things ye must give most humble and hearty thanks to God, the Father, the Son, and the Holy Ghost, for the redemption of the world by the death and passion of our Saviour Christ, both God and man; who did humble himself, even to the death upon the Cross, for us, miserable sinners, who lay in darkness and the shadow of death; that he might make us the children of God, and exalt us to everlasting life. And to the end that we should always remember the exceeding great love of our Master, and only Saviour, Jesus Christ, thus dying for us, and the innumerable benefits which by his precious blood-shedding he hath obtained for us; he hath instituted and ordained holy mysteries, as pledges of his love, and for a continual remembrance of his death, to our great and endless comfort. To him therefore, with the Father and the Holy Ghost, let us give, as we are most bounden, continual thanks; submitting ourselves wholly to his holy will and pleasure, and studying to serve him in true holiness and righteousness all the days of our life. *Amen.*

¶ *When the Minister giveth warning for the Celebration of the Holy Communion, (which he shall always do upon the Sunday, or some Holy Day, immediately preceding,) he shall read this Exhortation following; or so much thereof as, in his discretion, he may think convenient.*

DEARLY beloved, on —— day next I purpose, through God's assistance, to administer to all such as shall be religiously and devoutly disposed the most comfortable Sacrament of the Body and Blood of Christ; to be by them received in remembrance of his meritorious Cross and Passion; whereby alone we obtain remission of our sins, and are made partakers of the Kingdom of heaven. Wherefore it is our duty to render most humble and hearty thanks to Al-

Holy Communion

mighty God, our heavenly Father, for that he hath given his Son our Saviour Jesus Christ, not only to die for us, but also to be our spiritual food and sustenance in that holy Sacrament. Which being so divine and comfortable a thing to them who receive it worthily, and so dangerous to those who will presume to receive it unworthily; my duty is to exhort you, in the mean season to consider the dignity of that holy mystery, and the great peril of the unworthy receiving thereof; and so to search and examine your own consciences, and that not lightly, and after the manner of dissemblers with God; but so that ye may come holy and clean to such a heavenly Feast, in the marriage-garment required by God in holy Scripture, and be received as worthy partakers of that holy Table.

The way and means thereto is: First, to examine your lives and conversations by the rule of God's commandments; and whereinsoever ye shall perceive yourselves to have offended, either by will, word, or deed, there to bewail your own sinfulness, and to confess yourselves to Almighty God, with full purpose of amendment of life. And if ye shall perceive your offences to be such as are not only against God, but also against your neighbours; then ye shall reconcile yourselves unto them; being ready to make restitution and satisfaction, according to the uttermost of your powers, for all injuries and wrongs done by you to any other; and being likewise ready to forgive others who have offended you, as ye would have forgiveness of your offences at God's hand: for otherwise the receiving of the holy Communion doth nothing else but increase your condemnation. Therefore, if any of you be a blasphemer of God, an hinderer or slanderer of his Word, an adulterer, or be in malice, or envy, or in any other grievous crime; repent you of your sins, or else come not to that holy Table.

And because it is requisite that no man should come to

the holy Communion, but with a full trust in God's mercy, and with a quiet conscience; therefore, if there be any of you, who by this means cannot quiet his own conscience herein, but requireth further comfort or counsel, let him come to me, or to some other Minister of God's Word, and open his grief; that he may receive such godly counsel and advice, as may tend to the quieting of his conscience, and the removing of all scruple and doubtfulness.

¶ *Or, in case he shall see the People negligent to come to the Holy Communion, instead of the former, he may use this Exhortation.*

DEARLY beloved brethren, on —— I intend, by God's grace, to celebrate the Lord's Supper: unto which, in God's behalf, I bid you all who are here present; and beseech you, for the Lord Jesus Christ's sake, that ye will not refuse to come thereto, being so lovingly called and bidden by God himself. Ye know how grievous and unkind a thing it is, when a man hath prepared a rich feast, decked his table with all kind of provision, so that there lacketh nothing but the guests to sit down; and yet they who are called, without any cause, most unthankfully refuse to come. Which of you in such a case would not be moved? Who would not think a great injury and wrong done unto him? Wherefore, most dearly beloved in Christ, take ye good heed, lest ye, withdrawing yourselves from this holy Supper, provoke God's indignation against you. It is an easy matter for a man to say, I will not communicate, because I am otherwise hindered with worldly business. But such excuses are not so easily accepted and allowed before God. If any man say, I am a grievous sinner, and therefore am afraid to come: wherefore then do ye not repent and amend? When God calleth you, are ye not ashamed to say ye will not come? When ye should return to God, will ye excuse yourselves, and say ye are not ready? Consider earnestly with yourselves how little such feigned excuses will avail before God. Those who refused the feast in the Gospel, because they had bought a farm, or would try their yokes of oxen, or because they were married, were not so excused, but counted unworthy of the heavenly feast. Wherefore, according to mine office, I bid you in the Name of God, I call you in Christ's behalf, I exhort you, as ye love your own salvation, that ye will be partakers of this holy Communion. And as the Son of God did vouchsafe to yield up his soul by death upon the Cross for your salvation; so it is your duty to receive the Communion in remembrance of the sacrifice of his death, as he himself hath commanded: which if ye shall neglect to do, consider with yourselves how great is your ingratitude to God, and how sore punishment hangeth over your heads for the same; when ye wilfully abstain from the Lord's Table, and separate from your brethren, who come to feed on the banquet of that most heavenly food. These things if ye earnestly consider, ye will by God's grace return to a better mind: for the obtaining whereof we shall not cease to make our humble petitions unto Almighty God, our heavenly Father.

The Collects, Epistles, and Gospels

To be used throughout the Year.

¶ *The Collect, Epistle, and Gospel, appointed for the Sunday, shall serve all the Week after, where it is not in this Book otherwise ordered.*

¶ *The Collect appointed for any Sunday or other Feast may be used at the Evening Service of the day before.*

ADVENT SEASON.

The First Sunday in Advent.

The Collect.

ALMIGHTY God, give us grace that we may cast away the works of darkness, and put upon us the armour of light, now in the time of this mortal life, in which thy Son Jesus Christ came to visit us in great humility; that in the last day, when he shall come again in his glorious majesty to judge both the quick and the dead, we may rise to the life immortal, through him who liveth and reigneth with thee and the Holy Ghost, now and ever. *Amen.*

¶ *This Collect is to be repeated every day, after the other Collects in Advent, until Christmas Day.*

The Epistle. Romans xiii. 8.

OWE no man any thing, but to love one another: for he that loveth another hath fulfilled the law. For this, Thou shalt not commit adultery, Thou shalt not kill, Thou shalt not steal, Thou shalt not bear false witness, Thou shalt not covet; and if there be any other commandment, it is briefly comprehended in this saying, namely, Thou shalt love thy neighbour as thyself. Love worketh no ill to his neighbour: therefore love is the fulfilling of the law. And that, knowing the time, that now it is high time to awake

The First Sunday in Advent

out of sleep: for now is our salvation nearer than when we believed. The night is far spent, the day is at hand: let us therefore cast off the works of darkness, and let us put on the armour of light. Let us walk honestly, as in the day; not in rioting and drunkenness, not in chambering and wantonness, not in strife and envying. But put ye on the Lord Jesus Christ, and make not provision for the flesh, to fulfil the lusts thereof.

The Gospel. St. Matthew xxi. 1.

WHEN they drew nigh unto Jerusalem, and were come to Bethphage, unto the mount of Olives, then sent Jesus two disciples, saying unto them, Go into the village over against you, and straightway ye shall find an ass tied, and a colt with her: loose them, and bring them unto me. And if any man say ought unto you, ye shall say, The Lord hath need of them; and straightway he will send them. All this was done, that it might be fulfilled which was spoken by the prophet, saying, Tell ye the daughter of Sion, Behold, thy King cometh unto thee, meek, and sitting upon an ass, and a colt the foal of an ass. And the disciples went, and did as Jesus commanded them, and brought the ass, and the colt, and put on them their clothes, and they set him thereon. And a very great multitude spread their garments in the way; others cut down branches from the trees, and strawed them in the way. And the multitudes that went before, and that followed, cried, saying, Hosanna to the son of David: Blessed is he that cometh in the name of the Lord; Hosanna in the highest. And when he was come into Jerusalem, all the city was moved, saying, Who is this? And the multitude said, This is Jesus the prophet of Nazareth of Galilee. And Jesus went into the temple of God, and cast out all them that sold and bought in the temple, and overthrew the tables of the money-changers, and the seats of them that sold doves, and said unto them, It is written, My house shall be called the house of prayer; but ye have made it a den of thieves.

The Second Sunday in Advent.

The Collect.

BLESSED Lord, who hast caused all holy Scriptures to be written for our learning; Grant that we may in such wise hear them, read, mark, learn, and inwardly digest them, that by patience and comfort of thy holy Word, we may embrace, and ever hold fast, the blessed hope of everlasting life, which thou hast given us in our Saviour Jesus Christ. *Amen.*

The Epistle. Romans xv. 4.

WHATSOEVER things were written aforetime were written for our learning, that we through patience and comfort of the scriptures might have hope. Now the God of patience and consolation grant you to be like-minded one toward another according to Christ Jesus: that ye may with one mind and one mouth glorify God, even the Father of our Lord Jesus Christ. Wherefore receive ye one another, as Christ also received us to the glory of God. Now I say that Jesus Christ was a minister of the circumcision for the truth of God, to confirm the promises made unto the fathers: and that the Gentiles might glorify God for his mercy; as it is written, For this cause I will confess to thee among the Gentiles, and sing unto thy name. And again he saith, Rejoice, ye Gentiles, with his people. And again, Praise the Lord, all ye Gentiles; and laud him, all ye people. And again, Esaias saith, There shall be a root of Jesse, and he that shall rise to reign over the Gentiles; in him shall the Gentiles trust. Now the God of hope fill you

The Third Sunday in Advent

with all joy and peace in believing, that ye may abound in hope, through the power of the Holy Ghost.

The Gospel. St. Luke xxi. 25.

AND there shall be signs in the sun, and in the moon, and in the stars; and upon the earth distress of nations, with perplexity; the sea and the waves roaring; men's hearts failing them for fear, and for looking after those things which are coming on the earth: for the powers of heaven shall be shaken. And then shall they see the Son of man coming in a cloud with power and great glory. And when these things begin to come to pass, then look up, and lift up your heads; for your redemption draweth nigh. And he spake to them a parable; Behold the fig tree, and all the trees; when they now shoot forth, ye see and know of your own selves that summer is now nigh at hand. So likewise ye, when ye see these things come to pass, know ye that the kingdom of God is nigh at hand. Verily I say unto you, This generation shall not pass away, till all be fulfilled. Heaven and earth shall pass away: but my words shall not pass away.

The Third Sunday in Advent.

The Collect.

O LORD Jesus Christ, who at thy first coming didst send thy messenger to prepare thy way before thee; Grant that the ministers and stewards of thy mysteries may likewise so prepare and make ready thy way, by turning the hearts of the disobedient to the wisdom of the just, that at thy second coming to judge the world we may be found an acceptable people in thy sight, who livest and reignest with the Father and the Holy Spirit ever, one God, world without end. *Amen.*

The Third Sunday in Advent

The Epistle. 1 Corinthians iv. 1.

LET a man so account of us, as of the ministers of Christ, and stewards of the mysteries of God. Moreover it is required in stewards, that a man be found faithful. But with me it is a very small thing that I should be judged of you, or of man's judgment: yea, I judge not mine own self. For I know nothing against myself; yet am I not hereby justified: but he that judgeth me is the Lord. Therefore judge nothing before the time, until the Lord come, who both will bring to light the hidden things of darkness, and will make manifest the counsels of the hearts: and then shall every man have praise of God.

The Gospel. St. Matthew xi. 2.

NOW when John had heard in the prison the works of Christ, he sent two of his disciples, and said unto him, Art thou he that should come, or do we look for another? Jesus answered and said unto them, Go and shew John again those things which ye do hear and see: the blind receive their sight, and the lame walk, the lepers are cleansed, and the deaf hear, the dead are raised up, and the poor have the gospel preached to them. And blessed is he, whosoever shall not be offended in me. And as they departed, Jesus began to say unto the multitudes concerning John, What went ye out into the wilderness to see? A reed shaken with the wind? But what went ye out for to see? A man clothed in soft raiment? behold, they that wear soft clothing are in kings' houses. But what went ye out for to see? A prophet? yea, I say unto you, and more than a prophet. For this is he, of whom it is written, Behold, I send my messenger before thy face, which shall prepare thy way before thee.

The Fourth Sunday in Advent

The Fourth Sunday in Advent.

The Collect.

O LORD, raise up, we pray thee, thy power, and come among us, and with great might succour us; that whereas, through our sins and wickedness, we are sore let and hindered in running the race that is set before us, thy bountiful grace and mercy may speedily help and deliver us; through Jesus Christ our Lord, to whom, with thee and the Holy Ghost, be honour and glory, world without end. *Amen.*

The Epistle. Philippians iv. 4.

REJOICE in the Lord alway: and again I say, Rejoice. Let your moderation be known unto all men. The Lord is at hand. Be careful for nothing; but in every thing by prayer and supplication with thanksgiving let your requests be made known unto God. And the peace of God, which passeth all understanding, shall keep your hearts and minds through Christ Jesus.

The Gospel. St. John i. 19.

THIS is the record of John, when the Jews sent priests and Levites from Jerusalem to ask him, Who art thou? And he confessed, and denied not; but confessed, I am not the Christ. And they asked him, What then? Art thou Elias? And he saith, I am not. Art thou that prophet? And he answered, No. Then said they unto him, Who art thou? that we may give an answer to them that sent us. What sayest thou of thyself? He said, I am the voice of one crying in the wilderness, Make straight the way of the Lord, as said the prophet Esaias. And they which were sent were of the Pharisees. And they asked him, and said unto him, Why baptizest thou then, if thou be not that Christ, nor Elias, neither that prophet? John answered them, saying, I baptize with water: but there standeth one among you, whom ye know not; he it is, who coming after me is preferred before me, whose shoe's latchet I am not worthy to unloose. These things were done in Bethabara beyond Jordan, where John was baptizing.

CHRISTMASTIDE.

The Nativity of our Lord, or the Birthday of Christ, commonly called Christmas Day.

[December 25.]

The Collect.

ALMIGHTY God, who hast given us thy only-begotten Son to take our nature upon him, and as at this time to be born of a pure virgin; Grant that we being regenerate, and made thy children by adoption and grace, may daily be renewed by thy Holy Spirit; through the same our Lord Jesus Christ, who liveth and reigneth with thee and the same Spirit ever, one God, world without end. *Amen.*

¶ *This Collect is to be said daily throughout the Octave.*

The Epistle. Hebrews i. 1.

GOD, who at sundry times and in divers manners spake in time past unto the fathers by the prophets, hath in these last days spoken unto us by his Son, whom he hath appointed heir of all things, by whom also he made the worlds; who being the brightness of his glory, and the express image of his person, and upholding all things by the word of his power, when he had by himself purged our sins, sat down on the right hand of the Majesty on high; being made so much better than the angels, as he hath by inheritance obtained a more excellent name than they. For

Christmas Day

unto which of the angels said he at any time, Thou art my Son, this day have I begotten thee? And again, I will be to him a Father, and he shall be to me a Son? And again, when he bringeth in the first-begotten into the world, he saith, And let all the angels of God worship him. And of the angels he saith, Who maketh his angels spirits, and his ministers a flame of fire. But unto the Son he saith, Thy throne, O God, is for ever and ever: a sceptre of righteousness is the sceptre of thy kingdom. Thou hast loved righteousness, and hated iniquity; therefore God, even thy God, hath anointed thee with the oil of gladness above thy fellows. And, Thou, Lord, in the beginning hast laid the foundation of the earth; and the heavens are the works of thine hands: they shall perish; but thou remainest; and they all shall wax old as doth a garment; and as a vesture shalt thou fold them up, and they shall be changed: but thou art the same, and thy years shall not fail.

The Gospel. St. John i. 1.

IN the beginning was the Word, and the Word was with God, and the Word was God. The same was in the beginning with God. All things were made by him; and without him was not any thing made that was made. In him was life; and the life was the light of men. And the light shineth in darkness; and the darkness comprehended it not. There was a man sent from God, whose name was John. The same came for a witness, to bear witness of the Light, that all men through him might believe. He was not that Light, but was sent to bear witness of that Light. That was the true Light, which lighteth every man that cometh into the world. He was in the world, and the world was made by him, and the world knew him not. He came unto his own, and his own received him not. But as many as received him, to them gave he power to become the sons of God,

Christmas Day

even to them that believe on his name: which were born, not of blood, nor of the will of the flesh, nor of the will of man, but of God. And the Word was made flesh, and dwelt among us, (and we beheld his glory, the glory as of the only begotten of the Father,) full of grace and truth.

¶ *If in any Church the Holy Communion be twice celebrated on Christmas Day, the following Collect, Epistle, and Gospel may be used at the first Communion.*

The Collect.

O GOD, who makest us glad with the yearly remembrance of the birth of thine only Son Jesus Christ; Grant that as we joyfully receive him for our Redeemer, so we may with sure confidence behold him when he shall come to be our Judge, who liveth and reigneth with thee and the Holy Ghost, one God, world without end. *Amen.*

The Epistle. Titus ii. 11.

THE grace of God that bringeth salvation hath appeared to all men, teaching us that, denying ungodliness and worldly lusts, we should live soberly, righteously, and godly, in this present world; looking for that blessed hope, and the glorious appearing of the great God and our Saviour Jesus Christ; who gave himself for us, that he might redeem us from all iniquity, and purify unto himself a peculiar people, zealous of good works. These things speak, and exhort, and rebuke with all authority. Let no man despise thee.

The Gospel. St. Luke ii. 1.

AND it came to pass in those days, that there went out a decree from Cæsar Augustus, that all the world should be taxed. (And this taxing was first made when Cyrenius was governor of Syria.) And all went to be taxed, every one into his own city. And Joseph also went up from

Saint Stephen

Galilee, out of the city of Nazareth, into Judæa, unto the city of David, which is called Bethlehem; (because he was of the house and lineage of David:) to be taxed with Mary his espoused wife, being great with child. And so it was, that, while they were there, the days were accomplished that she should be delivered. And she brought forth her firstborn son, and wrapped him in swaddling clothes, and laid him in a manger; because there was no room for them in the inn. And there were in the same country shepherds abiding in the field, keeping watch over their flock by night. And, lo, the angel of the Lord came upon them, and the glory of the Lord shone round about them: and they were sore afraid. And the angel said unto them, Fear not: for, behold, I bring you good tidings of great joy, which shall be to all people. For unto you is born this day in the city of David a Saviour, which is Christ the Lord. And this shall be a sign unto you; Ye shall find the babe wrapped in swaddling clothes, lying in a manger. And suddenly there was with the angel a multitude of the heavenly host praising God, and saying, Glory to God in the highest, and on earth peace, good will toward men.

Saint Stephen, Deacon and Martyr.

[December 26.]

The Collect.

GRANT, O Lord, that, in all our sufferings here upon earth for the testimony of thy truth, we may stedfastly look up to heaven, and by faith behold the glory that shall be revealed; and, being filled with the Holy Ghost, may learn to love and bless our persecutors by the example of thy first Martyr Saint Stephen, who prayed for his murderers to thee, O blessed Jesus, who standest at the right

Saint Stephen

hand of God to succour all those who suffer for thee, our only Mediator and Advocate. *Amen.*

For the Epistle. Acts vii. 55.

STEPHEN, being full of the Holy Ghost, looked up stedfastly into heaven, and saw the glory of God, and Jesus standing on the right hand of God, and said, Behold, I see the heavens opened, and the Son of man standing on the right hand of God. Then they cried out with a loud voice, and stopped their ears, and ran upon him with one accord, and cast him out of the city, and stoned him: and the witnesses laid down their clothes at a young man's feet, whose name was Saul. And they stoned Stephen, calling upon God, and saying, Lord Jesus, receive my spirit. And he kneeled down, and cried with a loud voice, Lord, lay not this sin to their charge. And when he had said this, he fell asleep.

The Gospel. St. Matthew xxiii. 34.

BEHOLD, I send unto you prophets, and wise men, and scribes: and some of them ye shall kill and crucify; and some of them shall ye scourge in your synagogues, and persecute them from city to city: that upon you may come all the righteous blood shed upon the earth, from the blood of righteous Abel unto the blood of Zacharias son of Barachias, whom ye slew between the temple and the altar. Verily I say unto you, All these things shall come upon this generation. O Jerusalem, Jerusalem, thou that killest the prophets, and stonest them which are sent unto thee, how often would I have gathered thy children together, even as a hen gathereth her chickens under her wings, and ye would not! Behold, your house is left unto you desolate. For I say unto you, Ye shall not see me henceforth, till ye shall say, Blessed is he that cometh in the name of the Lord.

Saint John Evangelist

Saint John, Apostle and Evangelist.

[December 27.]

The Collect.

MERCIFUL Lord, we beseech thee to cast thy bright beams of light upon thy Church, that it, being illumined by the doctrine of thy blessed Apostle and Evangelist Saint John, may so walk in the light of thy truth, that it may at length attain to life everlasting; through Jesus Christ our Lord. *Amen.*

The Epistle. 1 St. John i. 1.

THAT which was from the beginning, which we have heard, which we have seen with our eyes, which we have looked upon, and our hands have handled, of the Word of life; (for the life was manifested, and we have seen it, and bear witness, and shew unto you that eternal life, which was with the Father, and was manifested unto us;) that which we have seen and heard declare we unto you, that ye also may have fellowship with us: and truly our fellowship is with the Father, and with his Son Jesus Christ. And these things write we unto you, that your joy may be full. This then is the message which we have heard of him, and declare unto you, that God is light, and in him is no darkness at all. If we say that we have fellowship with him, and walk in darkness, we lie, and do not the truth: but if we walk in the light, as he is in the light, we have fellowship one with another, and the blood of Jesus Christ his Son cleanseth us from all sin. If we say that we have no sin, we deceive ourselves, and the truth is not in us. If we confess our sins, he is faithful and just to forgive us our sins, and to cleanse us from all unrighteousness. If we say that we have not sinned, we make him a liar, and his word is not in us.

The Gospel. St. John xxi. 19.

JESUS saith unto Peter, Follow me. Then Peter, turning about, seeth the disciple whom Jesus loved following; which also leaned on his breast at supper, and said, Lord, which is he that betrayeth thee? Peter seeing him saith to Jesus, Lord, and what shall this man do? Jesus saith unto him, If I will that he tarry till I come, what is that to thee? Follow thou me. Then went this saying abroad among the brethren, that that disciple should not die: yet Jesus said not unto him, He shall not die; but, If I will that he tarry till I come, what is that to thee? This is the disciple which testifieth of these things, and wrote these things: and we know that his testimony is true. And there are also many other things which Jesus did, the which, if they should be written every one, I suppose that even the world itself could not contain the books that should be written.

The Holy Innocents.

[December 28.]

The Collect.

O ALMIGHTY God, who out of the mouths of babes and sucklings hast ordained strength, and madest infants to glorify thee by their deaths; Mortify and kill all vices in us, and so strengthen us by thy grace, that by the innocency of our lives, and constancy of our faith even unto death, we may glorify thy holy Name; through Jesus Christ our Lord. *Amen.*

For the Epistle. Revelation xiv. 1.

I LOOKED, and, lo, a Lamb stood on the mount Sion, and with him an hundred forty and four thousand, having his Father's name written in their foreheads. And I heard a voice from heaven, as the voice of many waters, and as the voice of a great thunder: and I heard the voice of harpers harping with their harps: and they sung as it were a new song before the throne, and before the four living creatures, and the elders: and no man could learn that song but the hundred and forty and four thousand, which were redeemed from the earth. These are they which were not defiled with women; for they are virgins. These are they which follow the Lamb whithersoever he goeth. These were redeemed from among men, being the first-fruits unto God and to the Lamb. And in their mouth was found no guile: for they are without fault before the throne of God.

The Gospel. St. Matthew ii. 13.

THE angel of the Lord appeareth to Joseph in a dream, saying, Arise, and take the young child and his mother, and flee into Egypt, and be thou there until I bring thee word: for Herod will seek the young child to destroy him. When he arose, he took the young child and his mother by night, and departed into Egypt: and was there until the death of Herod: that it might be fulfilled which was spoken of the Lord by the prophet, saying, Out of Egypt have I called my son. Then Herod, when he saw that he was mocked of the wise men, was exceeding wroth, and sent forth, and slew all the children that were in Bethlehem, and in all the coasts thereof, from two years old and under, according to the time which he had diligently enquired of the wise men. Then was fulfilled that which was spoken by Jeremy the prophet, saying, In Rama was there a voice heard, lamentation, and weeping, and great mourning, Rachel weeping for her children, and would not be comforted, because they are not.

¶ *If there be any more days before the Sunday following Christmas*

The First Sunday after Christmas

Day, the first Epistle and Gospel for Christmas Day shall serve for them.

The First Sunday after Christmas Day.

The Collect.

ALMIGHTY God, who hast given us thy only-begotten Son to take our nature upon him, and as at this time to be born of a pure virgin; Grant that we being regenerate, and made thy children by adoption and grace, may daily be renewed by thy Holy Spirit; through the same our Lord Jesus Christ, who liveth and reigneth with thee and the same Spirit ever, one God, world without end. *Amen.*

The Epistle. Galatians iv. 1.

NOW I say, That the heir, as long as he is a child, differeth nothing from a servant, though he be lord of all; but is under tutors and governors until the time appointed of the father. Even so we, when we were children, were in bondage under the elements of the world: but when the fulness of the time was come, God sent forth his Son, made of a woman, made under the law, to redeem them that were under the law, that we might receive the adoption of sons. And because ye are sons, God hath sent forth the Spirit of his Son into your hearts, crying, Abba, Father. Wherefore thou art no more a servant, but a son; and if a son, then an heir of God through Christ.

The Gospel. St. Matthew i. 18.

THE birth of Jesus Christ was on this wise: When as his mother Mary was espoused to Joseph, before they came together, she was found with child of the Holy Ghost. Then Joseph her husband, being a just man, and not willing to make her a publick example, was minded to put her away privily. But while he thought on these things, behold, the angel of the Lord appeared unto him in a dream, saying, Joseph, thou son of David, fear not to take unto thee Mary thy wife: for that which is conceived in her is of the Holy Ghost. And she shall bring forth a son, and thou shalt call his name JESUS: for he shall save his people from their sins. Now all this was done, that it might be fulfilled which was spoken of the Lord by the prophet, saying, Behold, a virgin shall be with child, and shall bring forth a son, and they shall call his name Emmanuel, which being interpreted is, God with us. Then Joseph being raised from sleep did as the angel of the Lord had bidden him, and took unto him his wife: and knew her not till she had brought forth her firstborn son: and he called his name JESUS.

The Circumcision of Christ.

[January 1.]

The Collect.

ALMIGHTY God, who madest thy blessed Son to be circumcised, and obedient to the law for man; Grant us the true circumcision of the Spirit; that, our hearts, and all our members, being mortified from all worldly and carnal lusts, we may in all things obey thy blessed will; through the same thy Son Jesus Christ our Lord. *Amen.*

The Epistle. Philippians ii. 9.

GOD also hath highly exalted him, and given him a name which is above every name: that at the name of Jesus every knee should bow, of things in heaven, and things in earth, and things under the earth; and that every tongue should confess that Jesus Christ is Lord, to the glory of God the Father. Wherefore, my beloved, as ye have al-

The Second Sunday after Christmas

ways obeyed, not as in my presence only, but now much more in my absence, work out your own salvation with fear and trembling. For it is God which worketh in you both to will and to do of his good pleasure.

The Gospel. St. Luke ii. 15.

AND it came to pass, as the angels were gone away from them into heaven, the shepherds said one to another, Let us now go even unto Bethlehem, and see this thing which is come to pass, which the Lord hath made known unto us. And they came with haste, and found Mary, and Joseph, and the babe lying in a manger. And when they had seen it, they made known abroad the saying which was told them concerning this child. And all they that heard it wondered at those things which were told them by the shepherds. But Mary kept all these things, and pondered them in her heart. And the shepherds returned, glorifying and praising God for all the things that they had heard and seen, as it was told unto them. And when eight days were accomplished for the circumcising of the child, his name was called JESUS, which was so named of the angel before he was conceived in the womb.

The Second Sunday after Christmas Day.

The Collect.

ALMIGHTY God, who hast poured upon us the new light of thine incarnate Word; Grant that the same light enkindled in our hearts may shine forth in our lives; through Jesus Christ our Lord. *Amen.*

For the Epistle. Isaiah lxi. 1.

THE Spirit of the Lord GOD is upon me; because the LORD hath anointed me to preach good tidings unto the meek; he hath sent me to bind up the brokenhearted, to proclaim liberty to the captives, and the opening of the prison to them that are bound; to proclaim the acceptable year of the LORD, and the day of vengeance of our God; to comfort all that mourn; to appoint unto them that mourn in Zion, to give unto them beauty for ashes, the oil of joy for mourning, the garment of praise for the spirit of heaviness; that they might be called trees of righteousness, the planting of the LORD, that he might be glorified.

The Gospel. St. Matthew ii. 19.

WHEN Herod was dead, behold, an angel of the Lord appeareth in a dream to Joseph in Egypt, saying, Arise, and take the young child and his mother, and go into the land of Israel: for they are dead which sought the young child's life. And he arose, and took the young child and his mother, and came into the land of Israel. But when he heard that Archelaus did reign in Judæa in the room of his father Herod, he was afraid to go thither: notwithstanding, being warned of God in a dream, he turned aside into the parts of Galilee: and he came and dwelt in a city called Nazareth: that it might be fulfilled which was spoken by the prophets, He shall be called a Nazarene.

EPIPHANY SEASON.

The Epiphany, or the Manifestation of Christ to the Gentiles.

[January 6.]

The Collect.

O GOD, who by the leading of a star didst manifest thy only-begotten Son to the Gentiles; Mercifully grant that we, who know thee now by faith, may after this life

The Epiphany

have the fruition of thy glorious Godhead; through the same thy Son Jesus Christ our Lord. *Amen.*

¶ *This Collect is to be said daily throughout the Octave.*

The Epistle. Ephesians iii. 1.

FOR this cause I Paul, the prisoner of Jesus Christ for you Gentiles, if ye have heard of the dispensation of the grace of God, which is given me to you-ward: how that by revelation he made known unto me the mystery; (as I wrote afore in few words, whereby, when ye read, ye may understand my knowledge in the mystery of Christ) which in other ages was not made known unto the sons of men, as it is now revealed unto his holy apostles and prophets by the Spirit; that the Gentiles should be fellow-heirs, and of the same body, and partakers of his promise in Christ by the gospel: whereof I was made a minister, according to the gift of the grace of God given unto me by the effectual working of his power. Unto me, who am less than the least of all saints, is this grace given, that I should preach among the Gentiles the unsearchable riches of Christ; and to make all men see what is the fellowship of the mystery, which from the beginning of the world hath been hid in God, who created all things by Jesus Christ: to the intent that now unto the principalities and powers in heavenly places might be known by the church the manifold wisdom of God, according to the eternal purpose which he purposed in Christ Jesus our Lord: in whom we have boldness and access with confidence by the faith of him.

The Gospel. St. Matthew ii. 1.

WHEN Jesus was born in Bethlehem of Judæa, in the days of Herod the king, behold, there came wise men from the east to Jerusalem, saying, Where is he that is born King of the Jews? for we have seen his star in the east,

The First Sunday after Epiphany

and are come to worship him. When Herod the king had heard these things, he was troubled, and all Jerusalem with him. And when he had gathered all the chief priests and scribes of the people together, he demanded of them where Christ should be born. And they said unto him, In Bethlehem of Judæa: for thus it is written by the prophet, And thou Bethlehem, in the land of Juda, art not the least among the princes of Juda: for out of thee shall come a Governor, that shall rule my people Israel. Then Herod, when he had privily called the wise men, enquired of them diligently what time the star appeared. And he sent them to Bethlehem, and said, Go and search diligently for the young child; and when ye have found him, bring me word again, that I may come and worship him also. When they had heard the king, they departed; and, lo, the star, which they saw in the east, went before them, till it came and stood over where the young child was. When they saw the star, they rejoiced with exceeding great joy. And when they were come into the house, they saw the young child with Mary his mother, and fell down, and worshipped him: and when they had opened their treasures, they presented unto him gifts; gold, and frankincense, and myrrh. And being warned of God in a dream that they should not return to Herod, they departed into their own country another way.

¶ *The same Epistle and Gospel shall serve unto the next Sunday.*

The First Sunday after the Epiphany.

The Collect.

O LORD, we beseech thee mercifully to receive the prayers of thy people who call upon thee; and grant that they may both perceive and know what things they ought to do, and also may have grace and power faithfully to fulfil the same; through Jesus Christ our Lord. *Amen.*

The First Sunday after Epiphany

The Epistle. Romans xii. 1.

I BESEECH you therefore, brethren, by the mercies of God, that ye present your bodies a living sacrifice, holy, acceptable unto God, which is your reasonable service. And be not conformed to this world: but be ye transformed by the renewing of your mind, that ye may prove what is that good, and acceptable, and perfect, will of God. For I say, through the grace given unto me, to every man that is among you, not to think of himself more highly than he ought to think; but to think soberly, according as God hath dealt to every man the measure of faith. For as we have many members in one body, and all members have not the same office: so we, being many, are one body in Christ, and every one members one of another.

The Gospel. St. Luke ii. 41.

NOW his parents went to Jerusalem every year at the feast of the passover. And when he was twelve years old, they went up to Jerusalem after the custom of the feast. And when they had fulfilled the days, as they returned, the child Jesus tarried behind in Jerusalem; and Joseph and his mother knew not of it. But they, supposing him to have been in the company, went a day's journey; and they sought him among their kinsfolk and acquaintance. And when they found him not, they turned back again to Jerusalem, seeking him. And it came to pass, that after three days they found him in the temple, sitting in the midst of the doctors, both hearing them, and asking them questions. And all that heard him were astonished at his understanding and answers. And when they saw him, they were amazed: and his mother said unto him, Son, why hast thou thus dealt with us? behold, thy father and I have sought thee sorrowing. And he said unto them, How is it that ye

The Second Sunday after Epiphany

sought me? wist ye not that I must be about my Father's business? And they understood not the saying which he spake unto them. And he went down with them, and came to Nazareth, and was subject unto them: but his mother kept all these sayings in her heart. And Jesus increased in wisdom and stature, and in favour with God and man.

The Second Sunday after the Epiphany.

The Collect.

ALMIGHTY and everlasting God, who dost govern all things in heaven and earth; Mercifully hear the supplications of thy people, and grant us thy peace all the days of our life; through Jesus Christ our Lord. *Amen.*

The Epistle. Romans xii. 6.

HAVING then gifts differing according to the grace that is given to us, whether prophecy, let us prophesy according to the proportion of faith; or ministry, let us wait on our ministering; or he that teacheth, on teaching; or he that exhorteth, on exhortation: he that giveth, let him do it with simplicity; he that ruleth, with diligence; he that sheweth mercy, with cheerfulness. Let love be without dissimulation. Abhor that which is evil; cleave to that which is good. Be kindly affectioned one to another with brotherly love; in honour preferring one another; not slothful in business; fervent in spirit; serving the Lord; rejoicing in hope; patient in tribulation; continuing instant in prayer; distributing to the necessity of saints; given to hospitality. Bless them which persecute you: bless, and curse not. Rejoice with them that do rejoice, and weep with them that weep. Be of the same mind one toward another. Mind not high things, but condescend to men of low estate.

The Third Sunday after Epiphany

The Gospel. St. Mark i. 1.

THE beginning of the gospel of Jesus Christ, the Son of God; as it is written in the prophets, Behold, I send my messenger before thy face, which shall prepare thy way before thee. The voice of one crying in the wilderness, Prepare ye the way of the Lord, make his paths straight. John did baptize in the wilderness, and preach the baptism of repentance for the remission of sins. And there went out unto him all the land of Judæa, and they of Jerusalem, and were all baptized of him in the river of Jordan, confessing their sins. And John was clothed with camel's hair, and with a girdle of a skin about his loins; and he did eat locusts and wild honey; and preached, saying, There cometh one mightier than I after me, the latchet of whose shoes I am not worthy to stoop down and unloose. I indeed have baptized you with water: but he shall baptize you with the Holy Ghost. And it came to pass in those days, that Jesus came from Nazareth of Galilee, and was baptized of John in Jordan. And straightway coming up out of the water, he saw the heavens opened, and the Spirit, like a dove, descending upon him: and there came a voice from heaven, saying, Thou art my beloved Son, in whom I am well pleased.

The Third Sunday after the Epiphany.

The Collect.

ALMIGHTY and everlasting God, mercifully look upon our infirmities, and in all our dangers and necessities stretch forth thy right hand to help and defend us; through Jesus Christ our Lord. *Amen.*

The Epistle. Romans xii. 16.

BE not wise in your own conceits. Recompense to no man evil for evil. Provide things honest in the sight of

The Third Sunday after Epiphany

all men. If it be possible, as much as lieth in you, live peaceably with all men. Dearly beloved, avenge not yourselves, but rather give place unto wrath: for it is written, Vengeance is mine; I will repay, saith the Lord. Therefore if thine enemy hunger, feed him; if he thirst, give him drink: for in so doing thou shalt heap coals of fire on his head. Be not overcome of evil, but overcome evil with good.

The Gospel. St. John ii. 1.

AND the third day there was a marriage in Cana of Galilee; and the mother of Jesus was there: and both Jesus was called, and his disciples, to the marriage. And when they wanted wine, the mother of Jesus saith unto him, They have no wine. Jesus saith unto her, Woman, what have I to do with thee? mine hour is not yet come. His mother saith unto the servants, Whatsoever he saith unto you, do it. And there were set there six water-pots of stone, after the manner of the purifying of the Jews, containing two or three firkins apiece. Jesus saith unto them, Fill the water-pots with water. And they filled them up to the brim. And he saith unto them, Draw out now, and bear unto the governor of the feast. And they bare it. When the ruler of the feast had tasted the water that was made wine, and knew not whence it was: (but the servants which drew the water knew;) the governor of the feast called the bridegroom, and saith unto him, Every man at the beginning doth set forth good wine; and when men have well drunk, then that which is worse: but thou hast kept the good wine until now. This beginning of miracles did Jesus in Cana of Galilee, and manifested forth his glory; and his disciples believed on him.

The Fourth Sunday after Epiphany

The Fourth Sunday after the Epiphany.

The Collect.

O GOD, who knowest us to be set in the midst of so many and great dangers, that by reason of the frailty of our nature we cannot always stand upright; Grant to us such strength and protection, as may support us in all dangers, and carry us through all temptations; through Jesus Christ our Lord. *Amen.*

The Epistle. Romans xiii. 1.

LET every soul be subject unto the higher powers. For there is no power but of God: the powers that be are ordained of God. Whosoever therefore resisteth the power, resisteth the ordinance of God; and they that resist shall receive to themselves condemnation. For rulers are not a terror to good works, but to the evil. Wilt thou then not be afraid of the power? do that which is good, and thou shalt have praise of the same: for he is the minister of God to thee for good. But if thou do that which is evil, be afraid; for he beareth not the sword in vain: for he is the minister of God, a revenger to execute wrath upon him that doeth evil. Wherefore ye must needs be subject, not only for wrath, but also for conscience sake. For for this cause pay ye tribute also: for they are God's ministers, attending continually upon this very thing. Render therefore to all their dues: tribute to whom tribute is due; custom to whom custom; fear to whom fear; honour to whom honour.

The Gospel. St. Matthew viii. 1.

WHEN he was come down from the mountain, great multitudes followed him. And, behold, there came a leper and worshipped him, saying, Lord, if thou wilt, thou canst make me clean. And Jesus put forth his hand, and

The Fifth Sunday after Epiphany

touched him, saying, I will; be thou clean. And immediately his leprosy was cleansed. And Jesus saith unto him, See thou tell no man; but go thy way, shew thyself to the priest, and offer the gift that Moses commanded, for a testimony unto them. And when Jesus was entered into Capernaum, there came unto him a centurion, beseeching him, and saying, Lord, my servant lieth at home sick of the palsy, grievously tormented. And Jesus saith unto him, I will come and heal him. The centurion answered and said, Lord, I am not worthy that thou shouldest come under my roof: but speak the word only, and my servant shall be healed. For I am a man under authority, having soldiers under me: and I say to this man, Go, and he goeth; and to another, Come, and he cometh; and to my servant, Do this, and he doeth it. When Jesus heard it, he marvelled, and said to them that followed, Verily I say unto you, I have not found so great faith, no, not in Israel. And I say unto you, that many shall come from the east and west, and shall sit down with Abraham, and Isaac, and Jacob, in the kingdom of heaven. But the children of the kingdom shall be cast out into outer darkness: there shall be weeping and gnashing of teeth. And Jesus said unto the centurion, Go thy way; and as thou hast believed, so be it done unto thee. And his servant was healed in the selfsame hour.

The Fifth Sunday after the Epiphany.

The Collect.

O LORD, we beseech thee to keep thy Church and household continually in thy true religion; that they who do lean only upon the hope of thy heavenly grace may evermore be defended by thy mighty power; through Jesus Christ our Lord. *Amen.*

The Fifth Sunday after Epiphany

The Epistle. Colossians iii. 12.

PUT on therefore, as the elect of God, holy and beloved, a heart of compassion, kindness, humbleness of mind, meekness, long-suffering; forbearing one another, and forgiving one another, if any man have a quarrel against any: even as Christ forgave you, so also do ye. And above all these things put on charity, which is the bond of perfectness. And let the peace of God rule in your hearts, to the which also ye are called in one body; and be ye thankful. Let the word of Christ dwell in you richly in all wisdom; teaching and admonishing one another in psalms and hymns and spiritual songs, singing with grace in your hearts to the Lord. And whatsoever ye do in word or deed, do all in the name of the Lord Jesus, giving thanks to God and the Father by him.

The Gospel. St. Matthew xiii. 24.

THE kingdom of heaven is likened unto a man which sowed good seed in his field: but while men slept, his enemy came and sowed tares among the wheat, and went his way. But when the blade was sprung up, and brought forth fruit, then appeared the tares also. So the servants of the householder came and said unto him, Sir, didst not thou sow good seed in thy field? from whence then hath it tares? He said unto them, An enemy hath done this. The servants said unto him, Wilt thou then that we go and gather them up? But he said, Nay; lest while ye gather up the tares, ye root up also the wheat with them. Let both grow together until the harvest: and in the time of harvest I will say to the reapers, Gather ye together first the tares, and bind them in bundles to burn them: but gather the wheat into my barn.

The Sixth Sunday after Epiphany

The Sixth Sunday after the Epiphany.

The Collect.

O GOD, whose blessed Son was manifested that he might destroy the works of the devil, and make us the sons of God, and heirs of eternal life; Grant us, we beseech thee, that, having this hope, we may purify ourselves, even as he is pure; that, when he shall appear again with power and great glory, we may be made like unto him in his eternal and glorious kingdom; where with thee, O Father, and thee, O Holy Ghost, he liveth and reigneth ever, one God, world without end. *Amen.*

The Epistle. 1 St. John iii. 1.

BEHOLD, what manner of love the Father hath bestowed upon us, that we should be called the sons of God: therefore the world knoweth us not, because it knew him not. Beloved, now are we the sons of God, and it doth not yet appear what we shall be: but we know that, when he shall appear, we shall be like him; for we shall see him as he is. And every man that hath this hope in him purifieth himself, even as he is pure. Whosoever committeth sin transgresseth also the law: for sin is the transgression of the law. And ye know that he was manifested to take away our sins; and in him is no sin. Whosoever abideth in him sinneth not: whosoever sinneth hath not seen him, neither known him. Little children, let no man deceive you: he that doeth righteousness is righteous, even as he is righteous. He that committeth sin is of the devil; for the devil sinneth from the beginning. For this purpose the Son of God was manifested, that he might destroy the works of the devil.

Septuagesima

The Gospel. St. Matthew xxiv. 23.

THEN if any man shall say unto you, Lo, here is Christ, or there; believe it not. For there shall arise false Christs, and false prophets, and shall shew great signs and wonders; insomuch that, if it were possible, they shall deceive the very elect. Behold, I have told you before. Wherefore if they shall say unto you, Behold, he is in the desert; go not forth: behold, he is in the secret chambers; believe it not. For as the lightning cometh out of the east, and shineth even unto the west; so shall also the coming of the Son of man be. For wheresoever the carcase is, there will the eagles be gathered together. Immediately after the tribulation of those days shall the sun be darkened, and the moon shall not give her light, and the stars shall fall from heaven, and the powers of the heavens shall be shaken: and then shall appear the sign of the Son of man in heaven: and then shall all the tribes of the earth mourn, and they shall see the Son of man coming in the clouds of heaven with power and great glory. And he shall send his angels with a great sound of a trumpet, and they shall gather together his elect from the four winds, from one end of heaven to the other.

PRE-LENTEN SEASON.

The Sunday called Septuagesima, or the third Sunday before Lent.

The Collect.

O LORD, we beseech thee favourably to hear the prayers of thy people; that we, who are justly punished for our offences, may be mercifully delivered by thy goodness, for the glory of thy Name; through Jesus Christ

Septuagesima

our Saviour, who liveth and reigneth with thee and the
Holy Ghost ever, one God, world without end. *Amen.*

The Epistle. 1 Corinthians ix. 24.

KNOW ye not that they which run in a race run all, but
one receiveth the prize? So run, that ye may obtain.
And every man that striveth for the mastery is temperate
in all things. Now they do it to obtain a corruptible crown;
but we an incorruptible. I therefore so run, not as uncer-
tainly; so fight I, not as one that beateth the air: but I keep
under my body, and bring it into subjection; lest that by
any means, when I have preached to others, I myself
should be a castaway.

The Gospel. St. Matthew xx. 1.

THE kingdom of heaven is like unto a man that is an
householder, which went out early in the morning to
hire labourers into his vineyard. And when he had agreed
with the labourers for a penny a day, he sent them into his
vineyard. And he went out about the third hour, and saw
others standing idle in the market-place, and said unto them;
Go ye also into the vineyard, and whatsoever is right I will
give you. And they went their way. Again he went out
about the sixth and ninth hour, and did likewise. And about
the eleventh hour he went out, and found others standing
idle, and saith unto them, Why stand ye here all the day
idle? They say unto him, Because no man hath hired us.
He saith unto them, Go ye also into the vineyard; and
whatsoever is right, that shall ye receive. So when even
was come, the lord of the vineyard saith unto his steward,
Call the labourers, and give them their hire, beginning from
the last unto the first. And when they came that were hired
about the eleventh hour, they received every man a penny.
But when the first came, they supposed that they should

have received more; and they likewise received every man a penny. And when they had received it, they murmured against the goodman of the house, saying, These last have wrought but one hour, and thou hast made them equal unto us, which have borne the burden and heat of the day. But he answered one of them, and said, Friend, I do thee no wrong: didst not thou agree with me for a penny? Take that thine is, and go thy way: I will give unto this last, even as unto thee. Is it not lawful for me to do what I will with mine own? Is thine eye evil, because I am good? So the last shall be first, and the first last: for many be called, but few chosen.

The Sunday called Sexagesima, or the second Sunday before Lent.

The Collect.

O LORD God, who seest that we put not our trust in any thing that we do; Mercifully grant that by thy power we may be defended against all adversity; through Jesus Christ our Lord. *Amen.*

The Epistle. 2 Corinthians xi. 19.

YE suffer fools gladly, seeing ye yourselves are wise. For ye suffer, if a man bring you into bondage, if a man devour you, if a man take of you, if a man exalt himself, if a man smite you on the face. I speak as concerning reproach, as though we had been weak. Howbeit wheresoever any is bold, (I speak foolishly,) I am bold also. Are they Hebrews? so am I. Are they Israelites? so am I. Are they the seed of Abraham? so am I. Are they ministers of Christ? (I speak as a fool) I am more; in labours more abundant, in stripes above measure, in prisons more frequent, in deaths oft. Of the Jews five times received I forty stripes save one. Thrice was I beaten with rods, once was I stoned, thrice I suffered shipwreck, a night and a day I have been in the deep; in journeyings often, in perils of waters, in perils of robbers, in perils by mine own countrymen, in perils by the heathen, in perils in the city, in perils in the wilderness, in perils in the sea, in perils among false brethren; in weariness and painfulness, in watchings often, in hunger and thirst, in fastings often, in cold and nakedness. Beside those things that are without, that which cometh upon me daily, the care of all the churches. Who is weak, and I am not weak? who is offended, and I burn not? If I must needs glory, I will glory of the things which concern mine infirmities. The God and Father of our Lord Jesus Christ, which is blessed for evermore, knoweth that I lie not.

The Gospel. St. Luke viii. 4.

WHEN much people were gathered together, and were come to him out of every city, he spake by a parable: A sower went out to sow his seed: and as he sowed, some fell by the way-side; and it was trodden down, and the fowls of the air devoured it. And some fell upon a rock; and as soon as it was sprung up, it withered away, because it lacked moisture. And some fell among thorns; and the thorns sprang up with it, and choked it. And other fell on good ground, and sprang up, and bare fruit an hundredfold. And when he had said these things, he cried, He that hath ears to hear, let him hear. And his disciples asked him, saying, What might this parable be? And he said, Unto you it is given to know the mysteries of the kingdom of God: but to others in parables; that seeing they might not see, and hearing they might not understand. Now the parable is this: The seed is the word of God. Those by the way-side are they that hear; then cometh the devil, and taketh away the word out of their hearts, lest they should believe and be saved. They on the rock are they, which, when they hear, receive the word with joy; and these have no root, which for a while believe, and in time of temptation fall away. And that which fell among thorns are they, which, when they have heard, go forth, and are choked with cares and riches and pleasures of this life, and bring no fruit to perfection. But that on the good ground are they, which in an honest and good heart, having heard the word, keep it, and bring forth fruit with patience.

The Sunday called Quinquagesima, or the Sunday next before Lent.

The Collect.

O LORD, who hast taught us that all our doings without charity are nothing worth; Send thy Holy Ghost, and pour into our hearts that most excellent gift of charity, the very bond of peace and of all virtues, without which whosoever liveth is counted dead before thee. Grant this for thine only Son Jesus Christ's sake. *Amen.*

The Epistle. 1 Corinthians xiii. 1.

THOUGH I speak with the tongues of men and of angels, and have not charity, I am become as sounding brass, or a tinkling cymbal. And though I have the gift of prophecy, and understand all mysteries, and all knowledge; and though I have all faith, so that I could remove mountains, and have not charity, I am nothing. And though I bestow all my goods to feed the poor, and though I give my body to be burned, and have not charity, it profiteth me nothing. Charity suffereth long, and is kind; charity envieth not; charity vaunteth not itself, is not puffed up, doth not behave itself unseemly, seeketh not her own, is not easily provoked, thinketh no evil; rejoiceth not in iniquity, but rejoiceth in the truth; beareth all things, believeth all things, hopeth all things, endureth all things. Charity never faileth: but whether there be prophecies, they shall fail; whether there be tongues, they shall cease; whether there be knowledge, it shall vanish away. For we know in part, and we prophesy in part. But when that which is perfect is come, then that which is in part shall be done away. When I was a child, I spake as a child, I understood as a child, I thought as a child: but when I became a man, I put away childish things. For now we see through a glass, darkly; but then face to face: now I know in part; but then shall I know even as also I am known. And now abideth faith, hope, charity, these three; but the greatest of these is charity.

The Gospel. St. Luke xviii. 31.

THEN Jesus took unto him the twelve, and said unto them, Behold, we go up to Jerusalem, and all things that are written by the prophets concerning the Son of man shall be accomplished. For he shall be delivered unto the Gentiles, and shall be mocked, and spitefully entreated, and spitted on: and they shall scourge him, and put him to death: and the third day he shall rise again. And they understood none of these things: and this saying was hid from them, neither knew they the things which were spoken. And it came to pass, that as he was come nigh unto Jericho, a certain blind man sat by the way-side begging: and hearing the multitude pass by, he asked what it meant. And they told him, that Jesus of Nazareth passeth by. And he cried, saying, Jesus, thou son of David, have mercy on me. And they which went before rebuked him, that he should hold his peace: but he cried so much the more, Thou son of David, have mercy on me. And Jesus stood, and commanded him to be brought unto him: and when he was come near, he asked him, saying, What wilt thou that I shall do unto

Ash Wednesday

thee? And he said, Lord, that I may receive my sight. And Jesus said unto him, Receive thy sight: thy faith hath saved thee. And immediately he received his sight, and followed him, glorifying God: and all the people, when they saw it, gave praise unto God.

LENTEN SEASON.

The first day of Lent, commonly called Ash Wednesday.

The Collect.

ALMIGHTY and everlasting God, who hatest nothing that thou hast made, and dost forgive the sins of all those who are penitent; Create and make in us new and contrite hearts, that we, worthily lamenting our sins and acknowledging our wretchedness, may obtain of thee, the God of all mercy, perfect remission and forgiveness; through Jesus Christ our Lord. *Amen.*

¶ *This Collect is to be said every day in Lent, after the Collect appointed for the day, until Palm Sunday.*

For the Epistle. Joel ii. 12.

TURN ye even to me, saith the LORD, with all your heart, and with fasting, and with weeping, and with mourning: and rend your heart, and not your garments, and turn unto the LORD your God: for he is gracious and merciful, slow to anger, and of great kindness, and repenteth him of the evil. Who knoweth if he will return and repent, and leave a blessing behind him; even a meat-offering and a drink-offering unto the LORD your God? Blow the trumpet in Zion, sanctify a fast, call a solemn assembly: gather the people, sanctify the congregation, assemble the elders, gather the children, and those that suck the breasts: let the bridegroom go forth of his chamber, and the bride out of her closet. Let the priests, the ministers of the LORD, weep between the porch and the altar, and let them say, Spare thy people, O LORD, and give not thine heritage to reproach, that the heathen should rule over them: wherefore should they say among the people, Where is their God?

The Gospel. St. Matthew vi. 16.

WHEN ye fast, be not, as the hypocrites, of a sad countenance: for they disfigure their faces, that they may appear unto men to fast. Verily I say unto you, They have their reward. But thou, when thou fastest, anoint thine head, and wash thy face; that thou appear not unto men to fast, but unto thy Father which is in secret: and thy Father, which seeth in secret, shall reward thee openly. Lay not up for yourselves treasures upon earth, where moth and rust doth corrupt, and where thieves break through and steal: but lay up for yourselves treasures in heaven, where neither moth nor rust doth corrupt, and where thieves do not break through nor steal: for where your treasure is, there will your heart be also.

¶ *The same Collect, Epistle, and Gospel shall serve for every day after, unto the next Sunday, except upon the Feast of St. Matthias.*

The First Sunday in Lent.

The Collect.

O LORD, who for our sake didst fast forty days and forty nights; Give us grace to use such abstinence, that, our flesh being subdued to the Spirit, we may ever obey thy godly motions in righteousness, and true holiness, to thy honour and glory, who livest and reignest with the Father and the Holy Ghost, one God, world without end. *Amen.*

The First Sunday in Lent

The Epistle. 2 Corinthians vi. 1.

WE then, as workers together with him, beseech you also that ye receive not the grace of God in vain; (for he saith, I have heard thee in a time accepted, and in the day of salvation have I succoured thee: behold, now is the accepted time; behold, now is the day of salvation;) giving no offence in any thing, that the ministry be not blamed: but in all things approving ourselves as the ministers of God, in much patience, in afflictions, in necessities, in distresses, in stripes, in imprisonments, in tumults, in labours, in watchings, in fastings; by pureness, by knowledge, by long-suffering, by kindness, by the Holy Ghost, by love unfeigned, by the word of truth, by the power of God, by the armour of righteousness on the right hand and on the left, by honour and dishonour, by evil report and good report: as deceivers, and yet true; as unknown, and yet well known; as dying, and, behold, we live; as chastened, and not killed; as sorrowful, yet alway rejoicing; as poor, yet making many rich; as having nothing, and yet possessing all things.

The Gospel. St. Matthew iv. 1.

THEN was Jesus led up of the spirit into the wilderness to be tempted of the devil. And when he had fasted forty days and forty nights, he was afterward an hungred. And when the tempter came to him, he said, If thou be the Son of God, command that these stones be made bread. But he answered and said, It is written, Man shall not live by bread alone, but by every word that proceedeth out of the mouth of God. Then the devil taketh him up into the holy city, and setteth him on a pinnacle of the temple, and saith unto him, If thou be the Son of God, cast thyself down: for it is written, He shall give his angels charge concerning thee: and in their hands they shall bear

The Second Sunday in Lent

thee up, lest at any time thou dash thy foot against a stone. Jesus said unto him, It is written again, Thou shalt not tempt the Lord thy God. Again, the devil taketh him up into an exceeding high mountain, and sheweth him all the kingdoms of the world, and the glory of them; and saith unto him, All these things will I give thee, if thou wilt fall down and worship me. Then saith Jesus unto him, Get thee hence, Satan: for it is written, Thou shalt worship the Lord thy God, and him only shalt thou serve. Then the devil leaveth him, and, behold, angels came and ministered unto him.

The Second Sunday in Lent.

The Collect.

ALMIGHTY God, who seest that we have no power of ourselves to help ourselves; Keep us both outwardly in our bodies, and inwardly in our souls; that we may be defended from all adversities which may happen to the body, and from all evil thoughts which may assault and hurt the soul; through Jesus Christ our Lord. *Amen.*

The Epistle. 1 Thessalonians iv. 1.

WE beseech you, brethren, and exhort you by the Lord Jesus, that as ye have received of us how ye ought to walk and to please God, so ye would abound more and more. For ye know what commandments we gave you by the Lord Jesus. For this is the will of God, even your sanctification, that ye should abstain from fornication: that every one of you should know how to possess his vessel in sanctification and honour; not in the lust of concupiscence, even as the Gentiles which know not God: that no man go beyond and defraud his brother in any matter: because that the Lord is the avenger of all such, as we also have forewarned you and testified. For God hath not called us unto uncleanness, but unto holiness. He therefore that despiseth, despiseth not man, but God, who hath also given unto us his holy Spirit.

The Gospel. St. Matthew xv. 21.

JESUS went thence, and departed into the coasts of Tyre and Sidon. And, behold, a woman of Canaan came out of the same coasts, and cried unto him, saying, Have mercy on me, O Lord, thou son of David; my daughter is grievously vexed with a devil. But he answered her not a word. And his disciples came and besought him, saying, Send her away; for she crieth after us. But he answered and said, I am not sent but unto the lost sheep of the house of Israel. Then came she and worshipped him, saying, Lord, help me. But he answered and said, It is not meet to take the children's bread, and to cast it to dogs. And she said, Truth, Lord: yet the dogs eat of the crumbs which fall from their masters' table. Then Jesus answered and said unto her, O woman, great is thy faith: be it unto thee even as thou wilt. And her daughter was made whole from that very hour.

The Third Sunday in Lent.

The Collect.

WE beseech thee, Almighty God, look upon the hearty desires of thy humble servants, and stretch forth the right hand of thy Majesty, to be our defence against all our enemies; through Jesus Christ our Lord. *Amen.*

The Epistle. Ephesians v. 1.

BE ye therefore followers of God, as dear children; and walk in love, as Christ also hath loved us, and hath given himself for us an offering and a sacrifice to God for a sweet-smelling savour. But fornication, and all uncleanness, or covetousness, let it not be once named among you, as becometh saints; neither filthiness, nor foolish talking, nor jesting, which are not convenient: but rather giving of thanks. For this ye know, that no whoremonger, nor unclean person, nor covetous man, who is an idolater, hath any inheritance in the kingdom of Christ and of God. Let no man deceive you with vain words: for because of these things cometh the wrath of God upon the children of disobedience. Be not ye therefore partakers with them. For ye were sometimes darkness, but now are ye light in the Lord: walk as children of light: (for the fruit of the Spirit is in all goodness and righteousness and truth;) proving what is acceptable unto the Lord. And have no fellowship with the unfruitful works of darkness, but rather reprove them. For it is a shame even to speak of those things which are done of them in secret. But all things that are reproved are made manifest by the light: for whatsoever doth make manifest is light. Wherefore he saith, Awake thou that sleepest, and arise from the dead, and Christ shall give thee light.

The Gospel. St. Luke xi. 14.

JESUS was casting out a devil, and it was dumb. And it came to pass, when the devil was gone out, the dumb spake; and the people wondered. But some of them said, He casteth out devils through Beelzebub the chief of the devils. And others, tempting him, sought of him a sign from heaven. But he, knowing their thoughts, said unto them, Every kingdom divided against itself is brought to desolation; and a house divided against a house falleth. If Satan also be divided against himself, how shall his kingdom stand? because ye say that I cast out devils through Beelzebub. And if I by Beelzebub cast out devils, by whom do

The Fourth Sunday in Lent

your sons cast them out? therefore shall they be your judges. But if I with the finger of God cast out devils, no doubt the kingdom of God is come upon you. When a strong man armed keepeth his palace, his goods are in peace: but when a stronger than he shall come upon him, and overcome him, he taketh from him all his armour wherein he trusted, and divideth his spoils. He that is not with me is against me: and he that gathereth not with me scattereth. When the unclean spirit is gone out of a man, he walketh through dry places, seeking rest; and finding none, he saith, I will return unto my house whence I came out. And when he cometh, he findeth it swept and garnished. Then goeth he, and taketh to him seven other spirits more wicked than himself; and they enter in, and dwell there: and the last state of that man is worse than the first. And it came to pass, as he spake these things, a certain woman of the company lifted up her voice, and said unto him, Blessed is the womb that bare thee, and the paps which thou hast sucked. But he said, Yea rather, blessed are they that hear the word of God, and keep it.

The Fourth Sunday in Lent.

The Collect.

GRANT, we beseech thee, Almighty God, that we, who for our evil deeds do worthily deserve to be punished, by the comfort of thy grace may mercifully be relieved; through our Lord and Saviour Jesus Christ. *Amen.*

The Epistle. Galatians iv. 21.

TELL me, ye that desire to be under the law, do ye not hear the law? For it is written, that Abraham had two sons, the one by a bondmaid, the other by a freewoman. But he who was of the bondwoman was born after the

The Fourth Sunday in Lent

flesh; but he of the freewoman was by promise. Which things are an allegory: for these are the two covenants; the one from the mount Sinai, which gendereth to bondage, which is Agar. For this Agar is mount Sinai in Arabia, and answereth to Jerusalem which now is, and is in bondage with her children. But Jerusalem which is above is free, which is the mother of us all. For it is written, Rejoice, thou barren that bearest not: break forth and cry, thou that travailest not: for the desolate hath many more children than she which hath an husband. Now we, brethren, as Isaac was, are the children of promise. But as then he that was born after the flesh persecuted him that was born after the Spirit, even so it is now. Nevertheless what saith the scripture? Cast out the bondwoman and her son: for the son of the bondwoman shall not be heir with the son of the freewoman. So then, brethren, we are not children of the bondwoman, but of the free.

The Gospel. St. John vi. 1.

JESUS went over the sea of Galilee, which is the sea of Tiberias. And a great multitude followed him, because they saw his miracles which he did on them that were diseased. And Jesus went up into a mountain, and there he sat with his disciples. And the passover, a feast of the Jews, was nigh. When Jesus then lifted up his eyes, and saw a great company come unto him, he saith unto Philip, Whence shall we buy bread, that these may eat? And this he said to prove him: for he himself knew what he would do. Philip answered him, Two hundred pennyworth of bread is not sufficient for them, that every one of them may take a little. One of his disciples, Andrew, Simon Peter's brother, saith unto him, There is a lad here, which hath five barley loaves, and two small fishes: but what are they among so many? And Jesus said, Make the men sit down. Now there was much grass in the place. So the men sat down, in number about five thousand. And Jesus took the loaves; and when he had given thanks, he distributed to the disciples, and the disciples to them that were set down; and likewise of the fishes as much as they would. When they were filled, he said unto his disciples, Gather up the fragments that remain, that nothing be lost. Therefore they gathered them together, and filled twelve baskets with the fragments of the five barley loaves, which remained over and above unto them that had eaten. Then those men, when they had seen the miracle that Jesus did, said, This is of a truth that prophet that should come into the world.

PASSIONTIDE.

The Fifth Sunday in Lent, commonly called Passion Sunday.

The Collect.

WE beseech thee, Almighty God, mercifully to look upon thy people; that by thy great goodness they may be governed and preserved evermore, both in body and soul; through Jesus Christ our Lord. *Amen.*

The Epistle. Hebrews ix. 11.

CHRIST being come an high priest of good things to come, by a greater and more perfect tabernacle, not made with hands, that is to say, not of this building; neither by the blood of goats and calves, but by his own blood he entered in once into the holy place, having obtained eternal redemption for us. For if the blood of bulls and of goats, and the ashes of an heifer sprinkling the unclean, sanctifieth to the purifying of the flesh: how much more shall the blood of Christ, who through the eternal Spirit offered

Passion Sunday

himself without spot to God, purge your conscience from dead works to serve the living God? And for this cause he is the mediator of the new testament, that by means of death, for the redemption of the transgressions that were under the first testament, they which are called might receive the promise of eternal inheritance.

The Gospel. St. John viii. 46.

JESUS said, Which of you convinceth me of sin? And if I say the truth, why do ye not believe me? He that is of God heareth God's words: ye therefore hear them not, because ye are not of God. Then answered the Jews, and said unto him, Say we not well that thou art a Samaritan, and hast a devil? Jesus answered, I have not a devil; but I honour my Father, and ye do dishonour me. And I seek not mine own glory: there is one that seeketh and judgeth. Verily, verily, I say unto you, If a man keep my saying, he shall never see death. Then said the Jews unto him, Now we know that thou hast a devil. Abraham is dead, and the prophets; and thou sayest, If a man keep my saying, he shall never taste of death. Art thou greater than our father Abraham, which is dead? and the prophets are dead: whom makest thou thyself? Jesus answered, If I honour myself, my honour is nothing: it is my Father that honoureth me; of whom ye say, that he is your God: yet ye have not known him; but I know him: and if I should say, I know him not, I shall be a liar like unto you; but I know him, and keep his saying. Your father Abraham rejoiced to see my day: and he saw it, and was glad. Then said the Jews unto him, Thou art not yet fifty years old, and hast thou seen Abraham? Jesus said unto them, Verily, verily, I say unto you, Before Abraham was, I am. Then took they up stones to cast at him: but Jesus hid himself, and went out of the temple.

Palm Sunday

The Sunday next before Easter, commonly called Palm Sunday.

The Collect.

ALMIGHTY and everlasting God, who, of thy tender love towards mankind, hast sent thy Son, our Saviour Jesus Christ, to take upon him our flesh, and to suffer death upon the cross, that all mankind should follow the example of his great humility; Mercifully grant, that we may both follow the example of his patience, and also be made partakers of his resurrection; through the same Jesus Christ our Lord. *Amen.*

¶ *This Collect is to be said every day, after the Collect appointed for the day, until Good Friday.*

The Epistle. Philippians ii. 5.

LET this mind be in you, which was also in Christ Jesus: who, being in the form of God, thought it not robbery to be equal with God: but made himself of no reputation, and took upon him the form of a servant, and was made in the likeness of men: and being found in fashion as a man, he humbled himself, and became obedient unto death, even the death of the cross. Wherefore God also hath highly exalted him, and given him a name which is above every name: that at the name of Jesus every knee should bow, of things in heaven, and things in earth, and things under the earth; and that every tongue should confess that Jesus Christ is Lord, to the glory of God the Father.

The Gospel. St. Matthew xxvii. 1.

WHEN the morning was come, all the chief priests and elders of the people took counsel against Jesus to put him to death: and when they had bound him, they led him away, and delivered him to Pontius Pilate the gov-

Palm Sunday

ernor. Then Judas, which had betrayed him, when he saw that he was condemned, repented himself, and brought again the thirty pieces of silver to the chief priests and elders, saying, I have sinned in that I have betrayed the innocent blood. And they said, What is that to us? see thou to that. And he cast down the pieces of silver in the temple, and departed, and went and hanged himself. And the chief priests took the silver pieces, and said, It is not lawful for to put them into the treasury, because it is the price of blood. And they took counsel, and bought with them the potter's field, to bury strangers in. Wherefore that field was called, The field of blood, unto this day. Then was fulfilled that which was spoken by Jeremy the prophet, saying, And they took the thirty pieces of silver, the price of him that was valued, whom they of the children of Israel did value; and gave them for the potter's field, as the Lord appointed me. And Jesus stood before the governor: and the governor asked him, saying, Art thou the King of the Jews? And Jesus said unto him, Thou sayest. And when he was accused of the chief priests and elders, he answered nothing. Then said Pilate unto him, Hearest thou not how many things they witness against thee? And he answered him to never a word; insomuch that the governor marvelled greatly. Now at that feast the governor was wont to release unto the people a prisoner, whom they would. And they had then a notable prisoner, called Barabbas. Therefore when they were gathered together, Pilate said unto them, Whom will ye that I release unto you? Barabbas, or Jesus which is called Christ? For he knew that for envy they had delivered him. When he was set down on the judgment-seat, his wife sent unto him, saying, Have thou nothing to do with that just man: for I have suffered many things this day in a dream because of him. But the chief priests and elders persuaded the multitude that they should ask Barabbas, and destroy Jesus. The governor answered and said unto them, Whether of the twain will ye that I release unto you? They said, Barabbas. Pilate saith unto them, What shall I do then with Jesus which is called Christ? They all say unto him, Let him be crucified. And the governor said, Why, what evil hath he done? But they cried out the more, saying, Let him be crucified. When Pilate saw that he could prevail nothing, but that rather a tumult was made, he took water, and washed his hands before the multitude, saying, I am innocent of the blood of this just person: see ye to it. Then answered all the people, and said, His blood be on us, and on our children. Then released he Barabbas unto them: and when he had scourged Jesus, he delivered him to be crucified. Then the soldiers of the governor took Jesus into the common hall, and gathered unto him the whole band of soldiers. And they stripped him, and put on him a scarlet robe. And when they had platted a crown of thorns, they put it upon his head, and a reed in his right hand: and they bowed the knee before him, and mocked him, saying, Hail, King of the Jews! And they spit upon him, and took the reed, and smote him on the head. And after that they had mocked him, they took the robe off from him, and put his own raiment on him, and led him away to crucify him. And as they came out, they found a man of Cyrene, Simon by name: him they compelled to bear his cross. And when they were come unto a place called Golgotha, that is to say, a place of a skull, they gave him vinegar to drink mingled with gall: and when he had tasted thereof, he would not drink. And they crucified him, and parted his garments, casting lots: that it might be fulfilled which was spoken by the prophet, They parted my garments among them, and upon my vesture did they cast lots. And sitting down they watched him there; and set

Palm Sunday

up over his head his accusation written, THIS IS JESUS THE KING OF THE JEWS. Then were there two thieves crucified with him, one on the right hand, and another on the left. And they that passed by reviled him, wagging their heads, and saying, Thou that destroyest the temple, and buildest it in three days, save thyself. If thou be the Son of God, come down from the cross. Likewise also the chief priests mocking him, with the scribes and elders, said, He saved others; himself he cannot save. If he be the King of Israel, let him now come down from the cross, and we will believe him. He trusted in God; let him deliver him now, if he will have him: for he said, I am the Son of God. The thieves also, which were crucified with him, cast the same in his teeth. Now from the sixth hour there was darkness over all the land unto the ninth hour. And about the ninth hour Jesus cried with a loud voice, saying, *Eli, Eli, lama sabachthani?* that is to say, My God, my God, why hast thou forsaken me? Some of them that stood there, when they heard that, said, This man calleth for Elias. And straightway one of them ran, and took a spunge, and filled it with vinegar, and put it on a reed, and gave him to drink. The rest said, Let be, let us see whether Elias will come to save him. Jesus, when he had cried again with a loud voice, yielded up the ghost. And, behold, the veil of the temple was rent in twain from the top to the bottom; and the earth did quake, and the rocks rent; and the graves were opened; and many bodies of the saints which slept arose, and came out of the graves after his resurrection, and went into the holy city, and appeared unto many. Now when the centurion, and they that were with him, watching Jesus, saw the earthquake, and those things that were done, they feared greatly, saying, Truly this was the Son of God.

Monday before Easter

Monday before Easter.

The Collect.

ALMIGHTY God, whose most dear Son went not up to joy but first he suffered pain, and entered not into glory before he was crucified; Mercifully grant that we, walking in the way of the cross, may find it none other than the way of life and peace; through the same thy Son Jesus Christ our Lord. *Amen.*

For the Epistle. Isaiah lxiii. 1.

WHO is this that cometh from Edom, with dyed garments from Bozrah? this that is glorious in his apparel, travelling in the greatness of his strength? I that speak in righteousness, mighty to save. Wherefore art thou red in thine apparel, and thy garments like him that treadeth in the winefat? I have trodden the winepress alone; and of the people there was none with me: for I will tread them in mine anger, and trample them in my fury; and their blood shall be sprinkled upon my garments, and I will stain all my raiment. For the day of vengeance is in mine heart, and the year of my redeemed is come. And I looked, and there was none to help; and I wondered that there was none to uphold: therefore mine own arm brought salvation unto me; and my fury, it upheld me. And I will tread down the people in mine anger, and make them drunk in my fury, and I will bring down their strength to the earth. I will mention the lovingkindnesses of the LORD, and the praises of the LORD, according to all that the LORD hath bestowed on us, and the great goodness toward the house of Israel, which he hath bestowed on them according to his mercies, and according to the multitude of his lovingkindnesses. For he said, Surely they are my people, children that will not lie: so he was their Saviour. In all their

Monday before Easter

affliction he was afflicted, and the angel of his presence saved them: in his love and in his pity he redeemed them; and he bare them, and carried them all the days of old. But they rebelled, and vexed his holy Spirit; therefore he was turned to be their enemy, and he fought against them. Then he remembered the days of old, Moses, and his people, saying, Where is he that brought them up out of the sea with the shepherd of his flock? where is he that put his holy Spirit within him? that led them by the right hand of Moses with his glorious arm, dividing the water before them, to make himself an everlasting name? that led them through the deep, as an horse in the wilderness, that they should not stumble? As a beast goeth down into the valley, the Spirit of the LORD caused him to rest: so didst thou lead thy people, to make thyself a glorious name. Look down from heaven, and behold from the habitation of thy holiness and of thy glory: where is thy zeal and thy strength, the sounding of thy bowels and of thy mercies toward me? are they restrained? Doubtless thou art our father, though Abraham be ignorant of us, and Israel acknowledge us not: thou, O LORD, art our father, our redeemer; thy name is from everlasting. O LORD, why hast thou made us to err from thy ways, and hardened our heart from thy fear? Return for thy servants' sake, the tribes of thine inheritance. The people of thy holiness have possessed it but a little while: our adversaries have trodden down thy sanctuary. We are thine: thou never barest rule over them; they were not called by thy name.

The Gospel. St. Mark xiv. 1.

AFTER two days was the feast of the passover, and of unleavened bread: and the chief priests and the scribes sought how they might take him by craft, and put him to death. But they said, Not on the feast day, lest there be an uproar of the people. And being in Bethany in the house of Simon the leper, as he sat at meat, there came a woman having an alabaster box of ointment of spikenard very precious; and she brake the box, and poured it on his head. And there were some that had indignation within themselves, and said, Why was this waste of the ointment made? for it might have been sold for more than three hundred pence, and have been given to the poor. And they murmured against her. And Jesus said, Let her alone; why trouble ye her? she hath wrought a good work on me. For ye have the poor with you always, and whensoever ye will ye may do them good: but me ye have not always. She hath done what she could: she is come aforehand to anoint my body to the burying. Verily I say unto you, Wheresoever this gospel shall be preached throughout the whole world, this also that she hath done shall be spoken of for a memorial of her. And Judas Iscariot, one of the twelve, went unto the chief priests, to betray him unto them. And when they heard it, they were glad, and promised to give him money. And he sought how he might conveniently betray him. And the first day of unleavened bread, when they killed the passover, his disciples said unto him, Where wilt thou that we go and prepare that thou mayest eat the passover? And he sendeth forth two of his disciples, and saith unto them, Go ye into the city, and there shall meet you a man bearing a pitcher of water: follow him. And wheresoever he shall go in, say ye to the goodman of the house, The Master saith, Where is the guest-chamber, where I shall eat the passover with my disciples? And he will shew you a large upper room furnished and prepared: there make ready for us. And his disciples went forth, and came into the city, and found as he had said unto them: and they made ready the passover. And in the evening he cometh with the twelve. And as they sat and did eat, Jesus said, Verily I say unto you, One of you which eateth with me shall betray me. And they began to be sorrowful, and to say unto him one by one, Is it I? and another said, Is it I? And he answered and said unto them, It is one of the twelve, that dippeth with me in the dish. The Son of man indeed goeth, as it is written of him: but woe to that man by whom the Son cf man is betrayed! good were it for that man if he had never been born. And as they did eat, Jesus took bread, and blessed, and brake it, and gave to them, and said, Take, eat: this is my body. And he took the cup, and when he had given thanks, he gave it to them: and they all drank of it. And he said unto them, This is my blood of the new testament, which is shed for many. Verily I say unto you, I will drink no more of the fruit of the vine, until that day that I drink it new in the kingdom of God. And when they had sung an hymn, they went out into the mount of Olives. And Jesus saith unto them, All ye shall be offended because of me this night: for it is written, I will smite the shepherd, and the sheep shall be scattered. But after that I am risen, I will go before you into Galilee. But Peter said unto him, Although all shall be offended, yet will not I. And Jesus saith unto him, Verily I say unto thee, That this day, even in this night, before the cock crow twice, thou shalt deny me thrice. But he spake the more vehemently, If I should die with thee, I will not deny thee in any wise. Likewise also said they all. And they came to a place which was named Gethsemane: and he saith to his disciples, Sit ye here, while I shall pray. And he taketh with him Peter and James and John, and began to be sore amazed, and to be very heavy; and saith unto them, My soul is exceeding sorrowful unto death: tarry ye here, and watch. And he went forward a little, and fell on the ground, and prayed that, if it were possible, the hour might pass from him. And he said, Abba, Father, all things are possible unto thee; take away this cup from me: nevertheless not what I will, but what thou wilt. And he cometh, and findeth them sleeping, and saith unto Peter, Simon, sleepest thou? couldest not thou watch one hour? Watch ye and pray, lest ye enter into temptation. The spirit truly is ready, but the flesh is weak. And again he went away, and prayed, and spake the same words. And when he returned, he found them asleep again, (for their eyes were heavy,) neither wist they what to answer him. And he cometh the third time, and saith unto them, Sleep on now, and take your rest: it is enough, the hour is come; behold, the Son of man is betrayed into the hands of sinners. Rise up, let us go; lo, he that betrayeth me is at hand. And immediately, while he yet spake, cometh Judas, one of the twelve, and with him a great multitude with swords and staves, from the chief priests and the scribes and the elders. And he that betrayed him had given them a token, saying, Whomsoever I shall kiss, that same is he; take him, and lead him away safely. And as soon as he was come, he goeth straightway to him, and saith, Master, master; and kissed him. And they laid their hands on him, and took him. And one of them that stood by drew a sword, and smote a servant of the high priest, and cut off his ear. And Jesus answered and said unto them, Are ye come out, as against a thief, with swords and with staves, to take me? I was daily with you in the temple teaching, and ye took me not: but the scriptures must be fulfilled. And they all forsook him, and fled. And there followed him a certain young man, having a linen cloth cast about his naked body; and the young men laid hold on him: and he left the linen cloth, and fled from them naked. And they led Jesus away to the high priest: and with him were assembled all the chief priests and the elders and the scribes. And Peter followed him afar off, even into the palace of the high priest: and he sat with the servants, and warmed himself at the fire.

Monday before Easter

And the chief priests and all the council sought for witness against Jesus to put him to death; and found none. For many bare false witness against him, but their witness agreed not together. And there arose certain, and bare false witness against him, saying, We heard him say, I will destroy this temple that is made with hands, and within three days I will build another made without hands. But neither so did their witness agree together. And the high priest stood up in the midst, and asked Jesus, saying, Answerest thou nothing? what is it which these witness against thee? But he held his peace, and answered nothing. Again the high priest asked him, and said unto him, Art thou the Christ, the Son of the Blessed? And Jesus said, I am: and ye shall see the Son of man sitting on the right hand of power, and coming in the clouds of heaven. Then the high priest rent his clothes, and saith, What need we any further witnesses? ye have heard the blasphemy: what think ye? And they all condemned him to be guilty of death. And some began to spit on him, and to cover his face, and to buffet him, and to say unto him, Prophesy: and the servants did strike him with the palms of their hands. And as Peter was beneath in the palace, there cometh one of the maids of the high priest: and when she saw Peter warming himself, she looked upon him, and said, And thou also wast with Jesus of Nazareth. But he denied, saying, I know not, neither understand I what thou sayest. And he went out into the porch; and the cock crew. And a maid saw him again, and began to say to them that stood by, This is one of them. And he denied it again. And a little after, they that stood by said again to Peter, Surely thou art one of them: for thou art a Galilæan, and thy speech agreeth thereto. But he began to curse and to swear, saying, I know not this man of whom ye speak. And the second time the cock crew. And Peter called to mind the word that Jesus said unto him, Be-

Tuesday before Easter

fore the cock crow twice, thou shalt deny me thrice. And when he thought thereon, he wept.

Tuesday before Easter.

The Collect.

O LORD God, whose blessed Son, our Saviour, gave his back to the smiters and hid not his face from shame; Grant us grace to take joyfully the sufferings of the present time, in full assurance of the glory that shall be revealed; through the same thy Son Jesus Christ our Lord. *Amen.*

For the Epistle. Isaiah l. 5.

THE Lord GOD hath opened mine ear, and I was not rebellious, neither turned away back. I gave my back to the smiters, and my cheeks to them that plucked off the hair: I hid not my face from shame and spitting. For the Lord GOD will help me; therefore shall I not be confounded: therefore have I set my face like a flint, and I know that I shall not be ashamed. He is near that justifieth me; who will contend with me? let us stand together: who is mine adversary? let him come near to me. Behold, the Lord GOD will help me; who is he that shall condemn me? lo, they all shall wax old as a garment; the moth shall eat them up. Who is among you that feareth the LORD, that obeyeth the voice of his servant, that walketh in darkness, and hath no light? let him trust in the name of the LORD, and stay upon his God. Behold, all ye that kindle a fire, that compass yourselves about with sparks: walk in the light of your fire, and in the sparks that ye have kindled. This shall ye have of mine hand; ye shall lie down in sorrow.

Tuesday before Easter

The Gospel. St. Mark xv. 1.

AND straightway in the morning the chief priests held a consultation with the elders and scribes and the whole council, and bound Jesus, and carried him away, and delivered him to Pilate. And Pilate asked him, Art thou the King of the Jews? And he answering said unto him, Thou sayest it. And the chief priests accused him of many things: but he answered nothing. And Pilate asked him again, saying, Answerest thou nothing? behold how many things they witness against thee. But Jesus yet answered nothing; so that Pilate marvelled. Now at that feast he released unto them one prisoner, whomsoever they desired. And there was one named Barabbas, which lay bound with them that had made insurrection with him, who had committed murder in the insurrection. And the multitude crying aloud began to desire him to do as he had ever done unto them. But Pilate answered them, saying, Will ye that I release unto you the King of the Jews? For he knew that the chief priests had delivered him for envy. But the chief priests moved the people, that he should rather release Barabbas unto them. And Pilate answered and said again unto them, What will ye then that I shall do unto him whom ye call the King of the Jews? And they cried out again, Crucify him. Then Pilate said unto them, Why, what evil hath he done? And they cried out the more exceedingly, Crucify him. And so Pilate, willing to content the people, released Barabbas unto them, and delivered Jesus, when he had scourged him, to be crucified. And the soldiers led him away into the hall, called Prætorium; and they call together the whole band. And they clothed him with purple, and platted a crown of thorns, and put it about his head, and began to salute him, Hail, King of the Jews! And they smote him on the head with a reed, and did spit upon him, and bowing their knees worshipped him. And when they had mocked him, they took off the purple from him, and put his own clothes on him, and led him out to crucify him. And they compel one Simon a Cyrenian, who passed by, coming out of the country, the father of Alexander and Rufus, to bear his cross. And they bring him unto the place Golgotha, which is, being interpreted, The place of a skull. And they gave him to drink wine mingled with myrrh: but he received it not. And when they had crucified him, they parted his garments, casting lots upon them, what every man should take. And it was the third hour, and they crucified him. And the superscription of his accusation was written over, THE KING OF THE JEWS. And with him they crucify two thieves; the one on his right hand, and the other on his left. And the scripture was fulfilled, which saith, And he was numbered with the transgressors. And they that passed by railed on him, wagging their heads, and saying, Ah, thou that destroyest the temple, and buildest it in three days, save thyself, and come down from the cross. Likewise also the chief priests mocking said among themselves with the scribes, He saved others; himself he cannot save. Let Christ the King of Israel descend now from the cross, that we may see and believe. And they that were crucified with him reviled him. And when the sixth hour was come, there was darkness over the whole land until the ninth hour. And at the ninth hour Jesus cried with a loud voice, saying, *Eloi, Eloi, lama sabachthani?* which is, being interpreted, My God, my God, why hast thou forsaken me? And some of them that stood by, when they heard it, said, Behold, he calleth Elias. And one ran and filled a spunge full of vinegar, and put it on a reed, and gave him to drink, saying, Let alone; let us see whether Elias will come to take him down. And Jesus cried with a loud voice, and gave up the ghost. And the veil of the temple was rent in twain from the top to the bottom. And when the centurion, which stood over against him, saw that he so cried out, and gave up the ghost, he said, Truly this man was the Son of God.

Wednesday before Easter.

The Collect.

ASSIST us mercifully with thy help, O Lord God of our salvation; that we may enter with joy upon the meditation of those mighty acts, whereby thou hast given unto us life and immortality; through Jesus Christ our Lord. *Amen.*

The Epistle. Hebrews ix. 16.

WHERE a testament is, there must also of necessity be the death of the testator. For a testament is of force after men are dead: otherwise it is of no strength at all while the testator liveth. Whereupon neither the first testament was dedicated without blood. For when Moses had spoken every precept to all the people according to the law, he took the blood of calves and of goats, with water, and scarlet wool, and hyssop, and sprinkled both the book and all the people, saying, This is the blood of the testament which God hath enjoined unto you. Moreover, he sprinkled with blood both the tabernacle, and all the vessels of the ministry. And almost all things are by the law purged with blood; and without shedding of blood is no remission. It was therefore necessary that the patterns of things in the heavens should be purified with these; but the heavenly things themselves with better sacrifices than these. For Christ is not entered into the holy places made with hands, which are the figures of the true; but into heaven itself, now to appear in the presence of God for us: nor yet that he should offer himself often, as the high priest entereth into the holy place every year with blood of others; for then must he often have suffered since the foundation of the world: but now once in the end of the world hath he appeared to put away sin by the sacrifice of himself. And as it is appointed unto men once to die, but after this the judgment: so Christ was once offered to bear the sins of many; and unto them that look for him shall he appear the second time without sin unto salvation.

The Gospel. St. Luke xxii. 1.

NOW the feast of unleavened bread drew nigh, which is called the Passover. And the chief priests and scribes sought how they might kill him; for they feared the people. Then entered Satan into Judas surnamed Iscariot, being of the number of the twelve. And he went his way, and communed with the chief priests and captains, how he might betray him unto them. And they were glad, and covenanted to give him money. And he promised, and sought opportunity to betray him unto them in the absence of the multitude. Then came the day of unleavened bread, when the passover must be killed. And he sent Peter and John, saying, Go and prepare us the passover, that we may eat. And they said unto him, Where wilt thou that we prepare? And he said unto them, Behold, when ye are entered into the city, there shall a man meet you, bearing a pitcher of water; follow him into the house where he entereth in. And ye shall say unto the goodman of the house, The Master saith unto thee, Where is the guest-chamber, where I shall eat the passover with my disciples? And he shall shew you a large upper room furnished: there make ready. And they went, and found as he had said unto them: and they made ready the passover. And when the hour was come, he sat down, and the twelve apostles with him. And

Wednesday before Easter

he said unto them, With desire I have desired to eat this passover with you before I suffer: for I say unto you, I will not any more eat thereof, until it be fulfilled in the kingdom of God. And he took the cup, and gave thanks, and said, Take this, and divide it among yourselves: for I say unto you, I will not drink of the fruit of the vine, until the kingdom of God shall come. And he took bread, and gave thanks, and brake it, and gave unto them, saying, This is my body which is given for you: this do in remembrance of me. Likewise also the cup after supper, saying, This cup is the new testament in my blood, which is shed for you. But, behold, the hand of him that betrayeth me is with me on the table. And truly the Son of man goeth, as it was determined: but woe unto that man by whom he is betrayed! And they began to enquire among themselves, which of them it was that should do this thing. And there was also a strife among them, which of them should be accounted the greatest. And he said unto them, The kings of the Gentiles exercise lordship over them; and they that exercise authority upon them are called benefactors. But ye shall not be so: but he that is greatest among you, let him be as the younger; and he that is chief, as he that doth serve. For whether is greater, he that sitteth at meat, or he that serveth? is not he that sitteth at meat? but I am among you as he that serveth. Ye are they which have continued with me in my temptations. And I appoint unto you a kingdom, as my Father hath appointed unto me; that ye may eat and drink at my table in my kingdom, and sit on thrones, judging the twelve tribes of Israel. And the Lord said, Simon, Simon, behold, Satan hath desired to have you, that he may sift you as wheat: but I have prayed for thee, that thy faith fail not; and when thou art converted, strengthen thy brethren. And he said unto him, Lord, I am ready to go with thee, both into prison, and to death. And he said, I tell thee, Peter, the cock shall not crow this day, before that thou shalt thrice deny that thou knowest me. And he said unto them, When I sent you without purse, and scrip, and shoes, lacked ye any thing? And they said, Nothing. Then said he unto them, But now, he that hath a purse, let him take it, and likewise his scrip: and he that hath no sword, let him sell his garment, and buy one. For I say unto you, that this that is written must yet be accomplished in me, And he was reckoned among the transgressors: for the things concerning me have an end. And they said, Lord, behold, here are two swords. And he said unto them, It is enough. And he came out, and went, as he was wont, to the mount of Olives; and his disciples also followed him. And when he was at the place, he said unto them, Pray that ye enter not into temptation. And he was withdrawn from them about a stone's cast, and kneeled down, and prayed, saying, Father, if thou be willing, remove this cup from me: nevertheless not my will, but thine, be done. And there appeared an angel unto him from heaven, strengthening him. And being in an agony he prayed more earnestly: and his sweat was as it were great drops of blood falling down to the ground. And when he rose up from prayer, and was come to his disciples, he found them sleeping for sorrow, and said unto them, Why sleep ye? rise and pray, lest ye enter into temptation. And while he yet spake, behold a multitude, and he that was called Judas, one of the twelve, went before them, and drew near unto Jesus to kiss him. But Jesus said unto him, Judas, betrayest thou the Son of man with a kiss? When they which were about him saw what would follow, they said unto him, Lord, shall we smite with the sword? And one of them smote the servant of the high priest, and cut off his right ear. And Jesus answered and said, Suffer ye thus far. And he touched his ear, and healed him. Then Jesus said unto the chief priests, and captains of the temple, and the elders, which were come to him, Be ye come out, as against a thief, with swords and staves? When I was daily with you in the temple, ye stretched forth no hands against me: but this is your hour, and the power of darkness. Then took they him, and led him, and brought him into the high priest's house. And Peter followed afar off. And when they had kindled a fire in the midst of the hall, and were set down together, Peter sat down among them. But a certain maid beheld him as he sat by the fire, and earnestly looked upon him, and said, This man was also with him. And he denied him, saying, Woman, I know him not. And after a little while another saw him, and said, Thou art also of them. And Peter said, Man, I am not. And about the space of one hour after another confidently affirmed, saying, Of a truth this fellow also was with him: for he is a Galilæan. And Peter said, Man, I know not what thou sayest. And immediately, while he yet spake, the cock crew. And the Lord turned, and looked upon Peter. And Peter remembered the word of the Lord, how he had said unto him, Before the cock crow, thou shalt deny me thrice. And Peter went out, and wept bitterly. And the men that held Jesus mocked him, and smote him. And when they had blindfolded him, they struck him on the face, and asked him, saying, Prophesy, who is it that smote thee? And many other things blasphemously spake they against him. And as soon as it was day, the elders of the people and the chief priests and the scribes came together, and led him into their council, saying, Art thou the Christ? tell us. And he said unto them, If I tell you, ye will not believe: and if I also ask you, ye will not answer me, nor let me go. Hereafter shall the Son of man sit on the right hand of the power of God. Then said they all, Art thou then the Son of God? And he said unto them, Ye say that I am. And they said, What need we any further witness? for we ourselves have heard of his own mouth.

Thursday before Easter, commonly called Maundy Thursday.

The Collect.

ALMIGHTY Father, whose dear Son, on the night before he suffered, did institute the Sacrament of his Body and Blood; Mercifully grant that we may thankfully receive the same in remembrance of him, who in these holy mysteries giveth us a pledge of life eternal; the same thy Son Jesus Christ our Lord, who now liveth and reigneth with thee and the Holy Spirit ever, one God, world without end. *Amen.*

The Epistle. 1 Corinthians xi. 23.

I HAVE received of the Lord that which also I delivered unto you, That the Lord Jesus the same night in which he was betrayed took bread: and when he had given thanks, he brake it, and said, Take, eat: this is my body, which is broken for you: this do in remembrance of me. After the same manner also he took the cup, when he had supped, saying, This cup is the new testament in my blood: this do ye, as oft as ye drink it, in remembrance of me. For as often as ye eat this bread, and drink this cup, ye do shew the Lord's death till he come.

The Gospel. St. Luke xxiii. 1.

THE whole multitude of them arose, and led him unto Pilate. And they began to accuse him, saying, We found this fellow perverting the nation, and forbidding to give tribute to Cæsar, saying that he himself is Christ a King. And Pilate asked him, saying, Art thou the King of the

Jews? And he answered him and said, Thou sayest it. Then said Pilate to the chief priests and to the people, I find no fault in this man. And they were the more fierce, saying, He stirreth up the people, teaching throughout all Jewry, beginning from Galilee to this place. When Pilate heard of Galilee, he asked whether the man were a Galilæan. And as soon as he knew that he belonged unto Herod's jurisdiction, he sent him to Herod, who himself also was at Jerusalem at that time. And when Herod saw Jesus, he was exceeding glad: for he was desirous to see him of a long season, because he had heard many things of him; and he hoped to have seen some miracle done by him. Then he questioned with him in many words; but he answered him nothing. And the chief priests and scribes stood and vehemently accused him. And Herod with his men of war set him at nought, and mocked him, and arrayed him in a gorgeous robe, and sent him again to Pilate. And the same day Pilate and Herod were made friends together: for before they were at enmity between themselves. And Pilate, when he had called together the chief priests and the rulers and the people, said unto them, Ye have brought this man unto me, as one that perverteth the people: and, behold, I, having examined him before you, have found no fault in this man touching those things whereof ye accuse him: no, nor yet Herod: for I sent you to him; and, lo, nothing worthy of death is done unto him. I will therefore chastise him, and release him. (For of necessity he must release one unto them at the feast.) And they cried out all at once, saying, Away with this man, and release unto us Barabbas: (who for a certain sedition made in the city, and for murder, was cast into prison.) Pilate therefore, willing to release Jesus, spake again to them. But they cried, saying, Crucify him, crucify him. And he said unto them the third time, Why, what evil hath he done? I have found no cause of death in

Maundy Thursday

him: I will therefore chastise him, and let him go. And they were instant with loud voices, requiring that he might be crucified. And the voices of them and of the chief priests prevailed. And Pilate gave sentence that it should be as they required. And he released unto them him that for sedition and murder was cast into prison, whom they had desired; but he delivered Jesus to their will. And as they led him away, they laid hold upon one Simon, a Cyrenian, coming out of the country, and on him they laid the cross, that he might bear it after Jesus. And there followed him a great company of people, and of women, which also bewailed and lamented him. But Jesus turning unto them said, Daughters of Jerusalem, weep not for me, but weep for yourselves, and for your children. For, behold, the days are coming, in the which they shall say, Blessed are the barren, and the wombs that never bare, and the paps which never gave suck. Then shall they begin to say to the mountains, Fall on us; and to the hills, Cover us. For if they do these things in a green tree, what shall be done in the dry? And there were also two other, malefactors, led with him to be put to death. And when they were come to the place which is called Calvary, there they crucified him, and the malefactors, one on the right hand, and the other on the left. Then said Jesus, Father, forgive them; for they know not what they do. And they parted his raiment, and cast lots. And the people stood beholding. And the rulers also with them derided him, saying, He saved others; let him save himself, if he be Christ, the chosen of God. And the soldiers also mocked him, coming to him, and offering him vinegar, and saying, If thou be the king of the Jews, save thyself. And a superscription also was written over him, in letters of Greek, and Latin, and Hebrew, THIS IS THE KING OF THE JEWS. And one of the malefactors which were hanged railed on him, saying, If thou be Christ, save thyself and us. But the other answering rebuked him, saying, Dost not thou fear God, seeing thou art in the same condemnation? And we indeed justly; for we receive the due reward of our deeds: but this man hath done nothing amiss. And he said unto Jesus, Lord, remember me when thou comest into thy kingdom. And Jesus said unto him, Verily I say unto thee, To-day shalt thou be with me in paradise. And it was about the sixth hour, and there was a darkness over all the earth until the ninth hour. And the sun was darkened, and the veil of the temple was rent in the midst. And when Jesus had cried with a loud voice, he said, Father, into thy hands I commend my spirit: and having said thus, he gave up the ghost. Now when the centurion saw what was done, he glorified God, saying, Certainly this was a righteous man. And all the people that came together to that sight, beholding the things which were done, smote their breasts, and returned. And all his acquaintance, and the women that followed him from Galilee, stood afar off, beholding these things.

¶ *Or else this that followeth.*

The Gospel. St. John xiii. 1.

NOW before the feast of the passover, when Jesus knew that his hour was come that he should depart out of this world unto the Father, having loved his own which were in the world, he loved them unto the end. And supper being ended, the devil having now put into the heart of Judas Iscariot, Simon's son, to betray him; Jesus knowing that the Father had given all things into his hands, and that he was come from God, and went to God; he riseth from supper, and laid aside his garments; and took a towel, and girded himself. After that he poureth water into a bason, and began to wash the disciples' feet, and to wipe them with the towel wherewith he was girded. Then cometh he

Good Friday

to Simon Peter: and Peter saith unto him, Lord, dost thou wash my feet? Jesus answered and said unto him, What I do thou knowest not now; but thou shalt know hereafter. Peter saith unto him, Thou shalt never wash my feet. Jesus answered him, If I wash thee not, thou hast no part with me. Simon Peter saith unto him, Lord, not my feet only, but also my hands and my head. Jesus saith to him, He that is washed needeth not save to wash his feet, but is clean every whit: and ye are clean, but not all. For he knew who should betray him; therefore said he, Ye are not all clean. So after he had washed their feet, and had taken his garments, and was set down again, he said unto them, Know ye what I have done to you? Ye call me Master and Lord: and ye say well; for so I am. If I then, your Lord and Master, have washed your feet; ye also ought to wash one another's feet. For I have given you an example, that ye should do as I have done to you.

Good Friday.

The Collects.

ALMIGHTY God, we beseech thee graciously to behold this thy family, for which our Lord Jesus Christ was contented to be betrayed, and given up into the hands of wicked men, and to suffer death upon the cross; who now liveth and reigneth with thee and the Holy Ghost ever, one God, world without end. *Amen.*

ALMIGHTY and everlasting God, by whose Spirit the whole body of the Church is governed and sanctified; Receive our supplications and prayers, which we offer before thee for all estates of men in thy holy Church, that every member of the same, in his vocation and ministry,

Good Friday

may truly and godly serve thee; through our Lord and Saviour Jesus Christ. *Amen.*

O MERCIFUL God, who hast made all men, and hatest nothing that thou hast made, nor desirest the death of a sinner, but rather that he should be converted and live; Have mercy upon all who know thee not as thou art revealed in the Gospel of thy Son. Take from them all ignorance, hardness of heart, and contempt of thy Word; and so fetch them home, blessed Lord, to thy fold, that they may be made one flock under one shepherd, Jesus Christ our Lord, who liveth and reigneth with thee and the Holy Spirit, one God, world without end. *Amen.*

The Epistle. Hebrews x. 1.

THE law having a shadow of good things to come, and not the very image of the things, can never with those sacrifices, which they offered year by year continually, make the comers thereunto perfect. For then would they not have ceased to be offered? because that the worshippers once purged should have had no more conscience of sins. But in those sacrifices there is a remembrance again made of sins every year. For it is not possible that the blood of bulls and of goats should take away sins. Wherefore when he cometh into the world, he saith, Sacrifice and offering thou wouldest not, but a body hast thou prepared me: in burnt-offerings and sacrifices for sin thou hast had no pleasure. Then said I, Lo, I come (in the volume of the book it is written of me,) to do thy will, O God. Above when he said, Sacrifice and offering and burnt-offerings and offering for sin thou wouldest not, neither hadst pleasure therein; which are offered by the law; then said he, Lo, I come to do thy will, O God: he taketh away the first, that he may establish the second. By the which will we are sanctified through the offering of the body of Jesus Christ once for all. And every priest standeth daily ministering and offering oftentimes the same sacrifices, which can never take away sins: but this man, after he had offered one sacrifice for sins for ever, sat down on the right hand of God; from henceforth expecting till his enemies be made his footstool. For by one offering he hath perfected for ever them that are sanctified. Whereof the Holy Ghost also is a witness to us: for after that he had said before, This is the covenant that I will make with them after those days, saith the Lord, I will put my laws into their hearts, and in their minds will I write them; then saith he, And their sins and iniquities will I remember no more. Now where remission of these is, there is no more offering for sin. Having therefore, brethren, boldness to enter into the holiest by the blood of Jesus, by a new and living way, which he hath consecrated for us, through the veil, that is to say, his flesh; and having an high priest over the house of God; let us draw near with a true heart in full assurance of faith, having our hearts sprinkled from an evil conscience, and our bodies washed with pure water. Let us hold fast the profession of our faith without wavering; (for he is faithful that promised;) and let us consider one another to provoke unto love and to good works: not forsaking the assembling of ourselves together, as the manner of some is; but exhorting one another: and so much the more, as ye see the day approaching.

The Gospel. St. John xix. 1.

PILATE therefore took Jesus, and scourged him. And the soldiers platted a crown of thorns, and put it on his head, and they put on him a purple robe, and said, Hail, King of the Jews! and they smote him with their hands. Pilate therefore went forth again, and saith unto them, Be-

Good Friday

hold, I bring him forth to you, that ye may know that I find no fault in him. Then came Jesus forth, wearing the crown of thorns, and the purple robe. And Pilate saith unto them, Behold the man! When the chief priests therefore and officers saw him, they cried out, saying, Crucify him, crucify him. Pilate saith unto them, Take ye him, and crucify him: for I find no fault in him. The Jews answered him, We have a law, and by our law he ought to die, because he made himself the Son of God. When Pilate therefore heard that saying, he was the more afraid; and went again into the judgment hall, and saith unto Jesus, Whence art thou? But Jesus gave him no answer. Then saith Pilate unto him, Speakest thou not unto me? knowest thou not that I have power to crucify thee, and have power to release thee? Jesus answered, Thou couldest have no power at all against me, except it were given thee from above: therefore he that delivered me unto thee hath the greater sin. And from thenceforth Pilate sought to release him: but the Jews cried out, saying, If thou let this man go, thou art not Cæsar's friend: whosoever maketh himself a king, speaketh against Cæsar. When Pilate therefore heard that saying, he brought Jesus forth, and sat down in the judgment-seat in a place that is called the Pavement, but in the Hebrew, Gabbatha. And it was the preparation of the passover, and about the sixth hour: and he saith unto the Jews, Behold your King! But they cried out, Away with him, away with him, crucify him. Pilate saith unto them, Shall I crucify your King? The chief priests answered, We have no king but Cæsar. Then delivered he him therefore unto them to be crucified. And they took Jesus, and led him away. And he bearing his cross went forth into a place called the place of a skull, which is called in the Hebrew Golgotha: where they crucified him, and two other with him, on either side one, and Jesus in the midst. And Pilate wrote a title, and put it on the cross.

Good Friday

And the writing was, JESUS OF NAZARETH THE KING OF THE JEWS. This title then read many of the Jews: for the place where Jesus was crucified was nigh to the city; and it was written in Hebrew, and Greek, and Latin. Then said the chief priests of the Jews to Pilate, Write not, The King of the Jews; but that he said, I am King of the Jews. Pilate answered, What I have written I have written. Then the soldiers, when they had crucified Jesus, took his garments, and made four parts, to every soldier a part; and also his coat: now the coat was without seam, woven from the top throughout. They said therefore among themselves, Let us not rend it, but cast lots for it, whose it shall be: that the scripture might be fulfilled, which saith, They parted my raiment among them, and for my vesture they did cast lots. These things therefore the soldiers did. Now there stood by the cross of Jesus his mother, and his mother's sister, Mary the wife of Cleophas, and Mary Magdalene. When Jesus therefore saw his mother, and the disciple standing by, whom he loved, he saith unto his mother, Woman, behold thy son! Then saith he to the disciple, Behold thy mother! And from that hour that disciple took her unto his own home. After this, Jesus knowing that all things were now accomplished, that the scripture might be fulfilled, saith, I thirst. Now there was set a vessel full of vinegar: and they filled a spunge with vinegar, and put it upon hyssop, and put it to his mouth. When Jesus therefore had received the vinegar, he said, It is finished: and he bowed his head, and gave up the ghost. The Jews therefore, because it was the preparation, that the bodies should not remain upon the cross on the sabbath day, (for that sabbath day was an high day,) besought Pilate that their legs might be broken, and that they might be taken away. Then came the soldiers, and brake the legs of the first, and of the other which was crucified with him.

Easter Even

But when they came to Jesus, and saw that he was dead already, they brake not his legs: but one of the soldiers with a spear pierced his side, and forthwith came there out blood and water. And he that saw it bare record, and his record is true: and he knoweth that he saith true, that ye might believe. For these things were done, that the scripture should be fulfilled, A bone of him shall not be broken. And again another scripture saith, They shall look on him whom they pierced.

Easter Even.

The Collect.

GRANT, O Lord, that as we are baptized into the death of thy blessed Son, our Saviour Jesus Christ, so by continual mortifying our corrupt affections we may be buried with him; and that through the grave, and gate of death, we may pass to our joyful resurrection; for his merits, who died, and was buried, and rose again for us, the same thy Son Jesus Christ our Lord. *Amen.*

The Epistle. 1 St. Peter iii. 17.

IT is better, if the will of God be so, that ye suffer for well doing, than for evil doing. For Christ also hath once suffered for sins, the just for the unjust, that he might bring us to God, being put to death in the flesh, but quickened by the Spirit: by which also he went and preached unto the spirits in prison; which sometime were disobedient, when once the long-suffering of God waited in the days of Noah, while the ark was a preparing, wherein few, that is, eight souls were saved by water. The like figure where-unto, even baptism, doth also now save us (not the putting away of the filth of the flesh, but the answer of a good conscience toward God,) by the resurrection of Jesus

Easter Day

Christ: who is gone into heaven, and is on the right hand of God; angels and authorities and powers being made subject unto him.

The Gospel. St. Matthew xxvii. 57.

WHEN the even was come, there came a rich man of Arimathæa, named Joseph, who also himself was Jesus' disciple: he went to Pilate, and begged the body of Jesus. Then Pilate commanded the body to be delivered. And when Joseph had taken the body, he wrapped it in a clean linen cloth, and laid it in his own new tomb, which he had hewn out in the rock: and he rolled a great stone to the door of the sepulchre, and departed. And there was Mary Magdalene, and the other Mary, sitting over against the sepulchre. Now the next day, that followed the day of the preparation, the chief priests and Pharisees came together unto Pilate, saying, Sir, we remember that that deceiver said, while he was yet alive, After three days I will rise again. Command therefore that the sepulchre be made sure until the third day, lest his disciples come by night, and steal him away, and say unto the people, He is risen from the dead: so the last error shall be worse than the first. Pilate said unto them, Ye have a watch: go your way, make it as sure as ye can. So they went, and made the sepulchre sure, sealing the stone, and setting a watch.

EASTERTIDE.

Easter Day.

¶ *At Morning Prayer, instead of the Venite, the following shall be said, and may be said throughout the Octave.*

CHRIST our Passover is sacrificed for us: * therefore let us keep the feast,

Not with old leaven, neither with the leaven of malice

Easter Day

and wickedness; * but with the unleavened bread of sincerity and truth. 1 *Cor.* v. 7.

CHRIST being raised from the dead dieth no more; * death hath no more dominion over him.

For in that he died, he died unto sin once: * but in that he liveth, he liveth unto God.

Likewise reckon ye also yourselves to be dead indeed unto sin, * but alive unto God through Jesus Christ our Lord. *Rom.* vi. 9.

CHRIST is risen from the dead, * and become the first-fruits of them that slept.

For since by man came death, * by man came also the resurrection of the dead.

For as in Adam all die, * even so in Christ shall all be made alive. 1 *Cor.* xv. 20.

Glory be to the Father, and to the Son, * and to the Holy Ghost;

As it was in the beginning, is now, and ever shall be, * world without end. Amen.

The Collect.

ALMIGHTY God, who through thine only-begotten Son Jesus Christ hast overcome death, and opened unto us the gate of everlasting life; We humbly beseech thee that, as by thy special grace preventing us thou dost put into our minds good desires, so by thy continual help we may bring the same to good effect; through the same Jesus Christ our Lord, who liveth and reigneth with thee and the Holy Ghost ever, one God, world without end. *Amen.*

¶ *This Collect is to be said daily throughout Easter Week.*

Easter Day

The Epistle. Colossians iii. 1.

IF ye then be risen with Christ, seek those things which are above, where Christ sitteth on the right hand of God. Set your affection on things above, not on things on the earth. For ye are dead, and your life is hid with Christ in God. When Christ, who is our life, shall appear, then shall ye also appear with him in glory.

The Gospel. St. John xx. 1.

THE first day of the week cometh Mary Magdalene early, when it was yet dark, unto the sepulchre, and seeth the stone taken away from the sepulchre. Then she runneth, and cometh to Simon Peter, and to the other disciple, whom Jesus loved, and saith unto them, They have taken away the Lord out of the sepulchre, and we know not where they have laid him. Peter therefore went forth, and that other disciple, and came to the sepulchre. So they ran both together: and the other disciple did outrun Peter, and came first to the sepulchre. And he stooping down, and looking in, saw the linen clothes lying; yet went he not in. Then cometh Simon Peter following him, and went into the sepulchre, and seeth the linen clothes lie, and the napkin, that was about his head, not lying with the linen clothes, but wrapped together in a place by itself. Then went in also that other disciple, which came first to the sepulchre, and he saw, and believed. For as yet they knew not the scripture, that he must rise again from the dead. Then the disciples went away again unto their own home.

¶ *If in any Church the Holy Communion be twice celebrated on Easter Day, the following Collect, Epistle, and Gospel may be used at the first Communion.*

164

Easter Day

The Collect.

O GOD, who for our redemption didst give thine only-begotten Son to the death of the Cross, and by his glorious resurrection hast delivered us from the power of our enemy; Grant us so to die daily from sin, that we may evermore live with him in the joy of his resurrection; through the same thy Son Christ our Lord. *Amen.*

The Epistle. 1 Corinthians v. 6.

KNOW ye not that a little leaven leaveneth the whole lump? Purge out therefore the old leaven, that ye may be a new lump, as ye are unleavened. For even Christ our passover is sacrificed for us: therefore let us keep the feast, not with old leaven, neither with the leaven of malice and wickedness; but with the unleavened bread of sincerity and truth.

The Gospel. St. Mark xvi. 1.

WHEN the sabbath was past, Mary Magdalene, and Mary the Mother of James, and Salome, had bought sweet spices, that they might come and anoint him. And very early in the morning the first day of the week, they came unto the sepulchre at the rising of the sun. And they said among themselves, Who shall roll us away the stone from the door of the sepulchre? And when they looked, they saw that the stone was rolled away: for it was very great. And entering into the sepulchre, they saw a young man sitting on the right side, clothed in a long white garment; and they were affrighted. And he saith unto them, Be not affrighted: Ye seek Jesus of Nazareth, which was crucified: he is risen; he is not here: behold the place where they laid him. But go your way, tell his disciples and Peter that he goeth before you into Galilee: there shall ye see him, as he said unto you. And they went out quickly, and fled from the sepulchre; for they trembled and were amazed: neither said they any thing to any man; for they were afraid.

Monday in Easter Week.

The Collect.

O GOD, whose blessed Son did manifest himself to his disciples in the breaking of bread; Open, we pray thee, the eyes of our faith, that we may behold thee in all thy works; through the same thy Son Jesus Christ our Lord. *Amen.*

For the Epistle. Acts x. 34.

PETER opened his mouth, and said, Of a truth I perceive that God is no respecter of persons: but in every nation he that feareth him, and worketh righteousness, is accepted with him. The word which God sent unto the children of Israel, preaching peace by Jesus Christ: (he is Lord of all:) that word, I say, ye know, which was published throughout all Judæa, and began from Galilee, after the baptism which John preached; how God anointed Jesus of Nazareth with the Holy Ghost and with power: who went about doing good, and healing all that were oppressed of the devil; for God was with him. And we are witnesses of all things which he did both in the land of the Jews, and in Jerusalem; whom they slew and hanged on a tree: him God raised up the third day, and shewed him openly; not to all the people, but unto witnesses chosen before of God, even to us, who did eat and drink with him after he rose from the dead. And he commanded us to preach unto the people, and to testify that it is he which was ordained of God to be the Judge of quick and dead. To him give all the prophets witness, that through his name whosoever believeth in him shall receive remission of sins.

Easter Monday

The Gospel. St. Luke xxiv. 13.

BEHOLD, two of his disciples went that same day to a village called Emmaus, which was from Jerusalem about threescore furlongs. And they talked together of all these things which had happened. And it came to pass, that, while they communed together and reasoned, Jesus himself drew near, and went with them. But their eyes were holden that they should not know him. And he said unto them, What manner of communications are these that ye have one to another, as ye walk, and are sad? And the one of them, whose name was Cleopas, answering said unto him, Art thou only a stranger in Jerusalem, and hast not known the things which are come to pass there in these days? And he said unto them, What things? And they said unto him, Concerning Jesus of Nazareth, which was a prophet mighty in deed and word before God and all the people: and how the chief priests and our rulers delivered him to be condemned to death, and have crucified him. But we trusted that it had been he which should have redeemed Israel: and beside all this, to-day is the third day since these things were done. Yea, and certain women also of our company made us astonished, which were early at the sepulchre; and when they found not his body, they came, saying, that they had also seen a vision of angels, which said that he was alive. And certain of them which were with us went to the sepulchre, and found it even so as the women had said: but him they saw not. Then he said unto them, O fools, and slow of heart to believe all that the prophets have spoken: ought not Christ to have suffered these things, and to enter into his glory? And beginning at Moses and all the prophets, he expounded unto them in all the scriptures the things concerning himself. And they drew nigh unto the village, whither they went: and he made as though he would have gone further. But they constrained him, saying, Abide with us: for it is toward evening, and the day is far spent. And he went in to tarry with them. And it came to pass, as he sat at meat with them, he took bread, and blessed it, and brake, and gave to them. And their eyes were opened, and they knew him; and he vanished out of their sight. And they said one to another, Did not our heart burn within us, while he talked with us by the way, and while he opened to us the scriptures? And they rose up the same hour, and returned to Jerusalem, and found the eleven gathered together, and them that were with them, saying, The Lord is risen indeed, and hath appeared to Simon. And they told what things were done in the way, and how he was known of them in breaking of bread.

Tuesday in Easter Week.

The Collect.

GRANT, we beseech thee, Almighty God, that we who celebrate with reverence the Paschal feast, may be found worthy to attain to everlasting joys; through Jesus Christ our Lord. *Amen.*

For the Epistle. Acts xiii. 26.

MEN and brethren, children of the stock of Abraham, and whosoever among you feareth God, to you is the word of this salvation sent. For they that dwell at Jerusalem, and their rulers, because they knew him not, nor yet the voices of the prophets which are read every sabbath day, they have fulfilled them in condemning him. And though they found no cause of death in him, yet desired they Pilate that he should be slain. And when they had fulfilled all that was written of him, they took him down from the tree, and laid him in a sepulchre. But God raised him from the dead: and he was seen many days of them which came up with him from Galilee to Jerusalem, who are his witnesses unto the people. And we declare unto you glad tidings, how that the promise which was made unto the fathers, God hath fulfilled the same unto us their children, in that he hath raised up Jesus again; as it is also written in the second psalm, Thou art my Son, this day have I begotten thee. And as concerning that he raised him up from the dead, now no more to return to corruption, he said on this wise, I will give you the sure mercies of David. Wherefore he saith also in another psalm, Thou shalt not suffer thine Holy One to see corruption. For David, after he had served his own generation by the will of God, fell on sleep, and was laid unto his fathers, and saw corruption: but he, whom God raised again, saw no corruption. Be it known unto you therefore, men and brethren, that through this man is preached unto you the forgiveness of sins: and by him all that believe are justified from all things, from which ye could not be justified by the law of Moses. Beware therefore, lest that come upon you, which is spoken of in the prophets; Behold, ye despisers, and wonder, and perish: for I work a work in your days, a work which ye shall in no wise believe, though a man declare it unto you.

The Gospel. St. Luke xxiv. 36.

JESUS himself stood in the midst of them, and saith unto them, Peace be unto you. But they were terrified and affrighted, and supposed that they had seen a spirit. And he said unto them, Why are ye troubled? and why do thoughts arise in your hearts? Behold my hands and my feet, that it is I myself: handle me, and see; for a spirit hath not flesh and bones, as ye see me have. And when he had thus spoken, he shewed them his hands and his feet. And while they yet believed not for joy, and wondered, he said unto them, Have ye here any meat? And they gave him a piece of a broiled fish, and of an honeycomb. And he took it, and did eat before them. And he said unto them, These are the words which I spake unto you, while I was yet with you, that all things must be fulfilled, which were written in the law of Moses, and in the prophets, and in the psalms, concerning me. Then opened he their understanding, that they might understand the scriptures, and said unto them, Thus it is written, and thus it behoved Christ to suffer, and to rise from the dead the third day: and that repentance and remission of sins should be preached in his name among all nations, beginning at Jerusalem. And ye are witnesses of these things.

The First Sunday after Easter.

The Collect.

ALMIGHTY Father, who hast given thine only Son to die for our sins, and to rise again for our justification; Grant us so to put away the leaven of malice and wickedness, that we may always serve thee in pureness of living and truth; through the merits of the same thy Son Jesus Christ our Lord. *Amen.*

The Epistle. 1 St. John v. 4.

WHATSOEVER is born of God overcometh the world: and this is the victory that overcometh the world, even our faith. Who is he that overcometh the world, but he that believeth that Jesus is the Son of God? This is he that came by water and blood, even Jesus Christ; not by water only, but by water and blood. And it is the Spirit that beareth witness, because the Spirit is truth. For there are three that bear witness, the Spirit, and the water, and the blood: and these three agree in one. If we receive the witness of men, the witness of God is greater: for this is the witness of God which he hath testified of his Son. He that believeth on the Son of God hath the witness in himself: he that believeth not God hath made him a liar; because he believeth not the record that God gave of his Son. And this is the record, that God hath given to us eternal life, and this life is in his Son. He that hath the Son hath life; and he that hath not the Son of God hath not life.

The Gospel. St. John xx. 19.

THE same day at evening, being the first day of the week, when the doors were shut where the disciples were assembled for fear of the Jews, came Jesus and stood in the midst, and saith unto them, Peace be unto you. And when he had so said, he shewed unto them his hands and his side. Then were the disciples glad when they saw the Lord. Then said Jesus to them again, Peace be unto you: as my Father hath sent me, even so send I you. And when he had said this, he breathed on them, and saith unto them, Receive ye the Holy Ghost: whosoever sins ye remit, they are remitted unto them; and whosoever sins ye retain, they are retained.

The Second Sunday after Easter.

The Collect.

ALMIGHTY God, who hast given thine only Son to be unto us both a sacrifice for sin, and also an ensample of godly life; Give us grace that we may always most thankfully receive that his inestimable benefit, and also daily endeavour ourselves to follow the blessed steps of his most holy life; through the same thy Son Jesus Christ our Lord. *Amen.*

The Epistle. 1 St. Peter ii. 19.

THIS is thankworthy, if a man for conscience toward God endure grief, suffering wrongfully. For what glory is it, if, when ye be buffeted for your faults, ye shall take it patiently? but if, when ye do well, and suffer for it, ye take it patiently, this is acceptable with God. For even hereunto were ye called: because Christ also suffered for us, leaving us an example, that ye should follow his steps: who did no sin, neither was guile found in his mouth: who, when he was reviled, reviled not again; when he suffered, he threatened not; but committed himself to him that judgeth righteously: who his own self bare our sins in his own body on the tree, that we, being dead to sins, should live unto righteousness: by whose stripes ye were healed. For ye were as sheep going astray; but are now returned unto the Shepherd and Bishop of your souls.

The Gospel. St. John x. 11.

JESUS said, I am the good shepherd: the good shepherd giveth his life for the sheep. But he that is an hireling, and not the shepherd, whose own the sheep are not, seeth the wolf coming, and leaveth the sheep, and fleeth: and the wolf catcheth them, and scattereth the sheep. The hireling fleeth, because he is an hireling, and careth not for the sheep. I am the good shepherd; and know my sheep, and am known of mine, even as the Father knoweth me, and I know the Father; and I lay down my life for the sheep. And other sheep I have, which are not of this fold: them also I must bring, and they shall hear my voice; and there shall be one flock, and one shepherd.

The Third Sunday after Easter

The Third Sunday after Easter.

The Collect.

ALMIGHTY God, who showest to them that are in error the light of thy truth, to the intent that they may return into the way of righteousness; Grant unto all those who are admitted into the fellowship of Christ's Religion, that they may avoid those things that are contrary to their profession, and follow all such things as are agreeable to the same; through our Lord Jesus Christ. *Amen.*

The Epistle. 1 St. Peter ii. 11.

DEARLY beloved, I beseech you as strangers and pilgrims, abstain from fleshly lusts, which war against the soul; having your conversation honest among the Gentiles: that, whereas they speak against you as evildoers, they may by your good works, which they shall behold, glorify God in the day of visitation. Submit yourselves to every ordinance of man for the Lord's sake: whether it be to the king, as supreme; or unto governors, as unto them that are sent by him for the punishment of evildoers, and for the praise of them that do well. For so is the will of God, that with well doing ye may put to silence the ignorance of foolish men: as free, and not using your liberty for a cloke of maliciousness, but as the servants of God. Honour all men. Love the brotherhood. Fear God. Honour the king.

The Gospel. St. John xvi. 16.

JESUS said to his disciples, A little while, and ye shall not see me: and again, a little while, and ye shall see me, because I go to the Father. Then said some of his disciples among themselves, What is this that he saith unto us, A little while, and ye shall not see me: and again, a little while, and ye shall see me: and, Because I go to the

Father? They said therefore, What is this that he saith, A little while? we cannot tell what he saith. Now Jesus knew that they were desirous to ask him, and said unto them, Do ye enquire among yourselves of that I said, A little while, and ye shall not see me: and again, a little while, and ye shall see me? Verily, verily, I say unto you, That ye shall weep and lament, but the world shall rejoice: and ye shall be sorrowful, but your sorrow shall be turned into joy. A woman when she is in travail hath sorrow, because her hour is come: but as soon as she is delivered of the child, she remembereth no more the anguish, for joy that a man is born into the world. And ye now therefore have sorrow: but I will see you again, and your heart shall rejoice, and your joy no man taketh from you.

The Fourth Sunday after Easter.

The Collect.

O ALMIGHTY God, who alone canst order the unruly wills and affections of sinful men; Grant unto thy people, that they may love the thing which thou commandest, and desire that which thou dost promise; that so, among the sundry and manifold changes of the world, our hearts may surely there be fixed, where true joys are to be found; through Jesus Christ our Lord. *Amen.*

The Epistle. St. James i. 17.

EVERY good gift and every perfect gift is from above, and cometh down from the Father of lights, with whom is no variableness, neither shadow of turning. Of his own will begat he us with the word of truth, that we should be a kind of firstfruits of his creatures. Wherefore, my beloved brethren, let every man be swift to hear, slow to speak, slow to wrath: for the wrath of man worketh not

Rogation Sunday

the righteousness of God. Wherefore lay apart all filthiness and superfluity of naughtiness, and receive with meekness the engrafted word, which is able to save your souls.

The Gospel. St. John xvi. 5.

JESUS said unto his disciples, Now I go my way to him that sent me; and none of you asketh me, Whither goest thou? But because I have said these things unto you, sorrow hath filled your heart. Nevertheless I tell you the truth; It is expedient for you that I go away: for if I go not away, the Comforter will not come unto you; but if I depart, I will send him unto you. And when he is come, he will reprove the world of sin, and of righteousness, and of judgment: of sin, because they believe not on me; of righteousness, because I go to my Father, and ye see me no more; of judgment, because the prince of this world is judged. I have yet many things to say unto you, but ye cannot bear them now. Howbeit when he, the Spirit of truth, is come, he will guide you into all truth: for he shall not speak of himself; but whatsoever he shall hear, that shall he speak: and he will shew you things to come. He shall glorify me: for he shall receive of mine, and shall shew it unto you. All things that the Father hath are mine: therefore said I, that he shall take of mine, and shall shew it unto you.

The Fifth Sunday after Easter, commonly called Rogation Sunday.

The Collect.

O LORD, from whom all good things do come; Grant to us thy humble servants, that by thy holy inspiration we may think those things that are good, and by thy merciful guiding may perform the same; through our Lord Jesus Christ. *Amen.*

The Epistle. St. James i. 22.

BE ye doers of the word, and not hearers only, deceiving your own selves. For if any be a hearer of the word, and not a doer, he is like unto a man beholding his natural face in a glass: for he beholdeth himself, and goeth his way, and straightway forgetteth what manner of man he was. But whoso looketh into the perfect law of liberty, and continueth therein, he being not a forgetful hearer, but a doer of the work, this man shall be blessed in his deed. If any man among you seem to be religious, and bridleth not his tongue, but deceiveth his own heart, this man's religion is vain. Pure religion and undefiled before God and the Father is this, To visit the fatherless and widows in their affliction, and to keep himself unspotted from the world.

The Gospel. St. John xvi. 23.

VERILY, verily, I say unto you, Whatsoever ye shall ask the Father in my name, he will give it you. Hitherto have ye asked nothing in my name: ask, and ye shall receive, that your joy may be full. These things have I spoken unto you in proverbs: but the time cometh, when I shall no more speak unto you in proverbs, but I shall shew you plainly of the Father. At that day ye shall ask in my name: and I say not unto you, that I will pray the Father for you: for the Father himself loveth you, because ye have loved me, and have believed that I came out from God. I came forth from the Father, and am come into the world: again, I leave the world, and go to the Father. His disciples said unto him, Lo, now speakest thou plainly, and speakest no proverb. Now are we sure that thou knowest

Ascension Day

all things, and needest not that any man should ask thee: by this we believe that thou camest forth from God. Jesus answered them, Do ye now believe? Behold, the hour cometh, yea, is now come, that ye shall be scattered, every man to his own, and shall leave me alone: and yet I am not alone, because the Father is with me. These things I have spoken unto you, that in me ye might have peace. In the world ye shall have tribulation: but be of good cheer; I have overcome the world.

ASCENSIONTIDE.

The Ascension Day.

The Collect.

GRANT, we beseech thee, Almighty God, that like as we do believe thy only-begotten Son our Lord Jesus Christ to have ascended into the heavens; so we may also in heart and mind thither ascend, and with him continually dwell, who liveth and reigneth with thee and the Holy Ghost, one God, world without end. *Amen.*

¶ *This Collect is to be said daily throughout the Octave.*

For the Epistle. Acts i. 1.

THE former treatise have I made, O Theophilus, of all that Jesus began both to do and teach, until the day in which he was taken up, after that he through the Holy Ghost had given commandments unto the apostles whom he had chosen: to whom also he shewed himself alive after his passion by many infallible proofs, being seen of them forty days, and speaking of the things pertaining to the kingdom of God: and, being assembled together with them, commanded them that they should not depart from Jerusalem, but wait for the promise of the Father, which, saith

Ascension Day

he, ye have heard of me. For John truly baptized with water; but ye shall be baptized with the Holy Ghost not many days hence. When they therefore were come together, they asked of him, saying, Lord, wilt thou at this time restore again the kingdom to Israel? And he said unto them, It is not for you to know the times or the seasons, which the Father hath put in his own power. But ye shall receive power, after that the Holy Ghost is come upon you: and ye shall be witnesses unto me both in Jerusalem, and in all Judæa, and in Samaria, and unto the uttermost part of the earth. And when he had spoken these things, while they beheld, he was taken up; and a cloud received him out of their sight. And while they looked stedfastly toward heaven as he went up, behold, two men stood by them in white apparel; which also said, Ye men of Galilee, why stand ye gazing up into heaven? this same Jesus, which is taken up from you into heaven, shall so come in like manner as ye have seen him go into heaven.

The Gospel. St. Luke xxiv. 49.

JESUS said, Behold, I send the promise of my Father upon you: but tarry ye in the city of Jerusalem, until ye be endued with power from on high. And he led them out as far as to Bethany, and he lifted up his hands, and blessed them. And it came to pass, while he blessed them, he was parted from them, and carried up into heaven. And they worshipped him, and returned to Jerusalem with great joy: and were continually in the temple, praising and blessing God.

¶ *The same Collect, Epistle, and Gospel shall serve for every day after, unto the next Sunday, except upon the Feast of St. Philip and St. James.*

Sunday after Ascension

The Sunday after Ascension Day.

The Collect.

O GOD, the King of glory, who hast exalted thine only Son Jesus Christ with great triumph unto thy kingdom in heaven; We beseech thee, leave us not comfortless; but send to us thine Holy Ghost to comfort us, and exalt us unto the same place whither our Saviour Christ is gone before, who liveth and reigneth with thee and the same Holy Ghost, one God, world without end. *Amen.*

The Epistle. 1 St. Peter iv. 7.

THE end of all things is at hand: be ye therefore sober, and watch unto prayer. And above all things have fervent charity among yourselves: for charity shall cover the multitude of sins. Use hospitality one to another without grudging. As every man hath received the gift, even so minister the same one to another, as good stewards of the manifold grace of God. If any man speak, let him speak as the oracles of God; if any man minister, let him do it as of the ability which God giveth: that God in all things may be glorified through Jesus Christ, to whom be praise and dominion for ever and ever. Amen.

The Gospel. St. John xv. 26, *and part of* Chap. xvi.

WHEN the Comforter is come, whom I will send unto you from the Father, even the Spirit of truth, which proceedeth from the Father, he shall testify of me: and ye also shall bear witness, because ye have been with me from the beginning. These things have I spoken unto you, that ye should not be offended. They shall put you out of the synagogues: yea, the time cometh, that whosoever killeth you will think that he doeth God service. And these things will they do unto you, because they have not known the Father, nor me. But these things have I told you, that when the time shall come, ye may remember that I told you of them.

WHITSUNTIDE.

Pentecost, commonly called Whitsunday.

The Collect.

O GOD, who as at this time didst teach the hearts of thy faithful people, by sending to them the light of thy Holy Spirit; Grant us by the same Spirit to have a right judgment in all things, and evermore to rejoice in his holy comfort; through the merits of Christ Jesus our Saviour, who liveth and reigneth with thee, in the unity of the same Spirit, one God, world without end. *Amen.*

¶ *This Collect is to be said daily throughout Whitsun Week.*

For the Epistle. Acts ii. 1.

WHEN the day of Pentecost was fully come, they were all with one accord in one place. And suddenly there came a sound from heaven as of a rushing mighty wind, and it filled all the house where they were sitting. And there appeared unto them cloven tongues like as of fire, and it sat upon each of them. And they were all filled with the Holy Ghost, and began to speak with other tongues, as the Spirit gave them utterance. And there were dwelling at Jerusalem Jews, devout men, out of every nation under heaven. Now when this was noised abroad, the multitude came together, and were confounded, because that every man heard them speak in his own language. And they were all amazed and marvelled, saying one to another, Behold, are not all these which speak Galilæans? And how hear we every man in our own tongue, wherein we were born? Parthians, and Medes, and Elamites, and the dwellers

Whitsunday

in Mesopotamia, and in Judæa, and Cappadocia, in Pontus, and Asia, Phrygia, and Pamphylia, in Egypt, and in the parts of Libya about Cyrene, and strangers of Rome, Jews and proselytes, Cretes and Arabians, we do hear them speak in our tongues the wonderful works of God.

The Gospel. St. John xiv. 15.

JESUS said unto his disciples, If ye love me, keep my commandments. And I will pray the Father, and he shall give you another Comforter, that he may abide with you for ever; even the Spirit of truth; whom the world cannot receive, because it seeth him not, neither knoweth him: but ye know him; for he dwelleth with you, and shall be in you. I will not leave you comfortless: I will come to you. Yet a little while, and the world seeth me no more; but ye see me: because I live, ye shall live also. At that day ye shall know that I am in my Father, and ye in me, and I in you. He that hath my commandments, and keepeth them, he it is that loveth me: and he that loveth me shall be loved of my Father, and I will love him, and will manifest myself to him. Judas saith unto him, not Iscariot, Lord, how is it that thou wilt manifest thyself unto us, and not unto the world? Jesus answered and said unto him, If a man love me, he will keep my words; and my Father will love him, and we will come unto him, and make our abode with him. He that loveth me not keepeth not my sayings: and the word which ye hear is not mine, but the Father's which sent me. These things have I spoken unto you, being yet present with you. But the Comforter, which is the Holy Ghost, whom the Father will send in my name, he shall teach you all things, and bring all things to your remembrance, whatsoever I have said unto you. Peace I leave with you, my peace I give unto you: not as the world giveth, give I unto you. Let not your heart be troubled,

Whitsunday

neither let it be afraid. Ye have heard how I said unto you, I go away, and come again unto you. If ye loved me, ye would rejoice, because I said, I go unto the Father: for my Father is greater than I. And now I have told you before it come to pass, that, when it is come to pass, ye might believe. Hereafter I will not talk much with you: for the prince of this world cometh, and hath nothing in me. But that the world may know that I love the Father; and as the Father gave me commandment, even so I do.

¶ *If in any Church the Holy Communion be twice celebrated on Whitsunday, the following Collect, Epistle, and Gospel may be used at the first Communion.*

The Collect.

ALMIGHTY and most merciful God, grant, we beseech thee, that by the indwelling of thy Holy Spirit, we may be enlightened and strengthened for thy service; through Jesus Christ our Lord, who liveth and reigneth with thee in the unity of the same Spirit ever, one God, world without end. *Amen.*

The Epistle. 1 Corinthians xii. 4.

NOW there are diversities of gifts, but the same Spirit. And there are differences of administrations, but the same Lord. And there are diversities of operations, but it is the same God which worketh all in all. But the manifestation of the Spirit is given to every man to profit withal. For to one is given by the Spirit the word of wisdom; to another the word of knowledge by the same Spirit; to another faith by the same Spirit; to another the gifts of healing by the same Spirit; to another the working of miracles; to another prophecy; to another discerning of spirits; to another divers kinds of tongues; to another the interpretation of tongues: but all these worketh that one and the selfsame Spirit, dividing to every man severally as

Monday in Whitsun Week

he will. For as the body is one, and hath many members, and all the members of that one body, being many, are one body: so also is Christ. For by one Spirit are we all baptized into one body, whether we be Jews or Gentiles, whether we be bond or free; and have been all made to drink into one Spirit. For the body is not one member, but many.

The Gospel. St. Luke xi. 9.

JESUS said to his disciples, Ask, and it shall be given you; seek, and ye shall find; knock, and it shall be opened unto you. For every one that asketh receiveth; and he that seeketh findeth; and to him that knocketh it shall be opened. If a son shall ask bread of any of you that is a father, will he give him a stone? or if he ask a fish, will he for a fish give him a serpent? or if he shall ask an egg, will he offer him a scorpion? If ye then, being evil, know how to give good gifts unto your children: how much more shall your heavenly Father give the Holy Spirit to them that ask him?

Monday in Whitsun Week.

The Collect.

SEND, we beseech thee, Almighty God, thy Holy Spirit into our hearts, that he may direct and rule us according to thy will, comfort us in all our afflictions, defend us from all error, and lead us into all truth; through Jesus Christ our Lord, who with thee and the same Holy Spirit liveth and reigneth, one God, world without end. *Amen.*

For the Epistle. Acts x. 34.

THEN Peter opened his mouth, and said, Of a truth I perceive that God is no respecter of persons: but in every nation he that feareth him, and worketh righteousness is accepted with him. The word which God sent unto the children of Israel, preaching peace by Jesus Christ: (he is Lord of all:) that word, I say, ye know, which was published throughout all Judæa, and began from Galilee, after the baptism which John preached; how God anointed Jesus of Nazareth with the Holy Ghost and with power: who went about doing good, and healing all that were oppressed of the devil; for God was with him. And we are witnesses of all things which he did both in the land of the Jews, and in Jerusalem; whom they slew and hanged on a tree: him God raised up the third day, and shewed him openly; not to all the people, but unto witnesses chosen before of God, even to us, who did eat and drink with him after he rose from the dead. And he commanded us to preach unto the people, and to testify that it is he which was ordained of God to be the Judge of quick and dead. To him give all the prophets witness, that through his name whosoever believeth in him shall receive remission of sins. While Peter yet spake these words, the Holy Ghost fell on all them which heard the word. And they of the circumcision which believed were astonished, as many as came with Peter, because that on the Gentiles also was poured out the gift of the Holy Ghost. For they heard them speak with tongues, and magnify God. Then answered Peter, Can any man forbid water, that these should not be baptized, which have received the Holy Ghost as well as we? And he commanded them to be baptized in the name of the Lord. Then prayed they him to tarry certain days.

The Gospel. St. John iii. 16.

GOD so loved the world, that he gave his only-begotten Son, that whosoever believeth in him should not perish, but have everlasting life. For God sent not his Son into the world to condemn the world; but that the world through him might be saved. He that believeth on him is not condemned: but he that believeth not is condemned already, because he hath not believed in the name of the only-begotten Son of God. And this is the condemnation, that light is come into the world, and men loved darkness rather than light, because their deeds were evil. For every one that doeth evil hateth the light, neither cometh to the light, lest his deeds should be reproved. But he that doeth truth cometh to the light, that his deeds may be made manifest, that they are wrought in God.

Tuesday in Whitsun Week.

The Collect.

GRANT, we beseech thee, merciful God, that thy Church, being gathered together in unity by thy Holy Spirit, may manifest thy power among all peoples, to the glory of thy Name; through Jesus Christ our Lord, who liveth and reigneth with thee and the same Spirit, one God, world without end. *Amen.*

For the Epistle. Acts viii. 14.

WHEN the apostles which were at Jerusalem heard that Samaria had received the word of God, they sent unto them Peter and John: who, when they were come down, prayed for them, that they might receive the Holy Ghost: for as yet he was fallen upon none of them: only they were baptized in the name of the Lord Jesus. Then laid they their hands on them, and they received the Holy Ghost.

The Gospel. St. John x. 1.

VERILY, verily, I say unto you, He that entereth not by the door into the sheepfold, but climbeth up some

185

other way, the same is a thief and a robber. But he that entereth in by the door is the shepherd of the sheep. To him the porter openeth; and the sheep hear his voice; and he calleth his own sheep by name, and leadeth them out. And when he putteth forth his own sheep, he goeth before them, and the sheep follow him: for they know his voice. And a stranger will they not follow, but will flee from him: for they know not the voice of strangers. This parable spake Jesus unto them: but they understood not what things they were which he spake unto them. Then said Jesus unto them again, Verily, verily, I say unto you, I am the door of the sheep. All that ever came before me are thieves and robbers: but the sheep did not hear them. I am the door: by me if any man enter in, he shall be saved, and shall go in and out, and find pasture. The thief cometh not, but for to steal, and to kill, and to destroy: I am come that they might have life, and that they might have it more abundantly.

TRINITY SEASON.

Trinity Sunday.

The Collect.

ALMIGHTY and everlasting God, who hast given unto us thy servants grace, by the confession of a true faith, to acknowledge the glory of the eternal Trinity, and in the power of the Divine Majesty to worship the Unity; We beseech thee that thou wouldest keep us stedfast in this faith, and evermore defend us from all adversities, who livest and reignest, one God, world without end. *Amen.*

For the Epistle. Revelation iv. 1.

AFTER this I looked, and, behold, a door was opened in heaven: and the first voice which I heard was as it

were of a trumpet talking with me; which said, Come up
hither, and I will shew thee things which must be hereafter. And immediately I was in the spirit: and, behold, a
throne was set in heaven, and one sat on the throne. And
he that sat was to look upon like a jasper and a sardine
stone: and there was a rainbow round about the throne, in
sight like unto an emerald. And round about the throne
were four and twenty seats: and upon the seats I saw four
and twenty elders sitting, clothed in white raiment; and
they had on their heads crowns of gold. And out of the
throne proceeded lightnings and thunderings and voices:
and there were seven lamps of fire burning before the
throne, which are the seven Spirits of God. And before
the throne there was a sea of glass like unto crystal: and
in the midst of the throne, and round about the throne,
were four living creatures full of eyes before and behind.
And the first was like a lion, and the second like a calf,
and the third had a face as a man, and the fourth was like
a flying eagle. And the four living creatures had each of
them six wings about him; and they were full of eyes
within: and they rest not day and night, saying, Holy,
holy, holy, Lord God Almighty, which was, and is, and is
to come. And when those living creatures give glory and
honour and thanks to him that sat on the throne, who
liveth for ever and ever, the four and twenty elders fall
down before him that sat on the throne, and worship
him that liveth for ever and ever, and cast their crowns
before the throne, saying, Thou art worthy, O Lord, to
receive glory and honour and power: for thou hast
created all things, and for thy pleasure they are, and were
created.

The Gospel. St. John iii. 1.

THERE was a man of the Pharisees, named Nicodemus,
a ruler of the Jews: the same came to Jesus by night,

The First Sunday after Trinity

and said unto him, Rabbi, we know that thou art a teacher come from God: for no man can do these miracles that thou doest, except God be with him. Jesus answered and said unto him, Verily, verily, I say unto thee, Except a man be born again, he cannot see the kingdom of God. Nicodemus saith unto him, How can a man be born when he is old? can he enter the second time into his mother's womb, and be born? Jesus answered, Verily, verily, I say unto thee, Except a man be born of water and of the Spirit, he cannot enter into the kingdom of God. That which is born of the flesh is flesh; and that which is born of the Spirit is spirit. Marvel not that I said unto thee, Ye must be born again. The wind bloweth where it listeth, and thou hearest the sound thereof, but canst not tell whence it cometh, and whither it goeth: so is every one that is born of the Spirit. Nicodemus answered and said unto him, How can these things be? Jesus answered and said unto him, Art thou a master of Israel, and knowest not these things? Verily, verily, I say unto thee, We speak that we do know, and testify that we have seen; and ye receive not our witness. If I have told you earthly things, and ye believe not, how shall ye believe, if I tell you of heavenly things? And no man hath ascended up to heaven, but he that came down from heaven, even the Son of man which is in heaven. And as Moses lifted up the serpent in the wilderness, even so must the Son of man be lifted up: that whosoever believeth in him should not perish, but have eternal life.

The First Sunday after Trinity.

The Collect.

O GOD, the strength of all those who put their trust in thee; Mercifully accept our prayers; and because,

The First Sunday after Trinity

through the weakness of our mortal nature, we can do no good thing without thee, grant us the help of thy grace, that in keeping thy commandments we may please thee, both in will and deed; through Jesus Christ our Lord. *Amen.*

The Epistle. 1 St. John iv. 7.

BELOVED, let us love one another: for love is of God; and every one that loveth is born of God, and knoweth God. He that loveth not knoweth not God; for God is love. In this was manifested the love of God toward us, because that God sent his only-begotten Son into the world, that we might live through him. Herein is love, not that we loved God, but that he loved us, and sent his Son to be the propitiation for our sins. Beloved, if God so loved us, we ought also to love one another. No man hath seen God at any time. If we love one another, God dwelleth in us, and his love is perfected in us. Hereby know we that we dwell in him, and he in us, because he hath given us of his Spirit. And we have seen and do testify that the Father sent the Son to be the Saviour of the world. Whosoever shall confess that Jesus is the Son of God, God dwelleth in him, and he in God. And we have known and believed the love that God hath to us. God is love; and he that dwelleth in love dwelleth in God, and God in him. Herein is our love made perfect, that we may have boldness in the day of judgment: because as he is, so are we in this world. There is no fear in love; but perfect love casteth out fear: because fear hath torment. He that feareth is not made perfect in love. We love him, because he first loved us. If a man say, I love God, and hateth his brother, he is a liar: for he that loveth not his brother whom he hath seen, how can he love God whom he hath not seen? And this commandment have we from him, That he who loveth God love his brother also.

The First Sunday after Trinity

The Gospel. St. Luke xvi. 19.

THERE was a certain rich man, which was clothed in purple and fine linen, and fared sumptuously every day: and there was a certain beggar named Lazarus, which was laid at his gate, full of sores, and desiring to be fed with the crumbs which fell from the rich man's table: moreover the dogs came and licked his sores. And it came to pass, that the beggar died, and was carried by the angels into Abraham's bosom: the rich man also died, and was buried; and in hell he lift up his eyes, being in torments, and seeth Abraham afar off, and Lazarus in his bosom. And he cried and said, Father Abraham, have mercy on me, and send Lazarus, that he may dip the tip of his finger in water, and cool my tongue; for I am tormented in this flame. But Abraham said, Son, remember that thou in thy lifetime receivedst thy good things, and likewise Lazarus evil things: but now he is comforted, and thou art tormented. And beside all this, between us and you there is a great gulf fixed: so that they which would pass from hence to you cannot; neither can they pass to us, that would come from thence. Then he said, I pray thee therefore, father, that thou wouldest send him to my father's house: for I have five brethren; that he may testify unto them, lest they also come into this place of torment. Abraham saith unto him, They have Moses and the prophets; let them hear them. And he said, Nay, father Abraham: but if one went unto them from the dead, they will repent. And he said unto him, If they hear not Moses and the prophets, neither will they be persuaded, though one rose from the dead.

The Second Sunday after Trinity

The Second Sunday after Trinity.

The Collect.

O LORD, who never failest to help and govern those whom thou dost bring up in thy stedfast fear and love; Keep us, we beseech thee, under the protection of thy good providence, and make us to have a perpetual fear and love of thy holy Name; through Jesus Christ our Lord. *Amen.*

The Epistle. 1 St. John iii. 13.

MARVEL not, my brethren, if the world hate you. We know that we have passed from death unto life, because we love the brethren. He that loveth not his brother abideth in death. Whosoever hateth his brother is a murderer: and ye know that no murderer hath eternal life abiding in him. Hereby perceive we the love of God, because he laid down his life for us: and we ought to lay down our lives for the brethren. But whoso hath this world's good, and seeth his brother have need, and shutteth up his bowels of compassion from him, how dwelleth the love of God in him? My little children, let us not love in word, neither in tongue; but in deed and in truth. And hereby we know that we are of the truth, and shall assure our hearts before him. For if our heart condemn us, God is greater than our heart, and knoweth all things. Beloved, if our heart condemn us not, then have we confidence toward God. And whatsoever we ask, we receive of him, because we keep his commandments, and do those things that are pleasing in his sight. And this is his commandment, That we should believe on the name of his Son Jesus Christ, and love one another, as he gave us commandment. And he that keepeth his commandments dwelleth in him, and he in him. And hereby we know that he abideth in us, by the Spirit which he hath given us.

The Third Sunday after Trinity

The Gospel. St. Luke xiv. 16.

A CERTAIN man made a great supper, and bade many: and sent his servant at supper time to say to them that were bidden, Come; for all things are now ready. And they all with one consent began to make excuse. The first said unto him, I have bought a piece of ground, and I must needs go and see it: I pray thee have me excused. And another said, I have bought five yoke of oxen, and I go to prove them: I pray thee have me excused. And another said, I have married a wife, and therefore I cannot come. So that servant came, and shewed his lord these things. Then the master of the house being angry said to his servant, Go out quickly into the streets and lanes of the city, and bring in hither the poor, and the maimed, and the halt, and the blind. And the servant said, Lord, it is done as thou hast commanded, and yet there is room. And the lord said unto the servant, Go out into the highways and hedges, and compel them to come in, that my house may be filled. For I say unto you, that none of those men which were bidden shall taste of my supper.

The Third Sunday after Trinity.

The Collect.

O LORD, we beseech thee mercifully to hear us; and grant that we, to whom thou hast given an hearty desire to pray, may, by thy mighty aid, be defended and comforted in all dangers and adversities; through Jesus Christ our Lord. *Amen.*

The Epistle. 1 St. Peter v. 5.

A LL of you be subject one to another, and be clothed with humility: for God resisteth the proud, and giveth grace to the humble. Humble yourselves therefore under the mighty hand of God, that he may exalt you in due time: casting all your care upon him; for he careth for you. Be sober, be vigilant; because your adversary the devil, as a roaring lion, walketh about, seeking whom he may devour: whom resist stedfast in the faith, knowing that the same afflictions are accomplished in your brethren that are in the world. But the God of all grace, who hath called us unto his eternal glory by Christ Jesus, after that ye have suffered a while, make you perfect, stablish, strengthen, settle you. To him be glory and dominion for ever and ever. Amen.

The Gospel. St. Luke xv. 1.

THEN drew near unto him all the publicans and sinners for to hear him. And the Pharisees and scribes murmured, saying, This man receiveth sinners, and eateth with them. And he spake this parable unto them, saying, What man of you, having an hundred sheep, if he lose one of them, doth not leave the ninety and nine in the wilderness, and go after that which is lost, until he find it? And when he hath found it, he layeth it on his shoulders, rejoicing. And when he cometh home, he calleth together his friends and neighbours, saying unto them, Rejoice with me; for I have found my sheep which was lost. I say unto you, that likewise joy shall be in heaven over one sinner that repenteth, more than over ninety and nine just persons, which need no repentance. Either what woman having ten pieces of silver, if she lose one piece, doth not light a candle, and sweep the house, and seek diligently till she find it? And when she hath found it, she calleth her friends and her neighbours together, saying, Rejoice with me; for I have found the piece which I had lost. Likewise, I say unto you, there is joy in the presence of the angels of God over one sinner that repenteth.

The Fourth Sunday after Trinity

The Fourth Sunday after Trinity.

The Collect.

O GOD, the protector of all that trust in thee, without whom nothing is strong, nothing is holy; Increase and multiply upon us thy mercy; that, thou being our ruler and guide, we may so pass through things temporal, that we finally lose not the things eternal. Grant this, O heavenly Father, for the sake of Jesus Christ our Lord. *Amen.*

The Epistle. Romans viii. 18.

I RECKON that the sufferings of this present time are not worthy to be compared with the glory which shall be revealed in us. For the earnest expectation of the creature waiteth for the manifestation of the sons of God. For the creature was made subject to vanity, not willingly, but by reason of him who hath subjected the same in hope, because the creature itself also shall be delivered from the bondage of corruption into the glorious liberty of the children of God. For we know that the whole creation groaneth and travaileth in pain together until now. And not only they, but ourselves also, which have the firstfruits of the Spirit, even we ourselves groan within ourselves, waiting for the adoption, to wit, the redemption of our body.

The Gospel. St. Luke vi. 36.

BE ye therefore merciful, as your Father also is merciful. Judge not, and ye shall not be judged: condemn not, and ye shall not be condemned: forgive, and ye shall be forgiven: give, and it shall be given unto you; good measure, pressed down, and shaken together, and running over, shall men give into your bosom. For with the same measure that ye mete withal it shall be measured to you

The Fifth Sunday after Trinity

again. And he spake a parable unto them, Can the blind lead the blind? shall they not both fall into the ditch? The disciple is not above his master: but every one that is perfect shall be as his master. And why beholdest thou the mote that is in thy brother's eye, but perceivest not the beam that is in thine own eye? Either how canst thou say to thy brother, Brother, let me pull out the mote that is in thine eye, when thou thyself beholdest not the beam that is in thine own eye? Thou hypocrite, cast out first the beam out of thine own eye, and then shalt thou see clearly to pull out the mote that is in thy brother's eye.

The Fifth Sunday after Trinity.

The Collect.

GRANT, O Lord, we beseech thee, that the course of this world may be so peaceably ordered by thy governance, that thy Church may joyfully serve thee in all godly quietness; through Jesus Christ our Lord. *Amen.*

The Epistle. 1 St. Peter iii. 8.

BE ye all of one mind, having compassion one of another, love as brethren, be pitiful, be courteous: not rendering evil for evil, or railing for railing: but contrariwise blessing; knowing that ye are thereunto called, that ye should inherit a blessing. For he that will love life, and see good days, let him refrain his tongue from evil, and his lips that they speak no guile: let him eschew evil, and do good; let him seek peace, and ensue it. For the eyes of the Lord are over the righteous, and his ears are open unto their prayers: but the face of the Lord is against them that do evil. And who is he that will harm you, if ye be followers of that which is good? But and if ye suffer for

righteousness' sake, happy are ye: and be not afraid of
their terror, neither be troubled; but sanctify the Lord
God in your hearts.

The Gospel. St. Luke v. 1.

IT came to pass, that, as the people pressed upon him to
hear the word of God, he stood by the lake of Gen-
nesaret, and saw two ships standing by the lake: but the
fishermen were gone out of them, and were washing their
nets. And he entered into one of the ships, which was
Simon's, and prayed him that he would thrust out a little
from the land. And he sat down, and taught the people
out of the ship. Now when he had left speaking, he said
unto Simon, Launch out into the deep, and let down your
nets for a draught. And Simon answering said unto him,
Master, we have toiled all the night, and have taken nothing: nevertheless at thy word I will let down the net. And
when they had this done, they inclosed a great multitude of
fishes: and their net brake. And they beckoned unto their
partners, which were in the other ship, that they should
come and help them. And they came, and filled both the
ships, so that they began to sink. When Simon Peter saw
it, he fell down at Jesus' knees, saying, Depart from me;
for I am a sinful man, O Lord. For he was astonished, and
all that were with him, at the draught of the fishes which
they had taken: and so was also James, and John, the sons
of Zebedee, which were partners with Simon. And Jesus
said unto Simon, Fear not; from henceforth thou shalt
catch men. And when they had brought their ships to land,
they forsook all, and followed him.

The Sixth Sunday after Trinity

The Sixth Sunday after Trinity.

The Collect.

O GOD, who hast prepared for those who love thee such good things as pass man's understanding; Pour into our hearts such love toward thee, that we, loving thee above all things, may obtain thy promises, which exceed all that we can desire; through Jesus Christ our Lord. *Amen.*

The Epistle. Romans vi. 3.

KNOW ye not, that so many of us as were baptized into Jesus Christ were baptized into his death? Therefore we are buried with him by baptism into death: that like as Christ was raised up from the dead by the glory of the Father, even so we also should walk in newness of life. For if we have been planted together in the likeness of his death, we shall be also in the likeness of his resurrection: knowing this, that our old man is crucified with him, that the body of sin might be destroyed, that henceforth we should not serve sin. For he that is dead is freed from sin. Now if we be dead with Christ, we believe that we shall also live with him: knowing that Christ being raised from the dead dieth no more; death hath no more dominion over him. For in that he died, he died unto sin once: but in that he liveth, he liveth unto God. Likewise reckon ye also yourselves to be dead indeed unto sin, but alive unto God through Jesus Christ our Lord.

The Gospel. St. Matthew v. 20.

JESUS said unto his disciples, Except your righteousness shall exceed the righteousness of the scribes and Pharisees, ye shall in no case enter into the kingdom of heaven. Ye have heard that it was said by them of old time, Thou

The Seventh Sunday after Trinity

shalt not kill; and whosoever shall kill shall be in danger of the judgment: but I say unto you, that whosoever is angry with his brother without a cause shall be in danger of the judgment: and whosoever shall say to his brother, Raca, shall be in danger of the council: but whosoever shall say, Thou fool, shall be in danger of hell-fire. Therefore if thou bring thy gift to the altar, and there rememberest that thy brother hath ought against thee; leave there thy gift before the altar, and go thy way; first be reconciled to thy brother, and then come and offer thy gift. Agree with thine adversary quickly, whiles thou art in the way with him; lest at any time the adversary deliver thee to the judge, and the judge deliver thee to the officer, and thou be cast into prison. Verily I say unto thee, Thou shalt by no means come out thence, till thou hast paid the uttermost farthing.

The Seventh Sunday after Trinity.

The Collect.

LORD of all power and might, who art the author and giver of all good things; Graft in our hearts the love of thy Name, increase in us true religion, nourish us with all goodness, and of thy great mercy keep us in the same; through Jesus Christ our Lord. *Amen.*

The Epistle. Romans vi. 19.

I SPEAK after the manner of men because of the infirmity of your flesh: for as ye have yielded your members servants to uncleanness and to iniquity unto iniquity; even so now yield your members servants to righteousness unto holiness. For when ye were the servants of sin, ye were free from righteousness. What fruit had ye then in those things whereof ye are now ashamed? for the end of those things is death. But now being made free from sin, and become servants to God, ye have your fruit unto holiness, and the end everlasting life. For the wages of sin is death; but the gift of God is eternal life through Jesus Christ our Lord.

The Gospel. St. Mark viii. i.

IN those days the multitude being very great, and having nothing to eat, Jesus called his disciples unto him, and saith unto them, I have compassion on the multitude, be-, cause they have now been with me three days, and have nothing to eat: and if I send them away fasting to their own houses, they will faint by the way: for divers of them came from far. And his disciples answered him, From whence can a man satisfy these men with bread here in the wilderness? And he asked them, How many loaves have ye? And they said, Seven. And he commanded the people to sit down on the ground: and he took the seven loaves, and gave thanks, and brake, and gave to his disciples to set before them; and they did set them before the people. And they had a few small fishes: and he blessed, and commanded to set them also before them. So they did eat, and were filled: and they took up of the broken meat that was left seven baskets. And they that had eaten were about four thousand: and he sent them away.

The Eighth Sunday after Trinity.

The Collect.

O GOD, whose never-failing providence ordereth all things both in heaven and earth; We humbly beseech thee to put away from us all hurtful things, and to give us those things which are profitable for us; through Jesus Christ our Lord. *Amen.*

The Ninth Sunday after Trinity

The Epistle. Romans viii. 12.

BRETHREN, we are debtors, not to the flesh, to live after the flesh. For if ye live after the flesh, ye shall die: but if ye through the Spirit do mortify the deeds of the body, ye shall live. For as many as are led by the Spirit of God, they are the sons of God. For ye have not received the spirit of bondage again to fear; but ye have received the Spirit of adoption, whereby we cry, Abba, Father. The Spirit himself beareth witness with our spirit, that we are the children of God: and if children, then heirs; heirs of God, and joint-heirs with Christ; if so be that we suffer with him, that we may be also glorified together.

The Gospel. St. Matthew vii. 15.

BEWARE of false prophets, which come to you in sheep's clothing, but inwardly they are ravening wolves. Ye shall know them by their fruits. Do men gather grapes of thorns, or figs of thistles? Even so every good tree bringeth forth good fruit; but a corrupt tree bringeth forth evil fruit. A good tree cannot bring forth evil fruit, neither can a corrupt tree bring forth good fruit. Every tree that bringeth not forth good fruit is hewn down, and cast into the fire. Wherefore by their fruits ye shall know them. Not every one that saith unto me, Lord, Lord, shall enter into the kingdom of heaven; but he that doeth the will of my Father which is in heaven.

The Ninth Sunday after Trinity.

The Collect.

GRANT to us, Lord, we beseech thee, the spirit to think and do always such things as are right; that we, who cannot do any thing that is good without thee, may

The Ninth Sunday after Trinity

by thee be enabled to live according to thy will; through Jesus Christ our Lord. *Amen.*

The Epistle. 1 Corinthians x. 1.

BRETHREN, I would not that ye should be ignorant, how that all our fathers were under the cloud, and all passed through the sea; and were all baptized unto Moses in the cloud and in the sea; and did all eat the same spiritual meat; and did all drink the same spiritual drink: for they drank of that spiritual Rock that followed them: and that Rock was Christ. But with many of them God was not well pleased: for they were overthrown in the wilderness. Now these things were our examples, to the intent we should not lust after evil things, as they also lusted. Neither be ye idolaters, as were some of them; as it is written, The people sat down to eat and drink, and rose up to play. Neither let us commit fornication, as some of them committed, and fell in one day three and twenty thousand. Neither let us tempt Christ, as some of them also tempted, and were destroyed of serpents. Neither murmur ye, as some of them also murmured, and were destroyed of the destroyer. Now all these things happened unto them for ensamples: and they are written for our admonition, upon whom the ends of the world are come. Wherefore let him that thinketh he standeth take heed lest he fall. There hath no temptation taken you but such as is common to man: but God is faithful, who will not suffer you to be tempted above that ye are able; but will with the temptation also make a way to escape, that ye may be able to bear it.

The Gospel. St. Luke xv. 11.

JESUS said, A certain man had two sons: and the younger of them said to his father, Father, give me the portion of goods that falleth to me. And he divided unto them his

The Ninth Sunday after Trinity

living. And not many days after the younger son gathered all together, and took his journey into a far country, and there wasted his substance with riotous living. And when he had spent all, there arose a mighty famine in that land; and he began to be in want. And he went and joined himself to a citizen of that country; and he sent him into his fields to feed swine. And he would fain have filled his belly with the husks that the swine did eat: and no man gave unto him. And when he came to himself, he said, How many hired servants of my father's have bread enough and to spare, and I perish with hunger! I will arise and go to my father, and will say unto him, Father, I have sinned against heaven, and before thee, and am no more worthy to be called thy son: make me as one of thy hired servants. And he arose, and came to his father. But when he was yet a great way off, his father saw him, and had compassion, and ran, and fell on his neck, and kissed him. And the son said unto him, Father, I have sinned against heaven, and in thy sight, and am no more worthy to be called thy son. But the father said to his servants, Bring forth the best robe, and put it on him; and put a ring on his hand, and shoes on his feet: and bring hither the fatted calf, and kill it; and let us eat, and be merry: for this my son was dead, and is alive again; he was lost, and is found. And they began to be merry. Now his elder son was in the field: and as he came and drew nigh to the house, he heard musick and dancing. And he called one of the servants, and asked what these things meant. And he said unto him, Thy brother is come; and thy father hath killed the fatted calf, because he hath received him safe and sound. And he was angry, and would not go in: therefore came his father out, and intreated him. And he answering said to his father, Lo, these many years do I serve thee, neither transgressed I at any time thy commandment: and yet thou never gavest me a

The Tenth Sunday after Trinity

kid, that I might make merry with my friends: but as soon as this thy son was come, which hath devoured thy living with harlots, thou hast killed for him the fatted calf. And he said unto him, Son, thou art ever with me, and all that I have is thine. It was meet that we should make merry, and be glad: for this thy brother was dead, and is alive again; and was lost, and is found.

The Tenth Sunday after Trinity.

The Collect.

LET thy merciful ears, O Lord, be open to the prayers of thy humble servants; and, that they may obtain their petitions, make them to ask such things as shall please thee; through Jesus Christ our Lord. *Amen.*

The Epistle. 1 Corinthians xii. 1.

CONCERNING spiritual gifts, brethren, I would not have you ignorant. Ye know that ye were Gentiles, carried away unto these dumb idols, even as ye were led. Wherefore I give you to understand, that no man speaking by the Spirit of God calleth Jesus accursed: and that no man can say that Jesus is the Lord, but by the Holy Ghost. Now there are diversities of gifts, but the same Spirit. And there are differences of administrations, but the same Lord. And there are diversities of operations, but it is the same God which worketh all in all. But the manifestation of the Spirit is given to every man to profit withal. For to one is given by the Spirit the word of wisdom; to another the word of knowledge by the same Spirit; to another faith by the same Spirit; to another the gifts of healing by the same Spirit; to another the working of miracles; to another prophecy; to another discerning of spirits; to another divers kinds of tongues; to another the interpretation of tongues: but all these worketh that one and the selfsame Spirit, dividing to every man severally as he will.

The Gospel. St. Luke xix. 41.

AND when he was come near, he beheld the city, and wept over it, saying, If thou hadst known, even thou, at least in this thy day, the things which belong unto thy peace! but now they are hid from thine eyes. For the days shall come upon thee, that thine enemies shall cast a trench about thee, and compass thee round, and keep thee in on every side, and shall lay thee even with the ground, and thy children within thee; and they shall not leave in thee one stone upon another; because thou knewest not the time of thy visitation. And he went into the temple, and began to cast out them that sold therein, and them that bought; saying unto them, It is written, My house is the house of prayer: but ye have made it a den of thieves. And he taught daily in the temple.

The Eleventh Sunday after Trinity.

The Collect.

O GOD, who declarest thy almighty power chiefly in showing mercy and pity; Mercifully grant unto us such a measure of thy grace, that we, running the way of thy commandments, may obtain thy gracious promises, and be made partakers of thy heavenly treasure; through Jesus Christ our Lord. *Amen.*

The Epistle. 1 Corinthians xv. 1.

BRETHREN, I declare unto you the gospel which I preached unto you, which also ye have received, and wherein ye stand; by which also ye are saved, if ye keep

The Eleventh Sunday after Trinity

in memory what I preached unto you, unless ye have believed in vain. For I delivered unto you first of all that which I also received, how that Christ died for our sins according to the scriptures; and that he was buried, and that he rose again the third day according to the scriptures: and that he was seen of Cephas, then of the twelve: after that, he was seen of above five hundred brethren at once; of whom the greater part remain unto this present, but some are fallen asleep. After that, he was seen of James; then of all the apostles. And last of all he was seen of me also, as of one born out of due time. For I am the least of the apostles, that am not meet to be called an apostle, because I persecuted the church of God. But by the grace of God I am what I am: and his grace which was bestowed upon me was not in vain; but I laboured more abundantly than they all: yet not I, but the grace of God which was with me. Therefore whether it were I or they, so we preach, and so ye believed.

The Gospel. St. Luke xviii. 9.

JESUS spake this parable unto certain which trusted in themselves that they were righteous, and despised others: Two men went up into the temple to pray; the one a Pharisee, and the other a publican. The Pharisee stood and prayed thus with himself, God, I thank thee, that I am not as other men are, extortioners, unjust, adulterers, or even as this publican. I fast twice in the week, I give tithes of all that I possess. And the publican, standing afar off, would not lift up so much as his eyes unto heaven, but smote upon his breast, saying, God be merciful to me a sinner. I tell you, this man went down to his house justified rather than the other: for every one that exalteth himself shall be abased; and he that humbleth himself shall be exalted.

The Twelfth Sunday after Trinity

The Twelfth Sunday after Trinity.

The Collect.

ALMIGHTY and everlasting God, who art always more ready to hear than we to pray, and art wont to give more than either we desire or deserve; Pour down upon us the abundance of thy mercy; forgiving us those things whereof our conscience is afraid, and giving us those good things which we are not worthy to ask, but through the merits and mediation of Jesus Christ, thy Son, our Lord. *Amen.*

The Epistle. 2 Corinthians iii. 4.

SUCH trust have we through Christ to God-ward: not that we are sufficient of ourselves to think any thing as of ourselves; but our sufficiency is of God; who also hath made us able ministers of the new testament; not of the letter, but of the spirit: for the letter killeth, but the spirit giveth life. But if the ministration of death, written and engraven in stones, was glorious, so that the children of Israel could not stedfastly behold the face of Moses for the glory of his countenance; which glory was to be done away: how shall not the ministration of the spirit be rather glorious? For if the ministration of condemnation be glory, much more doth the ministration of righteousness exceed in glory.

The Gospel. St. Mark vii. 31.

JESUS, departing from the coasts of Tyre and Sidon, came unto the sea of Galilee, through the midst of the coasts of Decapolis. And they bring unto him one that was deaf, and had an impediment in his speech; and they beseech him to put his hand upon him. And he took him aside from the multitude, and put his fingers into his ears, and he spit, and touched his tongue; and looking up to

The Thirteenth Sunday after Trinity

heaven, he sighed, and saith unto him, Ephphatha, that is, Be opened. And straightway his ears were opened, and the string of his tongue was loosed, and he spake plain. And he charged them that they should tell no man: but the more he charged them, so much the more a great deal they published it; and were beyond measure astonished, saying, He hath done all things well: he maketh both the deaf to hear, and the dumb to speak.

The Thirteenth Sunday after Trinity.

The Collect.

ALMIGHTY and merciful God, of whose only gift it cometh that thy faithful people do unto thee true and laudable service; Grant, we beseech thee, that we may so faithfully serve thee in this life, that we fail not finally to attain thy heavenly promises; through the merits of Jesus Christ our Lord. *Amen.*

The Epistle. Galatians iii. 16.

TO Abraham and his seed were the promises made. He saith not, And to seeds, as of many; but as of one, And to thy seed, which is Christ. And this I say, that the covenant, that was confirmed before of God in Christ, the law, which was four hundred and thirty years after, cannot disannul, that it should make the promise of none effect. For if the inheritance be of the law, it is no more of promise: but God gave it to Abraham by promise. Wherefore then serveth the law? It was added because of transgressions, till the seed should come to whom the promise was made; and it was ordained by angels in the hand of a mediator. Now a mediator is not a mediator of one, but God is one. Is the law then against the promises of God? God forbid: for if there had been a law given which could have given life, verily righteousness should have been by the law. But the scripture hath concluded all under sin, that the promise by faith of Jesus Christ might be given to them that believe.

The Gospel. St. Luke x. 23.

BLESSED are the eyes which see the things that ye see: for I tell you, that many prophets and kings have desired to see those things which ye see, and have not seen them; and to hear those things which ye hear, and have not heard them. And, behold, a certain lawyer stood up, and tempted him, saying, Master, what shall I do to inherit eternal life? He said unto him, What is written in the law? how readest thou? And he answering said, Thou shalt love the Lord thy God with all thy heart, and with all thy soul, and with all thy strength, and with all thy mind; and thy neighbour as thyself. And he said unto him, Thou hast answered right: this do, and thou shalt live. But he, willing to justify himself, said unto Jesus, And who is my neighbour? And Jesus answering said, A certain man went down from Jerusalem to Jericho, and fell among thieves, which stripped him of his raiment, and wounded him, and departed, leaving him half dead. And by chance there came down a certain priest that way: and when he saw him, he passed by on the other side. And likewise a Levite, when he was at the place, came and looked on him, and passed by on the other side. But a certain Samaritan, as he journeyed, came where he was: and when he saw him, he had compassion on him, and went to him, and bound up his wounds, pouring in oil and wine, and set him on his own beast, and brought him to an inn, and took care of him. And on the morrow when he departed, he took out two pence, and gave them to the host, and said unto him, Take care of him; and whatsoever thou spendest more, when I come again, I

The Fourteenth Sunday after Trinity

will repay thee. Which now of these three, thinkest thou, was neighbour unto him that fell among the thieves? And he said, He that shewed mercy on him. Then said Jesus unto him, Go, and do thou likewise.

The Fourteenth Sunday after Trinity.

The Collect.

ALMIGHTY and everlasting God, give unto us the increase of faith, hope, and charity; and, that we may obtain that which thou dost promise, make us to love that which thou dost command; through Jesus Christ our Lord. *Amen.*

The Epistle. Galatians v. 16.

I SAY then, Walk in the Spirit, and ye shall not fulfil the lust of the flesh. For the flesh lusteth against the Spirit, and the Spirit against the flesh: and these are contrary the one to the other: so that ye cannot do the things that ye would. But if ye be led of the Spirit, ye are not under the law. Now the works of the flesh are manifest, which are these; Adultery, fornication, uncleanness, lasciviousness, idolatry, witchcraft, hatred, variance, emulations, wrath, strife, seditions, heresies, envyings, murders, drunkenness, revellings, and such like: of the which I tell you before, as I have also told you in time past, that they which do such things shall not inherit the kingdom of God. But the fruit of the Spirit is love, joy, peace, long-suffering, gentleness, goodness, faith, meekness, temperance: against such there is no law. And they that are Christ's have crucified the flesh with the affections and lusts.

The Gospel. St. Luke xvii. 11.

AND it came to pass, as Jesus went to Jerusalem, that he passed through the midst of Samaria and Galilee. And as he entered into a certain village, there met him ten men that were lepers, which stood afar off: and they lifted up their voices, and said, Jesus, Master, have mercy on us. And when he saw them, he said unto them, Go shew your-selves unto the priests. And it came to pass, that, as they went, they were cleansed. And one of them, when he saw that he was healed, turned back, and with a loud voice glorified God, and fell down on his face at his feet, giving him thanks: and he was a Samaritan. And Jesus answer-ing said, Were there not ten cleansed? but where are the nine? There are not found that returned to give glory to God, save this stranger. And he said unto him, Arise, go thy way: thy faith hath made thee whole.

The Fifteenth Sunday after Trinity.

The Collect.

KEEP, we beseech thee, O Lord, thy Church with thy perpetual mercy; and, because the frailty of man without thee cannot but fall, keep us ever by thy help from all things hurtful, and lead us to all things profitable to our salvation; through Jesus Christ our Lord. *Amen.*

The Epistle. Galatians vi. 11.

YE see how large a letter I have written unto you with mine own hand. As many as desire to make a fair shew in the flesh, they constrain you to be circumcised; only lest they should suffer persecution for the cross of Christ. For neither they themselves who are circumcised keep the law; but desire to have you circumcised, that they may glory in your flesh. But God forbid that I should glory, save in the cross of our Lord Jesus Christ, by whom the world is crucified unto me, and I unto the world. For in Christ Jesus neither circumcision availeth any thing, nor

The Fifteenth Sunday after Trinity

uncircumcision, but a new creature. And as many as walk according to this rule, peace be on them, and mercy, and upon the Israel of God. From henceforth let no man trouble me: for I bear in my body the marks of the Lord Jesus. Brethren, the grace of our Lord Jesus Christ be with your spirit. Amen.

The Gospel. St. Matthew vi. 24.

NO man can serve two masters: for either he will hate the one, and love the other; or else he will hold to the one, and despise the other. Ye cannot serve God and mammon. Therefore I say unto you, Be not anxious for your life, what ye shall eat, or what ye shall drink; nor yet for your body, what ye shall put on. Is not the life more than the food, and the body than the raiment? Behold the birds of the heaven, that they sow not, neither do they reap, nor gather into barns; and your heavenly Father feedeth them. Are not ye of much more value than they? And which of you by being anxious can add one cubit unto the measure of his life? And why are ye anxious concerning raiment? Consider the lilies of the field, how they grow; they toil not, neither do they spin: yet I say unto you, that even Solomon in all his glory was not arrayed like one of these. But if God doth so clothe the grass of the field, which to-day is, and to-morrow is cast into the oven, shall he not much more clothe you, O ye of little faith? Be not therefore anxious, saying, What shall we eat? or, What shall we drink? or, Wherewithal shall we be clothed? For after all these things do the Gentiles seek; for your heavenly Father knoweth that ye have need of all these things. But seek ye first his kingdom, and his righteousness; and all these things shall be added unto you. Be not therefore anxious for the morrow: for the morrow will be anxious for itself. Sufficient unto the day is the evil thereof.

The Sixteenth Sunday after Trinity

The Sixteenth Sunday after Trinity.

The Collect.

O LORD, we beseech thee, let thy continual pity cleanse and defend thy Church; and, because it cannot continue in safety without thy succour, preserve it evermore by thy help and goodness; through Jesus Christ our Lord. *Amen.*

The Epistle. Ephesians iii. 13.

I DESIRE that ye faint not at my tribulations for you, which is your glory. For this cause I bow my knees unto the Father of our Lord Jesus Christ, of whom the whole family in heaven and earth is named, that he would grant you, according to the riches of his glory, to be strengthened with might by his Spirit in the inner man; that Christ may dwell in your hearts by faith; that ye, being rooted and grounded in love, may be able to comprehend with all saints what is the breadth, and length, and depth, and height; and to know the love of Christ, which passeth knowledge, that ye might be filled with all the fulness of God. Now unto him that is able to do exceeding abundantly above all that we ask or think, according to the power that worketh in us, unto him be glory in the church by Christ Jesus throughout all ages, world without end. Amen.

The Gospel. St. Luke vii. 11.

A ND it came to pass the day after, that Jesus went into a city called Nain; and many of his disciples went with him, and much people. Now when he came nigh to the gate of the city, behold, there was a dead man carried out, the only son of his mother, and she was a widow: and much people of the city was with her. And when the

The Seventeenth Sunday after Trinity

Lord saw her, he had compassion on her, and said unto her, Weep not. And he came and touched the bier: and they that bare him stood still. And he said, Young man, I say unto thee, Arise. And he that was dead sat up, and began to speak. And he delivered him to his mother. And there came a fear on all: and they glorified God, saying, That a great prophet is risen up among us; and, That God hath visited his people. And this rumour of him went forth throughout all Judæa, and throughout all the region round about.

The Seventeenth Sunday after Trinity.

The Collect.

LORD, we pray thee that thy grace may always prevent and follow us, and make us continually to be given to all good works; through Jesus Christ our Lord. *Amen.*

The Epistle. Ephesians iv. 1.

I THEREFORE, the prisoner of the Lord, beseech you that ye walk worthy of the vocation wherewith ye are called, with all lowliness and meekness, with long-suffering, forbearing one another in love; endeavouring to keep the unity of the Spirit in the bond of peace. There is one body, and one Spirit, even as ye are called in one hope of your calling; one Lord, one faith, one baptism, one God and Father of all, who is above all, and through all, and in you all.

The Gospel. St. Luke xiv. 1.

IT came to pass, as Jesus went into the house of one of the chief Pharisees to eat bread on the sabbath day, that they watched him. And, behold, there was a certain man before him which had the dropsy. And Jesus answering

The Eighteenth Sunday after Trinity

spake unto the lawyers and Pharisees, saying, Is it lawful to heal on the sabbath day? And they held their peace. And he took him, and healed him, and let him go; and answered them, saying, Which of you shall have an ass or an ox fallen into a pit, and will not straightway pull him out on the sabbath day? And they could not answer him again to these things. And he put forth a parable to those which were bidden, when he marked how they chose out the chief seats; saying unto them, When thou art bidden of any man to a wedding, sit not down in the highest seat; lest a more honourable man than thou be bidden of him; and he that bade thee and him come and say to thee, Give this man place; and thou begin with shame to take the lowest place. But when thou art bidden, go and sit down in the lowest place; that when he that bade thee cometh, he may say unto thee, Friend, go up higher: then shalt thou have worship in the presence of them that sit at meat with thee. For whosoever exalteth himself shall be abased; and he that humbleth himself shall be exalted.

The Eighteenth Sunday after Trinity.

The Collect.

LORD, we beseech thee, grant thy people grace to withstand the temptations of the world, the flesh, and the devil; and with pure hearts and minds to follow thee, the only God; through Jesus Christ our Lord. *Amen.*

The Epistle. 1 Corinthians i. 4.

I THANK my God always on your behalf, for the grace of God which is given you by Jesus Christ; that in every thing ye are enriched by him, in all utterance, and in all knowledge; even as the testimony of Christ was confirmed in you: so that ye come behind in no gift; waiting

The Nineteenth Sunday after Trinity

for the coming of our Lord Jesus Christ: who shall also confirm you unto the end, that ye may be blameless in the day of our Lord Jesus Christ.

The Gospel. St. Matthew xxii. 34.

WHEN the Pharisees had heard that Jesus had put the Sadducees to silence, they were gathered together. Then one of them, which was a lawyer, asked him a question, tempting him, and saying, Master, which is the great commandment in the law? Jesus said unto him, Thou shalt love the Lord thy God with all thy heart, and with all thy soul, and with all thy mind. This is the first and great commandment. And the second is like unto it, Thou shalt love thy neighbour as thyself. On these two commandments hang all the law and the prophets. While the Pharisees were gathered together, Jesus asked them, saying, What think ye of Christ? whose son is he? They say unto him, The son of David. He saith unto them, How then doth David in spirit call him Lord, saying, The LORD said unto my Lord, Sit thou on my right hand, till I make thine enemies thy footstool? If David then call him Lord, how is he his son? And no man was able to answer him a word, neither durst any man from that day forth ask him any more questions.

The Nineteenth Sunday after Trinity.

The Collect.

O GOD, forasmuch as without thee we are not able to please thee; Mercifully grant that thy Holy Spirit may in all things direct and rule our hearts; through Jesus Christ our Lord. *Amen.*

The Nineteenth Sunday after Trinity

The Epistle. Ephesians iv. 17.

THIS I say therefore, and testify in the Lord, that ye henceforth walk not as other Gentiles walk, in the vanity of their mind, having the understanding darkened, being alienated from the life of God through the ignorance that is in them, because of the blindness of their heart: who being past feeling have given themselves over unto lasciviousness, to work all uncleanness with greediness. But ye have not so learned Christ; if so be that ye have heard him, and have been taught by him, as the truth is in Jesus: that ye put off concerning the former conversation the old man, which is corrupt according to the deceitful lusts; and be renewed in the spirit of your mind; and that ye put on the new man, which after God is created in righteousness and true holiness. Wherefore putting away lying, speak every man truth with his neighbour: for we are members one of another. Be ye angry, and sin not: let not the sun go down upon your wrath: neither give place to the devil. Let him that stole steal no more: but rather let him labour, working with his hands the thing which is good, that he may have to give to him that needeth. Let no corrupt communication proceed out of your mouth, but that which is good to the use of edifying, that it may minister grace unto the hearers. And grieve not the holy Spirit of God, whereby ye are sealed unto the day of redemption. Let all bitterness, and wrath, and anger, and clamour, and evil speaking, be put away from you, with all malice: and be ye kind one to another, tender-hearted, forgiving one another, even as God for Christ's sake hath forgiven you.

The Gospel. St. Matthew ix. 1.

JESUS entered into a ship, and passed over, and came into his own city. And, behold, they brought to him a man sick of the palsy, lying on a bed: and Jesus, seeing their faith, said unto the sick of the palsy; Son, be of good cheer; thy sins be forgiven thee. And, behold, certain of the scribes said within themselves, This man blasphemeth. And Jesus knowing their thoughts said, Wherefore think ye evil in your hearts? For whether is easier, to say, Thy sins be forgiven thee; or to say, Arise, and walk? But that ye may know that the Son of man hath power on earth to forgive sins, (then saith he to the sick of the palsy,) Arise, take up thy bed, and go unto thine house. And he arose, and departed to his house. But when the multitudes saw it, they marvelled, and glorified God, which had given such power unto men.

The Twentieth Sunday after Trinity.

The Collect.

O ALMIGHTY and most merciful God, of thy bountiful goodness keep us, we beseech thee, from all things that may hurt us; that we, being ready both in body and soul, may cheerfully accomplish those things which thou commandest; through Jesus Christ our Lord. *Amen.*

The Epistle. Ephesians v. 15.

S EE then that ye walk circumspectly, not as fools, but as wise, redeeming the time, because the days are evil. Wherefore be ye not unwise, but understanding what the will of the Lord is. And be not drunk with wine, wherein is excess; but be filled with the Spirit; speaking to yourselves in psalms and hymns and spiritual songs, singing and making melody in your heart to the Lord; giving thanks always for all things unto God and the Father in the name of our Lord Jesus Christ; submitting yourselves one to another in the fear of God.

The Twenty-first Sunday after Trinity

The Gospel. St. Matthew xxii. 1.

JESUS said, The kingdom of heaven is like unto a certain king, which made a marriage for his son, and sent forth his servants to call them that were bidden to the wedding: and they would not come. Again, he sent forth other servants, saying, Tell them which are bidden, Behold, I have prepared my dinner: my oxen and my fatlings are killed, and all things are ready: come unto the marriage. But they made light of it, and went their ways, one to his farm, another to his merchandise: and the remnant took his servants, and entreated them spitefully, and slew them. But when the king heard thereof, he was wroth: and he sent forth his armies, and destroyed those murderers, and burned up their city. Then saith he to his servants, The wedding is ready, but they which were bidden were not worthy. Go ye therefore into the highways, and as many as ye shall find, bid to the marriage. So those servants went out into the highways, and gathered together all as many as they found, both bad and good: and the wedding was furnished with guests. And when the king came in to see the guests, he saw there a man which had not on a wedding-garment: and he saith unto him, Friend, how camest thou in hither not having a wedding-garment? And he was speechless. Then said the king to the servants, Bind him hand and foot, and take him away, and cast him into outer darkness; there shall be weeping and gnashing of teeth. For many are called, but few are chosen.

The Twenty-first Sunday after Trinity.

The Collect.

GRANT, we beseech thee, merciful Lord, to thy faithful people pardon and peace, that they may be

The Twenty-first Sunday after Trinity

cleansed from all their sins, and serve thee with a quiet mind; through Jesus Christ our Lord. *Amen.*

The Epistle. Ephesians vi. 10.

MY brethren, be strong in the Lord, and in the power of his might. Put on the whole armour of God, that ye may be able to stand against the wiles of the devil. For we wrestle not against flesh and blood, but against principalities, against powers, against the rulers of the darkness of this world, against spiritual wickedness in high places. Wherefore take unto you the whole armour of God, that ye may be able to withstand in the evil day, and having done all, to stand. Stand therefore, having your loins girt about with truth, and having on the breastplate of righteousness; and your feet shod with the preparation of the gospel of peace; above all, taking the shield of faith, wherewith ye shall be able to quench all the fiery darts of the wicked. And take the helmet of salvation, and the sword of the Spirit, which is the word of God: praying always with all prayer and supplication in the Spirit, and watching thereunto with all perseverance and supplication for all saints; and for me, that utterance may be given unto me, that I may open my mouth boldly, to make known the mystery of the gospel, for which I am an ambassador in bonds: that therein I may speak boldly, as I ought to speak.

The Gospel. St. John iv. 46.

THERE was a certain nobleman, whose son was sick at Capernaum. When he heard that Jesus was come out of Judæa into Galilee, he went unto him, and besought him that he would come down, and heal his son: for he was at the point of death. Then said Jesus unto him, Except ye see signs and wonders, ye will not believe. The nobleman

The Twenty-second Sunday after Trinity

saith unto him, Sir, come down ere my child die. Jesus saith unto him, Go thy way; thy son liveth. And the man believed the word that Jesus had spoken unto him, and he went his way. And as he was now going down, his servants met him, and told him, saying, Thy son liveth. Then enquired he of them the hour when he began to amend. And they said unto him, Yesterday at the seventh hour the fever left him. So the father knew that it was at the same hour, in the which Jesus said unto him, Thy son liveth: and himself believed, and his whole house. This is again the second miracle that Jesus did, when he was come out of Judæa into Galilee.

The Twenty-second Sunday after Trinity.

The Collect.

LORD, we beseech thee to keep thy household the Church in continual godliness; that through thy protection it may be free from all adversities, and devoutly given to serve thee in good works, to the glory of thy Name; through Jesus Christ our Lord. *Amen.*

The Epistle. Philippians i. 3.

I THANK my God upon every remembrance of you, always in every prayer of mine for you all making request with joy, for your fellowship in the gospel from the first day until now; being confident of this very thing, that he which hath begun a good work in you will perform it until the day of Jesus Christ: even as it is meet for me to think this of you all, because I have you in my heart; inasmuch as both in my bonds, and in the defence and confirmation of the gospel, ye all are partakers of my grace. For God is my record, how greatly I long after you all in the tender mercies of Christ Jesus. And this I pray, that

The Twenty-second Sunday after Trinity

your love may abound yet more and more in knowledge and in all judgment; that ye may approve things that are excellent; that ye may be sincere and without offence till the day of Christ; being filled with the fruits of righteousness, which are by Jesus Christ, unto the glory and praise of God.

The Gospel. St. Matthew xviii. 21.

PETER said unto Jesus, Lord, how oft shall my brother sin against me, and I forgive him? till seven times? Jesus saith unto him, I say not unto thee, Until seven times: but, Until seventy times seven. Therefore is the kingdom of heaven likened unto a certain king, which would take account of his servants. And when he had begun to reckon, one was brought unto him, which owed him ten thousand talents. But forasmuch as he had not to pay, his lord commanded him to be sold, and his wife, and children, and all that he had, and payment to be made. The servant therefore fell down, and worshipped him, saying, Lord, have patience with me, and I will pay thee all. Then the lord of that servant was moved with compassion, and loosed him, and forgave him the debt. But the same servant went out, and found one of his fellow-servants, which owed him an hundred pence: and he laid hands on him, and took him by the throat, saying, Pay me that thou owest. And his fellow-servant fell down at his feet, and besought him, saying, Have patience with me, and I will pay thee all. And he would not: but went and cast him into prison, till he should pay the debt. So when his fellow-servants saw what was done, they were very sorry, and came and told unto their lord all that was done. Then his lord, after that he had called him, said unto him, O thou wicked servant, I forgave thee all that debt, because thou desiredst me: shouldest not thou also have had compassion on thy

fellow-servant, even as I had pity on thee? And his lord
was wroth, and delivered him to the tormentors, till he
should pay all that was due unto him. So likewise shall
my heavenly Father do also unto you, if ye from your
hearts forgive not every one his brother their trespasses.

The Twenty-third Sunday after Trinity.

The Collect.

O GOD, our refuge and strength, who art the author
of all godliness; Be ready, we beseech thee, to hear
the devout prayers of thy Church; and grant that those
things which we ask faithfully we may obtain effectually;
through Jesus Christ our Lord. *Amen.*

The Epistle. Philippians iii. 17.

BRETHREN, be followers together of me, and mark
them which walk so as ye have us for an ensample.
(For many walk, of whom I have told you often, and now
tell you even weeping, that they are the enemies of the
cross of Christ: whose end is destruction, whose god is
their belly, and whose glory is in their shame, who mind
earthly things.) For our citizenship is in heaven; from
whence also we look for the Saviour, the Lord Jesus Christ:
who shall change the body of our humiliation that it may
be conformed unto the body of his glory, according to the
working whereby he is able even to subject all things unto
himself.

The Gospel. St. Matthew xxii. 15.

THEN went the Pharisees, and took counsel how they
might entangle him in his talk. And they sent out
unto him their disciples with the Herodians, saying, Master,
we know that thou art true, and teachest the way of God

The Twenty-fourth Sunday after Trinity

in truth, neither carest thou for any man: for thou regardest not the person of men. Tell us therefore, What thinkest thou? Is it lawful to give tribute unto Cæsar, or not? But Jesus perceived their wickedness, and said, Why tempt ye me, ye hypocrites? Shew me the tribute money. And they brought unto him a penny. And he saith unto them, Whose is this image and superscription? They say unto him, Cæsar's. Then saith he unto them, Render therefore unto Cæsar the things which are Cæsar's; and unto God the things that are God's. When they had heard these words, they marvelled, and left him, and went their way.

The Twenty-fourth Sunday after Trinity.

The Collect.

O LORD, we beseech thee, absolve thy people from their offences; that through thy bountiful goodness we may all be delivered from the bands of those sins, which by our frailty we have committed. Grant this, O heavenly Father, for the sake of Jesus Christ, our blessed Lord and Saviour. *Amen.*

The Epistle. Colossians i. 3.

WE give thanks to God and the Father of our Lord Jesus Christ, praying always for you, since we heard of your faith in Christ Jesus, and of the love which ye have to all the saints, for the hope which is laid up for you in heaven, whereof ye heard before in the word of the truth of the gospel; which is come unto you, as it is in all the world; and bringeth forth fruit, as it doth also in you, since the day ye heard of it, and knew the grace of God in truth: as ye also learned of Epaphras our dear fellow-servant, who is for you a faithful minister of Christ; who also declared unto us your love in the Spirit. For this cause we also, since the day we heard it, do not cease to pray for

The Twenty-fourth Sunday after Trinity

you, and to desire that ye might be filled with the knowledge of his will in all wisdom and spiritual understanding; that ye might walk worthy of the Lord unto all pleasing, being fruitful in every good work, and increasing in the knowledge of God; strengthened with all might, according to his glorious power, unto all patience and long-suffering with joyfulness; giving thanks unto the Father, which hath made us meet to be partakers of the inheritance of the saints in light.

The Gospel. St. Matthew ix. 18.

WHILE Jesus spake these things unto John's disciples, behold, there came a certain ruler, and worshipped him, saying, My daughter is even now dead: but come and lay thy hand upon her, and she shall live. And Jesus arose, and followed him, and so did his disciples. And, behold, a woman, which was diseased with an issue of blood twelve years, came behind him, and touched the hem of his garment: for she said within herself, If I may but touch his garment, I shall be whole. But Jesus turned him about, and when he saw her, he said, Daughter, be of good comfort; thy faith hath made thee whole. And the woman was made whole from that hour. And when Jesus came into the ruler's house, and saw the minstrels and the people making a noise, he said unto them, Give place: for the maid is not dead, but sleepeth. And they laughed him to scorn. But when the people were put forth, he went in, and took her by the hand, and the maid arose. And the fame hereof went abroad into all that land.

¶ *If in any year there be twenty-six Sundays after Trinity, the service for the Sixth Sunday after the Epiphany shall be used on the Twenty-fifth Sunday. If there be twenty-seven, the service for the Sixth Sunday after the Epiphany shall be used on the Twenty-sixth, and the service for the Fifth Sunday after the Epiphany on the Twenty-fifth. If there be fewer than twenty-five Sundays, the overplus shall be omitted.*

Sunday before Advent

The Sunday next before Advent.

The Collect.

STIR up, we beseech thee, O Lord, the wills of thy faithful people; that they, plenteously bringing forth the fruit of good works, may by thee be plenteously rewarded; through Jesus Christ our Lord. *Amen.*

For the Epistle. Jeremiah xxiii. 5.

BEHOLD, the days come, saith the LORD, that I will raise unto David a righteous Branch, and a King shall reign and prosper, and shall execute judgment and justice in the earth. In his days Judah shall be saved, and Israel shall dwell safely: and this is his name whereby he shall be called, THE LORD OUR RIGHTEOUSNESS. Therefore, behold, the days come, saith the LORD, that they shall no more say, The LORD liveth, which brought up the children of Israel out of the land of Egypt; but, The LORD liveth, which brought up and which led the seed of the house of Israel out of the north country, and from all countries whither I had driven them; and they shall dwell in their own land.

The Gospel. St. John vi. 5.

WHEN Jesus then lifted up his eyes, and saw a great company come unto him, he saith unto Philip, Whence shall we buy bread, that these may eat? And this he said to prove him: for he himself knew what he would do. Philip answered him, Two hundred pennyworth of bread is not sufficient for them, that every one of them may take a little. One of his disciples, Andrew, Simon Peter's brother, saith unto him, There is a lad here, which hath five barley loaves, and two small fishes: but what are they among so many? And Jesus said, Make the men sit down. Now there was much grass in the place. So the men sat down, in number about five thousand. And Jesus took the loaves; and when he had given thanks, he distributed to the disciples, and the disciples to them that were set down; and likewise of the fishes as much as they would. When they were filled, he said unto his disciples, Gather up the fragments that remain, that nothing be lost. Therefore they gathered them together, and filled twelve baskets with the fragments of the five barley loaves, which remained over and above unto them that had eaten. Then those men, when they had seen the miracle that Jesus did, said, This is of a truth that prophet that should come into the world.

HOLY DAYS.

Saint Andrew the Apostle.

[November 30.]

The Collect.

ALMIGHTY God, who didst give such grace unto thy holy Apostle Saint Andrew, that he readily obeyed the calling of thy Son Jesus Christ, and followed him without delay; Grant unto us all, that we, being called by thy holy Word, may forthwith give up ourselves obediently to fulfil thy holy commandments; through the same Jesus Christ our Lord. *Amen.*

The Epistle. Romans x. 9.

IF thou shalt confess with thy mouth the Lord Jesus, and shalt believe in thine heart that God hath raised him from the dead, thou shalt be saved. For with the heart man believeth unto righteousness; and with the mouth confession is made unto salvation. For the scripture saith, Whosoever believeth on him shall not be ashamed. For there is no difference between the Jew and the Greek: for the same Lord over all is rich unto all that call upon him. For whosoever shall call upon the name of the Lord shall be saved. How then shall they call on him in whom they have not believed? and how shall they believe in him of whom they have not heard? and how shall they hear without a preacher? and how shall they preach, except they be sent? as it is written, How beautiful are the feet of them that preach the gospel of peace, and bring glad tidings of good things! But they have not all obeyed the gospel. For Esaias saith, Lord, who hath believed our report? So then faith cometh by hearing, and hearing by the word of God. But I say, Have they not heard? Yes verily, their sound went into all the earth, and their words unto the ends of the world. But I say, Did not Israel know? First Moses saith, I will provoke you to jealousy by them that are no people, and by a foolish nation I will anger you. But Esaias is very bold, and saith, I was found of them that sought me not; I was made manifest unto them that asked not after me. But to Israel he saith, All day long I have stretched forth my hands unto a disobedient and gainsaying people.

The Gospel. St. Matthew iv. 18.

JESUS, walking by the sea of Galilee, saw two brethren, Simon called Peter, and Andrew his brother, casting a net into the sea: for they were fishers. And he saith unto them, Follow me, and I will make you fishers of men. And they straightway left their nets, and followed him. And going on from thence, he saw other two brethren, James the son of Zebedee, and John his brother, in a ship with Zebedee their father, mending their nets; and he called them. And they immediately left the ship and their father, and followed him.

Saint Thomas the Apostle.

[December 21.]

The Collect.

ALMIGHTY and everliving God, who, for the greater confirmation of the faith, didst suffer thy holy Apostle Thomas to be doubtful in thy Son's resurrection; Grant us so perfectly, and without all doubt, to believe in thy Son Jesus Christ, that our faith in thy sight may never be reproved. Hear us, O Lord, through the same Jesus Christ, to whom, with thee and the Holy Ghost, be all honour and glory, now and for evermore. *Amen.*

The Epistle. Hebrews x. 35, *and part of* Chap. xi.

CAST not away therefore your confidence, which hath great recompence of reward. For ye have need of patience, that, after ye have done the will of God, ye might receive the promise. For yet a little while, and he that shall come will come, and will not tarry. Now the just shall live by faith: but if any man draw back, my soul shall have no pleasure in him. But we are not of them who draw back unto perdition; but of them that believe to the saving of the soul. Now faith is the substance of things hoped for, the evidence of things not seen.

The Gospel. St. John xx. 24.

THOMAS, one of the twelve, called Didymus, was not with them when Jesus came. The other disciples therefore said unto him, We have seen the Lord. But he said unto them, Except I shall see in his hands the print of the nails, and put my finger into the print of the nails, and thrust my hand into his side, I will not believe. And after eight days again his disciples were within, and Thomas with them: then came Jesus, the doors being shut, and stood in the midst, and said, Peace be unto you. Then saith he to Thomas, Reach hither thy finger, and behold my hands; and reach hither thy hand, and thrust it into my side: and be not faithless, but believing. And Thomas answered and said unto him, My Lord and my God. Jesus saith unto him, Thomas, because thou hast seen me, thou hast believed: blessed are they that have not seen, and yet have believed. And many other signs truly did Jesus in the presence of his disciples, which are not written in this book: but these are written, that ye might believe that Jesus is the Christ, the Son of God; and that believing ye might have life through his name.

The Conversion of Saint Paul.

[January 25.]

The Collect.

O GOD, who, through the preaching of the blessed Apostle Saint Paul, hast caused the light of the Gospel to shine throughout the world; Grant, we beseech thee, that we, having his wonderful conversion in remembrance, may show forth our thankfulness unto thee for the same, by following the holy doctrine which he taught; through Jesus Christ our Lord. *Amen.*

For the Epistle. Acts ix. 1.

A ND Saul, yet breathing out threatenings and slaughter against the disciples of the Lord, went unto the high priest, and desired of him letters to Damascus to the synagogues, that if he found any of this way, whether they were men or women, he might bring them bound unto Jerusalem. And as he journeyed, he came near Damascus: and suddenly there shined round about him a light from heaven: and he fell to the earth, and heard a voice saying

Conversion of Saint Paul

unto him, Saul, Saul, why persecutest thou me? And he said, Who art thou, Lord? And the Lord said, I am Jesus whom thou persecutest: it is hard for thee to kick against the pricks. And he trembling and astonished said, Lord, what wilt thou have me to do? And the Lord said unto him, Arise, and go into the city, and it shall be told thee what thou must do. And the men which journeyed with him stood speechless, hearing a voice, but seeing no man. And Saul arose from the earth; and when his eyes were opened, he saw no man: but they led him by the hand, and brought him into Damascus. And he was three days without sight, and neither did eat nor drink. And there was a certain disciple at Damascus, named Ananias; and to him said the Lord in a vision, Ananias. And he said, Behold, I am here, Lord. And the Lord said unto him, Arise, and go into the street which is called Straight, and enquire in the house of Judas for one called Saul, of Tarsus: for, behold, he prayeth, and hath seen in a vision a man named Ananias coming in, and putting his hand on him, that he might receive his sight. Then Ananias answered, Lord, I have heard by many of this man, how much evil he hath done to thy saints at Jerusalem: and here he hath authority from the chief priests to bind all that call on thy name. But the Lord said unto him, Go thy way: for he is a chosen vessel unto me, to bear my name before the Gentiles, and kings, and the children of Israel: for I will shew him how great things he must suffer for my name's sake. And Ananias went his way, and entered into the house; and putting his hands on him said, Brother Saul, the Lord, even Jesus, that appeared unto thee in the way as thou camest, hath sent me, that thou mightest receive thy sight, and be filled with the Holy Ghost. And immediately there fell from his eyes as it had been scales: and he received sight forthwith, and arose, and was baptized. And when he had received meat, he was strengthened. Then was Saul certain days with the disciples which were at Damascus. And straightway he preached Christ in the synagogues, that he is the Son of God. But all that heard him were amazed, and said; Is not this he that destroyed them which called on this name in Jerusalem, and came hither for that intent, that he might bring them bound unto the chief priests? But Saul increased the more in strength, and confounded the Jews which dwelt at Damascus, proving that this is very Christ.

The Gospel. St. Matthew xix. 27.

PETER answered and said unto Jesus, Behold, we have forsaken all, and followed thee; what shall we have therefore? And Jesus said unto them, Verily I say unto you, That ye which have followed me, in the regeneration when the Son of man shall sit in the throne of his glory, ye also shall sit upon twelve thrones, judging the twelve tribes of Israel. And every one that hath forsaken houses, or brethren, or sisters, or father, or mother, or wife, or children, or lands, for my name's sake, shall receive an hundredfold, and shall inherit everlasting life. But many that are first shall be last; and the last shall be first.

The Presentation of Christ in the Temple, commonly called
The Purification of Saint Mary the Virgin.

[February 2.]

The Collect.

ALMIGHTY and everliving God, we humbly beseech thy Majesty, that, as thy only-begotten Son was this day presented in the temple in substance of our flesh, so we may be presented unto thee with pure and clean hearts, by the same thy Son Jesus Christ our Lord. *Amen.*

The Purification

For the Epistle. Malachi iii. 1.

BEHOLD, I will send my messenger, and he shall prepare the way before me: and the Lord, whom ye seek, shall suddenly come to his temple, even the messenger of the covenant, whom ye delight in: behold, he shall come, saith the LORD of hosts. But who may abide the day of his coming? and who shall stand when he appeareth? for he is like a refiner's fire, and like fullers' sope: and he shall sit as a refiner and purifier of silver: and he shall purify the sons of Levi, and purge them as gold and silver, that they may offer unto the LORD an offering in righteousness. Then shall the offering of Judah and Jerusalem be pleasant unto the LORD, as in the days of old, and as in former years. And I will come near to you to judgment; and I will be a swift witness against the sorcerers, and against the adulterers, and against false swearers, and against those that oppress the hireling in his wages, the widow, and the fatherless, and that turn aside the stranger from his right, and fear not me, saith the LORD of hosts.

The Gospel. St. Luke ii. 22.

AND when the days of her purification according to the law of Moses were accomplished, they brought him to Jerusalem, to present him to the Lord; (as it is written in the law of the Lord, Every male that openeth the womb shall be called holy to the Lord;) and to offer a sacrifice according to that which is said in the law of the Lord, A pair of turtle-doves, or two young pigeons. And, behold, there was a man in Jerusalem, whose name was Simeon; and the same man was just and devout, waiting for the consolation of Israel: and the Holy Ghost was upon him. And it was revealed unto him by the Holy Ghost, that he should not see death, before he had seen the Lord's Christ. And he came by the Spirit into the temple: and when the parents brought in the child Jesus, to do for him after the custom of the law, then took he him up in his arms, and blessed God, and said, Lord, now lettest thou thy servant depart in peace, according to thy word: for mine eyes have seen thy salvation, which thou hast prepared before the face of all people; a light to lighten the Gentiles, and the glory of thy people Israel. And Joseph and his mother marvelled at those things which were spoken of him. And Simeon blessed them, and said unto Mary his mother, Behold, this child is set for the fall and rising again of many in Israel; and for a sign which shall be spoken against; (yea, a sword shall pierce through thy own soul also,) that the thoughts of many hearts may be revealed. And there was one Anna, a prophetess, the daughter of Phanuel, of the tribe of Aser: she was of a great age, and had lived with an husband seven years from her virginity; and she was a widow of about fourscore and four years, which departed not from the temple, but served God with fastings and prayers night and day. And she coming in that instant gave thanks likewise unto the Lord, and spake of him to all them that looked for redemption in Jerusalem. And when they had performed all things according to the law of the Lord, they returned into Galilee, to their own city Nazareth. And the child grew, and waxed strong in spirit, filled with wisdom: and the grace of God was upon him.

Saint Matthias the Apostle.

[February 24.]

The Collect.

O ALMIGHTY God, who into the place of the traitor Judas didst choose thy faithful servant Matthias to be of the number of the twelve Apostles; Grant that thy

Saint Matthias

Church, being alway preserved from false Apostles, may be ordered and guided by faithful and true pastors; through Jesus Christ our Lord. *Amen*.

For the Epistle. Acts i. 15.

IN those days Peter stood up in the midst of the disciples, and said, (the number of names together were about an hundred and twenty,) Men and brethren, this scripture must needs have been fulfilled, which the Holy Ghost by the mouth of David spake before concerning Judas, which was guide to them that took Jesus. For he was numbered with us, and had obtained part of this ministry. Now this man purchased a field with the reward of iniquity; and falling headlong, he burst asunder in the midst, and all his bowels gushed out. And it was known unto all the dwellers at Jerusalem; insomuch as that field is called in their proper tongue, Aceldama, that is to say, The field of blood. For it is written in the book of Psalms, Let his habitation be desolate, and let no man dwell therein: and his bishoprick let another take. Wherefore of these men which have companied with us all the time that the Lord Jesus went in and out among us, beginning from the baptism of John, unto that same day that he was taken up from us, must one be ordained to be a witness with us of his resurrection. And they appointed two, Joseph called Barsabas, who was surnamed Justus, and Matthias. And they prayed, and said, Thou, Lord, which knowest the hearts of all men, shew whether of these two thou hast chosen, that he may take part of this ministry and apostleship, from which Judas by transgression fell, that he might go to his own place. And they gave forth their lots; and the lot fell upon Matthias; and he was numbered with the eleven apostles.

The Annunciation

The Gospel. St. Matthew xi. 25.

AT that time Jesus answered and said, I thank thee, O Father, Lord of heaven and earth, because thou hast hid these things from the wise and prudent, and hast revealed them unto babes. Even so, Father: for so it seemed good in thy sight. All things are delivered unto me of my Father: and no man knoweth the Son, but the Father; neither knoweth any man the Father, save the Son, and he to whomsoever the Son will reveal him. Come unto me, all ye that labour and are heavy laden, and I will give you rest. Take my yoke upon you, and learn of me; for I am meek and lowly in heart: and ye shall find rest unto your souls. For my yoke is easy, and my burden is light.

The Annunciation of the blessed Virgin Mary.

[March 25.]

The Collect.

WE beseech thee, O Lord, pour thy grace into our hearts; that, as we have known the incarnation of thy Son Jesus Christ by the message of an angel, so by his cross and passion we may be brought unto the glory of his resurrection; through the same Jesus Christ our Lord. *Amen.*

For the Epistle. Isaiah vii. 10.

MOREOVER the LORD spake again unto Ahaz, saying, Ask thee a sign of the LORD thy God; ask it either in the depth, or in the height above. But Ahaz said, I will not ask, neither will I tempt the LORD. And he said, Hear ye now, O house of David; Is it a small thing for you to weary men, but will ye weary my God also? Therefore the Lord himself shall give you a sign; Behold, a virgin shall conceive, and bear a son, and shall call his name Immanuel.

The Annunciation

Butter and honey shall he eat, that he may know to refuse the evil, and choose the good.

AND in the sixth month the angel Gabriel was sent from God unto a city of Galilee, named Nazareth, to a virgin espoused to a man whose name was Joseph, of the house of David; and the virgin's name was Mary. And the angel came in unto her, and said, Hail, thou that art highly favoured, the Lord is with thee: blessed art thou among women. And when she saw him, she was troubled at his saying, and cast in her mind what manner of salutation this should be. And the angel said unto her, Fear not, Mary: for thou hast found favour with God. And, behold, thou shalt conceive in thy womb, and bring forth a son, and shalt call his name JESUS. He shall be great, and shall be called the Son of the Highest: and the Lord God shall give unto him the throne of his father David: and he shall reign over the house of Jacob for ever; and of his kingdom there shall be no end. Then said Mary unto the angel, How shall this be, seeing I know not a man? And the angel answered and said unto her, The Holy Ghost shall come upon thee, and the power of the Highest shall overshadow thee: therefore also that holy thing which shall be born of thee shall be called the Son of God. And, behold, thy cousin Elisabeth, she hath also conceived a son in her old age: and this is the sixth month with her, who was called barren. For with God nothing shall be impossible. And Mary said, Behold the handmaid of the Lord; be it unto me according to thy word. And the angel departed from her.

Saint Mark the Evangelist.

[April 25.]

The Collect.

O ALMIGHTY God, who hast instructed thy holy Church with the heavenly doctrine of thy Evangelist Saint Mark; Give us grace that, being not like children carried away with every blast of vain doctrine, we may be established in the truth of thy holy Gospel; through Jesus Christ our Lord. *Amen.*

The Epistle. Ephesians iv. 7.

UNTO every one of us is given grace according to the measure of the gift of Christ. Wherefore he saith, When he ascended up on high, he led captivity captive, and gave gifts unto men. (Now that he ascended, what is it but that he also descended first into the lower parts of the earth? He that descended is the same also that ascended up far above all heavens, that he might fill all things.) And he gave some, apostles; and some, prophets; and some, evangelists; and some, pastors and teachers; for the perfecting of the saints, for the work of the ministry, for the edifying of the body of Christ: till we all come in the unity of the faith, and of the knowledge of the Son of God, unto a perfect man, unto the measure of the stature of the fulness of Christ: that we henceforth be no more children, tossed to and fro, and carried about with every wind of doctrine, by the sleight of men, and cunning craftiness, whereby they lie in wait to deceive; but speaking the truth in love, may grow up into him in all things, which is the head, even Christ: from whom the whole body fitly joined together and compacted by that which every joint supplieth, according to the effectual working in the measure of every part,

maketh increase of the body unto the edifying of itself
in love.

The Gospel. St. John xv. 1.

I AM the true vine, and my Father is the husbandman.
Every branch in me that beareth not fruit he taketh
away: and every branch that beareth fruit, he purgeth it,
that it may bring forth more fruit. Now ye are clean
through the word which I have spoken unto you. Abide in
me, and I in you. As the branch cannot bear fruit of itself,
except it abide in the vine; no more can ye, except ye
abide in me. I am the vine, ye are the branches: he that
abideth in me, and I in him, the same bringeth forth much
fruit: for without me ye can do nothing. If a man abide
not in me, he is cast forth as a branch, and is withered;
and men gather them, and cast them into the fire, and
they are burned. If ye abide in me, and my words abide
in you, ye shall ask what ye will, and it shall be done unto
you. Herein is my Father glorified, that ye bear much
fruit; so shall ye be my disciples. As the Father hath loved
me, so have I loved you: continue ye in my love. If ye
keep my commandments, ye shall abide in my love; even
as I have kept my Father's commandments, and abide in
his love. These things have I spoken unto you, that my
joy might remain in you, and that your joy might be full.

Saint Philip and Saint James, Apostles.

[May 1.]

The Collect.

O ALMIGHTY God, whom truly to know is everlasting life; Grant us perfectly to know thy Son Jesus
Christ to be the way, the truth, and the life; that, following the steps of thy holy Apostles, Saint Philip and Saint

St. Philip and St. James

James, we may stedfastly walk in the way that leadeth to eternal life; through the same thy Son Jesus Christ our Lord. *Amen.*

The Epistle. St. James i. 1.

JAMES, a servant of God and of the Lord Jesus Christ, to the twelve tribes which are scattered abroad, greeting. My brethren, count it all joy when ye fall into divers temptations; knowing this, that the trying of your faith worketh patience. But let patience have her perfect work, that ye may be perfect and entire, wanting nothing. If any of you lack wisdom, let him ask of God, that giveth to all men liberally, and upbraideth not; and it shall be given him. But let him ask in faith, nothing wavering. For he that wavereth is like a wave of the sea driven with the wind and tossed. For let not that man think that he shall receive any thing of the Lord. A double-minded man is unstable in all his ways. Let the brother of low degree rejoice in that he is exalted: but the rich, in that he is made low: because as the flower of the grass he shall pass away. For the sun is no sooner risen with a burning heat, but it withereth the grass, and the flower thereof falleth, and the grace of the fashion of it perisheth: so also shall the rich man fade away in his ways. Blessed is the man that endureth temptation: for when he is tried, he shall receive the crown of life, which the Lord hath promised to them that love him.

The Gospel. St. John xiv. 1.

AND Jesus said unto his disciples, Let not your heart be troubled: ye believe in God, believe also in me. In my Father's house are many mansions: if it were not so, I would have told you. I go to prepare a place for you. And if I go and prepare a place for you, I will come again, and receive you unto myself; that where I am, there ye may be also. And whither I go ye know, and the way ye know. Thomas saith unto him, Lord, we know not whither thou goest; and how can we know the way? Jesus saith unto him, I am the way, the truth, and the life: no man cometh unto the Father, but by me. If ye had known me, ye should have known my Father also: and from henceforth ye know him, and have seen him. Philip saith unto him, Lord, shew us the Father, and it sufficeth us. Jesus saith unto him, Have I been so long time with you, and yet hast thou not known me, Philip? he that hath seen me hath seen the Father; and how sayest thou then, Shew us the Father? Believest thou not that I am in the Father, and the Father in me? the words that I speak unto you I speak not of myself: but the Father that dwelleth in me, he doeth the works. Believe me that I am in the Father, and the Father in me: or else believe me for the very works' sake. Verily, verily, I say unto you, He that believeth on me, the works that I do shall he do also; and greater works than these shall he do; because I go unto my Father. And whatsoever ye shall ask in my name, that will I do, that the Father may be glorified in the Son. If ye shall ask any thing in my name, I will do it.

Saint Barnabas the Apostle.

[June 11.]

The Collect.

O LORD God Almighty, who didst endue thy holy Apostle Barnabas with singular gifts of the Holy Ghost; Leave us not, we beseech thee, destitute of thy manifold gifts, nor yet of grace to use them alway to thy honour and glory; through Jesus Christ our Lord. *Amen.*

Saint Barnabas

For the Epistle. Acts xi. 22.

TIDINGS of these things came unto the ears of the church which was in Jerusalem: and they sent forth Barnabas, that he should go as far as Antioch. Who, when he came, and had seen the grace of God, was glad, and exhorted them all, that with purpose of heart they would cleave unto the Lord. For he was a good man, and full of the Holy Ghost and of faith: and much people was added unto the Lord. Then departed Barnabas to Tarsus, for to seek Saul: and when he had found him, he brought him unto Antioch. And it came to pass, that a whole year they assembled themselves with the church, and taught much people. And the disciples were called Christians first in Antioch. And in these days came prophets from Jerusalem unto Antioch. And there stood up one of them named Agabus, and signified by the spirit that there should be great dearth throughout all the world: which came to pass in the days of Claudius Cæsar. Then the disciples, every man according to his ability, determined to send relief unto the brethren which dwelt in Judæa: which also they did, and sent it to the elders by the hands of Barnabas and Saul.

The Gospel. St. John xv. 12.

THIS is my commandment, That ye love one another, as I have loved you. Greater love hath no man than this, that a man lay down his life for his friends. Ye are my friends, if ye do whatsoever I command you. Henceforth I call you not servants; for the servant knoweth not what his lord doeth: but I have called you friends; for all things that I have heard of my Father I have made known unto you. Ye have not chosen me, but I have chosen you, and ordained you, that ye should go and bring forth fruit, and that your fruit should remain: that whatsoever ye shall ask of the Father in my name, he may give it you.

Saint John Baptist.

[June 24.]

The Collect.

ALMIGHTY God, by whose providence thy servant John Baptist was wonderfully born, and sent to prepare the way of thy Son our Saviour by preaching repentance; Make us so to follow his doctrine and holy life, that we may truly repent according to his preaching; and after his example constantly speak the truth, boldly rebuke vice, and patiently suffer for the truth's sake; through the same thy Son Jesus Christ our Lord. *Amen.*

For the Epistle. Isaiah xl. 1.

COMFORT ye, comfort ye my people, saith your God. Speak ye comfortably to Jerusalem, and cry unto her, that her warfare is accomplished, that her iniquity is pardoned: for she hath received of the LORD's hand double for all her sins. The voice of him that crieth in the wilderness, Prepare ye the way of the LORD, make straight in the desert a highway for our God. Every valley shall be exalted, and every mountain and hill shall be made low: and the crooked shall be made straight, and the rough places plain: and the glory of the LORD shall be revealed, and all flesh shall see it together: for the mouth of the LORD hath spoken it. The voice said, Cry. And he said, What shall I cry? All flesh is grass, and all the goodliness thereof is as the flower of the field: the grass withereth, the flower fadeth: because the spirit of the LORD bloweth upon it: surely the people is grass. The grass withereth, the flower fadeth: but the word of our God shall stand for ever. O

Saint John Baptist

Zion, that bringest good tidings, get thee up into the high mountain; O Jerusalem, that bringest good tidings, lift up thy voice with strength; lift it up, be not afraid; say unto the cities of Judah, Behold your God! Behold, the Lord GOD will come with strong hand, and his arm shall rule for him: behold, his reward is with him, and his work before him. He shall feed his flock like a shepherd: he shall gather the lambs with his arm, and carry them in his bosom, and shall gently lead those that are with young.

The Gospel. St. Luke i. 57.

ELISABETH'S full time came that she should be delivered; and she brought forth a son. And her neighbours and her cousins heard how the Lord had shewed great mercy upon her; and they rejoiced with her. And it came to pass, that on the eighth day they came to circumcise the child; and they called him Zacharias, after the name of his father. And his mother answered and said, Not so; but he shall be called John. And they said unto her, There is none of thy kindred that is called by this name. And they made signs to his father, how he would have him called. And he asked for a writing table, and wrote, saying, His name is John. And they marvelled all. And his mouth was opened immediately, and his tongue loosed, and he spake, and praised God. And fear came on all that dwelt round about them: and all these sayings were noised abroad throughout all the hill country of Judæa. And all they that heard them laid them up in their hearts, saying, What manner of child shall this be! And the hand of the Lord was with him. And his father Zacharias was filled with the Holy Ghost, and prophesied, saying, Blessed be the Lord God of Israel; for he hath visited and redeemed his people, and hath raised up an horn of salvation for us in the house of his servant David; as he spake by the mouth of his holy prophets, which have been since the world began: that we should be saved from our enemies, and from the hand of all that hate us; to perform the mercy promised to our fathers, and to remember his holy covenant; the oath which he sware to our father Abraham, that he would grant unto us, that we being delivered out of the hand of our enemies might serve him without fear, in holiness and righteousness before him, all the days of our life. And thou, child, shalt be called the prophet of the Highest: for thou shalt go before the face of the Lord to prepare his ways; to give knowledge of salvation unto his people by the remission of their sins, through the tender mercy of our God; whereby the dayspring from on high hath visited us, to give light to them that sit in darkness and in the shadow of death, to guide our feet into the way of peace. And the child grew, and waxed strong in spirit, and was in the deserts till the day of his shewing unto Israel.

Saint Peter the Apostle.

[June 29.]

The Collect.

O ALMIGHTY God, who by thy Son Jesus Christ didst give to thy Apostle Saint Peter many excellent gifts, and commandedst him earnestly to feed thy flock; Make, we beseech thee, all Bishops and Pastors diligently to preach thy holy Word, and the people obediently to follow the same, that they may receive the crown of everlasting glory; through the same thy Son Jesus Christ our Lord. *Amen.*

For the Epistle. Acts xii. 1.

A BOUT that time Herod the king stretched forth his hands to vex certain of the church. And he killed James the brother of John with the sword. And because

Saint Peter

he saw it pleased the Jews, he proceeded further to take Peter also. (Then were the days of unleavened bread.) And when he had apprehended him, he put him in prison, and delivered him to four quaternions of soldiers to keep him; intending after Easter to bring him forth to the people. Peter therefore was kept in prison: but prayer was made without ceasing of the church unto God for him. And when Herod would have brought him forth, the same night Peter was sleeping between two soldiers, bound with two chains: and the keepers before the door kept the prison. And, behold, the angel of the Lord came upon him, and a light shined in the prison: and he smote Peter on the side, and raised him up, saying, Arise up quickly. And his chains fell off from his hands. And the angel said unto him, Gird thyself, and bind on thy sandals. And so he did. And he saith unto him, Cast thy garment about thee, and follow me. And he went out, and followed him; and wist not that it was true which was done by the angel; but thought he saw a vision. When they were past the first and the second ward, they came unto the iron gate that leadeth unto the city; which opened to them of his own accord: and they went out, and passed on through one street; and forthwith the angel departed from him. And when Peter was come to himself, he said, Now I know of a surety, that the Lord hath sent his angel, and hath delivered me out of the hand of Herod, and from all the expectation of the people of the Jews.

The Gospel. St. Matthew xvi. 13.

WHEN Jesus came into the coasts of Cæsarea Philippi, he asked his disciples, saying, Whom do men say that I the Son of man am? And they said, Some say that thou art John the Baptist: some, Elias; and others, Jeremias, or one of the prophets. He saith unto them, But whom say ye that I am? And Simon Peter answered and said, Thou art the Christ, the Son of the living God. And Jesus answered and said unto him, Blessed art thou, Simon Bar-jona: for flesh and blood hath not revealed it unto thee, but my Father which is in heaven. And I say also unto thee, That thou art Peter, and upon this rock I will build my church; and the gates of hell shall not prevail against it. And I will give unto thee the keys of the kingdom of heaven: and whatsoever thou shalt bind on earth shall be bound in heaven: and whatsoever thou shalt loose on earth shall be loosed in heaven.

Saint James the Apostle.

[July 25.]

The Collect.

G RANT, O merciful God, that, as thine holy Apostle Saint James, leaving his father and all that he had, without delay was obedient unto the calling of thy Son Jesus Christ, and followed him; so we, forsaking all worldly and carnal affections, may be evermore ready to follow thy holy commandments; through the same Jesus Christ our Lord. *Amen.*

For the Epistle. Acts xi. 27, *and part of* Chap. xii.

I N these days came prophets from Jerusalem unto Antioch. And there stood up one of them named Agabus, and signified by the spirit that there should be great dearth throughout all the world: which came to pass in the days of Claudius Cæsar. Then the disciples, every man according to his ability, determined to send relief unto the brethren which dwelt in Judæa: which also they did, and sent it to the elders by the hands of Barnabas and Saul. Now about that time Herod the king stretched forth his hands to vex certain of the church. And he killed James the brother of John with the sword. And because he saw it pleased the Jews, he proceeded further to take Peter also.

The Gospel. St. Matthew xx. 20.

THEN came to him the mother of Zebedee's children with her sons, worshipping him, and desiring a certain thing of him. And he said unto her, What wilt thou? She saith unto him, Grant that these my two sons may sit, the one on thy right hand, and the other on the left, in thy kingdom. But Jesus answered and said, Ye know not what ye ask. Are ye able to drink of the cup that I shall drink of, and to be baptized with the baptism that I am baptized with? They say unto him, We are able. And he saith unto them, Ye shall drink indeed of my cup, and be baptized with the baptism that I am baptized with: but to sit on my right hand, and on my left, is not mine to give, but it shall be given to them for whom it is prepared of my Father. And when the ten heard it, they were moved with indignation against the two brethren. But Jesus called them unto him, and said, Ye know that the princes of the Gentiles exercise dominion over them, and they that are great exercise authority upon them. But it shall not be so among you: but whosoever will be great among you, let him be your minister; and whosoever will be chief among you, let him be your servant: even as the Son of man came not to be ministered unto, but to minister, and to give his life a ransom for many.

The Transfiguration of Christ.

[August 6.]

The Collect.

O GOD, who on the mount didst reveal to chosen witnesses thine only-begotten Son wonderfully transfig-

The Transfiguration

ured, in raiment white and glistering; Mercifully grant that we, being delivered from the disquietude of this world, may be permitted to behold the King in his beauty, who with thee, O Father, and thee, O Holy Ghost, liveth and reigneth, one God, world without end. *Amen.*

The Epistle. 2 St. Peter i. 13.

I THINK it meet, as long as I am in this tabernacle, to stir you up by putting you in remembrance; knowing that shortly I must put off this my tabernacle, even as our Lord Jesus Christ hath shewed me. Moreover I will endeavour that ye may be able after my decease to have these things always in remembrance. For we have not followed cunningly devised fables, when we made known unto you the power and coming of our Lord Jesus Christ, but were eyewitnesses of his majesty. For he received from God the Father honour and glory, when there came such a voice to him from the excellent glory, This is my beloved Son, in whom I am well pleased. And this voice which came from heaven we heard, when we were with him in the holy mount.

The Gospel. St. Luke ix. 28.

A ND it came to pass about an eight days after these sayings, he took Peter and John and James, and went up into a mountain to pray. And as he prayed, the fashion of his countenance was altered, and his raiment was white and glistering. And, behold, there talked with him two men, which were Moses and Elias: who appeared in glory, and spake of his decease which he should accomplish at Jerusalem. But Peter and they that were with him were heavy with sleep: and when they were awake, they saw his glory, and the two men that stood with him. And it came to pass, as they departed from him, Peter said unto Jesus,

Master, it is good for us to be here: and let us make three tabernacles; one for thee, and one for Moses, and one for Elias: not knowing what he said. While he thus spake, there came a cloud, and overshadowed them: and they feared as they entered into the cloud. And there came a voice out of the cloud, saying, This is my beloved Son: hear him. And when the voice was past, Jesus was found alone. And they kept it close, and told no man in those days any of those things which they had seen.

Saint Bartholomew the Apostle.

[August 24.]

The Collect.

O ALMIGHTY and everlasting God, who didst give to thine Apostle Bartholomew grace truly to believe and to preach thy Word; Grant, we beseech thee, unto thy Church, to love that Word which he believed, and both to preach and receive the same; through Jesus Christ our Lord. *Amen.*

For the Epistle. Acts v. 12.

BY the hands of the apostles were many signs and wonders wrought among the people; (and they were all with one accord in Solomon's porch. And of the rest durst no man join himself to them: but the people magnified them. And believers were the more added to the Lord, multitudes both of men and women.) Insomuch that they brought forth the sick into the streets, and laid them on beds and couches, that at the least the shadow of Peter passing by might overshadow some of them. There came also a multitude out of the cities round about unto Jerusalem, bringing sick folks, and them which were vexed with unclean spirits: and they were healed every one.

The Gospel. St. Luke xxii. 24.

AND there was also a strife among them, which of them should be accounted the greatest. And he said unto them, The kings of the Gentiles exercise lordship over them; and they that exercise authority upon them are called benefactors. But ye shall not be so: but he that is greatest among you, let him be as the younger; and he that is chief, as he that doth serve. For whether is greater, he that sitteth at meat, or he that serveth? is not he that sitteth at meat? but I am among you as he that serveth. Ye are they which have continued with me in my temptations. And I appoint unto you a kingdom, as my Father hath appointed unto me; that ye may eat and drink at my table in my kingdom, and sit on thrones judging the twelve tribes of Israel.

Saint Matthew, Apostle and Evangelist.

[September 21.]

The Collect.

O ALMIGHTY God, who by thy blessed Son didst call Matthew from the receipt of custom to be an Apostle and Evangelist; Grant us grace to forsake all covetous desires, and inordinate love of riches, and to follow the same 'hy Son Jesus Christ, who liveth and reigneth with thee and the Holy Ghost, one God, world without end. *Amen.*

The Epistle. 2 Corinthians iv. 1.

THEREFORE seeing we have this ministry, as we have received mercy, we faint not; but have renounced the hidden things of dishonesty, not walking in craftiness, nor handling the word of God deceitfully; but by manifestation of the truth commending ourselves to every man's conscience in the sight of God. But if our gospel be hid, it is hid to them that are lost: in whom the god of this world hath blinded the minds of them which believe not, lest the light of the glorious gospel of Christ, who is the image of God, should shine unto them. For we preach not ourselves, but Christ Jesus the Lord; and ourselves your servants for Jesus' sake. For God, who commanded the light to shine out of darkness, hath shined in our hearts, to give the light of the knowledge of the glory of God in the face of Jesus Christ.

The Gospel. St. Matthew ix. 9.

AND as Jesus passed forth from thence, he saw a man, named Matthew, sitting at the receipt of custom: and he saith unto him, Follow me. And he arose, and followed him. And it came to pass, as Jesus sat at meat in the house, behold, many publicans and sinners came and sat down with him and his disciples. And when the Pharisees saw it, they said unto his disciples, Why eateth your Master with publicans and sinners? But when Jesus heard that, he said unto them, They that be whole need not a physician, but they that are sick. But go ye and learn what that meaneth, I will have mercy, and not sacrifice: for I am not come to call the righteous, but sinners to repentance.

Saint Michael and all Angels.

[September 29.]

The Collect.

O EVERLASTING God, who hast ordained and constituted the services of Angels and men in a wonderful order; Mercifully grant that, as thy holy Angels always do thee service in heaven, so, by thy appointment, they may succour and defend us on earth; through Jesus Christ our Lord. *Amen.*

St. Michael and all Angels

For the Epistle. Revelation xii. 7.

THERE was war in heaven: Michael and his angels fought against the dragon; and the dragon fought and his angels, and prevailed not; neither was their place found any more in heaven. And the great dragon was cast out, that old serpent, called the Devil, and Satan, which deceiveth the whole world: he was cast out into the earth, and his angels were cast out with him. And I heard a loud voice saying in heaven, Now is come salvation, and strength, and the kingdom of our God, and the power of his Christ: for the accuser of our brethren is cast down, which accused them before our God day and night. And they overcame him by the blood of the Lamb, and by the word of their testimony; and they loved not their lives unto the death. Therefore rejoice, ye heavens, and ye that dwell in them. Woe to the inhabiters of the earth and of the sea! for the devil is come down unto you, having great wrath, because he knoweth that he hath but a short time.

The Gospel. St. Matthew xviii. 1.

AT the same time came the disciples unto Jesus, saying, Who is the greatest in the kingdom of heaven? And Jesus called a little child unto him, and set him in the midst of them, and said, Verily I say unto you, Except ye be converted, and become as little children, ye shall not enter into the kingdom of heaven. Whosoever therefore shall humble himself as this little child, the same is greatest in the kingdom of heaven. And whoso shall receive one such little child in my name receiveth me. But whoso shall offend one of these little ones which believe in me, it were better for him that a millstone were hanged about his neck, and that he were drowned in the depth of the sea. Woe unto the world because of offences! for it must needs be that offences come; but woe to that man by whom the offence cometh! Wherefore if thy hand or thy foot offend thee, cut them off, and cast them from thee: it is better for thee to enter into life halt or maimed, rather than having two hands or two feet to be cast into everlasting fire. And if thine eye offend thee, pluck it out, and cast it from thee: it is better for thee to enter into life with one eye, rather than having two eyes to be cast into hell-fire. Take heed that ye despise not one of these little ones; for I say unto you, That in heaven their angels do always behold the face of my Father which is in heaven.

Saint Luke the Evangelist.

[October 18.]

The Collect.

ALMIGHTY God, who didst inspire thy servant Saint Luke the Physician, to set forth in the Gospel the love and healing power of thy Son; Manifest in thy Church the like power and love, to the healing of our bodies and our souls; through the same thy Son Jesus Christ our Lord. *Amen.*

The Epistle. 2 Timothy iv. 5.

WATCH thou in all things, endure afflictions, do the work of an evangelist, make full proof of thy ministry. For I am now ready to be offered, and the time of my departure is at hand. I have fought a good fight, I have finished my course, I have kept the faith: henceforth there is laid up for me a crown of righteousness, which the Lord, the righteous judge, shall give me at that day: and not to me only, but unto all them also that love his appearing. Do thy diligence to come shortly unto me: for Demas hath forsaken me, having loved this present world, and is departed unto Thessalonica; Crescens to Galatia, Titus unto

Dalmatia. Only Luke is with me. Take Mark, and bring him with thee: for he is profitable to me for the ministry. And Tychicus have I sent to Ephesus. The cloke that I left at Troas with Carpus, when thou comest, bring with thee, and the books, but especially the parchments. Alexander the coppersmith did me much evil: the Lord reward him according to his works: of whom be thou ware also; for he hath greatly withstood our words.

The Gospel. St. Luke x. 1.

THE Lord appointed other seventy also, and sent them two and two before his face into every city and place, whither he himself would come. Therefore said he unto them, The harvest truly is great, but the labourers are few: pray ye therefore the Lord of the harvest, that he would send forth labourers into his harvest. Go your ways: behold, I send you forth as lambs among wolves. Carry neither purse, nor scrip, nor shoes: and salute no man by the way. And into whatsoever house ye enter, first say, Peace be to this house. And if the son of peace be there, your peace shall rest upon it: if not, it shall turn to you again. And in the same house remain, eating and drinking such things as they give: for the labourer is worthy of his hire.

Saint Simon and Saint Jude, Apostles.

[October 28.]

The Collect.

O ALMIGHTY God, who hast built thy Church upon the foundation of the Apostles and Prophets, Jesus Christ himself being the head corner-stone; Grant us so to be joined together in unity of spirit by their doctrine, that we may be made an holy temple acceptable unto thee; through the same Jesus Christ our Lord. *Amen.*

St. Simon and St. Jude

The Epistle. Ephesians ii. 19.

NOW therefore ye are no more strangers and foreigners, but fellow-citizens with the saints, and of the household of God; and are built upon the foundation of the apostles and prophets, Jesus Christ himself being the chief corner-stone; in whom all the building fitly framed together groweth unto an holy temple in the Lord: in whom ye also are builded together for an habitation of God through the Spirit.

The Gospel. St. John xv. 17.

THESE things I command you, that ye love one another. If the world hate you, ye know that it hated me before it hated you. If ye were of the world, the world would love his own: but because ye are not of the world, but I have chosen you out of the world, therefore the world hateth you. Remember the word that I said unto you, The servant is not greater than his lord. If they have persecuted me, they will also persecute you; if they have kept my saying, they will keep your's also. But all these things will they do unto you for my name's sake, because they know not him that sent me. If I had not come and spoken unto them, they had not had sin: but now they have no cloke for their sin. He that hateth me hateth my Father also. If I had not done among them the works which none other man did, they had not had sin: but now have they both seen and hated both me and my Father. But this cometh to pass, that the word might be fulfilled that is written in their law, They hated me without a cause. But when the Comforter is come, whom I will send unto you from the Father, even the Spirit of truth, which proceedeth from the Father, he shall testify of me: and ye also shall bear witness, because ye have been with me from the beginning.

All Saints' Day.

[November 1.]

The Collect.

O ALMIGHTY God, who hast knit together thine
elect in one communion and fellowship, in the mystical body of thy Son Christ our Lord; Grant us grace
so to follow thy blessed Saints in all virtuous and godly
living, that we may come to those unspeakable joys which
thou hast prepared for those who unfeignedly love thee;
through the same thy Son Jesus Christ our Lord. *Amen.*

¶ *This Collect is to be said daily throughout the Octave.*

For the Epistle. Revelation vii. 2.

A ND I saw another angel ascending from the east, having the seal of the living God: and he cried with a
loud voice to the four angels, to whom it was given to
hurt the earth and the sea, saying, Hurt not the earth,
neither the sea, nor the trees, till we have sealed the servants of our God in their foreheads. And I heard the number of them which were sealed: and there were sealed an
hundred and forty and four thousand of all the tribes of
the children of Israel.

After this I beheld, and, lo, a great multitude, which no
man could number, of all nations, and kindreds, and peoples,
and tongues, stood before the throne, and before the Lamb,
clothed with white robes, and palms in their hands; and
cried with a loud voice, saying, Salvation to our God which
sitteth upon the throne, and unto the Lamb. And all the
angels stood round about the throne, and about the elders
and the four living creatures, and fell before the throne on
their faces, and worshipped God, saying, Amen: Blessing,
and glory, and wisdom, and thanksgiving, and honour, and

All Saints' Day

power, and might, be unto our God for ever and ever. Amen.

And one of the elders answered, saying unto me, What are these which are arrayed in white robes? and whence came they? And I said unto him, Sir, thou knowest. And he said to me, These are they which came out of great tribulation, and have washed their robes, and made them white in the blood of the Lamb. Therefore are they before the throne of God, and serve him day and night in his temple: and he that sitteth on the throne shall dwell among them. They shall hunger no more, neither thirst any more; neither shall the sun light on them, nor any heat. For the Lamb which is in the midst of the throne shall feed them, and shall lead them unto living fountains of waters: and God shall wipe away all tears from their eyes.

The Gospel. St. Matthew v. 1.

JESUS seeing the multitudes, went up into a mountain: and when he was set, his disciples came unto him: and he opened his mouth, and taught them, saying, Blessed are the poor in spirit: for their's is the kingdom of heaven. Blessed are they that mourn: for they shall be comforted. Blessed are the meek: for they shall inherit the earth. Blessed are they which do hunger and thirst after righteousness: for they shall be filled. Blessed are the merciful: for they shall obtain mercy. Blessed are the pure in heart: for they shall see God. Blessed are the peacemakers: for they shall be called the children of God. Blessed are they which are persecuted for righteousness' sake: for their's is the kingdom of heaven. Blessed are ye, when men shall revile you, and persecute you, and shall say all manner of evil against you falsely, for my sake. Rejoice, and be exceeding glad: for great is your reward in heaven: for so persecuted they the prophets which were before you.

A Saint's Day

A Saint's Day.

The Collect.

ALMIGHTY and everlasting God, who dost enkindle the flame of thy love in the hearts of the Saints; Grant to us, thy humble servants, the same faith and power of love; that, as we rejoice in their triumphs, we may profit by their examples; through Jesus Christ our Lord. *Amen.*

¶ *Or this.*

O ALMIGHTY God, who hast called us to faith in thee, and hast compassed us about with so great a cloud of witnesses; Grant that we, encouraged by the good examples of thy Saints, and especially of thy servant [Saint ———], may persevere in running the race that is set before us, until at length, through thy mercy, we, with them, attain to thine eternal joy; through him who is the author and finisher of our faith, thy Son Jesus Christ our Lord. *Amen.*

The Epistle. Hebrews xii. 1.

SEEING we also are compassed about with so great a cloud of witnesses, let us lay aside every weight, and the sin which doth so easily beset us, and let us run with patience the race that is set before us, looking unto Jesus the author and finisher of our faith; who for the joy that was set before him endured the cross, despising the shame, and is set down at the right hand of the throne of God.

The Gospel. St. Matthew xxv. 31.

WHEN the Son of man shall come in his glory, and all the holy angels with him, then shall he sit upon the throne of his glory: and before him shall be gathered all nations: and he shall separate them one from another, as a shepherd divideth his sheep from the goats: and he shall set the sheep on his right hand, but the goats on the left. Then shall the King say unto them on his right hand, Come, ye blessed of my Father, inherit the kingdom prepared for you from the foundation of the world: for I was an hungred, and ye gave me meat: I was thirsty, and ye gave me drink: I was a stranger, and ye took me in: naked, and ye clothed me: I was sick, and ye visited me: I was in prison, and ye came unto me. Then shall the righteous answer him, saying, Lord, when saw we thee an hungred, and fed thee? or thirsty, and gave thee drink? When saw we thee a stranger, and took thee in? or naked, and clothed thee? Or when saw we thee sick, or in prison, and came unto thee? And the King shall answer and say unto them, Verily I say unto you, Inasmuch as ye have done it unto one of the least of these my brethren, ye have done it unto me.

Feast of the Dedication of a Church.

The Collect.

O GOD, whom year by year we praise for the dedication of this church; Hear, we beseech thee, the prayers of thy people, and grant that whosoever shall worship before thee in this place, may obtain thy merciful aid and protection; through Jesus Christ our Lord. *Amen.*

The Epistle. 1 St. Peter ii. 1.

LAYING aside all malice, and all guile, and hypocrisies, and envies, and all evil speakings, as newborn babes, desire the sincere milk of the word, that ye may grow thereby: if so be ye have tasted that the Lord is gracious. To whom coming, as unto a living stone, disallowed indeed of men, but chosen of God, and precious, ye also, as lively stones, are built up a spiritual house, an holy priesthood, to offer up spiritual sacrifices, acceptable to God by Jesus Christ.

Ember Days

The Gospel. St. Matthew xxi. 12.

JESUS went into the temple of God, and cast out all them that sold and bought in the temple, and overthrew the tables of the money-changers, and the seats of them that sold doves, and said unto them, It is written, My house shall be called the house of prayer; but ye have made it a den of thieves. And the blind and the lame came to him in the temple; and he healed them. And when the chief priests and scribes saw the wonderful things that he did, and the children crying in the temple, and saying, Hosanna to the son of David; they were sore displeased, and said unto him, Hearest thou what these say? And Jesus saith unto them, Yea; have ye never read, Out of the mouth of babes and sucklings thou hast perfected praise?

The Ember Days

At the Four Seasons.

The Collect.

O ALMIGHTY God, who hast committed to the hands of men the ministry of reconciliation; We humbly beseech thee, by the inspiration of thy Holy Spirit, to put it into the hearts of many to offer themselves for this ministry; that thereby mankind may be drawn to thy blessed kingdom; through Jesus Christ our Lord. *Amen.*

For the Epistle. Acts xiii. 44.

THE next sabbath day came almost the whole city together to hear the word of God. But when the Jews saw the multitudes, they were filled with envy, and spake against those things which were spoken by Paul, contradicting and blaspheming. Then Paul and Barnabas waxed bold, and said, It was necessary that the word of God should first have been spoken to you: but seeing ye put it from you, and judge yourselves unworthy of everlasting life, lo, we turn to the Gentiles. For so hath the Lord commanded us, saying, I have set thee to be a light of the Gentiles, that thou shouldest be for salvation unto the ends of the earth. And when the Gentiles heard this, they were glad, and glorified the word of the Lord: and as many as were ordained to eternal life believed. And the word of the Lord was published throughout all the region.

The Gospel. St. Luke iv. 16.

JESUS came to Nazareth, where he had been brought up: and, as his custom was, he went into the synagogue on the sabbath day, and stood up for to read. And there was delivered unto him the book of the prophet Esaias. And when he had opened the book, he found the place where it was written, The Spirit of the Lord is upon me, because he hath anointed me to preach the gospel to the poor; he hath sent me to heal the brokenhearted, to preach deliverance to the captives, and recovering of sight to the blind, to set at liberty them that are bruised, to preach the acceptable year of the Lord. And he closed the book, and he gave it again to the minister, and sat down. And the eyes of all them that were in the synagogue were fastened on him. And he began to say unto them, This day is this scripture fulfilled in your ears.

The Rogation Days

Being the Three Days before Ascension Day.

The Collect.

ALMIGHTY God, Lord of heaven and earth; We beseech thee to pour forth thy blessing upon this land, and to give us a fruitful season; that we, constantly receiving thy bounty, may evermore give thanks unto thee

Rogation Days

in thy holy Church; through Jesus Christ our Lord. *Amen.*

For the Epistle. Ezekiel xxxiv. 25.

I WILL make with them a covenant of peace, and will cause the evil beasts to cease out of the land: and they shall dwell safely in the wilderness, and sleep in the woods. And I will make them and the places round about my hill a blessing; and I will cause the shower to come down in his season; there shall be showers of blessing. And the tree of the field shall yield her fruit, and the earth shall yield her increase, and they shall be safe in their land, and shall know that I am the LORD, when I have broken the bands of their yoke, and delivered them out of the hand of those that served themselves of them. And they shall no more be a prey to the heathen, neither shall the beast of the land devour them; but they shall dwell safely, and none shall make them afraid. And I will raise up for them a plant of renown, and they shall be no more consumed with hunger in the land, neither bear the shame of the heathen any more. Thus shall they know that I the LORD their God am with them, and that they, even the house of Israel, are my people, saith the Lord GOD. And ye my flock, the flock of my pasture, are men, and I am your God, saith the Lord GOD.

The Gospel. St. Luke xi. 5.

JESUS said unto them, Which of you shall have a friend, and shall go unto him at midnight, and say unto him, Friend, lend me three loaves; for a friend of mine in his journey is come to me, and I have nothing to set before him? and he from within shall answer and say, Trouble me not: the door is now shut, and my children are with me in bed; I cannot rise and give thee. I say unto you, Though he will not rise and give him, because he is his friend, yet because of his importunity he will rise and give him as many as he needeth. And I say unto you, Ask, and it shall be given you; seek, and ye shall find; knock, and it shall be opened unto you. For every one that asketh receiveth; and he that seeketh findeth; and to him that knocketh it shall be opened. If a son shall ask bread of any of you that is a father, will he give him a stone? or if he ask a fish, will he for a fish give him a serpent? or if he shall ask an egg, will he offer him a scorpion? If ye then, being evil, know how to give good gifts unto your children: how much more shall your heavenly Father give the Holy Spirit to them that ask him?

Independence Day.

[July 4.]

The Collect.

O ETERNAL God, through whose mighty power our fathers won their liberties of old; Grant, we beseech thee, that we and all the people of this land may have grace to maintain these liberties in righteousness and peace; through Jesus Christ our Lord. *Amen.*

For the Epistle. Deuteronomy x. 17.

THE LORD your God is God of gods, and Lord of lords, a great God, a mighty, and a terrible, which regardeth not persons, nor taketh reward: he doth execute the judgment of the fatherless and widow, and loveth the stranger, in giving him food and raiment. Love ye therefore the stranger: for ye were strangers in the land of Egypt. Thou shalt fear the LORD thy God; him shalt thou serve, and to him shalt thou cleave, and swear by his name. He is thy praise, and he is thy God, that hath done for thee these great and terrible things, which thine eyes have seen.

Thanksgiving Day

The Gospel. St. Matthew v. 43,

JESUS said, Ye have heard that it hath been said, Thou shalt love thy neighbour, and hate thine enemy. But I say unto you, Love your enemies, bless them that curse you, do good to them that hate you, and pray for them which despitefully use you, and persecute you; that ye may be the children of your Father which is in heaven: for he maketh his sun to rise on the evil and on the good, and sendeth rain on the just and on the unjust. For if ye love them which love you, what reward have ye? do not even the publicans the same? And if ye salute your brethren only, what do ye more than others? do not even the publicans so? Be ye therefore perfect, even as your Father which is in heaven is perfect.

Thanksgiving Day.

¶ *Instead of the Venite, the following shall be said or sung.*

O PRAISE the LORD, for it is a good thing to sing praises unto our God; * yea, a joyful and pleasant thing it is to be thankful.

The LORD doth build up Jerusalem, * and gather together the outcasts of Israel.

He healeth those that are broken in heart, * and giveth medicine to heal their sickness.

O sing unto the LORD with thanksgiving; * sing praises upon the harp unto our God:

Who covereth the heaven with clouds, and prepareth rain for the earth; * and maketh the grass to grow upon the mountains, and herb for the use of men;

Who giveth fodder unto the cattle, * and feedeth the young ravens that call upon him.

Praise the LORD, O Jerusalem; * praise thy God, O Sion.

Thanksgiving Day

For he hath made fast the bars of thy gates, * and hath blessed thy children within thee.

He maketh peace in thy borders, * and filleth thee with the flour of wheat.

Glory be to the Father, and to the Son, * and to the Holy Ghost;

As it was in the beginning, is now, and ever shall be, * world without end. Amen.

The Collect.

O MOST merciful Father, who hast blessed the labours of the husbandman in the returns of the fruits of the earth; We give thee humble and hearty thanks for this thy bounty; beseeching thee to continue thy loving-kindness to us, that our land may still yield her increase, to thy glory and our comfort; through Jesus Christ our Lord. *Amen.*

The Epistle. St. James i. 16.

DO not err, my beloved brethren. Every good gift and every perfect gift is from above, and cometh down from the Father of lights, with whom is no variableness, neither shadow of turning. Of his own will begat he us with the word of truth, that we should be a kind of firstfruits of his creatures. Wherefore, my beloved brethren, let every man be swift to hear, slow to speak, slow to wrath: for the wrath of man worketh not the righteousness of God. Wherefore lay apart all filthiness and superfluity of naughtiness, and receive with meekness the engrafted word, which is able to save your souls. But be ye doers of the word, and not hearers only, deceiving your own selves. For if any be a hearer of the word, and not a doer, he is like unto a man beholding his natural face in a glass: for he beholdeth himself, and goeth his way, and straightway forgetteth what manner of man he was. But whoso looketh into the perfect

265

Thanksgiving Day

law of liberty, and continueth therein, he being not a forgetful hearer, but a doer of the work, this man shall be blessed in his deed. If any man among you seem to be religious, and bridleth not his tongue, but deceiveth his own heart, this man's religion is vain. Pure religion and undefiled before God and the Father is this, To visit the fatherless and widows in their affliction, and to keep himself unspotted from the world.

The Gospel. St. Matthew vi. 25.

JESUS said, Be not anxious for your life, what ye shall eat, or what ye shall drink; nor yet for your body, what ye shall put on. Is not the life more than food, and the body than raiment? Behold the fowls of the air: for they sow not, neither do they reap, nor gather into barns; yet your heavenly Father feedeth them. Are ye not much better than they? Which of you by being anxious can add one cubit unto the measure of his life? And why are ye anxious for raiment? Consider the lilies of the field, how they grow; they toil not, neither do they spin: and yet I say unto you, That even Solomon in all his glory was not arrayed like one of these. Wherefore, if God so clothe the grass of the field, which to-day is, and to-morrow is cast into the oven, shall he not much more clothe you, O ye of little faith? Therefore be not anxious, saying, What shall we eat? or, What shall we drink? or, Wherewithal shall we be clothed? (For after all these things do the Gentiles seek:) for your heavenly Father knoweth that ye have need of all these things. But seek ye first the kingdom of God, and his righteousness; and all these things shall be added unto you. Be not therefore anxious for the morrow: for the morrow shall take thought for the things of itself. Sufficient unto the day is the evil thereof.

At a Marriage

At a Marriage.

The Collect.

O ETERNAL God, we humbly beseech thee, favourably to behold these thy servants now (*or* about to be)
joined in wedlock according to thy holy ordinance; and
grant that they, seeking first thy kingdom and thy righteousness, may obtain the manifold blessings of thy grace;
through Jesus Christ our Lord. *Amen.*

The Epistle. Ephesians v. 20.

GIVE thanks always for all things unto God and the
Father in the name of our Lord Jesus Christ; submitting yourselves one to another in the fear of God. Wives,
submit yourselves unto your own husbands, as unto the
Lord. For the husband is the head of the wife, even as
Christ is the head of the church: and he is the saviour of
the body. Therefore as the church is subject unto Christ,
so let the wives be to their own husbands in every thing.
Husbands, love your wives, even as Christ also loved the
church, and gave himself for it; that he might sanctify and
cleanse it with the washing of water by the word, that he
might present it to himself a glorious church, not having
spot, or wrinkle, or any such thing; but that it should be
holy and without blemish. So ought men to love their
wives as their own bodies. He that loveth his wife loveth
himself. For no man ever yet hated his own flesh; but
nourisheth and cherisheth it, even as the Lord the church:
for we are members of his body, of his flesh, and of his
bones. For this cause shall a man leave his father and mother,
and shall be joined unto his wife, and they two shall be
one flesh. This is a great mystery: but I speak concerning
Christ and the church. Nevertheless let every one of you in

At a Burial

particular so love his wife even as himself; and the wife see that she reverence her husband.

The Gospel. St. Matthew xix. 4.

JESUS answered and said unto them, Have ye not read, that he which made them at the beginning made them male and female, and said, For this cause shall a man leave father and mother, and shall cleave to his wife: and they twain shall be one flesh? Wherefore they are no more twain, but one flesh. What therefore God hath joined to-gether, let not man put asunder.

At the Burial of the Dead.

The Collect.

O ETERNAL Lord God, who holdest all souls in life; Vouchsafe, we beseech thee, to thy whole Church in paradise and on earth, thy light and thy peace; and grant that we, following the good examples of those who have served thee here and are now at rest, may at the last enter with them into thine unending joy; through Jesus Christ our Lord. *Amen.*

¶ *Or this.*

O GOD, whose mercies cannot be numbered; Accept our prayers on behalf of the soul of thy servant de-parted, and grant *him* an entrance into the land of light and joy, in the fellowship of thy saints; through Jesus Christ our Lord. *Amen.*

The Epistle. 1 Thessalonians iv. 13.

I WOULD not have you to be ignorant, brethren, con-cerning them which are asleep, that ye sorrow not, even as others which have no hope. For if we believe that Jesus died and rose again, even so them also which sleep in Jesus

At a Burial

will God bring with him. For this we say unto you by the word of the Lord, that we which are alive and remain unto the coming of the Lord shall not prevent them which are asleep. For the Lord himself shall descend from heaven with a shout, with the voice of the archangel, and with the trump of God: and the dead in Christ shall rise first: then we which are alive and remain shall be caught up together with them in the clouds, to meet the Lord in the air: and so shall we ever be with the Lord. Wherefore comfort one another with these words.

The Gospel. St. John vi. 37.

JESUS said unto them, All that the Father giveth me shall come to me; and him that cometh to me I will in no wise cast out. For I came down from heaven, not to do mine own will, but the will of him that sent me. And this is the Father's will which hath sent me, that of all which he hath given me I should lose nothing, but should raise it up again at the last day. And this is the will of him that sent me, that every one which seeth the Son, and believeth on him, may have everlasting life: and I will raise him up at the last day.

The Ministration of
Holy Baptism

together with

The Offices of Instruction

The Order of Confirmation

The Solemnization of Matrimony

The Thanksgiving after Child-birth

The Visitation of the Sick

The Communion of the Sick

The Burial of the Dead

The Ministration of Holy Baptism

¶ *The Minister of every Parish shall often admonish the People, that they defer not the Baptism of their Children, and that it is most convenient that Baptism should be administered upon Sundays and other Holy Days. Nevertheless, if necessity so require, Baptism may be administered upon any other day. And also he shall warn them that, except for urgent cause, they seek not to have their Children baptized in their houses.*

¶ *There shall be for every Male-child to be baptized, when they can be had, two Godfathers and one Godmother; and for every Female, one Godfather and two Godmothers; and Parents shall be admitted as Sponsors, if it be desired.*

¶ *When there are Children to be baptized, the Parents or Sponsors shall give knowledge thereof to the Minister. And then the Godfathers and Godmothers, and the People with the Children, must be ready at the Font, either immediately after the Second Lesson at Morning or Evening Prayer, or at such other time as the Minister shall appoint.*

¶ *When any such Persons as are of riper years are to be baptized, timely notice shall be given to the Minister; that so due care may be taken for their examination, whether they be sufficiently instructed in the Principles of the Christian Religion; and that they may be exhorted to prepare themselves, with Prayers and Fasting, for the receiving of this holy Sacrament. And* NOTE, *That at the time of the Baptism of an Adult, there shall be present with him at the Font at least two Witnesses.*

¶ *The Minister, having come to the Font, which is then to be filled with pure Water, shall say as followeth, the People all standing,*

HATH this Child (Person) been already baptized, or no?

¶ *If they answer,* No: *then shall the Minister proceed as followeth.*

DEARLY beloved, forasmuch as our Saviour Christ saith, None can enter into the kingdom of God, except he be regenerate and born anew of Water and of the Holy Ghost; I beseech you to call upon God the Father, through

273

Holy Baptism

our Lord Jesus Christ, that of his bounteous mercy he will grant to *this Child* (*this Person*) that which by nature *he* cannot have; that *he* may be baptized with Water and the Holy Ghost, and received into Christ's holy Church, and be made *a* living *member* of the same.

¶ *Then shall the Minister say,*

Let us pray.

ALMIGHTY and immortal God, the aid of all who need, the helper of all who flee to thee for succour, the life of those who believe, and the resurrection of the dead; We call upon thee for *this Child* (*this* thy *Servant*), that *he,* coming to thy holy Baptism, may receive remission of sin, by spiritual regeneration. Receive *him,* O Lord, as thou hast promised by thy well-beloved Son, saying, Ask, and ye shall have; seek, and ye shall find; knock, and it shall be opened unto you. So give now unto us who ask; let us who seek, find; open the gate unto us who knock; that *this Child* (*this* thy *Servant*) may enjoy the everlasting benediction of thy heavenly washing, and may come to the eternal kingdom which thou hast promised by Christ our Lord. *Amen.*

¶ *Then the Minister shall say as followeth.*

Hear the words of the Gospel, written by Saint Mark, in the tenth Chapter, at the thirteenth Verse.

THEY brought young children to Christ, that he should touch them: and his disciples rebuked those that brought them. But when Jesus saw it, he was much displeased, and said unto them, Suffer the little children to come unto me, and forbid them not: for of such is the kingdom of God. Verily I say unto you, Whosoever shall not receive the kingdom of God as a little child, he shall not enter therein. And he took them up in his arms, put his hands upon them, and blessed them.

Holy Baptism

¶ *Or this.*

Hear the words of the Gospel, written by Saint John, in the third Chapter, at the first Verse.

THERE was a man of the Pharisees, named Nicodemus, a ruler of the Jews: the same came to Jesus by night, and said unto him, Rabbi, we know that thou art a teacher come from God: for no man can do these miracles that thou doest, except God be with him. Jesus answered and said unto him, Verily, verily, I say unto thee, Except a man be born again, he cannot see the kingdom of God. Nicodemus saith unto him, How can a man be born when he is old? can he enter the second time into his mother's womb, and be born? Jesus answered, Verily, verily, I say unto thee, Except a man be born of water and of the Spirit, he cannot enter into the kingdom of God. That which is born of the flesh is flesh; and that which is born of the Spirit is spirit. Marvel not that I said unto thee, Ye must be born again. The wind bloweth where it listeth, and thou hearest the sound thereof, but canst not tell whence it cometh, and whither it goeth: so is every one that is born of the Spirit.

¶ *Or this.*

Hear the words of the Gospel, written by Saint Matthew, in the twenty-eighth Chapter, at the eighteenth Verse.

JESUS came and spake unto them, saying, All power is given unto me in heaven and in earth. Go ye therefore, and make disciples of all nations, baptizing them in the name of the Father, and of the Son, and of the Holy Ghost: teaching them to observe all things whatsoever I have commanded you: and, lo, I am with you alway, even unto the end of the world.

Holy Baptism

¶ *Then shall the Minister say,*

AND now, being persuaded of the good will of our heavenly Father toward *this Child* (*this Person*), declared by his Son Jesus Christ; let us faithfully and devoutly give thanks unto him, and say,

ALMIGHTY and everlasting God, heavenly Father, We give thee humble thanks, That thou ¶ *Minister* hast vouchsafed to call us To the knowledge of *and People.* thy grace, and faith in thee: Increase this knowledge, And confirm this faith in us evermore. Give thy Holy Spirit to *this Child* (*this* thy *Servant*), That *he* may be born again, And be made *an heir* of everlasting salvation; Through our Lord Jesus Christ, Who liveth and reigneth with thee and the same Holy Spirit, Now and for ever. Amen.

¶ *When the Office is used for Children, the Minister shall speak unto the Godfathers and Godmothers on this wise.*

DEARLY beloved, ye have brought *this Child* here to be baptized; ye have prayed that our Lord Jesus Christ would vouchsafe to receive *him*, to release *him* from sin, to sanctify *him* with the Holy Ghost, to give *him* the kingdom of heaven, and everlasting life.

Dost thou, therefore, in the name of this Child, renounce the devil and all his works, the vain pomp and glory of the world, with all covetous desires of the same, and the sinful desires of the flesh, so that thou wilt not follow, nor be led by them?

Answer. I renounce them all; and, by God's help, will endeavour not to follow, nor be led by them.

Minister. Dost thou believe all the Articles of the Christian Faith, as contained in the Apostles' Creed?

Answer. I do.

Holy Baptism

Minister. Wilt thou be baptized in this Faith?

Answer. That is my desire.

Minister. Wilt thou then obediently keep God's holy will and commandments, and walk in the same all the days of thy life?

Answer. I will, by God's help.

Minister. Having now, in the name of this Child, made these promises, wilt thou also on thy part take heed that this Child learn the Creed, the Lord's Prayer, and the Ten Commandments, and all other things which a Christian ought to know and believe to his soul's health?

Answer. I will, by God's help.

Minister. Wilt thou take heed that this Child, so soon as sufficiently instructed, be brought to the Bishop to be confirmed by him?

Answer. I will, God being my helper.

¶ *When the Office is used for Adults, the Minister shall address them on this wise, the Persons to be baptized answering the questions for themselves.*

WELL–BELOVED, you have come hither desiring to receive holy Baptism. We have prayed that our Lord Jesus Christ would vouchsafe to receive you, to release you from sin, to sanctify you with the Holy Ghost, to give you the kingdom of heaven, and everlasting life.

DOST thou renounce the devil and all his works, the vain pomp and glory of the world, with all covetous desires of the same, and the sinful desires of the flesh, so that thou wilt not follow, nor be led by them?

Answer. I renounce them all; and, by God's help, will endeavour not to follow, nor be led by them.

Holy Baptism

Minister. Dost thou believe in Jesus the Christ, the Son of the Living God?

Answer. I do.

Minister. Dost thou accept him, and desire to follow him as thy Saviour and Lord?

Answer. I do.

Minister. Dost thou believe all the Articles of the Christian Faith, as contained in the Apostles' Creed?

Answer. I do.

Minister. Wilt thou be baptized in this Faith?

Answer. That is my desire.

Minister. Wilt thou then obediently keep God's holy will and commandments, and walk in the same all the days of thy life?

Answer. I will, by God's help.

¶ *Then shall the Minister say,*

O MERCIFUL God, grant that like as Christ died and rose again, so *this Child* (*this* thy *Servant*) may die to sin and rise to newness of life. *Amen.*

Grant that all sinful affections may die in *him,* and that all things belonging to the Spirit may live and grow in *him. Amen.*

Grant that *he* may have power and strength to have victory, and to triumph, against the devil, the world, and the flesh. *Amen.*

Grant that whosoever is here dedicated to thee by our office and ministry, may also be endued with heavenly virtues, and everlastingly rewarded, through thy mercy, O blessed Lord God, who dost live, and govern all things, world without end. *Amen.*

Minister. The Lord be with you.

Answer. And with thy spirit.

Holy Baptism

Minister. Lift up your hearts.
Answer. We lift them up unto the Lord.
Minister. Let us give thanks unto our Lord God.
Answer. It is meet and right so to do.

¶ *Then the Minister shall say,*

IT is very meet, right, and our bounden duty, that we should give thanks unto thee, O Lord, Holy Father, Almighty, Everlasting God, for that thy dearly beloved Son Jesus Christ, for the forgiveness of our sins, did shed out of his most precious side both water and blood; and gave commandment to his disciples, that they should go teach all nations, and baptize them In the Name of the Father, and of the Son, and of the Holy Ghost. Regard, we beseech thee, the supplications of thy congregation; sanctify this Water to the mystical washing away of sin; and grant that *this Child* (*this* thy *Servant*), now to be baptized therein, may receive the fulness of thy grace, and ever remain in the number of thy faithful children; through the same Jesus Christ our Lord, to whom, with thee, in the unity of the Holy Spirit, be all honour and glory, now and evermore. *Amen.*

¶ *Then the Minister shall take the Child into his arms, and shall say to the Godfathers and Godmothers,*

Name this Child.

¶ *And then, naming the Child after them, he shall dip him in the Water discreetly, or shall pour Water upon him, saying,*

N. I baptize thee In the Name of the Father, and of the Son, and of the Holy Ghost. Amen.

¶ *But* NOTE, *That if the Person to be baptized be an Adult, the Minister shall take him by the hand, and shall ask the Witnesses the Name; and then shall dip him in the Water, or pour Water upon him, using the same form of words.*

Holy Baptism

¶ Then the Minister shall say,

WE receive this Child (Person) into the congregation of Christ's flock; and do * sign *him* with the sign of the Cross, in token that here- ** Here the Minister shall make a Cross upon the Child's (or Person's) forehead.* after *he* shall not be ashamed to confess the faith of Christ crucified, and manfully to fight under his banner, against sin, the world, and the devil; and to continue Christ's faith- ful soldier and servant unto *his* life's end. Amen.

¶ Then shall the Minister say,

SEEING now, dearly beloved brethren, that *this Child* (*this Person*) *is* regenerate, and grafted into the body of Christ's Church, let us give thanks unto Almighty God for these benefits; and with one accord make our prayers unto him, that *this Child* (*this Person*) may lead the rest of *his* life according to this beginning.

¶ Then shall be said,

OUR Father, who art in heaven, Hallowed be thy Name. Thy kingdom come. Thy will be done, On earth as it is in heaven. Give us this day our daily bread. And forgive us our trespasses, As we forgive those who trespass against us. And lead us not into temptation, But deliver us from evil. For thine is the kingdom, and the power, and the glory, for ever and ever. Amen.

¶ Then shall the Minister say,

WE yield thee hearty thanks, most merciful Father, that it hath pleased thee to regenerate *this Child* (*this* thy *Servant*) with thy Holy Spirit, to receive *him* for thine own *Child*, and to incorporate *him* into thy holy Church. And humbly we beseech thee to grant, that *he*, be- ing dead unto sin, may live unto righteousness, and being

280

Holy Baptism

buried with Christ in his death, may also be *partaker* of his resurrection; so that finally, with the residue of thy holy Church, *he* may be *an inheritor* of thine everlasting kingdom; through Christ our Lord. *Amen.*

¶ Then the Minister shall add,

THE Almighty God, the Father of our Lord Jesus Christ, of whom the whole family in heaven and earth is named; Grant you to be strengthened with might by his Spirit in the inner man; that, Christ dwelling in your hearts by faith, ye may be filled with all the fulness of God. *Amen.*

¶ It is expedient that every Adult, thus baptized, should be confirmed by the Bishop, so soon after his Baptism as conveniently may be; that so he may be admitted to the Holy Communion.

PRIVATE BAPTISM.

¶ When, in consideration of extreme sickness, necessity may require, then the following form shall suffice:

¶ The Child (or Person) being named by some one who is present, the Minister shall pour Water upon him, saying these words:

N. I baptize thee In the Name of the Father, and of the Son, and of the Holy Ghost. Amen.

¶ After which shall be said the Lord's Prayer, and the Thanksgiving from this Office, beginning, We yield thee hearty thanks, *etc.*

¶ But NOTE, *That in the case of an Adult, the Minister shall first ask the questions provided in this Office for the Baptism of Adults.*

¶ In cases of extreme sickness, or any imminent peril, if a Minister cannot be procured, then any baptized person present may administer holy Baptism, using the foregoing form. Such Baptism shall be promptly reported to the Parish authorities.

THE RECEIVING OF ONE PRIVATELY BAPTIZED.

¶ It is expedient that a Child or Person so baptized be afterward

Holy Baptism

brought to the Church, at which time these parts of the foregoing service shall be used:

The Gospel, the Questions (omitting the question Wilt thou be baptized in this Faith? *and the answer thereto), the Declaration,* We receive this Child (*or* Person), etc., *and the remainder of the Office.*

CONDITIONAL BAPTISM.

¶ *If there be reasonable doubt whether any person was baptized with Water, In the Name of the Father, and of the Son, and of the Holy Ghost, (which are essential parts of Baptism), such person may be baptized in the form before appointed in this Office; saving that, at the immersion or the pouring of water, the Minister shall use this form of words:*

IF thou art not already baptized, *N.*, I baptize thee In the Name of the Father, and of the Son, and of the Holy Ghost. Amen.

Offices of Instruction

FIRST OFFICE.

¶ *After the singing of a Hymn, shall be said by the Minister and People together, all kneeling, the following Prayer, the Minister first pronouncing,*

The Lord be with you.
Answer. And with thy spirit.

Let us pray.

LORD of all power and might, Who art the author and giver of all good things; Graft in our hearts the love of thy Name, Increase in us true religion, Nourish us with all goodness, And of thy great mercy keep us in the same; Through Jesus Christ our Lord. Amen.

¶ *Then, the People being seated, the Minister shall ask them the Questions which follow, the People reading or repeating the Answers as appointed.*

Question. What is your Christian Name?
Answer. My Christian Name is ——.
Question. Who gave you this Name?
Answer. My Sponsors gave me this Name in Baptism; wherein I was made a member of Christ, the child of God, and an inheritor of the kingdom of heaven.
Question. What did your Sponsors then promise for you?
Answer. My Sponsors did promise and vow three things in my name: First, that I should renounce the devil and all his works, the pomps and vanity of this wicked world, and all the sinful lusts of the flesh; Secondly, that I should believe all the Articles of the Christian Faith; And Thirdly, that I should keep God's holy will and commandments, and walk in the same all the days of my life.
Question. Do you not think that you are bound so to do?
Answer. Yes, verily; and by God's help so I will. And

Offices of Instruction

I heartily thank our heavenly Father, that he hath called me to this state of salvation, through Jesus Christ our Saviour. And I pray unto God to give me his grace, that I may continue in the same unto my life's end.

¶ *Then the Minister shall say,*

YOU said that your Sponsors promised and vowed that you should believe all the Articles of the Christian Faith. Recite the Articles of the Christian Faith as contained in the Apostles' Creed.

¶ *Then, all standing, shall be said the Apostles' Creed by the Minister and People.*

I BELIEVE in God the Father Almighty, Maker of heaven and earth:

And in Jesus Christ his only Son our Lord: Who was conceived by the Holy Ghost, Born of the Virgin Mary: Suffered under Pontius Pilate, Was crucified, dead, and buried: He descended into hell; The third day he rose again from the dead: He ascended into heaven, And sitteth on the right hand of God the Father Almighty: From thence he shall come to judge the quick and the dead.

I believe in the Holy Ghost: The holy Catholic Church; The Communion of Saints: The Forgiveness of sins: The Resurrection of the body: And the Life everlasting. Amen.

¶ *Then, the Minister, turning to the People, shall ask the Question following, the People responding.*

Question. What do you chiefly learn in these Articles of your Belief?

Answer. First, I learn to believe in God the Father, who hath made me, and all the world.

Secondly, in God the Son, who hath redeemed me, and all mankind.

284

Offices of Instruction

Thirdly, in God the Holy Ghost, who sanctifieth me, and all the people of God.

And this Holy Trinity, One God, I praise and magnify, saying,

GLORY be to the Father, and to the Son, and to the Holy Ghost; ¶ *Minister and People.*

As it was in the beginning, is now, and ever shall be, world without end. Amen.

¶ *Here may be sung a Hymn, after which the Minister, turning to the People, shall say,*

YOU said that your Sponsors promised and vowed that you should keep God's holy will and commandments. Tell me how many Commandments there are.

Answer. There are Ten Commandments, given in old time by God to the people of Israel.

¶ *Then shall the Minister say,*

Let us ask God's help to know and to keep them.

The Lord be with you.
Answer. And with thy spirit.

Let us pray.

¶ *Then shall be said this Prayer by the Minister and People together, all kneeling.*

O ALMIGHTY God, Who alone canst order the unruly wills and affections of sinful men; Grant unto thy people, That they may love the thing which thou commandest, And desire that which thou dost promise; That so, among the sundry and manifold changes of the world, Our hearts may surely there be fixed, Where true joys are to be found; Through Jesus Christ our Lord. Amen.

¶ *Then shall the Minister repeat the Ten Commandments, and after every Commandment the People shall say the response. But* NOTE,

Offices of Instruction

That where so instructed, the People may repeat the Commandments, the Minister saying the response. And NOTE *further, That the part of the Commandment which is inset may be omitted.*

I. Thou shalt have none other gods but me.

Lord, have mercy upon us, and incline our hearts to keep this law.

II. Thou shalt not make to thyself any graven image, nor the likeness of any thing that is in heaven above, or in the earth beneath, or in the water under the earth; thou shalt not bow down to them, nor worship them;

> for I the LORD thy God am a jealous God, and visit the sins of the fathers upon the children, unto the third and fourth generation of them that hate me; and show mercy unto thousands in them that love me and keep my commandments.

Lord, have mercy upon us, and incline our hearts to keep this law.

III. Thou shalt not take the Name of the LORD thy God in vain;

> for the LORD will not hold him guiltless, that taketh his Name in vain.

Lord, have mercy upon us, and incline our hearts to keep this law.

IV. Remember that thou keep holy the Sabbath-day.

> Six days shalt thou labour, and do all that thou hast to do; but the seventh day is the Sabbath of the LORD thy God. In it thou shalt do no manner of work; thou, and thy son, and thy daughter, thy man-servant, and thy maid-servant, thy cattle, and the stranger that is within thy gates. For in six days the LORD made heaven and earth, the sea, and all that in them is, and rested the seventh day: wherefore the LORD blessed the seventh day, and hallowed it.

Lord, have mercy upon us, and incline our hearts to keep this law.

V. Honour thy father and thy mother;

Offices of Instruction

that thy days may be long in the land which the LORD thy God giveth thee.

Lord, have mercy upon us, and incline our hearts to keep this law.

VI. Thou shalt do no murder.

Lord, have mercy upon us, and incline our hearts to keep this law.

VII. Thou shalt not commit adultery.

Lord, have mercy upon us, and incline our hearts to keep this law.

VIII. Thou shalt not steal.

Lord, have mercy upon us, and incline our hearts to keep this law.

IX. Thou shalt not bear false witness against thy neighbour.

Lord, have mercy upon us, and incline our hearts to keep this law.

X. Thou shalt not covet

thy neighbour's house, thou shalt not covet thy neighbour's wife, nor his servant, nor his maid, nor his ox, nor his ass, nor any thing that is his.

Lord, have mercy upon us, and write all these thy laws in our hearts, we beseech thee.

¶ *Then shall the Minister say,*

GRANT to us, Lord, we beseech thee, the spirit to think and do always such things as are right; that we, who cannot do any thing that is good without thee, may by thee be enabled to live according to thy will; through Jesus Christ our Lord. *Amen.*

¶ *After this, the People being seated, the Minister, turning to them, shall ask the Questions which follow, the People reading or repeating the Answers.*

Offices of Instruction

Question. What does our Lord Jesus Christ teach us about these Commandments?

Answer. Our Lord Jesus Christ teaches us that they are summed up in these two Commandments: Thou shalt love the Lord thy God with all thy heart, with all thy mind, with all thy soul, and with all thy strength; this is the first and great Commandment. And the second is: Thou shalt love thy neighbour as thyself.

Question. What then do you chiefly learn from the Ten Commandments?

Answer. I learn two things from these Commandments; my duty towards God, and my duty towards my Neighbour.

Question. What is your duty towards God?

Answer. My duty towards God is To believe in him, to fear him, And to love him with all my heart, with all my mind, with all my soul, and with all my strength:

I., II. To worship him, to give him thanks: To put my whole trust in him, to call upon him:

III. To honour his holy Name and his Word:

IV. And to serve him truly all the days of my life.

Question. What is your duty towards your Neighbour?

Answer. My duty towards my Neighbour is To love him as myself, and to do to all men as I would they should do unto me:

V. To love, honour, and help my father and mother: To honour and obey the civil authority: To submit myself to all my governors, teachers, spiritual pastors and masters: And to order myself in that lowliness and reverence which becometh a servant of God:

VI. To hurt nobody by word or deed: To bear no malice nor hatred in my heart:

Offices of Instruction

VII. To keep my body in temperance, soberness, and chastity:

VIII. To keep my hands from picking and stealing: To be true and just in all my dealings:

IX. To keep my tongue from evil speaking, lying, and slandering:

X. Not to covet nor desire other men's goods; But to learn and labour truly to earn mine own living, And to do my duty in that state of life unto which it shall please God to call me.

¶ *Then shall be sung a Hymn, after which the Minister shall say as followeth.*

KNOW this; that you are not able to do these things of yourself, nor to walk in the Commandments of God, and to serve him, without his special grace; which you must learn at all times to call for by diligent prayer. What is the prayer that our Lord taught us to pray?

Answer. The Lord's Prayer.

Minister. Let us pray, as our Saviour Christ hath taught us, and say,

¶ *Then shall be said by the Minister and People together, all kneeling,*

OUR Father, who art in heaven, Hallowed be thy Name. Thy kingdom come. Thy will be done, On earth as it is in heaven. Give us this day our daily bread. And forgive us our trespasses, As we forgive those who trespass against us. And lead us not into temptation, But deliver us from evil. For thine is the kingdom, and the power, and the glory, for ever and ever. Amen.

THE grace of our Lord Jesus Christ, and the love of God, and the fellowship of the Holy Ghost, be with us all evermore. *Amen.*

Offices of Instruction

SECOND OFFICE.

¶ *After the singing of a Hymn, there shall be said the following Sentence by the Minister and People together.*

COME ye, and let us walk in the light of the Lord. And he will teach us of his ways, and we will walk in his paths.

Minister. Show thy servants thy work;
People.   And their children thy glory.
Minister. Let thy merciful kindness, O Lord, be upon us;
People.   As we do put our trust in thee.
Minister. Not unto us, O Lord, not unto us,
People.   But unto thy Name be the praise.
Minister. Lord, hear our prayer.
People.   And let our cry come unto thee.
Minister. The Lord be with you.
People.   And with thy spirit.
Minister. Let us pray.

O ALMIGHTY God, who hast built thy Church upon the foundation of the Apostles and Prophets, Jesus Christ himself being the head corner-stone; Grant us so to be joined together in unity of spirit by their doctrine, that we may be made an holy temple acceptable unto thee; through the same Jesus Christ our Lord. *Amen.*

¶ *Here may be sung a Hymn, after which, the People being seated, the Minister shall ask them the Questions concerning the Church which follow, the People responding.*

WHEN were you made a member of the Church?
       Answer. I was made a member of the Church when I was baptized.

Question. What is the Church?

Answer. The Church is the Body of which Jesus Christ is the Head, and all baptized people are the members.

Offices of Instruction

Question. How is the Church described in the Apostles'
and Nicene Creeds?

Answer. The Church is described in the Creeds as One,
Holy, Catholic, and Apostolic.

Question. What do we mean by these words?

Answer. We mean that the Church is

One; because it is one Body under one Head;

Holy; because the Holy Spirit dwells in it, and sanctifies
its members;

Catholic; because it is universal, holding earnestly the
Faith for all time, in all countries, and for all people; and
is sent to preach the Gospel to the whole world;

Apostolic; because it continues stedfastly in the Apostles'
teaching and fellowship.

Question. What is your bounden duty as a member of
the Church?

Answer. My bounden duty is to follow Christ, to worship God every Sunday in his Church; and to work and
pray and give for the spread of his kingdom.

Question. What special means does the Church provide
to help you to do all these things?

Answer. The Church provides the Laying on of Hands,
or Confirmation, wherein, after renewing the promises and
vows of my Baptism, and declaring my loyalty and devotion to Christ as my Master, I receive the strengthening
gifts of the Holy Spirit.

Question. After you have been confirmed, what great
privilege doth our Lord provide for you?

Answer. Our Lord provides the Sacrament of the
Lord's Supper, or Holy Communion, for the continual
strengthening and refreshing of my soul.

Offices of Instruction

¶ *After another Hymn, the Minister shall proceed with the Questions on the Sacraments, as followeth.*

HOW many Sacraments hath Christ ordained in his Church?

Answer. Christ hath ordained two Sacraments only, as generally necessary to salvation; that is to say, Baptism, and the Supper of the Lord.

Question. What do you mean by this word Sacrament?

Answer. I mean by this word Sacrament an outward and visible sign of an inward and spiritual grace given unto us; ordained by Christ himself, as a means whereby we receive this grace, and a pledge to assure us thereof.

Question. How many parts are there in a Sacrament?

Answer. There are two parts in a Sacrament; the outward and visible sign, and the inward and spiritual grace.

Question. What is the outward and visible sign or form in Baptism?

Answer. The outward and visible sign or form in Baptism is Water; wherein the person is baptized, *In the Name of the Father, and of the Son, and of the Holy Ghost.*

Question. What is the inward and spiritual grace in Baptism?

Answer. The inward and spiritual grace in Baptism is a death unto sin, and a new birth unto righteousness; whereby we are made the children of grace.

Question. What is required of persons to be baptized?

Answer. Repentance, whereby they forsake sin; and Faith, whereby they stedfastly believe the promises of God to them in that Sacrament.

Question. Why then are infants baptized, when by reason of their tender age they cannot perform them?

Answer. Because, by the faith of their Sponsors, infants are received into Christ's Church, become the recipients of his grace, and are trained in the household of faith.

Offices of Instruction

Question. Why was the Sacrament of the Lord's Supper ordained?

Answer. The Sacrament of the Lord's Supper was ordained for the continual remembrance of the sacrifice of the death of Christ, and of the benefits which we receive thereby.

Question. What is the outward part or sign of the Lord's Supper?

Answer. The outward part or sign of the Lord's Supper is, Bread and Wine, which the Lord hath commanded to be received.

Question. What is the inward part, or thing signified?

Answer. The inward part, or thing signified, is the Body and Blood of Christ, which are spiritually taken and received by the faithful in the Lord's Supper.

Question. What are the benefits whereof we are partakers in the Lord's Supper?

Answer. The benefits whereof we are partakers in the Lord's Supper are the strengthening and refreshing of our souls by the Body and Blood of Christ, as our bodies are strengthened and refreshed by the Bread and Wine.

Question. What is required of those who come to the Lord's Supper?

Answer. It is required of those who come to the Lord's Supper to examine themselves, whether they repent them truly of their former sins, with stedfast purpose to lead a new life; to have a lively faith in God's mercy through Christ, with a thankful remembrance of his death; and to be in charity with all men.

Offices of Instruction

¶ *Here may be sung a Hymn, after which the Minister shall ask the People the following Questions concerning the Ministry, the People responding.*

WHAT orders of Ministers are there in the Church? *Answer*. Bishops, Priests, and Deacons; which orders have been in the Church from the earliest times.

Question. What is the office of a Bishop?

Answer. The office of a Bishop is, to be a chief pastor in the Church; to confer Holy Orders; and to administer Confirmation.

Question. What is the office of a Priest?

Answer. The office of a Priest is, to minister to the people committed to his care; to preach the Word of God; to baptize; to celebrate the Holy Communion; and to pronounce Absolution and Blessing in God's Name.

Question. What is the office of a Deacon?

Answer. The office of a Deacon is, to assist the Priest in Divine Service, and in his other ministrations, under the direction of the Bishop.

¶ *Then shall the Minister add,*

The Lord be with you.

People. And with thy spirit.

Let us pray.

GRANT, O Lord, that they who shall renew the promises and vows of their Baptism, and be confirmed by the Bishop, may receive such a measure of thy Holy Spirit, that they may grow in grace unto their life's end; through Jesus Christ our Lord. *Amen*.

GRANT, O Father, that when we receive the blessed Sacrament of the Body and Blood of Christ, coming to those holy mysteries in faith, and love, and true repentance, we may receive remission of our sins, and be

Offices of Instruction

filled with thy grace and heavenly benediction; through Jesus Christ our Lord. *Amen.*

THE grace of our Lord Jesus Christ, and the love of God, and the fellowship of the Holy Ghost, be with us all evermore. *Amen.*

¶ *The Minister of every Parish shall diligently, upon Sundays and Holy Days, or on some other convenient occasions, openly in the Church, instruct or examine the Youth of his Parish.*

¶ *And all Fathers, Mothers, Guardians, and Sponsors shall bring those, for whose religious nurture they are responsible, to the Church at the time appointed, to receive instruction by the Minister.*

¶ *So soon as Children are come to a competent age, and can say the Creed, the Lord's Prayer, and the Ten Commandments, and are sufficiently instructed in the matter contained in these Offices, they shall be brought to the Bishop to be confirmed by him.*

The Order of Confirmation

Or Laying on of Hands upon Those that are Baptized, and come to Years of Discretion.

¶ *Upon the day appointed, all that are to be confirmed shall stand in order before the Bishop, sitting in his chair near to the Holy Table, the People all standing until the Lord's Prayer; and the Minister shall say,*

REVEREND Father in God, I present unto you these persons to receive the Laying on of Hands.

¶ *Then the Bishop, or some Minister appointed by him, may say,*

Hear the words of the Evangelist Saint Luke, in the eighth Chapter of the Acts of the Apostles.

WHEN the apostles which were at Jerusalem heard that Samaria had received the word of God, they sent unto them Peter and John: who, when they were come down, prayed for them, that they might receive the Holy Ghost: for as yet he was fallen upon none of them: only they were baptized in the name of the Lord Jesus. Then laid they their hands on them, and they received the Holy Ghost.

¶ *Then shall the Bishop say,*

DO ye here, in the presence of God, and of this congregation, renew the solemn promise and vow that ye made, or that was made in your name, at your Baptism; ratifying and confirming the same; and acknowledging yourselves bound to believe and to do all those things which ye then undertook, or your Sponsors then undertook for you?

¶ *And every one shall audibly answer,*

I do.

Confirmation

¶ *Then shall the Bishop say,*

DO ye promise to follow Jesus Christ as your Lord and Saviour?

¶ *And every one shall answer,*

I do.

Bishop. Our help is in the Name of the Lord;
Answer. Who hath made heaven and earth.
Bishop. Blessed be the Name of the Lord;
Answer. Henceforth, world without end.
Bishop. Lord, hear our prayer.
Answer. And let our cry come unto thee.

Bishop. Let us pray.

ALMIGHTY and everliving God, who hast vouchsafed to regenerate these thy servants by Water and the Holy Ghost, and hast given unto them forgiveness of all their sins; Strengthen them, we beseech thee, O Lord, with the Holy Ghost, the Comforter, and daily increase in them thy manifold gifts of grace: the spirit of wisdom and understanding, the spirit of counsel and ghostly strength, the spirit of knowledge and true godliness; and fill them, O Lord, with the spirit of thy holy fear, now and for ever. *Amen.*

¶ *Then all of them in order kneeling before the Bishop, he shall lay his hand upon the head of every one severally, saying,*

DEFEND, O Lord, this thy Child with thy heavenly grace; that *he* may continue thine for ever; and daily increase in thy Holy Spirit more and more, until *he* come unto thy everlasting kingdom. Amen.

¶ *Then shall the Bishop say,*

The Lord be with you.
Answer. And with thy spirit.

Confirmation

Bishop. Let us pray.

¶ Then shall the Bishop say the Lord's Prayer, the People kneeling and repeating it with him.

OUR Father, who art in heaven, Hallowed be thy Name. Thy kingdom come. Thy will be done, On earth as it is in heaven. Give us this day our daily bread. And forgive us our trespasses, As we forgive those who trespass against us. And lead us not into temptation, But deliver us from evil. For thine is the kingdom, and the power, and the glory, for ever and ever. Amen.

¶ Then shall the Bishop say,

ALMIGHTY and everliving God, who makest us both to will and to do those things which are good, and acceptable unto thy Divine Majesty; We make our humble supplications unto thee for these thy servants, upon whom, after the example of thy holy Apostles, we have now laid our hands, to certify them, by this sign, of thy favour and gracious goodness towards them. Let thy fatherly hand, we beseech thee, ever be over them; let thy Holy Spirit ever be with them; and so lead them in the knowledge and obedience of thy Word, that in the end they may obtain everlasting life; through our Lord Jesus Christ, who with thee and the same Holy Spirit liveth and reigneth ever, one God, world without end. *Amen.*

O ALMIGHTY Lord, and everlasting God, vouchsafe, we beseech thee, to direct, sanctify, and govern, both our hearts and bodies, in the ways of thy laws, and in the works of thy commandments; that, through thy most mighty protection, both here and ever, we may be preserved in body and soul; through our Lord and Saviour Jesus Christ. *Amen.*

Confirmation

¶ Then the Bishop shall bless them, saying thus,

THE Blessing of God Almighty, the Father, the Son, and the Holy Ghost, be upon you, and remain with you for ever. *Amen.*

¶ The Minister shall not omit earnestly to move the Persons confirmed to come, without delay, to the Lord's Supper.

¶ And there shall none be admitted to the Holy Communion, until such time as he be confirmed, or be ready and desirous to be confirmed.

The Form of
Solemnization of Matrimony

¶ *At the day and time appointed for Solemnization of Matrimony, the
Persons to be married shall come into the body of the Church, or shall
be ready in some proper house, with their friends and neighbours; and
there standing together, the Man on the right hand, and the Woman on
the left, the Minister shall say,*

DEARLY beloved, we are gathered together here in
the sight of God, and in the face of this company,
to join together this Man and this Woman in holy Matrimony; which is an honourable estate, instituted of God,
signifying unto us the mystical union that is betwixt Christ
and his Church: which holy estate Christ adorned and
beautified with his presence and first miracle that he
wrought in Cana of Galilee, and is commended of Saint
Paul to be honourable among all men: and therefore is
not by any to be entered into unadvisedly or lightly; but
reverently, discreetly, advisedly, soberly, and in the fear
of God. Into this holy estate these two persons present
come now to be joined. If any man can show just cause,
why they may not lawfully be joined together, let him
now speak, or else hereafter for ever hold his peace.

¶ *And also speaking unto the Persons who are to be married, he shall say,*

I REQUIRE and charge you both, as ye will answer at
the dreadful day of judgment when the secrets of all
hearts shall be disclosed, that if either of you know any
impediment, why ye may not be lawfully joined together in
Matrimony, ye do now confess it. For be ye well assured,
that if any persons are joined together otherwise than as
God's Word doth allow, their marriage is not lawful.

Matrimony

¶ *The Minister, if he shall have reason to doubt of the lawfulness of the proposed Marriage, may demand sufficient surety for his indemnification: but if no impediment shall be alleged, or suspected, the Minister shall say to the Man,*

N. WILT thou have this Woman to thy wedded wife, to live together after God's ordinance in the holy estate of Matrimony? Wilt thou love her, comfort her, honour, and keep her in sickness and in health; and, forsaking all others, keep thee only unto her, so long as ye both shall live?

¶ *The Man shall answer,*

I will.

¶ *Then shall the Minister say unto the Woman,*

N. WILT thou have this Man to thy wedded husband, to live together after God's ordinance in the holy estate of Matrimony? Wilt thou love him, comfort him, honour, and keep him in sickness and in health; and, forsaking all others, keep thee only unto him, so long as ye both shall live?

¶ *The Woman shall answer,*

I will.

¶ *Then shall the Minister say,*

Who giveth this Woman to be married to this Man?

¶ *Then shall they give their troth to each other in this manner. The Minister, receiving the Woman at her father's or friend's hands, shall cause the Man with his right hand to take the Woman by her right hand, and to say after him as followeth.*

I *N.* take thee *N.* to my wedded Wife, to have and to hold from this day forward, for better for worse, for richer for poorer, in sickness and in health, to love and to cherish, till death us do part, according to God's holy ordinance; and thereto I plight thee my troth.

301

Matrimony

¶ Then shall they loose their hands; and the Woman with her right hand taking the Man by his right hand, shall likewise say after the Minister,

I N. take thee N. to my wedded Husband, to have and to hold from this day forward, for better for worse, for richer for poorer, in sickness and in health, to love and to cherish, till death us do part, according to God's holy ordinance; and thereto I give thee my troth.

¶ Then shall they again loose their hands; and the Man shall give unto the Woman a Ring on this wise: the Minister taking the Ring shall deliver it unto the Man, to put it upon the fourth finger of the Woman's left hand. And the Man holding the Ring there, and taught by the Minister, shall say,

W ITH this Ring I thee wed: In the Name of the Father, and of the Son, and of the Holy Ghost. Amen.

¶ And, before delivering the Ring to the Man, the Minister may say as followeth.

B LESS, O Lord, this Ring, that he who gives it and she who wears it may abide in thy peace, and continue in thy favour, unto their life's end; through Jesus Christ our Lord. Amen.

¶ Then, the Man leaving the Ring upon the fourth finger of the Woman's left hand, the Minister shall say,

Let us pray.

¶ Then shall the Minister and the People, still standing, say the Lord's Prayer.

O UR Father, who art in heaven, Hallowed be thy Name. Thy kingdom come. Thy will be done, On earth as it is in heaven. Give us this day our daily bread. And forgive us our trespasses, As we forgive those who trespass against us. And lead us not into temptation, But deliver us from evil. For thine is the kingdom, and the power, and the glory, for ever and ever. Amen.

Matrimony

¶ Then shall the Minister add,

O ETERNAL God, Creator and Preserver of all mankind, Giver of all spiritual grace, the Author of everlasting life; Send thy blessing upon these thy servants, this man and this woman, whom we bless in thy Name; that they, living faithfully together, may surely perform and keep the vow and covenant betwixt them made, (whereof this Ring given and received is a token and pledge,) and may ever remain in perfect love and peace together, and live according to thy laws; through Jesus Christ our Lord. *Amen.*

¶ The Minister may add one or both of the following prayers.

O ALMIGHTY God, Creator of mankind, who only art the well-spring of life; Bestow upon these thy servants, if it be thy will, the gift and heritage of children; and grant that they may see their children brought up in thy faith and fear, to the honour and glory of thy Name; through Jesus Christ our Lord. *Amen.*

O GOD, who hast so consecrated the state of Matrimony that in it is represented the spiritual marriage and unity betwixt Christ and his Church; Look mercifully upon these thy servants, that they may love, honour, and cherish each other, and so live together in faithfulness and patience, in wisdom and true godliness, that their home may be a haven of blessing and of peace; through the same Jesus Christ our Lord, who liveth and reigneth with thee and the Holy Spirit ever, one God, world without end. *Amen.*

¶ Then shall the Minister join their right hands together, and say,

Those whom God hath joined together let no man put asunder.

Matrimony

¶ *Then shall the Minister speak unto the company.*

FORASMUCH as *N.* and *N.* have consented together in holy wedlock, and have witnessed the same before God and this company, and thereto have given and pledged their troth, each to the other, and have declared the same by giving and receiving a Ring, and by joining hands; I pronounce that they are Man and Wife, In the Name of the Father, and of the Son, and of the Holy Ghost. Amen.

¶ *The Man and Wife kneeling, the Minister shall add this Blessing.*

GOD the Father, God the Son, God the Holy Ghost, bless, preserve, and keep you; the Lord mercifully with his favour look upon you, and fill you with all spiritual benediction and grace; that ye may so live together in this life, that in the world to come ye may have life everlasting. *Amen.*

¶ *The laws respecting Matrimony, whether by publishing the Banns in Churches, or by Licence, being different in the several States, every Minister is left to the direction of those laws, in every thing that regards the civil contract between the parties.*

¶ *And when the Banns are published, it shall be in the following form:* I publish the Banns of Marriage between *N.* of —, and *N.* of —. If any of you know cause, or just impediment, why these two persons should not be joined together in holy Matrimony, ye are to declare it. This is the first [second *or* third] time of asking.

The Thanksgiving of Women after Child-birth

Commonly called the Churching of Women.

¶ *This Service, or the concluding prayer alone, as it stands among the Occasional Prayers and Thanksgivings, may be used at the discretion of the Minister.*

¶ *The Woman, at the usual time after her delivery, shall come into the Church decently apparelled, and there shall kneel down in some convenient place, as hath been accustomed, or as the Ordinary shall direct.*

¶ *The Minister shall then say unto her,*

FORASMUCH as it hath pleased Almighty God, of his goodness, to give you safe deliverance, and to preserve you in the great danger of Child-birth; you shall therefore give hearty thanks unto God, and say,

¶ *Then shall be said by both of them the following Hymn, the Woman still kneeling.*

Dilexi, quoniam. Psalm cxvi.

MY delight is in the LORD; because he hath heard the voice of my prayer;

Because he hath inclined his ear unto me; therefore will I call upon him as long as I live.

I found trouble and heaviness; then called I upon the Name of the LORD; O LORD, I beseech thee, deliver my soul.

Gracious is the LORD, and righteous; yea, our God is \merciful.

What reward shall I give unto the LORD for all the benefits that he hath done unto me?

I will receive the cup of salvation, and call upon the Name of the LORD.

I will pay my vows now in the presence of all his people,

in the courts of the LORD's house; even in the midst of thee, O Jerusalem. Praise the LORD.

Glory be to the Father, and to the Son, and to the Holy Ghost;

As it was in the beginning, is now, and ever shall be, world without end. Amen.

¶ *Then shall the Minister say the Lord's Prayer, with what followeth: but the Lord's Prayer may be omitted, if this be used with the Morning or Evening Prayer.*

OUR Father, who art in heaven, Hallowed be thy Name. Thy kingdom come. Thy will be done, On earth as it is in heaven. Give us this day our daily bread. And forgive us our trespasses, As we forgive those who trespass against us. And lead us not into temptation, But deliver us from evil. Amen.

Minister. O Lord, save this woman thy servant;
Answer. Who putteth her trust in thee.
Minister. Be thou to her a strong tower;
Answer. From the face of her enemy.
Minister. Lord, hear our prayer.
Answer. And let our cry come unto thee.

Minister. Let us pray.

O ALMIGHTY God, we give thee humble thanks for that thou hast been graciously pleased to preserve, through the great pain and peril of child-birth, this woman, thy servant, who desireth now to offer her praises and thanksgivings unto thee. Grant, we beseech thee, most merciful Father, that she, through thy help, may faithfully live according to thy will in this life, and also may be partaker of everlasting glory in the life to come; through Jesus Christ our Lord. *Amen.*

Churching of Women

¶ *Then may be said,*

GRANT, we beseech thee, O heavenly Father, that the child of this thy servant may daily increase in wisdom and stature, and grow in thy love and service, until *he* come to thy eternal joy; through Jesus Christ our Lord. *Amen.*

¶ *The Woman, that cometh to give her Thanks, must offer accustomed offerings, which shall be applied by the Minister and the Church-wardens to the relief of distressed women in child-bed; and if there be a Communion, it is convenient that she receive the Holy Communion.*

The Order for
the Visitation of the Sick

¶ *The following Service, or any part thereof, may be used at the discretion of the Minister.*

¶ *When any person is sick, notice shall be given thereof to the Minister of the Parish; who, coming into the sick person's presence, shall say,*

PEACE be to this house, and to all that dwell in it.

¶ *After which he shall say the Antiphon following, and then, according to his discretion, one of the Penitential Psalms.*

Antiphon. Remember not, Lord, our iniquities; Nor the iniquities of our forefathers.

¶ *Then the Minister shall say,*

Let us pray.
Lord, have mercy upon us.
Christ, have mercy upon us.
Lord, have mercy upon us.

OUR Father, who art in heaven, Hallowed be thy Name. Thy kingdom come. Thy will be done, On earth as it is in heaven. Give us this day our daily bread. And forgive us our trespasses, As we forgive those who trespass against us. And lead us not into temptation, But deliver us from evil. Amen.

Minister. O Lord, save thy servant;
Answer. Who putteth *his* trust in thee.
Minister. Send *him* help from thy holy place;
Answer. And evermore mightily defend *him.*
Minister. Let the enemy have no advantage of *him;*
Answer. Nor the wicked approach to hurt *him.*
Minister. Be unto *him,* O Lord, a strong tower;
Answer. From the face of *his* enemy.
Minister. O Lord, hear our prayer.

Visitation of the Sick

Answer. And let our cry come unto thee.

Minister.

O LORD, look down from heaven, behold, visit, and relieve this thy servant. Look upon *him* with the eyes of thy mercy, give *him* comfort and sure confidence in thee, defend *him* in all danger, and keep *him* in perpetual peace and safety; through Jesus Christ our Lord. *Amen.*

¶ *Here may be said any one or more of the Psalms following, with Antiphon and Collect.*

Antiphon. I did call upon the LORD with my voice; And he heard me out of his holy hill.

Domine, quid multiplicati? Psalm iii.

LORD, how are they increased that trouble me! many are they that rise against me.

Many one there be that say of my soul, There is no help for him in his God.

But thou, O LORD, art my defender; thou art my worship, and the lifter up of my head.

I did call upon the LORD with my voice, and he heard me out of his holy hill.

I laid me down and slept, and rose up again; for the LORD sustained me.

Salvation belongeth unto the LORD; and thy blessing is upon thy people.

The Collect.

HEAR us, Almighty and most merciful God and Saviour; extend thy accustomed goodness to this thy servant who is grieved with sickness. Visit *him*, O Lord, with thy loving mercy, and so restore *him* to *his* former health, that *he* may give thanks unto thee in thy holy Church; through Jesus Christ our Lord. *Amen.*

Visitation of the Sick

Antiphon. I will go unto the altar of God; Unto the God of my joy and gladness.

Judica me, Deus. Psalm xliii.

GIVE sentence with me, O God, and defend my cause against the ungodly people; O deliver me from the deceitful and wicked man.

For thou art the God of my strength; why hast thou put me from thee? and why go I so heavily, while the enemy oppresseth me?

O send out thy light and thy truth, that they may lead me, and bring me unto thy holy hill, and to thy dwelling;

And that I may go unto the altar of God, even unto the God of my joy and gladness; and upon the harp will I give thanks unto thee, O God, my God.

Why art thou so heavy, O my soul? and why art thou so disquieted within me?

O put thy trust in God; for I will yet give him thanks, which is the help of my countenance, and my God.

The Collect.

SANCTIFY, we beseech thee, O Lord, the sickness of this thy servant; that the sense of *his* weakness may add strength to *his* faith, and seriousness to *his* repentance; and grant that *he* may dwell with thee in life everlasting; through Jesus Christ our Lord. *Amen.*

Antiphon. I have considered the days of old; And the years that are past.

Voce mea ad Dominum. Psalm lxxvii.

I WILL cry unto God with my voice; even unto God will I cry with my voice, and he shall hearken unto me.

In the time of my trouble I sought the Lord: I stretched

Visitation of the Sick

forth my hands unto him, and ceased not in the night season; my soul refused comfort.

When I am in heaviness, I will think upon God; when my heart is vexed, I will complain.

Thou holdest mine eyes waking: I am so feeble that I cannot speak.

I have considered the days of old, and the years that are past.

I call to remembrance my song, and in the night I commune with mine own heart, and search out my spirit.

Will the Lord absent himself for ever? and will he be no more intreated?

Is his mercy clean gone for ever? and is his promise come utterly to an end for evermore?

Hath God forgotten to be gracious? and will he shut up his loving-kindness in displeasure?

And I said, It is mine own infirmity; but I will remember the years of the right hand of the Most Highest.

The Collect.

HEAR, O Lord, we beseech thee, these our prayers, as we call upon thee on behalf of this thy servant; and bestow upon *him* the help of thy merciful consolation; through Jesus Christ our Lord. *Amen.*

Antiphon. Though I walk in the midst of trouble; Yet shalt thou refresh me.

Confitebor tibi. Psalm cxxxviii.

I WILL give thanks unto thee, O Lord, with my whole heart; even before the gods will I sing praise unto thee.

I will worship toward thy holy temple, and praise thy Name, because of thy loving-kindness and truth; for thou hast magnified thy Name, and thy word, above all things.

Visitation of the Sick

When I called upon thee, thou heardest me; and enduedst my soul with much strength.

Though I walk in the midst of trouble, yet shalt thou refresh me; thou shalt stretch forth thy hand upon the furiousness of mine enemies, and thy right hand shall save me.

The LORD shall make good his loving-kindness toward me; yea, thy mercy, O LORD, endureth for ever; despise not then the works of thine own hands.

The Collect.

O GOD, the strength of the weak and the comfort of sufferers; Mercifully accept our prayers, and grant to thy servant the help of thy power, that *his* sickness may be turned into health, and our sorrow into joy; through Jesus Christ our Lord. *Amen.*

Antiphon. The LORD saveth thy life from destruction; And crowneth thee with mercy and loving-kindness.

Benedic, anima mea. Psalm ciii.

PRAISE the LORD, O my soul; and all that is within me, praise his holy Name.

Praise the LORD, O my soul, and forget not all his benefits:

Who forgiveth all thy sin, and healeth all thine infirmities;

Who saveth thy life from destruction, and crowneth thee with mercy and loving-kindness.

O praise the LORD, ye angels of his, ye that excel in strength; ye that fulfil his commandment, and hearken unto the voice of his word.

O praise the LORD, all ye his hosts; ye servants of his that do his pleasure.

Visitation of the Sick

O speak good of the LORD, all ye works of his, in all places of his dominion: praise thou the LORD, O my soul.

The Collect.

ACCEPT, we beseech thee, merciful Lord, the devout praise of thy humble servant; and grant *him* an abiding sense of thy loving-kindness; through Jesus Christ our Lord. *Amen.*

¶ *Any of the following Psalms, 20, 27, 42, 91, 121, 146, may, at the discretion of the Minister, be substituted for any of those given above.*

¶ *Here shall be said,*

O SAVIOUR of the world, who by thy Cross and precious Blood hast redeemed us; Save us, and help us, we humbly beseech thee, O Lord.

¶ *As occasion demands, the Minister shall address the sick person on the meaning and use of the time of sickness, and the opportunity it affords for spiritual profit.*

¶ *Here may the Minister inquire of the sick person as to his acceptance of the Christian Faith, and as to whether he repent him truly of his sins, and be in charity with all the world; exhorting him to forgive, from the bottom of his heart, all persons that have offended him; and if he hath offended any other, to ask them forgiveness; and where he hath done injury or wrong to any man, that he make amends to the uttermost of his power.*

¶ *Then shall the sick person be moved to make a special confession of his sins, if he feel his conscience troubled with any matter; after which confession, on evidence of his repentance, the Minister shall assure him of God's mercy and forgiveness.*

¶ *Then the Minister shall say,*

Let us pray.

O MOST merciful God, who, according to the multitude of thy mercies, dost so put away the sins of those who truly repent, that thou rememberest them no more; Open thine eye of mercy upon this thy servant, who most earnestly desireth pardon and forgiveness. Renew in *him*, most loving Father, whatsoever hath been decayed by the fraud and malice of the devil, or by *his* own carnal will and frailness; preserve and continue this sick member in the unity of the Church; consider *his* contrition, accept *his* tears, assuage *his* pain, as shall seem to thee most expedient for *him*. And forasmuch as *he* putteth *his* full trust only in thy mercy, impute not unto *him his* former sins, but strengthen *him* with thy blessed Spirit; and, when thou art pleased to take *him* hence, take *him* unto thy favour; through the merits of thy most dearly beloved Son, Jesus Christ our Lord. *Amen.*

¶ Then shall the Minister say,

THE Almighty Lord, who is a most strong tower to all those who put their trust in him, to whom all things in heaven, in earth, and under the earth, do bow and obey; Be now and evermore thy defence; and make thee know and feel, that there is none other Name under heaven given to man, in whom, and through whom, thou mayest receive health and salvation, but only the Name of our Lord Jesus Christ. Amen.

¶ Here the Minister may use any part of the service of this Book, which, in his discretion, he shall think convenient to the occasion; and after that shall say,

UNTO God's gracious mercy and protection we commit thee. The LORD bless thee, and keep thee. The LORD make his face to shine upon thee, and be gracious unto thee. The LORD lift up his countenance upon thee, and give thee peace, both now and evermore. *Amen.*

Visitation of the Sick

PRAYERS.

¶ *These Prayers may be said with the foregoing Service, or any part thereof, at the discretion of the Minister.*

A Prayer for Recovery.

O GOD of heavenly powers, who, by the might of thy command, drivest away from men's bodies all sickness and all infirmity; Be present in thy goodness with this thy servant, that *his* weakness may be banished and *his* strength recalled; that *his* health being thereupon restored, *he* may bless thy holy Name; through Jesus Christ our Lord. *Amen.*

A Prayer for Healing.

O ALMIGHTY God, who art the giver of all health, and the aid of them that turn to thee for succour; We entreat thy strength and goodness in behalf of this thy servant, that *he* may be healed of *his* infirmities, to thine honour and glory; through Jesus Christ our Lord. *Amen.*

A Thanksgiving for the Beginning of a Recovery.

GREAT and mighty God, who bringest down to the grave, and bringest up again; We bless thy wonderful goodness, for having turned our heaviness into joy and our mourning into gladness, by restoring this our *brother* to some degree of *his* former health. Blessed be thy Name that thou didst not forsake *him* in *his* sickness; but didst visit *him* with comforts from above; didst support *him* in patience and submission to thy will; and at last didst send *him* seasonable relief. Perfect, we beseech thee, this thy mercy towards *him;* and prosper the means which shall be made use of for *his* cure: that, being restored to health of body, vigour of mind, and cheerfulness of spirit, *he* may be able to go to thine house, to offer thee an oblation with great gladness, and to bless thy holy Name for all thy goodness towards *him;* through Jesus Christ our Saviour, to whom, with thee and the Holy Spirit, be all honour and glory, world without end. *Amen.*

A Prayer for a Sick Person, when there appeareth but small hope of Recovery.

O FATHER of mercies, and God of all comfort, our only help in time of need; We fly unto thee for succour in behalf of this thy servant, here lying in great weakness of body. Look graciously upon *him,* O Lord; and the more the outward man decayeth, strengthen *him,* we beseech thee, so much the more continually with thy grace and Holy Spirit in the inner man. Give *him* unfeigned repentance for all the errors of *his* life past, and stedfast faith in thy Son Jesus; that *his* sins may be done away by thy mercy, and *his* pardon sealed in heaven; through the same thy Son, our Lord and Saviour. *Amen.*

A Prayer for the Despondent.

COMFORT, we beseech thee, most gracious God, this thy servant, cast down and faint of heart amidst the sorrows and difficulties of the world; and grant that, by the power of thy Holy Spirit, *he* may be enabled to go upon *his* way rejoicing, and give thee continual thanks for thy sustaining providence; through Jesus Christ our Lord. *Amen.*

A Prayer which may be said by the Minister in behalf of all present at the Visitation.

O GOD, whose days are without end, and whose mercies cannot be numbered; Make us, we beseech thee, deeply sensible of the shortness and uncertainty of human life; and let thy Holy Spirit lead us in holiness and righteousness, all our days: that, when we shall have served thee

Visitation of the Sick

in our generation, we may be gathered unto our fathers, having the testimony of a good conscience; in the communion of the Catholic Church; in the confidence of a certain faith; in the comfort of a reasonable, religious, and holy hope; in favour with thee our God, and in perfect charity with the world. All which we ask through Jesus Christ our Lord. *Amen.*

A Commendatory Prayer for a Sick Person
at the point of Departure.

O ALMIGHTY God, with whom do live the spirits of just men made perfect, after they are delivered from their earthly prisons; We humbly commend the soul of this thy servant, our dear *brother*, into thy hands, as into the hands of a faithful Creator, and most merciful Saviour; beseeching thee, that it may be precious in thy sight. Wash it, we pray thee, in the blood of that immaculate Lamb, that was slain to take away the sins of the world; that whatsoever defilements it may have contracted, through the lusts of the flesh or the wiles of Satan, being purged and done away, it may be presented pure and without spot before thee; through the merits of Jesus Christ thine only Son our Lord. *Amen.*

LITANY FOR THE DYING.

O GOD the Father;
Have mercy upon the soul of thy servant.
O God the Son;
Have mercy upon the soul of thy servant.
O God the Holy Ghost;
Have mercy upon the soul of thy servant.
O holy Trinity, one God;
Have mercy upon the soul of thy servant.

Visitation of the Sick

From all evil, from all sin, from all tribulation;
Good Lord, deliver him.

By thy holy Incarnation, by thy Cross and Passion, by thy precious Death and Burial;
Good Lord, deliver him.

By thy glorious Resurrection and Ascension, and by the coming of the Holy Ghost;
Good Lord, deliver him.

We sinners do beseech thee to hear us, O Lord God; That it may please thee to deliver the soul of thy servant from the power of the evil one, and from eternal death;
We beseech thee to hear us, good Lord.

That it may please thee mercifully to pardon all *his* sins.
We beseech thee to hear us, good Lord.

That it may please thee to grant *him* a place of refreshment and everlasting blessedness;
We beseech thee to hear us, good Lord.

That it may please thee to give *him* joy and gladness in thy kingdom, with thy saints in light;
We beseech thee to hear us, good Lord.

O Lamb of God, who takest away the sins of the world;
Have mercy upon him.

O Lamb of God, who takest away the sins of the world;
Have mercy upon him.

O Lamb of God, who takest away the sins of the world;
Grant him *thy peace.*

Lord, have mercy.
Christ, have mercy.
Lord, have mercy.

OUR Father, who art in heaven, Hallowed be thy Name. Thy kingdom come. Thy will be done, On earth as it is in heaven. Give us this day our daily bread. And forgive us our trespasses, As we forgive those who trespass against us. And lead us not into temptation, But deliver us from evil. Amen.

Let us pray.

O SOVEREIGN Lord, who desirest not the death of a sinner; We beseech thee to loose the spirit of this thy servant from every bond, and set *him* free from all evil; that *he* may rest with all thy saints in the eternal habitations; through Jesus Christ our Lord, who liveth and reigneth with thee and the Holy Ghost, one God, world without end. *Amen.*

An Absolution to be said by the Priest.

THE Almighty and merciful Lord grant thee pardon and remission of all thy sins, and the grace and comfort of the Holy Spirit. *Amen.*

A Commendation.

DEPART, O Christian soul, out of this world,
In the Name of God the Father Almighty who created thee.
In the Name of Jesus Christ who redeemed thee.
In the Name of the Holy Ghost who sanctifieth thee.
May thy rest be this day in peace, and thy dwelling-place in the Paradise of God.

A Commendatory Prayer when the Soul is Departed.

INTO thy hands, O merciful Saviour, we commend the soul of thy servant, now departed from the body. Acknowledge, we humbly beseech thee, a sheep of thine own fold, a lamb of thine own flock, a sinner of thine own redeeming. Receive *him* into the arms of thy mercy, into the blessed rest of everlasting peace, and into the glorious company of the saints in light. *Amen.*

UNCTION OF THE SICK.

¶ *When any sick person shall in humble faith desire the ministry of healing through Anointing or Laying on of Hands, the Minister may use such portion of the foregoing Office as he shall think fit, and the following:*

O BLESSED Redeemer, relieve, we beseech thee, by thy indwelling power, the distress of this thy servant; release *him* from sin, and drive away all pain of soul and body, that being restored to soundness of health, *he* may offer thee praise and thanksgiving; who livest and reignest with the Father and the Holy Ghost, one God, world without end. *Amen.*

I ANOINT thee with oil (*or* I lay my hand upon thee), In the Name of the Father, and of the Son, and of the Holy Ghost; beseeching the mercy of our Lord Jesus Christ, that all thy pain and sickness of body being put to flight, the blessing of health may be restored unto thee. Amen.

¶ *The Minister is ordered, from time to time, to advise the People, whilst they are in health, to make Wills arranging for the disposal of their temporal goods, and, when of ability, to leave Bequests for religious and charitable uses.*

The Communion of the Sick

¶ *Forasmuch as all mortal men are subject to many sudden perils, diseases,*
and sicknesses, and ever uncertain what time they shall depart out of this
life; therefore, to the intent they may be always in readiness to die, whenso-
ever it shall please Almighty God to call them, the Ministers shall diligently
from time to time, but especially in the time of pestilence, or other infectious
sickness, exhort their parishioners to the often receiving of the Holy Com-
munion of the Body and Blood of our Saviour Christ, when it shall be
publicly administered in the Church; that so doing, they may, in case of
sudden visitation, have the less cause to be disquieted for lack of the same.
But if the sick person be not able to come to the Church, and yet is desirous
to receive the Communion in his house; then he must give timely notice to
the Minister, signifying also how many there are to communicate with
him; and all things necessary being prepared, the Minister shall there
celebrate the Holy Communion, beginning with the Collect, Epistle, and
Gospel, here following.

The Collect.

ALMIGHTY, everliving God, Maker of mankind, who
dost correct those whom thou dost love, and chastise every one whom thou dost receive; We beseech thee
to have mercy upon this thy servant visited with thine
hand, and to grant that *he* may take *his* sickness patiently,
and recover *his* bodily health, if it be thy gracious will;
and that, whensoever *his* soul shall depart from the body,
it may be without spot presented unto thee; through Jesus
Christ our Lord. *Amen.*

The Epistle. Hebrews xii. 5.

MY son, despise not thou the chastening of the Lord,
nor faint when thou art rebuked of him: for whom
the Lord loveth he chasteneth, and scourgeth every son
whom he receiveth.

The Gospel. St. John v. 24.

VERILY, verily, I say unto you, He that heareth my
word, and believeth on him that sent me, hath ever-

Communion of the Sick

lasting life, and shall not come into condemnation; but is passed from death unto life.

¶ *Or the following Collect, Epistle, and Gospel.*

The Collect.

O LORD, holy Father, by whose loving-kindness our souls and bodies are renewed; Mercifully look upon this thy servant, that, every cause of sickness being removed, *he* may be restored to soundness of health; through Jesus Christ our Lord. *Amen.*

The Epistle. 1 St. John v. 13.

THESE things have I written unto you that believe on the name of the Son of God; that ye may know that ye have eternal life, and that ye may believe on the name of the Son of God. And this is the confidence that we have in him, that, if we ask any thing according to his will, he heareth us: and if we know that he hear us, whatsoever we ask, we know that we have the petitions that we desired of him.

The Gospel. St. John vi. 47.

JESUS said, Verily, verily, I say unto you, He that believeth on me hath everlasting life. I am that bread of life. Your fathers did eat manna in the wilderness, and are dead. This is the bread which cometh down from heaven, that a man may eat thereof, and not die. I am the living bread which came down from heaven: if any man eat of this bread, he shall live for ever: and the bread that I will give is my flesh, which I will give for the life of the world.

¶ *After which the Minister shall proceed according to the form before prescribed for the Holy Communion, beginning at these words,* Ye who do truly, *etc.*

¶ *At the time of the distribution of the holy Sacrament, the Minister shall first receive the Communion himself, and after minister unto*

Communion of the Sick

those who are appointed to communicate with the sick, and last of all to the sick person.

¶ *When circumstances render it expedient to shorten the Service, the following form shall suffice:*

The Confession and the Absolution; Lift up your hearts, *etc., through the Sanctus; The Prayer of Consecration, ending with these words,* partakers of his most blessed Body and Blood; *The Prayer of Humble Access; The Communion; The Lord's Prayer; The Blessing. And* NOTE, *That for the Confession and Absolution the following may be used.*

The Confession.

O ALMIGHTY Father, Lord of heaven and earth, we confess that we have sinned against thee in thought, word, and deed. Have mercy upon us, O God, after thy great goodness; according to the multitude of thy mercies, do away our offences and cleanse us from our sins; for Jesus Christ's sake. Amen.

The Absolution.

THE Almighty and merciful Lord grant you Absolution and Remission of all your sins, true repentance, amendment of life, and the grace and consolation of his Holy Spirit. *Amen.*

¶ *But if a man, either by reason of extremity of sickness, or for want of warning in due time to the Minister, or by any other just impediment, do not receive the Sacrament of Christ's Body and Blood, the Minister shall instruct him, that if he do truly repent him of his sins, and stedfastly believe that Jesus Christ hath suffered death upon the Cross for him, and shed his Blood for his redemption, earnestly remembering the benefits he hath thereby, and giving him hearty thanks therefor, he doth eat and drink the Body and Blood of our Saviour Christ profitably to his soul's health, although he do not receive the Sacrament with his mouth.*

¶ *This Office may be used with aged and bed-ridden persons, or such as are not able to attend the public Ministration in Church, substituting the Collect, Epistle, and Gospel for the Day, for those appointed above.*

The Order for
The Burial of the Dead

¶ *The Minister, meeting the Body, and going before it, either into the Church or towards the Grave, shall say or sing,*

I AM the resurrection and the life, saith the Lord: he that believeth in me, though he were dead, yet shall he live: and whosoever liveth and believeth in me, shall never die.

I know that my redeemer liveth, and that he shall stand at the latter day upon the earth: and though this body be destroyed, yet shall I see God: whom I shall see for myself, and mine eyes shall behold, and not as a stranger.

We brought nothing into this world, and it is certain we can carry nothing out. The LORD gave, and the LORD hath taken away; blessed be the name of the LORD.

¶ *After they are come into the Church, shall be said one or more of the following Selections, taken from the Psalms. The Gloria Patri may be omitted except at the end of the whole portion or selection from the Psalter.*

Dixi, custodiam. Psalm xxxix.

LORD, let me know mine end, and the number of my days; * that I may be certified how long I have to live.

Behold, thou hast made my days as it were a span long, and mine age is even as nothing in respect of thee; * and verily every man living is altogether vanity.

For man walketh in a vain shadow, and disquieteth himself in vain; * he heapeth up riches, and cannot tell who shall gather them.

And now, Lord, what is my hope? * truly my hope is even in thee.

Deliver me from all mine offences; * and make me not a rebuke unto the foolish.

When thou with rebukes dost chasten man for sin, thou makest his beauty to consume away, like as it were a moth fretting a garment: * every man therefore is but vanity.

Hear my prayer, O LORD, and with thine ears consider my calling; * hold not thy peace at my tears;

For I am a stranger with thee, and a sojourner, * as all my fathers were.

O spare me a little, that I may recover my strength, * before I go hence, and be no more seen.

Domine, refugium. Psalm xc.

LORD, thou hast been our refuge, * from one generation to another.

Before the mountains were brought forth, or ever the earth and the world were made, * thou art God from everlasting, and world without end.

Thou turnest man to destruction; * again thou sayest, Come again, ye children of men.

For a thousand years in thy sight are but as yesterday, when it is past, * and as a watch in the night.

As soon as thou scatterest them they are even as a sleep; * and fade away suddenly like the grass.

In the morning it is green, and groweth up; * but in the evening it is cut down, dried up, and withered.

For we consume away in thy displeasure, * and are afraid at thy wrathful indignation.

Thou hast set our misdeeds before thee; * and our secret sins in the light of thy countenance.

For when thou art angry all our days are gone: * we bring our years to an end, as it were a tale that is told.

The days of our age are threescore years and ten; and though men be so strong that they come to fourscore years, * yet is their strength then but labour and sorrow; so soon passeth it away, and we are gone.

Burial of the Dead

So teach us to number our days, * that we may apply our hearts unto wisdom.

Dominus illuminatio. Psalm xxvii.

THE LORD is my light and my salvation; whom then shall I fear? * the LORD is the strength of my life; of whom then shall I be afraid?

One thing have I desired of the LORD, which I will require; * even that I may dwell in the house of the LORD all the days of my life, to behold the fair beauty of the LORD, and to visit his temple.

For in the time of trouble he shall hide me in his tabernacle; * yea, in the secret place of his dwelling shall he hide me, and set me up upon a rock of stone.

And now shall he lift up mine head * above mine enemies round about me.

Therefore will I offer in his dwelling an oblation, with great gladness: * I will sing and speak praises unto the LORD.

Hearken unto my voice, O LORD, when I cry unto thee; * have mercy upon me, and hear me.

My heart hath talked of thee, Seek ye my face: * Thy face, LORD, will I seek.

O hide not thou thy face from me, * nor cast thy servant away in displeasure.

Thou hast been my succour; * leave me not, neither forsake me, O God of my salvation.

I should utterly have fainted, * but that I believe verily to see the goodness of the LORD in the land of the living.

O tarry thou the LORD'S leisure; * be strong, and he shall comfort thine heart; and put thou thy trust in the LORD.

Burial of the Dead

Deus noster refugium. Psalm xlvi.

GOD is our hope and strength, * a very present help in trouble.

Therefore will we not fear, though the earth be moved, * and though the hills be carried into the midst of the sea;

Though the waters thereof rage and swell, * and though the mountains shake at the tempest of the same.

There is a river, the streams whereof make glad the city of God; * the holy place of the tabernacle of the Most Highest.

God is in the midst of her, therefore shall she not be removed; * God shall help her, and that right early.

Be still then, and know that I am God: * I will be exalted among the nations, and I will be exalted in the earth.

The LORD of hosts is with us; * the God of Jacob is our refuge.

Levavi oculos. Psalm cxxi.

I WILL lift up mine eyes unto the hills; * from whence cometh my help?

My help cometh even from the LORD, * who hath made heaven and earth.

He will not suffer thy foot to be moved; * and he that keepeth thee will not sleep.

Behold, he that keepeth Israel * shall neither slumber nor sleep.

The LORD himself is thy keeper; * the LORD is thy defence upon thy right hand;

So that the sun shall not burn thee by day, * neither the moon by night.

The LORD shall preserve thee from all evil; * yea, it is even he that shall keep thy soul.

The LORD shall preserve thy going out, and thy coming in, * from this time forth for evermore

Burial of the Dead

De profundis. Psalm cxxx.

OUT of the deep have I called unto thee, O LORD; * Lord, hear my voice.

O let thine ears consider well * the voice of my complaint.

If thou, LORD, wilt be extreme to mark what is done amiss, * O Lord, who may abide it?

For there is mercy with thee; * therefore shalt thou be feared.

I look for the LORD; my soul doth wait for him; * in his word is my trust.

My soul fleeth unto the Lord before the morning watch; * I say, before the morning watch.

O Israel, trust in the LORD, for with the LORD there is mercy, * and with him is plenteous redemption.

And he shall redeem Israel * from all his sins.

¶ *Then shall follow the Lesson, taken out of the fifteenth Chapter of the first Epistle of St. Paul to the Corinthians.*

1 Corinthians xv. 20.

NOW is Christ risen from the dead, and become the firstfruits of them that slept. For since by man came death, by man came also the resurrection of the dead. For as in Adam all die, even so in Christ shall all be made alive. But every man in his own order: Christ the firstfruits; afterward they that are Christ's at his coming. Then cometh the end, when he shall have delivered up the kingdom to God, even the Father; when he shall have put down all rule and all authority and power. For he must reign, till he hath put all enemies under his feet. The last enemy that shall be destroyed is death. For he hath put all things under his feet. But when he saith all things are put under him, it is manifest that he is excepted, which did put all things under him. And when all things shall be subdued

328

unto him, then shall the Son also himself be subject unto him that put all things under him, that God may be all in all.

But some man will say, How are the dead raised up? and with what body do they come? Thou foolish one, that which thou sowest is not quickened, except it die: and that which thou sowest, thou sowest not that body that shall be, but bare grain, it may chance of wheat, or of some other grain: but God giveth it a body as it hath pleased him, and to every seed its own body. All flesh is not the same flesh: but there is one kind of flesh of men, another flesh of beasts, another of fishes, and another of birds. There are also celestial bodies, and bodies terrestrial: but the glory of the celestial is one, and the glory of the terrestrial is another. There is one glory of the sun, and another glory of the moon, and another glory of the stars: for one star differeth from another star in glory. So also is the resurrection of the dead. It is sown in corruption; it is raised in incorruption: it is sown in dishonour; it is raised in glory: it is sown in weakness; it is raised in power: it is sown a natural body; it is raised a spiritual body. There is a natural body, and there is a spiritual body. And so it is written, The first man Adam was made a living soul; the last Adam was made a quickening spirit. Howbeit that was not first which is spiritual, but that which is natural; and afterward that which is spiritual. The first man is of the earth, earthy: the second man is the Lord from heaven. As is the earthy, such are they also that are earthy: and as is the heavenly, such are they also that are heavenly. And as we have borne the image of the earthy, we shall also bear the image of the heavenly.

Now this I say, brethren, that flesh and blood cannot inherit the kingdom of God; neither doth corruption inherit incorruption. Behold, I shew you a mystery; We shall not all sleep, but we shall all be changed, in a moment, in the twinkling of an eye, at the last trump: for the trumpet shall sound, and the dead shall be raised incorruptible, and we shall be changed. For this corruptible must put on incorruption, and this mortal must put on immortality. So when this corruptible shall have put on incorruption, and this mortal shall have put on immortality, then shall be brought to pass the saying that is written, Death is swallowed up in victory. O death, where is thy sting? O grave, where is thy victory? The sting of death is sin; and the strength of sin is the law. But thanks be to God, which giveth us the victory through our Lord Jesus Christ. Therefore, my beloved brethren, be ye stedfast, unmoveable, always abounding in the work of the Lord, forasmuch as ye know that your labour is not in vain in the Lord.

¶ *Or this.*

Romans viii. 14.

AS many as are led by the Spirit of God, they are the sons of God. For ye have not received the spirit of bondage again to fear; but ye have received the Spirit of adoption, whereby we cry, Abba, Father. The Spirit himself beareth witness with our spirit, that we are the children of God: and if children, then heirs; heirs of God, and jointheirs with Christ; if so be that we suffer with him, that we may be also glorified together. For I reckon that the sufferings of this present time are not worthy to be compared with the glory which shall be revealed in us. For the earnest expectation of the creature waiteth for the manifestation of the sons of God. We know that all things work together for good to them that love God, to them who are the called according to his purpose. What shall we then say to these things? If God be for us, who can be against us? He that spared not his own Son, but delivered him up for us all, how shall he not with him also freely give us all things? Who is he that condemneth? It is Christ that died, yea rather, that is risen again, who is even at the right hand of God, who also maketh intercession for us. Who shall separate us from the love of Christ? shall tribulation, or distress, or persecution, or famine, or nakedness, or peril, or sword? Nay, in all these things we are more than conquerors through him that loved us. For I am persuaded, that neither death, nor life, nor angels, nor principalities, nor powers, nor things present, nor things to come, nor height, nor depth, nor any other creature, shall be able to separate us from the love of God, which is in Christ Jesus our Lord.

¶ *Or this.*

St. John xiv. 1.

JESUS said, Let not your heart be troubled: ye believe in God, believe also in me. In my Father's house are many mansions: if it were not so, I would have told you. I go to prepare a place for you. And if I go and prepare a place for you, I will come again, and receive you unto myself; that where I am, there ye may be also. And whither I go ye know, and the way ye know. Thomas saith unto him, Lord, we know not whither thou goest; and how can we know the way? Jesus saith unto him, I am the way, the truth, and the life: no man cometh unto the Father, but by me.

¶ *Here may be sung a Hymn or Anthem; and, at the discretion of the Minister, the Creed, the Lord's Prayer, the Prayer which followeth, and such other fitting Prayers as are elsewhere provided in this Book, ending with the Blessing; the Minister, before the Prayers, first pronouncing,*

The Lord be with you.
Answer. And with thy spirit.

Burial of the Dead

Let us pray.

REMEMBER thy servant, O Lord, according to the favour which thou bearest unto thy people, and grant that, increasing in knowledge and love of thee, *he* may go from strength to strength, in the life of perfect service, in thy heavenly kingdom; through Jesus Christ our Lord, who liveth and reigneth with thee and the Holy Ghost ever, one God, world without end. *Amen.*

UNTO God's gracious mercy and protection we commit you. The LORD bless you and keep you. The LORD make his face to shine upon you, and be gracious unto you. The LORD lift up his countenance upon you, and give you peace, both now and evermore. *Amen.*

AT THE GRAVE.

¶ *When they come to the Grave, while the Body is made ready to be laid into the earth, shall be sung or said,*

MAN, that is born of a woman, hath but a short time to live, and is full of misery. He cometh up, and is cut down, like a flower; he fleeth as it were a shadow, and never continueth in one stay.

In the midst of life we are in death; of whom may we seek for succour, but of thee, O Lord, who for our sins art justly displeased?

Yet, O Lord God most holy, O Lord most mighty, O holy and most merciful Saviour, deliver us not into the bitter pains of eternal death.

Thou knowest, Lord, the secrets of our hearts; shut not thy merciful ears to our prayer; but spare us, Lord most holy, O God most mighty, O holy and merciful Saviour, thou most worthy Judge eternal, suffer us not, at our last hour, for any pains of death, to fall from thee.

Burial of the Dead

¶ *Or this.*

ALL that the Father giveth me shall come to me; and him that cometh to me I will in no wise cast out.

He that raised up Jesus from the dead will also quicken our mortal bodies, by his Spirit that dwelleth in us.

Wherefore my heart is glad, and my glory rejoiceth: my flesh also shall rest in hope.

Thou shalt show me the path of life; in thy presence is the fulness of joy, and at thy right hand there is pleasure for evermore.

¶ *Then, while the earth shall be cast upon the Body by some standing by, the Minister shall say,*

UNTO Almighty God we commend the soul of our *brother* departed, and we commit *his* body to the ground; earth to earth, ashes to ashes, dust to dust; in sure and certain hope of the Resurrection unto eternal life, through our Lord Jesus Christ; at whose coming in glorious majesty to judge the world, the earth and the sea shall give up their dead; and the corruptible bodies of those who sleep in him shall be changed, and made like unto his own glorious body; according to the mighty working whereby he is able to subdue all things unto himself.

¶ *Then shall be said or sung,*

I HEARD a voice from heaven, saying unto me, Write, From henceforth blessed are the dead who die in the Lord: even so saith the Spirit; for they rest from their labours.

¶ *Then the Minister shall say,*

The Lord be with you.
Answer. And with thy spirit.

333

Burial of the Dead

Let us pray.

Lord, have mercy upon us.
Christ, have mercy upon us.
Lord, have mercy upon us.

OUR Father, who art in heaven, Hallowed be thy Name. Thy kingdom come. Thy will be done, On earth as it is in heaven. Give us this day our daily bread. And forgive us our trespasses, As we forgive those who trespass against us. And lead us not into temptation, But deliver us from evil. Amen.

¶ *Then the Minister shall say one or more of the following Prayers, at his discretion.*

O GOD, whose mercies cannot be numbered; Accept our prayers on behalf of the soul of thy servant departed, and grant *him* an entrance into the land of light and joy, in the fellowship of thy saints; through Jesus Christ our Lord. *Amen.*

ALMIGHTY God, with whom do live the spirits of those who depart hence in the Lord, and with whom the souls of the faithful, after they are delivered from the burden of the flesh, are in joy and felicity; We give thee hearty thanks for the good examples of all those thy servants, who, having finished their course in faith, do now rest from their labours. And we beseech thee, that we, with all those who are departed in the true faith of thy holy Name, may have our perfect consummation and bliss, both in body and soul, in thy eternal and everlasting glory; through Jesus Christ our Lord. *Amen.*

O MERCIFUL God, the Father of our Lord Jesus Christ, who is the Resurrection and the Life; in whom whosoever believeth, shall live, though he die; and

Burial of the Dead

whosoever liveth, and believeth in him, shall not die eternally; who also hath taught us, by his holy Apostle Saint Paul, not to be sorry, as men without hope, for those who sleep in him; We humbly beseech thee, O Father, to raise us from the death of sin unto the life of righteousness; that, when we shall depart this life, we may rest in him; and that, at the general Resurrection in the last day, we may be found acceptable in thy sight; and receive that blessing, which thy well-beloved Son shall then pronounce to all who love and fear thee, saying, Come, ye blessed children of my Father, receive the kingdom prepared for you from the beginning of the world. Grant this, we beseech thee, O merciful Father, through Jesus Christ, our Mediator and Redeemer. *Amen.*

THE God of peace, who brought again from the dead our Lord Jesus Christ, the great Shepherd of the sheep, through the blood of the everlasting covenant; Make you perfect in every good work to do his will, working in you that which is well pleasing in his sight; through Jesus Christ, to whom be glory for ever and ever. *Amen.*

¶ *The Minister, at his discretion, may also use any of the following Prayers before the final Blessing.*

O ALMIGHTY God, the God of the spirits of all flesh, who by a voice from heaven didst proclaim, Blessed are the dead who die in the Lord; Multiply, we beseech thee, to those who rest in Jesus, the manifold blessings of thy love, that the good work which thou didst begin in them may be perfected unto the day of Jesus Christ. And of thy mercy, O heavenly Father, vouchsafe that we, who now serve thee here on earth, may at last, together with them, be found meet to be partakers of the inheritance of

Burial of the Dead

the saints in light; for the sake of the same thy Son Jesus Christ our Lord. *Amen.*

MOST merciful Father, who hast been pleased to take unto thyself the soul of this thy servant (*or* this thy child); Grant to us who are still in our pilgrimage, and who walk as yet by faith, that having served thee with constancy on earth, we may be joined hereafter with thy blessed saints in glory everlasting; through Jesus Christ our Lord. *Amen.*

O LORD Jesus Christ, who by thy death didst take away the sting of death; Grant unto us thy servants so to follow in faith where thou hast led the way, that we may at length fall asleep peacefully in thee, and awake up after thy likeness; through thy mercy, who livest with the Father and the Holy Ghost, one God, world without end. *Amen.*

ALMIGHTY and everliving God, we yield unto thee most high praise and hearty thanks, for the wonderful grace and virtue declared in all thy saints, who have been the choice vessels of thy grace, and the lights of the world in their several generations; most humbly beseeching thee to give us grace so to follow the example of their stedfastness in thy faith, and obedience to thy holy commandments, that at the day of the general Resurrection, we, with all those who are of the mystical body of thy Son, may be set on his right hand, and hear that his most joyful voice: Come, ye blessed of my Father, inherit the kingdom prepared for you from the foundation of the world. Grant this, O Father, for the sake of the same, thy Son Jesus Christ, our only Mediator and Advocate. *Amen.*

¶ *Inasmuch as it may sometimes be expedient to say under shelter of the Church the whole or a part of the service appointed to be said at the Grave, the same is hereby allowed for weighty cause.*

Burial of the Dead

¶ *It is to be noted that this Office is appropriate to be used only for the faithful departed in Christ, provided that in any other case the Minister may, at his discretion, use such part of this Office, or such devotions taken from other parts of this Book, as may be fitting.*

At the Burial of the Dead at Sea.

¶ *The same Office may be used; but instead of the Sentence of Committal, the Minister shall say,*

UNTO Almighty God we commend the soul of our *brother* departed, and we commit *his* body to the deep; in sure and certain hope of the Resurrection unto eternal life, through our Lord Jesus Christ; at whose coming in glorious majesty to judge the world, the sea shall give up her dead; and the corruptible bodies of those who sleep in him shall be changed, and made like unto his glorious body; according to the mighty working whereby he is able to subdue all things unto himself.

Burial of a Child

AT THE BURIAL OF A CHILD.

¶ *The Minister, meeting the Body, and going before it, either into the Church or towards the Grave, shall say,*

I AM the resurrection and the life, saith the Lord: he that believeth in me, though he were dead, yet shall he live: and whosoever liveth and believeth in me, shall never die.

JESUS called them unto him and said, Suffer the little children to come unto me, and forbid them not: for of such is the kingdom of God.

HE shall feed his flock like a shepherd: he shall gather the lambs with his arms, and carry them in his bosom.

¶ *When they are come into the Church, shall be said the following Psalms; and at the end of each Psalm shall be said the Gloria Patri.*

Dominus regit me. Psalm xxiii.

THE LORD is my shepherd; * therefore can I lack nothing.

He shall feed me in a green pasture, * and lead me forth beside the waters of comfort.

He shall convert my soul, * and bring me forth in the paths of righteousness for his Name's sake.

Yea, though I walk through the valley of the shadow of death, I will fear no evil; * for thou art with me; thy rod and thy staff comfort me.

Thou shalt prepare a table before me in the presence of them that trouble me; * thou hast anointed my head with oil, and my cup shall be full.

Surely thy loving-kindness and mercy shall follow me all the days of my life; * and I will dwell in the house of the LORD for ever.

Burial of a Child

Levavi oculos. Psalm cxxi.

I WILL lift up mine eyes unto the hills; * from whence cometh my help?

My help cometh even from the LORD, * who hath made heaven and earth.

He will not suffer thy foot to be moved; * and he that keepeth thee will not sleep.

Behold, he that keepeth Israel * shall neither slumber nor sleep.

The LORD himself is thy keeper; * the LORD is thy defence upon thy right hand;

So that the sun shall not burn thee by day, * neither the moon by night.

The LORD shall preserve thee from all evil; * yea, it is even he that shall keep thy soul.

The LORD shall preserve thy going out, and thy coming in, * from this time forth for evermore.

¶ *Then shall follow the Lesson taken out of the eighteenth Chapter of the Gospel according to St. Matthew.*

AT the same time came the disciples unto Jesus, saying, Who is the greatest in the kingdom of heaven? And Jesus called a little child unto him, and set him in the midst of them, and said, Verily I say unto you, Except ye be converted, and become as little children, ye shall not enter into the kingdom of heaven. Whosoever therefore shall humble himself as this little child, the same is greatest in the kingdom of heaven. And whoso shall receive one such little child in my name receiveth me. Take heed that ye despise not one of these little ones; for I say unto you, That in heaven their angels do always behold the face of my Father which is in heaven.

Burial of a Child

¶ *Here may be sung a Hymn or an Anthem; then shall the Minister say.*

The Lord be with you.
Answer. And with thy spirit.

Let us pray.
Lord, have mercy upon us.
Christ, have mercy upon us.
Lord, have mercy upon us.

¶ *Then shall be said by the Minister and People,*

OUR Father, who art in heaven, Hallowed be thy
Name. Thy kingdom come. Thy will be done, On
earth as it is in heaven. Give us this day our daily bread.
And forgive us our trespasses, As we forgive those who
trespass against us. And lead us not into temptation, But
deliver us from evil. Amen.

Minister. Blessed are the pure in heart;
Answer. For they shall see God.
Minister. Blessed be the Name of the Lord;
Answer. Henceforth, world without end.
Minister. Lord, hear our prayer;
Answer. And let our cry come unto thee.

¶ *Here shall be said the following Prayers, or other fitting Prayers from this Book.*

O MERCIFUL Father, whose face the angels of thy
little ones do always behold in heaven; Grant us
stedfastly to believe that this thy child hath been taken
into the safe keeping of thine eternal love; through Jesus
Christ our Lord. *Amen.*

A LMIGHTY and merciful Father, who dost grant to
children an abundant entrance into thy kingdom;
Grant us grace so to conform our lives to their innocency

Burial of a Child

and perfect faith, that at length, united with them, we may stand in thy presence in fulness of joy; through Jesus Christ our Lord. *Amen.*

THE grace of our Lord Jesus Christ, and the love of God, and the fellowship of the Holy Ghost, be with us all evermore. *Amen.*

¶ *When they are come to the Grave shall be said or sung,*

JESUS saith to his disciples, Ye now therefore have sorrow: but I will see you again, and your heart shall rejoice, and your joy no man taketh from you.

¶ *While the earth is being cast upon the Body, the Minister shall say,*

IN sure and certain hope of the Resurrection to eternal life through our Lord Jesus Christ, we commit the body of this child to the ground. The LORD bless *him* and keep *him*, the LORD make his face to shine upon *him* and be gracious unto *him*, the LORD lift up his countenance upon *him*, and give *him* peace, both now and evermore.

¶ *Then shall be said or sung,*

THEREFORE are they before the throne of God, and serve him day and night in his temple: and he that sitteth on the throne shall dwell among them.

They shall hunger no more, neither thirst any more; neither shall the sun light on them, nor any heat.

For the Lamb which is in the midst of the throne shall feed them, and shall lead them unto living fountains of waters: and God shall wipe away all tears from their eyes.

¶ *Then shall the Minister say,*

The Lord be with you.
Answer. And with thy spirit.

Burial of a Child

Let us pray.

O GOD, whose most dear Son did take little children into his arms and bless them; Give us grace, we beseech thee, to entrust the soul of this child to thy never-failing care and love, and bring us all to thy heavenly kingdom; through the same thy Son, Jesus Christ our Lord. *Amen.*

ALMIGHTY God, Father of mercies and giver of all comfort; Deal graciously, we pray thee, with all those who mourn, that, casting every care on thee, they may know the consolation of thy love; through Jesus Christ our Lord. *Amen.*

MAY Almighty God, the Father, the Son, and the Holy Ghost, bless you and keep you, now and for evermore. *Amen.*

The Psalter

The Psalter

The Psalter
or Psalms of David

BOOK I

The First Day.
Morning Prayer.

Psalm 1. *Beatus vir qui non abiit.*

BLESSED is the man that hath not walked in the counsel of the ungodly, nor stood in the way of sinners, * and hath not sat in the seat of the scornful.

2 But his delight is in the law of the LORD; * and in his law will he exercise himself day and night.

3 And he shall be like a tree planted by the water-side, * that will bring forth his fruit in due season.

4 His leaf also shall not wither; * and look, whatsoever he doeth, it shall prosper.

5 As for the ungodly, it is not so with them; * but they are like the chaff, which the wind scattereth away from the face of the earth.

6 Therefore the ungodly shall not be able to stand in the judgment, * neither the sinners in the congregation of the righteous.

7 But the LORD knoweth the way of the righteous; * and the way of the ungodly shall perish.

Psalm 2. *Quare fremuerunt gentes?*

WHY do the heathen so furiously rage together? * and why do the people imagine a vain thing?

2 The kings of the earth stand up, and the rulers take counsel together * against the LORD, and against his Anointed:

345

3 Let us break their bonds asunder, * and cast away their cords from us.

4 He that dwelleth in heaven shall laugh them to scorn: * the Lord shall have them in derision.

5 Then shall he speak unto them in his wrath, * and vex them in his sore displeasure:

6 Yet have I set my King * upon my holy hill of Sion.

7 I will rehearse the decree; * the LORD hath said unto me, Thou art my Son, this day have I begotten thee.

8 Desire of me, and I shall give thee the nations for thine inheritance, * and the utmost parts of the earth for thy possession.

9 Thou shalt bruise them with a rod of iron, * and break them in pieces like a potter's vessel.

10 Be wise now therefore, O ye kings; * be instructed, ye that are judges of the earth.

11 Serve the LORD in fear, * and rejoice unto him with reverence.

12 Kiss the Son, lest he be angry, and so ye perish from the right way, if his wrath be kindled, yea but a little. * Blessed are all they that put their trust in him.

Psalm 3. *Domine, quid multiplicati?*

LORD, how are they increased that trouble me! * many are they that rise against me.

2 Many one there be that say of my soul, * There is no help for him in his God.

3 But thou, O LORD, art my defender; * thou art my worship, and the lifter up of my head.

4 I did call upon the LORD with my voice, * and he heard me out of his holy hill.

5 I laid me down and slept, and rose up again; * for the LORD sustained me.

6 I will not be afraid for ten thousands of the people, * that have set themselves against me round about.

7 Up, LORD, and help me, O my God, * for thou smitest all mine enemies upon the cheek-bone; thou hast broken the teeth of the ungodly.

8 Salvation belongeth unto the LORD; * and thy blessing is upon thy people.

Psalm 4. *Cum invocarem.*

HEAR me when I call, O God of my righteousness: * thou hast set me at liberty when I was in trouble; have mercy upon me, and hearken unto my prayer.

2 O ye sons of men, how long will ye blaspheme mine honour, * and have such pleasure in vanity, and seek after falsehood?

3 Know this also, that the LORD hath chosen to himself the man that is godly; * when I call upon the LORD he will hear me.

4 Stand in awe, and sin not; * commune with your own heart, and in your chamber, and be still.

5 Offer the sacrifice of righteousness, * and put your trust in the LORD.

6 There be many that say. * Who will show us any good?

7 LORD, lift thou up * the light of thy countenance upon us.

8 Thou hast put gladness in my heart; * yea, more than when their corn and wine and oil increase.

9 I will lay me down in peace, and take my rest; * for it is thou, LORD, only, that makest me dwell in safety.

Psalm 5. *Verba mea auribus.*

PONDER my words, O LORD, * consider my meditation.
2 O hearken thou unto the voice of my calling, my

King and my God: * for unto thee will I make my prayer.

3 My voice shalt thou hear betimes, O LORD; * early in the morning will I direct my prayer unto thee, and will look up.

4 For thou art the God that hast no pleasure in wickedness; * neither shall any evil dwell with thee.

5 Such as be foolish shall not stand in thy sight; * for thou hatest all them that work iniquity.

6 Thou shalt destroy them that speak lies: * the LORD will abhor both the blood-thirsty and deceitful man.

7 But as for me, in the multitude of thy mercy I will come into thine house; * and in thy fear will I worship toward thy holy temple.

8 Lead me, O LORD, in thy righteousness, because of mine enemies; * make thy way plain before my face.

9 For there is no faithfulness in their mouth; * their inward parts are very wickedness.

10 Their throat is an open sepulchre; * they flatter with their tongue.

11 Destroy thou them, O God; let them perish through their own imaginations; * cast them out in the multitude of their ungodliness; for they have rebelled against thee.

12 And let all them that put their trust in thee rejoice: * they shall ever be giving of thanks, because thou defendest them; they that love thy Name shall be joyful in thee;

13 For thou, LORD, wilt give thy blessing unto the righteous, * and with thy favourable kindness wilt thou defend him as with a shield.

Evening Prayer.

Psalm 6. *Domine, ne in furore.*

O LORD, rebuke me not in thine indignation, * neither chasten me in thy displeasure.

2 Have mercy upon me, O LORD, for I am weak; * O LORD, heal me, for my bones are vexed.

3 My soul also is sore troubled: * but, LORD, how long wilt thou punish me?

4 Turn thee, O LORD, and deliver my soul; * O save me, for thy mercy's sake.

5 For in death no man remembereth thee; * and who will give thee thanks in the pit?

6 I am weary of my groaning; * every night wash I my bed, and water my couch with my tears.

7 My beauty is gone for very trouble, * and worn away because of all mine enemies.

8 Away from me, all ye that work iniquity; * for the LORD hath heard the voice of my weeping.

9 The LORD hath heard my petition; * the LORD will receive my prayer.

10 All mine enemies shall be confounded, and sore vexed; * they shall be turned back, and put to shame suddenly.

Psalm 7. *Domine, Deus meus.*

O LORD my God, in thee have I put my trust: * save me from all them that persecute me, and deliver me;

2 Lest he devour my soul like a lion, and tear it in pieces, * while there is none to help.

3 O LORD my God, if I have done any such thing; * or if there be any wickedness in my hands;

4 If I have rewarded evil unto him that dealt friendly with me; * (yea, I have delivered him that without any cause is mine enemy;)

5 Then let mine enemy persecute my soul, and take me; * yea, let him tread my life down upon the earth, and lay mine honour in the dust.

6 Stand up, O LORD, in thy wrath, and lift up thyself,

because of the indignation of mine enemies; * arise up for me in the judgment that thou hast commanded.

7 And so shall the congregation of the peoples come about thee: * for their sakes therefore lift up thyself again.

8 The LORD shall judge the peoples: give sentence with me, O LORD, * according to my righteousness, and according to the innocency that is in me.

9 O let the wickedness of the ungodly come to an end; * but guide thou the just.

10 For the righteous God * trieth the very hearts and reins.

11 My help cometh of God, * who preserveth them that are true of heart.

12 God is a righteous Judge, strong, and patient; * and God is provoked every day.

13 If a man will not turn, he will whet his sword; * he hath bent his bow, and made it ready.

14 He hath prepared for him the instruments of death; * he ordaineth his arrows against the persecutors.

15 Behold, the ungodly travaileth with iniquity; * he hath conceived mischief, and brought forth falsehood.

16 He hath graven and digged up a pit, * and is fallen himself into the destruction that he made for other.

17 For his travail shall come upon his own head, * and his wickedness shall fall on his own pate.

18 I will give thanks unto the LORD, according to his righteousness; * and I will praise the Name of the LORD Most High.

Psalm 8. *Domine, Dominus noster.*

O LORD our Governor, how excellent is thy Name in all the world; * thou that hast set thy glory above the heavens!

2 Out of the mouth of very babes and sucklings hast

thou ordained strength, because of thine enemies, * that thou mightest still the enemy and the avenger.

3 When I consider thy heavens, even the work of thy fingers; * the moon and the stars which thou hast ordained;

4 What is man, that thou art mindful of him? * and the son of man, that thou visitest him?

5 Thou madest him lower than the angels, * to crown him with glory and worship.

6 Thou makest him to have dominion of the works of thy hands; * and thou hast put all things in subjection under his feet:

7 All sheep and oxen; * yea, and the beasts of the field;

8 The fowls of the air, and the fishes of the sea; * and whatsoever walketh through the paths of the seas.

9 O LORD our Governor, * how excellent is thy Name in all the world!

The Second Day.

Morning Prayer.

Psalm 9. *Confitebor tibi.*

I WILL give thanks unto thee, O LORD, with my whole heart; * I will speak of all thy marvellous works.

2 I will be glad and rejoice in thee; * yea, my songs will I make of thy Name, O thou Most Highest.

3 While mine enemies are driven back, * they shall fall and perish at thy presence.

4 For thou hast maintained my right and my cause; * thou art set in the throne that judgest right.

5 Thou hast rebuked the heathen, and destroyed the ungodly; * thou hast put out their name for ever and ever.

6 O thou enemy, thy destructions are come to a perpetual end; * even as the cities which thou hast destroyed, whose memorial is perished with them.

351

7 But the LORD shall endure for ever; * he hath also prepared his seat for judgment.

8 For he shall judge the world in righteousness, * and minister true judgment unto the people.

9 The LORD also will be a defence for the oppressed, * even a refuge in due time of trouble.

10 And they that know thy Name will put their trust in thee; * for thou, LORD, hast never failed them that seek thee.

11 O praise the LORD which dwelleth in Sion; * show the people of his doings.

12 For when he maketh inquisition for blood, he remembereth them, * and forgetteth not the complaint of the poor.

13 Have mercy upon me, O LORD; consider the trouble which I suffer of them that hate me, * thou that liftest me up from the gates of death;

14 That I may show all thy praises within the gates of the daughter of Sion: * I will rejoice in thy salvation.

15 The heathen are sunk down in the pit that they made; * in the same net which they hid privily is their foot taken.

16 The LORD is known to execute judgment; * the ungodly is trapped in the work of his own hands.

17 The wicked shall be turned to destruction, * and all the people that forget God.

18 For the poor shall not alway be forgotten; * the patient abiding of the meek shall not perish for ever.

19 Up, LORD, and let not man have the upper hand; * let the heathen be judged in thy sight.

20 Put them in fear, O LORD, * that the heathen may know themselves to be but men.

Psalm 10. *Ut quid, Domine?*

WHY standest thou so far off, O LORD, * and hidest thy face in the needful time of trouble?

2 The ungodly, for his own lust, doth persecute the poor: * let them be taken in the crafty wiliness that they have imagined.

3 For the ungodly hath made boast of his own heart's desire, * and speaketh good of the covetous, whom the LORD abhorreth.

4 The ungodly is so proud, that he careth not for God, * neither is God in all his thoughts.

5 His ways are alway grievous; * thy judgments are far above out of his sight, and therefore defieth he all his enemies.

6 For he hath said in his heart, Tush, I shall never be cast down, * there shall no harm happen unto me.

7 His mouth is full of cursing, deceit, and fraud; * under his tongue is ungodliness and vanity.

8 He sitteth lurking in the thievish corners of the streets, * and privily in his lurking dens doth he murder the innocent; his eyes are set against the poor.

9 For he lieth waiting secretly; even as a lion lurketh he in his den, * that he may ravish the poor.

10 He doth ravish the poor, * when he getteth him into his net.

11 He falleth down, and humbleth himself, * that the congregation of the poor may fall into the hands of his captains.

12 He hath said in his heart, Tush, God hath forgotten; * he hideth away his face, and he will never see it.

13 Arise, O LORD God, and lift up thine hand; * forget not the poor.

14 Wherefore should the wicked blaspheme God, *

while he doth say in his heart, Tush, thou God carest not for it?

15 Surely thou hast seen it; * for thou beholdest ungodliness and wrong, that thou mayest take the matter into thy hand.

16 The poor committeth himself unto thee; * for thou art the helper of the friendless.

17 Break thou the power of the ungodly and malicious; * search out his ungodliness, until thou find none.

18 The Lord is King for ever and ever, * and the heathen are perished out of the land.

19 Lord, thou hast heard the desire of the poor; * thou preparest their heart, and thine ear hearkeneth;

20 To help the fatherless and poor unto their right, * that the man of the earth be no more exalted against them.

Psalm 11. *In Domino confido.*

IN the Lord put I my trust; * how say ye then to my soul, that she should flee as a bird unto the hill?

2 For lo, the ungodly bend their bow, and make ready their arrows within the quiver, * that they may privily shoot at them which are true of heart.

3 If the foundations be destroyed, * what can the righteous do?

4 The Lord is in his holy temple; * the Lord's seat is in heaven.

5 His eyes consider the poor, * and his eyelids try the children of men.

6 The Lord approveth the righteous: * but the ungodly, and him that delighteth in wickedness, doth his soul abhor.

7 Upon the ungodly he shall rain snares, fire and brimstone, storm and tempest: * this shall be their portion to drink.

8 For the righteous LORD loveth righteousness; * his countenance will behold the thing that is just.

Evening Prayer.

Psalm 12. *Salvum me fac.*

HELP me, LORD, for there is not one godly man left; * for the faithful are minished from among the children of men.

2 They talk of vanity every one with his neighbour; * they do but flatter with their lips, and dissemble in their double heart.

3 The LORD shall root out all deceitful lips, * and the tongue that speaketh proud things;

4 Which have said, With our tongue will we prevail; * we are they that ought to speak; who is lord over us?

5 Now, for the comfortless troubles' sake of the needy, * and because of the deep sighing of the poor,

6 I will up, saith the LORD; * and will help every one from him that swelleth against him, and will set him at rest.

7 The words of the LORD are pure words; * even as the silver which from the earth is tried, and purified seven times in the fire.

8 Thou shalt keep them, O LORD; * thou shalt preserve them from this generation for ever.

9 The ungodly walk on every side: * when they are exalted, the children of men are put to rebuke.

Psalm 13. *Usquequo, Domine?*

HOW long wilt thou forget me, O LORD; for ever? * how long wilt thou hide thy face from me?

2 How long shall I seek counsel in my soul, and be so vexed in my heart? * how long shall mine enemy triumph over me?

3 Consider, and hear me, O LORD my God; * lighten mine eyes, that I sleep not in death;

4 Lest mine enemy say, I have prevailed against him: * for if I be cast down, they that trouble me will rejoice at it.

5 But my trust is in thy mercy, * and my heart is joyful in thy salvation.

6 I will sing of the LORD, because he hath dealt so lovingly with me; * yea, I will praise the Name of the Lord Most Highest.

Psalm 14. *Dixit insipiens.*

THE fool hath said in his heart, * There is no God.

2 They are corrupt, and become abominable in their doings; * there is none that doeth good, no not one.

3 The LORD looked down from heaven upon the children of men, * to see if there were any that would understand, and seek after God.

4 But they are all gone out of the way, they are altogether become abominable; * there is none that doeth good, no not one.

5 Have they no knowledge, that they are all such workers of mischief, * eating up my people as it were bread, and call not upon the LORD?

6 There were they brought in great fear, even where no fear was; * for God is in the generation of the righteous.

7 As for you, ye have made a mock at the counsel of the poor; * because he putteth his trust in the LORD.

8 Who shall give salvation unto Israel out of Sion? * When the LORD turneth the captivity of his people, then shall Jacob rejoice, and Israel shall be glad.

The Third Day.

Morning Prayer.

Psalm 15. *Domine, quis habitabit?*

LORD, who shall dwell in thy tabernacle? * or who shall rest upon thy holy hill?

2 Even he that leadeth an uncorrupt life, * and doeth the thing which is right, and speaketh the truth from his heart.

3 He that hath used no deceit in his tongue, nor done evil to his neighbour, * and hath not slandered his neighbour.

4 He that setteth not by himself, but is lowly in his own eyes, * and maketh much of them that fear the LORD.

5 He that sweareth unto his neighbour, and disappointeth him not, * though it were to his own hindrance.

6 He that hath not given his money upon usury, * nor taken reward against the innocent.

7 Whoso doeth these things * shall never fall.

Psalm 16. *Conserva me, Domine.*

PRESERVE me, O God; * for in thee have I put my trust.

2 O my soul, thou hast said unto the LORD, * Thou art my God; I have no good like unto thee.

3 All my delight is upon the saints that are in the earth, * and upon such as excel in virtue.

4 But they that run after another god * shall have great trouble.

5 Their drink-offerings of blood will I not offer, * neither make mention of their names within my lips.

6 The LORD himself is the portion of mine inheritance, and of my cup; * thou shalt maintain my lot.

357

7 The lot is fallen unto me in a fair ground; * yea, I have a goodly heritage.

8 I will thank the LORD for giving me warning; * my reins also chasten me in the night season.

9 I have set the LORD alway before me; * for he is on my right hand, therefore I shall not fall.

10 Wherefore my heart is glad, and my glory rejoiceth: * my flesh also shall rest in hope.

11 For why? thou shalt not leave my soul in hell; * neither shalt thou suffer thy Holy One to see corruption.

12 Thou shalt show me the path of life: in thy presence is the fulness of joy, * and at thy right hand there is pleasure for evermore.

Psalm 17. *Exaudi, Domine.*

HEAR the right, O LORD, consider my complaint, * and hearken unto my prayer, that goeth not out of feigned lips.

2 Let my sentence come forth from thy presence; * and let thine eyes look upon the thing that is equal.

3 Thou hast proved and visited mine heart in the night season; thou hast tried me, and shalt find no wickedness in me; * for I am utterly purposed that my mouth shall not offend.

4 As for the works of men, * by the word of thy lips I have kept me from the ways of the destroyer.

5 O hold thou up my goings in thy paths, * that my footsteps slip not.

6 I have called upon thee, O God, for thou shalt hear me: * incline thine ear to me, and hearken unto my words.

7 Show thy marvellous loving-kindness, thou that art the Saviour of them which put their trust in thee, * from such as resist thy right hand.

8 Keep me as the apple of an eye; * hide me under the shadow of thy wings,

9 From the ungodly, that trouble me; * mine enemies compass me round about, to take away my soul.

10 They are inclosed in their own fat, * and their mouth speaketh proud things.

11 They lie waiting in our way on every side, * watching to cast us down to the ground;

12 Like as a lion that is greedy of his prey, * and as it were a lion's whelp lurking in secret places.

13 Up, LORD, disappoint him, and cast him down; * deliver my soul from the ungodly, by thine own sword;

14 Yea, by thy hand, O LORD; from the men of the evil world; * which have their portion in this life, whose bellies thou fillest with thy hid treasure.

15 They have children at their desire, * and leave the rest of their substance for their babes.

16 But as for me, I shall behold thy presence in righteousness; * and when I awake up after thy likeness, I shall be satisfied.

Evening Prayer.

Psalm 18. *Diligam te, Domine.*

I WILL love thee, O LORD, my strength. * The LORD is my stony rock, and my defence;

2 My Saviour, my God, and my might, in whom I will trust; * my buckler, the horn also of my salvation, and my refuge.

3 I will call upon the LORD, which is worthy to be praised; * so shall I be safe from mine enemies.

4 The sorrows of death compassed me, * and the overflowings of ungodliness made me afraid.

5 The pains of hell came about me; * the snares of death overtook me.

6 In my trouble I called upon the LORD, * and complained unto my God:

7 So he heard my voice out of his holy temple, * and my complaint came before him; it entered even into his ears.

8 The earth trembled and quaked, * the very foundations also of the hills shook, and were removed, because he was wroth.

9 There went a smoke out in his presence, * and a consuming fire out of his mouth, so that coals were kindled at it.

10 He bowed the heavens also, and came down, * and it was dark under his feet.

11 He rode upon the Cherubim, and did fly; * he came flying upon the wings of the wind.

12 He made darkness his secret place, * his pavilion round about him with dark water, and thick clouds to cover him.

13 At the brightness of his presence his clouds removed; * hailstones and coals of fire.

14 The LORD also thundered out of heaven, and the Highest gave his thunder; * hailstones and coals of fire.

15 He sent out his arrows, and scattered them; * he cast forth lightnings, and destroyed them.

16 The springs of waters were seen, and the foundations of the round world were discovered, * at thy chiding, O LORD, at the blasting of the breath of thy displeasure.

17 He sent down from on high to fetch me, * and took me out of many waters.

18 He delivered me from my strongest enemy, and from them which hate me; * for they were too mighty for me.

19 They came upon me in the day of my trouble; * but the LORD was my upholder.

20 He brought me forth also into a place of liberty; * he brought me forth, even because he had a favour unto me.

21 The LORD rewarded me after my righteous dealing, * according to the cleanness of my hands did he recompense me.

22 Because I have kept the ways of the LORD, * and have not forsaken my God, as the wicked doth.

23 For I have an eye unto all his laws, * and will not cast out his commandments from me.

24 I was also uncorrupt before him, * and eschewed mine own wickedness.

25 Therefore the LORD rewarded me after my righteous dealing, * and according unto the cleanness of my hands in his eyesight.

26 With the holy thou shalt be holy, * and with a perfect man thou shalt be perfect.

27 With the clean thou shalt be clean, * and with the froward thou shalt be froward.

28 For thou shalt save the people that are in adversity, * and shalt bring down the high looks of the proud.

29 Thou also shalt light my candle; * the LORD my God shall make my darkness to be light.

30 For in thee I shall discomfit an host of men, * and with the help of my God I shall leap over the wall.

31 The way of God is an undefiled way: * the word of the LORD also is tried in the fire; he is the defender of all them that put their trust in him.

32 For who is God, but the LORD? * or who hath any strength, except our God?

33 It is God that girdeth me with strength of war, * and maketh my way perfect.

34 He maketh my feet like harts' feet, * and setteth me up on high.

35 He teacheth mine hands to fight, * and mine arms shall bend even a bow of steel.

36 Thou hast given me the defence of thy salvation; * thy right hand also shall hold me up, and thy loving correction shall make me great.

37 Thou shalt make room enough under me for to go, * that my footsteps shall not slide.

38 I will follow upon mine enemies, and overtake them; * neither will I turn again till I have destroyed them.

39 I will smite them, that they shall not be able to stand, * but fall under my feet.

40 Thou hast girded me with strength unto the battle; * thou shalt throw down mine enemies under me.

41 Thou hast made mine enemies also to turn their backs upon me, * and I shall destroy them that hate me.

42 They shall cry, but there shall be none to help them; * yea, even unto the LORD shall they cry, but he shall not hear them.

43 I will beat them as small as the dust before the wind: * I will cast them out as the clay in the streets.

44 Thou shalt deliver me from the strivings of the people, * and thou shalt make me the head of the nations; a people whom I have not known shall serve me.

45 As soon as they hear of me, they shall obey me; * the strangers shall feign obedience unto me.

46 The strangers shall fail, * and come trembling out of their strongholds.

47 The LORD liveth; and blessed be my strong helper, * and praised be the God of my salvation;

48 Even the God that seeth that I be avenged, * and subdueth the people unto me.

49 It is he that delivereth me from my cruel enemies, and setteth me up above mine adversaries: * thou shalt rid me from the wicked man.

50 For this cause will I give thanks unto thee, O LORD, among the Gentiles, * and sing praises unto thy Name.

51 Great prosperity giveth he unto his King, * and showeth loving-kindness unto David his anointed, and unto his seed for evermore.

The Fourth Day.

Morning Prayer.

Psalm 19. *Cæli enarrant.*

THE heavens declare the glory of God; * and the firmament showeth his handy-work.

2 One day telleth another; * and one night certifieth another.

3 There is neither speech nor language; * but their voices are heard among them.

4 Their sound is gone out into all lands; * and their words into the ends of the world.

5 In them hath he set a tabernacle for the sun; * which cometh forth as a bridegroom out of his chamber, and rejoiceth as a giant to run his course.

6 It goeth forth from the uttermost part of the heaven, and runneth about unto the end of it again; * and there is nothing hid from the heat thereof.

7 The law of the LORD is an undefiled law, converting the soul; * the testimony of the LORD is sure, and giveth wisdom unto the simple.

8 The statutes of the LORD are right, and rejoice the heart; * the commandment of the LORD is pure, and giveth light unto the eyes.

9 The fear of the LORD is clean, and endureth for ever; *

the judgments of the LORD are true, and righteous altogether.

10 More to be desired are they than gold, yea, than much fine gold; * sweeter also than honey, and the honeycomb.

11 Moreover, by them is thy servant taught; * and in keeping of them there is great reward.

12 Who can tell how oft he offendeth? * O cleanse thou me from my secret faults.

13 Keep thy servant also from presumptuous sins, lest they get the dominion over me; * so shall I be undefiled, and innocent from the great offence.

14 Let the words of my mouth, and the meditation of my heart, be alway acceptable in thy sight, * O LORD, my strength and my redeemer.

Psalm 20. *Exaudiat te Dominus.*

THE LORD hear thee in the day of trouble; * the Name of the God of Jacob defend thee:

2 Send thee help from the sanctuary, * and strengthen thee out of Sion:

3 Remember all thy offerings, * and accept thy burnt-sacrifice:

4 Grant thee thy heart's desire, * and fulfil all thy mind.

5 We will rejoice in thy salvation, and triumph in the Name of the Lord our God: * the LORD perform all thy petitions.

6 Now know I that the LORD helpeth his anointed, and will hear him from his holy heaven, * even with the wholesome strength of his right hand.

7 Some put their trust in chariots, and some in horses; * but we will remember the Name of the LORD our God.

8 They are brought down and fallen; * but we are risen and stand upright.

9 Save, LORD; and hear us, O King of heaven, * when we call upon thee.

Psalm 21. *Domine, in virtute tua.*

THE King shall rejoice in thy strength, O LORD; * exceeding glad shall he be of thy salvation.

2 Thou hast given him his heart's desire, * and hast not denied him the request of his lips.

3 For thou shalt meet him with the blessings of goodness, * and shalt set a crown of pure gold upon his head.

4 He asked life of thee; and thou gavest him a long life, * even for ever and ever.

5 His honour is great in thy salvation; * glory and great worship shalt thou lay upon him.

6 For thou shalt give him everlasting felicity, * and make him glad with the joy of thy countenance.

7 And why? because the King putteth his trust in the LORD; * and in the mercy of the Most Highest he shall not miscarry.

8 All thine enemies shall feel thine hand; * thy right hand shall find out them that hate thee.

9 Thou shalt make them like a fiery oven in time of thy wrath: * the LORD shall destroy them in his displeasure, and the fire shall consume them.

10 Their fruit shalt thou root out of the earth, * and their seed from among the children of men.

11 For they intended mischief against thee, * and imagined such a device as they are not able to perform.

12 Therefore shalt thou put them to flight, * and the strings of thy bow shalt thou make ready against the face of them.

13 Be thou exalted, LORD, in thine own strength; * so will we sing, and praise thy power.

Evening Prayer.

Psalm 22. *Deus, Deus meus.*

MY God, my God, look upon me; why hast thou for-saken me? * and art so far from my health, and from the words of my complaint?

2 O my God, I cry in the day-time, but thou hearest not; * and in the night season also I take no rest.

3 And thou continuest holy, * O thou Worship of Israel.

4 Our fathers hoped in thee; * they trusted in thee, and thou didst deliver them.

5 They called upon thee, and were holpen; * they put their trust in thee, and were not confounded.

6 But as for me, I am a worm, and no man; * a very scorn of men, and the outcast of the people.

7 All they that see me laugh me to scorn; * they shoot out their lips, and shake their heads, saying,

8 He trusted in the LORD, that he would deliver him; * let him deliver him, if he will have him.

9 But thou art he that took me out of my mother's womb; * thou wast my hope, when I hanged yet upon my mother's breasts.

10 I have been left unto thee ever since I was born; * thou art my God even from my mother's womb.

11 O go not from me; for trouble is hard at hand, * and there is none to help me.

12 Many oxen are come about me; * fat bulls of Bashan close me in on every side.

13 They gape upon me with their mouths, * as it were a ramping and a roaring lion.

14 I am poured out like water, and all my bones are out of joint; * my heart also in the midst of my body is even like melting wax.

15 My strength is dried up like a potsherd, and my

tongue cleaveth to my gums, * and thou bringest me into the dust of death.

16 For many dogs are come about me, * and the council of the wicked layeth siege against me.

17 They pierced my hands and my feet: I may tell all my bones: * they stand staring and looking upon me.

18 They part my garments among them, * and cast lots upon my vesture.

19 But be not thou far from me, O LORD; * thou art my succour, haste thee to help me.

20 Deliver my soul from the sword, * my darling from the power of the dog.

21 Save me from the lion's mouth; * thou hast heard me also from among the horns of the unicorns.

22 I will declare thy Name unto my brethren; * in the midst of the congregation will I praise thee.

23 O praise the LORD, ye that fear him: * magnify him, all ye of the seed of Jacob; and fear him, all ye seed of Israel.

24 For he hath not despised nor abhorred the low estate of the poor; * he hath not hid his face from him; but when he called unto him he heard him.

25 My praise is of thee in the great congregation; * my vows will I perform in the sight of them that fear him.

26 The poor shall eat, and be satisfied; they that seek after the LORD shall praise him: * your heart shall live for ever.

27 All the ends of the world shall remember themselves, and be turned unto the LORD; * and all the kindreds of the nations shall worship before him.

28 For the kingdom is the LORD's, * and he is the Governor among the nations.

29 All such as be fat upon earth * have eaten, and worshipped.

30 All they that go down into the dust shall kneel before him; * and no man hath quickened his own soul.

31 My seed shall serve him: * they shall be counted unto the Lord for a generation.

32 They shall come, and shall declare his righteousness * unto a people that shall be born, whom the Lord hath made.

Psalm 23. *Dominus regit me.*

THE LORD is my shepherd; * therefore can I lack nothing.

2 He shall feed me in a green pasture, * and lead me forth beside the waters of comfort.

3 He shall convert my soul, * and bring me forth in the paths of righteousness for his Name's sake.

4 Yea, though I walk through the valley of the shadow of death, I will fear no evil; * for thou art with me; thy rod and thy staff comfort me.

5 Thou shalt prepare a table before me in the presence of them that trouble me; * thou hast anointed my head with oil, and my cup shall be full.

6 Surely thy loving-kindness and mercy shall follow me all the days of my life; * and I will dwell in the house of the LORD for ever.

The Fifth Day.

Morning Prayer.

Psalm 24. *Domini est terra.*

THE earth is the LORD'S, and all that therein is; * the compass of the world, and they that dwell therein.

2 For he hath founded it upon the seas, * and stablished it upon the floods.

3 Who shall ascend into the hill of the LORD? * or who shall rise up in his holy place?

4 Even he that hath clean hands, and a pure heart; * and that hath not lift up his mind unto vanity, nor sworn to deceive his neighbour.

5 He shall receive the blessing from the LORD, * and righteousness from the God of his salvation.

6 This is the generation of them that seek him; * even of them that seek thy face, O God of Jacob.

7 Lift up your heads, O ye gates; and be ye lift up, ye everlasting doors; * and the King of glory shall come in.

8 Who is this King of glory? * It is the LORD strong and mighty, even the LORD mighty in battle.

9 Lift up your heads, O ye gates; and be ye lift up, ye everlasting doors; * and the King of glory shall come in.

10 Who is this King of glory? * Even the LORD of hosts, he is the King of glory.

Psalm 25. *Ad te, Domine, levavi.*

UNTO thee, O LORD, will I lift up my soul; my God, I have put my trust in thee: * O let me not be confounded, neither let mine enemies triumph over me.

2 For all they that hope in thee shall not be ashamed; * but such as transgress without a cause shall be put to confusion.

3 Show me thy ways, O LORD, * and teach me thy paths.

4 Lead me forth in thy truth, and learn me: * for thou art the God of my salvation; in thee hath been my hope all the day long.

5 Call to remembrance, O LORD, thy tender mercies, * and thy loving-kindnesses, which have been ever of old.

6 O remember not the sins and offences of my youth; * but according to thy mercy think thou upon me, O LORD, for thy goodness.

7 Gracious and righteous is the LORD; * therefore will he teach sinners in the way.

8 Them that are meek shall he guide in judgment; *
and such as are gentle, them shall he learn his way.

9 All the paths of the LORD are mercy and truth, * unto
such as keep his covenant and his testimonies.

10 For thy Name's sake, O LORD, * be merciful unto my
sin; for it is great.

11 What man is he that feareth the LORD? * him shall
he teach in the way that he shall choose.

12 His soul shall dwell at ease, * and his seed shall inherit the land.

13 The secret of the LORD is among them that fear
him; * and he will show them his covenant.

14 Mine eyes are ever looking unto the LORD; * for he
shall pluck my feet out of the net.

15 Turn thee unto me, and have mercy upon me; * for
I am desolate, and in misery.

16 The sorrows of my heart are enlarged: * O bring
thou me out of my troubles.

17 Look upon my adversity and misery, * and forgive
me all my sin.

18 Consider mine enemies, how many they are; * and
they bear a tyrannous hate against me.

19 O keep my soul, and deliver me: * let me not be
confounded, for I have put my trust in thee.

20 Let perfectness and righteous dealing wait upon
me; * for my hope hath been in thee.

21 Deliver Israel, O God, * out of all his troubles.

Psalm 26. *Judica me, Domine.*

BE thou my Judge, O LORD, for I have walked innocently: * my trust hath been also in the LORD, therefore shall I not fall.

2 Examine me, O LORD, and prove me; * try out my
reins and my heart.

3 For thy loving-kindness is ever before mine eyes; * and I will walk in thy truth.

4 I have not dwelt with vain persons; * neither will I have fellowship with the deceitful.

5 I have hated the congregation of the wicked; * and will not sit among the ungodly.

6 I will wash my hands in innocency, O LORD; * and so will I go to thine altar;

7 That I may show the voice of thanksgiving, * and tell of all thy wondrous works.

8 LORD, I have loved the habitation of thy house, * and the place where thine honour dwelleth.

9 O shut not up my soul with the sinners, * nor my life with the blood-thirsty;

10 In whose hands is wickedness, * and their right hand is full of gifts.

11 But as for me, I will walk innocently: * O deliver me, and be merciful unto me.

12 My foot standeth right: * I will praise the LORD in the congregations.

Evening Prayer.

Psalm 27. *Dominus illuminatio.*

THE LORD is my light and my salvation; whom then shall I fear? * the LORD is the strength of my life; of whom then shall I be afraid?

2 When the wicked, even mine enemies and my foes, came upon me to eat up my flesh, * they stumbled and fell.

3 Though an host of men were laid against me, yet shall not my heart be afraid; * and though there rose up war against me, yet will I put my trust in him.

4 One thing have I desired of the LORD, which I will require; * even that I may dwell in the house of the LORD

all the days of my life, to behold the fair beauty of the LORD, and to visit his temple.

5 For in the time of trouble he shall hide me in his tabernacle; * yea, in the secret place of his dwelling shall he hide me, and set me up upon a rock of stone.

6 And now shall he lift up mine head * above mine enemies round about me.

7 Therefore will I offer in his dwelling an oblation, with great gladness: * I will sing and speak praises unto the LORD.

8 Hearken unto my voice, O LORD, when I cry unto thee; * have mercy upon me, and hear me.

9 My heart hath talked of thee, Seek ye my face: * Thy face, LORD, will I seek.

10 O hide not thou thy face from me, * nor cast thy servant away in displeasure.

11 Thou hast been my succour; * leave me not, neither forsake me, O God of my salvation.

12 When my father and my mother forsake me, * the LORD taketh me up.

13 Teach me thy way, O LORD, * and lead me in the right way, because of mine enemies.

14 Deliver me not over into the will of mine adversaries: * for there are false witnesses risen up against me, and such as speak wrong.

15 I should utterly have fainted, * but that I believe verily to see the goodness of the LORD in the land of the living.

16 O tarry thou the LORD's leisure; * be strong, and he shall comfort thine heart; and put thou thy trust in the LORD.

Psalm 28. *Ad te, Domine.*

UNTO thee will I cry, O LORD, my strength: * think no scorn of me; lest, if thou make as though thou hearest not, I become like them that go down into the pit.

2 Hear the voice of my humble petitions, when I cry unto thee; * when I hold up my hands towards the mercy-seat of thy holy temple.

3 O pluck me not away, neither destroy me with the ungodly and wicked doers, * which speak friendly to their neighbours, but imagine mischief in their hearts.

4 Reward them according to their deeds, * and according to the wickedness of their own inventions.

5 Recompense them after the work of their hands; * pay them that they have deserved.

6 For they regard not in their mind the works of the LORD, nor the operation of his hands; * therefore shall he break them down, and not build them up.

7 Praised be the LORD; * for he hath heard the voice of my humble petitions.

8 The LORD is my strength, and my shield; my heart hath trusted in him, and I am helped; * therefore my heart danceth for joy, and in my song will I praise him.

9 The LORD is my strength, * and he is the wholesome defence of his anointed.

10 O save thy people, and give thy blessing unto thine inheritance: * feed them, and set them up for ever.

Psalm 29. *Afferte Domino.*

ASCRIBE unto the LORD, O ye mighty, * ascribe unto the LORD worship and strength.

2 Ascribe unto the LORD the honour due unto his Name; * worship the LORD with holy worship.

3 The voice of the LORD is upon the waters; * it is the glorious God that maketh the thunder.

4 It is the LORD that ruleth the sea; the voice of the LORD is mighty in operation; * the voice of the LORD is a glorious voice.

5 The voice of the LORD breaketh the cedar-trees; * yea, the LORD breaketh the cedars of Lebanon.

6 He maketh them also to skip like a calf; * Lebanon also, and Sirion, like a young unicorn.

7 The voice of the LORD divideth the flames of fire; the voice of the LORD shaketh the wilderness; * yea, the LORD shaketh the wilderness of Kadesh.

8 The voice of the LORD maketh the hinds to bring forth young, and strippeth bare the forests: * in his temple doth every thing speak of his honour.

9 The LORD sitteth above the water-flood, * and the LORD remaineth a King for ever.

10 The LORD shall give strength unto his people; * the LORD shall give his people the blessing of peace.

The Sixth Day.

Morning Prayer.

Psalm 30. *Exaltabo te, Domine.*

I WILL magnify thee, O LORD; for thou hast set me up, * and not made my foes to triumph over me.

2 O LORD my God, I cried unto thee; * and thou hast healed me.

3 Thou, LORD, hast brought my soul out of hell: * thou hast kept my life, that I should not go down into the pit.

4 Sing praises unto the LORD, O ye saints of his; * and give thanks unto him, for a remembrance of his holiness.

5 For his wrath endureth but the twinkling of an eye,

and in his pleasure is life; * heaviness may endure for a night, but joy cometh in the morning.

6 And in my prosperity I said, I shall never be removed: * thou, LORD, of thy goodness, hast made my hill so strong.

7 Thou didst turn thy face from me, * and I was troubled.

8 Then cried I unto thee, O LORD; * and gat me to my LORD right humbly.

9 What profit is there in my blood, * when I go down into the pit?

10 Shall the dust give thanks unto thee? * or shall it declare thy truth?

11 Hear, O LORD, and have mercy upon me; * LORD, be thou my helper.

12 Thou hast turned my heaviness into joy; * thou hast put off my sackcloth, and girded me with gladness:

13 Therefore shall every good man sing of thy praise without ceasing. * O my God, I will give thanks unto thee for ever.

Psalm 31. *In te, Domine, speravi.*

IN thee, O LORD, have I put my trust; let me never be put to confusion; * deliver me in thy righteousness.

2 Bow down thine ear to me; * make haste to deliver me.

3 And be thou my strong rock, and house of defence, * that thou mayest save me.

4 For thou art my strong rock, and my castle: * be thou also my guide, and lead me for thy Name's sake.

5 Draw me out of the net that they have laid privily for me; * for thou art my strength.

6 Into thy hands I commend my spirit; * for thou hast redeemed me, O LORD, thou God of truth.

7 I have hated them that hold of lying vanities, * and my trust hath been in the LORD.

8 I will be glad and rejoice in thy mercy; * for thou hast considered my trouble, and hast known my soul in adversities.

9 Thou hast not shut me up into the hand of the enemy; * but hast set my feet in a large room.

10 Have mercy upon me, O LORD, for I am in trouble, * and mine eye is consumed for very heaviness; yea, my soul and my body.

11 For my life is waxen old with heaviness, * and my years with mourning.

12 My strength faileth me, because of mine iniquity, * and my bones are consumed.

13 I became a reproach among all mine enemies, but especially among my neighbours; * and they of mine acquaintance were afraid of me; and they that did see me without, conveyed themselves from me.

14 I am clean forgotten as a dead man out of mind; * I am become like a broken vessel.

15 For I have heard the blasphemy of the multitude, and fear is on every side; * while they conspire together against me, and take their counsel to take away my life.

16 But my hope hath been in thee, O LORD; * I have said, Thou art my God.

17 My times are in thy hand; deliver me from the hand of mine enemies, * and from them that persecute me.

18 Show thy servant the light of thy countenance, * and save me for thy mercy's sake.

19 Let me not be confounded, O LORD, for I have called upon thee; * let the ungodly be put to confusion, and be put to silence in the grave.

20 Let the lying lips be put to silence, * which cruelly, disdainfully, and despitefully speak against the righteous.

21 O how plentiful is thy goodness, which thou hast laid up for them that fear thee, * and that thou hast prepared for them that put their trust in thee, even before the sons of men!

22 Thou shalt hide them in the covert of thine own presence from the plottings of men: * thou shalt keep them secretly in thy tabernacle from the strife of tongues.

23 Thanks be to the LORD; * for he hath showed me marvellous great kindness in a strong city.

24 But in my haste I said, * I am cast out of the sight of thine eyes.

25 Nevertheless, thou heardest the voice of my prayer, * when I cried unto thee.

26 O love the LORD, all ye his saints; * for the LORD preserveth them that are faithful, and plenteously rewardeth the proud doer.

27 Be strong, and he shall establish your heart, * all ye that put your trust in the LORD.

Evening Prayer.

Psalm 32. *Beati quorum.*

BLESSED is he whose unrighteousness is forgiven, * and whose sin is covered.

2 Blessed is the man unto whom the LORD imputeth no sin, * and in whose spirit there is no guile.

3 For whilst I held my tongue, * my bones consumed away through my daily complaining.

4 For thy hand was heavy upon me day and night, * and my moisture was like the drought in summer.

5 I acknowledged my sin unto thee; * and mine unrighteousness have I not hid.

6 I said, I will confess my sins unto the LORD; * and so thou forgavest the wickedness of my sin.

7 For this shall every one that is godly make his prayer unto thee, in a time when thou mayest be found; * surely the great water-floods shall not come nigh him.

8 Thou art a place to hide me in; thou shalt preserve me from trouble; * thou shalt compass me about with songs of deliverance.

9 I will inform thee, and teach thee in the way wherein thou shalt go; * and I will guide thee with mine eye.

10 Be ye not like to horse and mule, which have no understanding; * whose mouths must be held with bit and bridle, else they will not obey thee.

11 Great plagues remain for the ungodly; * but whoso putteth his trust in the LORD, mercy embraceth him on every side.

12 Be glad, O ye righteous, and rejoice in the LORD; * and be joyful, all ye that are true of heart.

Psalm 33. *Exultate, justi.*

REJOICE in the LORD, O ye righteous; * for it becometh well the just to be thankful.

2 Praise the LORD with harp; * sing praises unto him with the lute, and instrument of ten strings.

3 Sing unto the Lord a new song; * sing praises lustily unto him with a good courage.

4 For the word of the LORD is true; * and all his works are faithful.

5 He loveth righteousness and judgment; * the earth is full of the goodness of the LORD.

6 By the word of the LORD were the heavens made; * and all the host of them by the breath of his mouth.

7 He gathereth the waters of the sea together, as it were upon an heap; * and layeth up the deep, as in a treasure-house.

8 Let all the earth fear the LORD: * stand in awe of him, all ye that dwell in the world.

9 For he spake, and it was done; * he commanded, and it stood fast.

10 The LORD bringeth the counsel of the heathen to nought, * and maketh the devices of the people to be of none effect, and casteth out the counsels of princes.

11 The counsel of the LORD shall endure for ever, * and the thoughts of his heart from generation to generation.

12 Blessed are the people whose God is the Lord JEHOVAH; * and blessed are the folk that he hath chosen to him, to be his inheritance.

13 The LORD looketh down from heaven, and beholdeth all the children of men; * from the habitation of his dwelling, he considereth all them that dwell on the earth.

14 He fashioneth all the hearts of them, * and understandeth all their works.

15 There is no king that can be saved by the multitude of an host; * neither is any mighty man delivered by much strength.

16 A horse is counted but a vain thing to save a man; * neither shall he deliver any man by his great strength.

17 Behold, the eye of the LORD is upon them that fear him, * and upon them that put their trust in his mercy;

18 To deliver their soul from death, * and to feed them in the time of dearth.

19 Our soul hath patiently tarried for the LORD; * for he is our help and our shield.

20 For our heart shall rejoice in him; * because we have hoped in his holy Name.

21 Let thy merciful kindness, O LORD, be upon us, * like as we do put our trust in thee.

379

Psalm 34. *Benedicam Dominum.*

I WILL alway give thanks unto the LORD; * his praise
shall ever be in my mouth.

2 My soul shall make her boast in the LORD; * the
humble shall hear thereof, and be glad.

3 O praise the LORD with me, * and let us magnify his
Name together.

4 I sought the LORD, and he heard me; * yea, he delivered me out of all my fear.

5 They had an eye unto him, and were lightened; * and
their faces were not ashamed.

6 Lo, the poor crieth, and the LORD heareth him; *
yea, and saveth him out of all his troubles.

7 The angel of the LORD tarrieth round about them that
fear him, * and delivereth them.

8 O taste, and see, how gracious the LORD is: * blessed
is the man that trusteth in him.

9 O fear the LORD, ye that are his saints; * for they
that fear him lack nothing.

10 The lions do lack, and suffer hunger; * but they who
seek the LORD shall want no manner of thing that is good.

11 Come, ye children, and hearken unto me; * I will
teach you the fear of the LORD.

12 What man is he that lusteth to live, * and would fain
see good days?

13 Keep thy tongue from evil, * and thy lips, that they
speak no guile.

14 Eschew evil, and do good; * seek peace, and ensue it.

15 The eyes of the LORD are over the righteous, * and
his ears are open unto their prayers.

16 The countenance of the LORD is against them that
do evil, * to root out the remembrance of them from the
earth.

17 The righteous cry, and the LORD heareth them, * and delivereth them out of all their troubles.

18 The LORD is nigh unto them that are of a contrite heart, * and will save such as be of an humble spirit.

19 Great are the troubles of the righteous; * but the LORD delivereth him out of all.

20 He keepeth all his bones, * so that not one of them is broken.

21 But misfortune shall slay the ungodly; * and they that hate the righteous shall be desolate.

22 The LORD delivereth the souls of his servants; * and all they that put their trust in him shall not be destitute.

The Seventh Day.

Morning Prayer.

Psalm 35. *Judica, Domine.*

PLEAD thou my cause, O LORD, with them that strive with me, * and fight thou against them that fight against me.

2 Lay hand upon the shield and buckler, * and stand up to help me.

3 Bring forth the spear, and stop the way against them that pursue me: * say unto my soul, I am thy salvation.

4 Let them be confounded, and put to shame, that seek after my soul; * let them be turned back, and brought to confusion, that imagine mischief for me.

5 Let them be as the dust before the wind, * and the angel of the LORD scattering them.

6 Let their way be dark and slippery, * and let the angel of the LORD pursue them.

7 For they have privily laid their net to destroy me

without a cause; * yea, even without a cause have they made a pit for my soul.

8 Let a sudden destruction come upon him unawares, and his net that he hath laid privily catch himself; * that he may fall into his own mischief.

9 And my soul shall be joyful in the LORD; * it shall rejoice in his salvation.

10 All my bones shall say, LORD, who is like unto thee, who deliverest the poor from him that is too strong for him; * yea, the poor, and him that is in misery, from him that spoileth him?

11 False witnesses did rise up: * they laid to my charge things that I knew not.

12 They rewarded me evil for good, * to the great discomfort of my soul.

13 Nevertheless, when they were sick, I put on sackcloth, and humbled my soul with fasting; * and my prayer shall turn into mine own bosom.

14 I behaved myself as though it had been my friend or my brother; * I went heavily, as one that mourneth for his mother.

15 But in mine adversity they rejoiced, and gathered themselves together; * yea, the very abjects came together against me unawares, making mouths at me, and ceased not.

16 With the flatterers were busy mockers, * who gnashed upon me with their teeth.

17 Lord, how long wilt thou look upon this? * O deliver my soul from the calamities which they bring on me, and my darling from the lions.

18 So will I give thee thanks in the great congregation; * I will praise thee among much people.

19 O let not them that are mine enemies triumph over me ungodly; * neither let them wink with their eyes, that hate me without a cause.

20 And why? their communing is not for peace; * but they imagine deceitful words against them that are quiet in the land.

21 They gaped upon me with their mouths, and said, * Fie on thee! fie on thee! we saw it with our eyes.

22 This thou hast seen, O LORD; * hold not thy tongue then; go not far from me, O Lord.

23 Awake, and stand up to judge my quarrel; * avenge thou my cause, my God and my Lord.

24 Judge me, O LORD my God, according to thy righteousness; * and let them not triumph over me.

25 Let them not say in their hearts, There! there! so would we have it; * neither let them say, We have devoured him.

26 Let them be put to confusion and shame together, that rejoice at my trouble; * let them be clothed with rebuke and dishonour, that boast themselves against me.

27 Let them be glad and rejoice, that favour my righteous dealing; * yea, let them say alway, Blessed be the LORD, who hath pleasure in the prosperity of his servant.

28 And as for my tongue, it shall be talking of thy righteousness, * and of thy praise, all the day long.

Psalm 36. *Dixit injustus.*

MY heart showeth me the wickedness of the ungodly, * that there is no fear of God before his eyes.

2 For he flattereth himself in his own sight, * until his abominable sin be found out.

3 The words of his mouth are unrighteous and full of deceit: * he hath left off to behave himself wisely, and to do good.

4 He imagineth mischief upon his bed, and hath set

himself in no good way; * neither doth he abhor any thing that is evil.

5 Thy mercy, O LORD, reacheth unto the heavens, * and thy faithfulness unto the clouds.

6 Thy righteousness standeth like the strong mountains: * thy judgments are like the great deep.

7 Thou, LORD, shalt save both man and beast: how excellent is thy mercy, O God! * and the children of men shall put their trust under the shadow of thy wings.

8 They shall be satisfied with the plenteousness of thy house; * and thou shalt give them drink of thy pleasures, as out of the river.

9 For with thee is the well of life; * and in thy light shall we see light.

10 O continue forth thy loving-kindness unto them that know thee, * and thy righteousness unto them that are true of heart.

11 O let not the foot of pride come against me; * and let not the hand of the ungodly cast me down.

12 There are they fallen, all that work wickedness; * they are cast down, and shall not be able to stand.

Evening Prayer.

Psalm 37. *Noli æmulari.*

FRET not thyself because of the ungodly; * neither be thou envious against the evil doers.

2 For they shall soon be cut down like the grass, * and be withered even as the green herb.

3 Put thou thy trust in the LORD, and be doing good; * dwell in the land, and verily thou shalt be fed.

4 Delight thou in the LORD, * and he shall give thee thy heart's desire.

5 Commit thy way unto the LORD, and put thy trust in him, * and he shall bring it to pass.

6 He shall make thy righteousness as clear as the light, * and thy just dealing as the noon-day.

7 Hold thee still in the LORD, and abide patiently upon him: * but grieve not thyself at him whose way doth prosper, against the man that doeth after evil counsels.

8 Leave off from wrath, and let go displeasure: * fret not thyself, else shalt thou be moved to do evil.

9 Wicked doers shall be rooted out; * and they that patiently abide the LORD, those shall inherit the land.

10 Yet a little while, and the ungodly shall be clean gone: * thou shalt look after his place, and he shall be away.

11 But the meek-spirited shall possess the earth, * and shall be refreshed in the multitude of peace.

12 The ungodly seeketh counsel against the just, * and gnasheth upon him with his teeth.

13 The Lord shall laugh him to scorn; * for he hath seen that his day is coming.

14 The ungodly have drawn out the sword, and have bent their bow, * to cast down the poor and needy, and to slay such as be upright in their ways.

15 Their sword shall go through their own heart, * and their bow shall be broken.

16 A small thing that the righteous hath, * is better than great riches of the ungodly.

17 For the arms of the ungodly shall be broken, * and the LORD upholdeth the righteous.

18 The LORD knoweth the days of the godly; * and their inheritance shall endure for ever.

19 They shall not be confounded in the perilous time; * and in the days of dearth they shall have enough.

20 As for the ungodly, they shall perish, and the enemies

of the LORD shall consume as the fat of lambs: * yea, even as the smoke shall they consume away.

21 The ungodly borroweth, and payeth not again; * but the righteous is merciful and liberal.

22 Such as are blessed of God, shall possess the land; * and they that are cursed of him, shall be rooted out.

23 The LORD ordereth a good man's going, * and maketh his way acceptable to himself.

24 Though he fall, he shall not be cast away; * for the LORD upholdeth him with his hand.

25 I have been young, and now am old; * and yet saw I never the righteous forsaken, nor his seed begging their bread.

26 The righteous is ever merciful, and lendeth; * and his seed is blessed.

27 Flee from evil, and do the thing that is good; * and dwell for evermore.

28 For the LORD loveth the thing that is right; * he forsaketh not his that be godly, but they are preserved for ever.

29 The unrighteous shall be punished; * as for the seed of the ungodly, it shall be rooted out.

30 The righteous shall inherit the land, * and dwell therein for ever.

31 The mouth of the righteous is exercised in wisdom, * and his tongue will be talking of judgment.

32 The law of his God is in his heart, * and his goings shall not slide.

33 The ungodly watcheth the righteous, * and seeketh occasion to slay him.

34 The LORD will not leave him in his hand, * nor condemn him when he is judged.

35 Hope thou in the LORD, and keep his way, and he

shall promote thee, that thou shalt possess the land: *
when the ungodly shall perish, thou shalt see it.

36 I myself have seen the ungodly in great power, *
and flourishing like a green bay-tree.

37 I went by, and lo, he was gone: * I sought him, but
his place could no where be found.

38 Keep innocency, and take heed unto the thing that
is right; * for that shall bring a man peace at the last.

39 As for the transgressors, they shall perish together; *
and the end of the ungodly is, they shall be rooted out at
the last.

40 But the salvation of the righteous cometh of the
LORD; * who is also their strength in the time of trouble.

41 And the LORD shall stand by them, and save them: *
he shall deliver them from the ungodly, and shall save
them, because they put their trust in him.

The Eighth Day.

Morning Prayer.

Psalm 38. *Domine, ne in furore.*

PUT me not to rebuke, O LORD, in thine anger; *
neither chasten me in thy heavy displeasure:

2 For thine arrows stick fast in me, * and thy hand
presseth me sore.

3 There is no health in my flesh, because of thy displeasure; * neither is there any rest in my bones, by reason
of my sin.

4 For my wickednesses are gone over my head, * and
are like a sore burden, too heavy for me to bear.

5 My wounds stink, and are corrupt, * through my
foolishness.

6 I am brought into so great trouble and misery, * that I go mourning all the day long.

7 For my loins are filled with a sore disease, * and there is no whole part in my body.

8 I am feeble and sore smitten; * I have roared for the very disquietness of my heart.

9 Lord, thou knowest all my desire; * and my groaning is not hid from thee.

10 My heart panteth, my strength hath failed me, * and the light of mine eyes is gone from me.

11 My lovers and my neighbours did stand looking upon my trouble, * and my kinsmen stood afar off.

12 They also that sought after my life laid snares for me; * and they that went about to do me evil talked of wickedness, and imagined deceit all the day long.

13 As for me, I was like a deaf man, and heard not; * and as one that is dumb, who doth not open his mouth.

14 I became even as a man that heareth not, * and in whose mouth are no reproofs.

15 For in thee, O LORD, have I put my trust; * thou shalt answer for me, O Lord my God.

16 I have required that they, even mine enemies, should not triumph over me; * for when my foot slipt, they rejoiced greatly against me.

17 And I truly am set in the plague, * and my heaviness is ever in my sight.

18 For I will confess my wickedness, * and be sorry for my sin.

19 But mine enemies live, and are mighty; * and they that hate me wrongfully are many in number.

20 They also that reward evil for good are against me; * because I follow the thing that good is.

21 Forsake me not, O LORD my God; * be not thou far from me.

22 Haste thee to help me, * O Lord God of my salvation.

Psalm 39. *Dixi, Custodiam.*

I SAID, I will take heed to my ways, * that I offend not in my tongue

2 I will keep my mouth as it were with a bridle, * while the ungodly is in my sight.

3 I held my tongue, and spake nothing: * I kept silence, yea, even from good words; but it was pain and grief to me.

4 My heart was hot within me: and while I was thus musing the fire kindled, * and at the last I spake with my tongue:

5 LORD, let me know mine end, and the number of my days; * that I may be certified how long I have to live.

6 Behold, thou hast made my days as it were a span long, and mine age is even as nothing in respect of thee; * and verily every man living is altogether vanity.

7 For man walketh in a vain shadow, and disquieteth himself in vain; * he heapeth up riches, and cannot tell who shall gather them.

8 And now, Lord, what is my hope? * truly my hope is even in thee.

9 Deliver me from all mine offences; * and make me not a rebuke unto the foolish.

10 I became dumb, and opened not my mouth; * for it was thy doing.

11 Take thy plague away from me: * I am even consumed by the means of thy heavy hand.

12 When thou with rebukes dost chasten man for sin, thou makest his beauty to consume away, like as it were a moth fretting a garment: * every man therefore is but vanity.

13 Hear my prayer, O LORD, and with thine ears consider my calling; * hold not thy peace at my tears;

14 For I am a stranger with thee, and a sojourner, * as all my fathers were.

15 O spare me a little, that I may recover my strength, * before I go hence, and be no more seen.

Psalm 40. *Expectans expectavi.*

I WAITED patiently for the LORD, * and he inclined unto me, and heard my calling.

2 He brought me also out of the horrible pit, out of the mire and clay, * and set my feet upon the rock, and ordered my goings.

3 And he hath put a new song in my mouth, * even a thanksgiving unto our God.

4 Many shall see it, and fear, * and shall put their trust in the LORD.

5 Blessed is the man that hath set his hope in the LORD, * and turned not unto the proud, and to such as go about with lies.

6 O LORD my God, great are the wondrous works which thou hast done, like as be also thy thoughts, which are to us-ward; * and yet there is no man that ordereth them unto thee.

7 If I should declare them, and speak of them, * they should be more than I am able to express.

8 Sacrifice and offering thou wouldest not, * but mine ears hast thou opened.

9 Burnt-offering and sacrifice for sin hast thou not required: * then said I, Lo, I come;

10 In the volume of the book it is written of me, that I should fulfil thy will, O my God: * I am content to do it; yea, thy law is within my heart.

11 I have declared thy righteousness in the great con-

gregation: * lo, I will not refrain my lips, O LORD, and that thou knowest.

12 I have not hid thy righteousness within my heart; * my talk hath been of thy truth, and of thy salvation.

13 I have not kept back thy loving mercy and truth * from the great congregation.

14 Withdraw not thou thy mercy from me, O LORD; * let thy loving-kindness and thy truth alway preserve me.

15 For innumerable troubles are come about me; my sins have taken such hold upon me, that I am not able to look up; * yea, they are more in number than the hairs of my head, and my heart hath failed me.

16 O LORD, let it be thy pleasure to deliver me; * make haste, O LORD, to help me.

17 Let them be ashamed, and confounded together, that seek after my soul to destroy it; * let them be driven backward, and put to rebuke, that wish me evil.

18 Let them be desolate, and rewarded with shame, * that say unto me, Fie upon thee! fie upon thee!

19 Let all those that seek thee, be joyful and glad in thee; * and let such as love thy salvation, say alway, The LORD be praised.

20 As for me, I am poor and needy; * but the Lord careth for me.

21 Thou art my helper and redeemer; * make no long tarrying, O my God.

Evening Prayer.

Psalm 41. *Beatus qui intelligit.*

BLESSED is he that considereth the poor and needy; the LORD shall deliver him in the time of trouble.

2 The LORD preserve him, and keep him alive, that he

may be blessed upon earth; * and deliver not thou him into the will of his enemies.

3 The LORD comfort him when he lieth sick upon his bed; * make thou all his bed in his sickness.

4 I said, LORD, be merciful unto me; * heal my soul, for I have sinned against thee.

5 Mine enemies speak evil of me, * When shall he die, and his name perish?

6 And if he come to see me, he speaketh vanity, * and his heart conceiveth falsehood within himself; and when he cometh forth, he telleth it.

7 All mine enemies whisper together against me; * even against me do they imagine this evil.

8 An evil disease, say they, cleaveth fast unto him; * and now that he lieth, he shall rise up no more.

9 Yea, even mine own familiar friend whom I trusted, * who did also eat of my bread, hath laid great wait for me.

10 But be thou merciful unto me, O LORD; * raise thou me up again, and I shall reward them.

11 By this I know thou favourest me, * that mine enemy doth not triumph against me.

12 And in my innocency thou upholdest me, * and shalt set me before thy face for ever.

13 Blessed be the LORD God of Israel, * world without end. Amen.

BOOK II.

Psalm 42. *Quemadmodum.*

LIKE as the hart desireth the water-brooks, * so longeth my soul after thee, O God.

2 My soul is athirst for God, yea, even for the living

God: * when shall I come to appear before the presence of God?

3 My tears have been my meat day and night, * while they daily say unto me, Where is now thy God?

4 Now when I think thereupon, I pour out my heart by myself; * for I went with the multitude, and brought them forth into the house of God;

5 In the voice of praise and thanksgiving, * among such as keep holy-day.

6 Why art thou so full of heaviness, O my soul? * and why art thou so disquieted within me?

7 O put thy trust in God; * for I will yet thank him, which is the help of my countenance, and my God.

8 My soul is vexed within me; * therefore will I remember thee from the land of Jordan, from Hermon and the little hill.

9 One deep calleth another, because of the noise of thy water-floods; * all thy waves and storms are gone over me.

10 The LORD will grant his loving-kindness in the day-time; * and in the night season will I sing of him, and make my prayer unto the God of my life.

11 I will say unto the God of my strength, Why hast thou forgotten me? * why go I thus heavily, while the enemy oppresseth me?

12 My bones are smitten asunder as with a sword, * while mine enemies that trouble me cast me in the teeth;

13 Namely, while they say daily unto me, * Where is now thy God?

14 Why art thou so vexed, O my soul? * and why art thou so disquieted within me?

15 O put thy trust in God; * for I will yet thank him, which is the help of my countenance, and my God.

Psalm 43. *Judica me, Deus.*

GIVE sentence with me, O God, and defend my cause against the ungodly people; * O deliver me from the deceitful and wicked man.

2 For thou art the God of my strength; why hast thou put me from thee? * and why go I so heavily, while the enemy oppresseth me?

3 O send out thy light and thy truth, that they may lead me, * and bring me unto thy holy hill, and to thy dwelling;

4 And that I may go unto the altar of God, even unto the God of my joy and gladness; * and upon the harp will I give thanks unto thee, O God, my God.

5 Why art thou so heavy, O my soul? * and why art thou so disquieted within me?

6 O put thy trust in God; * for I will yet give him thanks, which is the help of my countenance, and my God.

The Ninth Day.

Morning Prayer.

Psalm 44. *Deus, auribus.*

WE have heard with our ears, O God, our fathers have told us * what thou hast done in their time of old:

2 How thou hast driven out the heathen with thy hand, and planted our fathers in; * how thou hast destroyed the nations, and made thy people to flourish.

3 For they gat not the land in possession through their own sword, * neither was it their own arm that helped them;

4 But thy right hand, and thine arm, and the light of thy countenance; * because thou hadst a favour unto them.

5 Thou art my King, O God; * send help unto Jacob.

6 Through thee will we overthrow our enemies, * and in thy Name will we tread them under that rise up against us.

7 For I will not trust in my bow, * it is not my sword that shall help me;

8 But it is thou that savest us from our enemies, * and puttest them to confusion that hate us.

9 We make our boast of God all day long, * and will praise thy Name for ever.

10 But now thou art far off, and puttest us to confusion, * and goest not forth with our armies.

11 Thou makest us to turn our backs upon our enemies, * so that they which hate us spoil our goods.

12 Thou lettest us be eaten up like sheep, * and hast scattered us among the heathen.

13 Thou sellest thy people for nought, * and takest no money for them.

14 Thou makest us to be rebuked of our neighbours, * to be laughed to scorn, and had in derision of them that are round about us.

15 Thou makest us to be a by-word among the nations, * and that the peoples shake their heads at us.

16 My confusion is daily before me, * and the shame of my face hath covered me;

17 For the voice of the slanderer and blasphemer, * for the enemy and avenger.

18 And though all this be come upon us, yet do we not forget thee, * nor behave ourselves frowardly in thy covenant.

19 Our heart is not turned back, * neither our steps gone out of thy way;

20 No, not when thou hast smitten us into the place of dragons, * and covered us with the shadow of death.

21 If we have forgotten the Name of our God, and

holden up our hands to any strange god, * shall not God search it out? for he knoweth the very secrets of the heart.

22 For thy sake also are we killed all the day long, * and are counted as sheep appointed to be slain.

23 Up, Lord, why sleepest thou? * awake, and be not absent from us for ever.

24 Wherefore hidest thou thy face, * and forgettest our misery and trouble?

25 For our soul is brought low, even unto the dust; * our belly cleaveth unto the ground.

26 Arise, and help us, * and deliver us, for thy mercy's sake.

Psalm 45. *Eructavit cor meum.*

M Y heart overfloweth with a good matter; I speak the things which I have made concerning the King. * My tongue is the pen of a ready writer.

2 Thou art fairer than the children of men; * full of grace are thy lips, because God hath blessed thee for ever.

3 Gird thee with thy sword upon thy thigh, O thou Most Mighty, * according to thy worship and renown.

4 Good luck have thou with thine honour: * ride on, because of the word of truth, of meekness, and righteousness; and thy right hand shall teach thee terrible things.

5 Thy arrows are very sharp in the heart of the King's enemies, * and the people shall be subdued unto thee.

6 Thy seat, O God, endureth for ever; * the sceptre of thy kingdom is a right sceptre.

7 Thou hast loved righteousness, and hated iniquity; * wherefore God, even thy God, hath anointed thee with the oil of gladness above thy fellows.

8 All thy garments smell of myrrh, aloes, and cassia; * out of the ivory palaces, whereby they have made thee glad.

9 Kings' daughters are among thy honourable women; * upon thy right hand doth stand the queen in a vesture of gold, wrought about with divers colours.

10 Hearken, O daughter, and consider; incline thine ear; * forget also thine own people, and thy father's house.

11 So shall the King have pleasure in thy beauty; * for he is thy Lord, and worship thou him.

12 And the daughter of Tyre shall be there with a gift; * like as the rich also among the people shall make their supplication before thee.

13 The King's daughter is all glorious within; * her clothing is of wrought gold.

14 She shall be brought unto the King in raiment of needlework: * the virgins that be her fellows shall bear her company, and shall be brought unto thee.

15 With joy and gladness shall they be brought, * and shall enter into the King's palace.

16 Instead of thy fathers, thou shalt have children, * whom thou mayest make princes in all lands.

17 I will make thy Name to be remembered from one generation to another; * therefore shall the people give thanks unto thee, world without end.

Psalm 46. *Deus noster refugium.*

GOD is our hope and strength, * a very present help in trouble.

2 Therefore will we not fear, though the earth be moved, * and though the hills be carried into the midst of the sea;

3 Though the waters thereof rage and swell, * and though the mountains shake at the tempest of the same.

4 There is a river, the streams whereof make glad the city of God; * the holy place of the tabernacle of the Most Highest.

5 God is in the midst of her, therefore shall she not be removed; * God shall help her, and that right early.

6 The nations make much ado, and the kingdoms are moved; * but God hath showed his voice, and the earth shall melt away.

7 The LORD of hosts is with us; * the God of Jacob is our refuge.

8 O come hither, and behold the works of the LORD, * what destruction he hath brought upon the earth.

9 He maketh wars to cease in all the world; * he breaketh the bow, and knappeth the spear in sunder, and burneth the chariots in the fire.

10 Be still then, and know that I am God: * I will be exalted among the nations, and I will be exalted in the earth.

11 The LORD of hosts is with us; * the God of Jacob is our refuge.

Evening Prayer.

Psalm 47. *Omnes gentes, plaudite.*

O CLAP your hands together, all ye peoples: * O sing unto God with the voice of melody.

2 For the LORD is high, and to be feared; * he is the great King upon all the earth.

3 He shall subdue the peoples under us, * and the nations under our feet.

4 He shall choose out an heritage for us, * even the excellency of Jacob, whom he loved.

5 God is gone up with a merry noise, * and the LORD with the sound of the trump.

6 O sing praises, sing praises unto our God; * O sing praises, sing praises unto our King.

7 For God is the King of all the earth: * sing ye praises with understanding.

8 God reigneth over the nations; * God sitteth upon his holy seat.

9 The princes of the peoples are joined unto the people of the God of Abraham; * for God, which is very high exalted, doth defend the earth, as it were with a shield.

Psalm 48. *Magnus Dominus.*

GREAT is the LORD, and highly to be praised * in the city of our God, even upon his holy hill.

2 The hill of Sion is a fair place, and the joy of the whole earth; * upon the north side lieth the city of the great King: God is well known in her palaces as a sure refuge.

3 For lo, the kings of the earth * were gathered, and gone by together.

4 They marvelled to see such things; * they were astonished, and suddenly cast down.

5 Fear came there upon them; and sorrow, * as upon a woman in her travail.

6 Thou dost break the ships of the sea * through the east-wind.

7 Like as we have heard, so have we seen in the city of the LORD of hosts, in the city of our God; * God upholdeth the same for ever.

8 We wait for thy loving-kindness, O God, * in the midst of thy temple.

9 O God, according to thy Name, so is thy praise unto the world's end; * thy right hand is full of righteousness.

10 Let the mount Sion rejoice, and the daughters of Judah be glad, * because of thy judgments.

11 Walk about Sion, and go round about her; * and tell the towers thereof.

12 Mark well her bulwarks, consider her palaces, * that ye may tell them that come after.

13 For this God is our God for ever and ever: * he shall be our guide unto death.

Psalm 49. *Audite hæc, omnes.*

O HEAR ye this, all ye people; * ponder it with your ears, all ye that dwell in the world;

2 High and low, rich and poor, * one with another.

3 My mouth shall speak of wisdom, * and my heart shall muse of understanding.

4 I will incline mine ear to the parable, * and show my dark speech upon the harp.

5 Wherefore should I fear in the days of evil, * when wickedness at my heels compasseth me round about?

6 There be some that put their trust in their goods, * and boast themselves in the multitude of their riches.

7 But no man may deliver his brother, * nor give a ransom unto God for him,

8 (For it cost more to redeem their souls, * so that he must let that alone for ever;)

9 That he shall live alway, * and not see the grave.

10 For he seeth that wise men also die and perish together, * as well as the ignorant and foolish, and leave their riches for other.

11 And yet they think that their houses shall continue for ever, and that their dwelling-places shall endure from one generation to another; * and call the lands after their own names.

12 Nevertheless, man being in honour abideth not, * seeing he may be compared unto the beasts that perish;

13 This their way is very foolishness; * yet their posterity praise their saying.

14 They lie in the grave like sheep; death is their shep-

herd; and the righteous shall have dominion over them in the morning: * their beauty shall consume in the sepulchre, and have no abiding.

15 But God hath delivered my soul from the power of the grave; * for he shall receive me.

16 Be not thou afraid, though one be made rich, * or if the glory of his house be increased;

17 For he shall carry nothing away with him when he dieth, * neither shall his pomp follow him.

18 For while he lived, he counted himself an happy man; * and so long as thou doest well unto thyself, men will speak good of thee.

19 He shall follow the generation of his fathers, * and shall never see light.

20 Man that is in honour but hath no understanding * is compared unto the beasts that perish.

The Tenth Day.

Morning Prayer.

Psalm 50. *Deus deorum.*

THE LORD, even the Most Mighty God, hath spoken, * and called the world, from the rising up of the sun unto the going down thereof.

2 Out of Sion hath God appeared * in perfect beauty.

3 Our God shall come, and shall not keep silence; * there shall go before him a consuming fire, and a mighty tempest shall be stirred up round about him.

4 He shall call the heaven from above, * and the earth, that he may judge his people.

5 Gather my saints together unto me; * those that have made a covenant with me with sacrifice.

6 And the heavens shall declare his righteousness; *
for God is Judge himself.

7 Hear, O my people, and I will speak; * I myself will
testify against thee, O Israel; for I am God, even thy God.

8 I will not reprove thee because of thy sacrifices; * as
for thy burnt-offerings, they are alway before me.

9 I will take no bullock out of thine house, * nor he-
goats out of thy folds.

10 For all the beasts of the forest are mine, * and so
are the cattle upon a thousand hills.

11 I know all the fowls upon the mountains, * and the
wild beasts of the field are in my sight.

12 If I be hungry, I will not tell thee; * for the whole
world is mine, and all that is therein.

13 Thinkest thou that I will eat bulls' flesh, * and drink
the blood of goats?

14 Offer unto God thanksgiving, * and pay thy vows
unto the Most Highest.

15 And call upon me in the time of trouble; * so will I
hear thee, and thou shalt praise me.

16 But unto the ungodly saith God, * Why dost thou
preach my laws, and takest my covenant in thy mouth;

17 Whereas thou hatest to be reformed, * and hast cast
my words behind thee?

18 When thou sawest a thief, thou consentedst unto
him; * and hast been partaker with the adulterers.

19 Thou hast let thy mouth speak wickedness, * and
with thy tongue thou hast set forth deceit.

20 Thou sattest and spakest against thy brother; * yea,
and hast slandered thine own mother's son.

21 These things hast thou done, and I held my tongue,
and thou thoughtest wickedly, that I am even such a one
as thyself; * but I will reprove thee, and set before thee
the things that thou hast done.

22 O consider this, ye that forget God, * lest I pluck you away, and there be none to deliver you.

23 Whoso offereth me thanks and praise, he honoureth me; * and to him that ordereth his way aright, will I show the salvation of God.

Psalm 51. *Miserere mei, Deus.*

HAVE mercy upon me, O God, after thy great goodness; * according to the multitude of thy mercies do away mine offences.

2 Wash me throughly from my wickedness, * and cleanse me from my sin.

3 For I acknowledge my faults, * and my sin is ever before me.

4 Against thee only have I sinned, and done this evil in thy sight; * that thou mightest be justified in thy saying, and clear when thou shalt judge.

5 Behold, I was shapen in wickedness, * and in sin hath my mother conceived me.

6 But lo, thou requirest truth in the inward parts, * and shalt make me to understand wisdom secretly.

7 Thou shalt purge me with hyssop, and I shall be clean; * thou shalt wash me, and I shall be whiter than snow.

8 Thou shalt make me hear of joy and gladness, * that the bones which thou hast broken may rejoice.

9 Turn thy face from my sins, * and put out all my misdeeds.

10 Make me a clean heart, O God, * and renew a right spirit within me.

11 Cast me not away from thy presence, * and take not thy holy Spirit from me.

12 O give me the comfort of thy help again, * and stablish me with thy free Spirit.

13 Then shall I teach thy ways unto the wicked, * and sinners shall be converted unto thee.

14 Deliver me from blood-guiltiness, O God, thou that art the God of my health; * and my tongue shall sing of thy righteousness.

15 Thou shalt open my lips, O Lord, * and my mouth shall show thy praise.

16 For thou desirest no sacrifice, else would I give it thee; * but thou delightest not in burnt-offerings.

17 The sacrifice of God is a troubled spirit: * a broken and contrite heart, O God, shalt thou not despise.

18 O be favourable and gracious unto Sion; * build thou the walls of Jerusalem.

19 Then shalt thou be pleased with the sacrifice of righteousness, with the burnt-offerings and oblations; * then shall they offer young bullocks upon thine altar.

Psalm 52. *Quid gloriaris?*

WHY boastest thou thyself, thou tyrant, * that thou canst do mischief;

2 Whereas the goodness of God * endureth yet daily?

3 Thy tongue imagineth wickedness, * and with lies thou cuttest like a sharp razor.

4 Thou hast loved unrighteousness more than goodness, * and falsehood more than righteousness.

5 Thou hast loved to speak all words that may do hurt, * O thou false tongue.

6 Therefore shall God destroy thee for ever; * he shall take thee, and pluck thee out of thy dwelling, and root thee out of the land of the living.

7 The righteous also shall see this, and fear, * and shall laugh him to scorn:

8 Lo, this is the man that took not God for his

strength; * but trusted unto the multitude of his riches, and strengthened himself in his wickedness.

9 As for me, I am like a green olive-tree in the house of God; * my trust is in the tender mercy of God for ever and ever.

10 I will alway give thanks unto thee for that thou hast done; * and I will hope in thy Name, for thy saints like it well.

Evening Prayer.

Psalm 53. *Dixit insipiens.*

THE foolish body hath said in his heart, * There is no God.

2 Corrupt are they, and become abominable in their wickedness; * there is none that doeth good.

3 God looked down from heaven upon the children of men, * to see if there were any that would understand, and seek after God.

4 But they are all gone out of the way, they are altogether become abominable; * there is also none that doeth good, no not one.

5 Are not they without understanding that work wickedness, * eating up my people as if they would eat bread? they have not called upon God.

6 They were afraid where no fear was; * for God hath broken the bones of him that besieged thee; thou hast put them to confusion, because God hath despised them.

7 O that the salvation were given unto Israel out of Sion! * O that the Lord would deliver his people out of captivity!

8 Then should Jacob rejoice, * and Israel should be right glad.

Psalm 54. *Deus, in Nomine.*

SAVE me, O God, for thy Name's sake, * and avenge me in thy strength.

2 Hear my prayer, O God, * and hearken unto the words of my mouth.

3 For strangers are risen up against me; * and tyrants, which have not God before their eyes, seek after my soul.

4 Behold, God is my helper; * the Lord is with them that uphold my soul.

5 He shall reward evil unto mine enemies: * destroy thou them in thy truth.

6 An offering of a free heart will I give thee, and praise thy Name, O LORD; * because it is so comfortable.

7 For he hath delivered me out of all my trouble; * and mine eye hath seen his desire upon mine enemies.

Psalm 55. *Exaudi, Deus.*

HEAR my prayer, O God, * and hide not thyself from my petition.

2 Take heed unto me, and hear me, * how I mourn in my prayer, and am vexed;

3 The enemy crieth so, and the ungodly cometh on so fast; * for they are minded to do me some mischief, so maliciously are they set against me.

4 My heart is disquieted within me, * and the fear of death is fallen upon me.

5 Fearfulness and trembling are come upon me, * and an horrible dread hath overwhelmed me.

6 And I said, O that I had wings like a dove! * for then would I flee away, and be at rest.

7 Lo, then would I get me away far off, * and remain in the wilderness.

8 I would make haste to escape, * because of the stormy wind and tempest.

9 Destroy their tongues, O Lord, and divide them; * for I have spied unrighteousness and strife in the city.

10 Day and night they go about within the walls thereof: * mischief also and sorrow are in the midst of it.

11 Wickedness is therein; * deceit and guile go not out of her streets.

12 For it is not an open enemy that hath done me this dishonour; * for then I could have borne it;

13 Neither was it mine adversary that did magnify himself against me; * for then peradventure I would have hid myself from him;

14 But it was even thou, my companion, * my guide, and mine own familiar friend.

15 We took sweet counsel together, * and walked in the house of God as friends.

16 Let death come hastily upon them, and let them go down alive into the pit; * for wickedness is in their dwellings, and among them.

17 As for me, I will call upon God, * and the LORD shall save me.

18 In the evening, and morning, and at noon-day will I pray, and that instantly; * and he shall hear my voice.

19 It is he that hath delivered my soul in peace from the battle that was against me; * for there were many that strove with me.

20 Yea, even God, that endureth for ever, shall hear me, and bring them down; * for they will not turn, nor fear God.

21 He laid his hands upon such as be at peace with him, * and he brake his covenant.

22 The words of his mouth were softer than butter,

having war in his heart; * his words were smoother than oil, and yet be they very swords.

23 O cast thy burden upon the LORD, and he shall nourish thee, * and shall not suffer the righteous to fall for ever.

24 And as for them, * thou, O God, shalt bring them into the pit of destruction.

25 The blood-thirsty and deceitful men shall not live out half their days: * nevertheless, my trust shall be in thee, O Lord.

The Eleventh Day.

Morning Prayer.

Psalm 56. *Miserere mei, Deus.*

BE merciful unto me, O God, for man goeth about to devour me; * he is daily fighting, and troubling me.

2 Mine enemies are daily at hand to swallow me up; * for they be many that fight against me, O thou Most Highest.

3 Nevertheless, though I am sometime afraid, * yet put I my trust in thee.

4 I will praise God, because of his word: * I have put my trust in God, and will not fear what flesh can do unto me.

5 They daily mistake my words; * all that they imagine is to do me evil.

6 They hold all together, and keep themselves close, * and mark my steps, when they lay wait for my soul.

7 Shall they escape for their wickedness? * thou, O God, in thy displeasure shalt cast them down.

8 Thou tellest my wanderings; put my tears into thy bottle: * are not these things noted in thy book?

9 Whensoever I call upon thee, then shall mine enemies be put to flight: * this I know; for God is on my side.

10 In God's word will I rejoice; * in the LORD's word will I comfort me.

11 Yea, in God have I put my trust; * I will not be afraid what man can do unto me.

12 Unto thee, O God, will I pay my vows; * unto thee will I give thanks.

13 For thou hast delivered my soul from death, and my feet from falling, * that I may walk before God in the light of the living.

Psalm 57. *Miserere mei, Deus.*

BE merciful unto me, O God, be merciful unto me; for my soul trusteth in thee; * and under the shadow of thy wings shall be my refuge, until this tyranny be overpast.

2 I will call unto the Most High God, * even unto the God that shall perform the cause which I have in hand.

3 He shall send from heaven, * and save me from the reproof of him that would eat me up.

4 God shall send forth his mercy and truth: * my soul is among lions;

5 And I lie even among the children of men, that are set on fire, * whose teeth are spears and arrows, and their tongue a sharp sword.

6 Set up thyself, O God, above the heavens; * and thy glory above all the earth.

7 They have laid a net for my feet, and pressed down my soul; * they have digged a pit before me, and are fallen into the midst of it themselves.

8 My heart is fixed, O God, my heart is fixed; * I will sing and give praise.

9 Awake up, my glory; awake, lute and harp: * I myself will awake right early.

10 I will give thanks unto thee, O Lord, among the peoples; * and I will sing unto thee among the nations.

11 For the greatness of thy mercy reacheth unto the heavens, * and thy truth unto the clouds.

12 Set up thyself, O God, above the heavens; * and thy glory above all the earth.

Psalm 58. *Si vere utique.*

ARE your minds set upon righteousness, O ye congregation? * and do ye judge the thing that is right, O ye sons of men?

2 Yea, ye imagine mischief in your heart upon the earth, * and your hands deal with wickedness.

3 The ungodly are froward, even from their mother's womb; * as soon as they are born, they go astray, and speak lies.

4 They are as venomous as the poison of a serpent, * even like the deaf adder, that stoppeth her ears;

5 Which refuseth to hear the voice of the charmer, * charm he never so wisely.

6 Break their teeth, O God, in their mouths; * smite the jaw-bones of the lions, O LORD.

7 Let them fall away like water that runneth apace; * when they shoot their arrows, let them be rooted out.

8 Let them consume away like a snail, and be like the untimely fruit of a woman; * and let them not see the sun.

9 Or ever your pots be made hot with thorns, * he shall take them away with a whirlwind, the green and the burning alike.

10 The righteous shall rejoice when he seeth the vengeance; * he shall wash his footsteps in the blood of the ungodly.

11 So that a man shall say, Verily there is a reward for the righteous; * doubtless there is a God that judgeth the earth.

Evening Prayer.

Psalm 59. *Eripe me de inimicis.*

DELIVER me from mine enemies, O God; * defend me from them that rise up against me.

2 O deliver me from the wicked doers, * and save me from the blood-thirsty men.

3 For lo, they lie waiting for my soul; * the mighty men are gathered against me, without any offence or fault of me, O LORD.

4 They run and prepare themselves without my fault; * arise thou therefore to help me, and behold.

5 Stand up, O LORD God of hosts, thou God of Israel, to visit all the heathen, * and be not merciful unto them that offend of malicious wickedness.

6 They go to and fro in the evening, * they grin like a dog, and run about through the city.

7 Behold, they speak with their mouth, and swords are in their lips; * for who doth hear?

8 But thou, O LORD, shalt have them in derision, * and thou shalt laugh all the heathen to scorn.

9 My strength will I ascribe unto thee; * for thou art the God of my refuge.

10 God showeth me his goodness plenteously; * and God shall let me see my desire upon mine enemies.

11 Slay them not, lest my people forget it; * but scatter them abroad among the people, and put them down, O Lord our defence.

12 For the sin of their mouth, and for the words of their lips, they shall be taken in their pride: * and why? their talk is of cursing and lies.

13 Consume them in thy wrath, consume them, that they may perish; * and know that it is God that ruleth in Jacob, and unto the ends of the world.

14 And in the evening they will return, * grin like a dog, and will go about the city.

15 They will run here and there for meat, * and grudge if they be not satisfied.

16 As for me, I will sing of thy power, and will praise thy mercy betimes in the morning; * for thou hast been my defence and refuge in the day of my trouble.

17 Unto thee, O my strength, will I sing; * for thou, O God, art my refuge, and my merciful God.

Psalm 60. *Deus, repulisti nos.*

O GOD, thou hast cast us out, and scattered us abroad; * thou hast also been displeased: O turn thee unto us again.

2 Thou hast moved the land, and divided it: * heal the sores thereof, for it shaketh.

3 Thou hast showed thy people heavy things; * thou hast given us a drink of deadly wine.

4 Thou hast given a token for such as fear thee, * that they may triumph because of the truth.

5 Therefore were thy beloved delivered: * help me with thy right hand, and hear me.

6 God hath spoken in his holiness, I will rejoice, and divide Shechem, * and mete out the valley of Succoth.

7 Gilead is mine, and Manasseh is mine; * Ephraim also is the strength of my head; Judah is my law-giver;

8 Moab is my wash-pot; over Edom will I cast out my shoe; * Philistia, be thou glad of me.

9 Who will lead me into the strong city? * who will bring me into Edom?

10 Hast not thou cast us out, O God? * wilt not thou, O God, go out with our hosts?

11 O be thou our help in trouble; * for vain is the help of man.

12 Through God will we do great acts; * for it is he that shall tread down our enemies.

Psalm 61. *Exaudi, Deus.*

HEAR my crying, O God, * give ear unto my prayer.
2 From the ends of the earth will I call upon thee, * when my heart is in heaviness.

3 O set me up upon the rock that is higher than I; * for thou hast been my hope, and a strong tower for me against the enemy.

4 I will dwell in thy tabernacle for ever, * and my trust shall be under the covering of thy wings.

5 For thou, O Lord, hast heard my desires, * and hast given an heritage unto those that fear thy Name.

6 Thou shalt grant the King a long life, * that his years may endure throughout all generations.

7 He shall dwell before God for ever: * O prepare thy loving mercy and faithfulness, that they may preserve him.

8 So will I alway sing praise unto thy Name, * that I may daily perform my vows.

The Twelfth Day.

Morning Prayer.

Psalm 62. *Nonne Deo?*

MY soul truly waiteth still upon God; * for of him cometh my salvation.

2 He verily is my strength and my salvation; * he is my defence, so that I shall not greatly fall.

3 How long will ye imagine mischief against every

man? * Ye shall be slain all the sort of you; yea, as a tottering wall shall ye be, and like a broken hedge.

4 Their device is only how to put him out whom God will exalt; * their delight is in lies; they give good words with their mouth, but curse with their heart.

5 Nevertheless, my soul, wait thou still upon God; * for my hope is in him.

6 He truly is my strength and my salvation; * he is my defence, so that I shall not fall.

7 In God is my health and my glory; * the rock of my might; and in God is my trust.

8 O put your trust in him alway, ye people; * pour out your hearts before him, for God is our hope.

9 As for the children of men, they are but vanity; the children of men are deceitful; * upon the weights they are altogether lighter than vanity itself.

10 O trust not in wrong and robbery; give not yourselves unto vanity: * if riches increase, set not your heart upon them.

11 God spake once, and twice I have also heard the same, * that power belongeth unto God;

12 And that thou, Lord, art merciful; * for thou rewardest every man according to his work.

Psalm 63. *Deus, Deus meus.*

O GOD, thou art my God; * early will I seek thee.

2 My soul thirsteth for thee, my flesh also longeth after thee, * in a barren and dry land where no water is.

3 Thus have I looked for thee in the sanctuary, * that I might behold thy power and glory.

4 For thy loving-kindness is better than the life itself: * my lips shall praise thee.

5 As long as I live will I magnify thee in this manner, * and lift up my hands in thy Name.

6 My soul shall be satisfied, even as it were with marrow and fatness, * when my mouth praiseth thee with joyful lips.

7 Have I not remembered thee in my bed, * and thought upon thee when I was waking?

8 Because thou hast been my helper; * therefore under the shadow of thy wings will I rejoice.

9 My soul hangeth upon thee; * thy right hand hath upholden me.

10 These also that seek the hurt of my soul, * they shall go under the earth.

11 Let them fall upon the edge of the sword, * that they may be a portion for foxes.

12 But the King shall rejoice in God; all they also that swear by him shall be commended; * for the mouth of them that speak lies shall be stopped.

Psalm 64. *Exaudi, Deus.*

HEAR my voice, O God, in my prayer; * preserve my life from fear of the enemy.

2 Hide me from the gathering together of the froward, * and from the insurrection of wicked doers;

3 Who have whet their tongue like a sword, * and shoot out their arrows, even bitter words;

4 That they may privily shoot at him that is perfect: * suddenly do they hit him, and fear not.

5 They encourage themselves in mischief, * and commune among themselves, how they may lay snares; and say, that no man shall see them.

6 They imagine wickedness, and practise it; * that they keep secret among themselves, every man in the deep of his heart.

7 But God shall suddenly shoot at them with a swift arrow, * that they shall be wounded.

8 Yea, their own tongues shall make them fall; * insomuch that whoso seeth them shall laugh them to scorn.

9 And all men that see it shall say, This hath God done; * for they shall perceive that it is his work.

10 The righteous shall rejoice in the LORD, and put his trust in him; * and all they that are true of heart shall be glad.

Evening Prayer.

Psalm 65. *Te decet hymnus.*

THOU, O God, art praised in Sion; * and unto thee shall the vow be performed in Jerusalem.

2 Thou that hearest the prayer, * unto thee shall all flesh come.

3 My misdeeds prevail against me: * O be thou merciful unto our sins.

4 Blessed is the man whom thou choosest, and receivest unto thee: * he shall dwell in thy court, and shall be satisfied with the pleasures of thy house, even of thy holy temple.

5 Thou shalt show us wonderful things in thy righteousness, O God of our salvation; * thou that art the hope of all the ends of the earth, and of them that remain in the broad sea.

6 Who in his strength setteth fast the mountains, * and is girded about with power.

7 Who stilleth the raging of the sea, * and the noise of his waves, and the madness of the peoples.

8 They also that dwell in the uttermost parts of the earth shall be afraid at thy tokens, * thou that makest the out-goings of the morning and evening to praise thee.

9 Thou visitest the earth, and blessest it; * thou makest it very plenteous.

10 The river of God is full of water: * thou preparest their corn, for so thou providest for the earth.

11 Thou waterest her furrows; thou sendest rain into the little valleys thereof; * thou makest it soft with the drops of rain, and blessest the increase of it.

12 Thou crownest the year with thy goodness; * and thy clouds drop fatness.

13 They shall drop upon the dwellings of the wilderness; * and the little hills shall rejoice on every side.

14 The folds shall be full of sheep; * the valleys also shall stand so thick with corn, that they shall laugh and sing.

Psalm 66. *Jubilate Deo.*

O BE joyful in God, all ye lands; * sing praises unto the honour of his Name; make his praise to be glorious.

2 Say unto God, O how wonderful art thou in thy works! * through the greatness of thy power shall thine enemies bow down unto thee.

3 For all the world shall worship thee, * sing of thee, and praise thy Name.

4 O come hither, and behold the works of God; * how wonderful he is in his doing toward the children of men.

5 He turned the sea into dry land, * so that they went through the water on foot; there did we rejoice thereof.

6 He ruleth with his power for ever; his eyes behold the nations: * and such as will not believe shall not be able to exalt themselves.

7 O praise our God, ye peoples, * and make the voice of his praise to be heard;

8 Who holdeth our soul in life; * and suffereth not our feet to slip.

9 For thou, O God, hast proved us; * thou also hast tried us, like as silver is tried.

10 Thou broughtest us into the snare; * and laidest trouble upon our loins.

11 Thou sufferedst men to ride over our heads; * we went through fire and water, and thou broughtest us out into a wealthy place.

12 I will go into thine house with burnt-offerings, and will pay thee my vows, * which I promised with my lips, and spake with my mouth, when I was in trouble.

13 I will offer unto thee fat burnt-sacrifices, with the incense of rams; * I will offer bullocks and goats.

14 O come hither, and hearken, all ye that fear God; * and I will tell you what he hath done for my soul.

15 I called unto him with my mouth, * and gave him praises with my tongue.

16 If I incline unto wickedness with mine heart, * the Lord will not hear me.

17 But God hath heard me; * and considered the voice of my prayer.

18 Praised be God, who hath not cast out my prayer, * nor turned his mercy from me.

Psalm 67. *Deus misereatur.*

GOD be merciful unto us, and bless us, * and show us the light of his countenance, and be merciful unto us;

2 That thy way may be known upon earth, * thy saving health among all nations.

3 Let the peoples praise thee, O God; * yea, let all the peoples praise thee.

4 O let the nations rejoice and be glad; * for thou shalt judge the folk righteously, and govern the nations upon earth.

5 Let the peoples praise thee, O God; * yea, let all the peoples praise thee.

6 Then shall the earth bring forth her increase; * and God, even our own God, shall give us his blessing.

7 God shall bless us; * and all the ends of the world shall fear him.

The Thirteenth Day.

Morning Prayer.

Psalm 68. *Exsurgat Deus.*

LET God arise, and let his enemies be scattered; * let them also that hate him flee before him.

2 Like as the smoke vanisheth, so shalt thou drive them away; * and like as wax melteth at the fire, so let the ungodly perish at the presence of God.

3 But let the righteous be glad, and rejoice before God; * let them also be merry and joyful.

4 O sing unto God, and sing praises unto his Name; magnify him that rideth upon the heavens; * praise him in his Name JAH, and rejoice before him.

5 He is a Father of the fatherless, and defendeth the cause of the widows; * even God in his holy habitation.

6 He is the God that maketh men to be of one mind in an house, and bringeth the prisoners out of captivity; * but letteth the runagates continue in scarceness.

7 O God, when thou wentest forth before the people; * when thou wentest through the wilderness,

8 The earth shook, and the heavens dropped at the presence of God; * even as Sinai also was moved at the presence of God, who is the God of Israel.

9 Thou, O God, sentest a gracious rain upon thine inheritance, * and refreshedst it when it was weary.

10 Thy congregation shall dwell therein; * for thou, O God, hast of thy goodness prepared for the poor.

11 The Lord gave the word; * great was the company of women that bare the tidings.

12 Kings with their armies did flee, and were discomfited, * and they of the household divided the spoil.

13 Though ye have lain among the sheep-folds, yet shall ye be as the wings of a dove * that is covered with silver wings, and her feathers like gold.

14 When the Almighty scattered kings for their sake, * then were they as white as snow in Salmon.

15 As the hill of Bashan, so is God's hill; * even an high hill, as the hill of Bashan.

16 Why mock ye so, ye high hills? this is God's hill, in the which it pleaseth him to dwell; * yea, the LORD will abide in it for ever.

17 The chariots of God are twenty thousand, even thousands of angels; * and the Lord is among them as in the holy place of Sinai.

18 Thou art gone up on high, thou hast led captivity captive, and received gifts from men; * yea, even from thine enemies, that the LORD God might dwell among them.

19 Praised be the Lord daily, * even the God who helpeth us, and poureth his benefits upon us.

20 He is our God, even the God of whom cometh salvation: * GOD is the Lord, by whom we escape death.

21 God shall wound the head of his enemies, * and the hairy scalp of such a one as goeth on still in his wickedness.

22 The Lord hath said, I will bring my people again, as I did from Bashan; * mine own will I bring again, as I did sometime from the deep of the sea.

23 That thy foot may be dipped in the blood of thine enemies, * and that the tongue of thy dogs may be red through the same.

24 It is well seen, O God, how thou goest; * how thou, my God and King, goest in the sanctuary.

25 The singers go before, the minstrels follow after, * in the midst of the damsels playing with the timbrels.

26 Give thanks unto God the Lord in the congregation, * ye that are of the fountain of Israel.

27 There is little Benjamin their ruler, and the princes of Judah their council; * the princes of Zebulon, and the princes of Naphthali.

28 Thy God hath sent forth strength for thee; * stablish the thing, O God, that thou hast wrought in us,

29 For thy temple's sake at Jerusalem; * so shall kings bring presents unto thee.

30 Rebuke thou the dragon and the bull, with the leaders of the heathen, so that they humbly bring pieces of silver; * scatter thou the peoples that delight in war;

31 Then shall the princes come out of Egypt; * the Morians' land shall soon stretch out her hands unto God.

32 Sing unto God, O ye kingdoms of the earth; * O sing praises unto the Lord;

33 Who sitteth in the heavens over all, from the beginning: * lo, he doth send out his voice; yea, and that a mighty voice.

34 Ascribe ye the power to God over Israel; * his worship and strength is in the clouds.

35 O God, wonderful art thou in thy holy places: * even the God of Israel, he will give strength and power unto his people. Blessed be God.

Evening Prayer.

Psalm 69. *Salvum me fac.*

SAVE me, O God; * for the waters are come in, even unto my soul.

2 I stick fast in the deep mire, where no ground is; * I am come into deep waters, so that the floods run over me.

3 I am weary of crying; my throat is dry; * my sight faileth me for waiting so long upon my God.

4 They that hate me without a cause are more than the hairs of my head; * they that are mine enemies, and would destroy me guiltless, are mighty.

5 I paid them the things that I never took: * God, thou knowest my simpleness, and my faults are not hid from thee.

6 Let not them that trust in thee, O Lord GOD of hosts, be ashamed for my cause; * let not those that seek thee be confounded through me, O Lord God of Israel.

7 And why? for thy sake have I suffered reproof; * shame hath covered my face.

8 I am become a stranger unto my brethren, * even an alien unto my mother's children.

9 For the zeal of thine house hath even eaten me; * and the rebukes of them that rebuked thee are fallen upon me.

10 I wept, and chastened myself with fasting, * and that was turned to my reproof.

11 I put on sackcloth also, * and they jested upon me.

12 They that sit in the gate speak against me, * and the drunkards make songs upon me.

13 But, LORD, I make my prayer unto thee * in an acceptable time.

14 Hear me, O God, in the multitude of thy mercy, * even in the truth of thy salvation.

15 Take me out of the mire, that I sink not; * O let me be delivered from them that hate me, and out of the deep waters.

16 Let not the water-flood drown me, neither let the

deep swallow me up; * and let not the pit shut her mouth upon me.

17 Hear me, O LORD, for thy loving-kindness is comfortable; * turn thee unto me according to the multitude of thy mercies.

18 And hide not thy face from thy servant; for I am in trouble: * O haste thee, and hear me.

19 Draw nigh unto my soul, and save it; * O deliver me, because of mine enemies.

20 Thou hast known my reproach, my shame, and my dishonour: * mine adversaries are all in thy sight.

21 Reproach hath broken my heart; I am full of heaviness: * I looked for some to have pity on me, but there was no man, neither found I any to comfort me.

22 They gave me gall to eat; * and when I was thirsty they gave me vinegar to drink.

23 Let their table be made a snare to take themselves withal; * and let the things that should have been for their wealth be unto them an occasion of falling.

24 Let their eyes be blinded, that they see not; * and ever bow thou down their backs.

25 Pour out thine indignation upon them, * and let thy wrathful displeasure take hold of them.

26 Let their habitation be void, * and no man to dwell in their tents.

27 For they persecute him whom thou hast smitten; * and they talk how they may vex them whom thou hast wounded.

28 Let them fall from one wickedness to another, * and not come into thy righteousness.

29 Let them be wiped out of the book of the living, * and not be written among the righteous.

30 As for me, when I am poor and in heaviness, * thy help, O God, shall lift me up.

31 I will praise the Name of God with a song, * and magnify it with thanksgiving.

32 This also shall please the LORD * better than a bullock that hath horns and hoofs.

33 The humble shall consider this, and be glad: * seek ye after God, and your soul shall live.

34 For the LORD heareth the poor, * and despiseth not his prisoners.

35 Let heaven and earth praise him: * the sea, and all that moveth therein.

36 For God will save Sion, and build the cities of Judah, * that men may dwell there, and have it in possession.

37 The posterity also of his servants shall inherit it; * and they that love his Name shall dwell therein.

Psalm 70. *Deus, in adjutorium.*

HASTE thee, O God, to deliver me; * make haste to help me, O LORD.

2 Let them be ashamed and confounded that seek after my soul; * let them be turned backward and put to confusion that wish me evil.

3 Let them for their reward be soon brought to shame, * that cry over me, There! there!

4 But let all those that seek thee be joyful and glad in thee: * and let all such as delight in thy salvation say alway, The Lord be praised.

5 As for me, I am poor and in misery: * haste thee unto me, O God.

6 Thou art my helper, and my redeemer: * O LORD, make no long tarrying.

The Fourteenth Day.

Morning Prayer.

Psalm 71. *In te, Domine, speravi.*

IN thee, O LORD, have I put my trust; let me never be put to confusion, * but rid me and deliver me in thy righteousness; incline thine ear unto me, and save me.

2 Be thou my stronghold, whereunto I may alway resort: * thou hast promised to help me, for thou art my house of defence, and my castle.

3 Deliver me, O my God, out of the hand of the ungodly, * out of the hand of the unrighteous and cruel man.

4 For thou, O Lord GOD, art the thing that I long for: * thou art my hope, even from my youth.

5 Through thee have I been holden up ever since I was born: * thou art he that took me out of my mother's womb: my praise shall be alway of thee.

6 I am become as it were a monster unto many, * but my sure trust is in thee.

7 O let my mouth be filled with thy praise, * that I may sing of thy glory and honour all the day long.

8 Cast me not away in the time of age; * forsake me not when my strength faileth me.

9 For mine enemies speak against me; * and they that lay wait for my soul take their counsel together, saying,

10 God hath forsaken him; * persecute him, and take him, for there is none to deliver him.

11 Go not far from me, O God; * my God, haste thee to help me.

12 Let them be confounded and perish that are against my soul; * let them be covered with shame and dishonour that seek to do me evil.

13 As for me, I will patiently abide alway, * and will praise thee more and more.

14 My mouth shall daily speak of thy righteousness and salvation; * for I know no end thereof.

15 I will go forth in the strength of the Lord GOD, * and will make mention of thy righteousness only.

16 Thou, O God, hast taught me from my youth up until now; * therefore will I tell of thy wondrous works.

17 Forsake me not, O God, in mine old age, when I am gray-headed, * until I have showed thy strength unto this generation, and thy power to all them that are yet for to come.

18 Thy righteousness, O God, is very high, * and great things are they that thou hast done: O God, who is like unto thee!

19 O what great troubles and adversities hast thou showed me! and yet didst thou turn and refresh me; * yea, and broughtest me from the deep of the earth again.

20 Thou hast brought me to great honour, * and comforted me on every side:

21 Therefore will I praise thee, and thy faithfulness, O God, playing upon an instrument of music: * unto thee will I sing upon the harp, O thou Holy One of Israel.

22 My lips will be glad when I sing unto thee; * and so will my soul whom thou hast delivered.

23 My tongue also shall talk of thy righteousness all the day long; * for they are confounded and brought unto shame that seek to do me evil.

Psalm 72. *Deus, judicium.*

GIVE the King thy judgments, O God, * and thy righteousness unto the King's son.

2 Then shall he judge thy people according unto right, * and defend the poor.

3 The mountains also shall bring peace, * and the little hills righteousness unto the people.

4 He shall keep the simple folk by their right, * defend the children of the poor, and punish the wrong doer.

5 They shall fear thee, as long as the sun and moon endureth, * from one generation to another.

6 He shall come down like the rain upon the mown grass, * even as the drops that water the earth.

7 In his time shall the righteous flourish; * yea, and abundance of peace, so long as the moon endureth.

8 His dominion shall be also from the one sea to the other, * and from the River unto the world's end.

9 They that dwell in the wilderness shall kneel before him; * his enemies shall lick the dust.

10 The kings of Tarshish and of the isles shall give presents; * the kings of Arabia and Saba shall bring gifts.

11 All kings shall fall down before him; * all nations shall do him service.

12 For he shall deliver the poor when he crieth; * the needy also, and him that hath no helper.

13 He shall be favourable to the simple and needy, * and shall preserve the souls of the poor.

14 He shall deliver their souls from falsehood and wrong; * and dear shall their blood be in his sight.

15 He shall live, and unto him shall be given of the gold of Arabia; * prayer shall be made ever unto him, and daily shall he be praised.

16 There shall be an heap of corn in the earth, high upon the hills; the fruit thereof shall shake like Lebanon: * and they of the city shall flourish like grass upon the earth.

17 His Name shall endure for ever; his Name shall remain under the sun among the posterities, which shall be blessed in him; * and all the nations shall praise him.

18 Blessed be the LORD God, even the God of Israel, * which only doeth wondrous things;

19 And blessed be the Name of his majesty for ever: * and all the earth shall be filled with his majesty. Amen, Amen.

BOOK III.

Evening Prayer.

Psalm 73. *Quam bonus Israel!*

TRULY God is loving unto Israel: * even unto such as are of a clean heart.

2 Nevertheless, my feet were almost gone, * my treadings had well-nigh slipt.

3 And why? I was grieved at the wicked: * I do also see the ungodly in such prosperity.

4 For they are in no peril of death; * but are lusty and strong.

5 They come in no misfortune like other folk; * neither are they plagued like other men.

6 And this is the cause that they are so holden with pride, * and cruelty covereth them as a garment.

7 Their eyes swell with fatness, * and they do even what they lust.

8 They corrupt other, and speak of wicked blasphemy; * their talking is against the Most High.

9 For they stretch forth their mouth unto the heaven, * and their tongue goeth through the world.

10 Therefore fall the people unto them, * and thereout suck they no small advantage.

11 Tush, say they, how should God perceive it? * is there knowledge in the Most High?

12 Lo, these are the ungodly, * these prosper in the world, and these have riches in possession:

13 And I said, Then have I cleansed my heart in vain, * and washed my hands in innocency.

14 All the day long have I been punished, * and chastened every morning.

15 Yea, and I had almost said even as they; * but lo, then I should have condemned the generation of thy children.

16 Then thought I to understand this; * but it was too hard for me,

17 Until I went into the sanctuary of God: * then understood I the end of these men;

18 Namely, how thou dost set them in slippery places, * and castest them down, and destroyest them.

19 O how suddenly do they consume, * perish, and come to a fearful end!

20 Yea, even like as a dream when one awaketh; * so shalt thou make their image to vanish out of the city.

21 Thus my heart was grieved, * and it went even through my reins.

22 So foolish was I, and ignorant, * even as it were a beast before thee.

23 Nevertheless, I am alway by thee; * for thou hast holden me by my right hand.

24 Thou shalt guide me with thy counsel, * and after that receive me with glory.

25 Whom have I in heaven but thee? * and there is none upon earth that I desire in comparison of thee.

26 My flesh and my heart faileth; * but God is the strength of my heart, and my portion for ever.

27 For lo, they that forsake thee shall perish; * thou hast destroyed all them that are unfaithful unto thee.

28 But it is good for me to hold me fast by God, to put my trust in the Lord GOD, * and to speak of all thy works in the gates of the daughter of Sion.

Psalm 74. *Ut quid, Deus?*

O GOD, wherefore art thou absent from us so long? *
why is thy wrath so hot against the sheep of thy
pasture?

2 O think upon thy congregation, * whom thou hast
purchased, and redeemed of old.

3 Think upon the tribe of thine inheritance, * and Mount
Sion, wherein thou hast dwelt.

4 Lift up thy feet, that thou mayest utterly destroy
every enemy, * which hath done evil in thy sanctuary.

5 Thine adversaries roar in the midst of thy congregations, * and set up their banners for tokens.

6 He that hewed timber afore out of the thick trees, *
was known to bring it to an excellent work.

7 But now they break down all the carved work thereof * with axes and hammers.

8 They have set fire upon thy holy places, * and have
defiled the dwelling-place of thy Name, even unto the
ground.

9 Yea, they said in their hearts, Let us make havoc of
them altogether: * thus have they burnt up all the houses
of God in the land.

10 We see not our tokens; there is not one prophet
more; * no, not one is there among us, that understandeth
any more.

11 O God, how long shall the adversary do this dishonour? * shall the enemy blaspheme thy Name for ever?

12 Why withdrawest thou thy hand? * why pluckest
thou not thy right hand out of thy bosom to consume the
enemy?

13 For God is my King of old; * the help that is done
upon earth, he doeth it himself.

14 Thou didst divide the sea through thy power; * thou brakest the heads of the dragons in the waters.

15 Thou smotest the heads of leviathan in pieces, * and gavest him to be meat for the people of the wilderness.

16 Thou broughtest out fountains and waters out of the hard rocks; * thou driedst up mighty waters.

17 The day is thine, and the night is thine; * thou hast prepared the light and the sun.

18 Thou hast set all the borders of the earth; * thou hast made summer and winter.

19 Remember this, O LORD, how the enemy hath rebuked; * and how the foolish people hath blasphemed thy Name.

20 O deliver not the soul of thy turtle-dove unto the multitude of the enemies; * and forget not the congregation of the poor for ever.

21 Look upon the covenant; * for all the earth is full of darkness and cruel habitations.

22 O let not the simple go away ashamed; * but let the poor and needy give praise unto thy Name.

23 Arise, O God, maintain thine own cause; * remember how the foolish man blasphemeth thee daily.

24 Forget not the voice of thine enemies: * the presumption of them that hate thee increaseth ever more and more.

The Fifteenth Day.

Morning Prayer.

Psalm 75. *Confitebimur tibi.*

UNTO thee, O God, do we give thanks; * yea, unto thee do we give thanks.

2 Thy Name also is so nigh; * and that do thy wondrous works declare.

3 In the appointed time, saith God, * I shall judge according unto right.

4 The earth is weak, and all the inhabiters thereof: * I bear up the pillars of it.

5 I said unto the fools, Deal not so madly; * and to the ungodly, Set not up your horn.

6 Set not up your horn on high, * and speak not with a stiff neck.

7 For promotion cometh neither from the east, nor from the west, * nor yet from the south.

8 And why? God is the Judge; * he putteth down one, and setteth up another.

9 For in the hand of the LORD there is a cup, and the wine is red; * it is full mixt, and he poureth out of the same.

10 As for the dregs thereof, * all the ungodly of the earth shall drink them, and suck them out.

11 But I will talk of the God of Jacob, * and praise him for ever.

12 All the horns of the ungodly also will I break, * and the horns of the righteous shall be exalted.

Psalm 76. *Notus in Judæa.*

IN Judah is God known; * his Name is great in Israel.
2 At Salem is his tabernacle, * and his dwelling in Sion.

3 There brake he the arrows of the bow, * the shield, the sword, and the battle.

4 Thou art glorious in might, * when thou comest from the hills of the robbers.

5 The proud are robbed, they have slept their sleep; * and all the men whose hands were mighty have found nothing.

6 At thy rebuke, O God of Jacob, * both the chariot and horse are fallen.

7 Thou, even thou art to be feared; * and who may stand in thy sight when thou art angry?

8 Thou didst cause thy judgment to be heard from heaven; * the earth trembled, and was still,

9 When God arose to judgment, * and to help all the meek upon earth.

10 The fierceness of man shall turn to thy praise; * and the fierceness of them shalt thou refrain.

11 Promise unto the LORD your God, and keep it, all ye that are round about him; * bring presents unto him that ought to be feared.

12 He shall refrain the spirit of princes, * and is wonderful among the kings of the earth.

Psalm 77. *Voce mea ad Dominum.*

I WILL cry unto God with my voice; * even unto God will I cry with my voice, and he shall hearken unto me.

2 In the time of my trouble I sought the Lord: * I stretched forth my hands unto him, and ceased not in the night season; my soul refused comfort.

3 When I am in heaviness, I will think upon God; * when my heart is vexed, I will complain.

4 Thou holdest mine eyes waking: * I am so feeble that I cannot speak.

5 I have considered the days of old, * and the years that are past.

6 I call to remembrance my song, * and in the night I commune with mine own heart, and search out my spirit.

7 Will the Lord absent himself for ever? * and will he be no more intreated?

8 Is his mercy clean gone for ever? * and is his promise come utterly to an end for evermore?

9 Hath God forgotten to be gracious? * and will he shut up his loving-kindness in displeasure?

433

10 And I said, It is mine own infirmity; * but I will remember the years of the right hand of the Most Highest.

11 I will remember the works of the LORD, * and call to mind thy wonders of old time.

12 I will think also of all thy works, * and my talking shall be of thy doings.

13 Thy way, O God, is holy: * who is so great a God as our God?

14 Thou art the God that doest wonders, * and hast declared thy power among the peoples.

15 Thou hast mightily delivered thy people, * even the sons of Jacob and Joseph.

16 The waters saw thee, O God, the waters saw thee, and were afraid; * the depths also were troubled.

17 The clouds poured out water, the air thundered, * and thine arrows went abroad.

18 The voice of thy thunder was heard round about: * the lightnings shone upon the ground; the earth was moved, and shook withal.

19 Thy way is in the sea, and thy paths in the great waters, * and thy footsteps are not known.

20 Thou leddest thy people like sheep, * by the hand of Moses and Aaron.

Evening Prayer.

Psalm 78. *Attendite, popule.*

HEAR my law, O my people; * incline your ears unto the words of my mouth.

2 I will open my mouth in a parable; * I will declare hard sentences of old;

3 Which we have heard and known, * and such as our fathers have told us;

4 That we should not hide them from the children of

the generations to come; * but to show the honour of the LORD, his mighty and wonderful works that he hath done.

5 He made a covenant with Jacob, and gave Israel a law, * which he commanded our forefathers to teach their children;

6 That their posterity might know it, * and the children which were yet unborn;

7 To the intent that when they came up, * they might show their children the same;

8 That they might put their trust in God; * and not to forget the works of God, but to keep his commandments;

9 And not to be as their forefathers, a faithless and stubborn generation; * a generation that set not their heart aright, and whose spirit clave not stedfastly unto God;

10 Like as the children of Ephraim; * who being harnessed, and carrying bows, turned themselves back in the day of battle.

11 They kept not the covenant of God, * and would not walk in his law;

12 But forgat what he had done, * and the wonderful works that he had showed for them.

13 Marvellous things did he in the sight of our forefathers, in the land of Egypt, * even in the field of Zoan.

14 He divided the sea, and let them go through; * he made the waters to stand on an heap.

15 In the day-time also he led them with a cloud, * and all the night through with a light of fire.

16 He clave the hard rocks in the wilderness, * and gave them drink thereof, as it had been out of the great depth.

17 He brought waters out of the stony rock, * so that it gushed out like the rivers.

18 Yet for all this they sinned more against him, * and provoked the Most Highest in the wilderness.

19 They tempted God in their hearts, * and required meat for their lust.

20 They spake against God also, saying, * Shall God prepare a table in the wilderness?

21 He smote the stony rock indeed, that the water gushed out, and the streams flowed withal; * but can he give bread also, or provide flesh for his people?

22 When the LORD heard this, he was wroth; * so the fire was kindled in Jacob, and there came up heavy displeasure against Israel;

23 Because they believed not in God, * and put not their trust in his help.

24 So he commanded the clouds above, * and opened the doors of heaven.

25 He rained down manna also upon them for to eat, * and gave them food from heaven.

26 So man did eat angels' food; * for he sent them meat enough.

27 He caused the east-wind to blow under heaven; * and through his power he brought in the southwest-wind.

28 He rained flesh upon them as thick as dust, * and feathered fowls like as the sand of the sea.

29 He let it fall among their tents, * even round about their habitation.

30 So they did eat, and were well filled; for he gave them their own desire: * they were not disappointed of their lust.

31 But while the meat was yet in their mouths, the heavy wrath of God came upon them, and slew the wealthiest of them; * yea, and smote down the chosen men that were in Israel.

32 But for all this they sinned yet more, * and believed not his wondrous works.

33 Therefore their days did he consume in vanity, * and their years in trouble.

34 When he slew them, they sought him, * and turned them early, and inquired after God.

35 And they remembered that God was their strength, * and that the High God was their redeemer.

36 Nevertheless, they did but flatter him with their mouth, * and dissembled with him in their tongue.

37 For their heart was not whole with him, * neither continued they stedfast in his covenant.

38 But he was so merciful, that he forgave their misdeeds, * and destroyed them not.

39 Yea, many a time turned he his wrath away, * and would not suffer his whole displeasure to arise.

40 For he considered that they were but flesh, * and that they were even a wind that passeth away, and cometh not again.

41 Many a time did they provoke him in the wilderness, * and grieved him in the desert.

42 They turned back, and tempted God, * and provoked the Holy One in Israel.

43 They thought not of his hand, * and of the day when he delivered them from the hand of the enemy;

44 How he had wrought his miracles in Egypt, * and his wonders in the field of Zoan.

45 He turned their waters into blood, * so that they might not drink of the rivers.

46 He sent flies among them, and devoured them up; * and frogs to destroy them.

47 He gave their fruit unto the caterpillar, * and their labour unto the grasshopper.

48 He destroyed their vines with hailstones, * and their mulberry-trees with the frost.

49 He smote their cattle also with hailstones, * and their flocks with hot thunderbolts.

50 He cast upon them the furiousness of his wrath, anger, displeasure, and trouble: * and sent evil angels among them.

51 He made a way to his indignation, and spared not their soul from death; * but gave their life over to the pestilence;

52 And smote all the firstborn in Egypt, * the most principal and mightiest in the dwellings of Ham.

53 But as for his own people, he led them forth like sheep, * and carried them in the wilderness like a flock.

54 He brought them out safely, that they should not fear, * and overwhelmed their enemies with the sea.

55 And brought them within the borders of his sanctuary, * even to this mountain, which he purchased with his right hand.

56 He cast out the heathen also before them, * caused their land to be divided among them for an heritage, and made the tribes of Israel to dwell in their tents.

57 Yet they tempted and displeased the Most High God, * and kept not his testimonies.

58 They turned their backs, and fell away like their forefathers; * starting aside like a broken bow.

59 For they grieved him with their hill-altars, * and provoked him to displeasure with their images.

60 When God heard this, he was wroth, * and took sore displeasure at Israel;

61 So that he forsook the tabernacle in Shiloh, * even the tent that he had pitched among men.

62 He delivered their power into captivity, * and their beauty into the enemy's hand.

63 He gave his people over also unto the sword, * and was wroth with his inheritance.

64 The fire consumed their young men, * and their maidens were not given in marriage.

65 Their priests were slain with the sword, * and there were no widows to make lamentation.

66 So the Lord awaked as one out of sleep, * and like a giant refreshed with wine.

67 He drave his enemies backward, * and put them to a perpetual shame.

68 He refused the tabernacle of Joseph, * and chose not the tribe of Ephraim;

69 But chose the tribe of Judah, * even the hill of Sion which he loved.

70 And there he built his temple on high, * and laid the foundation of it like the ground which he hath made continually.

71 He chose David also his servant, * and took him away from the sheep-folds:

72 As he was following the ewes with their young he took him, * that he might feed Jacob his people, and Israel his inheritance.

73 So he fed them with a faithful and true heart, * and ruled them prudently with all his power.

The Sixteenth Day.

Morning Prayer.

Psalm 79. *Deus, venerunt.*

O GOD, the heathen are come into thine inheritance; * thy holy temple have they defiled, and made Jerusalem an heap of stones.

2 The dead bodies of thy servants have they given to

be meat unto the fowls of the air, * and the flesh of thy saints unto the beasts of the land.

3 Their blood have they shed like water on every side of Jerusalem, * and there was no man to bury them.

4 We are become an open shame to our enemies, * a very scorn and derision unto them that are round about us.

5 LORD, how long wilt thou be angry? * shall thy jealousy burn like fire for ever?

6 Pour out thine indignation upon the heathen that have not known thee; * and upon the kingdoms that have not called upon thy Name.

7 For they have devoured Jacob, * and laid waste his dwelling-place.

8 O remember not our old sins, but have mercy upon us, and that soon; * for we are come to great misery.

9 Help us, O God of our salvation, for the glory of thy Name: * O deliver us, and be merciful unto our sins, for thy Name's sake.

10 Wherefore do the heathen say, * Where is now their God?

11 O let the vengeance of thy servants' blood that is shed, * be openly showed upon the heathen, in our sight.

12 O let the sorrowful sighing of the prisoners come before thee; * according to the greatness of thy power, preserve thou those that are appointed to die.

13 And for the blasphemy wherewith our neighbours have blasphemed thee, * reward thou them, O Lord, sevenfold into their bosom.

14 So we, that are thy people, and sheep of thy pasture, shall give thee thanks for ever, * and will alway be showing forth thy praise from generation to generation.

Psalm 80. *Qui regis Israel.*

HEAR, O thou Shepherd of Israel, thou that leadest Joseph like a flock; * show thyself also, thou that sittest upon the Cherubim.

2 Before Ephraim, Benjamin, and Manasseh, * stir up thy strength, and come and help us.

3 Turn us again, O God; * show the light of thy countenance, and we shall be whole.

4 O LORD God of hosts, * how long wilt thou be angry with thy people that prayeth?

5 Thou feedest them with the bread of tears, * and givest them plenteousness of tears to drink.

6 Thou hast made us a very strife unto our neighbours, * and our enemies laugh us to scorn.

7 Turn us again, thou God of hosts; * show the light of thy countenance, and we shall be whole.

8 Thou hast brought a vine out of Egypt; * thou hast cast out the heathen, and planted it.

9 Thou madest room for it; * and when it had taken root, it filled the land.

10 The hills were covered with the shadow of it, * and the boughs thereof were like the goodly cedar-trees.

11 She stretched out her branches unto the sea, * and her boughs unto the River.

12 Why hast thou then broken down her hedge, * that all they that go by pluck off her grapes?

13 The wild boar out of the wood doth root it up, * and the wild beasts of the field devour it.

14 Turn thee again, thou God of hosts, look down from heaven, * behold, and visit this vine;

15 And the place of the vineyard that thy right hand hath planted, * and the branch that thou madest so strong for thyself.

441

16 It is burnt with fire, and cut down; * and they shall perish at the rebuke of thy countenance.

17 Let thy hand be upon the man of thy right hand, * and upon the son of man, whom thou madest so strong for thine own self.

18 And so will not we go back from thee: * O let us live, and we shall call upon thy Name.

19 Turn us again, O LORD God of hosts; * show the light of thy countenance, and we shall be whole.

Psalm 81. *Exultate Deo.*

SING we merrily unto God our strength; * make a cheerful noise unto the God of Jacob.

2 Take the psalm, bring hither the tabret, * the merry harp with the lute.

3 Blow up the trumpet in the new moon, * even in the time appointed, and upon our solemn feast-day.

4 For this was made a statute for Israel, * and a law of the God of Jacob.

5 This he ordained in Joseph for a testimony, * when he came out of the land of Egypt, and had heard a strange language.

6 I eased his shoulder from the burden, * and his hands were delivered from making the pots.

7 Thou calledst upon me in troubles, and I delivered thee; * and heard thee what time as the storm fell upon thee.

8 I proved thee also * at the waters of strife.

9 Hear, O my people; and I will assure thee, O Israel, * if thou wilt hearken unto me,

10 There shall no strange god be in thee, * neither shalt thou worship any other god.

11 I am the LORD thy God, who brought thee out of the land of Egypt: * open thy mouth wide, and I shall fill it.

12 But my people would not hear my voice; * and Israel would not obey me;

13 So I gave them up unto their own hearts' lusts, * and let them follow their own imaginations.

14 O that my people would have hearkened unto me! * for if Israel had walked in my ways,

15 I should soon have put down their enemies, * and turned my hand against their adversaries.

16 The haters of the LORD should have submitted themselves unto him; * but their time should have endured for ever.

17 I would have fed them also with the finest wheat-flour; * and with honey out of the stony rock would I have satisfied thee.

Evening Prayer.

Psalm 82. *Deus stetit.*

GOD standeth in the congregation of princes; * he is a Judge among gods.

2 How long will ye give wrong judgment, * and accept the persons of the ungodly?

3 Defend the poor and fatherless; * see that such as are in need and necessity have right.

4 Deliver the outcast and poor; * save them from the hand of the ungodly.

5 They know not, neither do they understand, but walk on still in darkness: * all the foundations of the earth are out of course.

6 I have said, Ye are gods, * and ye are all the children of the Most Highest.

7 But ye shall die like men, * and fall like one of the princes.

8 Arise, O God, and judge thou the earth; * for thou shalt take all nations to thine inheritance.

Psalm 83. *Deus, quis similis?*

HOLD not thy tongue, O God, keep not still silence: * refrain not thyself, O God.

2 For lo, thine enemies make a murmuring; * and they that hate thee have lift up their head.

3 They have imagined craftily against thy people, * and taken counsel against thy secret ones.

4 They have said, Come, and let us root them out, that they be no more a people, * and that the name of Israel may be no more in remembrance.

5 For they have cast their heads together with one consent, * and are confederate against thee:

6 The tabernacles of the Edomites, and the Ishmaelites; * the Moabites, and Hagarenes;

7 Gebal, and Ammon, and Amalek; * the Philistines, with them that dwell at Tyre.

8 Assyria also is joined with them; * they have holpen the children of Lot.

9 But do thou to them as unto the Midianites; * unto Sisera, and unto Jabin at the brook of Kishon;

10 Who perished at Endor, * and became as the dung of the earth.

11 Make them and their princes like Oreb and Zeëb; * yea, make all their princes like as Zebah and Zalmunna;

12 Who say, Let us take to ourselves * the houses of God in possession.

13 O my God, make them like unto the whirling dust, * and as the stubble before the wind;

14 Like as the fire that burneth up the forest, * and as the flame that consumeth the mountains;

15 Pursue them even so with thy tempest, * and make them afraid with thy storm.

16 Make their faces ashamed, O LORD, * that they may seek thy Name.

17 Let them be confounded and vexed ever more and more; * let them be put to shame, and perish.

18 And they shall know that thou, whose Name is JEHOVAH, * art only the Most Highest over all the earth.

Psalm 84. *Quam dilecta!*

O HOW amiable are thy dwellings, * thou LORD of hosts!

2 My soul hath a desire and longing to enter into the courts of the LORD; * my heart and my flesh rejoice in the living God.

3 Yea, the sparrow hath found her an house, and the swallow a nest, where she may lay her young; * even thy altars, O LORD of hosts, my King and my God.

4 Blessed are they that dwell in thy house; * they will be alway praising thee.

5 Blessed is the man whose strength is in thee; * in whose heart are thy ways.

6 Who going through the vale of misery use it for a well; * and the pools are filled with water.

7 They will go from strength to strength, * and unto the God of gods appeareth every one of them in Sion.

8 O LORD God of hosts, hear my prayer; * hearken, O God of Jacob.

9 Behold, O God our defender, * and look upon the face of thine anointed.

10 For one day in thy courts * is better than a thousand.

11 I had rather be a door-keeper in the house of my God, * than to dwell in the tents of ungodliness.

12 For the LORD God is a light and defence; * the LORD
will give grace and worship; and no good thing shall he
withhold from them that live a godly life.

13 O LORD God of hosts, * blessed is the man that
putteth his trust in thee.

Psalm 85. *Benedixisti, Domine.*

LORD, thou art become gracious unto thy land; * thou
hast turned away the captivity of Jacob.

2 Thou hast forgiven the offence of thy people, * and
covered all their sins.

3 Thou hast taken away all thy displeasure, * and turned
thyself from thy wrathful indignation.

4 Turn us then, O God our Saviour, * and let thine
anger cease from us.

5 Wilt thou be displeased at us for ever? * and wilt thou
stretch out thy wrath from one generation to another?

6 Wilt thou not turn again, and quicken us, * that thy
people may rejoice in thee?

7 Show us thy mercy, O LORD, * and grant us thy salvation.

8 I will hearken what the LORD God will say; * for he
shall speak peace unto his people, and to his saints, that
they turn not again unto foolishness.

9 For his salvation is nigh them that fear him; * that
glory may dwell in our land.

10 Mercy and truth are met together: * righteousness
and peace have kissed each other.

11 Truth shall flourish out of the earth, * and righteousness hath looked down from heaven.

12 Yea, the LORD shall show loving-kindness; * and our
land shall give her increase.

13 Righteousness shall go before him, * and shall direct
his going in the way.

The Seventeenth Day.

Morning Prayer.

Psalm 86. *Inclina, Domine.*

BOW down thine ear, O LORD, and hear me; * for I am poor, and in misery.

2 Preserve thou my soul, for I am holy: * my God, save thy servant that putteth his trust in thee.

3 Be merciful unto me, O Lord; * for I will call daily upon thee.

4 Comfort the soul of thy servant; * for unto thee, O Lord, do I lift up my soul.

5 For thou, Lord, art good and gracious, * and of great mercy unto all them that call upon thee.

6 Give ear, LORD, unto my prayer, * and ponder the voice of my humble desires.

7 In the time of my trouble I will call upon thee; * for thou hearest me.

8 Among the gods there is none like unto thee, O Lord; * there is not one that can do as thou doest.

9 All nations whom thou hast made shall come and worship thee, O Lord; * and shall glorify thy Name.

10 For thou art great, and doest wondrous things: * thou art God alone.

11 Teach me thy way, O LORD, and I will walk in thy truth: * O knit my heart unto thee, that I may fear thy Name.

12 I will thank thee, O Lord my God, with all my heart; * and will praise thy Name for evermore.

13 For great is thy mercy toward me; * and thou hast delivered my soul from the nethermost hell.

14 O God, the proud are risen against me; * and the

congregations of violent men have sought after my soul, and have not set thee before their eyes.

15 But thou, O Lord God, art full of compassion and mercy, * long-suffering, plenteous in goodness and truth.

16 O turn thee then unto me, and have mercy upon me; * give thy strength unto thy servant, and help the son of thine handmaid.

17 Show some token upon me for good; that they who hate me may see it, and be ashamed, * because thou, LORD, hast holpen me, and comforted me.

Psalm 87. *Fundamenta ejus.*

HER foundations are upon the holy hills: * the LORD loveth the gates of Sion more than all the dwellings of Jacob.

2 Very excellent things are spoken of thee, * thou city of God.

3 I will make mention of Egypt and Babylon, * among them that know me.

4 Behold, Philistia also; and Tyre, with Ethiopia; * lo, in Sion were they born.

5 Yea, of Sion it shall be reported, this one and that one were born in her; * and the Most High shall stablish her.

6 The LORD shall record it, when he writeth up the peoples; * lo, in Sion were they born.

7 The singers also and trumpeters shall make answer: * All my fresh springs are in thee.

Psalm 88. *Domine, Deus.*

O LORD God of my salvation, I have cried day and night before thee: * O let my prayer enter into thy presence, incline thine ear unto my calling;

2 For my soul is full of trouble, * and my life draweth nigh unto the grave.

3 I am counted as one of them that go down into the pit, * and I am even as a man that hath no strength;

4 Cast off among the dead, like unto them that are slain, and lie in the grave, * who are out of remembrance, and are cut away from thy hand.

5 Thou hast laid me in the lowest pit, * in a place of darkness, and in the deep.

6 Thine indignation lieth hard upon me, * and thou hast vexed me with all thy storms.

7 Thou hast put away mine acquaintance far from me, * and made me to be abhorred of them.

8 I am so fast in prison * that I cannot get forth.

9 My sight faileth for very trouble; * LORD, I have called daily upon thee, I have stretched forth my hands unto thee.

10 Dost thou show wonders among the dead? * or shall the dead rise up again, and praise thee?

11 Shall thy loving-kindness be showed in the grave? * or thy faithfulness in destruction?

12 Shall thy wondrous works be known in the dark? * and thy righteousness in the land where all things are forgotten?

13 Unto thee have I cried, O LORD; * and early shall my prayer come before thee.

14 LORD, why abhorrest thou my soul, * and hidest thou thy face from me?

15 I am in misery, and like unto him that is at the point to die; * even from my youth up, thy terrors have I suffered with a troubled mind.

16 Thy wrathful displeasure goeth over me, * and the fear of thee hath undone me.

17 They came round about me daily like water, * and compassed me together on every side.

18 My lovers and friends hast thou put away from me, * and hid mine acquaintance out of my sight.

Evening Prayer.

Psalm 89. *Misericordias Domini.*

MY song shall be alway of the loving-kindness of the LORD; * with my mouth will I ever be showing thy truth from one generation to another.

2 For I have said, Mercy shall be set up for ever; * thy truth shalt thou stablish in the heavens.

3 I have made a covenant with my chosen; * I have sworn unto David my servant:

4 Thy seed will I stablish for ever, * and set up thy throne from one generation to another.

5 O LORD, the very heavens shall praise thy wondrous works; * and thy truth in the congregation of the saints.

6 For who is he among the clouds, * that shall be compared unto the LORD?

7 And what is he among the gods, * that shall be like unto the LORD?

8 God is very greatly to be feared in the council of the saints, * and to be had in reverence of all them that are round about him.

9 O Lord God of hosts, who is like unto thee? * thy truth, most mighty LORD, is on every side.

10 Thou rulest the raging of the sea; * thou stillest the waves thereof when they arise.

11 Thou hast subdued Egypt, and destroyed it; * thou hast scattered thine enemies abroad with thy mighty arm.

12 The heavens are thine, the earth also is thine; * thou hast laid the foundation of the round world, and all that therein is.

13 Thou hast made the north and the south; * Tabor and Hermon shall rejoice in thy Name.

14 Thou hast a mighty arm; * strong is thy hand, and high is thy right hand.

15 Righteousness and equity are the habitation of thy seat; * mercy and truth shall go before thy face.

16 Blessed is the people, O LORD, that can rejoice in thee; * they shall walk in the light of thy countenance.

17 Their delight shall be daily in thy Name; * and in thy righteousness shall they make their boast.

18 For thou art the glory of their strength, * and in thy loving-kindness thou shalt lift up our horns.

19 For the LORD is our defence; * the Holy One of Israel is our King.

20 Thou spakest sometime in visions unto thy saints, and saidst, * I have laid help upon one that is mighty, I have exalted one chosen out of the people.

21 I have found David my servant; * with my holy oil have I anointed him.

22 My hand shall hold him fast, * and my arm shall strengthen him.

23 The enemy shall not be able to do him violence; * the son of wickedness shall not hurt him.

24 I will smite down his foes before his face, * and plague them that hate him.

25 My truth also and my mercy shall be with him; * and in my Name shall his horn be exalted.

26 I will set his dominion also in the sea, * and his right hand in the floods.

27 He shall call me, Thou art my Father, * my God, and my strong salvation.

28 And I will make him my firstborn, * higher than the kings of the earth.

29 My mercy will I keep for him for evermore, * and my covenant shall stand fast with him.

30 His seed also will I make to endure for ever, * and his throne as the days of heaven.

31 But if his children forsake my law, * and walk not in my judgments;

32 If they break my statutes, and keep not my commandments; * I will visit their offences with the rod, and their sin with scourges.

33 Nevertheless, my loving-kindness will I not utterly take from him, * nor suffer my truth to fail.

34 My covenant will I not break, nor alter the thing that is gone out of my lips: * I have sworn once by my holiness, that I will not fail David.

35 His seed shall endure for ever, * and his throne is like as the sun before me.

36 He shall stand fast for evermore as the moon, * and as the faithful witness in heaven.

37 But thou hast abhorred and forsaken thine anointed, * and art displeased at him.

38 Thou hast broken the covenant of thy servant, * and cast his crown to the ground.

39 Thou hast overthrown all his hedges, * and broken down his strongholds.

40 All they that go by spoil him, * and he is become a reproach to his neighbours.

41 Thou hast set up the right hand of his enemies, * and made all his adversaries to rejoice.

42 Thou hast taken away the edge of his sword, * and givest him not victory in the battle.

43 Thou hast put out his glory, * and cast his throne down to the ground.

44 The days of his youth hast thou shortened, * and covered him with dishonour.

45 LORD, how long wilt thou hide thyself? for ever? * and shall thy wrath burn like fire?

46 O remember how short my time is; * wherefore hast thou made all men for nought?

47 What man is he that liveth, and shall not see death? * and shall he deliver his soul from the power of the grave?

48 Lord, where are thy old loving-kindnesses, * which thou swarest unto David in thy truth?

49 Remember, Lord, the rebuke that thy servants have, * and how I do bear in my bosom the rebukes of many people;

50 Wherewith thine enemies have blasphemed thee, * and slandered the footsteps of thine anointed.

51 Praised be the LORD for evermore. * Amen, and Amen.

BOOK IV.

The Eighteenth Day.

Morning Prayer.

Psalm 90. *Domine, refugium.*

LORD, thou hast been our refuge, * from one generation to another.

2 Before the mountains were brought forth, or ever the earth and the world were made, * thou art God from everlasting, and world without end.

3 Thou turnest man to destruction; * again thou sayest, Come again, ye children of men.

4 For a thousand years in thy sight are but as yesterday when it is past, * and as a watch in the night.

5 As soon as thou scatterest them they are even as a sleep; * and fade away suddenly like the grass.

6 In the morning it is green, and groweth up; * but in the evening it is cut down, dried up, and withered.

7 For we consume away in thy displeasure, * and are afraid at thy wrathful indignation.

8 Thou hast set our misdeeds before thee; * and our secret sins in the light of thy countenance.

9 For when thou art angry all our days are gone: * we bring our years to an end, as it were a tale that is told.

10 The days of our age are threescore years and ten; and though men be so strong that they come to fourscore years, * yet is their strength then but labour and sorrow; so soon passeth it away, and we are gone.

11 But who regardeth the power of thy wrath? * or feareth aright thy indignation?

12 So teach us to number our days, * that we may apply our hearts unto wisdom.

13 Turn thee again, O LORD, at the last, * and be gracious unto thy servants.

14 O satisfy us with thy mercy, and that soon: * so shall we rejoice and be glad all the days of our life.

15 Comfort us again now after the time that thou hast plagued us; * and for the years wherein we have suffered adversity.

16 Show thy servants thy work, * and their children thy glory.

17 And the glorious majesty of the LORD our God be upon us: * prosper thou the work of our hands upon us; O prosper thou our handy-work.

Psalm 91. *Qui habitat.*

WHOSO dwelleth under the defence of the Most High, * shall abide under the shadow of the Almighty.

2 I will say unto the LORD, Thou art my hope, and my stronghold; * my God, in him will I trust.

3 For he shall deliver thee from the snare of the hunter, * and from the noisome pestilence.

4 He shall defend thee under his wings, and thou shalt be safe under his feathers; * his faithfulness and truth shall be thy shield and buckler.

5 Thou shalt not be afraid for any terror by night, * nor for the arrow that flieth by day;

6 For the pestilence that walketh in darkness, * nor for the sickness that destroyeth in the noon-day.

7 A thousand shall fall beside thee, and ten thousand at thy right hand; * but it shall not come nigh thee.

8 Yea, with thine eyes shalt thou behold, * and see the reward of the ungodly.

9 For thou, LORD, art my hope; * thou hast set thine house of defence very high.

10 There shall no evil happen unto thee, * neither shall any plague come nigh thy dwelling.

11 For he shall give his angels charge over thee, * to keep thee in all thy ways.

12 They shall bear thee in their hands, * that thou hurt not thy foot against a stone.

13 Thou shalt go upon the lion and adder: * the young lion and the dragon shalt thou tread under thy feet.

14 Because he hath set his love upon me, therefore will I deliver him; * I will set him up, because he hath known my Name.

15 He shall call upon me, and I will hear him; * yea, I am with him in trouble; I will deliver him, and bring him to honour.

16 With long life will I satisfy him, * and show him my salvation.

Psalm 92. *Bonum est confiteri.*

IT is a good thing to give thanks unto the LORD, * and to sing praises unto thy Name, O Most Highest;

2 To tell of thy loving-kindness early in the morning, * and of thy truth in the night season;

3 Upon an instrument of ten strings, and upon the lute; * upon a loud instrument, and upon the harp.

4 For thou, LORD, hast made me glad through thy works; * and I will rejoice in giving praise for the operations of thy hands.

5 O LORD, how glorious are thy works! * thy thoughts are very deep.

6 An unwise man doth not well consider this, * and a fool doth not understand it.

7 When the ungodly are green as the grass, and when all the workers of wickedness do flourish, * then shall they be destroyed for ever; but thou, LORD, art the Most Highest for evermore.

8 For lo, thine enemies, O LORD, lo, thine enemies shall perish; * and all the workers of wickedness shall be destroyed.

9 But my horn shall be exalted like the horn of an unicorn; * for I am anointed with fresh oil.

10 Mine eye also shall see his lust of mine enemies, * and mine ear shall hear his desire of the wicked that arise up against me.

11 The righteous shall flourish like a palm-tree, * and shall spread abroad like a cedar in Lebanon.

12 Such as are planted in the house of the LORD, * shall flourish in the courts of the house of our God.

13 They also shall bring forth more fruit in their age, * and shall be fat and well-liking;

14 That they may show how true the LORD my strength is, * and that there is no unrighteousness in him.

Evening Prayer.

Psalm 93. *Dominus regnavit.*

THE LORD is King, and hath put on glorious apparel; * the LORD hath put on his apparel, and girded himself with strength.

2 He hath made the round world so sure, * that it cannot be moved.

3 Ever since the world began, hath thy seat been prepared: * thou art from everlasting.

4 The floods are risen, O LORD, the floods have lift up their voice; * the floods lift up their waves.

5 The waves of the sea are mighty, and rage horribly; * but yet the LORD, who dwelleth on high, is mightier.

6 Thy testimonies, O LORD, are very sure: * holiness becometh thine house for ever.

Psalm 94. *Deus ultionum.*

O LORD God, to whom vengeance belongeth, * thou God, to whom vengeance belongeth, show thyself.

2 Arise, thou Judge of the world, * and reward the proud after their deserving.

3 LORD, how long shall the ungodly, * how long shall the ungodly triumph?

4 How long shall all wicked doers speak so disdainfully, * and make such proud boasting?

5 They smite down thy people, O LORD, * and trouble thine heritage.

6 They murder the widow and the stranger, * and put the fatherless to death.

7 And yet they say, Tush, the LORD shall not see, * neither shall the God of Jacob regard it.

8 Take heed, ye unwise among the people: * O ye fools, when will ye understand?

9 He that planted the ear, shall he not hear? * or he that made the eye, shall he not see?

10 Or he that instructeth the heathen, * it is he that teacheth man knowledge; shall not he punish?

11 The LORD knoweth the thoughts of man, * that they are but vain.

12 Blessed is the man whom thou chastenest, O LORD, * and teachest him in thy law;

13 That thou mayest give him patience in time of adversity, * until the pit be digged up for the ungodly.

14 For the LORD will not fail his people; * neither will he forsake his inheritance;

15 Until righteousness turn again unto judgment: * all such as are true in heart shall follow it.

16 Who will rise up with me against the wicked? * or who will take my part against the evil doers?

17 If the LORD had not helped me, * it had not failed, but my soul had been put to silence.

18 But when I said, My foot hath slipt; * thy mercy, O LORD, held me up.

19 In the multitude of the sorrows that I had in my heart, * thy comforts have refreshed my soul.

20 Wilt thou have any thing to do with the throne of wickedness, * which imagineth mischief as a law?

21 They gather them together against the soul of the righteous, * and condemn the innocent blood.

22 But the LORD is my refuge, * and my God is the strength of my confidence.

23 He shall recompense them their wickedness, and destroy them in their own malice; * yea, the LORD our God shall destroy them.

The Nineteenth Day.

Morning Prayer.

Psalm 95. *Venite, exultemus.*

O COME, let us sing unto the LORD; * let us heartily rejoice in the strength of our salvation.

2 Let us come before his presence with thanksgiving; * and show ourselves glad in him with psalms.

3 For the LORD is a great God; * and a great King above all gods.

4 In his hand are all the corners of the earth; * and the strength of the hills is his also.

5 The sea is his, and he made it; * and his hands prepared the dry land.

6 O come, let us worship and fall down, * and kneel before the LORD our Maker.

7 For he is the Lord our God; * and we are the people of his pasture, and the sheep of his hand.

8 To-day if ye will hear his voice, harden not your hearts * as in the provocation, and as in the day of temptation in the wilderness;

9 When your fathers tempted me, * proved me, and saw my works.

10 Forty years long was I grieved with this generation, and said, * It is a people that do err in their hearts, for they have not known my ways:

11 Unto whom I sware in my wrath, * that they should not enter into my rest.

Psalm 96. *Cantate Domino.*

O SING unto the LORD a new song; * sing unto the LORD, all the whole earth.

2 Sing unto the LORD, and praise his Name; * be telling of his salvation from day to day.

3 Declare his honour unto the heathen, * and his wonders unto all peoples.

4 For the LORD is great, and cannot worthily be praised; * he is more to be feared than all gods.

5 As for all the gods of the heathen, they are but idols; * but it is the LORD that made the heavens.

6 Glory and worship are before him; * power and honour are in his sanctuary.

7 Ascribe unto the LORD, O ye kindreds of the peoples, * ascribe unto the LORD worship and power.

8 Ascribe unto the LORD the honour due unto his Name; * bring presents, and come into his courts.

9 O worship the LORD in the beauty of holiness; * let the whole earth stand in awe of him.

10 Tell it out among the heathen, that the LORD is King, and that it is he who hath made the round world so fast that it cannot be moved; * and how that he shall judge the peoples righteously.

11 Let the heavens rejoice, and let the earth be glad; * let the sea make a noise, and all that therein is.

12 Let the field be joyful, and all that is in it; * then shall all the trees of the wood rejoice before the LORD.

13 For he cometh, for he cometh to judge the earth; * and with righteousness to judge the world, and the peoples with his truth.

Psalm 97. *Dominus regnavit.*

THE LORD is King, the earth may be glad thereof; * yea, the multitude of the isles may be glad thereof.

2 Clouds and darkness are round about him: * righteousness and judgment are the habitation of his seat.

3 There shall go a fire before him, * and burn up his enemies on every side.

4 His lightnings gave shine unto the world: * the earth saw it, and was afraid.

5 The hills melted like wax at the presence of the LORD; * at the presence of the Lord of the whole earth.

6 The heavens have declared his righteousness, * and all the peoples have seen his glory.

7 Confounded be all they that worship carved images, and that delight in vain gods: * worship him, all ye gods.

8 Sion heard of it, and rejoiced; and the daughters of Judah were glad, * because of thy judgments, O LORD.

9 For thou, LORD, art higher than all that are in the earth: * thou art exalted far above all gods.

10 O ye that love the LORD, see that ye hate the thing which is evil: * the Lord preserveth the souls of his saints; he shall deliver them from the hand of the ungodly.

11 There is sprung up a light for the righteous, * and joyful gladness for such as are true-hearted.

12 Rejoice in the LORD, ye righteous; * and give thanks for a remembrance of his holiness.

Evening Prayer.

Psalm 98. *Cantate Domino.*

O SING unto the LORD a new song; * for he hath done marvellous things.

2 With his own right hand, and with his holy arm, * hath he gotten himself the victory.

3 The LORD declared his salvation; * his righteousness hath he openly showed in the sight of the heathen.

4 He hath remembered his mercy and truth toward the house of Israel; * and all the ends of the world have seen the salvation of our God.

5 Show yourselves joyful unto the LORD, all ye lands; * sing, rejoice, and give thanks.

6 Praise the LORD upon the harp; * sing to the harp with a psalm of thanksgiving.

7 With trumpets also and shawms, * O show yourselves joyful before the LORD, the King.

8 Let the sea make a noise, and all that therein is; * the round world, and they that dwell therein.

9 Let the floods clap their hands, and let the hills be joyful together before the LORD; * for he is come to judge the earth.

10 With righteousness shall he judge the world, * and the peoples with equity.

Psalm 99. *Dominus regnavit.*

THE LORD is King, be the people never so impatient; * he sitteth between the Cherubim, be the earth never so unquiet.

2 The LORD is great in Sion, * and high above all people.

3 They shall give thanks unto thy Name, * which is great, wonderful, and holy.

4 The King's power loveth judgment; thou hast prepared equity, * thou hast executed judgment and righteousness in Jacob.

5 O magnify the LORD our God, and fall down before his footstool; * for he is holy.

6 Moses and Aaron among his priests, and Samuel among such as call upon his Name: * these called upon the LORD, and he heard them.

7 He spake unto them out of the cloudy pillar; * for they kept his testimonies, and the law that he gave them.

8 Thou heardest them, O LORD our God; * thou forgavest them, O God, though thou didst punish their wicked doings.

9 O magnify the LORD our God, and worship him upon his holy hill; * for the LORD our God is holy.

Psalm 100. *Jubilate Deo.*

O BE joyful in the LORD, all ye lands: * serve the LORD with gladness, and come before his presence with a song.

2 Be ye sure that the LORD he is God; it is he that hath made us, and not we ourselves; * we are his people, and the sheep of his pasture.

3 O go your way into his gates with thanksgiving, and into his courts with praise; * be thankful unto him, and speak good of his Name.

4 For the LORD is gracious, his mercy is everlasting; * and his truth endureth from generation to generation.

Psalm 101. *Misericordiam et judicium.*

M Y song shall be of mercy and judgment; * unto thee, O LORD, will I sing.

2 O let me have understanding * in the way of godliness!

3 When wilt thou come unto me? * I will walk in my house with a perfect heart.

4 I will take no wicked thing in hand; I hate the sins of unfaithfulness; * there shall no such cleave unto me.

5 A froward heart shall depart from me; * I will not know a wicked person.

6 Whoso privily slandereth his neighbour, * him will I destroy.

7 Whoso hath also a haughty look and a proud heart, * I will not suffer him.

8 Mine eyes look upon such as are faithful in the land, * that they may dwell with me.

9 Whoso leadeth a godly life, * he shall be my servant.

10 There shall no deceitful person dwell in my house; *
he that telleth lies shall not tarry in my sight.

11 I shall soon destroy all the ungodly that are in the
land; * that I may root out all wicked doers from the city
of the LORD.

The Twentieth Day.

Morning Prayer.

Psalm 102. *Domine, exaudi.*

HEAR my prayer, O LORD, * and let my crying come
unto thee.

2 Hide not thy face from me in the time of my trouble; *
incline thine ear unto me when I call; O hear me, and
that right soon.

3 For my days are consumed away like smoke, * and
my bones are burnt up as it were a firebrand.

4 My heart is smitten down, and withered like grass; *
so that I forget to eat my bread.

5 For the voice of my groaning, * my bones will scarce
cleave to my flesh.

6 I am become like a pelican in the wilderness, * and
like an owl that is in the desert.

7 I have watched, and am even as it were a sparrow, *
that sitteth alone upon the housetop.

8 Mine enemies revile me all the day long; * and they
that are mad upon me are sworn together against me.

9 For I have eaten ashes as it were bread, * and mingled
my drink with weeping;

10 And that, because of thine indignation and wrath; *
for thou hast taken me up, and cast me down.

11 My days are gone like a shadow, * and I am withered like grass.

12 But thou, O LORD, shalt endure for ever, * and thy remembrance throughout all generations.

13 Thou shalt arise, and have mercy upon Sion; * for it is time that thou have mercy upon her, yea, the time is come.

14 And why? thy servants think upon her stones, * and it pitieth them to see her in the dust.

15 The nations shall fear thy Name, O LORD; * and all the kings of the earth thy majesty;

16 When the LORD shall build up Sion, * and when his glory shall appear;

17 When he turneth him unto the prayer of the poor destitute, * and despiseth not their desire.

18 This shall be written for those that come after, * and the people which shall be born shall praise the LORD.

19 For he hath looked down from his sanctuary; * out of the heaven did the LORD behold the earth;

20 That he might hear the mournings of such as are in captivity, * and deliver them that are appointed unto death;

21 That they may declare the Name of the LORD in Sion, * and his worship at Jerusalem;

22 When the peoples are gathered together, * and the kingdoms also, to serve the LORD.

23 He brought down my strength in my journey, * and shortened my days.

24 But I said, O my God, take me not away in the midst of mine age; * as for thy years, they endure throughout all generations.

25 Thou, Lord, in the beginning hast laid the foundation of the earth, * and the heavens are the work of thy hands.

26 They shall perish, but thou shalt endure: * they all shall wax old as doth a garment;

27 And as a vesture shalt thou change them, and they shall be changed; * but thou art the same, and thy years shall not fail.

28 The children of thy servants shall continue, * and their seed shall stand fast in thy sight.

Psalm 103. *Benedic, anima mea.*

PRAISE the LORD, O my soul; * and all that is within me, praise his holy Name.

2 Praise the LORD, O my soul, * and forget not all his benefits:

3 Who forgiveth all thy sin, * and healeth all thine infirmities;

4 Who saveth thy life from destruction, * and crowneth thee with mercy and loving-kindness;

5 Who satisfieth thy mouth with good things, * making thee young and lusty as an eagle.

6 The LORD executeth righteousness and judgment * for all them that are oppressed with wrong.

7 He showed his ways unto Moses, * his works unto the children of Israel.

8 The LORD is full of compassion and mercy, * long-suffering, and of great goodness.

9 He will not alway be chiding; * neither keepeth he his anger for ever.

10 He hath not dealt with us after our sins; * nor rewarded us according to our wickednesses.

11 For look how high the heaven is in comparison of the earth; * so great is his mercy also toward them that fear him.

12 Look how wide also the east is from the west; * so far hath he set our sins from us.

13 Yea, like as a father pitieth his own children; * even so is the LORD merciful unto them that fear him.

14 For he knoweth whereof we are made; * he remembereth that we are but dust.

15 The days of man are but as grass; * for he flourisheth as a flower of the field.

16 For as soon as the wind goeth over it, it is gone; * and the place thereof shall know it no more.

17 But the merciful goodness of the LORD endureth for ever and ever upon them that fear him; * and his righteousness upon children's children;

18 Even upon such as keep his covenant, * and think upon his commandments to do them.

19 The LORD hath prepared his seat in heaven, * and his kingdom ruleth over all.

20 O praise the LORD, ye angels of his, ye that excel in strength; * ye that fulfil his commandment, and hearken unto the voice of his word.

21 O praise the LORD, all ye his hosts; * ye servants of his that do his pleasure.

22 O speak good of the LORD, all ye works of his, in all places of his dominion: * praise thou the LORD, O my soul.

Evening Prayer.

Psalm 104. *Benedic, anima mea.*

PRAISE the LORD, O my soul: * O LORD my God, thou art become exceeding glorious; thou art clothed with majesty and honour.

2 Thou deckest thyself with light as it were with a garment, * and spreadest out the heavens like a curtain.

3 Who layeth the beams of his chambers in the waters, * and maketh the clouds his chariot, and walketh upon the wings of the wind.

4 He maketh his angels winds, * and his ministers a flaming fire.

5 He laid the foundations of the earth, * that it never should move at any time.

6 Thou coveredst it with the deep like as with a garment; * the waters stand above the hills.

7 At thy rebuke they flee; * at the voice of thy thunder they haste away.

8 They go up as high as the hills, and down to the valleys beneath; * even unto the place which thou hast appointed for them.

9 Thou hast set them their bounds, which they shall not pass, * neither turn again to cover the earth.

10 He sendeth the springs into the rivers, * which run among the hills.

11 All beasts of the field drink thereof, * and the wild asses quench their thirst.

12 Beside them shall the fowls of the air have their habitation, * and sing among the branches.

13 He watereth the hills from above; * the earth is filled with the fruit of thy works.

14 He bringeth forth grass for the cattle, * and green herb for the service of men;

15 That he may bring food out of the earth, and wine that maketh glad the heart of man; * and oil to make him a cheerful countenance, and bread to strengthen man's heart.

16 The trees of the LORD also are full of sap; * even the cedars of Lebanon which he hath planted;

17 Wherein the birds make their nests; * and the fir-trees are a dwelling for the stork.

18 The high hills are a refuge for the wild goats; * and so are the stony rocks for the conies.

19 He appointed the moon for certain seasons, * and the sun knoweth his going down.

20 Thou makest darkness that it may be night; * wherein all the beasts of the forest do move.

21 The lions, roaring after their prey, * do seek their meat from God.

22 The sun ariseth, and they get them away together, * and lay them down in their dens.

23 Man goeth forth to his work, and to his labour, * until the evening.

24 O LORD, how manifold are thy works! * in wisdom hast thou made them all; the earth is full of thy riches.

25 So is the great and wide sea also; * wherein are things creeping innumerable, both small and great beasts.

26 There go the ships, and there is that leviathan, * whom thou hast made to take his pastime therein.

27 These wait all upon thee, * that thou mayest give them meat in due season.

28 When thou givest it them, they gather it; * and when thou openest thy hand, they are filled with good.

29 When thou hidest thy face, they are troubled: * when thou takest away their breath, they die, and are turned again to their dust.

30 When thou lettest thy breath go forth, they shall be made; * and thou shalt renew the face of the earth.

31 The glorious majesty of the LORD shall endure for ever; * the LORD shall rejoice in his works.

32 The earth shall tremble at the look of him; * if he do but touch the hills, they shall smoke.

33 I will sing unto the LORD as long as I live; * I will praise my God while I have my being.

34 And so shall my words please him: * my joy shall be in the LORD.

35 As for sinners, they shall be consumed out of the earth, * and the ungodly shall come to an end.

36 Praise thou the LORD, O my soul. * Praise the LORD.

The Twenty-first Day.

Morning Prayer.

Psalm 105. *Confitemini Domino.*

O GIVE thanks unto the LORD, and call upon his Name; * tell the people what things he hath done.

2 O let your songs be of him, and praise him; * and let your talking be of all his wondrous works.

3 Rejoice in his holy Name; * let the heart of them rejoice that seek the LORD.

4 Seek the LORD and his strength; * seek his face evermore.

5 Remember the marvellous works that he hath done; * his wonders, and the judgments of his mouth;

6 O ye seed of Abraham his servant, * ye children of Jacob his chosen.

7 He is the LORD our God; * his judgments are in all the world.

8 He hath been alway mindful of his covenant and promise, * that he made to a thousand generations;

9 Even the covenant that he made with Abraham; * and the oath that he sware unto Isaac;

10 And appointed the same unto Jacob for a law, * and to Israel for an everlasting testament;

11 Saying, Unto thee will I give the land of Canaan, * the lot of your inheritance:

12 When there were yet but a few of them, * and they strangers in the land;

13 What time as they went from one nation to another, * from one kingdom to another people;

14 He suffered no man to do them wrong, * but reproved even kings for their sakes;

15 Touch not mine anointed, * and do my prophets no harm.

16 Moreover, he called for a dearth upon the land, * and destroyed all the provision of bread.

17 But he had sent a man before them, * even Joseph, who was sold to be a bond-servant;

18 Whose feet they hurt in the stocks; * the iron entered into his soul;

19 Until the time came that his cause was known: * the word of the LORD tried him.

20 The king sent, and delivered him; * the prince of the people let him go free.

21 He made him lord also of his house, * and ruler of all his substance;

22 That he might inform his princes after his will, * and teach his senators wisdom.

23 Israel also came into Egypt, * and Jacob was a stranger in the land of Ham.

24 And he increased his people exceedingly, * and made them stronger than their enemies;

25 Whose heart turned so, that they hated his people, * and dealt untruly with his servants.

26 Then sent he Moses his servant, * and Aaron whom he had chosen.

27 And these showed his tokens among them, * and wonders in the land of Ham.

28 He sent darkness, and it was dark; * and they were not obedient unto his word.

29 He turned their waters into blood, * and slew their fish.

30 Their land brought forth frogs; * yea, even in their kings' chambers.

31 He spake the word, and there came all manner of flies, * and lice in all their quarters.

32 He gave them hailstones for rain; * and flames of fire in their land.

33 He smote their vines also and fig-trees; * and destroyed the trees that were in their coasts.

34 He spake the word, and the grasshoppers came, and caterpillars innumerable, * and did eat up all the grass in their land, and devoured the fruit of their ground.

35 He smote all the firstborn in their land; * even the chief of all their strength.

36 He brought them forth also with silver and gold; * there was not one feeble person among their tribes.

37 Egypt was glad at their departing; * for they were afraid of them.

38 He spread out a cloud to be a covering, * and fire to give light in the night season.

39 At their desire he brought quails; * and he filled them with the bread of heaven.

40 He opened the rock of stone, and the waters flowed out, * so that rivers ran in the dry places.

41 For why? he remembered his holy promise; * and Abraham his servant.

42 And he brought forth his people with joy, * and his chosen with gladness;

43 And gave them the lands of the heathen; * and they took the labours of the people in possession;

44 That they might keep his statutes, * and observe his laws.

Evening Prayer.

Psalm 106. *Confitemini Domino.*

O GIVE thanks unto the LORD; for he is gracious, * and his mercy endureth for ever.

2 Who can express the noble acts of the LORD, * or show forth all his praise?

3 Blessed are they that alway keep judgment, * and do righteousness.

4 Remember me, O LORD, according to the favour that thou bearest unto thy people; * O visit me with thy salvation;

5 That I may see the felicity of thy chosen, * and rejoice in the gladness of thy people, and give thanks with thine inheritance.

6 We have sinned with our fathers; * we have done amiss, and dealt wickedly.

7 Our fathers regarded not thy wonders in Egypt, neither kept they thy great goodness in remembrance; * but were disobedient at the sea, even at the Red Sea.

8 Nevertheless, he helped them for his Name's sake, * that he might make his power to be known.

9 He rebuked the Red Sea also, and it was dried up; * so he led them through the deep, as through a wilderness.

10 And he saved them from the adversary's hand, * and delivered them from the hand of the enemy.

11 As for those that troubled them, the waters overwhelmed them; * there was not one of them left.

12 Then believed they his words, * and sang praise unto him.

13 But within a while they forgat his works, * and would not abide his counsel.

14 But lust came upon them in the wilderness, * and they tempted God in the desert.

15 And he gave them their desire, * and sent leanness withal into their soul.

16 They angered Moses also in the tents, * and Aaron the saint of the LORD.

17 So the earth opened, and swallowed up Dathan, * and covered the congregation of Abiram.

18 And the fire was kindled in their company; * the flame burnt up the ungodly.

19 They made a calf in Horeb, * and worshipped the molten image.

20 Thus they turned their glory * into the similitude of a calf that eateth hay.

21 And they forgat God their Saviour, * who had done so great things in Egypt;

22 Wondrous works in the land of Ham; * and fearful things by the Red Sea.

23 So he said he would have destroyed them, had not Moses his chosen stood before him in the gap, * to turn away his wrathful indignation, lest he should destroy them.

24 Yea, they thought scorn of that pleasant land, * and gave no credence unto his word;

25 But murmured in their tents, * and hearkened not unto the voice of the LORD.

26 Then lift he up his hand against them, * to overthrow them in the wilderness;

27 To cast out their seed among the nations, * and to scatter them in the lands.

28 They joined themselves unto Baal-peor, * and ate the offerings of the dead.

29 Thus they provoked him to anger with their own inventions; * and the plague was great among them.

30 Then stood up Phinehas, and interposed; * and so the plague ceased.

31 And that was counted unto him for righteousness, * among all posterities for evermore.

32 They angered him also at the waters of strife, * so that he punished Moses for their sakes;

33 Because they provoked his spirit, * so that he spake unadvisedly with his lips.

34 Neither destroyed they the heathen, * as the LORD commanded them;

35 But were mingled among the heathen, * and learned their works.

36 Insomuch that they worshipped their idols, which became a snare unto them; * yea, they offered their sons and their daughters unto devils;

37 And shed innocent blood, even the blood of their sons and of their daughters, * whom they offered unto the idols of Canaan; and the land was defiled with blood.

38 Thus were they stained with their own works, * and went a whoring with their own inventions.

39 Therefore was the wrath of the LORD kindled against his people, * insomuch that he abhorred his own inheritance.

40 And he gave them over into the hand of the heathen; * and they that hated them were lords over them.

41 Their enemies oppressed them, * and had them in subjection.

42 Many a time did he deliver them; * but they rebelled against him with their own inventions, and were brought down in their wickedness.

43 Nevertheless, when he saw their adversity, * he heard their complaint.

44 He thought upon his covenant, and pitied them, according unto the multitude of his mercies; * yea, he made all those that led them away captive to pity them.

45 Deliver us, O LORD our God, and gather us from among the heathen; * that we may give thanks unto thy holy Name, and make our boast of thy praise.

46 Blessed be the LORD God of Israel, from everlasting, and world without end; * And let all the people say, Amen.

BOOK V.

The Twenty-second Day.

Morning Prayer.

Psalm 107. *Confitemini Domino.*

O GIVE thanks unto the LORD, for he is gracious, *
and his mercy endureth for ever.

2 Let them give thanks whom the LORD hath redeemed, * and delivered from the hand of the enemy;

3 And gathered them out of the lands, from the east,
and from the west; * from the north, and from the south.

4 They went astray in the wilderness out of the way, *
and found no city to dwell in.

5 Hungry and thirsty, * their soul fainted in them.

6 So they cried unto the LORD in their trouble, * and
he delivered them from their distress.

7 He led them forth by the right way, * that they might
go to the city where they dwelt.

8 O that men would therefore praise the LORD for his
goodness; * and declare the wonders that he doeth for the
children of men!

9 For he satisfieth the empty soul, * and filleth the
hungry soul with goodness.

10 Such as sit in darkness, and in the shadow of death, *
being fast bound in misery and iron;

11 Because they rebelled against the words of the Lord, *
and lightly regarded the counsel of the Most Highest;

12 He also brought down their heart through heaviness: * they fell down, and there was none to help them.

13 So when they cried unto the LORD in their trouble, *
he delivered them out of their distress.

14 For he brought them out of darkness, and out of the shadow of death, * and brake their bonds in sunder.

15 O that men would therefore praise the LORD for his goodness; * and declare the wonders that he doeth for the children of men!

16 For he hath broken the gates of brass, * and smitten the bars of iron in sunder.

17 Foolish men are plagued for their offence, * and because of their wickedness.

18 Their soul abhorred all manner of meat, * and they were even hard at death's door.

19 So when they cried unto the LORD in their trouble, * he delivered them out of their distress.

20 He sent his word, and healed them; * and they were saved from their destruction.

21 O that men would therefore praise the LORD for his goodness; * and declare the wonders that he doeth for the children of men!

22 That they would offer unto him the sacrifice of thanksgiving, * and tell out his works with gladness!

23 They that go down to the sea in ships, * and occupy their business in great waters;

24 These men see the works of the LORD, * and his wonders in the deep.

25 For at his word the stormy wind ariseth, * which lifteth up the waves thereof.

26 They are carried up to the heaven, and down again to the deep; * their soul melteth away because of the trouble.

27 They reel to and fro, and stagger like a drunken man, * and are at their wit's end.

28 So when they cry unto the LORD in their trouble, * he delivereth them out of their distress.

29 For he maketh the storm to cease, * so that the waves thereof are still.

30 Then are they glad, because they are at rest; * and so he bringeth them unto the haven where they would be.

31 O that men would therefore praise the LORD for his goodness; * and declare the wonders that he doeth for the children of men!

32 That they would exalt him also in the congregation of the people, * and praise him in the seat of the elders!

33 He turneth the floods into a wilderness, * and drieth up the water-springs.

34 A fruitful land maketh he barren, * for the wickedness of them that dwell therein.

35 Again, he maketh the wilderness a standing water, * and water-springs of a dry ground.

36 And there he setteth the hungry, * that they may build them a city to dwell in;

37 That they may sow their land, and plant vineyards, * to yield them fruits of increase.

38 He blesseth them, so that they multiply exceedingly; * and suffereth not their cattle to decrease.

39 And again, when they are minished and brought low * through oppression, through any plague or trouble;

40 Though he suffer them to be evil entreated through tyrants, * and let them wander out of the way in the wilderness;

41 Yet helpeth he the poor out of misery, * and maketh him households like a flock of sheep.

42 The righteous will consider this, and rejoice; * and the mouth of all wickedness shall be stopped.

43 Whoso is wise, will ponder these things; * and they shall understand the loving-kindness of the LORD.

Evening Prayer.

Psalm 108. *Paratum cor meum.*

O GOD, my heart is ready, my heart is ready; * I will sing, and give praise with the best member that I have.

2 Awake, thou lute and harp; * I myself will awake right early.

3 I will give thanks unto thee, O LORD, among the peoples; * I will sing praises unto thee among the nations.

4 For thy mercy is greater than the heavens, * and thy truth reacheth unto the clouds.

5 Set up thyself, O God, above the heavens, * and thy glory above all the earth;

6 That thy beloved may be delivered: * let thy right hand save them, and hear thou me.

7 God hath spoken in his holiness; * I will rejoice therefore, and divide Shechem, and mete out the valley of Succoth.

8 Gilead is mine, and Manasseh is mine; * Ephraim also is the strength of my head; Judah is my lawgiver;

9 Moab is my wash-pot; over Edom will I cast out my shoe; * upon Philistia will I triumph.

10 Who will lead me into the strong city? * and who will bring me into Edom?

11 Hast not thou forsaken us, O God? * and wilt not thou, O God, go forth with our hosts?

12 O help us against the enemy: * for vain is the help of man.

13 Through God we shall do great acts; * and it is he that shall tread down our enemies.

Psalm 109. *Deus, laudem.*

HOLD not thy tongue, O God of my praise; * for the mouth of the ungodly, yea, the mouth of the deceitful is opened upon me.

2 And they have spoken against me with false tongues; * they compassed me about also with words of hatred, and fought against me without a cause.

3 For the love that I had unto them, lo, they take now my contrary part; * but I give myself unto prayer.

4 Thus have they rewarded me evil for good, * and hatred for my good will.

5 Set thou an ungodly man to be ruler over him, * and let an adversary stand at his right hand.

6 When sentence is given upon him, let him be condemned; * and let his prayer be turned into sin.

7 Let his days be few; * and let another take his office.

8 Let his children be fatherless, * and his wife a widow.

9 Let his children be vagabonds, and beg their bread; * let them seek it also out of desolate places.

10 Let the extortioner consume all that he hath; * and let the stranger spoil his labour.

11 Let there be no man to pity him, * nor to have compassion upon his fatherless children.

12 Let his posterity be destroyed; * and in the next generation let his name be clean put out.

13 Let the wickedness of his fathers be had in remembrance in the sight of the LORD; * and let not the sin of his mother be done away.

14 Let them alway be before the LORD, * that he may root out the memorial of them from off the earth;

15 And that, because his mind was not to do good; * but persecuted the poor helpless man, that he might slay him that was vexed at the heart.

16 His delight was in cursing, and it shall happen unto him; * he loved not blessing, therefore shall it be far from him.

17 He clothed himself with cursing like as with a raiment, * and it shall come into his bowels like water, and like oil into his bones.

18 Let it be unto him as the cloak that he hath upon him, * and as the girdle that he is alway girded withal.

19 Let it thus happen from the LORD unto mine enemies, * and to those that speak evil against my soul.

20 But deal thou with me, O LORD God, according unto thy Name; * for sweet is thy mercy.

21 O deliver me, for I am helpless and poor, * and my heart is wounded within me.

22 I go hence like the shadow that departeth, * and am driven away as the grasshopper.

23 My knees are weak through fasting; * my flesh is dried up for want of fatness.

24 I am become also a reproach unto them: * they that look upon me shake their heads.

25 Help me, O LORD my God; * O save me according to thy mercy;

26 And they shall know how that this is thy hand, * and that thou, LORD, hast done it.

27 Though they curse, yet bless thou; * and let them be confounded that rise up against me; but let thy servant rejoice.

28 Let mine adversaries be clothed with shame; * and let them cover themselves with their own confusion, as with a cloak.

29 As for me, I will give great thanks unto the LORD with my mouth, * and praise him among the multitude;

30 For he shall stand at the right hand of the poor, *
to save his soul from unrighteous judges.

The Twenty-third Day.

Morning Prayer.

Psalm 110. *Dixit Dominus.*

THE LORD said unto my Lord, * Sit thou on my right
hand, until I make thine enemies thy footstool.

2 The LORD shall send the rod of thy power out of
Sion: * be thou ruler, even in the midst among thine enemies.

3 In the day of thy power shall thy people offer themselves willingly with an holy worship: * thy young men
come to thee as dew from the womb of the morning.

4 The LORD sware, and will not repent, * Thou art a
Priest for ever after the order of Melchizedek.

5 The Lord upon thy right hand * shall wound even
kings in the day of his wrath.

6 He shall judge among the heathen; * he shall fill the
places with the dead bodies, and smite in sunder the heads
over divers countries.

7 He shall drink of the brook in the way; * therefore
shall he lift up his head.

Psalm 111. *Confitebor tibi.*

I WILL give thanks unto the LORD with my whole heart, *
secretly among the faithful, and in the congregation.

2 The works of the LORD are great, * sought out of all
them that have pleasure therein.

3 His work is worthy to be praised and had in honour, *
and his righteousness endureth for ever.

4 The merciful and gracious LORD hath so done his mar-

vellous works, * that they ought to be had in remembrance.

5 He hath given meat unto them that fear him; * he shall ever be mindful of his covenant.

6 He hath showed his people the power of his works, * that he may give them the heritage of the heathen.

7 The works of his hands are verity and judgment; * all his commandments are true.

8 They stand fast for ever and ever, * and are done in truth and equity.

9 He sent redemption unto his people; * he hath commanded his covenant for ever; holy and reverend is his Name.

10 The fear of the LORD is the beginning of wisdom; * a good understanding have all they that do thereafter; his praise endureth for ever.

Psalm 112. *Beatus vir.*

BLESSED is the man that feareth the LORD; * he hath great delight in his commandments.

2 His seed shall be mighty upon earth; * the generation of the faithful shall be blessed.

3 Riches and plenteousness shall be in his house; * and his righteousness endureth for ever.

4 Unto the godly there ariseth up light in the darkness; * he is merciful, loving, and righteous.

5 A good man is merciful, and lendeth; * and will guide his words with discretion.

6 For he shall never be moved: * and the righteous shall be had in everlasting remembrance.

·7 He will not be afraid of any evil tidings; * for his heart standeth fast, and believeth in the LORD.

8 His heart is stablished, and will not shrink, * until he see his desire upon his enemies.

9 He hath dispersed abroad, and given to the poor, *

and his righteousness remaineth for ever; his horn shall be exalted with honour.

10 The ungodly shall see it, and it shall grieve him; * he shall gnash with his teeth, and consume away; the desire of the ungodly shall perish.

Psalm 113. *Laudate, pueri.*

PRAISE the LORD, ye servants; * O praise the Name of the LORD.

2 Blessed be the Name of the LORD * from this time forth for evermore.

3 The LORD'S Name is praised * from the rising up of the sun unto the going down of the same.

4 The LORD is high above all nations, * and his glory above the heavens.

5 Who is like unto the LORD our God, that hath his dwelling so high, * and yet humbleth himself to behold the things that are in heaven and earth!

6 He taketh up the simple out of the dust, * and lifteth the poor out of the mire;

7 That he may set him with the princes, * even with the princes of his people.

8 He maketh the barren woman to keep house, * and to be a joyful mother of children.

Evening Prayer.

Psalm 114. *In exitu Israel.*

WHEN Israel came out of Egypt, * and the house of Jacob from among the strange people,

2 Judah was his sanctuary, * and Israel his dominion.

3 The sea saw that, and fled; * Jordan was driven back.

4 The mountains skipped like rams, * and the little hills like young sheep.

5 What aileth thee, O thou sea, that thou fleddest? * and thou Jordan, that thou wast driven back?

6 Ye mountains, that ye skipped like rams? * and ye little hills, like young sheep?

7 Tremble, thou earth, at the presence of the Lord: * at the presence of the God of Jacob;

8 Who turned the hard rock into a standing water, * and the flint-stone into a springing well.

Psalm 115. *Non nobis, Domine.*

NOT unto us, O Lord, not unto us, but unto thy Name give the praise; * for thy loving mercy, and for thy truth's sake.

2 Wherefore shall the heathen say, * Where is now their God?

3 As for our God, he is in heaven: * he hath done whatsoever pleased him.

4 Their idols are silver and gold, * even the work of men's hands.

5 They have mouths, and speak not; * eyes have they, and see not.

6 They have ears, and hear not; * noses have they, and smell not.

7 They have hands, and handle not; feet have they, and walk not; * neither speak they through their throat.

8 They that make them are like unto them; * and so are all such as put their trust in them.

9 But thou, house of Israel, trust thou in the Lord; * he is their helper and defender.

10 Ye house of Aaron, put your trust in the Lord; * he is their helper and defender.

11 Ye that fear the Lord, put your trust in the Lord; * he is their helper and defender.

12 The Lord hath been mindful of us, and he shall bless

us; * even he shall bless the house of Israel, he shall bless the house of Aaron.

13 He shall bless them that fear the LORD, * both small and great.

14 The LORD shall increase you more and more, * you and your children.

15 Ye are the blessed of the LORD, * who made heaven and earth.

16 All the whole heavens are the LORD'S; * the earth hath he given to the children of men.

17 The dead praise not thee, O LORD, * neither all they that go down into silence.

18 But we will praise the LORD, * from this time forth for evermore. Praise the LORD.

The Twenty-fourth Day.

Morning Prayer.

Psalm 116. *Dilexi, quoniam.*

MY delight is in the LORD; * because he hath heard the voice of my prayer;

2 Because he hath inclined his ear unto me; * therefore will I call upon him as long as I live.

3 The snares of death compassed me round about, * and the pains of hell gat hold upon me.

4 I found trouble and heaviness; then called I upon the Name of the LORD; * O LORD, I beseech thee, deliver my soul.

5 Gracious is the LORD, and righteous; * yea, our God is merciful.

6 The LORD preserveth the simple: * I was in misery, and he helped me.

7 Turn again then unto thy rest, O my soul; * for the LORD hath rewarded thee.

8 And why? thou hast delivered my soul from death, * mine eyes from tears, and my feet from falling.

9 I will walk before the LORD * in the land of the living.

10 I believed, and therefore will I speak; but I was sore troubled: * I said in my haste, All men are liars.

11 What reward shall I give unto the LORD * for all the benefits that he hath done unto me?

12 I will receive the cup of salvation, * and call upon the Name of the LORD.

13 I will pay my vows now in the presence of all his people: * right dear in the sight of the LORD is the death of his saints.

14 Behold, O LORD, how that I am thy servant; * I am thy servant, and the son of thine handmaid; thou hast broken my bonds in sunder.

15 I will offer to thee the sacrifice of thanksgiving, * and will call upon the Name of the LORD.

16 I will pay my vows unto the LORD, in the sight of all his people, * in the courts of the LORD'S house; even in the midst of thee, O Jerusalem. Praise the LORD.

Psalm 117. *Laudate Dominum.*

O PRAISE the LORD, all ye nations; * praise him, all ye peoples.

2 For his merciful kindness is ever more and more toward us; * and the truth of the LORD endureth for ever. Praise the LORD.

Psalm 118. *Confitemini Domino.*

O GIVE thanks unto the LORD, for he is gracious; * because his mercy endureth for ever.

2 Let Israel now confess that he is gracious, * and that his mercy endureth for ever.

3 Let the house of Aaron now confess, * that his mercy endureth for ever.

4 Yea, let them now that fear the LORD confess, * that his mercy endureth for ever.

5 I called upon the LORD in trouble; * and the LORD heard me at large.

6 The LORD is on my side; * I will not fear what man doeth unto me.

7 The LORD taketh my part with them that help me; * therefore shall I see my desire upon mine enemies.

8 It is better to trust in the LORD, * than to put any confidence in man.

9 It is better to trust in the LORD, * than to put any confidence in princes.

10 All nations compassed me round about; * but in the Name of the LORD will I destroy them.

11 They kept me in on every side, they kept me in, I say, on every side; * but in the Name of the LORD will I destroy them.

12 They came about me like bees, and are extinct even as the fire among the thorns; * for in the Name of the LORD I will destroy them.

13 Thou hast thrust sore at me, that I might fall; * but the LORD was my help.

14 The LORD is my strength, and my song; * and is become my salvation.

15 The voice of joy and health is in the dwellings of the righteous; * the right hand of the LORD bringeth mighty things to pass.

16 The right hand of the LORD hath the pre-eminence; * the right hand of the LORD bringeth mighty things to pass.

17 I shall not die, but live, * and declare the works of the LORD.

18 The LORD hath chastened and corrected me; * but he hath not given me over unto death.

19 Open me the gates of righteousness, * that I may go into them, and give thanks unto the LORD.

20 This is the gate of the LORD, * the righteous shall enter into it.

21 I will thank thee; for thou hast heard me, * and art become my salvation.

22 The same stone which the builders refused, * is become the head-stone in the corner.

23 This is the LORD'S doing, * and it is marvellous in our eyes.

24 This is the day which the LORD hath made; * we will rejoice and be glad in it.

25 Help me now, O LORD: * O LORD, send us now prosperity.

26 Blessed be he that cometh in the Name of the LORD: * we have wished you good luck, we that are of the house of the LORD.

27 God is the LORD, who hath showed us light: * bind the sacrifice with cords, yea, even unto the horns of the altar.

28 Thou art my God, and I will thank thee; * thou art my God, and I will praise thee.

29 O give thanks unto the LORD; for he is gracious, * and his mercy endureth for ever.

Evening Prayer.

Psalm 119. I. *Beati immaculati.*

BLESSED are those that are undefiled in the way, * and walk in the law of the LORD.

2 Blessed are they that keep his testimonies, * and seek him with their whole heart;

3 Even they who do no wickedness, * and walk in his ways.

4 Thou hast charged * that we shall diligently keep thy commandments.

5 O that my ways were made so direct, * that I might keep thy statutes!

6 So shall I not be confounded, * while I have respect unto all thy commandments.

7 I will thank thee with an unfeigned heart, * when I shall have learned the judgments of thy righteousness.

8 I will keep thy statutes; * O forsake me not utterly.

II. *In quo corrigit?*

WHEREWITHAL shall a young man cleanse his way? * even by ruling himself after thy word.

10 With my whole heart have I sought thee; * O let me not go wrong out of thy commandments.

11 Thy word have I hid within my heart, * that I should not sin against thee.

12 Blessed art thou, O LORD; * O teach me thy statutes.

13 With my lips have I been telling * of all the judgments of thy mouth.

14 I have had as great delight in the way of thy testimonies, * as in all manner of riches.

15 I will talk of thy commandments, * and have respect unto thy ways.

16 My delight shall be in thy statutes, * and I will not forget thy word.

III. *Retribue servo tuo.*

O DO well unto thy servant; * that I may live, and keep thy word.

18 Open thou mine eyes; * that I may see the wondrous things of thy law.

19 I am a stranger upon earth; * O hide not thy commandments from me.

20 My soul breaketh out for the very fervent desire * that it hath alway unto thy judgments.

21 Thou hast rebuked the proud; * and cursed are they that do err from thy commandments.

22 O turn from me shame and rebuke; * for I have kept thy testimonies.

23 Princes also did sit and speak against me; * but thy servant is occupied in thy statutes.

24 For thy testimonies are my delight, * and my counsellors.

iv. *Adhæsit pavimento.*

MY soul cleaveth to the dust; * O quicken thou me, according to thy word.

26 I have acknowledged my ways, and thou heardest me: * O teach me thy statutes.

27 Make me to understand the way of thy commandments; * and so shall I talk of thy wondrous works.

28 My soul melteth away for very heaviness; * comfort thou me according unto thy word.

29 Take from me the way of lying, * and cause thou me to make much of thy law.

30 I have chosen the way of truth, * and thy judgments have I laid before me.

31 I have stuck unto thy testimonies; * O LORD, confound me not.

32 I will run the way of thy commandments, * when thou hast set my heart at liberty.

The Twenty-fifth Day.

Morning Prayer.

v. *Legem pone.*

TEACH me, O LORD, the way of thy statutes, * and I shall keep it unto the end.

34 Give me understanding, and I shall keep thy law; * yea, I shall keep it with my whole heart.

35 Make me to go in the path of thy commandments; * for therein is my desire.

36 Incline my heart unto thy testimonies, * and not to covetousness.

37 O turn away mine eyes, lest they behold vanity; * and quicken thou me in thy way.

38 O stablish thy word in thy servant, * that I may fear thee.

39 Take away the rebuke that I am afraid of; * for thy judgments are good.

40 Behold, my delight is in thy commandments; * O quicken me in thy righteousness.

vi. *Et veniat super me.*

LET thy loving mercy come also unto me, O LORD, * even thy salvation, according unto thy word.

42 So shall I make answer unto my blasphemers; * for my trust is in thy word.

43 O take not the word of thy truth utterly out of my mouth; * for my hope is in thy judgments.

44 So shall I alway keep thy law; * yea, for ever and ever.

45 And I will walk at liberty; * for I seek thy commandments.

46 I will speak of thy testimonies also, even before kings, * and will not be ashamed.

47 And my delight shall be in thy commandments, * which I have loved.

48 My hands also will I lift up unto thy commandments, which I have loved; * and my study shall be in thy statutes.

VII. *Memor esto verbi tui.*

O THINK upon thy servant, as concerning thy word, * wherein thou hast caused me to put my trust.

50 The same is my comfort in my trouble; * for thy word hath quickened me.

51 The proud have had me exceedingly in derision; * yet have I not shrinked from thy law.

52 For I remembered thine everlasting judgments, O LORD, * and received comfort.

53 I am horribly afraid, * for the ungodly that forsake thy law.

54 Thy statutes have been my songs, * in the house of my pilgrimage.

55 I have thought upon thy Name, O LORD, in the night season, * and have kept thy law.

56 This I had, * because I kept thy commandments.

VIII. *Portio mea, Domine.*

THOU art my portion, O LORD; * I have promised to keep thy law.

58 I made my humble petition in thy presence with my whole heart; * O be merciful unto me, according to thy word.

59 I called mine own ways to remembrance, * and turned my feet unto thy testimonies.

60 I made haste, and prolonged not the time, * to keep thy commandments.

61 The snares of the ungodly have compassed me about; * but I have not forgotten thy law.

62 At midnight I will rise to give thanks unto thee, * because of thy righteous judgments.

63 I am a companion of all them that fear thee, * and keep thy commandments.

64 The earth, O LORD, is full of thy mercy: * O teach me thy statutes.

IX. *Bonitatem fecisti.*

O LORD, thou hast dealt graciously with thy servant, * according unto thy word.

66 O teach me true understanding and knowledge; * for I have believed thy commandments.

67 Before I was troubled, I went wrong; * but now have I kept thy word.

68 Thou art good and gracious; * O teach me thy statutes.

69 The proud have imagined a lie against me; * but I will keep thy commandments with my whole heart.

70 Their heart is as fat as brawn; * but my delight hath been in thy law.

71 It is good for me that I have been in trouble; * that I may learn thy statutes.

72 The law of thy mouth is dearer unto me * than thousands of gold and silver.

Evening Prayer.

x. *Manus tuæ fecerunt me.*

THY hands have made me and fashioned me: * O give me understanding, that I may learn thy commandments.

74 They that fear thee will be glad when they see me; * because I have put my trust in thy word.

75 I know, O LORD, that thy judgments are right, * and that thou of very faithfulness hast caused me to be troubled.

76 O let thy merciful kindness be my comfort, * according to thy word unto thy servant.

77 O let thy loving mercies come unto me, that I may live; * for thy law is my delight.

78 Let the proud be confounded, for they go wickedly about to destroy me; * but I will be occupied in thy commandments.

79 Let such as fear thee, and have known thy testimonies, * be turned unto me.

80 O let my heart be sound in thy statutes, * that I be not ashamed.

XI. *Deficit anima mea.*

MY soul hath longed for thy salvation, * and I have a good hope because of thy word.

82 Mine eyes long sore for thy word; * saying, O when wilt thou comfort me?

83 For I am become like a bottle in the smoke; * yet do I not forget thy statutes.

84 How many are the days of thy servant? * when wilt thou be avenged of them that persecute me?

85 The proud have digged pits for me, * which are not after thy law.

86 All thy commandments are true: * they persecute me falsely; O be thou my help.

87 They had almost made an end of me upon earth; * but I forsook not thy commandments.

88 O quicken me after thy loving-kindness; * and so shall I keep the testimonies of thy mouth.

XII. *In æternum, Domine.*

O LORD, thy word * endureth for ever in heaven.

90 Thy truth also remaineth from one generation to another; * thou hast laid the foundation of the earth, and it abideth.

91 They continue this day according to thine ordinance; * for all things serve thee.

92 If my delight had not been in thy law, * I should have perished in my trouble.

93 I will never forget thy commandments; * for with them thou hast quickened me.

94 I am thine: O save me, * for I have sought thy commandments.

95 The ungodly laid wait for me, to destroy me; * but I will consider thy testimonies.

96 I see that all things come to an end; * but thy commandment is exceeding broad.

XIII. *Quomodo dilexi!*

LORD, what love have I unto thy law! * all the day long is my study in it.

98 Thou, through thy commandments, hast made me wiser than mine enemies; * for they are ever with me.

99 I have more understanding than my teachers; * for thy testimonies are my study.

100 I am wiser than the aged; * because I keep thy commandments.

101 I have refrained my feet from every evil way, * that I may keep thy word.

102 I have not shrunk from thy judgments; * for thou teachest me.

103 O how sweet are thy words unto my throat; * yea, sweeter than honey unto my mouth!

104 Through thy commandments I get understanding: * therefore I hate all evil ways.

The Twenty-sixth Day.

Morning Prayer.

XIV. *Lucerna pedibus meis.*

THY word is a lantern unto my feet, * and a light unto my paths.

106 I have sworn, and am stedfastly purposed, * to keep thy righteous judgments.

107 I am troubled above measure: * quicken me, O LORD, according to thy word.

108 Let the free-will offerings of my mouth please thee, O LORD; * and teach me thy judgments.

109 My soul is alway in my hand; * yet do I not forget thy law.

110 The ungodly have laid a snare for me; * but yet I swerved not from thy commandments.

111 Thy testimonies have I claimed as mine heritage for ever; * and why? they are the very joy of my heart.

112 I have applied my heart to fulfil thy statutes alway, * even unto the end.

XV. *Iniquos odio habui.*

I HATE them that imagine evil things; * but thy law do I love.

114 Thou art my defence and shield; * and my trust is in thy word.

115 Away from me, ye wicked; * I will keep the commandments of my God.

116 O stablish me according to thy word, that I may live; * and let me not be disappointed of my hope.

117 Hold thou me up, and I shall be safe; * yea, my delight shall be ever in thy statutes.

118 Thou hast trodden down all them that depart from thy statutes; * for they imagine but deceit.

119 Thou puttest away all the ungodly of the earth like dross; * therefore I love thy testimonies.

120 My flesh trembleth for fear of thee; * and I am afraid of thy judgments.

XVI. *Feci judicium.*

I DEAL with the thing that is lawful and right; * O give me not over unto mine oppressors.

122 Make thou thy servant to delight in that which is good, * that the proud do me no wrong.

123 Mine eyes are wasted away with looking for thy health, * and for the word of thy righteousness.

124 O deal with thy servant according unto thy loving mercy, * and teach me thy statutes.

125 I am thy servant; O grant me understanding, * that I may know thy testimonies.

126 It is time for thee, LORD, to lay to thine hand; * for they have destroyed thy law.

127 For I love thy commandments * above gold and precious stones.

128 Therefore hold I straight all thy commandments; * and all false ways I utterly abhor.

XVII. *Mirabilia.*

THY testimonies are wonderful; * therefore doth my soul keep them.

130 When thy word goeth forth, * it giveth light and understanding unto the simple.

131 I opened my mouth, and drew in my breath; * for my delight was in thy commandments.

132 O look thou upon me, and be merciful unto me, * as thou usest to do unto those that love thy Name.

133 Order my steps in thy word; * and so shall no wickedness have dominion over me.

134 O deliver me from the wrongful dealings of men; * and so shall I keep thy commandments.

135 Show the light of thy countenance upon thy servant, * and teach me thy statutes.

136 Mine eyes gush out with water, * because men keep not thy law.

XVIII. *Justus es, Domine.*

RIGHTEOUS art thou, O LORD; * and true are thy judgments.

138 The testimonies that thou hast commanded * are exceeding righteous and true.

139 My zeal hath even consumed me; * because mine enemies have forgotten thy words.

140 Thy word is tried to the uttermost, * and thy servant loveth it.

141 I am small and of no reputation; * yet do I not forget thy commandments.

142 Thy righteousness is an everlasting righteousness, * and thy law is the truth.

143 Trouble and heaviness have taken hold upon me; * yet is my delight in thy commandments.

144 The righteousness of thy testimonies is everlasting: * O grant me understanding, and I shall live.

Evening Prayer.

XIX. *Clamavi in toto corde meo.*

I CALL with my whole heart; * hear me, O LORD; I will keep thy statutes.

146 Yea, even unto thee do I call; * help me, and I shall keep thy testimonies.

147 Early in the morning do I cry unto thee; * for in thy word is my trust.

148 Mine eyes prevent the night watches; * that I might be occupied in thy word.

149 Hear my voice, O LORD, according unto thy loving-kindness; * quicken me, according to thy judgments.

150 They draw nigh that of malice persecute me, * and are far from thy law.

151 Be thou nigh at hand, O LORD; * for all thy commandments are true.

152 As concerning thy testimonies, I have known long since, * that thou hast grounded them for ever.

xx. *Vide humilitatem.*

O CONSIDER mine adversity, and deliver me, * for I do not forget thy law.

154 Avenge thou my cause, and deliver me; * quicken me according to thy word.

155 Health is far from the ungodly; * for they regard not thy statutes.

156 Great is thy mercy, O LORD; * quicken me, as thou art wont.

157 Many there are that trouble me, and persecute me; * yet do I not swerve from thy testimonies.

158 It grieveth me when I see the transgressors; * because they keep not thy law.

159 Consider, O LORD, how I love thy commandments; * O quicken me, according to thy loving-kindness.

160 Thy word is true from everlasting; * all the judgments of thy righteousness endure for evermore.

XXI. *Principes persecuti sunt.*

PRINCES have persecuted me without a cause; * but my heart standeth in awe of thy word.

162 I am as glad of thy word, * as one that findeth great spoils.

163 As for lies, I hate and abhor them; * but thy law do I love.

164 Seven times a day do I praise thee; * because of thy righteous judgments.

165 Great is the peace that they have who love thy law; * and they have none occasion of stumbling.

166 LORD, I have looked for thy saving health, * and done after thy commandments.

167 My soul hath kept thy testimonies, * and loved them exceedingly.

168 I have kept thy commandments and testimonies; * for all my ways are before thee.

XXII. *Appropinquet deprecatio.*

LET my complaint come before thee, O LORD; * give me understanding according to thy word.

170 Let my supplication come before thee; * deliver me according to thy word.

171 My lips shall speak of thy praise, * when thou hast taught me thy statutes.

172 Yea, my tongue shall sing of thy word; * for all thy commandments are righteous.

173 Let thine hand help me; * for I have chosen thy commandments.

174 I have longed for thy saving health, O LORD; * and in thy law is my delight.

175 O let my soul live, and it shall praise thee; * and thy judgments shall help me.

176 I have gone astray like a sheep that is lost; * O seek thy servant, for I do not forget thy commandments.

The Twenty-seventh Day.

Morning Prayer.

Psalm 120. *Ad Dominum.*

WHEN I was in trouble, I called upon the LORD, * and he heard me.

2 Deliver my soul, O LORD, from lying lips, * and from a deceitful tongue.

3 What reward shall be given or done unto thee, thou false tongue? * even mighty and sharp arrows, with hot burning coals.

4 Woe is me, that I am constrained to dwell with Mesech, * and to have my habitation among the tents of Kedar!

5 My soul hath long dwelt among them * that are enemies unto peace.

6 I labour for peace; but when I speak unto them thereof, * they make them ready to battle.

Psalm 121. *Levavi oculos.*

I WILL lift up mine eyes unto the hills; * from whence cometh my help?

2 My help cometh even from the LORD, * who hath made heaven and earth.

3 He will not suffer thy foot to be moved; * and he that keepeth thee will not sleep.

4 Behold, he that keepeth Israel * shall neither slumber nor sleep.

5 The LORD himself is thy keeper; * the LORD is thy defence upon thy right hand;

6 So that the sun shall not burn thee by day, * neither the moon by night.

7 The LORD shall preserve thee from all evil; * yea, it is even he that shall keep thy soul.

8 The LORD shall preserve thy going out, and thy coming in, * from this time forth for evermore.

Psalm 122. *Lætatus sum.*

I WAS glad when they said unto me, * We will go into the house of the LORD.

2 Our feet shall stand in thy gates, * O Jerusalem.

3 Jerusalem is built as a city * that is at unity in itself.

4 For thither the tribes go up, even the tribes of the LORD, * to testify unto Israel, to give thanks unto the Name of the LORD.

5 For there is the seat of judgment, * even the seat of the house of David.

6 O pray for the peace of Jerusalem; * they shall prosper that love thee.

7 Peace be within thy walls, * and plenteousness within thy palaces.

8 For my brethren and companions' sakes, * I will wish thee prosperity.

9 Yea, because of the house of the LORD our God, * I will seek to do thee good.

Psalm 123. *Ad te levavi oculos meos.*

U NTO thee lift I up mine eyes, * O thou that dwellest in the heavens.

2 Behold, even as the eyes of servants look unto the hand of their masters, and as the eyes of a maiden unto the hand of her mistress, * even so our eyes wait upon the LORD our God, until he have mercy upon us.

3 Have mercy upon us, O LORD, have mercy upon us; * for we are utterly despised.

4 Our soul is filled with the scornful reproof of the wealthy, * and with the despitefulness of the proud.

Psalm 124. *Nisi quia Dominus.*

IF the LORD himself had not been on our side, now may Israel say; * if the LORD himself had not been on our side, when men rose up against us;

2 They had swallowed us up alive; * when they were so wrathfully displeased at us.

3 Yea, the waters had drowned us, * and the stream had gone over our soul.

4 The deep waters of the proud * had gone even over our soul.

5 But praised be the LORD, * who hath not given us over for a prey unto their teeth.

6 Our soul is escaped even as a bird out of the snare of the fowler; * the snare is broken, and we are delivered.

7 Our help standeth in the Name of the LORD, * who hath made heaven and earth.

Psalm 125. *Qui confidunt.*

THEY that put their trust in the LORD shall be even as the mount Sion, * which may not be removed, but standeth fast for ever.

2 The hills stand about Jerusalem; * even so standeth the LORD round about his people, from this time forth for evermore.

3 For the sceptre of the ungodly shall not abide upon the lot of the righteous; * lest the righteous put their hand unto wickedness.

4 Do well, O LORD, * unto those that are good and true of heart.

5 As for such as turn back unto their own wickedness, *
the LORD shall lead them forth with the evil doers; but
peace shall be upon Israel.

Evening Prayer.

Psalm 126. *In convertendo.*

WHEN the LORD turned again the captivity of Sion, *
then were we like unto them that dream.

2 Then was our mouth filled with laughter, * and our
tongue with joy.

3 Then said they among the heathen, * The LORD hath
done great things for them.

4 Yea, the LORD hath done great things for us already; *
whereof we rejoice.

5 Turn our captivity, O LORD, * as the rivers in the
south.

6 They that sow in tears * shall reap in joy.

7 He that now goeth on his way weeping, and beareth
forth good seed, * shall doubtless come again with joy, and
bring his sheaves with him.

Psalm 127. *Nisi Dominus.*

EXCEPT the LORD build the house, * their labour is
but lost that build it.

2 Except the LORD keep the city, * the watchman wak-
eth but in vain.

3 It is but lost labour that ye haste to rise up early, and
so late take rest, and eat the bread of carefulness; * for so
he giveth his beloved sleep.

4 Lo, children, and the fruit of the womb, * are an heritage and gift that cometh of the LORD.

5 Like as the arrows in the hand of the giant, * even so
are the young children.

6 Happy is the man that hath his quiver full of them; *
they shall not be ashamed when they speak with their
enemies in the gate.

Psalm 128. *Beati omnes.*

BLESSED are all they that fear the LORD, * and walk
in his ways.

2 For thou shalt eat the labours of thine hands: * O
well is thee, and happy shalt thou be.

3 Thy wife shall be as the fruitful vine * upon the
walls of thine house;

4 Thy children like the olive-branches * round about
thy table.

5 Lo, thus shall the man be blessed * that feareth the
LORD.

6 The LORD from out of Sion shall so bless thee, * that
thou shalt see Jerusalem in prosperity all thy life long;

7 Yea, that thou shalt see thy children's children, * and
peace upon Israel.

Psalm 129. *Sæpe expugnaverunt.*

MANY a time have they fought against me from my
youth up, * may Israel now say;

2 Yea, many a time have they vexed me from my
youth up; * but they have not prevailed against me.

3 The plowers plowed upon my back, * and made
long furrows.

4 But the righteous LORD * hath hewn the snares of
the ungodly in pieces.

5 Let them be confounded and turned backward, * as
many as have evil will at Sion.

6 Let them be even as the grass upon the housetops, *
which withereth afore it be grown up;

7 Whereof the mower filleth not his hand, * neither he that bindeth up the sheaves his bosom.

8 So that they who go by say not so much as, The LORD prosper you; * we wish you good luck in the Name of the LORD.

Psalm 130. *De profundis.*

OUT of the deep have I called unto thee, O LORD; * Lord, hear my voice.

2 O let thine ears consider well * the voice of my complaint.

3 If thou, LORD, wilt be extreme to mark what is done amiss, * O Lord, who may abide it?

4 For there is mercy with thee; * therefore shalt thou be feared.

5 I look for the LORD; my soul doth wait for him; * in his word is my trust.

6 My soul fleeth unto the Lord before the morning watch; * I say, before the morning watch.

7 O Israel, trust in the LORD; for with the LORD there is mercy, * and with him is plenteous redemption.

8 And he shall redeem Israel * from all his sins.

Psalm 131. *Domine, non est.*

LORD, I am not high-minded; * I have no proud looks.

2 I do not exercise myself in great matters * which are too high for me.

3 But I refrain my soul, and keep it low, like as a child that is weaned from his mother: * yea, my soul is even as a weaned child.

4 O Israel, trust in the LORD * from this time forth for evermore.

The Twenty-eighth Day.

Morning Prayer.

Psalm 132. *Memento, Domine.*

LORD, remember David, * and all his trouble:

2 How he sware unto the LORD, * and vowed a vow unto the Almighty God of Jacob:

3 I will not come within the tabernacle of mine house, * nor climb up into my bed;

4 I will not suffer mine eyes to sleep, nor mine eyelids to slumber; * neither the temples of my head to take any rest;

5 Until I find out a place for the temple of the LORD; * an habitation for the Mighty God of Jacob.

6 Lo, we heard of the same at Ephratah, * and found it in the wood.

7 We will go into his tabernacle, * and fall low on our knees before his footstool.

8 Arise, O LORD, into thy resting-place; * thou, and the ark of thy strength.

9 Let thy priests be clothed with righteousness; * and let thy saints sing with joyfulness.

10 For thy servant David's sake, * turn not away the face of thine anointed.

11 The LORD hath made a faithful oath unto David, * and he shall not shrink from it:

12 Of the fruit of thy body * shall I set upon thy throne.

13 If thy children will keep my covenant, and my testimonies that I shall teach them; * their children also shall sit upon thy throne for evermore.

14 For the LORD hath chosen Sion to be an habitation for himself; * he hath longed for her.

15 This shall be my rest for ever: * here will I dwell, for I have a delight therein.

16 I will bless her victuals with increase, * and will satisfy her poor with bread.

17 I will deck her priests with health, * and her saints shall rejoice and sing.

18 There shall I make the horn of David to flourish: * I have ordained a lantern for mine anointed.

19 As for his enemies, I shall clothe them with shame; * but upon himself shall his crown flourish.

Psalm 133. *Ecce, quam bonum!*

BEHOLD, how good and joyful a thing it is, * for brethren to dwell together in unity!

2 It is like the precious oil upon the head, that ran down unto the beard, * even unto Aaron's beard, and went down to the skirts of his clothing.

3 Like as the dew of Hermon, * which fell upon the hill of Sion.

4 For there the LORD promised his blessing, * and life for evermore.

Psalm 134. *Ecce nunc.*

BEHOLD now, praise the LORD, * all ye servants of the LORD;

2 Ye that by night stand in the house of the LORD, * even in the courts of the house of our God.

3 Lift up your hands in the sanctuary, * and praise the LORD.

4 The LORD that made heaven and earth * give thee blessing out of Sion.

Psalm 135. *Laudate Nomen.*

O PRAISE the LORD, laud ye the Name of the LORD; * praise it, O ye servants of the LORD;

2 Ye that stand in the house of the LORD, * in the courts of the house of our God.

3 O praise the LORD, for the LORD is gracious; * O sing praises unto his Name, for it is lovely.

4 For why? the LORD hath chosen Jacob unto himself, * and Israel for his own possession.

5 For I know that the LORD is great, * and that our Lord is above all gods.

6 Whatsoever the LORD pleased, that did he in heaven, and in earth; * and in the sea, and in all deep places.

7 He bringeth forth the clouds from the ends of the world, * and sendeth forth lightnings with the rain, bringing the winds out of his treasuries.

8 He smote the firstborn of Egypt, * both of man and beast.

9 He hath sent tokens and wonders into the midst of thee, O thou land of Egypt; * upon Pharaoh, and all his servants.

10 He smote divers nations, * and slew mighty kings:

11 Sihon, king of the Amorites; and Og, the king of Bashan; * and all the kingdoms of Canaan;

12 And gave their land to be an heritage, * even an heritage unto Israel his people.

13 Thy Name, O LORD, endureth for ever; * so doth thy memorial, O LORD, from one generation to another.

14 For the LORD will avenge his people, * and be gracious unto his servants.

15 As for the images of the heathen, they are but silver and gold; * the work of men's hands.

16 They have mouths, and speak not; * eyes have they, but they see not.

17 They have ears, and yet they hear not; * neither is there any breath in their mouths.

18 They that make them are like unto them; * and so are all they that put their trust in them.

19 Praise the LORD, ye house of Israel; * praise the LORD, ye house of Aaron.

20 Praise the LORD, ye house of Levi; * ye that fear the LORD, praise the LORD.

21 Praised be the LORD out of Sion, * who dwelleth at Jerusalem.

Evening Prayer.

Psalm 136. *Confitemini.*

O GIVE thanks unto the LORD, for he is gracious: * and his mercy endureth for ever.

2 O give thanks unto the God of all gods: * for his mercy endureth for ever.

3 O thank the Lord of all lords: * for his mercy endureth for ever.

4 Who only doeth great wonders: * for his mercy endureth for ever.

5 Who by his excellent wisdom made the heavens: * for his mercy endureth for ever.

6 Who laid out the earth above the waters: * for his mercy endureth for ever.

7 Who hath made great lights: * for his mercy endureth for ever:

8 The sun to rule the day: * for his mercy endureth for ever;

9 The moon and the stars to govern the night: * for his mercy endureth for ever.

10 Who smote Egypt, with their firstborn: * for his mercy endureth for ever;

11 And brought out Israel from among them: * for his mercy endureth for ever;

12 With a mighty hand and stretched-out arm: * for his mercy endureth for ever.

13 Who divided the Red Sea in two parts: * for his mercy endureth for ever;

14 And made Israel to go through the midst of it: * for his mercy endureth for ever.

15 But as for Pharaoh and his host, he overthrew them in the Red Sea: * for his mercy endureth for ever.

16 Who led his people through the wilderness: * for his mercy endureth for ever.

17 Who smote great kings: * for his mercy endureth for ever;

18 Yea, and slew mighty kings: * for his mercy endureth for ever:

19 Sihon, king of the Amorites: * for his mercy endureth for ever;

20 And Og, the king of Bashan: * for his mercy endureth for ever;

21 And gave away their land for an heritage: * for his mercy endureth for ever;

22 Even for an heritage unto Israel his servant: * for his mercy endureth for ever.

23 Who remembered us when we were in trouble: * for his mercy endureth for ever;

24 And hath delivered us from our enemies: * for his mercy endureth for ever.

25 Who giveth food to all flesh: * for his mercy endureth for ever.

26 O give thanks unto the God of heaven: * for his mercy endureth for ever.

27 O give thanks unto the Lord of lords: * for his mercy endureth for ever.

Psalm 137. *Super flumina.*

BY the waters of Babylon we sat down and wept, * when we remembered thee, O Sion.

2 As for our harps, we hanged them up * upon the trees that are therein.

3 For they that led us away captive, required of us then a song, and melody in our heaviness: * Sing us one of the songs of Sion.

4 How shall we sing the LORD's song * in a strange land?

5 If I forget thee, O Jerusalem, * let my right hand forget her cunning.

6 If I do not remember thee, let my tongue cleave to the roof of my mouth; * yea, if I prefer not Jerusalem above my chief joy.

7 Remember the children of Edom, O LORD, in the day of Jerusalem; * how they said, Down with it, down with it, even to the ground.

8 O daughter of Babylon, wasted with misery; * yea, happy shall he be that rewardeth thee as thou hast served us.

9 Blessed shall he be that taketh thy children, * and throweth them against the stones.

Psalm 138. *Confitebor tibi.*

I WILL give thanks unto thee, O Lord, with my whole heart; * even before the gods will I sing praise unto thee.

2 I will worship toward thy holy temple, and praise thy Name, because of thy loving-kindness and truth; * for thou hast magnified thy Name, and thy word, above all things.

3 When I called upon thee, thou heardest me; * and enduedst my soul with much strength.

4 All the kings of the earth shall praise thee, O LORD; * for they have heard the words of thy mouth.

5 Yea, they shall sing of the ways of the LORD, * that great is the glory of the LORD.

6 For though the LORD be high, yet hath he respect unto the lowly; * as for the proud, he beholdeth them afar off.

7 Though I walk in the midst of trouble, yet shalt thou refresh me; * thou shalt stretch forth thy hand upon the furiousness of mine enemies, and thy right hand shall save me.

8 The LORD shall make good his loving-kindness toward me; * yea, thy mercy, O LORD, endureth for ever; despise not then the works of thine own hands.

The Twenty-ninth Day.

Morning Prayer.

Psalm 139. *Domine, probasti.*

O LORD, thou hast searched me out, and known me. * Thou knowest my down-sitting, and mine up-rising; thou understandest my thoughts long before.

2 Thou art about my path, and about my bed; * and art acquainted with all my ways.

3 For lo, there is not a word in my tongue, * but thou, O LORD, knowest it altogether.

4 Thou hast beset me behind and before, * and laid thine hand upon me.

5 Such knowledge is too wonderful and excellent for me; * I cannot attain unto it.

6 Whither shall I go then from thy Spirit? * or whither shall I go then from thy presence?

7 If I climb up into heaven, thou art there; * if I go down to hell, thou art there also.

8 If I take the wings of the morning, * and remain in the uttermost parts of the sea;

9 Even there also shall thy hand lead me, * and thy right hand shall hold me.

10 If I say, Peradventure the darkness shall cover me; * then shall my night be turned to day.

11 Yea, the darkness is no darkness with thee, but the night is as clear as the day; * the darkness and light to thee are both alike.

12 For my reins are thine; * thou hast covered me in my mother's womb.

13 I will give thanks unto thee, for I am fearfully and wonderfully made: * marvellous are thy works, and that my soul knoweth right well.

14 My bones are not hid from thee, * though I be made secretly, and fashioned beneath in the earth.

15 Thine eyes did see my substance, yet being imperfect; * and in thy book were all my members written;

16 Which day by day were fashioned, * when as yet there was none of them.

17 How dear are thy counsels unto me, O God; * O how great is the sum of them!

18 If I tell them, they are more in number than the sand: * when I wake up, I am present with thee.

19 Wilt thou not slay the wicked, O God? * Depart from me, ye blood-thirsty men.

20 For they speak unrighteously against thee; * and thine enemies take thy Name in vain.

21 Do not I hate them, O Lord, that hate thee? * and am not I grieved with those that rise up against thee?

22 Yea, I hate them right sore; * even as though they were mine enemies.

23 Try me, O God, and seek the ground of my heart; * prove me, and examine my thoughts.

24 Look well if there be any way of wickedness in me; * and lead me in the way everlasting.

Psalm 140. *Eripe me, Domine.*

DELIVER me, O LORD, from the evil man; * and preserve me from the wicked man;

2 Who imagine mischief in their hearts, * and stir up strife all the day long.

3 They have sharpened their tongues like a serpent; * adder's poison is under their lips.

4 Keep me, O LORD, from the hands of the ungodly; * preserve me from the wicked men, who are purposed to overthrow my goings.

5 The proud have laid a snare for me, and spread a net abroad with cords; * yea, and set traps in my way.

6 I said unto the LORD, Thou art my God, * hear the voice of my prayers, O LORD.

7 O LORD God, thou strength of my health; * thou hast covered my head in the day of battle.

8 Let not the ungodly have his desire, O LORD; * let not his mischievous imagination prosper, lest they be too proud.

9 Let the mischief of their own lips fall upon the head of them * that compass me about.

10 Let hot burning coals fall upon them; * let them be cast into the fire, and into the pit, that they never rise up again.

11 A man full of words shall not prosper upon the earth: * evil shall hunt the wicked person to overthrow him.

12 Sure I am that the LORD will avenge the poor, * and maintain the cause of the helpless.

13 The righteous also shall give thanks unto thy Name; * and the just shall continue in thy sight.

Evening Prayer.

Psalm 141. *Domine, clamavi.*

LORD, I call upon thee; haste thee unto me, * and consider my voice, when I cry unto thee.

2 Let my prayer be set forth in thy sight as the incense; * and let the lifting up of my hands be an evening sacrifice.

3 Set a watch, O LORD, before my mouth, * and keep the door of my lips.

4 O let not mine heart be inclined to any evil thing; * let me not be occupied in ungodly works with the men that work wickedness, neither let me eat of such things as please them.

5 Let the righteous rather smite me friendly, and reprove me; * yea, let not my head refuse their precious balms.

6 As for the ungodly, * I will pray yet against their wickedness.

7 Let their judges be overthrown in stony places, * that they may hear my words; for they are sweet.

8 Our bones lie scattered before the pit, * like as when one breaketh and heweth wood upon the earth.

9 But mine eyes look unto thee, O LORD God; * in thee is my trust; O cast not out my soul.

10 Keep me from the snare that they have laid for me, * and from the traps of the wicked doers.

11 Let the ungodly fall into their own nets together, * and let me ever escape them.

Psalm 142. *Voce mea ad Dominum.*

I CRIED unto the LORD with my voice; * yea, even unto the LORD did I make my supplication.

2 I poured out my complaints before him, * and showed him of my trouble.

3 When my spirit was in heaviness, thou knewest my path; * in the way wherein I walked, have they privily laid a snare for me.

4 I looked also upon my right hand, * and saw there was no man that would know me.

5 I had no place to flee unto, * and no man cared for my soul.

6 I cried unto thee, O LORD, and said, * Thou art my hope, and my portion in the land of the living.

7 Consider my complaint; * for I am brought very low.

8 O deliver me from my persecutors; * for they are too strong for me.

9 Bring my soul out of prison, that I may give thanks unto thy Name; * which thing if thou wilt grant me, then shall the righteous resort unto my company.

Psalm 143. *Domine, exaudi.*

HEAR my prayer, O LORD, and consider my desire; * hearken unto me for thy truth and righteousness' sake.

2 And enter not into judgment with thy servant; * for in thy sight shall no man living be justified.

3 For the enemy hath persecuted my soul; he hath smitten my life down to the ground; * he hath laid me in the darkness, as the men that have been long dead.

4 Therefore is my spirit vexed within me, * and my heart within me is desolate.

5 Yet do I remember the time past; I muse upon all thy works; * yea, I exercise myself in the works of thy hands.

6 I stretch forth my hands unto thee; * my soul gaspeth unto thee as a thirsty land.

7 Hear me, O LORD, and that soon; for my spirit waxeth faint: * hide not thy face from me, lest I be like unto them that go down into the pit.

8 O let me hear thy loving-kindness betimes in the morning; for in thee is my trust: * show thou me the way that I should walk in; for I lift up my soul unto thee.

9 Deliver me, O LORD, from mine enemies; * for I flee unto thee to hide me.

10 Teach me to do the thing that pleaseth thee; for thou art my God: * let thy loving Spirit lead me forth into the land of righteousness.

11 Quicken me, O LORD, for thy Name's sake; * and for thy righteousness' sake bring my soul out of trouble.

12 And of thy goodness slay mine enemies, * and destroy all them that vex my soul; for I am thy servant.

The Thirtieth Day.

Morning Prayer.

Psalm 144. *Benedictus Dominus.*

BLESSED be the LORD my strength, * who teacheth my hands to war, and my fingers to fight:

2 My hope and my fortress, my castle and deliverer, my defender in whom I trust; * who subdueth my people that is under me.

3 LORD, what is man, that thou hast such respect unto him? * or the son of man, that thou so regardest him?

4 Man is like a thing of nought; * his time passeth away like a shadow.

5 Bow thy heavens, O LORD, and come down; * touch the mountains, and they shall smoke.

6 Cast forth thy lightning, and tear them; * shoot out thine arrows, and consume them.

7 Send down thine hand from above; * deliver me, and take me out of the great waters, from the hand of strangers;

8 Whose mouth talketh of vanity, * and their right hand is a right hand of wickedness.

9 I will sing a new song unto thee, O God; * and sing praises unto thee upon a ten-stringed lute.

10 Thou hast given victory unto kings, * and hast delivered David thy servant from the peril of the sword.

11 Save me, and deliver me from the hand of strangers, * whose mouth talketh of vanity, and their right hand is a right hand of iniquity:

12 That our sons may grow up as the young plants, * and that our daughters may be as the polished corners of the temple;

13 That our garners may be full and plenteous with all manner of store; * that our sheep may bring forth thousands, and ten thousands in our fields;

14 That our oxen may be strong to labour; that there be no decay, * no leading into captivity, and no complaining in our streets.

15 Happy are the people that are in such a case; * yea, blessed are the people who have the LORD for their God.

Psalm 145. *Exaltabo te, Deus.*

I WILL magnify thee, O God, my King; * and I will praise thy Name for ever and ever.

2 Every day will I give thanks unto thee; * and praise thy Name for ever and ever.

3 Great is the LORD, and marvellous worthy to be praised; * there is no end of his greatness.

4 One generation shall praise thy works unto another, * and declare thy power.

5 As for me, I will be talking of thy worship, * thy glory, thy praise, and wondrous works;

6 So that men shall speak of the might of thy marvellous acts; * and I will also tell of thy greatness.

7 The memorial of thine abundant kindness shall be showed; * and men shall sing of thy righteousness.

8 The LORD is gracious and merciful; * long-suffering, and of great goodness.

9 The LORD is loving unto every man; * and his mercy is over all his works.

10 All thy works praise thee, O LORD; * and thy saints give thanks unto thee.

11 They show the glory of thy kingdom, * and talk of thy power;

12 That thy power, thy glory, and mightiness of thy kingdom, * might be known unto men.

13 Thy kingdom is an everlasting kingdom, * and thy dominion endureth throughout all ages.

14 The LORD upholdeth all such as fall, * and lifteth up all those that are down.

15 The eyes of all wait upon thee, O Lord; * and thou givest them their meat in due season.

16 Thou openest thine hand, * and fillest all things living with plenteousness.

17 The LORD is righteous in all his ways, * and holy in all his works.

18 The LORD is nigh unto all them that call upon him; * yea, all such as call upon him faithfully.

19 He will fulfil the desire of them that fear him; * he also will hear their cry, and will help them.

20 The LORD preserveth all them that love him; * but scattereth abroad all the ungodly.

21 My mouth shall speak the praise of the LORD; * and let all flesh give thanks unto his holy Name for ever and ever.

Psalm 146. *Lauda, anima mea.*

PRAISE the LORD, O my soul: while I live, will I praise the LORD; * yea, as long as I have any being, I will sing praises unto my God.

2 O put not your trust in princes, nor in any child of man; * for there is no help in them.

3 For when the breath of man goeth forth, he shall turn again to his earth, * and then all his thoughts perish.

4 Blessed is he that hath the God of Jacob for his help, * and whose hope is in the LORD his God:

5 Who made heaven and earth, the sea, and all that therein is; * who keepeth his promise for ever;

6 Who helpeth them to right that suffer wrong; * who feedeth the hungry.

7 The LORD looseth men out of prison; * the LORD giveth sight to the blind.

8 The LORD helpeth them that are fallen; * the LORD careth for the righteous.

9 The LORD careth for the strangers; he defendeth the fatherless and widow: * as for the way of the ungodly, he turneth it upside down.

10 The LORD thy God, O Sion, shall be King for evermore, * and throughout all generations.

Evening Prayer.

Psalm 147. *Laudate Dominum.*

O PRAISE the LORD, for it is a good thing to sing praises unto our God; * yea, a joyful and pleasant thing it is to be thankful.

2 The LORD doth build up Jerusalem, * and gather together the outcasts of Israel.

3 He healeth those that are broken in heart, * and giveth medicine to heal their sickness.

4 He telleth the number of the stars, * and calleth them all by their names.

5 Great is our Lord, and great is his power; * yea, and his wisdom is infinite.

6 The LORD setteth up the meek, * and bringeth the ungodly down to the ground.

7 O sing unto the LORD with thanksgiving; * sing praises upon the harp unto our God:

8 Who covereth the heaven with clouds, and prepareth rain for the earth; * and maketh the grass to grow upon the mountains, and herb for the use of men;

9 Who giveth fodder unto the cattle, * and feedeth the young ravens that call upon him.

10 He hath no pleasure in the strength of an horse; * neither delighteth he in any man's legs.

11 But the LORD'S delight is in them that fear him, * and put their trust in his mercy.

12 Praise the LORD, O Jerusalem; * praise thy God, O Sion.

13 For he hath made fast the bars of thy gates, * and hath blessed thy children within thee.

14 He maketh peace in thy borders, * and filleth thee with the flour of wheat.

15 He sendeth forth his commandment upon earth, * and his word runneth very swiftly.

16 He giveth snow like wool, * and scattereth the hoarfrost like ashes.

17 He casteth forth his ice like morsels: * who is able to abide his frost?

18 He sendeth out his word, and melteth them: * he bloweth with his wind, and the waters flow.

19 He showeth his word unto Jacob, * his statutes and ordinances unto Israel.

20 He hath not dealt so with any nation; * neither have the heathen knowledge of his laws.

Psalm 148. *Laudate Dominum*.

O PRAISE the LORD from the heavens: * praise him in the heights.

2 Praise him, all ye angels of his: * praise him, all his host.

3 Praise him, sun and moon: * praise him, all ye stars and light.

4 Praise him, all ye heavens, * and ye waters that are above the heavens.

5 Let them praise the Name of the LORD: * for he spake the word, and they were made; he commanded, and they were created.

6 He hath made them fast for ever and ever: * he hath given them a law which shall not be broken.

7 Praise the LORD from the earth, * ye dragons and all deeps;

8 Fire and hail, snow and vapours, * wind and storm, fulfilling his word;

9 Mountains and all hills; * fruitful trees and all cedars;

10 Beasts and all cattle; * creeping things and flying fowls;

11 Kings of the earth, and all peoples; * princes, and all judges of the world;

12 Young men and maidens, old men and children, praise the Name of the LORD: * for his Name only is excellent, and his praise above heaven and earth.

13 He shall exalt the horn of his people: all his saints shall praise him; * even the children of Israel, even the people that serveth him.

Psalm 149. *Cantate Domino.*

O SING unto the LORD a new song; * let the congregation of saints praise him.

2 Let Israel rejoice in him that made him, * and let the children of Sion be joyful in their King.

3 Let them praise his Name in the dance: * let them sing praises unto him with tabret and harp.

4 For the LORD hath pleasure in his people, * and helpeth the meek-hearted.

5 Let the saints be joyful with glory; * let them rejoice in their beds.

6 Let the praises of God be in their mouth; * and a two-edged sword in their hands;

7 To be avenged of the nations, * and to rebuke the peoples;

8 To bind their kings in chains, * and their nobles with links of iron;

9 To execute judgment upon them; as it is written, * Such honour have all his saints.

Psalm 150. *Laudate Dominum.*

O PRAISE God in his sanctuary: * praise him in the firmament of his power.

2 Praise him in his noble acts: * praise him according to his excellent greatness.

3 Praise him in the sound of the trumpet: * praise him upon the lute and harp.

4 Praise him in the timbrels and dances: * praise him upon the strings and pipe.

5 Praise him upon the well-tuned cymbals: * praise him upon the loud cymbals.

6 Let every thing that hath breath * praise the LORD.

The End of the Psalter.

The Ordinal

being the

Form of Making, Ordaining, and Consecrating

Bishops, Priests, and Deacons

together with

The Form of Consecration of a Church

An Office of Institution of Ministers

The Form and Manner of
Making, Ordaining, and Consecrating
Bishops, Priests, and Deacons
according to the
Order of the Protestant Episcopal Church
in the United States of America,
as established by the Bishops, the Clergy, and Laity
of said Church, in General Convention,
September, A. D. 1792.

THE PREFACE.

IT is evident unto all men, diligently reading Holy Scripture and ancient Authors, that from the Apostles' time there have been these Orders of Ministers in Christ's Church,—Bishops, Priests, and Deacons. Which Offices were evermore had in such reverend estimation, that no man might presume to execute any of them, except he were first called, tried, examined, and known to have such qualities as are requisite for the same; and also by public Prayer, with Imposition of Hands, were approved and admitted thereunto by lawful Authority. And therefore, to the intent that these Orders may be continued, and reverently used and esteemed in this Church, no man shall be accounted or taken to be a lawful Bishop, Priest, or Deacon, in this Church, or suffered to execute any of the said Functions, except he be called, tried, examined, and admitted thereunto, according to the Form hereafter following, or hath had Episcopal Consecration or Ordination.

And none shall be admitted a Deacon, Priest, or Bishop, except he be of the age which the Canon in that case provided may require.

And the Bishop, knowing either by himself, or by sufficient testimony, any Person to be a man of virtuous conversation, and without crime; and, after examination and trial, finding him sufficiently instructed in the Holy Scripture, and otherwise learned as the Canons require, may, at the times appointed, or else, on urgent occasion, upon some other day, in the face of the Church, admit him a Deacon, in such manner and form as followeth.

529

The Form and Manner of Making Deacons

¶ *When the day appointed by the Bishop is come, there shall be a Sermon, or Exhortation, declaring the Duty and Office of such as come to be admitted Deacons; how necessary that Order is in the Church of Christ, and also, how the People ought to esteem them in their Office.*

¶ *The Sermon being ended, a Priest shall present unto the Bishop, sitting in his chair near to the Holy Table, such as desire to be ordained Deacons, each of them being decently habited, saying these words,*

REVEREND Father in God, I present unto you these persons present, to be admitted Deacons.

¶ *The Bishop.*

TAKE heed that the persons, whom ye present unto us, be apt and meet, for their learning and godly conversation, to exercise their Ministry duly, to the honour of God, and the edifying of his Church.

¶ *The Priest shall answer,*

I HAVE inquired concerning them, and also examined them, and think them so to be.

¶ *Then the Bishop shall say unto the People,*

BRETHREN, if there be any of you who knoweth any Impediment, or notable Crime, in any of these persons presented to be ordered Deacons, for the which he ought not to be admitted to that Office, let him come forth in the Name of God, and show what the Crime or Impediment is.

¶ *And if any great Crime or Impediment be objected, the Bishop shall cease from Ordering that person, until such time as the party accused shall be found clear of that Crime.*

¶ *Then the Bishop (commending such as shall be found meet to be Ordered, to the Prayers of the congregation) shall, with the Clergy and People present, say the Litany.*

The Ordering of Deacons

¶ *And* NOTE, *That after the Suffrage*, That it may please thee to **illuminate** all Bishops, *etc., shall be said the following Suffrage:*

THAT it may please thee to bless these thy servants, now to be admitted to the Order of Deacons, and to pour thy grace upon them; that they may duly execute their Office, to the edifying of thy Church, and the glory of thy holy Name;

¶ *And* NOTE *further, That in the discretion of the Bishop, instead of the Litany appointed, may be said the Litany for Ordinations.*

¶ *Then shall be said the Service for the Communion, with the Collect, Epistle, and Gospel, as followeth.*

The Collect.

ALMIGHTY God, who by thy divine providence hast appointed divers Orders of Ministers in thy Church, and didst inspire thine Apostles to choose into the Order of Deacons the first Martyr Saint Stephen, with others; Mercifully behold these thy servants now called to the like Office and Administration: so replenish them with the truth of thy Doctrine, and adorn them with innocency of life, that, both by word and good example, they may faithfully serve thee in this Office, to the glory of thy Name, and the edification of thy Church; through the merits of our Saviour Jesus Christ, who liveth and reigneth with thee and the Holy Ghost, now and for ever. *Amen.*

The Epistle. i Timothy iii. 8.

LIKEWISE must the deacons be grave, not doubletongued, not given to much wine, not greedy of filthy lucre; holding the mystery of the faith in a pure conscience. And let these also first be proved; then let them use the office of a deacon, being found blameless. Even so must their wives be grave, not slanderers, sober, faithful in all things. Let the deacons be the husbands of one wife, ruling their

The Ordering of Deacons

children and their own houses well. For they that have used the office of a deacon well purchase to themselves a good degree, and great boldness in the faith which is in Christ Jesus.

¶ *Or else.*

The Epistle. Acts vi. 2.

THEN the twelve called the multitude of the disciples unto them, and said, It is not reason that we should leave the word of God, and serve tables. Wherefore, brethren, look ye out among you seven men of honest report, full of the Holy Ghost and wisdom, whom we may appoint over this business. But we will give ourselves continually to prayer, and to the ministry of the word. And the saying pleased the whole multitude: and they chose Stephen, a man full of faith and of the Holy Ghost, and Philip, and Prochorus, and Nicanor, and Timon, and Parmenas, and Nicolas a proselyte of Antioch: whom they set before the apostles: and when they had prayed, they laid their hands on them. And the word of God increased; and the number of the disciples multiplied in Jerusalem greatly; and a great company of the priests were obedient to the faith.

¶ *Then, the People being seated, the Bishop shall examine every one of those who are to be Ordered, in the presence of the People, after this manner following.*

DO you trust that you are inwardly moved by the Holy Ghost to take upon you this Office and Ministration, to serve God for the promoting of his glory, and the edifying of his people?

Answer. I trust so.

Bishop. Do you think that you are truly called, according to the will of our Lord Jesus Christ, and according to the Canons of this Church, to the Ministry of the same?

Answer. I think so.

The Ordering of Deacons

Bishop. Are you persuaded that the Holy Scriptures contain all Doctrine required as necessary for eternal salvation through faith in Jesus Christ?

Answer. I am so persuaded.

Bishop. Will you diligently read the same unto the people assembled in the Church where you shall be appointed to serve?

Answer. I will.

Bishop. It appertaineth to the Office of a Deacon, in the Church where he shall be appointed to serve, to assist the Priest in Divine Service, and specially when he ministereth the Holy Communion, and to help him in the distribution thereof; and to read Holy Scriptures and Homilies in the Church; and to instruct the youth in the Catechism; in the absence of the Priest to baptize infants; and to preach, if he be admitted thereto by the Bishop. And furthermore, it is his Office, where provision is so made, to search for the sick, poor, and impotent people of the Parish, that they may be relieved with the alms of the Parishioners, or others. Will you do this gladly and willingly?

Answer. I will so do, by the help of God.

Bishop. Will you apply all your diligence to frame and fashion your own lives, and the lives of your families, according to the Doctrine of Christ; and to make both yourselves and them, as much as in you lieth, wholesome examples of the flock of Christ?

Answer. I will so do, the Lord being my helper.

Bishop. Will you reverently obey your Bishop, and other chief Ministers, who, according to the Canons of the Church, may have the charge and government over you; following with a glad mind and will their godly admonitions?

Answer. I will endeavour so to do, the Lord being my helper.

533

The Ordering of Deacons

¶ *Then, the People standing, the Bishop shall lay his Hands severally upon the Head of every one to be made Deacon, humbly kneeling before him, and shall say,*

TAKE thou Authority to execute the Office of a Deacon in the Church of God committed unto thee; In the Name of the Father, and of the Son, and of the Holy Ghost. Amen.

¶ *Then shall the Bishop deliver to every one of them the New Testament, saying,*

TAKE thou Authority to read the Gospel in the Church of God, and to preach the same, if thou be thereto licensed by the Bishop himself.

¶ *Then one of them, appointed by the Bishop, shall read the Gospel.*

The Gospel. St. Luke xii. 35.

LET your loins be girded about, and your lights burning; and ye yourselves like unto men that wait for their lord, when he will return from the wedding; that when he cometh and knocketh, they may open unto him immediately. Blessed are those servants, whom the lord when he cometh shall find watching: verily I say unto you, that he shall gird himself, and make them to sit down to meat, and will come forth and serve them. And if he shall come in the second watch, or come in the third watch, and find them so, blessed are those servants.

¶ *Then shall the Bishop proceed in the Communion; and all who are Ordered shall tarry, and receive the Holy Communion the same day, with the Bishop.*
¶ *The Communion ended, after the last Collect, and immediately before the Benediction, shall be said this Collect following.*

ALMIGHTY God, giver of all good things, who of thy great goodness hast vouchsafed to accept and take

The Ordering of Deacons

these thy servants unto the Office of Deacons in thy Church; Make them, we beseech thee, O Lord, to be modest, humble, and constant in their Ministration, to have a ready will to observe all spiritual Discipline; that they, having always the testimony of a good conscience, and continuing ever stable and strong in thy Son Christ, may so well behave themselves in this inferior Office, that they may be found worthy to be called unto the higher Ministries in thy Church; through the same thy Son our Saviour Jesus Christ, to whom be glory and honour, world without end. *Amen.*

THE Peace of God, which passeth all understanding, keep your hearts and minds in the knowledge and love of God, and of his Son Jesus Christ our Lord: And the Blessing of God Almighty, the Father, the Son, and the Holy Ghost, be amongst you, and remain with you always. *Amen.*

¶ *And here it must be declared unto the Deacon, that he must continue in that Office of a Deacon the space of a whole year, (except for reasonable causes it shall otherwise seem good unto the Bishop,) to the intent he may be perfect and well expert in the things appertaining to the Ecclesiastical Administration. In executing whereof if he be found faithful and diligent, he may be admitted by his Diocesan to the Order of Priesthood, at the times appointed in the Canon; or else, on urgent occasion, upon some other day, in the face of the Church, in such manner and form as hereafter followeth.*

The Form and Manner of
Ordering Priests

¶ *When the day appointed by the Bishop is come, there shall be a Sermon, or Exhortation, declaring the Duty and Office of such as come to be admitted Priests; how necessary that Order is in the Church of Christ, and also, how the People ought to esteem them in their Office.*

¶ *A Priest shall present unto the Bishop, sitting in his chair near to the Holy Table, all those who are to receive the Order of Priesthood that day, each of them being decently habited, and shall say,*

REVEREND Father in God, I present unto you these persons present, to be admitted to the Order of Priesthood.

¶ *The Bishop.*

TAKE heed that the persons, whom ye present unto us, be apt and meet, for their learning and godly conversation, to exercise their Ministry duly, to the honour of God, and the edifying of his Church.

¶ *The Priest shall answer,*

I HAVE inquired concerning them, and also examined them, and think them so to be.

¶ *Then the Bishop shall say unto the People,*

GOOD People, these are they whom we purpose, God willing, to receive this day unto the holy Office of Priesthood; for, after due examination, we find not to the contrary, but that they are lawfully called to their Function and Ministry, and that they are persons meet for the same. But yet, if there be any of you who knoweth any Impediment, or notable Crime, in any of them, for the which he ought not to be received into this holy Ministry, let him come forth in the Name of God, and show what the Crime or Impediment is.

536

The Ordering of Priests

¶ *And if any great Crime or Impediment be objected, the Bishop shall cease from Ordering that person, until such time as the party accused shall be found clear of that Crime.*

¶ *Then the Bishop (commending such as shall be found meet to be Ordered, to the Prayers of the congregation) shall, with the Clergy and People present, say the Litany.*

¶ *And* NOTE, *That after the Suffrage,* That it may please thee to illuminate all Bishops, *etc., shall be said the following Suffrage:*

THAT it may please thee to bless these thy servants, now to be admitted to the Order of Priests, and to pour thy grace upon them; that they may duly exercise their Office, to the edifying of thy Church, and the glory of thy holy Name;

¶ *And* NOTE *further, That in the discretion of the Bishop, instead of the Litany appointed, may be said the Litany for Ordinations.*

¶ *Then shall be said the Service for the Communion, with the Collect, Epistle, and Gospel, as followeth.*

The Collect.

ALMIGHTY God, giver of all good things, who by thy Holy Spirit hast appointed divers Orders of Ministers in thy Church; Mercifully behold these thy servants now called to the Office of Priesthood; and so replenish them with the truth of thy Doctrine, and adorn them with innocency of life, that, both by word and good example, they may faithfully serve thee in this Office, to the glory of thy Name, and the edification of thy Church; through the merits of our Saviour Jesus Christ, who liveth and reigneth with thee and the same Holy Spirit, world without end. *Amen.*

The Epistle. Ephesians iv. 7.

UNTO every one of us is given grace according to the measure of the gift of Christ. Wherefore he saith, When he ascended up on high, he led captivity captive, and gave gifts unto men. (Now that he ascended, what is it but that he also descended first into the lower parts of the earth? He that descended is the same also that ascended up far above all heavens, that he might fill all things.) And he gave some, apostles; and some, prophets; and some, evangelists; and some, pastors and teachers; for the perfecting of the saints, for the work of the ministry, for the edifying of the body of Christ: till we all come in the unity of the faith, and of the knowledge of the Son of God, unto a perfect man, unto the measure of the stature of the fulness of Christ.

The Gospel. St. Matthew ix. 36.

WHEN Jesus saw the multitudes, he was moved with compassion on them, because they fainted, and were scattered abroad as sheep having no shepherd. Then saith he unto his disciples, The harvest truly is plenteous, but the labourers are few; pray ye therefore the Lord of the harvest, that he will send forth labourers into his harvest.

¶ *Or else.*

The Gospel. St. John x. 1.

VERILY, verily, I say unto you, He that entereth not by the door into the sheepfold, but climbeth up some other way, the same is a thief and a robber. But he that entereth in by the door is the shepherd of the sheep. To him the porter openeth; and the sheep hear his voice: and he calleth his own sheep by name, and leadeth them out. And when he putteth forth his own sheep, he goeth before them, and the sheep follow him: for they know his voice. And a stranger will they not follow, but will flee from him: for they know not the voice of strangers. This parable spake Jesus unto them: but they understood not

The Ordering of Priests

what things they were which he spake unto them. Then said Jesus unto them again, Verily, verily, I say unto you, I am the door of the sheep. All that ever came before me are thieves and robbers: but the sheep did not hear them. I am the door: by me if any man enter in, he shall be saved, and shall go in and out, and find pasture. The thief cometh not, but for to steal, and to kill, and to destroy: I am come that they might have life, and that they might have it more abundantly. I am the good shepherd: the good shepherd giveth his life for the sheep. But he that is an hireling, and not the shepherd, whose own the sheep are not, seeth the wolf coming, and leaveth the sheep, and fleeth: and the wolf catcheth them, and scattereth the sheep. The hireling fleeth, because he is an hireling, and careth not for the sheep. I am the good shepherd; and know my sheep, and am known of mine, even as the Father knoweth me, and I know the Father; and I lay down my life for the sheep. And other sheep I have, which are not of this fold: them also I must bring, and they shall hear my voice; and there shall be one flock, and one shepherd.

¶ *Then, the People being seated, the Bishop shall say unto those who are to be ordained Priests as followeth.*

YE have heard, Brethren, as well in your private examination, as in the exhortation which was now made to you, and in the holy Lessons taken out of the Gospel, and the writings of the Apostles, of what dignity, and of how great importance this Office is, whereunto ye are called. And now again we exhort you, in the Name of our Lord Jesus Christ, that ye have in remembrance, into how high a Dignity, and to how weighty an Office and Charge ye are called: that is to say, to be Messengers, Watchmen, and Stewards of the Lord; to teach, and to premonish, to feed and provide for the Lord's family; to seek for Christ's sheep

539

that are dispersed abroad, and for his children who are in the midst of this naughty world, that they may be saved through Christ for ever.

Have always therefore printed in your remembrance, how great a treasure is committed to your charge. For they are the sheep of Christ, which he bought with his death, and for whom he shed his blood. The Church and Congregation whom you must serve, is his Spouse, and his Body. And if it shall happen that the same Church, or any Member thereof, do take any hurt or hindrance by reason of your negligence, ye know the greatness of the fault, and also the horrible punishment that will ensue. Wherefore consider with yourselves the end of the Ministry towards the children of God, towards the Spouse and Body of Christ; and see that ye never cease your labour, your care and diligence, until ye have done all that lieth in you, according to your bounden duty, to bring all such as are or shall be committed to your charge, unto that agreement in the faith and knowledge of God, and to that ripeness and perfectness of age in Christ, that there be no place left among you, either for error in religion, or for viciousness in life.

Forasmuch then as your Office is both of so great excellency, and of so great difficulty, ye see with how great care and study ye ought to apply yourselves, as well to show yourselves dutiful and thankful unto that Lord, who hath placed you in so high a dignity; as also to beware that neither you yourselves offend, nor be occasion that others offend. Howbeit, ye cannot have a mind and will thereto of yourselves; for that will and ability is given of God alone: therefore ye ought, and have need, to pray earnestly for his Holy Spirit. And seeing that ye cannot by any other means compass the doing of so weighty a work, pertaining to the salvation of man, but with doctrine and exhortation

The Ordering of Priests

taken out of the Holy Scriptures, and with a life agreeable
to the same; consider how studious ye ought to be in reading and learning the Scriptures, and in framing the manners
both of yourselves, and of them that specially pertain unto
you, according to the rule of the same Scriptures; and for
this self-same cause, how ye ought to forsake and set aside,
as much as ye may, all worldly cares and studies.

We have good hope that ye have well weighed these
things with yourselves, long before this time; and that ye
have clearly determined, by God's grace, to give yourselves
wholly to this Office, whereunto it hath pleased God to call
you: so that, as much as lieth in you, ye will apply yourselves wholly to this one thing, and draw all your cares and
studies this way; and that ye will continually pray to God
the Father, by the mediation of our only Saviour Jesus
Christ, for the heavenly assistance of the Holy Ghost; that,
by daily reading and weighing the Scriptures, ye may wax
riper and stronger in your Ministry; and that ye may so endeavour yourselves, from time to time, to sanctify the lives
of you and yours, and to fashion them after the Rule and
Doctrine of Christ, that ye may be wholesome and godly
examples and patterns for the people to follow.

And now, that this present Congregation of Christ may
also understand your minds and wills in these things, and
that this your promise may the more move you to do your
duties; ye shall answer plainly to these things, which we,
in the Name of God, and of his Church, shall demand of
you touching the same.

D O you think in your heart, that you are truly called,
according to the will of our Lord Jesus Christ, and
according to the Canons of this Church, to the Order and
Ministry of Priesthood?

Answer. I think it.

The Ordering of Priests

Bishop. Are you persuaded that the Holy Scriptures contain all Doctrine required as necessary for eternal salvation through faith in Jesus Christ? And are you determined, out of the said Scriptures to instruct the people committed to your charge; and to teach nothing, as necessary to eternal salvation, but that which you shall be persuaded may be concluded and proved by the Scripture?

Answer. I am so persuaded, and have so determined, by God's grace.

Bishop. Will you then give your faithful diligence always so to minister the Doctrine and Sacraments, and the Discipline of Christ, as the Lord hath commanded, and as this Church hath received the same, according to the Commandments of God; so that you may teach the people committed to your Cure and Charge with all diligence to keep and observe the same?

Answer. I will so do, by the help of the Lord.

Bishop. Will you be ready, with all faithful diligence, to banish and drive away from the Church all erroneous and strange doctrines contrary to God's Word; and to use both public and private monitions and exhortations, as well to the sick as to the whole, within your Cures, as need shall require, and occasion shall be given?

Answer. I will, the Lord being my helper.

Bishop. Will you be diligent in Prayers, and in reading the Holy Scriptures, and in such studies as help to the knowledge of the same, laying aside the study of the world and the flesh?

Answer. I will endeavour so to do, the Lord being my helper.

Bishop. Will you be diligent to frame and fashion your own selves, and your families, according to the Doctrine of Christ; and to make both yourselves and them, as much

The Ordering of Priests

as in you lieth, wholesome examples and patterns to the flock of Christ?

Answer. I will apply myself thereto, the Lord being my helper.

Bishop. Will you maintain and set forwards, as much as lieth in you, quietness, peace, and love, among all Christian people, and especially among them that are or shall be committed to your charge?

Answer. I will so do, the Lord being my helper.

Bishop. Will you reverently obey your Bishop, and other chief Ministers, who, according to the Canons of the Church, may have the charge and government over you; following with a glad mind and will their godly admonitions, and submitting yourselves to their godly judgments?

Answer. I will so do, the Lord being my helper.

¶ *Then, all standing, shall the Bishop say,*

ALMIGHTY God, who hath given you this will to do all these things; Grant also unto you strength and power to perform the same, that he may accomplish his work which he hath begun in you; through Jesus Christ our Lord. *Amen.*

¶ *After this, the Congregation shall be desired, secretly in their Prayers, to make their humble supplications to God for all these things; for the which Prayers there shall be silence kept for a space.*

¶ *After which, the Persons to be ordained Priests kneeling, and others standing, the Bishop shall sing or say the Veni, Creator Spiritus; the Bishop beginning, and the Priests, and others that are present, answering by verses, as followeth.*

Veni, Creator Spiritus.

COME, Holy Ghost, our souls inspire,
  And lighten with celestial fire.
Thou the anointing Spirit art,
  Who dost thy sevenfold gifts impart.

The Ordering of Priests

Thy blessed unction from above,
Is comfort, life, and fire of love.
Enable with perpetual light
The dulness of our blinded sight.

Anoint and cheer our soiled face
With the abundance of thy grace.
Keep far our foes, give peace at home;
Where thou art guide, no ill can come.

Teach us to know the Father, Son,
And thee, of both, to be but One;
That, through the ages all along,
This may be our endless song:
    Praise to thy eternal merit,
    Father, Son, and Holy Spirit.

¶ *Or this.*

COME, Holy Ghost, Creator blest,
    Vouchsafe within our souls to rest;
Come with thy grace and heavenly aid,
And fill the hearts which thou hast made.

To thee, the Comforter, we cry;
To thee, the Gift of God most high;
The Fount of life, the Fire of love,
The soul's Anointing from above.

The sevenfold gifts of grace are thine,
O Finger of the Hand Divine;
True Promise of the Father thou,
Who dost the tongue with speech endow.

The Ordering of Priests

Thy light to every sense impart,
And shed thy love in every heart;
Thine own unfailing might supply
To strengthen our infirmity.

Drive far away our ghostly foe,
And thine abiding peace bestow;
If thou be our preventing Guide,
No evil can our steps betide.

¶ *That done, the Bishop shall pray in this wise, and say,*

Let us pray.

ALMIGHTY God, and heavenly Father, who, of thine infinite love and goodness towards us, hast given to us thy only and most dearly beloved Son Jesus Christ, to be our Redeemer, and the Author of everlasting life; who, after he had made perfect our redemption by his death, and was ascended into heaven, sent abroad into the world his Apostles, Prophets, Evangelists, Doctors, and Pastors; by whose labour and ministry he gathered together a great flock in all the parts of the world, to set forth the eternal praise of thy holy Name: For these so great benefits of thy eternal goodness, and for that thou hast vouchsafed to call these thy servants here present to the same Office and Ministry, appointed for the salvation of mankind, we render unto thee most hearty thanks, we praise and worship thee; and we humbly beseech thee, by the same thy blessed Son, to grant unto all, which either here or elsewhere call upon thy holy Name, that we may continue to show ourselves thankful unto thee for these and all thy other benefits; and that we may daily increase and go forwards in the knowledge and faith of thee and thy Son, by the Holy Spirit. So that as well by these thy Ministers, as by them over whom they shall be appointed thy Ministers, thy holy Name may

The Ordering of Priests

be for ever glorified, and thy blessed kingdom enlarged; through the same thy Son Jesus Christ our Lord, who liveth and reigneth with thee in the unity of the same Holy Spirit, world without end. *Amen.*

¶ *When this Prayer is done, the Bishop with the Priests present, shall lay their Hands severally upon the Head of every one that receiveth the Order of Priesthood; the Receivers humbly kneeling, and the Bishop saying,*

RECEIVE the Holy Ghost for the Office and Work of a Priest in the Church of God, now committed unto thee by the Imposition of our hands. Whose sins thou dost forgive, they are forgiven; and whose sins thou dost retain, they are retained. And be thou a faithful Dispenser of the Word of God, and of his holy Sacraments; In the Name of the Father, and of the Son, and of the Holy Ghost. Amen.

¶ *Or this.*

TAKE thou Authority to execute the Office of a Priest in the Church of God, now committed to thee by the Imposition of our hands. And be thou a faithful Dispenser of the Word of God, and of his holy Sacraments; In the Name of the Father, and of the Son, and of the Holy Ghost. Amen.

¶ *Then the Bishop shall deliver to every one of them kneeling, the Bible into his hand, saying,*

TAKE thou Authority to preach the Word of God, and to minister the holy Sacraments in the Congregation, where thou shalt be lawfully appointed thereunto.

¶ *When this is done, the Nicene Creed shall be said, and the Bishop shall go on in the Service of the Communion, which all they who receive Orders shall take together, and remain in the same place where Hands were laid upon them, until such time as they have received the Communion.*

The Ordering of Priests

¶ *The Communion being done, after the last Collect, and immediately before the Benediction, shall be said this Collect.*

MOST merciful Father, we beseech thee to send upon these thy servants thy heavenly blessing; that they may be clothed with righteousness, and that thy Word spoken by their mouths may have such success, that it may never be spoken in vain. Grant also, that we may have grace to hear and receive what they shall deliver out of thy most holy Word, or agreeable to the same, as the means of our salvation; that in all our words and deeds we may seek thy glory, and the increase of thy kingdom; through Jesus Christ our Lord. *Amen.*

THE Peace of God, which passeth all understanding, keep your hearts and minds in the knowledge and love of God, and of his Son Jesus Christ our Lord: And the Blessing of God Almighty, the Father, the Son, and the Holy Ghost, be amongst you, and remain with you always. *Amen.*

¶ *And if, on the same day, the Order of Deacons be given to some, and the Order of Priesthood to others; the Deacons shall be first presented, and then the Priests; and it shall suffice that the Litany be once said for both. The Epistle shall be Ephesians iv. 7 to 13, as before in this Office. Immediately after which, they that are to be made Deacons, shall be examined and Ordained, as is above prescribed. Then one of them having read the Gospel, (which shall be either Saint Matthew ix. 36 to 38, as before in this Office; or else Saint Luke xii. 35 to 38, as before in the Form for the Ordering of Deacons,) they that are to be made Priests shall likewise be examined and Ordained, as is in this Office before appointed. The Collect shall be as followeth.*

The Collect.

ALMIGHTY God, giver of all good things, who by thy Holy Spirit hast appointed divers Orders of Ministers in thy Church; Mercifully behold these thy servants now called to the Office of Deacon and these thy servants now called to the Office of Priest; and so replenish them with the truth of thy Doctrine, and adorn them with innocency of life, that, both by word and good example, they may faithfully serve thee in their Ministry, to the glory of thyName, and the edification of thy Church; through the merits of our Saviour Jesus Christ, who liveth and reigneth with thee and the same Holy Spirit, world without end. *Amen.*

The Form of Ordaining or Consecrating a Bishop

¶ *When all things are duly prepared in the Church, and set in order, the Presiding Bishop, or some other Bishop appointed by the Bishops present, shall begin the Communion Service, in which this shall be*

The Collect.

ALMIGHTY God, who by thy Son Jesus Christ didst give to thy holy Apostles many excellent gifts, and didst charge them to feed thy flock; Give grace, we beseech thee, to all Bishops, the Pastors of thy Church, that they may diligently preach thy Word, and duly administer the godly Discipline thereof; and grant to the people, that they may obediently follow the same; that all may receive the crown of everlasting glory; through the same thy Son Jesus Christ our Lord. *Amen.*

¶ *And another Bishop shall read the Epistle.*

The Epistle. 1 Timothy iii. 1.

THIS is a true saying, If a man desire the office of a bishop, he desireth a good work. A bishop then must be blameless, the husband of one wife, vigilant, sober, of good behaviour, given to hospitality, apt to teach; not given to wine, no striker, not greedy of filthy lucre; but patient, not a brawler, not covetous; one that ruleth well his own house, having his children in subjection with all gravity; (for if a man know not how to rule his own house, how shall he take care of the church of God?) not a novice, lest being lifted up with pride he fall into the condemnation of the devil. Moreover he must have a good report of them which are without; lest he fall into reproach and the snare of the devil.

549

The Consecrating of Bishops

¶ *Or this.*

For the Epistle. Acts xx. 17.

FROM Miletus Paul sent to Ephesus, and called the elders of the church. And when they were come to him, he said unto them, Ye know, from the first day that I came into Asia, after what manner I have been with you at all seasons, serving the Lord with all humility of mind, and with many tears, and temptations, which befell me by the lying in wait of the Jews: and how I kept back nothing that was profitable unto you, but have shewed you, and have taught you publickly, and from house to house, testifying both to the Jews, and also to the Greeks, repentance toward God, and faith toward our Lord Jesus Christ. And now, behold, I go bound in the spirit unto Jerusalem, not knowing the things that shall befall me there: save that the Holy Ghost witnesseth in every city, saying that bonds and afflictions abide me. But none of these things move me, neither count I my life dear unto myself, so that I might finish my course with joy, and the ministry, which I have received of the Lord Jesus, to testify the gospel of the grace of God. And now, behold, I know that ye all, among whom I have gone preaching the kingdom of God, shall see my face no more. Wherefore I take you to record this day, that I am pure from the blood of all men. For I have not shunned to declare unto you all the counsel of God. Take heed therefore unto yourselves, and to all the flock, over the which the Holy Ghost hath made you overseers, to feed the church of God, which he hath purchased with his own blood. For I know this, that after my departing shall grievous wolves enter in among you, not sparing the flock. Also of your own selves shall men arise, speaking perverse things, to draw away disciples after them. Therefore watch, and remember, that by the space of three years I ceased not to warn every

The Consecrating of Bishops

one night and day with tears. And now, brethren, I commend you to God, and to the word of his grace, which is able to build you up, and to give you an inheritance among all them which are sanctified. I have coveted no man's silver, or gold, or apparel. Yea, ye yourselves know, that these hands have ministered unto my necessities, and to them that were with me. I have shewed you all things, how that so labouring ye ought to support the weak, and to remember the words of the Lord Jesus, how he said, It is more blessed to give than to receive.

¶ *Then another Bishop shall read the Gospel.*

The Gospel. St. John xxi. 15.

JESUS saith to Simon Peter, Simon, son of Jonas, lovest thou me more than these? He saith unto him, Yea, Lord; thou knowest that I love thee. He saith unto him, Feed my lambs. He saith to him again the second time, Simon, son of Jonas, lovest thou me? He saith unto him, Yea, Lord; thou knowest that I love thee. He saith unto him, Feed my sheep. He saith unto him the third time, Simon, son of Jonas, lovest thou me? Peter was grieved because he said unto him the third time, Lovest thou me? And he said unto him, Lord, thou knowest all things; thou knowest that I love thee. Jesus saith unto him, Feed my sheep.

¶ *Or this.*

The Gospel. St. John xx. 19.

THE same day at evening, being the first day of the week, when the doors were shut where the disciples were assembled for fear of the Jews, came Jesus, and stood in the midst, and saith unto them, Peace be unto you. And when he had so said, he shewed unto them his hands and his side. Then were the disciples glad, when they saw the Lord. Then saith Jesus to them again, Peace be unto you:

The Consecrating of Bishops

as my Father hath sent me, even so send I you. And when he had said this, he breathed on them, and saith unto them, Receive ye the Holy Ghost: whose soever sins ye remit, they are remitted unto them; and whose soever sins ye retain, they are retained.

¶ *Or this.*

The Gospel. St. Matthew xxviii. 18.

JESUS came and spake unto them, saying, All power is given unto me in heaven and in earth. Go ye therefore, and teach all nations, baptizing them in the name of the Father, and of the Son, and of the Holy Ghost: teaching them to observe all things whatsoever I have commanded you: and, lo, I am with you alway, even unto the end of the world.

¶ *Then shall follow the Nicene Creed, and after that the Sermon; which being ended, the Elected Bishop, vested with his Rochet, shall be presented by two Bishops of this Church unto the Presiding Bishop, or to the Bishop appointed, sitting in his chair, near the Holy Table; the Bishops who present him saying,*

REVEREND Father in God, we present unto you this godly and well-learned man, to be Ordained and Consecrated Bishop.

¶ *Then shall the Presiding Bishop demand Testimonials of the person presented for Consecration, and shall cause them to be read.*

¶ *He shall then require of him the following Promise of Conformity to the Doctrine, Discipline, and Worship of the Protestant Episcopal Church.*

IN the Name of God, Amen. I, *N.*, chosen Bishop of the Protestant Episcopal Church in *N.*, do promise conformity and obedience to the Doctrine, Discipline, and Worship of the Protestant Episcopal Church in the United States of America. So help me God, through Jesus Christ.

The Consecrating of Bishops

¶ *Then the Presiding Bishop shall move the Congregation present to pray, saying thus to them:*

BRETHREN, it is written in the Gospel of Saint Luke, that our Saviour Christ continued the whole night in prayer, before he chose and sent forth his twelve Apostles. It is written also, that the holy Apostles prayed before they ordained Matthias to be of the number of the Twelve. Let us, therefore, following the example of our Saviour Christ, and his Apostles, offer up our prayers to Almighty God, before we admit and send forth this person presented unto us, to the work whereunto we trust the Holy Ghost hath called him.

¶ *And then shall be said the Litany; save only, that after this place,* That it may please thee to illuminate all Bishops, *etc., the proper Suffrage shall be,*

THAT it may please thee to bless this our Brother elected, and to send thy grace upon him, that he may duly execute the Office whereunto he is called, to the edifying of thy Church, and to the honour, praise, and glory of thy Name;

Answer. We beseech thee to hear us, good Lord.

¶ *And* NOTE, *That in the discretion of the Presiding Bishop, instead of the Litany, may be said the Litany for Ordinations.*

¶ *Then shall be said this Prayer following.*

ALMIGHTY God, giver of all good things, who by thy Holy Spirit hast appointed divers Orders of Ministers in thy Church; Mercifully behold this thy servant, now called to the Work and Ministry of a Bishop; and so replenish him with the truth of thy Doctrine, and adorn him with innocency of life, that, both by word and deed, he may faithfully serve thee in this Office, to the glory of thy Name, and the edifying and well-governing of thy Church;

The Consecrating of Bishops

through the merits of our Saviour Jesus Christ, who liveth and reigneth with thee and the same Holy Spirit, world without end. *Amen.*

¶ *Then, the People being seated, the Presiding Bishop, sitting in his chair, shall say to him that is to be Consecrated,*

BROTHER, forasmuch as the Holy Scripture and the ancient Canons command, that we should not be hasty in laying on hands, and admitting any person to Government in the Church of Christ, which he hath purchased with no less price than the effusion of his own blood; before we admit you to this Administration, we will examine you in certain Articles, to the end that the Congregation present may have a trial, and bear witness, how you are minded to behave yourself in the Church of God.

ARE you persuaded that you are truly called to this Ministration, according to the will of our Lord Jesus Christ, and the order of this Church?

Answer. I am so persuaded.

Bishop. Are you persuaded that the Holy Scriptures contain all Doctrine required as necessary for eternal salvation through faith in Jesus Christ? And are you determined out of the same Holy Scriptures to instruct the people committed to your charge; and to teach or maintain nothing, as necessary to eternal salvation, but that which you shall be persuaded may be concluded and proved by the same?

Answer. I am so persuaded, and determined, by God's grace.

Bishop. Will you then faithfully exercise yourself in the Holy Scriptures, and call upon God by prayer for the true understanding of the same; so that you may be able by them to teach and exhort with wholesome Doctrine, and to withstand and convince the gainsayers?

Answer. I will so do, by the help of God.

The Consecrating of Bishops

Bishop. Are you ready, with all faithful diligence, to banish and drive away from the Church all erroneous and strange doctrine contrary to God's Word; and both privately and openly to call upon and encourage others to the same?

Answer. I am ready, the Lord being my helper.

Bishop. Will you deny all ungodliness and worldly lusts, and live soberly, righteously, and godly in this present world; that you may show yourself in all things an example of good works unto others, that the adversary may be ashamed, having nothing to say against you?

Answer. I will so do, the Lord being my helper.

Bishop. Will you maintain and set forward, as much as shall lie in you, quietness, love, and peace among all men; and diligently exercise such discipline as by the authority of God's Word, and by the order of this Church, is committed to you?

Answer. I will so do, by the help of God.

Bishop. Will you be faithful in Ordaining, sending, or laying hands upon others?

Answer. I will so be, by the help of God.

Bishop. Will you show yourself gentle, and be merciful for Christ's sake to poor and needy people, and to all strangers destitute of help?

Answer. I will so show myself, by God's help.

¶ *Then, all standing, the Presiding Bishop shall say,*

ALMIGHTY God, our heavenly Father, who hath given you a good will to do all these things; Grant also unto you strength and power to perform the same; that, he accomplishing in you the good work which he hath begun, you may be found perfect and irreprehensible at the latter day; through Jesus Christ our Lord. *Amen.*

The Consecrating of Bishops

¶ Then shall the Bishop elect put on the rest of the Episcopal habit, and shall kneel down; and the Veni, Creator Spiritus shall be sung or said over him; the Presiding Bishop shall begin, and the Bishops, and the others that are present, standing, shall answer by verses, as followeth.

COME, Holy Ghost, our souls inspire,
And lighten with celestial fire.
Thou the anointing Spirit art,
Who dost thy sevenfold gifts impart.

Thy blessed unction from above,
Is comfort, life, and fire of love.
Enable with perpetual light
The dulness of our blinded sight.

Anoint and cheer our soiled face
With the abundance of thy grace.
Keep far our foes, give peace at home;
Where thou art guide, no ill can come.

Teach us to know the Father, Son,
And thee, of both, to be but One;
That, through the ages all along,
This may be our endless song:
    Praise to thy eternal merit,
    Father, Son, and Holy Spirit.

¶ Or this.

COME, Holy Ghost, Creator blest,
Vouchsafe within our souls to rest;
Come with thy grace and heavenly aid,
And fill the hearts which thou hast made.

To thee, the Comforter, we cry;
To thee, the gift of God most high;

The Consecrating of Bishops

The Fount of life, the Fire of love,
The soul's Anointing from above.

The sevenfold gifts of grace are thine,
O Finger of the Hand Divine;
True Promise of the Father thou,
Who dost the tongue with speech endow.

Thy light to every sense impart,
And shed thy love in every heart;
Thine own unfailing might supply
To strengthen our infirmity.

Drive far away our ghostly foe,
And thine abiding peace bestow;
If thou be our preventing Guide,
No evil can our steps betide.

¶ *That ended, the Presiding Bishop shall say,*

Lord, hear our prayer.
Answer. And let our cry come unto thee.

Let us pray.

ALMIGHTY God, and most merciful Father, who, of thine infinite goodness, hast given thy only and dearly beloved Son Jesus Christ, to be our Redeemer, and the Author of everlasting life; who, after that he had made perfect our redemption by his death, and was ascended into heaven, poured down his gifts abundantly upon men, making some Apostles, some Prophets, some Evangelists, some Pastors and Doctors, to the edifying and making perfect his Church; Grant, we beseech thee, to this thy servant, such grace, that he may evermore be ready to spread abroad thy Gospel, the glad tidings of reconciliation with thee; and

557

The Consecrating of Bishops

use the authority given him, not to destruction, but to salvation; not to hurt, but to help: so that, as a wise and faithful servant, giving to thy family their portion in due season, he may at last be received into everlasting joy; through the same Jesus Christ our Lord, who, with thee and the Holy Ghost, liveth and reigneth, one God, world without end. *Amen.*

¶ *Then the Presiding Bishop and Bishops present shall lay their hands upon the head of the Elected Bishop, kneeling before them, the Presiding Bishop saying,*

RECEIVE the Holy Ghost for the Office and Work of a Bishop in the Church of God, now committed unto thee by the Imposition of our hands; In the Name of the Father, and of the Son, and of the Holy Ghost. Amen. And remember that thou stir up the grace of God, which is given thee by this Imposition of our hands; for God hath not given us the spirit of fear, but of power, and love, and soberness.

¶ *Then the Presiding Bishop shall deliver him the Bible, saying,*

GIVE heed unto reading, exhortation, and doctrine. Think upon the things contained in this Book. Be diligent in them, that the increase coming thereby may be manifest unto all men; for by so doing thou shalt both save thyself and them that hear thee. Be to the flock of Christ a shepherd, not a wolf; feed them, devour them not. Hold up the weak, heal the sick, bind up the broken, bring again the outcasts, seek the lost. Be so merciful, that you be not too remiss; so minister discipline, that you forget not mercy; that when the Chief Shepherd shall appear, you may receive the never-fading crown of glory; through Jesus Christ our Lord. *Amen.*

The Consecrating of Bishops

¶ *Then the Presiding Bishop shall proceed in the Communion Service; with whom the newly consecrated Bishop, with others, shall also communicate.*
¶ *And immediately before the Benediction, shall be said this Prayer.*

MOST merciful Father, send down, we beseech thee, upon this thy servant thy heavenly blessing; and so endue him with thy Holy Spirit, that he, preaching thy Word, may not only be earnest to reprove, beseech, and rebuke, with all patience and doctrine; but also may be, to such as believe, a wholesome example in word, in conversation, in love, in faith, in chastity, and in purity; that, faithfully fulfilling his course, at the latter day he may receive the crown of righteousness, laid up by the Lord Jesus, the righteous Judge, who liveth and reigneth with thee and the same Holy Spirit, one God, world without end. *Amen.*

THE Peace of God, which passeth all understanding, keep your hearts and minds in the knowledge and love of God, and of his Son Jesus Christ our Lord: And the Blessing of God Almighty, the Father, the Son, and the Holy Ghost, be amongst you, and remain with you always. *Amen.*

The Litany and Suffrages for Ordinations

O GOD the Father,
Have mercy upon us.
O God the Son,
Have mercy upon us.
O God the Holy Ghost,
Have mercy upon us.
O holy Trinity, one God,
Have mercy upon us.

WE beseech thee to hear us, good Lord; and that it may please thee to grant peace to the whole world, and to thy Church;
We beseech thee to hear us, good Lord.

That it may please thee to sanctify and bless thy holy Church throughout the world;
We beseech thee to hear us, good Lord.

That it may please thee to inspire all Bishops, Priests, and Deacons, with love of thee and of thy truth;
We beseech thee to hear us, good Lord.

That it may please thee to endue all Ministers of thy Church with devotion to thy glory and to the salvation of souls;
We beseech thee to hear us, good Lord.

¶ *Here, at the Ordination of Deacons or of Priests shall be said,*

That it may please thee to bless these thy servants, now to be admitted to the Order of Deacons (*or* Priests), and to pour thy grace upon them; that they may duly execute their Office to the edifying of thy Church, and to the glory of thy holy Name;
We beseech thee to hear us, good Lord.

¶ *Here, at the Consecration of a Bishop shall be said,*

The Litany for Ordinations

That it may please thee to bless this our Brother elected, and to send thy grace upon him, that he may duly execute the Office whereunto he is called, to the edifying of thy Church, and to the honour, praise, and glory of thy Name;
We beseech thee to hear us, good Lord.

That it may please thee to guide by thy indwelling Spirit those whom thou dost call to the Ministry of thy Church; that they may go forward with courage, and persevere unto the end;
We beseech thee to hear us, good Lord.

That it may please thee to increase the number of the Ministers of thy Church, that the Gospel may be preached to all people;
We beseech thee to hear us, good Lord.

That it may please thee to hasten the fulfilment of thy purpose, that thy Church may be one;
We beseech thee to hear us, good Lord.

That it may please thee to grant that we, with all thy saints, may be partakers of thy everlasting kingdom;
We beseech thee to hear us, good Lord.

Lord, have mercy upon us.
Christ, have mercy upon us.
Lord, have mercy upon us.

OUR Father, who art in heaven, Hallowed be thy Name. Thy kingdom come. Thy will be done, On earth as it is in heaven. Give us this day our daily bread. And forgive us our trespasses, As we forgive those who trespass against us. And lead us not into temptation, But deliver us from evil. Amen.

Minister. Hearken unto our voice, O Lord, when we cry unto thee;
Answer. Have mercy upon us and hear us.

The Litany for Ordinations

Minister. O Lord, arise, help us;

Answer. And deliver us for thy Name's sake.

Minister. Let thy priests be clothed with righteousness;

Answer. And let thy saints sing with joyfulness.

Minister. Lord, hear our prayer;

Answer. And let our cry come unto thee.

Let us pray.

O GOD, who dost ever hallow and protect thy Church; Raise up therein, through thy Spirit, good and faithful stewards of the mysteries of Christ, that by their ministry and example thy people may abide in thy favour and be guided in the way of truth; through Jesus Christ our Lord, who liveth and reigneth with thee in the unity of the same Spirit ever, one God, world without end. *Amen.*

Consecration of a Church

Glory be to the Father and to the Son, * and to the Holy Ghost;

¶ The Bishop

there recommend

by the secret

agreeably to

reverence for

pious works have

the Bishops and

will also

put this used

of religious

that he

incompr

faithful servants shall assemble

The Form of Consecration of a Church or Chapel

¶ *The following Office may be used with the Order for the Holy Communion, or at Morning Prayer or Evening Prayer, or separately.*

¶ *The Bishop is to be received at the entrance of the Church, or Chapel, by the Church-wardens and Vestrymen, or some other persons appointed for that purpose. The Bishop and the Clergy who are present shall go up the aisle of the Church, or Chapel, to the Holy Table, repeating the following Psalm alternately, the Bishop one verse and the Clergy another.*

Domini est terra. Psalm xxiv.

THE earth is the LORD'S, and all that therein is; * the compass of the world, and they that dwell therein.

2 For he hath founded it upon the seas, * and stablished it upon the floods.

3 Who shall ascend into the hill of the LORD? * or who shall rise up in his holy place?

4 Even he that hath clean hands, and a pure heart; * and that hath not lift up his mind unto vanity, nor sworn to deceive his neighbour.

5 He shall receive the blessing from the LORD, * and righteousness from the God of his salvation.

6 This is the generation of them that seek him; * even of them that seek thy face, O Jacob.

7 Lift up your heads, O ye gates; and be ye lift up, ye everlasting doors; * and the King of glory shall come in.

8 Who is this King of glory? * It is the LORD strong and mighty, even the LORD mighty in battle.

9 Lift up your heads, O ye gates; and be ye lift up, ye everlasting doors; * and the King of glory shall come in.

10 Who is this King of glory? * Even the LORD of hosts, he is the King of glory.

Consecration of a Church

Glory be to the Father, and to the Son, * and to the Holy Ghost;

As it was in the beginning, is now, and ever shall be, * world without end. Amen.

¶ *The Bishop shall go within the rails, with such of the Clergy as can be there accommodated. The Bishop, sitting in his chair, shall have the instruments of Donation and Endowment, if there be any, presented to him; and then standing up, and turning to the Congregation, he shall say,*

DEARLY beloved in the Lord; forasmuch as devout and holy men, as well under the Law as under the Gospel, moved either by the express command of God, or by the secret inspiration of the blessed Spirit, and acting agreeably to their own reason and sense of the natural decency of things, have erected houses for the public worship of God, and separated them from all unhallowed, worldly, and common uses, in order to fill men's minds with greater reverence for his glorious Majesty, and affect their hearts with more devotion and humility in his service; which pious works have been approved of and graciously accepted by our heavenly Father; Let us not doubt but that he will also favourably approve our godly purpose of setting apart this place in solemn manner, for the several Offices of religious worship, and let us faithfully and devoutly beg his blessing on this our undertaking.

¶ *Then the Bishop, kneeling, shall say the following Prayer.*

O ETERNAL God, mighty in power, and of majesty incomprehensible, whom the heaven of heavens cannot contain, much less the walls of temples made with hands; and who yet hast been graciously pleased to promise thy especial presence, wherever two or three of thy faithful servants shall assemble in thy Name, to offer up

Consecration of a Church

their praises and supplications unto thee; Vouchsafe, O Lord, to be present with us, who are here gathered together with all humility and readiness of heart, to consecrate this place to the honour of thy great Name; separating it henceforth from all unhallowed, ordinary, and common uses; and dedicating it to thy service, for reading thy holy Word, for celebrating thy holy Sacraments, for offering to thy glorious Majesty the sacrifices of prayer and thanksgiving, for blessing thy people in thy Name, and for all other holy offices: accept, O Lord, this service at our hands, and bless it with such success as may tend most to thy glory, and the furtherance of our happiness both temporal and spiritual; through Jesus Christ our blessed Lord and Saviour. *Amen.*

¶ *After this the Bishop shall stand up, and turning his face towards the Congregation, shall say,*

REGARD, O Lord, the supplications of thy servants, and grant that whosoever in this house shall be received by Baptism into the congregation of Christ's flock, may be sanctified by the Holy Ghost, and may continue Christ's faithful soldier and servant unto his life's end. *Amen.*

GRANT, O Lord, that they who at this place shall in their own persons renew the promises and vows of their Baptism, and be Confirmed by the Bishop, may receive such a measure of thy Holy Spirit, that they may grow in grace unto their life's end. *Amen.*

GRANT, O Lord, that whosoever shall receive in this place the blessed Sacrament of the Body and Blood of Christ, may come to that holy ordinance with faith, charity, and true repentance; and being filled with thy grace and heavenly benediction, may, to their great and endless comfort, obtain remission of their sins, and all other benefits of his passion. *Amen.*

Consecration of a Church

GRANT, O Lord, that by thy holy Word which shall be read and preached in this place, and by thy Holy Spirit grafting it inwardly in the heart, the hearers thereof may both perceive and know what things they ought to do, and may have power and strength to fulfil the same. *Amen.*

GRANT, O Lord, that whosoever shall be joined together in this place in the holy estate of Matrimony, may faithfully perform and keep the vow and covenant betwixt them made, and may remain in perfect love together unto their life's end. *Amen.*

GRANT, we beseech thee, blessed Lord, that whosoever shall draw near to thee in this place, to give thee thanks for the benefits which they have received at thy hands, to set forth thy most worthy praise, to confess their sins unto thee, and to ask such things as are requisite and necessary, as well for the body as for the soul, may do it with such steadiness of faith, and with such seriousness, affection, and devotion of mind, that thou mayest accept their bounden duty and service, and vouchsafe to give whatever in thy infinite wisdom thou shalt see to be most expedient for them. All which we beg for Jesus Christ's sake, our most blessed Lord and Saviour. *Amen.*

¶ *Then, the Bishop sitting in his chair, the Sentence of Consecration is to be read by some person appointed by him, and then laid by him upon the Communion Table; after which, the Bishop shall say,*

BLESSED be thy Name, O Lord, that it hath pleased thee to put it into the hearts of thy servants to appropriate and devote this house to thy honour and worship; and grant that all who shall enjoy the benefit of this pious work, may show forth their thankfulness, by making a right use of it, to the glory of thy blessed Name; through Jesus Christ our Lord. *Amen.*

Consecration of a Church

¶ *When there is a Communion, the following shall be the Collect, Epistle, and Gospel.*

The Collect.

O MOST glorious God, whom the heaven of heavens cannot contain; Graciously accept the Dedication of this place to thy service; and grant that all who shall call upon thee here may worship thee in spirit and in truth, and may in their lives show forth thy praise; through Jesus Christ our Lord. *Amen.*

For the Epistle. Revelation xxi. 2.

AND I John saw the holy city, new Jerusalem, coming down from God out of heaven, prepared as a bride adorned for her husband. And I heard a great voice out of heaven saying, Behold, the tabernacle of God is with men, and he will dwell with them, and they shall be his people, and God himself shall be with them, and be their God. And God shall wipe away all tears from their eyes; and there shall be no more death, neither sorrow, nor crying, neither shall there be any more pain: for the former things are passed away. And he that sat upon the throne said, Behold, I make all things new. And he said unto me, Write: for these words are true and faithful.

The Gospel. St. John ii. 13.

AND the Jews' passover was at hand, and Jesus went up to Jerusalem, and found in the temple those that sold oxen and sheep and doves, and the changers of money sitting: and when he had made a scourge of small cords, he drove them all out of the temple, and the sheep, and the oxen; and poured out the changers' money, and overthrew the tables; and said unto them that sold doves, Take these things hence; make not my Father's house an house of

Consecration of a Church

merchandise. And his disciples remembered that it was written, The zeal of thine house hath eaten me up.

¶ *And immediately before the final Blessing, the Bishop shall say this Prayer.*

BLESSED be thy Name, O Lord God, for that it hath pleased thee to have thy habitation among the sons of men, and to dwell in the midst of the assembly of the saints upon the earth; Grant, we beseech thee, that in this place now set apart to thy service, thy holy Name may be worshipped in truth and purity through all generations; through Jesus Christ our Lord. *Amen.*

THE Peace of God, which passeth all understanding, keep your hearts and minds in the knowledge and love of God, and of his Son Jesus Christ our Lord: And the Blessing of God Almighty, the Father, the Son, and the Holy Ghost, be amongst you, and remain with you always. *Amen.*

An Office of
Institution of Ministers
into Parishes or Churches.

¶ *The Bishop having received due Notice of the Election of a Minister into a Parish or Church, as prescribed by Canon, and being satisfied that the Person chosen is a qualified Minister of this Church, may proceed to institute him into the Parish.*

¶ *The following Office may be used with the Order for the Holy Communion, or at Morning Prayer or Evening Prayer, or separately.*

¶ *In any Diocese, the concluding Paragraph in the Letter of Institution may be omitted, where it interferes with the Usages, Laws, or Charters of the Church in the same.*

To our well-beloved in Christ, A. B., Presbyter, Greeting.

WE do by these Presents give and grant unto you, in whose Learning, Diligence, sound Doctrine, and Prudence, we do fully confide, our Licence and Authority to perform the Office of a Priest, in the Parish (*or* Church) of E. And also hereby do institute you into said Parish, (*or* Church,) possessed of full power to perform every Act of sacerdotal Function among the People of the same; you continuing in communion with us, and complying with the rubrics and canons of the Church, and with such lawful directions as you shall at any time receive from us. *Sigillum. Signat.*

And as a canonically instituted Priest into the Office of Rector of —— Parish, (*or* Church,) you are faithfully to feed that portion of the flock of Christ which is now intrusted to you; not as a man-pleaser, but as continually bearing in mind that you are accountable to us here, and to the Chief Bishop and Sovereign Judge of all, hereafter.

And as the Lord hath ordained that they who serve at the altar should live of the things belonging to the altar; so we authorize you to claim and enjoy all the accustomed temporalities appertaining to your cure, until some urgent reason or reasons occasion a wish in you, or in the congregation committed to your charge, to bring about a separation, and dissolution of all sacerdotal relation, between you and them; of all which you will give us due notice; and in case of any difference between you and your congregation, as to a separation and dissolution of all sacerdotal connection between you and them, we, your Bishop, with the advice of our Presbyters, are to be the ultimate arbiter and judge.

In witness whereof, we have hereunto affixed our episcopal seal and signature, at ——, this —— day of ——, A. D. ——, and in the —— year of our consecration.

569

Office of Institution

¶ *At the time designated for the new Incumbent's Institution, the Bishop, or the Institutor appointed by him, attended by the new Incumbent, and by the other Clergy present, shall enter the Chancel. Then all the Clergy present standing in the Chancel or Choir, except the Bishop, or the Priest who acts as Institutor, who shall go within the rails of the Altar; the Wardens (or, in case of their necessary absence, two members of the Vestry) standing on the right and left of the Altar, without the rails; the Senior Warden (or the member of the Vestry supplying his place) holding the keys of the Church in his hand, in open view, the Bishop, or the Priest who acts as the Institutor, shall say,*

DEARLY beloved in the Lord, we have assembled for the purpose of instituting the Rev. *A. B.* into this Parish, (*or* Church,) as Priest and Rector of the same; and we are possessed of your Vote that he has been so elected; as also of the prescribed Letter of Institution. But if any of you can show just cause why he may not be instituted, we proceed no further, because we would not that an unworthy person should minister among you.

¶ *If any objection be offered, the Bishop, or the Priest who acts as the Institutor, shall judge whether it afford just cause to suspend the Service.*

¶ *No objection being offered, or the Institutor choosing to go on with the Service, then shall be read the Letter of Institution.*

¶ *And then shall the Senior Warden (or the member of the Vestry supplying his place) present the keys of the Church to the new Incumbent, saying,*

IN the name and behalf of —— Parish (*or* Church) I do receive and acknowledge you, the Rev. *A. B.*, as Priest and Rector of the same; and in token thereof, give into your hands the keys of this Church.

¶ *Then the new Incumbent shall say,*

I *A. B.*, receive these keys of the House of God at your hands, as the pledges of my Institution, and of your parochial recognition, and promise to be a faithful shepherd

570

Office of Institution

over you; In the Name of the Father, and of the Son, and of the Holy Ghost.

¶ *Here the Institutor shall begin the Office.*

Minister. The Lord be with you.
Answer. And with thy spirit.

Let us pray.

DIRECT us, O Lord, in all our doings, with thy most gracious favour, and further us with thy continual help; that in all our works begun, continued, and ended in thee, we may glorify thy holy Name, and finally, by thy mercy, obtain everlasting life; through Jesus Christ our Lord, who hath taught us to pray unto thee, O Almighty Father, in his prevailing Name and words,

OUR Father, who art in heaven, Hallowed be thy Name. Thy kingdom come. Thy will be done, On earth as it is in heaven. Give us this day our daily bread. And forgive us our trespasses, As we forgive those who trespass against us. And lead us not into temptation, But deliver us from evil. For thine is the kingdom, and the power, and the glory, for ever and ever. Amen.

¶ *Then shall the Institutor receive the Incumbent within the rails of the Altar, and present him the Bible, Book of Common Prayer, and Books of Canons of the General and Diocesan Convention, saying as follows.*

RECEIVE these Books; and let them be the rule of thy conduct in dispensing the divine Word, in leading the Devotions of the People, and in exercising the Discipline of the Church; and be thou in all things a pattern to the flock committed to thy care.

¶ *Then shall be said or sung Exsurgat Deus, Psalm lxviii., or Judica me, Domine, Psalm xxvi.*

Minister. The Law was given by Moses;

Office of Institution

People. But Grace and Truth came by Jesus Christ:
Minister and People. Who is God over all, blessed for
evermore. Amen.

Let us pray.

MOST gracious Father, the giver of all good and perfect gifts, who of thy wise providence hast appointed divers Orders in thy Church; Give thy grace, we
beseech thee, to thy servant, to whom the charge of this
Congregation is now committed; and so replenish him
with the truth of thy doctrine, and endue him with innocency of life, that he may faithfully serve before thee, to
the glory of thy great Name, and the benefit of thy holy
Church; through Jesus Christ, our only Mediator and Redeemer. *Amen.*

O HOLY Jesus, who hast purchased to thyself an universal Church, and hast promised to be with the
Ministers of Apostolic Succession to the end of the world;
Be graciously pleased to bless the ministry and service of
him who is now appointed to offer the sacrifices of prayer
and praise to thee in this house, which is called by thy
Name. May the words of his mouth, and the meditation of
his heart, be alway acceptable in thy sight, O Lord, our
strength and our Redeemer. *Amen.*

O GOD, Holy Ghost, Sanctifier of the faithful, visit, we
pray thee, this Congregation with thy love and favour;
enlighten their minds more and more with the light of the
everlasting Gospel; graft in their hearts a love of the truth;
increase in them true religion; nourish them with all goodness; and of thy great mercy keep them in the same, O blessed
Spirit, whom, with the Father and the Son together, we worship and glorify as one God, world without end. *Amen.*

Office of Institution

Benediction.

THE God of peace, who brought again from the dead our Lord Jesus Christ, the great Shepherd of the sheep, through the blood of the everlasting covenant; Make you perfect in every good work to do his will, working in you that which is well pleasing in his sight; through Jesus Christ, to whom be glory for ever and ever. *Amen.*

¶ *Then shall the Instituted Minister kneel at the Altar, to present his supplication for himself, in this form.*

O LORD my God, I am not worthy that thou shouldest come under my roof; yet thou hast honoured thy servant with appointing him to stand in thy House, and to serve at thy holy Altar. To thee and to thy service I devote myself, body, soul, and spirit, with all their powers and faculties. Fill my memory with the words of thy Law; enlighten my understanding with the illumination of the Holy Ghost; and may all the wishes and desires of my will centre in what thou hast commanded. And, to make me instrumental in promoting the salvation of the people now committed to my charge, grant that I may faithfully administer thy holy Sacraments, and by my life and doctrine set forth thy true and lively Word. Be ever with me in the performance of all the duties of my ministry: in prayer, to quicken my devotion; in praises, to heighten my love and gratitude; and in preaching, to give a readiness of thought and expression suitable to the clearness and excellency of thy holy Word. Grant this for the sake of Jesus Christ thy Son our Saviour.

¶ *The Instituted Minister, standing up, shall say,*

The Lord be with you.
Answer. And with thy spirit.

Office of Institution

Let us pray.

O ALMIGHTY God, who hast built thy Church upon the foundation of the Apostles and Prophets, Jesus Christ himself being the chief corner-stone; Grant that, by the operation of the Holy Ghost, all Christians may be so joined together in unity of spirit, and in the bond of peace, that they may be an holy temple acceptable unto thee. And especially to this Congregation present, give the abundance of thy grace; that with one heart they may desire the prosperity of thy holy Apostolic Church, and with one mouth may profess the faith once delivered to the Saints. Defend them from the sins of heresy and schism; let not the foot of pride come nigh to hurt them, nor the hand of the ungodly to cast them down. And grant that the course of this world may be so peaceably ordered by thy governance, that thy Church may joyfully serve thee in all godly quietness; that so they may walk in the ways of truth and peace, and at last be numbered with thy Saints in glory everlasting; through the merits of the same thy blessed Son Jesus Christ, the gracious Bishop and Shepherd of our souls, who liveth and reigneth with thee and the same Holy Ghost, one God, world without end. *Amen.*

¶ *Then shall follow the Sermon. And after that, if there be a Communion, the Instituted Minister shall proceed to that Service, and to administer the holy Eucharist to his Congregation; and after the Benediction, (which he shall always pronounce,) the Wardens, Vestry, and others, shall salute and welcome him, bidding him God-speed.*

¶ *When the Bishop of the Diocese is present at the Institution of a Minister, he shall make to him the address, as prescribed in this Office in the form of a letter.*

A Catechism

A Catechism

A Catechism

that is to say, an Instruction,

to be Learned by Every Person before he

be brought to be Confirmed

by the Bishop.

QUESTION. What is your Name?

Answer. N. or N. N.

Question. Who gave you this Name?

Answer. My Sponsors in Baptism; wherein I was made a member of Christ, the child of God, and an inheritor of the kingdom of heaven.

Question. What did your Sponsors then for you?

Answer. They did promise and vow three things in my name: First, that I should renounce the devil and all his works, the pomps and vanity of this wicked world, and all the sinful lusts of the flesh; Secondly, that I should believe all the Articles of the Christian Faith; And Thirdly, that I should keep God's holy will and commandments, and walk in the same all the days of my life.

Question. Dost thou not think that thou art bound to believe, and to do, as they have promised for thee?

Answer. Yes, verily; and by God's help so I will. And I heartily thank our heavenly Father, that he hath called me to this state of salvation, through Jesus Christ our Saviour. And I pray unto God to give me his grace, that I may continue in the same unto my life's end.

Catechist. Rehearse the Articles of thy Belief.

Answer. I believe in God the Father Almighty, Maker of heaven and earth:

And in Jesus Christ his only Son our Lord: Who was conceived by the Holy Ghost, Born of the Virgin Mary: Suffered under Pontius Pilate, Was crucified, dead, and

577

buried: He descended into hell; The third day he rose again from the dead: He ascended into heaven, And sitteth on the right hand of God the Father Almighty: From thence he shall come to judge the quick and the dead.

I believe in the Holy Ghost: The holy Catholic Church; The Communion of Saints: The Forgiveness of sins: The Resurrection of the body: And the Life everlasting. Amen.

Question. What dost thou chiefly learn in these Articles of thy Belief?

Answer. First, I learn to believe in God the Father, who hath made me, and all the world.

Secondly, in God the Son, who hath redeemed me, and all mankind.

Thirdly, in God the Holy Ghost, who sanctifieth me, and all the people of God.

Question. You said that your Sponsors did promise for you, that you should keep God's Commandments. Tell me how many there are?

Answer. Ten.

Question. Which are they?

Answer. The same which God spake in the twentieth Chapter of Exodus, saying, I am the LORD thy God, who brought thee out of the land of Egypt, out of the house of bondage.

I. Thou shalt have none other gods but me.

II. Thou shalt not make to thyself any graven image, nor the likeness of any thing that is in heaven above, or in the earth beneath, or in the water under the earth; thou shalt not bow down to them, nor worship them; for I the LORD thy God am a jealous God, and visit the sins of the fathers upon the children, unto the third and fourth generation of them that hate me; and show mercy unto thousands in them that love me and keep my commandments.

III. Thou shalt not take the Name of the LORD thy God

A Catechism

in vain; for the LORD will not hold him guiltless, that taketh his Name in vain.

IV. Remember that thou keep holy the Sabbath-day. Six days shalt thou labour, and do all that thou hast to do; but the seventh day is the Sabbath of the LORD thy God. In it thou shalt do no manner of work; thou, and thy son, and thy daughter, thy man-servant, and thy maid-servant, thy cattle, and the stranger that is within thy gates. For in six days the LORD made heaven and earth, the sea, and all that in them is, and rested the seventh day: wherefore the LORD blessed the seventh day, and hallowed it.

V. Honour thy father and thy mother; that thy days may be long in the land which the LORD thy God giveth thee.

VI. Thou shalt do no murder.

VII. Thou shalt not commit adultery.

VIII. Thou shalt not steal.

IX. Thou shalt not bear false witness against thy neighbour.

X. Thou shalt not covet thy neighbour's house, thou shalt not covet thy neighbour's wife, nor his servant, nor his maid, nor his ox, nor his ass, nor any thing that is his.

Question. What dost thou chiefly learn by these Commandments?

Answer. I learn two things; my duty towards God, and my duty towards my Neighbour.

Question. What is thy duty towards God?

Answer. My duty towards God is To believe in him, to fear him, And to love him with all my heart, with all my mind, with all my soul, and with all my strength: To worship him, to give him thanks: To put my whole trust in him, to call upon him: To honour his holy Name and his Word: And to serve him truly all the days of my life.

Question. What is thy duty towards thy Neighbour?

Answer. My duty towards my Neighbour is To love

him as myself, and to do to all men as I would they should do unto me: To love, honour, and succour my father and mother: To honour and obey the civil authority: To submit myself to all my governors, teachers, spiritual pastors and masters: To order myself lowly and reverently to all my betters: To hurt nobody by word or deed: To be true and just in all my dealings: To bear no malice nor hatred in my heart: To keep my hands from picking and stealing, and my tongue from evil speaking, lying, and slandering: To keep my body in temperance, soberness, and chastity: Not to covet nor desire other men's goods; But to learn and labour truly to get mine own living, And to do my duty in that state of life unto which it shall please God to call me.

Catechist. My good Child, know this; that thou art not able to do these things of thyself, nor to walk in the Commandments of God, and to serve him, without his special grace; which thou must learn at all times to call for by diligent prayer. Let me hear, therefore, if thou canst say the Lord's Prayer.

Answer. Our Father, who art in heaven, Hallowed be thy Name. Thy kingdom come. Thy will be done, On earth as it is in heaven. Give us this day our daily bread. And forgive us our trespasses, As we forgive those who trespass against us. And lead us not into temptation, But deliver us from evil. Amen.

Question. What desirest thou of God in this Prayer?

Answer. I desire my Lord God, our heavenly Father, who is the giver of all goodness, to send his grace unto me, and to all people; that we may worship him, serve him, and obey him, as we ought to do. And I pray unto God, that he will send us all things that are needful both for our souls and bodies; and that he will be merciful unto us, and forgive us our sins; and that it will please him to

A Catechism

save and defend us in all dangers both of soul and body; and that he will keep us from all sin and wickedness, and from our spiritual enemy, and from everlasting death. And this I trust he will do of his mercy and goodness, through our Lord Jesus Christ. And therefore I say, Amen, So be it.

Question. How many Sacraments hath Christ ordained in his Church?

Answer. Two only, as generally necessary to salvation; that is to say, Baptism, and the Supper of the Lord.

Question. What meanest thou by this word *Sacrament?*

Answer. I mean an outward and visible sign of an inward and spiritual grace given unto us; ordained by Christ himself, as a means whereby we receive the same, and a pledge to assure us thereof.

Question. How many parts are there in a Sacrament?

Answer. Two; the outward visible sign, and the inward spiritual grace.

Question. What is the outward visible sign or form in Baptism?

Answer. Water; wherein the person is baptized, In the Name of the Father, and of the Son, and of the Holy Ghost.

Question. What is the inward and spiritual grace?

Answer. A death unto sin, and a new birth unto righteousness: for being by nature born in sin, and the children of wrath, we are hereby made the children of grace.

Question. What is required of persons to be baptized?

Answer. Repentance, whereby they forsake sin; and Faith, whereby they stedfastly believe the promises of God made to them in that Sacrament.

Question. Why then are Infants baptized, when by reason of their tender age they cannot perform them?

Answer. Because they promise them both by their Sureties; which promise, when they come to age, themselves are bound to perform.

A Catechism

Question. Why was the Sacrament of the Lord's Supper ordained?

Answer. For the continual remembrance of the sacrifice of the death of Christ, and of the benefits which we receive thereby.

Question. What is the outward part or sign of the Lord's Supper?

Answer. Bread and Wine, which the Lord hath commanded to be received.

Question. What is the inward part, or thing signified?

Answer. The Body and Blood of Christ, which are spiritually taken and received by the faithful in the Lord's Supper.

Question. What are the benefits whereof we are partakers thereby?

Answer. The strengthening and refreshing of our souls by the Body and Blood of Christ, as our bodies are by the Bread and Wine.

Question. What is required of those who come to the Lord's Supper?

Answer. To examine themselves, whether they repent them truly of their former sins, stedfastly purposing to lead a new life; have a lively faith in God's mercy through Christ, with a thankful remembrance of his death; and be in charity with all men.

¶ *The Minister of every Parish shall diligently, upon Sundays and Holy Days, or on some other convenient occasions, openly in the Church, instruct or examine so many Children of his Parish, sent unto him, as he shall think convenient, in some part of this Catechism.*

¶ *And all Fathers, Mothers, Masters, and Mistresses, shall cause their Children, Servants, and Apprentices, who have not learned their Catechism, to come to the Church at the time appointed, and obediently to hear and to be ordered by the Minister, until such time as they have learned all that is here appointed for them to learn.*

¶ *So soon as Children are come to a competent age, and can say the*

A Catechism

Creed, the Lord's Prayer, and the Ten Commandments, and can answer to the other questions of this short Catechism, they shall be brought to the Bishop.

¶ *And whensoever the Bishop shall give knowledge for Children to be brought unto him for their Confirmation, the Minister of every Parish shall either bring, or send in writing, with his hand subscribed thereunto the Names of all such Persons within his Parish, as he shall think fit to be presented to the Bishop to be confirmed.*

A Catechism

Family Prayer
Forms of Prayer to be used in Families
With Additional Prayers

Forms of Prayer
to be used in Families

MORNING PRAYER.

¶ *The Master or Mistress having called together as many of the Family as can conveniently be present, let one of them, or any other who may be appointed, say as followeth, all kneeling, and repeating with him the Lord's Prayer.*

OUR Father, who art in heaven, Hallowed be thy Name. Thy kingdom come. Thy will be done, On earth as it is in heaven. Give us this day our daily bread. And forgive us our trespasses, As we forgive those who trespass against us. And lead us not into temptation, But deliver us from evil. For thine is the kingdom, and the power, and the glory, for ever and ever. Amen.

¶ *Here may follow the Collect for the day.*

Acknowledgment of God's Mercy and Preservation, especially through the Night past.

ALMIGHTY and everlasting God, in whom we live and move and have our being; We, thy needy creatures, render thee our humble praises, for thy preservation of us from the beginning of our lives to this day, and especially for having delivered us from the dangers of the past night. For these thy mercies, we bless and magnify thy glorious Name; humbly beseeching thee to accept this our morning sacrifice of praise and thanksgiving; for his sake who lay down in the grave, and rose again for us, thy Son our Saviour Jesus Christ. *Amen.*

587

Family Prayer

AND since it is of thy mercy, O gracious Father, that
another day is added to our lives; We here dedicate
both our souls and our bodies to thee and thy service, in a
sober, righteous, and godly life: in which resolution, do
thou, O merciful God, confirm and strengthen us; that, as
we grow in age, we may grow in grace, and in the knowledge of our Lord and Saviour Jesus Christ. *Amen.*

Prayer for Grace to enable us to perform that Resolution.

BUT, O God, who knowest the weakness and corruption
of our nature, and the manifold temptations which we
daily meet with; We humbly beseech thee to have compassion on our infirmities, and to give us the constant
assistance of thy Holy Spirit; that we may be effectually
restrained from sin, and incited to our duty. Imprint upon
our hearts such a dread of thy judgments, and such a
grateful sense of thy goodness to us, as may make us both
afraid and ashamed to offend thee. And, above all, keep in
our minds a lively remembrance of that great day, in which
we must give a strict account of our thoughts, words, and
actions to him whom thou hast appointed the Judge of
quick and dead, thy Son Jesus Christ our Lord. *Amen.*

*For Grace to guide and keep us the following Day, and
for God's Blessing on the business of the Same.*

IN particular, we implore thy grace and protection for the
ensuing day. Keep us temperate in all things, and diligent in our several callings. Grant us patience under our
afflictions. Give us grace to be just and upright in all our
dealings; quiet and peaceable; full of compassion; and ready
to do good to all men, according to our abilities and oppor-

Family Prayer

tunities. Direct us in all our ways. Defend us from all dangers and adversities; and be graciously pleased to take us, and all who are dear to us, under thy fatherly care and protection. These things, and whatever else thou shalt see to be necessary and convenient to us, we humbly beg, through the merits and mediation of thy Son Jesus Christ, our Lord and Saviour. *Amen.*

THE grace of our Lord Jesus Christ, and the love of God, and the fellowship of the Holy Ghost, be with us all evermore. *Amen.*

EVENING PRAYER.

¶ *The Family being together, a little before bed-time, let the Master or Mistress, or any other who may be appointed, say as followeth, all kneeling, and repeating with him the Lord's Prayer.*

OUR Father, who art in heaven, Hallowed be thy Name. Thy kingdom come. Thy will be done, On earth as it is in heaven. Give us this day our daily bread. And forgive us our trespasses, As we forgive those who trespass against us. And lead us not into temptation, But deliver us from evil. For thine is the kingdom, and the power, and the glory, for ever and ever. Amen.

¶ *Here may follow the Collect for the day.*

Confession of Sins, with a Prayer for Contrition and Pardon.

MOST merciful God, who art of purer eyes than to behold iniquity, and hast promised forgiveness to all those who confess and forsake their sins; We come before thee in an humble sense of our own unworthiness, acknowledging our manifold transgressions of thy righteous laws.* But, O gracious Father, who desirest not the death of a sinner, look upon

* Here let him who reads make a short pause, that every one may secretly confess the sins and failings of that day.

Family Prayer

us, we beseech thee, in mercy, and forgive us all our transgressions. Make us deeply sensible of the great evil of them;
and work in us an hearty contrition; that we may obtain
forgiveness at thy hands, who art ever ready to receive
humble and penitent sinners; for the sake of thy Son Jesus
Christ, our only Saviour and Redeemer. *Amen.*

Prayer for Grace to reform and grow Better.

AND lest, through our own frailty, or the temptations
which encompass us, we be drawn again into sin,
vouchsafe us, we beseech thee, the direction and assistance
of thy Holy Spirit. Reform whatever is amiss in the tem-
per and disposition of our souls; that no unclean thoughts,
unlawful designs, or inordinate desires, may rest there.
Purge our hearts from envy, hatred, and malice; that we
may never suffer the sun to go down upon our wrath; but
may always go to our rest in peace, charity, and good-will,
with a conscience void of offence towards thee, and towards
men; that so we may be preserved pure and blameless, unto
the coming of our Lord and Saviour Jesus Christ. *Amen.*

The Intercession.

AND accept, O Lord, our intercessions for all mankind.
Let the light of thy Gospel shine upon all nations;
and may as many as have received it, live as becomes it.
Be gracious unto thy Church; and grant that every member of the same, in his vocation and ministry, may serve
thee faithfully. Bless all in authority over us; and so rule
their hearts and strengthen their hands, that they may punish wickedness and vice, and maintain thy true religion and
virtue. Send down thy blessings, temporal and spiritual,
upon all our relations, friends, and neighbours. Reward all
who have done us good, and pardon all those who have
done or wish us evil, and give them repentance and better

Family Prayer

minds. Be merciful to all who are in any trouble; and do thou, the God of pity, administer to them according to their several necessities; for his sake who went about doing good, thy Son our Saviour Jesus Christ. *Amen.*

The Thanksgiving.

TO our prayers, O Lord, we join our unfeigned thanks for all thy mercies; for our being, our reason, and all other endowments and faculties of soul and body; for our health, friends, food, and raiment, and all the other comforts and conveniences of life. Above all, we adore thy mercy in sending thy only Son into the world, to redeem us from sin and eternal death, and in giving us the knowledge and sense of our duty towards thee. We bless thee for thy patience with us, notwithstanding our many and great provocations; for all the directions, assistances, and comforts of thy Holy Spirit; for thy continual care and watchful providence over us through the whole course of our lives; and particularly for the mercies and benefits of the past day; beseeching thee to continue these thy blessings to us, and to give us grace to show our thankfulness in a sincere obedience to his laws, through whose merits and intercession we received them all, thy Son our Saviour Jesus Christ. *Amen.*

Prayer for God's Protection through the Night following.

IN particular, we beseech thee to continue thy gracious protection to us this night. Defend us from all dangers and mischiefs, and from the fear of them; that we may enjoy such refreshing sleep as may fit us for the duties of the coming day. And grant us grace always to live in such a state that we may never be afraid to die; so that, living and dying, we may be thine, through the merits and satisfaction of thy Son Christ Jesus, in whose Name we offer up these our imperfect prayers. *Amen.*

591

Family Prayer

THE grace of our Lord Jesus Christ, and the love of God, and the fellowship of the Holy Ghost, be with us all evermore. *Amen.*

¶ *On Sundays, and on other days when it may be convenient, it will be proper to begin with a Chapter, or part of a Chapter, from the New Testament.*

A SHORTER FORM.

MORNING.

¶ *After the reading of a brief portion of Holy Scripture, let the Head of the Household, or some other member of the family, say as followeth, all kneeling, and repeating with him the Lord's Prayer.*

OUR Father, who art in heaven, Hallowed be thy Name. Thy kingdom come. Thy will be done, On earth as it is in heaven. Give us this day our daily bread. And forgive us our trespasses, As we forgive those who trespass against us. And lead us not into temptation, But deliver us from evil. For thine is the kingdom, and the power, and the glory, for ever and ever. Amen.

O LORD, our heavenly Father, Almighty and everlasting God, who hast safely brought us to the beginning of this day; Defend us in the same with thy mighty power; and grant that this day we fall into no sin, neither run into any kind of danger; but that all our doings, being ordered by thy governance, may be righteous in thy sight; through Jesus Christ our Lord. *Amen.*

¶ *Here may be added any special Prayers.*

THE grace of our Lord Jesus Christ, and the love of God, and the fellowship of the Holy Ghost, be with us all evermore. *Amen.*

Family Prayer

EVENING.

¶ After the reading of a brief portion of Holy Scripture, let the Head of the Household, or some other member of the family, say as followeth, all kneeling, and repeating with him the Lord's Prayer.

OUR Father, who art in heaven, Hallowed be thy Name. Thy kingdom come. Thy will be done, On earth as it is in heaven. Give us this day our daily bread. And forgive us our trespasses, As we forgive those who trespass against us. And lead us not into temptation, But deliver us from evil. For thine is the kingdom, and the power, and the glory, for ever and ever. Amen.

LIGHTEN our darkness, we beseech thee, O Lord; and by thy great mercy defend us from all perils and dangers of this night; for the love of thy only Son, our Saviour, Jesus Christ. *Amen.*

¶ Here may be added any special Prayers.

THE Lord bless us and keep us. The Lord make his face to shine upon us, and be gracious unto us. The Lord lift up his countenance upon us, and give us peace, this night and evermore. *Amen.*

Family Prayer

ADDITIONAL PRAYERS.

For the Spirit of Prayer.

O ALMIGHTY God, who pourest out on all who desire it, the spirit of grace and of supplication; Deliver us, when we draw nigh to thee, from coldness of heart and wanderings of mind, that with stedfast thoughts and kindled affections, we may worship thee in spirit and in truth; through Jesus Christ our Lord. *Amen.*

In the Morning.

O GOD, the King eternal, who dividest the day from the darkness, and turnest the shadow of death into the morning; Drive far off from us all wrong desires, incline our hearts to keep thy law, and guide our feet into the way of peace; that having done thy will with cheerfulness while it was day, we may, when the night cometh, rejoice to give thee thanks; through Jesus Christ our Lord. *Amen.*

ALMIGHTY God, who alone gavest us the breath of life, and alone canst keep alive in us the holy desires thou dost impart; We beseech thee, for thy compassion's sake, to sanctify all our thoughts and endeavours; that we may neither begin an action without a pure intention nor continue it without thy blessing. And grant that, having the eyes of the mind opened to behold things invisible and unseen, we may in heart be inspired by thy wisdom, and in work be upheld by thy strength, and in the end be accepted of thee as thy faithful servants; through Jesus Christ our Saviour. *Amen.*

At Night.

O LORD, support us all the day long, until the shadows lengthen and the evening comes, and the busy world is hushed, and the fever of life is over, and our work is

Family Prayer

done. Then in thy mercy grant us a safe lodging, and a holy rest, and peace at the last. *Amen.*

O GOD, who art the life of mortal men, the light of the faithful, the strength of those who labour, and the repose of the dead; We thank thee for the timely blessings of the day, and humbly supplicate thy merciful protection all this night. Bring us, we beseech thee, in safety to the morning hours; through him who died for us and rose again, thy Son, our Saviour Jesus Christ. *Amen.*

Sunday Morning.

O GOD, who makest us glad with the weekly remembrance of the glorious resurrection of thy Son our Lord; Vouchsafe us this day such blessing through our worship of thee, that the days to come may be spent in thy service; through the same Jesus Christ our Lord. *Amen.*

For Quiet Confidence.

O GOD of peace, who hast taught us that in returning and rest we shall be saved, in quietness and in confidence shall be our strength; By the might of thy Spirit lift us, we pray thee, to thy presence, where we may be still and know that thou art God; through Jesus Christ our Lord. *Amen.*

For Guidance.

O GOD, by whom the meek are guided in judgment, and light riseth up in darkness for the godly; Grant us, in all our doubts and uncertainties, the grace to ask what thou wouldest have us to do, that the Spirit of Wisdom may save us from all false choices, and that in thy light we may see light, and in thy straight path may not stumble; through Jesus Christ our Lord. *Amen.*

Family Prayer

For Trustfulness.

O MOST loving Father, who willest us to give thanks for all things, to dread nothing but the loss of thee, and to cast all our care on thee, who carest for us; Preserve us from faithless fears and worldly anxieties, and grant that no clouds of this mortal life may hide from us the light of that love which is immortal, and which thou hast manifested unto us in thy Son, Jesus Christ our Lord. *Amen.*

O HEAVENLY Father, thou understandest all thy children; through thy gift of faith we bring our perplexities to the light of thy wisdom, and receive the blessed encouragement of thy sympathy, and a clearer knowledge of thy will. Glory be to thee for all thy gracious gifts. *Amen.*

For Joy in God's Creation.

O HEAVENLY Father, who hast filled the world with beauty; Open, we beseech thee, our eyes to behold thy gracious hand in all thy works; that rejoicing in thy whole creation, we may learn to serve thee with gladness; for the sake of him by whom all things were made, thy Son, Jesus Christ our Lord. *Amen.*

For the Children.

A LMIGHTY God, heavenly Father, who hast blessed us with the joy and care of children; Give us light and strength so to train them, that they may love whatsoever things are true and pure and lovely and of good report, following the example of their Saviour Jesus Christ. *Amen.*

For the Absent.

O GOD, whose fatherly care reacheth to the uttermost parts of the earth; We humbly beseech thee gra-

Family Prayer

ciously to behold and bless those whom we love, now absent from us. Defend them from all dangers of soul and body; and grant that both they and we, drawing nearer to thee, may be bound together by thy love in the communion of thy Holy Spirit, and in the fellowship of thy saints; through Jesus Christ our Lord. *Amen.*

For Those We Love.

ALMIGHTY God, we entrust all who are dear to us to thy never-failing care and love, for this life and the life to come; knowing that thou art doing for them better things than we can desire or pray for; through Jesus Christ our Lord. *Amen.*

For the Recovery of a Sick Person.

O MERCIFUL God, giver of life and health; Bless, we pray thee, thy servant, [*N.*], and those who administer to *him* of thy healing gifts; that *he* may be restored to health of body and of mind; through Jesus Christ our Lord. *Amen.*

For One about to undergo an Operation.

ALMIGHTY God our heavenly Father, we beseech thee graciously to comfort thy servant in *his* suffering, and to bless the means made use of for *his* cure. Fill *his* heart with confidence, that though *he* be sometime afraid, *he* yet may put *his* trust in thee; through Jesus Christ our Lord. *Amen.*

For a Birthday.

WATCH over thy child, O Lord, as *his* days increase; bless and guide *him* wherever *he* may be, keeping *him* unspotted from the world. Strengthen *him* when *he* stands; comfort *him* when discouraged or sorrowful; raise

Family Prayer

him up if *he* fall; and in *his* heart may thy peace which passeth understanding abide all the days of *his* life; through Jesus Christ our Lord. *Amen.*

For an Anniversary of One Departed.

ALMIGHTY God, we remember this day before thee thy faithful servant [*N.*], and we pray thee that, having opened to *him* the gates of larger life, thou wilt receive *him* more and more into thy joyful service; that *he* may win, with thee and thy servants everywhere, the eternal victory; through Jesus Christ our Lord. *Amen.*

For Those in Mental Darkness.

O HEAVENLY Father, we beseech thee to have mercy upon all thy children who are living in mental darkness. Restore them to strength of mind and cheerfulness of spirit, and give them health and peace; through Jesus Christ our Lord. *Amen.*

For a Blessing on the Families of the Land.

ALMIGHTY God, our heavenly Father, who settest the solitary in families; We commend to thy continual care the homes in which thy people dwell. Put far from them, we beseech thee, every root of bitterness, the desire of vain-glory, and the pride of life. Fill them with faith, virtue, knowledge, temperance, patience, godliness. Knit together in constant affection those who, in holy wedlock, have been made one flesh; turn the heart of the fathers to the children, and the heart of the children to the fathers; and so enkindle fervent charity among us all, that we be evermore kindly affectioned with brotherly love; through Jesus Christ our Lord. *Amen.*

Family Prayer

For all Poor, Homeless, and Neglected Folk.

O GOD, Almighty and merciful, who healest those that are broken in heart, and turnest the sadness of the sorrowful to joy; Let thy fatherly goodness be upon all that thou hast made. Remember in pity such as are this day destitute, homeless, or forgotten of their fellow-men. Bless the congregation of thy poor. Uplift those who are cast down. Mightily befriend innocent sufferers, and sanctify to them the endurance of their wrongs. Cheer with hope all discouraged and unhappy people, and by thy heavenly grace preserve from falling those whose penury tempteth them to sin; though they be troubled on every side, suffer them not to be distressed; though they be perplexed, save them from despair. Grant this, O Lord, for the love of him, who for our sakes became poor, thy Son, our Saviour Jesus Christ. *Amen.*

For Faithfulness in the Use of this World's Goods.

ALMIGHTY God, whose loving hand hath given us all that we possess; Grant us grace that we may honour thee with our substance, and remembering the account which we must one day give, may be faithful stewards of thy bounty; through Jesus Christ our Lord. *Amen.*

A General Intercession.

O GOD, at whose word man goeth forth to his work and to his labour until the evening; Be merciful to all whose duties are difficult or burdensome, and comfort them concerning their toil. Shield from bodily accident and harm the workmen at their work. Protect the efforts of sober and honest industry, and suffer not the hire of the labourers to be kept back by fraud. Incline the heart of employers and of those whom they employ to mutual forbearance,

Family Prayer

fairness, and good-will. Give the spirit of governance and of a sound mind to all in places of authority. Bless all those who labour in works of mercy or in schools of good learning. Care for all aged persons, and all little children, the sick and the afflicted, and those who travel by land or by sea. Remember all who by reason of weakness are overtasked, or because of poverty are forgotten. Let the sorrowful sighing of the prisoners come before thee; and according to the greatness of thy power, preserve thou those that are appointed to die. Give ear unto our prayer, O merciful and gracious Father, for the love of thy dear Son, our Saviour Jesus Christ. *Amen.*

Grace before Meat.

BLESS, O Father, thy gifts to our use and us to thy service; for Christ's sake. *Amen.*

GIVE us grateful hearts, our Father, for all thy mercies, and make us mindful of the needs of others; through Jesus Christ our Lord. *Amen.*

Articles of Religion

As established by the Bishops, the Clergy, and the Laity of the
Protestant Episcopal Church in the
United States of America,
in Convention, on the twelfth day of September,
in the Year of our Lord

1801

ARTICLES OF RELIGION.

I. Of Faith in the Holy Trinity.

THERE is but one living and true God, everlasting, without body, parts, or passions; of infinite power, wisdom, and goodness; the Maker, and Preserver of all things both visible and invisible. And in unity of this Godhead there be three Persons, of one substance, power, and eternity; the Father, the Son, and the Holy Ghost.

II. Of the Word or Son of God, which was made very Man.

THE Son, which is the Word of the Father, begotten from everlasting of the Father, the very and eternal God, and of one substance with the Father, took Man's nature in the womb of the blessed Virgin, of her substance: so that two whole and perfect Natures, that is to say, the Godhead and Manhood, were joined together in one Person, never to be divided, whereof is one Christ, very God, and very Man; who truly suffered, was crucified, dead, and buried, to reconcile his Father to us, and to be a sacrifice, not only for original guilt, but also for actual sins of men.

III. Of the going down of Christ into Hell.

As Christ died for us, and was buried; so also is it to be believed, that he went down into Hell.

IV. Of the Resurrection of Christ.

CHRIST did truly rise again from death, and took again his body, with flesh, bones, and all things appertaining to the perfection of Man's nature; wherewith he ascended into Heaven, and there sitteth, until he return to judge all Men at the last day.

V. Of the Holy Ghost.

THE Holy Ghost, proceeding from the Father and the Son, is of one substance, majesty, and glory, with the Father and the Son, very and eternal God.

VI. Of the Sufficiency of the Holy Scriptures for Salvation.

HOLY Scripture containeth all things necessary to salvation: so that whatsoever is not read therein, nor may be proved thereby, is not to be required of any man, that it should be believed as an article of the Faith, or be thought requisite or necessary to salvation. In the name of the Holy Scripture we do understand those canonical Books of the Old and New Testament, of whose authority was never any doubt in the Church.

Of the Names and Number of the Canonical Books.

Genesis,	The First Book of Samuel,	The Book of Esther,
Exodus,	The Second Book of Samuel,	The Book of Job,
Leviticus,	The First Book of Kings,	The Psalms,
Numbers,	The Second Book of Kings,	The Proverbs,
Deuteronomy,	The First Book of Chronicles,	Ecclesiastes or Preacher,
Joshua,	The Second Book of Chronicles,	Cantica, or Songs of Solomon,
Judges,	The First Book of Esdras,	Four Prophets the greater,
Ruth,	The Second Book of Esdras,	Twelve Prophets the less.

Articles of Religion

And the other Books (as Hierome saith) the Church doth read for example of life and instruction of manners; but yet doth it not apply them to establish any doctrine; such are these following:

The Third Book of Esdras,	Baruch the Prophet,
The Fourth Book of Esdras,	The Song of the Three Children,
The Book of Tobias,	The Story of Susanna,
The Book of Judith,	Of Bel and the Dragon,
The rest of the Book of Esther,	The Prayer of Manasses,
The Book of Wisdom,	The First Book of Maccabees,
Jesus the Son of Sirach,	The Second Book of Maccabees.

All the Books of the New Testament, as they are commonly received, we do receive, and account them Canonical.

VII. *Of the Old Testament.*

THE Old Testament is not contrary to the New: for both in the Old and New Testament everlasting life is offered to Mankind by Christ, who is the only Mediator between God and Man, being both God and Man. Wherefore they are not to be heard, which feign that the old Fathers did look only for transitory promises. Although the Law given from God by Moses, as touching Ceremonies and Rites, do not bind Christian men, nor the Civil precepts thereof ought of necessity to be received in any commonwealth; yet notwithstanding, no Christian man whatsoever is free from the obedience of the Commandments which are called Moral.

VIII. *Of the Creeds.*

THE Nicene Creed, and that which is commonly called the Apostles' Creed, ought thoroughly to be received and believed: for they may be proved by most certain warrants of Holy Scripture.

IX. *Of Original or Birth-Sin.*

ORIGINAL sin standeth not in the following of Adam, (as the Pelagians do vainly talk;) but it is the fault and corruption of the Nature of every man, that naturally is engendered of the offspring of Adam; whereby man is very far gone from original righteousness, and is of his own nature inclined to evil, so that the flesh lusteth always contrary to the Spirit; and therefore in every person born into this world, it deserveth God's wrath and damnation. And this infection of nature doth remain, yea in them that are regenerated; whereby the lust of the flesh, called in Greek, $\phi\rho\acute{o}\nu\eta\mu\alpha$ $\sigma\alpha\rho\kappa\acute{o}\varsigma$, (which some do expound the wisdom, some sensuality, some the affection, some the desire, of the flesh,) is not subject to the Law of God. And although there is no condemnation for them that believe and are baptized; yet the Apostle doth confess, that concupiscence and lust hath of itself the nature of sin.

X. *Of Free-Will.*

THE condition of Man after the fall of Adam is such, that he cannot turn and prepare himself, by his own natural strength and good works, to faith, and calling upon God. Wherefore we have no power to do good works pleasant

Articles of Religion

and acceptable to God, without the grace of God by Christ preventing us, that we may have a good will, and working with us, when we have that good will.

XI. *Of the Justification of Man.*

WE are accounted righteous before God, only for the merit of our Lord and Saviour Jesus Christ by Faith, and not for our own works or deservings. Wherefore, that we are justified by Faith only, is a most wholesome Doctrine, and very full of comfort, as more largely is expressed in the Homily of Justification.

XII. *Of Good Works.*

ALBEIT that Good Works, which are the fruits of Faith, and follow after Justification, cannot put away our sins, and endure the severity of God's judgment; yet are they pleasing and acceptable to God in Christ, and do spring out necessarily of a true and lively Faith; insomuch that by them a lively Faith may be as evidently known as a tree discerned by the fruit.

XIII. *Of Works before Justification.*

WORKS done before the grace of Christ, and the Inspiration of his Spirit, are not pleasant to God, forasmuch as they spring not of faith in Jesus Christ; neither do they make men meet to receive grace, or (as the School-authors say) deserve grace of congruity: yea rather, for that they are not done as God hath willed and commanded them to be done, we doubt not but they have the nature of sin.

XIV. *Of Works of Supererogation.*

VOLUNTARY Works besides, over and above, God's Commandments, which they call Works of Supererogation, cannot be taught without arrogancy and impiety: for by them men do declare, that they do not only render unto God as much as they are bound to do, but that they do more for his sake, than of bounden duty is required: whereas Christ saith plainly, When ye have done all that are commanded to you, say, We are unprofitable servants.

XV. *Of Christ alone without Sin.*

CHRIST in the truth of our nature was made like unto us in all things, sin only except, from which he was clearly void, both in his flesh, and in his spirit. He came to be the Lamb without spot, who, by sacrifice of himself once made, should take away the sins of the world; and sin (as Saint John saith) was not in him. But all we the rest, although baptized, and born again in Christ, yet offend in many things; and if we say we have no sin, we deceive ourselves, and the truth is not in us.

XVI. *Of Sin after Baptism.*

NOT every deadly sin willingly committed after Baptism is sin against the Holy Ghost, and unpardonable. Wherefore the grant of repentance is not to be denied to such as fall into sin after Baptism. After we have received the Holy Ghost, we may depart from grace given, and fall into sin, and by the grace of

God we may arise again, and amend our lives. And therefore they are to be condemned, which say, they can no more sin as long as they live here, or deny the place of forgiveness to such as truly repent.

XVII. *Of Predestination and Election.*

PREDESTINATION to Life is the everlasting purpose of God, whereby (before the foundations of the world were laid) he hath constantly decreed by his counsel secret to us, to deliver from curse and damnation those whom he hath chosen in Christ out of mankind, and to bring them by Christ to everlasting salvation, as vessels made to honour. Wherefore, they which be endued with so excellent a benefit of God, be called according to God's purpose by his Spirit working in due season: they through Grace obey the calling: they be justified freely: they be made sons of God by adoption: they be made like the image of his only-begotten Son Jesus Christ: they walk religiously in good works, and at length, by God's mercy, they attain to everlasting felicity.

As the godly consideration of Predestination, and our Election in Christ, is full of sweet, pleasant, and unspeakable comfort to godly persons, and such as feel in themselves the working of the Spirit of Christ, mortifying the works of the flesh, and their earthly members, and drawing up their mind to high and heavenly things, as well because it doth greatly establish and confirm their faith of eternal Salvation to be enjoyed through Christ, as because it doth fervently kindle their love towards God: So, for curious and carnal persons, lacking the Spirit of Christ, to have continually before their eyes the sentence of God's Predestination, is a most dangerous downfall, whereby the Devil doth thrust them either into desperation, or into wretchlessness of most unclean living, no less perilous than desperation.

Furthermore, we must receive God's promises in such wise, as they be generally set forth to us in Holy Scripture: and, in our doings, that Will of God is to be followed, which we have expressly declared unto us in the Word of God.

XVIII. *Of obtaining eternal Salvation only by the Name of Christ.*

THEY also are to be had accursed that presume to say, That every man shall be saved by the Law or Sect which he professeth, so that he be diligent to frame his life according to that Law, and the light of Nature. For Holy Scripture doth set out unto us only the Name of Jesus Christ, whereby men must be saved.

XIX. *Of the Church.*

THE visible Church of Christ is a congregation of faithful men, in the which the pure Word of God is preached, and the Sacraments be duly ministered according to Christ's ordinance, in all those things that of necessity are requisite to the same.

As the Church of Jerusalem, Alexandria, and Antioch, have erred; so also the Church of Rome hath erred, not only in their living and manner of Ceremonies, but also in matters of Faith.

Articles of Religion

XX. *Of the Authority of the Church.*

THE Church hath power to decree Rites or Ceremonies, and authority in Controversies of Faith: and yet it is not lawful for the Church to ordain any thing that is contrary to God's Word written, neither may it so expound one place of Scripture, that it be repugnant to another. Wherefore, although the Church be a witness and a keeper of Holy Writ, yet, as it ought not to decree any thing against the same, so besides the same ought it not to enforce any thing to be believed for necessity of Salvation.

XXI. *Of the Authority of General Councils.*

[The Twenty-first of the former Articles is omitted; because it is partly of a local and civil nature, and is provided for, as to the remaining parts of it, in other Articles.]

XXII. *Of Purgatory.*

THE Romish Doctrine concerning Purgatory, Pardons, Worshipping and Adoration, as well of Images as of Relics, and also Invocation of Saints, is a fond thing, vainly invented, and grounded upon no warranty of Scripture, but rather repugnant to the Word of God.

XXIII. *Of Ministering in the Congregation.*

IT is not lawful for any man to take upon him the office of public preaching, or ministering the Sacraments in the Congregation, before he be lawfully called, and sent to execute the same. And those we ought to judge lawfully called and sent, which be chosen and called to this work by men who have public authority given unto them in the Congregation, to call and send Ministers into the Lord's vineyard.

XXIV. *Of Speaking in the Congregation in such a Tongue as the people understandeth.*

IT is a thing plainly repugnant to the Word of God, and the custom of the Primitive Church, to have public Prayer in the Church, or to minister the Sacraments, in a tongue not understanded of the people.

XXV. *Of the Sacraments.*

SACRAMENTS ordained of Christ be not only badges or tokens of Christian men's profession, but rather they be certain sure witnesses, and effectual signs of grace, and God's good will towards us, by the which he doth work invisibly in us, and doth not only quicken, but also strengthen and confirm our Faith in him.

There are two Sacraments ordained of Christ our Lord in the Gospel, that is to say, Baptism, and the Supper of the Lord.

Those five commonly called Sacraments, that is to say, Confirmation, Penance, Orders, Matrimony, and Extreme Unction, are not to be counted for Sacraments of the Gospel, being such as have grown partly of the corrupt following of the Apostles, partly are states of life allowed in the Scriptures; but yet have not like nature of Sacraments with Baptism, and the Lord's Supper, for that they have not any visible sign or ceremony ordained of God.

Articles of Religion

The Sacraments were not ordained of Christ to be gazed upon, or to be carried about, but that we should duly use them. And in such only as worthily receive the same, they have a wholesome effect or operation: but they that receive them unworthily, purchase to themselves damnation, as Saint Paul saith.

XXVI. *Of the Unworthiness of the Ministers, which hinders not the effect of the Sacraments.*

ALTHOUGH in the visible Church the evil be ever mingled with the good, and sometimes the evil have chief authority in the Ministration of the Word and Sacraments, yet forasmuch as they do not the same in their own name, but in Christ's, and do minister by his commission and authority, we may use their Ministry, both in hearing the Word of God, and in receiving the Sacraments. Neither is the effect of Christ's ordinance taken away by their wickedness, nor the grace of God's gifts diminished from such as by faith, and rightly, do receive the Sacraments ministered unto them; which be effectual, because of Christ's institution and promise, although they be ministered by evil men.

Nevertheless, it appertaineth to the discipline of the Church, that inquiry be made of evil Ministers, and that they be accused by those that have knowledge of their offences; and finally, being found guilty, by just judgment be deposed.

XXVII. *Of Baptism.*

BAPTISM is not only a sign of profession, and mark of difference, whereby Christian men are discerned from others that be not christened, but it is also a sign of Regeneration or New-Birth, whereby, as by an instrument, they that receive Baptism rightly are grafted into the Church; the promises of the forgiveness of sin, and of our adoption to be the sons of God by the Holy Ghost, are visibly signed and sealed; Faith is confirmed, and Grace increased by virtue of prayer unto God.

The Baptism of young Children is in any wise to be retained in the Church, as most agreeable with the institution of Christ.

XXVIII. *Of the Lord's Supper.*

THE Supper of the Lord is not only a sign of the love that Christians ought to have among themselves one to another; but rather it is a Sacrament of our Redemption by Christ's death: insomuch that to such as rightly, worthily, and with faith, receive the same, the Bread which we break is a partaking of the Body of Christ; and likewise the Cup of Blessing is a partaking of the Blood of Christ.

Transubstantiation (or the change of the substance of Bread and Wine) in the Supper of the Lord, cannot be proved by Holy Writ; but is repugnant to the plain words of Scripture, overthroweth the nature of a Sacrament, and hath given occasion to many superstitions.

The Body of Christ is given, taken, and eaten, in the Supper, only after an heavenly and spiritual manner. And the mean whereby the Body of Christ is received and eaten in the Supper, is Faith.

The Sacrament of the Lord's Supper was not by Christ's ordinance reserved, carried about, lifted up, or worshipped.

Articles of Religion

XXIX. *Of the Wicked, which eat not the Body of Christ in the use of the Lord's Supper.*

THE Wicked, and such as be void of a lively faith, although they do carnally and visibly press with their teeth (as Saint Augustine saith) the Sacrament of the Body and Blood of Christ; yet in no wise are they partakers of Christ: but rather, to their condemnation, do eat and drink the sign or Sacrament of so great a thing.

XXX. *Of both Kinds.*

THE Cup of the Lord is not to be denied to the Lay-people: for both the parts of the Lord's Sacrament, by Christ's ordinance and commandment, ought to be ministered to all Christian men alike.

XXXI. *Of the one Oblation of Christ finished upon the Cross.*

THE Offering of Christ once made is that perfect redemption, propitiation, and satisfaction, for all the sins of the whole world, both original and actual; and there is none other satisfaction for sin, but that alone. Wherefore the sacrifices of Masses, in the which it was commonly said, that the Priest did offer Christ for the quick and the dead, to have remission of pain or guilt, were blasphemous fables, and dangerous deceits.

XXXII. *Of the Marriage of Priests.*

BISHOPS, Priests, and Deacons, are not commanded by God's Law, either to vow the estate of single life, or to abstain from marriage: therefore it is lawful for them, as for all other Christian men, to marry at their own discretion, as they shall judge the same to serve better to godliness.

XXXIII. *Of excommunicate Persons, how they are to be avoided.*

THAT person which by open denunciation of the Church is rightly cut off from the unity of the Church, and excommunicated, ought to be taken of the whole multitude of the faithful, as an Heathen and Publican, until he be openly reconciled by penance, and received into the Church by a Judge that hath authority thereunto.

XXXIV. *Of the Traditions of the Church.*

IT is not necessary that Traditions and Ceremonies be in all places one, or utterly like; for at all times they have been divers, and may be changed according to the diversity of countries, times, and men's manners, so that nothing be ordained against God's Word. Whosoever, through his private judgment, willingly and purposely, doth openly break the Traditions and Ceremonies of the Church, which be not repugnant to the Word of God, and be ordained and approved by common authority, ought to be rebuked openly, (that others may fear to do the like,) as he that offendeth against the common order of the Church, and hurteth the authority of the Magistrate, and woundeth the consciences of the weak brethren.

Every particular or national Church hath authority to ordain, change, and

Articles of Religion

abolish, Ceremonies or Rites of the Church ordained only by man's authority, so that all things be done to edifying.

XXXV. *Of the Homilies.*

THE Second Book of Homilies, the several titles whereof we have joined under this Article, doth contain a godly and wholesome Doctrine, and necessary for these times, as doth the former Book of Homilies, which were set forth in the time of Edward the Sixth; and therefore we judge them to be read in Churches by the Ministers, diligently and distinctly, that they may be understanded of the people.

Of the Names of the Homilies.

1 Of the right Use of the Church.
2 Against Peril of Idolatry.
3 Of repairing and keeping clean of Churches.
4 Of good Works: first of Fasting.
5 Against Gluttony and Drunkenness.
6 Against Excess of Apparel.
7 Of Prayer.
8 Of the Place and Time of Prayer.
9 That Common Prayers and Sacraments ought to be ministered in a known tongue.
10 Of the reverend Estimation of God's Word.
11 Of Alms-doing.
12 Of the Nativity of Christ.
13 Of the Passion of Christ.
14 Of the Resurrection of Christ.
15 Of the worthy receiving of the Sacrament of the Body and Blood of Christ.
16 Of the Gifts of the Holy Ghost.
17 For the Rogation-days.
18 Of the State of Matrimony.
19 Of Repentance.
20 Against Idleness.
21 Against Rebellion.

[This Article is received in this Church, so far as it declares the Books of Homilies to be an explication of Christian doctrine, and instructive in piety and morals. But all references to the constitution and laws of England are considered as inapplicable to the circumstances of this Church; which also suspends the order for the reading of said Homilies in churches, until a revision of them may be conveniently made, for the clearing of them, as well from obsolete words and phrases, as from the local references.]

XXXVI. *Of Consecration of Bishops and Ministers.*

THE Book of Consecration of Bishops, and Ordering of Priests and Deacons, as set forth by the General Convention of this Church in 1792, doth contain all things necessary to such Consecration and Ordering; neither hath it any thing that, of itself, is superstitious and ungodly. And, therefore, whosoever are consecrated or ordered according to said Form, we decree all such to be rightly, orderly, and lawfully consecrated and ordered.

XXXVII. *Of the Power of the Civil Magistrates.*

THE Power of the Civil Magistrate extendeth to all men, as well Clergy as Laity, in all things temporal; but hath no authority in things purely spiritual. And we hold it to be the duty of all men who are professors of the Gospel, to pay respectful obedience to the Civil Authority, regularly and legitimately constituted.

XXXVIII. *Of Christian Men's Goods, which are not common.*

THE Riches and Goods of Christians are not common, as touching the right, title, and possession of the same; as certain Anabaptists do falsely boast. Notwithstanding, every man ought, of such things as he possesseth, liberally to give alms to the poor, according to his ability.

XXXIX. *Of a Christian Man's Oath.*

As we confess that vain and rash Swearing is forbidden Christian men by our Lord Jesus Christ, and James his Apostle, so we judge, that Christian Religion doth not prohibit, but that a man may swear when the Magistrate requireth, in a cause of faith and charity, so it be done according to the Prophet's teaching, in justice, judgment, and truth.